WATERSHED HYDROLOGY

(PRINCIPLES OF HYDROLOGY)

WATERSHED HYDROLOGY

(PRINCIPLES OF HYDROLOGY)

Prof. R. SURESH, Ph.D.

Head, Department of Soil & Water Conservation Engineering,
College of Agricultural Engineering
Rajendra Agricultural University
Pusa, Samastipur (Bihar)

STANDARD PUBLISHERS DISTRIBUTORS

1705-B, Nai Sarak, Post Box No. 1066, Delhi-110006

email : stpub@vsnl.com **www.standardpublishers.com**

Published by :
A.K. Jain
For **Standard Publishers Distributors**
1705-B, Nai Sarak, Delhi-110006
Ph.: 23262700, 23285798 Fax.: 23243180

First Edition	: 1997
Second Revised & Enlarged Edition	: 2005
Reprint	: 2008
Reprint	: 2012
Reprint	: 2015
Reprint	: 2017
Reprint	: 2019

Price Rs: 300-00

ISBN 81-8014-056-3

Computer Typeset :
SOFTSERVE Computer Systems, Delhi-51

Printed at :
Lomus Offset Press, Delhi

Preface to the Second Edition

Second edition of the book "Watershed Hydrology" is in revised and enlarged form. All chapters have been thoroughly revised and enlarged by adding new and few advance contents as per demand of readers. In this edition, the **important points** on subject matter, **references and descriptive & objective type questions along with answers** have been incorporated. A large number of solved examples (about 500) and subject index which were not in first edition, have also been incorporated in second edition. Author has made his best effort for enriching the contents; however, constructive criticism will always be appreciated.

Author expresses his deep sense of gratitude to his teachers, i.e. Dr. Ghanshyam Das (retired Professor), Department of Soil & Water Conservation Engineering and Dr. H.S. Chauhan (retired Professor), Department of Irrigation & Drainage Engineering, G.B. Pant University of Agric & Technology, Pantnagar (Uttranchal), who directly or indirectly encouraged me from different corners.

R.A.U., Pusa
22.4.2005

R. Suresh

Preface to the First Edition

This book has been written for the purpose to fulfill the requirement of degree and diploma students of civil and agricultural engineering disciplines, studying in different Indian universities and institutions. It will also be more beneficial to those students who are willing to appear in GATE examination, ICAR examinations, forest services, bank examinations and others.

The book has been accomplished under 13 main chapters, completing a full syllabus of hydrology subject of different Indian Universities. Each and every chapters have been dealt with good number of solved examples and diagrams in simple way, which can be easily grasp by the readers. At the end of each chapter, several descriptive and objective type questions are also cited which is demand of students, now a days. Several appendices, essential to describe the subject matter, have also been included in the book.

The author expresses his sincere thanks to all individuals who inspired, provided fruitful suggestions and helped in different ways to make the manuscript able to publish. He is also thankful to his teachers of Allahabad and Ludhiana from where he was graduated and post graduated, respectively.

The author is thankful to M/s Standard Publishers Distributors, Delhi for taking keen interest to publish this book in very short time period.

Finally, his parents, wife, son, daughter and relatives are also highly thankful for their various sacrifices during preparation of manuscript of the book.

Constructive suggestions will always be acknowledged and appreciated.

Pusa
22nd, Oct. 1996

R. Suresh

Dedicated to

my

Wife Savita Verma,

Son Yash Verma

and

Daughter Rhea Verma

Contents

Chapter Name *Page No.*

Chapter Name *Page No.*

1

Introduction

The word "hydrology" is derived from Greek word "hydor" and "logos" (*i.e.* hydrology = hydor + logos), in which, "hydor" refers to water and "logos" to the science. Thus, as such hydrology represents the meaning of science of water. However, it does not represent the complete definition of the hydrology. Hydrologists have made wide study on this fact and defined the hydrology as "the science, which deals with the occurrence, distribution and circulation of atmospheric water through unending hydrologic cycle and simultancousely its physical, chemical and physiological reactions with the earth surface. As far as engineering hydrology is concerned, it includes those parts of hydrology, which play key role in design and operation of engineering projects for control as well as use of water.

The hydrology of a region is affected by its weather pattern and physical factors related to the topography, geology and vegetation, existing there. The advances in civilization, human activities etc. also change the dynamic equilibrium of the hydrologic cycle. It has been investigated that because of burning of fossil fuels, the amount of CO_2 is increasing day-by day in the atmosphere which could develop the effect of warming up of the earth and accordingly to the global hydrology.

1.1. Importance

The water is most essential requirement for human life and survial of plants & animals. In this respect, the hydrology provides a tool for assessment and development of water potential of a particular region. However, various importance of hydrology are listed as under :

1. It gives an estimate about water resource potential of the river basin.
2. It casts the informations on probability of flood occurrence, their pattern and magnitude.
3. The dependable yields for major irrigation projects and hydro-electric power stations can be determined.
4. The maximum expected flood discharge and its volume for reservoir storage can be evaluated.
5. Spillway's capacity, dam height, dam safety measures etc. can be designed.

6. It provides guideline to construct the flood control measures for any river basin.
7. It helps in improvement of navigation.
8. Gives a guideline for u/s erosion control, to prolong the reservoir's life, and
9. Flood forecasting based on rainfall data can also be done.

1.2. Scope and Application

Generally, the scope and application of hydrology are governed by the problems incurred in the hydrology.

The main problems are given as under :

1. Measurement and publication of hydrologic data.
2. Analysis of data for development of relationships, and
3. Application of empirical solutions for solving the problems related to the hydrology.

Hydrology is a broad base science which is related to the several fields and involves various data and theories. Hydrologic theories, are rather distinct from other fields.

Solution of above problems is based on the following points :

1. Collection and systematic presentation of hydrologic data.
2. Appropriate analysis and interpretation of data.

1.3. Division of Hydrology

The hydrology includes following sub-divisions :

1. **Hydro-meteorology :** It is that part of hydrology which studies about hydrology and meteorology.

2. **Liminology :** Studies about surface lakes etc.

3. **Gylogy :** It includes the study of sub-surface water.

4. **Geo-hydrology :** It deals the study of sub-surface water.

5. **Potamology :** The science, which studies about surface streams is called potamology.

1.4. Distribution of Water on Earth

The investigation record states that, of the total available water *i.e.* 1.4×10^{18} m^3 on the earth surface about 97% is found in the oceans as saline water. The distribution of fresh water on the earth is shown in table 1.1.

Table 1.1. Worldwide distribution of fresh water on the earth

S. No.	*Place*	*% Water available*
1.	Ice and glaciers	75 (approx.)
2.	Sub-soil	24 (approx.)
3.	Lakes	0.30
4.	Soil-moisture	0.06
5.	Atmosphere	0.035
6.	Rivers	0.03

Table 1.2. World wide distribution of runoff.

Continent (or others)	Pacific slope		Atlantic slope		Regions of interior drainage		Total land area	
	Area ($10^3 km^3$)	Runoff (cm)	Area ($10^3 km^3$)	Runoff (cm)	Area ($10^5 km^2$)	Runoff	Area ($x10^3 km^2$)	Runoff (cm)
Europe (including ice land)	—	—	7,970	29.7	1,710	10.9	9680	26.2
Asia including Japasese and Phillipine island	16,700	30.0	11,970	16.3	13,630	1.7	42,300	17.0
Africa including Medagaskar	5,470	21.8	13,250	35.5	11,130	1.4	29,850	20.3
Australia including Tasmania and N. Land)	4,230	14.0	—	—	3,740	0.6	7,970	7.6
South-America	1,340	44.4	15,600	47.5	988	6.6	17,928	45.0
North-America including W.Indese and C. America	4,960	48.5	14,400	27.4	835	1.1	20,195	31.4
Green land and Canadian Archipelage	—	—	3,880	18.0	—	—	3,880	18.0
Malayan Arhipelags	2,620	160.0	—	—	—	—	2,620	160.0
Total – average	35,320	39.3	64,070	32.4	32,033	2.1	1,31,423	25.0

The other details, such as total geographical area of the world, sea area, etc. are as follows :

Total geographical area of the world $= 1.36 \times 10^8$ km^2

Total sea area $= 3.74 \times 10^8$ km^2

Precipitation depth on land surface $= 7.5 \times 10^2$ mm/year

Evaporation from the land surface $= 7.5 \times 10^2$ mm/year

Precipitation depth on sea surface $= 8.7 \times 10^2$ mm/year

Evaporation from sea surface $= 9.4 \times 10^2$ mm/year

The world wide distribution of runoff is given in table 1.2 (L Wovich from Mutreja book) and for Indian sub continent, it is given in table 1.3. The zone wise surface water potential and ground water resources of India are also shown in tables 1.4 and 1.5, respectively. The estimated world water and world water balance are also given in tables 1.6 and 1.7 respectively.

Table 1.3. Runoff distribution under different river basins of India

S.N.o.	*Region*	*Catchment area (km^2)*	*Runoff (annual)*	
			Volume (m^3)	*Depth (cm)*
1.	River falling into Bay of Bengal and Ganga & Brahmputtra systems	1.21×10^6	4.11×10^{11}	34
2..	Ganga system	9.78×10^5	4.9×10^{11}	50
3.	Brahmputra system	5.06×10^5	3.81×10^{11}	75
4.	Rivers falling into Arabian Sea rather than Indus system	4.8×10^5	3.1×10^{11}	63
5.	Indus basin (India)	3.58×10^5	7.95×10^{11}	22

Table 1.4. Zonewise surface water potential of India

S.No.	*Water potential (Mm^3)*
1. *Zone-1 : (Rivers flowing towards West)*	
a) Narmada basin	40,088.10
b) Basins above Narmada	27,753.30
c) Tapti basin	19,735.68
d) River basins of Kerala	37,041.40
e) River basins of Tamil Nadu and Mumbai	1,80,852.83

Table Contd.

S.No.	Water potential (Mm^3)
2. *Zone-2 : (Rivers flowing towards East)*	
a) Kaveri basin	18,600.88
b) Godavari basin	1,15,355.04
c) Krishna basin	57,763.87
d) Pennar basin	6,858.15
e) Mahanadi and other basins between Ganga & Godavari rivers	1,31,390.28
f) Tambraparni and Vaigai river basins	8,733.04
g) Basin between Kaveri and Pennar rivers	16,898.68
3. *Zone-3*	
Indus basin	79,473.12
4. *Zone-4 : Ganga basin*	
a) Chambal river basin	24,311.89
b) Ramganga basin	18,635.55
c) Gomti basin	8,461.67
d) Ghaghra basin	1,14,281.92
e) Main Ganga basin	42,555.06
f) Tone basin	6,278.41
g) Yamuna basin	65,621.14
h) Sone and other basins between Sone and Tone rivers	50,140.96
i) Basins below Sone river	45,145.37
j) Basins above Sone river	1,74,660.76
Total	5,50,082.73
5. *Zone-5*	
Barhmputra and Barak basins	5,90,713.57
Total surface water potential of entire India	**18,81,340.67**

Table 1.5. Statewise ground water resources of India

S.No.	*State*	*G.W. Resource* (Mm^3)
1.	Andhra Pradesh	30,343.61
2.	Assam+Nagaland+Arunanchal	51,682.81
3.	Bihar	38,607.92
4.	Delhi	616.74

Contd.

S.No.	State	G.W. Resource (Mm^3)
5.	Gujrat	17,885.46
6.	Haryana	5,674.01
7.	Himachal Pradesh	2,837.00
8.	J & K	12,334.80
9.	Karnataka	20,475.77
10.	Kerala	13,198.24
11.	Maharashtra	25,903.08
12.	M.P.	54,889.86
13..	Orissa	28,123.34
14.	Punjab	11,224.67
15.	Rajasthan	7,154.18
16.	Tamilnadu + Pondichery	20,229.07
17.	U.P.	54,889.86
18.	West Bengal	28,370.04
	Total Ground Water Resource	4,24,440.46 Mm^3

Table 1.6. Estimated amounts of world water

Particular	*Area, (10^6 km^2)*	*Volum 10^6 km^3*	*Percent of total water*	*Percent of fresh water*
Oceans	361.3	1338	96.5	
Ground water				
Fresh	134.8	10.53	0.76	30.1
Saline	134.8	12.87	0.93	
Soil-moisture	82.0	0.0165	0.0012	0.05
Polar ice	16.0	24.0235	1.7	68.6
Other ice and snow	0.3	0.3406	0.025	1.0
Lakes				
Fresh	1.2	0.0910	0.007	0.26
Saline	0.8	0.0854	0.006	
Marshes	2.7	0.01147	0.0008	0.03
Rivers	148.8	0.00212	0.0002	0.006
Biological water	510.0	0.00112	0.0001	0.003
Atmospheric water	510.0	0.00129	0.001	0.04
Total water	510.0	1385.98461	100	
Fresh water	148.8	35.029210	2.5	100

Source : UNESCO (1978)

Table 1.7. Global water balance (annual)

Particular		*Ocean*	*Land*
Area	(km^2)	3613×10^5	1488×10^5
Precipitation	(mm/y)	1270	800
Evaporation	(mm/y)	1400	484
Runoff to ocean	(km^3/y)	—	—
Rivers	(km^3/y)	—	44700
Ground water	(km^3/y)	—	2200
Total runoff	(km^3/y)	—	46900
	(mm/y)	—	316

Source : UNESCO (1978)

1.5. Hydrologic Data

It refers to the data on available water and its quality both in time and space. The main types of hydrologic data are given as under :

1. **Historic data :** This types of data are also referred as chronological data. Historic data have special feature that, if they are not recorded at appropriate time, they get lost forever. Generally, runoff, river discharge, rainfall depth etc fall under histroric data.

2. **Field data :** Such data are recorded according to need or necessity. Generally, groundwater depth, sediment load along the river flow etc. are counted under field data. The field data can be generated at any time by conducting experiments.

3. **Laboratory and field experimental data :** The field and laboratory data related to the hydrology are generated in the same way as the data in hydraulic engineering. Use of these data is limited to basic or applied researches, only.

Sometimes, to develop the empirical relationship between different hydrological variables, the simultaneous measurements on two or more hydrologic variables is also conducted.

1.6. Hydrologic Cycle

It is defined as the water transfer cycle, in which water is transferred from the ocean or sea to the atmosphere, then from atmosphere to the earth and again to the sea. It always maintains the balance between water present on the earth surface and in the atmosphere.

Hydrologic cycle comprises following three main phases :

1. Evaporation and transpiration
2. Precipitation, and
3. Runoff

Evaporation and Transpiration : These two are the process by virtue of which, the water/moisture from water- body/soil surface is removed continuously under temperature effect.

The total water lost due to evaporation and transpiration in combined from is referred as evapo-transpiration loss. The transpiration loss is only from the plant's body during respiration process, while evaporation loss is from water and soil surface due to temperature influence. These two processes are mainly responsible for making availability of the moisture in the atmosphere. It is estimated that, in India about 80% of total precipitation is lost due to evaporation from the oceans.

Precipitation : It takes place due to lifting of moisture to the atmosphere and subsequently formation of cluds at some height. The water from clouds falls over the earth in form of precipitation which is circulated to the oceans, rivers, inland bodies etc.

Runoff : During precipitation, a part of precipitated water which is intercepted by the vegetative foliage, dry surfaces of buildings, ground surface etc. is ultimately lost to the atmosphere is known as interception loss. The rest amount of precipitation goes to the streams, rivers etc. is called surface runoff, which ultimately meets to the sea. Again, during rainfall or runoff, few part of the same also goes down into the soil and joins to the rivers, oceans or sea is called sub-surface runoff.

The above three phases of hydrologic cycle are always in function under influence of solar energy and complete an unending chain.

For inland areas, the hydrologic balance equation can be expressed as:

$$P = R + E \quad \text{...(1.1)}$$

where, P = precipitation R = runoff

E = losses through evaporation and transpiration

Figure 1.1 illlustrates the view of hydrologic cycle.

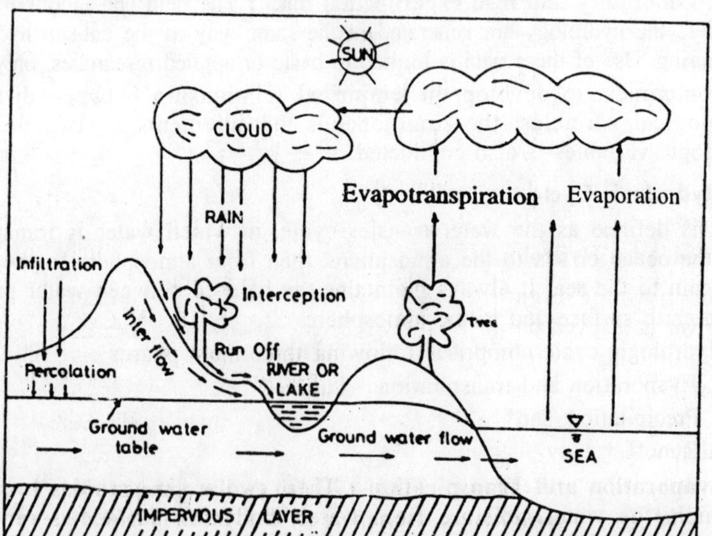

Fig. 1.1

Global Hydrologic Cycle

The hydrologic cycle may be treated as the dynamic system with the components of precipitation, evaporation, runoff etc. These components are further grouped into sub systems of overall cycle. The global hydrologic cycle as system is shown in Figure 1.2, in which dashed lines divide the entire cycle into three subsystems *i.e.* the atmospheric water system, surface water system and sub surface water system. The atmospheric water system comprises, the processes of precipitation, evaporation, interception and transpiration. The surface water system includes, the processes of overland flow, surface runoff, subsurface ground water outflow and runoff to streams, oceans etc. The third sub-system which is the sub- surface water system contains the processes of infiltration, ground water recharge, subsurface flow and ground water flow.

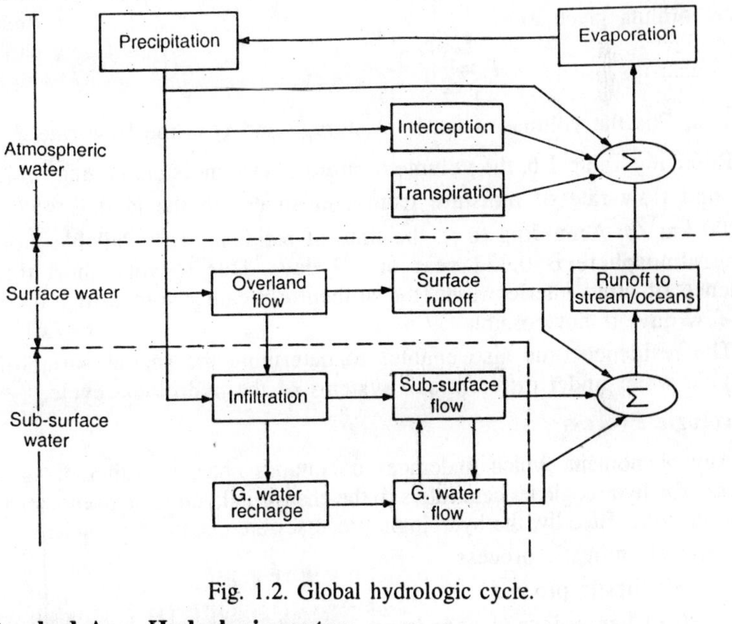

Fig. 1.2. Global hydrologic cycle.

Watershed As a Hydrologic system

It is shown in Figure 1.3. Watershed is the land draining into the stream/river at a given point. Watershed divide refers to the line dividing the land area draining towards a given stream. The system boundary is around the watershed which is drawn by projecting the watershed divide vertically upward and downward to the horizontal plane. The input to the watershed is the rainfall which gets distributed over the area of watershed. The output of watershed is the run-off *i.e.* stream flow which is concentrated to the outlet of watershed. Apart from runoff, the evaporation and sub-surface flow could also be counted as the output of the watershed system. However, as compared to runoff the significance of these two outputs is very less or negligible. Since, all associated processes of hydrologic cycle take place within the divide line of the watershed, therefore watershed is also considered as a hydrological entity.

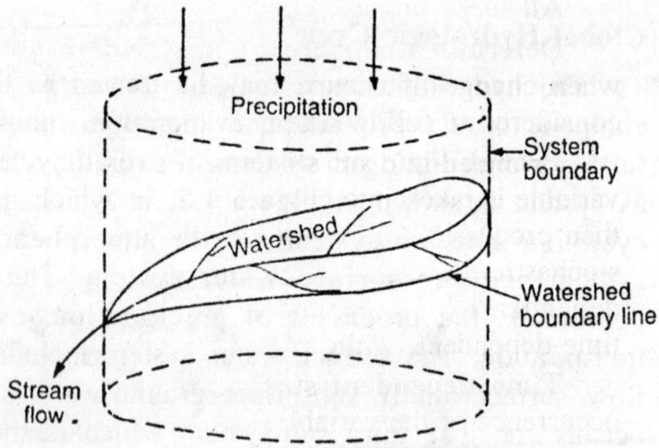

Fig. 1.3. Watershed as a hydrologic system.

Residence Time : It is the average duration of water molecule to pass through a sub-system of the hydrologic cycle. Residence time (T_r) is calculated by the formula given as :

$$T_r = \frac{S}{2} \quad \text{...(1.2)}$$

in which S is the volume of water in storage and Q is the flow rate.

Referring Table 1.6, the volume of atmospheric moisture content is 12900 km^3, and flow rate of moisture from atmosphere to the land is 458000 + 119000 km^3/y. According to it, the time of residence for available moisture in the atmosphere is 0.022 year or 8.2 days. Due to very short time of residence of atmospheric water, the authentic weather forecasting for more than few days is not possible.

The residence time also enables to determine the spatial variability of available water under different sub systems of the hydrologic cycle.

Hydrologic Process

Any phenomena which undergoes continuous changes with time is called process. The hydrologic process refers to the change in hydrologic phenomena with respect to time. Broadly, the hydrologic processes are classified as under :

1. Deterministic process
2. Stochastic process
   - (*a*) Chance dependent process
   - (*b*) Time dependent process
     - (*i*) Pure random process — Stationary process / Non-stationary process
     - (*ii*) Non-pure random process — Stationary process / Non-stationary process
3. Probabilistic process
   - Time independent process
     - (*i*) Pure random process.

All these processes are described below :

Deterministic process : A hydrologic process is said to be deterministic when change of occurrence of involved variables is ignored and process is considered to follow a definite law of certainty but not the law of probability.

Probabilistic or stochastic process : If the change of occurrence of variable is taken into consideration and process follows the law of probability, then process is known as probabilistic or stochastic. In strictly speaking, the stochastic process is different from the probabilistic process in respect of time dependence or independence. The stochastic processes are considered as time-dependent, while probabilistic processes are time independent.

Time dependent stochastic process : In this process, the sequence of occurrence of the variables is considered and variables are either pure random or non-pure random. Also, probability distribution of the variables may or may not vary with time.

Pure random stochastic process : In this stochastic processes, the variables of time series are independent among themselves, and constitute a random sequence.

Non-pure random stochastic process : In this process, the variables of time series are dependent among themselves, and constitute a non-random sequence. The non-random stochastic processes are composed of deterministic and pure random components.

Time independent probabilistic process : The sequence of occurrence of variables is ignored and chance of their occurrence is assumed to follow a definite probability distribution in which variables are considered to be as pure-random.

In real speaking, all hydrologic processes are generally stochastic. These are assumed as deterministic or probabilistic only for analysis simplicity. In mathematical terms, the stochastic processes are a family of random variables which may be the function of time (*i.e.* t) or some other parameters. Also, in quantitative respect, the stochastic process may be discrete or continuous and can be sampled continuously or at discrete or at uniform intervals.

Stationary process : If probability distribution of variables remains constant throughout the process, the process is said to be stationary.

Non-stationary process : If probability distribution of variables changes during the process, the process is called non-stationary.

Hydrologic System

An aggregation or assemblage of the objects, interlinked into by some specific form of regular interaction or independence is called system. The system may be dynamic if there is process in the system.

Stochastic system : The system which contains probabilistic or stochastic processes is called stochastic system.

Deterministic system : A system with deterministic process is called deterministic system.

Sequential system : A system is said to be sequential if it consists of input, output and some working medium (*i.e.* energy, matter or information).

The working medium is also known as 'throughput'. The hydrologic cycle or drainage basins are the sequential system containing throughput as the water.

The hydrological phenomenon are extremely complex ; they may not be completely understood. However, they can be represented in a simplified manner by means of system concept. Hydrologic cycle is a system, consisting the components of precipitation, evaporation, runoff and other phases. By analogy, the hydrologic system is a structure or volume in space surrounded by the boundary accepting water and other inputs, that operates on them internally and produces them inform of outputs. It is shown in Figure 1.4. The structure for surface or subsurface flow or atmospheric water of hydrologic system refers to the totality of the flow path through which water passes to the outlet from the point of its entry in the system. The boundary refers to the continuous surface enclosing the volume or structure. In hydrologic system, the working medium is the precipitation which enters as input and interacts with the structure and yields the output inform of runoff. The physical, chemical and biological processes operate on the working medium *i.e.* precipitation within the system.

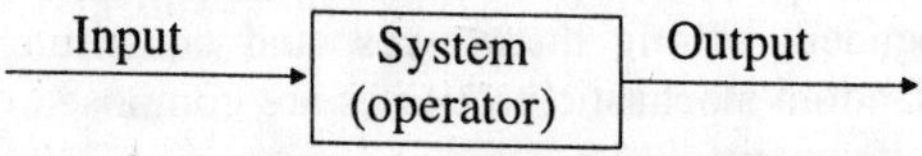

Fig. 1.4. Sequential system.

1.7. Hydrologic Equation

It is based on the law of conservation of mass, given as under :

$$I = O + S \qquad ...(1.3)$$

where, I = inflow

O = outflow

S = change in storage

This equation states that during a specified time period, the amount of total inflow into an area is always equal to the sum of outflow and change in storage volume made of that area. It enables to predict the available water in the drainage basin.

1.8. Measurement of Atmospheric Moisture

Atmospheric moisture is an important content for running the hydrologic cycle, as it is the only source of precipitation. It also affects the evaporation loss from land and water bodies. Atmospheric moisture denotes the presence of water vapour in the air, which spatially varies in the atmosphere depending on altitude. The condition at which air contains maximum amount of water vapour at a given temperature is called saturation and the temperature at which air is saturated if cooled at constant pressure, is termed as dew point temperature. For example, if air temperature near ground surface is 24°C and dew point temperature is 10°C, then it is essential to cool the air up to 10°C for reaching it to the saturation stage. Degree of saturation is denoted as the index of relative humidity.

Relative Humidity : It is used as an index for indicating the degree of saturation and is defined as the ratio of amount of moisture present in a given space to the total amount which that volume contains at saturation stage. In other way, it can also be defined as the ratio of actual vapour pressure (e) to the saturation vapour pressure (e_s), given as :

$$f = \frac{e}{e_s} \times 100 \qquad ...(1.4)$$

It is expressed in percent.

Also, if air temperature and dew point are known, then relative humidity can be directly computed by using the following formula :

$$\text{R.H.} = \frac{(112 - 0.1T + T_d)}{(112 + 0.9\,T)} \qquad ...(1.5)$$

where, T = air temperature (°C)

T_d = dew point temperature (°C)

Factors Affecting Relative Humidity

Various factors which affect the relative humidity are described as under :

1. **Altitude** : Relative humidity increases with increase in altitude and vice-versa.

2. **Vegetation** : It increases the relative humidity because it directly supplies the moisture to the air passing over. This is the reason that a belt of barren land contains comparitively less humidity as compared to the cropped land.

3. **Orographic effect** : In atmosphere the maximum amount of moisture is found upto the elevation of 8000 m from the ground surface. At higher elevation than 8000 m, the moisture is comparitively less to that of the sea level. Regarding orographic effect on relative humidity is concerned it is greater in mountaneous regions, than at the same elevation in plane lands.

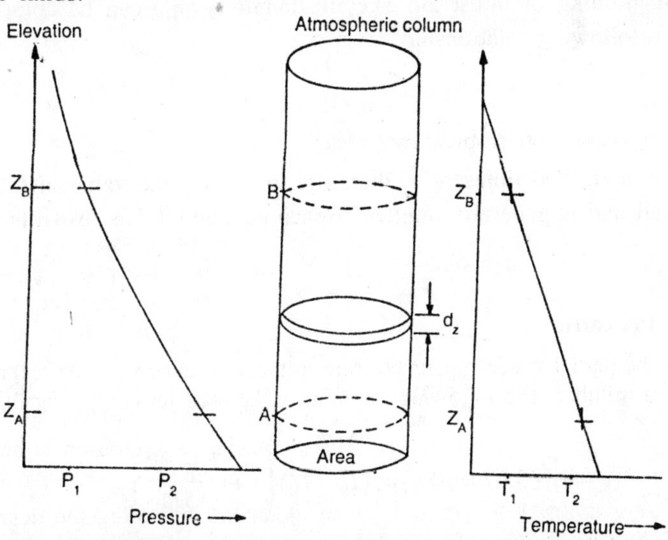

Fig. 1.5. Variations in temperature and pressure in the atmosphere.

4. **Land and water mass :** Relative humidity is greatly affected by the presence of water bodies on the land surface. If all the factors are kept constant then humidity is found greater over the water surface than the land surface. Due to this reason, the moisture content is relatively higher over the ocean than at some distance away from it in land areas.

5. **Annual variation :** It refers to the season-wise variations in the level of moisture content. In summer season, it is found maximum and minimum during winter season of the year. But at higher altitudes, the relative humidity is comparitively greater during winter season and lesser in summer season.

6. **Diurnal variation :** It indicates the variations in relative humidity with respect to different diurnals (*i.e.* morning, evening and night) of the day. In the early morning, the relative humidity is at maximum level, while minimum during early afternoon. In coastal areas, the level of relative humidity increases during day time and decreases to night hours.

Absolute Humidity

Absolute humidity is defined as the ratio of mass of water vapour to the unit volume of space. It is generally expressed as gram per m^3 (g/m^3) and can be computed by using the following formula :

$$a_h = \frac{e}{T_a} \times 217 \qquad ...(1.6)$$

where a_h = absolute humidity

e = vapour pressure

T_a = absolute temperature

Specific Humidity

It is the mass of water vapour in a unit mass of moist air, expressed in terms of gram/kg of moist air. Specific humidity (q_h) can be computed by using the following relationship :

$$q_h = 622 \frac{e}{p_a - 0.378\, e} \qquad ...(1.7)$$

where, p_a = atmospheric pressure (mbar)

Since p_a is 100 times of e, therefore in eq. 1.7 the value of 0.378 e is very small and is generally omitted. Hence equation 1.7 is rewritten as

$$q_h = 622 \frac{e}{p_a} \qquad ...(1.8)$$

Vapour Pressure

It is the partial water vapour pressure in the atmosphere, usually expressed in the unit of millibar. The following formula can be used for computing the vapour pressure :

$$e = e_s - 3.67 \times 10^{-4}\, p_a\, (T_a - T_w) \left(1 + \frac{T_w - 32}{1571}\right) \qquad ...(1.9)$$

where, e = vapour pressure (m.bar)

e_s = saturation vapour pressure at T_w

T_w = wet-bulb temperature (°F)

T_a = dry–bulb temperature (°F)

p_a = atmospheric pressure (m.bar)

Dew Point

It is the temperature at which the air containing constant water- vapour is saturated when allowed to cool under constant pressure. Dew point (T_d) is also defined as the temperature, at which saturation vapour pressure gets equilibriated to the existing vapour pressure.

Mixing Ratio

It is the ratio of mass of water vapour to the mass of dry air, usually expressed as gram per kilogram of dry air. The mixing ratio (W_r) can be computed by using the following formula :

$$W_r = 622 \frac{e}{p_a - e} \qquad ...(1.10)$$

On comparing the equations 1.8 and 1.10, it is found that there is little difference between mixing ratio and specific humidity, that is why sometimes mixing ratio is also considered equivalent to specific humidity.

Water vapour in Atmospheric column

The availability of water vapour in static column of atmosphere can be predicted by using the ideal gas law and hydrostatic pressure law. The ideal gas law is described by the formula *i.e.*

$$P = \rho_a R_a T \qquad ...(1.11)$$

and hydrostatic pressure is given by

$$\frac{dp}{dz} = \rho_a \cdot g \qquad ...(1.12)$$

Variations in air temperature with altitude is given as

$$\frac{dT}{dz} = -\alpha \qquad ...(1.13)$$

where ρ_a is the air density, R_a is the gas constant given by the equation, $R_a = R_d (1 + 0.608\, q_v)$ or $287 (1 + 0.608\, q_v)$ J/kg.K. R_a of moist air increases with specific humidity. T is the temperature (°C), p is the vapour pressure, S is the altitude and α is the lapse rate.

Substituting the value of ρ_a as $\frac{p}{R_a T}$ in the equation 1.12, we have

$$\frac{dp}{dz} = -\frac{p \cdot g}{R_a T}$$

or
$$\frac{dp}{p} = \left(-\frac{g}{R_a T}\right) \cdot dz$$

Putting the value of dz as $-\frac{dT}{\alpha}$ (from equation 1.13)

$$\frac{dp}{p} = \left(\frac{g}{\alpha R_a}\right)\frac{dT}{T} \quad \text{...(1.14)}$$

Integrating equation 1.14 with the limits p_1 to p_2 and T_1 to T_2 (Figure 1.4), we have

$$\int_{p_1}^{p_2} \frac{1}{p}\, dp = \frac{g}{\alpha R_a} \int_{T_1}^{T_2} \frac{1}{T}\, dT$$

$$[Ln\,(p)]_{p_1}^{p_2} = \frac{g}{\alpha R_a}\, [Ln\,(T)]_{T_1}^{T_2}$$

$$Ln\left(\frac{p_2}{p_1}\right) = \frac{g}{\alpha R_a}\, Ln\left(\frac{T_2}{T_1}\right)$$

or
$$p_2 = p_1 \left(\frac{T_2}{T_1}\right)^{g/\alpha R_a} \quad \text{...(1.15)}$$

Similarly, variations in temperature between Z_1 Z_2 is given by

$$\int_{T_1}^{T_2} dT = -\alpha \int_{z_1}^{z_2} dz$$

$$\left(T\right)_{T_1}^{T_2} = -\alpha \left(z\right)_{z_1}^{z_2}$$

$$(T_2 - T_1) = \alpha\,(Z_1 - Z_2)$$

or
$$T_2 = T_1 - \alpha\,(Z_1 - Z_2)$$

$$= T_1 - \alpha\,(Z_2 - Z_1) \quad \text{...(1.16)}$$

History of Indian Rainfall Data

In India, the measurement of rainfall was started in the eighteenth century. The first recorded rainfall data was obtained from Kolkata in the year 1784 followed by Madras, Bombay and Shimla in the years 1792, 1823 and 1840 respectively. The establishment of Indian Meteorological Department, Pune was made in 1875. In the year 1930, the government of India empowered the IMD to have overall control of rainfall registration. Under resolution, the state governments were assigned the responsibility to collect the rainfall data at different locations and their publication under technical guidance/control of IMD.

According to the surrey (1987) in India 5472 raingauge stations have been established, out of which 561 raingauge stations are operated under the control of IMD. Rests are under state government control. According to this database, the raingauge density of India is about 1 station per 600 km^2 area. In addition to the above raingauge stations, about 4650 other stations have also been established which are managed by different departments such as Railways, Irrigation, Civil aviation, Public Works Department, Agriculture, Forest Departments etc. The rainfall data generated by these departments are not published and also not easily available to the person concerned for any kind of hydrological analysis.

Furthermore, in India there are more than 522 self-recording type raingauge stations, in which about 323 stations are under control of IMD. The available network of recording type raingauge station is about 50% less to the recommended number of WMO.

Characteristics of Indian Precipitation

Indian sub-continent includes two major seasons and two transitional periods. These are as under :

1. South-west monsoon season (October to November)
2. Transition-I, post-monsoon (June to September)
3. Winter season (December to February) and
4. Transition-II, Summer (March to May)

South-west Monsoon : Its characteristics are as under :

1. It is from June to September.
2. It is popularly known as monsoon or rainy season of India.
3. In this season about 75% of the annual rainfall is received over major parts of the country.
4. Its source is Indian ocean.
5. Onset of monsoon is generally accompanied with high south westerly winds blowing at the speed of 30 to 70 kmph.
6. The monsoon winds advance across the country into Arabian sea branch and Bay of Bengal branch. In which, the Arabian sea branch setsin at the extreme southern part of the Kerala, and the Bay of Bengal branch covers the north-eastern regions first and thereafter turns westwards to cover the states of Bihar and U.P. The other states such as Karnataka, Gujrat and Maharastra also receive the monsoon by Arabian-sea branch. In Delhi, monsoon is received by both the branches during 4th week of the June.
7. During south-west monsoon, a monsoon trough (low-pressure region) is developed between the two branches, which is extended from Bay of Bengal to Rajasthan.
8. Precipitation pattern of India is generally governed by the monsoon.
9. During this season, the monsoon winds become stronger from June to July and get weaken in the month of September.
10. It ends in the month of September with substantial rainfall in northern parts of country.
11. During monsoon, the rainfall is not in continuous; however with frequent spell. And weather is cloudy.

Post-monsoon season : Its various features are as under :

1. Its time span is from October to November.
2. It starts after end of the south-west monsoon.
3. It is resulted due to formation of low pressure areas in the Bay of Bengal, from where the north-easterly wind picks up moisture. The formed air-mass, strikes the east-coast of southern peninsula (*i.e.* Tamilnadu) and releases the rainfall there.
4. During this period, especially in the month of November, the formations of tropical cyclones also happen in Bay of Bengal and Arabian sea, which strike the coastal areas and generate intense rainfall.

Winter season : It includes following features :

1. It extends from December to February.
2. Precipitation happens due to western-disturbance (*i.e.* extra tropical wind travelling across Afghanistan and Pakistan).
3. During this period, there happens moderate to heavy rainfall over Himalaya and J. & K. Occasionally, snowfall is also there.
4. Light rainfall also takes place in the northern plains during this period.
5. Low pressure areas are also formed in Bay of Bengal, which produce the rainfall (10 to 12 cm) in southern Tamilnadu.

Summer : Its features are as under :

1. It is also known as premonsoon.
2. Its time span is from March to May.
3. During this period, there is very little rainfall in the country.
4. In Kerala, West Bengal and Assam convective cells cause thunder storm during summer.
5. In east-coast areas, the cyclones are also formed and cause rainfall.

Annual Rainfall of India

Average annual rainfall of India is 1190 mm. However, there is considerable variation within the country, *e.g.* 2000 mm in Assam and north-eastern parts and western-ghats; scanty rainfall in eastern Rajasthan, Maharastra, Karnataka and few parts of Gujrat. The coefficient of variation (C_v) of annual rainfall of the country varies from 15 to 70%. Least variation in annual rainfall is found in the regions of high rainfall areas, while greater variation in the annual rainfall is in the areas of scanty rainfall *i.e.* Punjab, Gujarat, Haryana, and Rajasthan.

SOLVED PROBLEMS

Problem 1.1. At a weather station of Bihar on a day the pressure was measured as 100 kPa, air temperature as 21°C and wet-bulb or dew point temperature as 16.5°C. Determine the corresponding

1. vapour pressure
2. relative humidity ; and
3. sp. humidity

Solution. Given that,

(*a*) air pressure = 100 kpa

(*b*) air temperature = 21°C

(*c*) wet-bulb or dew point temperature = 16.5°C

Computation

(*i*) Saturated vapour pressure at 16.5°C is given by the relationship

$$e_s = 611 \exp\left(\frac{17.27\,T}{237.3 + T}\right)$$

(inwhich e_s is in pascal and T is in °C)

$$= 611 \exp\left(\frac{17.27 \times 21}{237.3 + 21}\right) = \mathbf{2487.66\ Pa} \quad \textbf{Ans.}$$

(*ii*) Relative humidity (R_h) :

$$R_h = \frac{e}{e_s}$$

inwhich e is the actual vapour pressure, is given by

$$e = 611 \exp\left(\frac{17.27\,T_d}{237.3 + T_d}\right)$$

(T_d is the dew point temperature)

$$= 611 \exp\left(\frac{17.27 \times 16.5}{237.3 + 16.5}\right) = \mathbf{1878.25\ Pa} \quad \textbf{Ans.}$$

Therefore $$R_h = \frac{e}{e_s} = \frac{1878.25}{2487.66} = 0.76$$

or **76% Ans.**

(*iii*) Specific humidity (q_v) :

$$q_v = 0.622\,\frac{e}{p}$$

(in which p is the air pressure)

$$q_v = 0.622 \times \frac{1878.25}{100 \times 1000}$$

$$= \mathbf{0.012}\ \text{Kg water/kg moist air} \quad \textbf{Ans.}$$

Problem 1.2. At a particular meteorological station, on a given date the air pressure, air temperature and wet bulb or dew point temperature are recorded as 75 KPa, 20°C and 15°C, respectively. Calculate the saturated vapour pressure

Solution. Using the formula

$$e_s = 611 \exp\left(\frac{17.27\,T}{237.3 + T}\right)$$

Substituting the value of T as 20°C (air temperature), we have

$$e_s = 611 \exp\left(\frac{17.27 \times 20}{237.3 + 20}\right)$$

$$= 2339\ Pa = \mathbf{2.339\ kPa} \quad \textbf{Ans.}$$

Problem 1.3. Using the data of problem 1.2, determine the actual vapour pressure of the prescribed place.

Solution. Using the formula

$$e = 611 \exp\left(\frac{17.27\, T_d}{237.3 + T_d}\right)$$

Substituting the value of T_d as 15°C (dew point temperature), we have

$$e = 611 \exp\left(\frac{17.27 \times 15}{237.3 + 15}\right)$$

$$= 611 \exp(1.02675) = 1706\ Pa = \mathbf{1.71\ kPa} \quad \textbf{Ans.}$$

Problem 1.4. Based on the data of the problem 1.2, compute the value of relative humidety of the prescribed place.

Solution. Using the formula

$$R_h = \frac{e}{e_s} \times 100 = \frac{1.706}{2.339} \times 100 = \mathbf{72.94\%} \quad \textbf{Ans.}$$

Problem 1.5. Calculate the specific humidity from the data given in problem 1.2.

Solution. Using the formula

$$q_v = 0.622 \frac{e}{p} = \frac{0.622 \times 1706}{75 \times 10^3}$$

$$= \mathbf{0.014\ kg\ water/kg\ of\ moist\ air} \quad \textbf{Ans.}$$

Problem 1.6. A thunder storm of 5.5 km diameter contains 1.2 km cloud base. If the air temperature is 25°C, pressure 100 kPa, wind velocity 1.5 m/s, average sp. humidity at top 0.0002 Kg/Kg, average air density 1.07 Kg/m^3 and average sp. humidity at base of cloud is 0.022 kg/kg, compute the intensity of precipitation likely to be occured from the thunderstorm. Assume the wind speed as 1.5 m/s.

Solution. Using the formula

Intensity of precipitation from thunderstorm cell :

$$i = \frac{4\, \rho_a \cdot V \cdot \Delta Z}{\rho_w \cdot D}\left(\frac{q_1 - q_2}{1 - q_2}\right)$$

in which

ρ_a (average air density)	= 1.07 kg/m^3
V (wind velocity)	= 1.5 m/s
ΔZ (cloud height)	= 1.2 km = 1200 m
ρ_w (density of water)	= 1000
D (dia of thunderstorm)	= 5500 m
q_1 (sp. humidity at base)	= 0.022 kg/kg
q_2 (sp. humidity at top)	= 0.0002 kg/kg

Therefore, we have

$$i = \frac{4 \times 1.07 \times 1.5 \times 1200}{100 \times 5500}\left(\frac{0.022 - 0.0002}{1 - 0.0002}\right) \text{m/s}$$

$$= 3.05 \times 10^{-4} \text{ m/s} = \mathbf{0.0305 \text{ cm/s}} \quad \textbf{Ans.}$$

Problem 1.7. Compute the mass flow rate of the precipitation from thunderstorm. Use the data of problem 1.6.

Solution. Using the formula,

$$m_p = \rho_w \, i \cdot A$$

in which, $\rho_w = 1000$

$$i = 0.0305 \text{ cm/s or } 3.05 \times 10^{-4} \text{ m/s}$$

$$A = \frac{\pi}{4} D^2 = \frac{\pi}{4}(5500)^2 = 2.376 \times 10^7 \text{ m}^2$$

Therefore, the mass of flow rate of precipitation (m_p) :

$$= 1000 \times 3.05 \times 10^{-4} \times 2.376 \times 10^7 \text{ kg/s}$$

$$= \mathbf{7.246 \times 10^6 \text{ kg/s}} \quad \textbf{Ans.}$$

Problem 1.8. Determine the mass flow rate of incoming moisture in the thunderstorm. Consider the data of problem 1.6.

Solution. Using the formula,

$$M_{v1} = \rho_a \cdot q_1 \cdot V \cdot \Delta Z \cdot \pi \cdot D$$

In which

$$\rho_a = 1.07 \text{ kg/m}^3,\ q_1 = 0.022 \text{ kg/kg},\ V = 1.5 \text{ m/s},\ \Delta Z = 1200 \text{ m}$$

and $D = 5500$ m

Therefore,

$$M_{v1} = 1.07 \times 0.022 \times 1.5 \times 1200 \times \pi \times 5500 \text{ kg/s}$$

$$= \mathbf{7.32 \times 10^5 \text{ kg/s}} \quad \textbf{Ans.}$$

Important Points

1. Scientific hydrology is concerned on acedemic aspects.
2. Engineering or applied hydrology is concerned with the enineering applications.
3. Hydrologic cycle is activated by solar energy.
4. Hydrologic cycle is the unending water circulation cycle in the atmosphere - earth continuoum.
5. Ocean is considered as the starting point of the hydrologic cycle.
6. Humidity is the measure of atmospheric moisture content.
7. Watershed is considered as the hydrologic system.
8. Of the total estimated world water, the contribution of oceans is 96.5%.
9. Availability of fresh ground water in the world is 0.76% of the total water.

10. Of the total estimated world water, the contribution of atmospher is 0.001%.
11. Total available fresh water on the earth is 2.5% of the total estimated world water.
12. Total precipitation over occans is 1270 mm/y.
13. Total precipitation over land is 800 mm/y.
14. Average annual evaporation from oceans (world level) is 1400 mm.
15. Average annual evaporation from land surface (world level) is 484 mm.

Bibiliography

1. Biswas A.K. History of Hydrology, North-Holland Publishing Co. Amslerdam. (1970)
2. Chow, V.T. Handbook of Applied Hydrology, McGraw-Hill, New York. (1964)
3. Dooge J.C.I. The Hydrologic cycle as a closed system, IAHS Bull. Vol. 13(1). (1968)
4. Eagleson, P.S. Dynamic Hydrology, McGraw Hill, New York. (1970)
5. Gray D.M. Principles of Hydrology, Water Information centre, New York. (1970)
6. Linsley, R.K. M.A. Kohler and J.L.H. Paulhus, Hydrology for Engineers, McGraw-Hill, New York. (1982)
7. Shaw E.M. Hydrology in Practice, Van Nostrand Reinhold (UK) England. (1983)
8. Subramanya. K. Engineering Hydrology, Tata McGraw-Hill Publishing company Ltd., New Delhi (1995)
9. UNESCO, studies and reports in Hydrology, Paris. (1978)
10. Van der Leeden Water Resource of the world, Water Information Centre, New York. (1975)
11. Wiesner, C.J. Hydrometeorology, Chapman and Hall, London. (1970)

DESCRIPTIVE TYPE QUESTIONS

1. Define hydrology and explain its importance and various scopes.
2. What is the hydrologic cycle; describe its different phases
3. Describe the divisions of hydrology
4. Explain that the hydrologic cycle is an unending process.
5. What are the types of hydrologic data, explain the field data.
6. Explain measurement techniques of atmospheric moisture.
7. Define relative humidity and write various factors affecting it.

OBJECTIVE TYPE QUESTIONS

TRUE/FALSE

1. The word "hydrology" is derived from Greek word hydor and logos. (T/F)
2. Hydrology represents the meaning of 'science of water'. (T/F)
3. Engineering hydrology deals that part of hydrology which is related to design and operation of engineering projects etc. (T/F)
4. Hydrology facilitates the flood forecasting. (T/F)
5. Geology is the science which studies about sub-surface water. (T/F)
6. The science which studies about surface streams is called potamology. (T/F)

7. Liminology studies about surface lakes. (T/F)
8. About 97% of total available water in the oceans is saline water. (T/F)
9. The hydrologic cycle is accomplished under the phases of evaporation & transpiration, precipitation and runoff. (T/F)
10. Relative humidity of a place is maximum during evening and minimum during early morning. (T/F)
11. Absolute and specific humidities are the same at constant temperature. (T/F)
12. Dew point is the temperature at which saturation vapour pressure is equal to the existing vapour pressure. (T/F)
13. Mixing ratio and specific humidity are the same. (T/F)

MULTIPLE CHOICE

1. Of the total global water, the Fresh water in lakes is about
   (*a*) 0.26% (*b*) 0.5%
   (*c*) 15% (*d*) 5 to 12%
2. Evaporation from land surface is about
   (*a*) 7.5×10^2 mm/year (*b*) 8.0×10^2 mm/year
   (*c*) 15810^3 mm/year (*d*) 9 cm/mm
3. Evaporation from sea is about
   (*a*) 10.5×10^2 mm/year (*b*) 9.4×10^2 mm/year
   (*c*) 5.5×1^2 mm/year (*d*) 3.5 cm/min
4. Precipitation on sea surface is about
   (*a*) 8.7×10^2 mm/year (*b*) 5.5×10^3 mm/year
   (*c*) 10.5×10^3 mm/year (*d*) 1.5×10^2 mm/year
5. Total sea area is about
   (*a*) 3.74×10^8 km^2 (*b*) 5000 km^2
   (*c*) 10.5×10^5 km^2 (*d*) 1000 km^2
6. Water potential of Narmada basin is about
   (*a*) 40,088 mm^3 (*b*) 10,000 mm^3
   (*c*) 45,005 mm^3 (*d*) 100 cm^2
7. Atmospheric pressure is
   (*a*) 100 times of vapour pressure
   (*b*) 10 times of vapour pressure
   (*c*) 75 times of vapour pressure.
   (*d*) 5 times of sea pressure
8. Rainfall intensity is the ratio of
   (*a*) effective rainfall to ϕ-index
   (*b*) rainfall depth to return period
   (*c*) rainfall depth to storm duration
   (*d*) return period to length of record

Answer (Multiple Choice)

1. (*a*)	**2.** (*a*)	**3.** (*b*)	**4.** (*a*)
5. (*a*)	**6.** (*a*)	**7.** (*a*)	**8.** (*c*)

2

Precipitation and its Occurrence

Precipitation

It is general form of atmospheric water, which emanates from the cloud and ultimately falls over the land surface. In other words, precipitation may be defined as the falling of water from the atmosphere in form of rain, snow, mist etc. on the earth, useful for human beings. It is measured in form of depth occurred on a horizontal land surface. Amount of precipitation occured during a particular day, month or year is designated as daily, monthly or yearly rainfall, respectively. The phenomena from cloud formation to its occurrence on the ground is counted under meterology and the phenomena after reaching the precipitation to the ground is tackled by the hydrology. In other way the meteorology deals the phenomena from occurrence of precipitation till its reaching over the ground surface and hydrology deals the phenomena after reaching of precipitation over the ground surface.

2.1. Forms of Precipitation

Based on the state, the precipitations are classified in following two forms :

1. Liquid precipitation ; and 2. Solid state precipitation.

The other forms of precipitation under above two are described as under :

Liquid precipitation : It refers to the rainfall, which is a most important form of precipitation regarding agricultural concern. In rain, the size of water droplets is more than 0.50 mm diameter and goes maximum up to 6 mm. Based on intensity, the rains are classified into following three forms :

1. **Light rain :** Its falling rate is up to 2.5 mm/h
2. **Moderate rain :** Intensity ranges from 2.5 to 7.5 mm/h
3. **Heavy rain :** Involves the intensity greater than 7.5 mm/h

Drizzle : It is also a liquid form of precipitation, in which size of water droplet is less than 0.5 mm diameter and intensity is also less than 1 mm/h. Generally, drizzles appear in floating form in the air.

Solid state precipitation : It is also known as frozen precipitation, generally found in following forms :

1. **Glaze :** It is a kind of frozen precipitation which is generally formed when drizzles or rain drops come in contact with the cold objects lying over the ground surface and get freezed, there. Glaze is found inform of coating of frozen water over the cold objects on ground surface.

2. **Sleet :** Sleet is the frozen rain drop, which is likely to form when rain drops are falling through the medium at sub-freezing temperature.

3. **Snow :** It occurs in irregular form of ice crystal, such as branched, hexagonal, stars etc. The snow falls either separately or in combination. Cluster of snow is called snow flake.

4. **Snow flake :** It is the ice crystal fused together during snow fall.

5. **Hail** : It is the small lump of ice, ranging from 5 to 10 mm or more in diameter. Hails are generally formed by alternate freezing and melting process, when ice lumpes are falling down by rapidly blowing turbulent air currents.

6. **Dew :** It is condensed moisture on the cold objects.

7. **Frost :** It is feathering deposit of ice, formed by dew or water vapour, that has been frozen on the ground or on the other surface objects.

8. **Fog :** A thin form of cloud of varying density, formed near the earth surface by condensation of atmospheric moisture is defined as the fog.

9. **Mist :** It is the thin fog.

2.2. Types of Precipitation

Cloud is the source of precipitation which is formed due to adiabadic cooling of upward lifted warm air masses. Lifting of air masse takes place by several ways, such as convection, orographic effect and by fronts. Accordingly, the precipitations are classified as :

1. Convective precipitation,
2. Orographic precipitation
3. Frontal precipitation, and
4. Cyclonic precipitation.

These are described as under :

Convective precipitation : In this type of precipitation, the lifting of air mass is done by convection process. The solar energy is the main source of supplying heat for development of convective currents in the air. This precipitation takes place in warm weather condition, under intense heating of earth surface and abundant supply of moisture to the air to create sufficient relative humidity.

The convective precipitation is accompanied by thunder-lighting along with local winds and in the form of rainfall. Sometimes, hails are also appeared in this type of precipitation.

Since this precipitation is resulted due to continuous heating of earth surface, therefore most favourable condition for its occurrence is found in summer season of the year. In brief, the convective precipitation can be characterized by the following points :

1. It occurs in hot weather condition.
2. Occurs in temperate zones at low latitudes.
3. It takes place for a short duration with intense rainfall.
4. Comulo-nimbus clouds are the source of this type of precipitation.
5. It is a peculier type precipitation in which sufficient amount of precipitation can be resulted from a little cloud.
6. It covers small area etc.

Orographic precipitation : It occurs due to lifting of moisture ladden air mass along the orographic plane and cooling of the same adiabadically to form cloud. The orographic precipitation depends on the elevation and rate of rise of air mass. This type of precipitation comprises following two parts.

1. Wind ward orographic precipitation, and
2. Leeward orographic precipitation.

The side of orographic plane, from where air masses are lifting is known as wind-ward side and occurring precipitation towards this side is called wind ward precipitation. This precipitation is intense in nature and sometimes also accompanied by snow fall.

The leeward side is the opposite of wind ward side. In this zone, rainfall amount is comparitively less to that of the windward side. The leeward orographic precipitation is also known as rain-shadow. Orographic precipitation is shown in figure 2.1

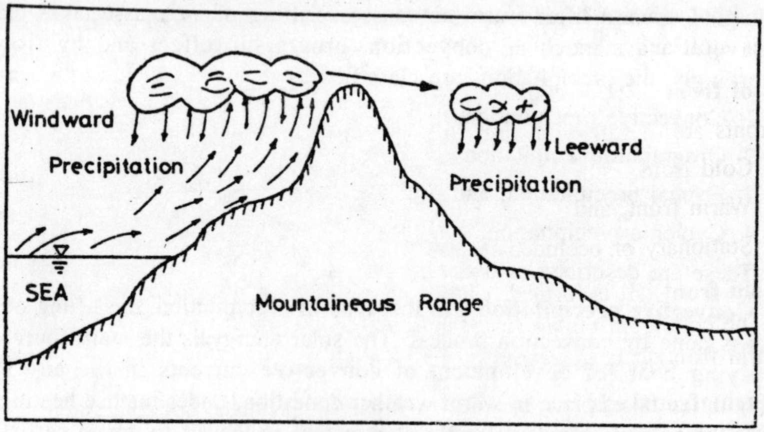

Fig. 2.1. Orographic Precipitation.

Difference between Orographic and Convective Precipitation

Orographic precipitation	Convective precipitation
1. It is function of elevation and rate of lifting of moist air.	1. It occurs in the afternoon or early evening of the day.
2. It has wide head as compared to the convective precipitation.	2. It covers smaller area.
3. Precipitation is not intensive type.	3. It has high rainfall intensity.
4. Duration prolongs as long as lifting of moisture is continued.	4. It is usually a design storm for smaller watersheds.

Frontal precipitation

This type of precipitation occurs, when lifting of air mass is carried out by fronts which is formed between two different kinds of air masses (*i.e.* warm and cold air). The frontal precipitation is usually in drizzle form. It occurs mainly in temperate regions. In brief, this precipitation can be characterized by the following two main points.

1. It is resulted from cauliflower shaped clouds of grey colour.
2. Precipitation is steady for long duration.

To have detail knowledge about frontal precipitation, it is very essential to know about the front which is described as under.

2.2.1. Front

It is an imaginary boundary line formed between two adjacent air masses with dissimilar temperature and moisture content. Frontal surfaces are actually layers or transition zones. Thickness of front is small as compared to the air masses. The line of intersection of frontal surface with the earth is called surface front. An upper-air front is formed by the intersection of two frontal surfaces aloft and mark a boundary between the air masses.

Types of front

Fronts are of following three types :

1. Cold front
2. Warm front, and
3. Stationary or occluded front.

Cold front : It is formed, when cold air mass pushes the warm air mass back. The cold front moves faster than the warm front and usually overtakes the warm front. It is expressed by the symbol, as shown in Fig. 2.2 (*a*).

Warm front : If the air masses are moving such that, the warm air displaces the cold air ; at this situation the formed front is called warm front. It is expressed by the symbol as shown in Fig. 2.2 (*b*).

(a) (b) (c)

Fig. 2.2. Types of Front.

Stationary front : If the cold air mass pushes the warm air mass under and there is the formation of front which does not move from its place is called stationary front. It is expressed by the combine symbol of cold and warm fronts, as shown in Fig. 2.2 (c).

Since, the cold front moves faster than the warm front and overtakes the warm front, therefore at this condition, the frontal surfaces of both fronts slide on each other. This action is called occlusion and resulting front due to this action is known as occluded front. When cold air replaces the warm air, then centre is filled and occlusion is destroyed. Generally, occlusion completes in 3 to 4 days from the time of wave initiation.

Types of Frontal Precipitation

The frontal precipitations are found in following three types :

1. Warm - front precipitation
2. Cold - front precipitation, and
3. Non - frontal precipitation.

Warm front precipitation : This type of precipitation takes place, when warm air mass moves gradually upward over a wedge of cold air mass *i.e.* warm air replaces the cold air. This precipitation generally occurs with light to moderate intensity on larger area than the cold front precipitation. It is generally extended up to 500 km ahead of surface of the front.

Cold-front precipitation : It takes place, when warm air masses are forced upward by an advancing wedge of cold air mass. Nature of this precipitation is generally showery and occurs adjacent to the area of surface front. It is extended up to 150 km or more from the frontal surface. The cold front precipitation consists of relatively narrow band of bad weather and passes quickly, because cold front moves at faster speed than the warm front.

Non-frontal precipitation : This type of precipitation is resulted due to lifting of air masses by any kind of barometric depression. Especially, when moving cold air mass strikes the stationary warm air-mass, the warm air is lifted upward over the cold air. At higher altitude, which (*i.e.* warm air) gets condensed and results precipitation, is called non-frontal precipitation. Various types of frontal precipitation are shown in Fig. 2.3.

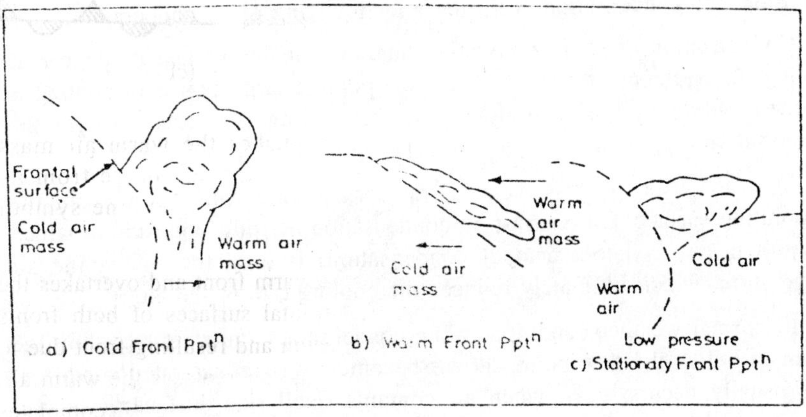

Fig. 2.3. Types of Frontal Precipitation.

Cyclonic precipitation

This precipitation is resulted by mechanical lifting of warm air mass due to pressure difference caused by unequal heating of earth surface. Movement of warm air takes place from the high pressure region to low pressure region.

Basically, there are two types of cyclones, *i.e.*

1. Tropical cyclone, and
2. Extra-tropical cyclone.

Tropical cyclone is also known by the name of hurrican or sometimes typhone, also. Its diameter is comparitively small, ranging from 300 to 1500 km. It is accompained with high wind velocity and intense storm.

The extra - tropical cyclone covers large diameter, which is up to 3000 km. It causes frontal precipitation.

2.3. Occurrence of Precipitaion

In atmosphere, the water vapours are found in varying amounts at all times and altitudes. However, it is less at lower altitudes. It is estimated that, about half of the total moisture is found below the altitude of 2000 m. The amount of water vapour hold by the air, varies with the temperature. Warm air contains relatively more amount of moisture as compared to the cold air, without tendency to get condensed. However, if air temperature is lowered, then at a certain point the available moisture tends to condense and forms the cloud, which falls down over the earth surface, as precipitation.

2.3.1. Condensation

It is the process by virtue of which the water vapour changes into liquid form. In condensation process, the air is allowed to cool below dew point, during which the available moisture in the air gets change into liquid form. When dew point falls below the freezing point (*i.e.* 0°C), then water vapours are directly converted into ice form by sublimation process. Under this condition, the condensation is started after lowering of its temperature.

Condensation depends on relative humidity of the air and its degree of cooling. In arid zones for reaching at dew point, a large degree of cooling is required, while in humid regions a lesser cooling is needed to start the condensation.

In evaporation process, heat is transformed into work for cooling the evaporating surface. On contrast, in condensation it is just opposite, in which released heat (*i.e* latent heat of condensation) is used for raising the air temperature, which ultimately reduces the cooling rate of the air.

In normal weather condition, when condensation starts after cooling the air much below the dew point, the air becomes in super-saturated condition. This usually occurs, only, when air contains small size dust particles (*i.e.* freezing nuclei).

2.3.2. Cooling Process for Condensation

Coling processess for producing condensation are given as under :

1. By expansion process.
2. Conduction of heat from air to the cold objects.
3. Radiation-cooling process, and
4. Mixing of saturated warm and cold air masses.

All these processes are acting in combination ; and are sub-classified as under :

1. Adiabatic process, and
2. Non-adiabatic process.

Adiabatic process has already been described earlier. In non- adiabatic process, the cooling is performed by the methods of radiation, conduction or mixing the saturated warm air mass to the cold air mass.

In radiation process, the cooling is achieved by making loss of heat through radiation from the warm air mass which results the formation of fogs or clouds in presence of hygroscopic nuclei. The cooling of warm air mass under conduction or advection process happens across the cold surface. During this, when warm air comes in contact with the cold surface, produces dew, frost or fog. It mainly depends on the atmospheric conditions.

The non-adiabatic cooling process has limitation that, it produces only dew, fog or frost, which are incapable of yielding the appreciable amount of precipitation, while in adiabatic cooling process, the warm air mass is lifted upward in the atmosphere, where it is expanded and cooled adiabadieally, and formed the conducive clouds which generate intese rainfall.

2.3.3. Requirements for Condensation

Condensation is the process of changing the water vapours into liquid state, which is ultimately converted in the form of dew, fog, frost or clouds. For condensation, mainly two things are most essential in which one is saturation of air and other is presence of some kinds of surfaces in the atmosphere to provide space for condensation of water vapours. The saturation of air can be brought either by adding the water vapours into the air or by reducing the air temperature. For producing the fog, frost or dew, the presence of solid objects on the ground surface is essential. But incase of cloud formation, for which condensation should be occurred at some height above the earth surface, requires dust, salt, carbon particles etc., called condensation nuclei. These particles are available in the lower zone of atmosphere. Condensation nuclei are also known as hygroscopic nuclei, as they have affinity to absorb the moisture. The hygroscopic nuclei are very powerful for attracting the water vapour, relatively at low humidity of about 75%. At 100% relative humidity, the condensation increases rapidly and water particles gain larger size, which results the formation of cloud in the sky. The clouds are supported by a small wind velocity.

Condensation Nuclei

As per observations and theory, it has been found that the condensation of water vapour into cloud droplets takes place on a certain types of hygroscopic particles, which are called as condensation nuclei. Although in absence of such nuclei, the condensation can also be initiated on certain large ions, but there would be required to have several hundred percent of relative humidity, while in natural air, the degree of super saturation is usually a fraction of one percent. The particles of sea salt and products of fuel combustion are found very active in condensation as these have sulphurous and nitrous acids. The diameter of customary nuclei is generally less than 1 micron. For cloud formation, the number of salt nuclei should be upto 1000 per cm^3. In atmosphere, generally the number of combustion born nuclei is less as compared to the sea salt nuclei. The common condensation nuclei, which are generally found in the sky are given as under :

1. Sea salt : it includes Chlorides of Calcium, Magnecium etc.
2. Sulpher-dioxide (SO_2): it changes into Sulpher trioxide (SO_3) by oxidation process, which again produces Sulphuric-acid when mixed with the water vapour.
3. Oxides of Nitrogen, particularly Nitric acid (NH_3).
4. Artificial hygroscopic nuclei, such as CO_2 and AgI are the most common. These are widely used for weather modification. CO_2 can easily produce the ice crystals at any temperature up to about 0°C in super cooled clouds, while Silver iodide (AgI) has ability to get nucleate at about-4°C.

2.3.4. Cloud

It is visible aggregate of water droplets or ice particles in the sky supported by blowing wind. According to Critchfield, the clouds are the condensed atmospheric moisture, resulted from lifting of warm air masses in the sky.

Clouds are the source of precipitation and also play an important role to control the atmospheric heat, as these are very succeptible to absorb the solar energy. Clouds absorb a part of terristrial radiations and re-radiate them back to the ground surface. Clouds radiate the heat in proporation to their temperature, like a black body. Generally, cloudless days are warmer than the nights, is the example of it. In winter season a thick cloud layer makes the night warmer and cool the day.

Growth of Cloud Droplets

The growth of cloud droplets can be explained based on the following two theories :

1. Theory of physical chemistry : According to this theory, the equilibrium vapour pressure gets reduced when salts or similar substances are available in the water. The reduction in vapour pressure is in following form :

$$\frac{e_1}{e_s} = 1 - CM \qquad ...(2.1)$$

where, e_s = saturation vapour pressure corresponding to pure water

e_1 = equilibrium pressure of molar aqueous salt solution with M moles of solute per litre.

C = factor known as temperature - variable factor. It varies with the characteristics of individual substance.

The above relationship revealed that if vapour condenses on a given condensation nucleus, the M decreases and causes an effect on solute. The solute effect ultimately results into growth of cloud droplets. Generally, when radius of droplets is increased to about 2 microns then effect of solute is negligible.

2. Theory of surface tension : This theory states that, the equilibrium vapour pressure over a curved shape droplet is greater than that which is over a plain surface. The relationship between droplet size and vapour pressure is given as under :

$$\frac{e_2}{e_s} = \left(1 - \frac{K}{r}\right)^{-1} \qquad ...(2.2)$$

where, e_2 = equilibrium vapour pressure over a curved water droplet

K = constant. It varies with temperature.

r = radius of droplet.

The value of K is very small and effect of curvature is generally negligible for the radius of droplet greater than 2 micron. The above two theories indicate that the effects of solute and curvature of the droplet are as consequence when size of cloud droplets is less than 2 microns.

Under normal condition, a nucleus takes few seconds to grow to a droplet size of 10 microns; a few minute to attain the size of 100 microns; 3 hours to reach 1000 microns or 1 mm size and about 24 hours to grow to a small raindrop of 3 mm diameter. When cloud droplets attain the size of 3 mm diameter then condensation becomes incapable to produce raindrops.

2.3.4.1. Cloud Classification

International Cloud Atlas proposed 10 main cloud families, which are again sub-divided into 14 sub-families based on their shape and structure. The main cloud families are listed below according to the altitudes,

1. High cloud (mean height 5 to 13 km)
   (*i*) Cirrus,
   (*ii*) Cirro-cumulus, and
   (*iii*) Cirro-stratus.
2. Middle cloud (mean height 2 to 7 km)
   (*i*) Alto-cumulus,
   (*ii*) Alto-stratus, and
   (*iii*) Nimbo-stratus
3. Low cloud (mean height 1 to 2 km)
   (*i*) Strato cumulus
   (*ii*) Stratus
   (*iii*) Cumulus, and
   (*iv*) Cumulonimbus.

All these clouds are described below :

Cirrus cloud

This types of cloud are lying at the mean height of 5 to 13 km from the earth surface in the sky. They appear in the form of white, narrow bands or white patches. The cirrus clouds contain ice crystals and do not yield precipitation. The shining of sun or moon makes hollow in this cloud. These clouds produce colours at the time of sunset and sun rise, both.

Cirro-cumulus cloud

These clouds are very small in the form of grains, ripple etc and look like small globule or flakes. These are arranged in the line or group. Cirro-cumulus clouds are the combine form of cirrus and cirro-stratus clouds, which are arranged in uniform sequence and make the sky in mackerel form.

Cirro-stratus cloud

These clouds appear at greater height, normally in transparent nature, whitish in colour and milky in appearance. They cover the sky fully or partly and produce the hole around the sun or moon. The cirro-stratus clouds often appear in the form of patches of cirrus or cirro-cumulus clouds. These clouds contain ice crystals.

Alto-cumulus cloud

Such types of cloud are found in white or grey or both white and grey in colours at a time. They produce a dark shadow on the ground surface and do not have halo effect. Alto-cumulus clouds are also known by the name of sheep or wool pack clouds. These appear in the form of patches, sheets or layers and are arranged in parallel or wavy sequence.

Alto-stratus cloud

These clouds are greyish or bluish in colour and are found either in the form of sheet or fiber. They cover the sky partly or fully in thin layer and reveal the sun in hazy outline. In this cloud, the hole around the sun or moon is not seen. The sun or moon appears as a bright spot behind the cloud. Alto-stratus clouds contain water droplets and produce precipitation either in the form of drizzle or snow.

Nimbo-stratus cloud

Nimbo-stratus clouds are found in the layer of grey colour with dark appearance. Such clouds are thick enough throughout their spread area. These are generally low clouds, may be up to 1000 feet height and are capable to result the rain or snow fall. They never accompanied with lighting or thunder hail.

Strato-cumulus cloud

Appear in grey or white or both in grey and white colours at a time ; generally in the form of patches, sheets or layers. These clouds always contain dark portions having tasselations, rounded masses etc. in non-fibrous form.

Stratus cloud

Stratus clouds are generally found in grey colour, and are arranged in the form of layers with uniform base. These clouds result the precipitation in form of drizzle, iceprism or snow grain. These clouds do not have hole effect, except at very low temperature. Sometimes, this cloud also appears like ragged patches. Generally, the thick fogs and stratus clouds are similar to each other and it is very difficult to distinguish them.

Cumulus cloud

These are detached clouds, which appear in the form of sharp outlines. Such clouds generally appear during day time and disappear to the night hours and cause light precipitation.

Cumulo-nimbus cloud

These are heavy and dense clouds, appear in the shape of mountain or huge tower. Base of cloud is very dark and results heavy precipitation, thunder, lighting, hails etc.

Process of Precipitation

The processes through which clouds release the precipitation are mainly following two, *i.e.*

1. Coalescence process, and 2. Ice- crystal process

Coalescence process : Water drops in air are exposed to two forces namely : gravity force and frictional drag force. As soon as these forces are balanced, the water drops gain maximum velocity, called terminal velocity. Which is directly proportional to the square of the radius of water droplets. Due to this fact, a large size rain drop falls at faster speed. The bigger size rain drops collect the smaller droplets on their forward path. Also, a falling rain drop leaves a turbulent wake, behind it, as result smaller droplets also fall at faster speed and overtake the heading droplets. In this way, the larger drops grow due to direct capture of smaller droplets on their forward path and smaller droplets grow due to wake capture of droplets of almost equal size. Experimentally, it has been found that a drop grows to the size of 7 mm in diameter and fall velocity increases maximum upto 10 m/s. At such high velocity, the drops are flatten and break up into several small size droplets called drizzle. These drizzles fall at faster speed than the cloud droplets. It causes repeating of capturing process. In thunder cloud, the water droplets fall and grow, splinter and rise several times, causing into increase in number of droplets, if the chain of process is in operation.

2. **Ice-crystal process :** The water droplets can remain in cloud mass at sub freezing temperature down to about – 40°C. At this temperature, there occurs solidification of freezing nuclei (*i.e.* clay minerals such as kaolin, montmorillonite, illite, pyrite, organic substances and common salts). During solidification, when ice elements are formed in the cooled cloud mass, then there is created imbalance because equilibrium vapour pressure over the water droplets is greater than the ice crystals/elements. This results into evaporation of water droplets and condensation over ice elements. In this way, in cloud mass, some cloud elements are continuously growing and some are shrinking, which cause uneven size distribution of cloud elements within the cloud ; this phenomena again favours for further growth of water droplets through collison and colascence actions.

In warm clouds *i.e.* clouds not at subfreezing temperature, the giant salt nuclei if present, they serve to develop some unusual large size water drops which cause precipitation through fragmentation process.

Formation of Rain

Following four mechanisms are essential for occurrence of rain fall from the cloud mass :

1. Mechanism to produce cooling of the air.
2. Mechanism to produce condensation.
3. Mechanism to produce growth of cloud droplets.
4. Mechanism to cause accumulation of sufficient moisture.

Cooling mechanism : Cooling action lowers the capacity of a given space to contain water vapours. Generally, the cooling of air mass happens under following methods.

(*i*) Adiabatic cooling
(*ii*) Radiational cooling
(*iii*) Cooling by contact with colder objects, and
(*iv*) Mixing of two different air-masses.

Amongst all four cooling methods, the methods from (*ii*) to (*iv*) are not much effective to cause precipitation but able to generate light drizzle or fog. In the first method *i.e.* adiabatic cooling, the cooling of air mass is due to its rising upward as the result of pressure drop in the atmosphere. It is effective mechanism to generate precipitation. The supply rate of vapour content essential for saturation during upward lifting is called the production rate of moisture excess over the saturation. When rate of production of moisture excess with high speed *i.e.* miles per hour at 10,000 to 20,000 ft altitude is equal to the rate of precipitation, then accompanied precipitation is at intense rate.

Condensation mechanism : Condensation takes place on hygroscopic nuclei which are the small particles of substance having affinity for water molecules even at unsaturated condition of air. The sodium chloride and sulphur trioxide substances are best for condensation of water molecules. The size of nuclei varies from 10^{-3} to 10 microns. The number of nuclei varies greatly from region to region, ranging from several millions per cubic cm in heavy polluted industrial air to only a few per cubic cm in mountaneous regions or at high altitudes.

The condensation also occurs very easily on the particles, whose surface has large curvature, because saturation vapour pressure increases as the surface curvature increases. The effect of curvature and hygroscopicity of particle becomes negligible, when size of droplet approaches to 10^{-4} cm. At the size of droplets greater than 10^{-4} cm, the growth of droplets is due to process of molecular diffusion. In diffusion process, the water changes from vapour state in the surrounding air to the liquid state over the droplets.

Growth mechanism : It has been described earlier.

Mechanism of moisture accumulation : For intense precipitation, there must be good amount of moisture content to over compensate the evaporation losses between cloud and ground. In this regard, one important point is that at the begining of rainfall, the amount of water vapour in vertical column of atmosphere should be less as compared to the rainfall amount and at the same time, the amount of water vapour in vertical column over the area of rainfall should either be same or greater during occurrence of rainfall. In this way, there should always sufficient horizontal inflow of water vapours into the atmosphere above rainfall zone. This process is referred as 'convergence', which may be defined as the net horizontal inflow of air mass per unit area.

IMPORTANT TERMS

Monsoon : The wind system with annual oscillations, blowing from oceans to the continents in summer and from continents to the oceans in winter is called monsoon. The oscillations in wind system affect the annual heating and cooling of the underlying surface. Indian monsoon is well known in terms of excessive dryness during winter and excessive rainfall during summer. In South-Asia, the monsoon starts in April or early May in Myanmar (Burma). In central India, the monsoon sweeps within 3-week period in the late May and early June, which is generally accompanied by heavy rain, squalls and occasional violent storms.

Airmass : It is a vast body of air having more or less uniform physical properties ; however there is abrupt change along the border between surrounding air masses. The physical properties of airmass reflect the climate of the region, where air is retained for long duration to acquire quasi-equilibrium with the underlying surface. Such regions are known as air-mass-source region. The followings are the regions, which have their own air-mass-source.

1. Arctic fields of snow and ice areas
2. Sub polar continents
3. Sub tropical ocean areas, and
4. Arid-sub tropical land areas

The moving air masses out of their source region are either cold air mass or warm air mass. A cold-air mass is colder than the surface over which it moves. Simlarly, the warm air-mass is warmer than the surface over which it moves. The cold air mass is often unstable and formed clouds are generally of cumulus family. Occurring precipitations due to cold-air mass are in showery nature. The warm-air mass develops a stable stratification and formed clouds are of stratus family and occurring precipitation is in intense form.

Cyclone : It is a low pressure region with attendant winds. Cyclones are accompanied with extensive cloud and thunder rainfall. The extratropical and tropical cyclones are the forms of cyclone. The extra-tropical cyclones are often used to distinguish the mid-latitude cyclones and the cyclones generated in intertropical regions. Special features of extra tropical cyclones are as under :

1. Tropical air contains large mass of moisture content and produce low stratus or drizzles.
2. Polar air contains vast air mass flowing southwards and produce numerous showers.
3. Polar fronts separate two different kinds of air masses and produce continuous precipitation.

The tropical cyclones are also known as hurricane, typhoon and tropical revolving storm. Hurricane is an extensive cyclone originated from tropics. Its coverage area is relatively small varies from 100 to 300 miles. In India tropical cyclone is called cyclone, and typhoon in the Far East.

Tornado : It is also a kind of cyclone. In north-America, tornadoes are called cyclones. It involves violent whirl of destructive wind and always accompanied with funnel shaped clouds facing down ward. The wind velocity is in excess of 100 mph and diameter varies upto few hundred yards.

Anticyclone : A large area of high pressure with attendant wind is called anticyclone. It is accompanied with fair weather and existing of clouds at low altitude over sea and costal areas. Wind speed is generally moderate, except towards boundary of cyclone.

Air-mass showers : It is the scattered rainfall associated to no synoptic pressure system (*i.e.* low pressure system).

Cloud seeding : It is the process of artificially nucleating of clouds to induce precipitation. Silver Iodide is very common nucleating agent to form cloud in the sky. It is seeded from the air craft during which Silver iodide solution is evaporated with propane flame to generate water particles. The generated particles are ultimately fall over the ground.

Design storm : This storm is required for estimation of design flood which is done by the use of unit hydrograph method. The design storms may the PMP producing storm for determining the PMF or SPS for deriving standard project flood (SPF). There are various methods for analysis of past rainfall data to determine the design flood. A commonly used method is described under following steps :

1. *Select the critical rainfall duration*, which is the basin lag if flood peak is of interest. However, if flood volume is of interest then longest storm duration is selected as critical rainfall duration.
2. *Select past major storms*, which have been occurred in the study area for deriving envelope curve representing the maximum-depth-duration relationship.
3. *Determine rainfall depths* for the convenient time interval — it is performed by using the envelope curve. The commonly used time interval is 6.0 h. Based on scaled rainfall depth, the increments are arranged to determine the critical sequence producing maximum flood peak. In other way, the sequence of incremental precipitation is also arranged in following forms :
   - (*i*) The maximum increment of rainfall and the maximum unit hydrograph ordinate.
   - (*ii*) The next highest rainfall increment and the second largest unit hydrograph ordinate.
   - (*iii*) Last item at first and vice-versa. This new sequence results design storm.
4. The determined design storm is adjusted for lowest initial losses and infiltration rate. It is essential for deriving the effective rainfall hyetograph.

Probable Maximum Precipitation : It is estimated limiting value of precipitation, which is defined as the analytically estimated greatest depth of precipitation for a given duration that is physically possible and reasonably characterized over a particular geographical region at a certain time of the year. PMP is not adjusted for long term effect of climatic change of the region. PMP is not completely reliable because it is probabilistic value, which exact occurrence is unknown.

In case of hydraulic structures, such as spillways, bridges, culverts etc., to keep their failure probability as low as possible or zero, the design is performed on the basis of probable maximum rainfall of the concerned watershed. Hydraulic engineers and Hydrologist consider it very seriously in design of such structures.

The computation of PMP is done based on the following two methods :

1. Meteorological method
2. Statistical study of rainfall data

Under meteorological approach, there are several models have been developed, can be used for estimation of PMP. For this, the reader can refer the reference Weisner C.J. (1970).

The computation of PMP based on statistical study of rainfall data, the following relationship can be used.

$$PMP = \overline{P_{\max}} + K \cdot \sigma \quad ...(2.3)$$

in which, $\overline{P_{\max}}$ is the mean of annual maximum rainfall series, K is the frequency factor which is the function of number of years of rainfall record, return period and statistical distribution of series and σ is the standard deviation of the rainfall series. The value of PMP for North-Indian plains varies from 37 to 100 cm for 1-day rainfall. The Indian Institute of Tropical Meteorology has published PMP atlas for India, which depicts 1-day PMP for different parts of India (Anonymous, 1989).

Excessive Precipitation : U.S. Weather Bureau defined the excessive precipitation as the precipitation which falls at the rate equal to or greater than the rate estimated for the durations of 5, 10, 15, 20, 30, 45, 60, 80, 100, 120, 150 and 180 minutes by the following formula.

$$P = t \div 20 \quad ...(2.4)$$

in which P is the precipitation in hundredth of an inch and t is the time in minutes.

Variability of Precipitation : Precipitation varies temporally and spatially according to the pattern of atmospheric condition and local factors. The long term average of weather variables is called normal value. It may be normal rainfall, normal temperature etc. The temporal variability of precipitation can be expressed in terms of

(*i*) Annual and mean annual precipitation

(*ii*) Seasonal precipitation

(*ii*) Monthly and mean monthly precipitation

(*iv*) Weekly and mean weekly precipitation

(*v*) Daily precipitation.

2.3.5. Precipitable Water

It is the total amount of water contained in a column of atmosphere extending upward from the earth surface.

Let, if the height of atmospheric column is 'Z' with the pressure P_o and p at lower and upper end of the column, respectively (Figure 2.4)

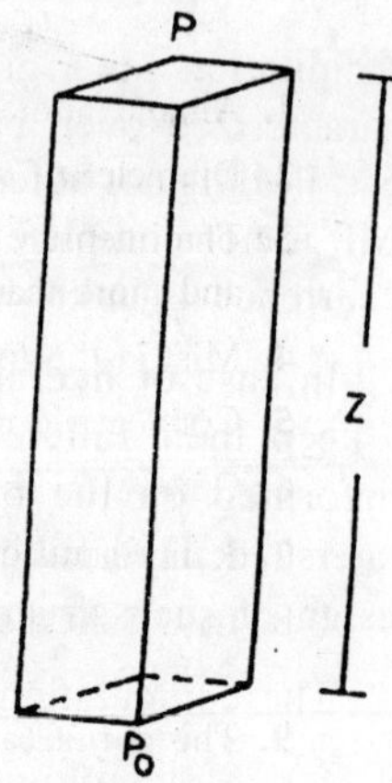

Fig. 2.4

Then, total mass of water in the column is given by

$$W = 1 \cdot Z \cdot \rho_w \quad \text{(for unit cross-sectional area)}$$

or
$$\int_0^z 1 \cdot \rho_w \cdot dz \qquad ...(2.5)$$

We know that, the hydrostatic pressure $(P) = h \cdot \rho \cdot g$ ...(2.6)

Differenciating equation 2.6 with respect to Z,

$$dp = -g \cdot \rho \cdot dz$$

or
$$dz = -\frac{dp}{\rho \cdot g} \qquad ...(2.7)$$

Substituting the value of dz in equation 2.5

$$\int_0^z -\frac{dp}{\rho g}\rho_w \qquad ...(2.8)$$

or
$$W = \int_{p_o}^{p} -\frac{dp}{(\rho_w + \rho_d) \cdot g} \cdot \rho_w \qquad ...(2.9)$$

$$(\rho = \rho_w + \rho_d)$$

in which ρ_d = density of dry gass

and
$$\left(\frac{\rho_w}{\rho_w + \rho_d}\right) = \frac{0.622e}{p}$$

Thus eq. (2.9) becomes as

$$\frac{1}{g}\int_{p_o}^{p} \frac{0.622e}{p} \cdot dp$$

or
$$\mathbf{W = \frac{0.622}{g}\int_{p_o}^{p} \frac{e}{p} \cdot dp} \qquad ...(2.10)$$

IMPORTANT POINTS

1. Annual rainfall of India is 1190 mm.
2. Diameter of water droplets in drizzle is less than 0.5 mm.
3. The intensity of light, moderate and heavy rains is 2.5 mm/h, 2.5 to 7.5 mm/h and more than 7.5 mm/h, respectively.
4. Mist is the form of thin fog.
5. Convective precipitation occurs in hot weather condition.
6. Cumulo-nimbus cloud results convective precipitation.
7. Rainshadow is the leeward orographic precipitation.
8. In U.S.A. the tropical cyclone is called hurricane, and typhon in south-east Asia.
9. The normal areal extent of cyclone is 100 to 200 km diameter.
10. Centre of storm is called 'eye' which diameter varies from 10 to 50 km.
11. Tropical cyclones generate the rainfall for the areal extent of about 10^3 km^2 for several weeks.
12. Areal extent of convective type precipitation is about 10 km diameter.
13. Monson trough is the low pressure region.
14. In India, the south-west monsoon is popularly known as *monsoon*.
15. In India, the south-west monsoon contributes 75% of the total rainfall.
16. The annual rainfall of Assam and North-eastern regions of India is 200 to 400 cm.
17. Annual rainfall of west coast and western ghats of India is 200 to 300 cm.
18. Annual rainfall of west Bengal is 120 to 400 cm.
19. Annual rainfall of U.P., Haryana and Punjab is 100 to 120 cm.
20. The coefficient of variation of annual rainfall of India is from 15 to 70%.

REFERENCES

1. Byers H.R. General Meteorology (3eds), McGraw-Hill Book Co. Inc, New York, 1959.
2. Chow V.T., Handbook of Applied Hydrology, McGraw-Hill, New York, 1964.
3. Das G., Hydrology and Soil Conservation Engineering, Prentice- Hall (India), 2000.
4. Indian Institute of Tropical Meteorology, Probable Maximum Precipitation, Atlas, IITM., Pune (India), 1989.
5. Mason B.J. The physics of clouds, Oxford University Press, London, 1957.
6. Mack Donald J.E. The physics and cloud modification, Advan, in Geophysics, Vol 5, 1958.
7. Pruppacher H.R. and J.D. Klett. Microphysics of cluds and precipitation, 1978.
8. Raudkivi A.J., Hydrology, Pergamon Press, Oxford (London), 1979.
9. Subramanya K., Engineering Hydrology, Tata McGraw-Hill Publishing Co. Ltd., New Delhi, 2000.
10. Weisner C.J. Hydrometeorology, Chapman and Hall, London, 1970.

DESCRIPTIVE TYPE QUESTIONS

1. Define precipitation and explain its mechanism of occurrence
2. List various forms of precipitation and write the difference between rainfall and drizzle.
3. List various types of precipitation and explain orographic precipitation.
4. Write the difference between cold and stationary fronts.
5. Explain cooling process of condensation.
6. Define condensation and list various types of condensation nuclei.
7. Define cloud and explain various types of clouds.
8. Derive the solution to compute precipiatable water.

OBJECTIVE TYPE QUESTIONS

1. The rainfall varies from
   (*a*) 0.50 to 6.0 mm (*b*) 0.50 to 5.5 mm
   (*c*) 0.25 to 6.0 mm. (*d*) 1 to 1.125 mm
2. The drop size of dizzle is
   (*a*) 0.25 mm or less than 0.50 mm
   (*b*) 0.50 mm
   (*c*) 1.0 mm.
   (*d*) less than 0.01 mm
3. Intensity of moderate rain is
   (*a*) 2.5 to 7.5 mm/h (*b*) 2.5 mm/h
   (*c*) more than 7.5 mm/h. (*d*) less than 0.25 mm/h
4. A thin fog is also termed as
   (*a*) dew (*b*) mist
   (*c*) glaze (*d*) sleet
5. The convective precipitation covers
   (*a*) larger area (*b*) small area
   (d) very small area (*d*) about 150 km^2 area
6. Convective precipitation occurs in
   (*a*) cold weather (*b*) warm weather
   (*c*) windy weather (*d*) cloudy weather
7. Leeward orographic precipitation receives
   (*a*) high intensity rainfall (*b*) low intensity rainfall
   (*c*) no rainfall (*d*) 1.25 cm/h rainfall
8. Frontal precipitation occurs for
   (*a*) long duration (*b*) short duration
   (*c*) steady and long duration (*d*) 2 hours
9. Diameter of topical cyclone varies from
   (*a*) 500 to 2000 km (*b*) 500 to 1500 km
   (*c*) 300 to 1500 km (*d*) 50 to 100 km
10. Diameter of extra-tropical cyclone is maximum upto
    (*a*) 2500 km (*b*) 3000 km
    (*c*) 1500 km. (*d*) 750 km

11. The condensation nuclei are
(*a*) rock pieces (*b*) dust particles
(*c*) glass pieces (*d*) warm air

12. The hygroscopic nucleus is
(*a*) CO_2 (*b*) NH_3
(*c*) H_2 (*d*) H_2S

13. The Cirrus clouds are lying at the height of
(*a*) 2 to 7 km (*b*) 5 to 13 km
(*c*) 1 to 2 km (*d*) 1500 m

14. Cumulo nimbus cloud results
(*a*) drizzle (*b*) low rainfall
(*c*) heavy rainfall without lightening
(*d*) hail

15. Alto-startus cloud results.
(*a*) drizzle or snow (*b*) low rainfall
(*c*) heavy rainfall (*d*) sleet

Answer (Objective Type)

1. (*a*) **2.** (*a*) **3.** (*a*) **4.** (*a*) **5.** (*b*) **6.** (*b*) **7.** (*b*) **8.** (*c*)
9. (*a*) **10.** (*a*) **11.** (*b*) **12.** (*b*) **13.** (*b*) **14.** (*d*) **15.** (*a*)

3

Precipitation Measurement and Analysis

Precipitation is measured in terms of depth of water, that accumulates over the land surface during its occurrence. It is generally expressed in millimeter. Measurement of precipitation is performed by using an instrument known as "raingauge". The details of rain gauge, such as its type, installation, optimum number of rain gauges to be required for a watershed etc., are described below.

Measurement : Generally, the measurement of rainfall is performed in terms of depth and intensity for hydrological analysis. These two modes of measurement are described as under :

Rainfall depth : The depth of rainfall is measured in terms of daily, which is converted to monthly, yearly etc. to express temporal distribution of the occurring rainfall. It is expressed in the unit of mm. The commonly used raingauge is non-recording type *i.e.* Symon type ; is considered as standard raingauge for measurement of rainfall. The other raingauge *i.e.* recording type, records the accumulated depth of rainfall over a day while storage raingauge measures the rainfall depth over a week or months.

Rainfall measured by the raingauge denotes the total depth of water that would stand on the soil surface during rainfall, e.g., if by the raingauge 1 cm depth of rainfall is recorded in the area, then it will result $10^6 \times \frac{1}{100}\ m^3 = 10^4\ m^3$ volume of rain water over the surface area of 1 ha land. In snow fall case, the equivalent depth of water that would be made after melting, is considered as the depth of rainfall or precipitation.

Rainfall intensity : It is the falling rate of rainwater over the ground surface, commonly expressed as mm/h. Intensity of occurring rainfall is determined from the mass-curve obtained from the weighing or siphon type raingauge. The slope of mass curve at any time is the rainfall intensity.

Measuring Instruments

3.1. Rain Gauge

It is an instrument, used for measuring the depth of precipitation at a particular point and time falling over the land surface. Raingauges are classified into two following categories :

1. Non-recording type rain gauge, and
2. Recording type rain gauge.

Non-recording type rain gauge

This type of rain gauge records the rainfall depth only and does not indicate the time of rainfall. Observations are taken at the end of 24 hours, mannualy. However in case of heavy rainfall, the observation time can be changed. In this type of rain gauge, the collected rain water in the 'can' is measured with the help of graduated measuring cylinder in terms of volume. The volume of rain water is converted in the form of depth by dividing with the aperture area of the gauge, given as under :

$$\text{Rainfall depth (cm)} = \frac{\text{Volume of collected water (cm}^3\text{)}}{\text{Aperture area of the gauge (cm}^2\text{)}}$$

There are various types of non recording raingauges ; however, Symon's type rain gauge is one of the most popular amongst them and is widely used for measuring the rainfall depth in the watershed.

Symon type rain gauge

It is one of the most common type non-recording raingauge, which consists of a cylindrical vessel of 12.7 cm diameter ; a funnel of exactly 12.7 cm internal diameter and a receiving bottle. At the top of cylindrical vessel, the funnel is kept in such a way that its shank should be above the mouth of receiving bottle. The whole parts are covered with cylindrical metal casing. The capacity of receiving bottle is being sufficient to collect the rainfall amount likely to be occurred during 24 hours period. The gauge is fixed vertically on the masonary foundation, 30.5 cm above the ground surface.

Measuring procedure of rainfall may be described as : when rainfall takes place, the rain drops fall directly in the funnel, from where they are collected into the bottle. The collected water is measured with graduated cylinder. A full receiving bottle indicates 1.25 cm rainfall depth, at a time. Symon type rain gauge is shown in Fig. 3.1.

Demerits

It has following demerits :

(*i*) It does not provide the informations on intensity and duration of rainfall.

(*ii*) It does not indicate the start and end of the rainfall.

(*iii*) The non-recording type rain gauge does not measure the rainfall so accurate that can be compared with the rainfall amounts, measured by the other types of raingauges.

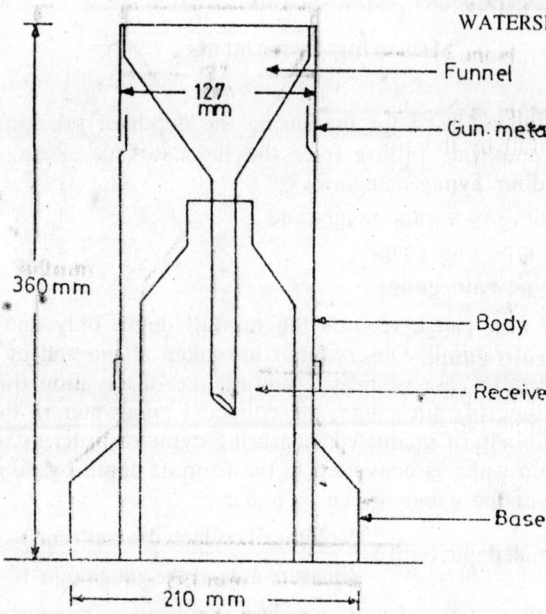

Fig. 3.1. Symon type rain gauge.

Recording type rain gauge

Recording type raingauges are also called as automatic, integrating or self recording rain gauge. These rain gauges record the rainfall amount and duration simultaneously during occurrence. In this raingauge, the collected rainfall is not measured by the graduated cylinder but recorded automatically by a mechanical arrangement provided in the system. A graph paper, known as rain gauge chart is wrapped over a clock-wise rotating drum, on which rainfall depth w.r.t. time is recorded in the form of curve, known as "mass curve." A such raingauge chart showing the mass curve is illustrated in Fig. 3.2. Using mass curve, the following informations can be furnished :

1. Depth of rainfall at any time.
2. Intensity of rainfall at any time during the rainfall.
3. Onset of rainfall, and 4. Cessation of rainfall

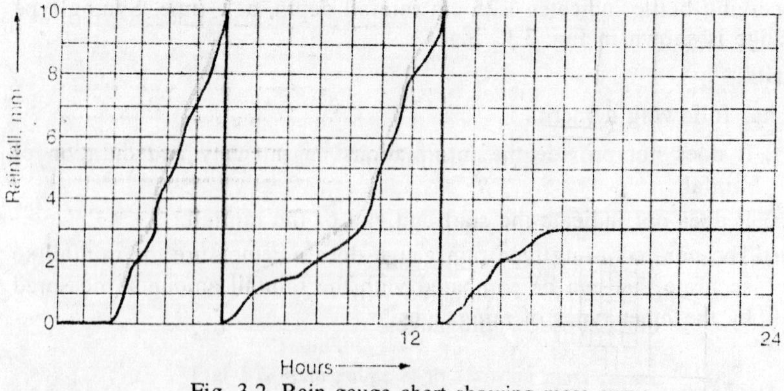

Fig. 3.2. Rain gauge chart showing mass curve.

Since, these raingauge record the cumulative rainfall depth, that is why they are also known by the name of integrating raingauge. Similarly, some times these are also known as continuous rain gauge due to continuous recording of rainfall by them.

Kinds of Recording Type Rain Gauge

Various kinds of recording rain gauge are as follows :

1. Weighing type
2. Tipping bucket type, and
3. Float type

Weighing type rain gauge

It is a common type raingauge for measuring the rainfall and moderate snow fall. The snow fall is measured by collecting the snow in the receiver, which is melted in the gauge itself by a heating device attached to the raingauge or by using some chemicals, such as calcium chloride, ethylene glycol etc. It gives the snowfall depth in terms of equivalent rainfall depth.

Its constructional feature consists of a receiver or bucket kept on the platform equipped with spring or lever balance. The rain water falls into the collector and deposited in the receiver. A recording mechanism is attached to the weighing system, which consists of a recording pen and clockwise rotating drum with raingauge chart.

When rainfall takes place, the rain water is collected into the bucket which depresses the weighing mechanism. At the same time, the depression is transmitted to the recording pen through lever. The pen traces the depression in the form of curve over the chart wrapped on clock-wise rotating drum. In this way, the rainfall measurement is obtained in the form of graph, indicating cumulative rainfall depth with respect to time. Weighing type raingauge is shown in Fig. 3.3.

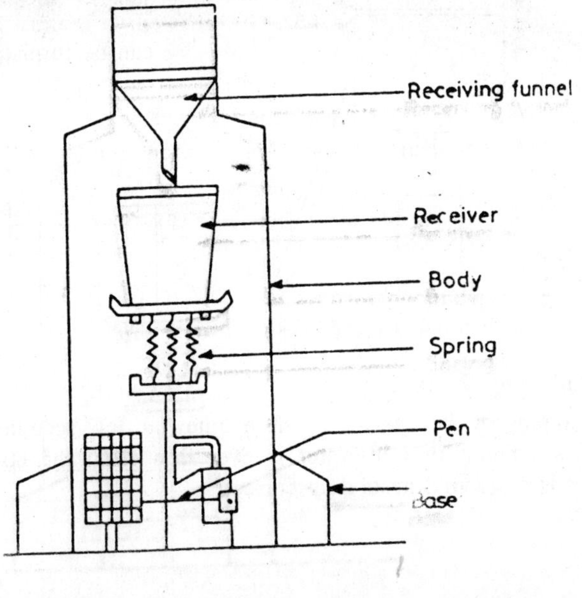

Tipping bucket type raingauge

This is an electrically operated raingauge. It is used for recording the rainfall of remote areas. It consists of 300 mm diameter sharp edged cylindrical receiver with a funnel inside. Below the funnel one pair of bucket is pivoted on fulcrum. The capacity of each bucket is equivalent to 0.25 mm rainfall depth. These buckets are so balanced that, when one bucket is filled with water by its full capacity (*i.e.* 0.25 mm depth), it tips down and empties the water into the storage 'can' placed just below the tipping bucket. And immediately the other bucket takes the position of first bucket. This process is continued during rainfall. During tipping action, there activates electrical current in the system, which causes the movement of pen to trace the mass curve on the raingauge chart, mounted on the clock-wise revolving drum.

The tipping time of bucket mainly depends on the rainfall intensity. For the rainfall intensity ranging from 1.25 to 1.5 cm/h, the tipping action is completed at every 6 to 7 seconds periods. The water collected in storage can is also measured at regular interval for determining the total rainfall amount and to verify the measurement. This rain gauge has limitation that, it can not measure the snow fall. View of rain gauge is shown in Fig. 3.4.

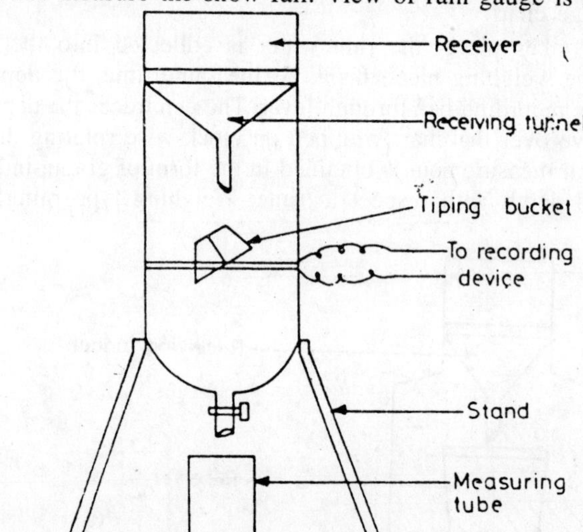

Fig. 3.4. Tipping bucket type rain gauge.

Limitations

It has following limitations :

1. The tipping bucket takes very little time (*i.e.* few seconds) to tip, as the result few amount of rain water is over flew from the bucket, hence measurement is not found absolutely correct.

2. By this rain gauge, it is very difficult to characterize the time of start and end of the rainfall.

3. For measurement of light showers, this raingauge is unsuitable.

4. Due to sophistications in its mechanism, this rain gauge requires a constant servicing at regular interval.

Float type rain gauge

It is also known as syphon type rain gauge; shown in Fig. 3.5. In this rain gauge, a float chamber is provided, which consists of a light hollow float. When rainfall takes place, the rain water falls over 127 mm size funnel, kept over the float chamber, which is ultimately collected in float chamber. The float is attached to the recording mechanism. As volume of rain water increases in the float chamber, the float gets lifted up and at the same time, movement of float is transmitted to the pen by a suitable arrangement. In the system, a clock wise rotating drum is provided, which completes its full rotation in 24 hours duration. Over the drum, a chart is wraped on which pen traces the rainfall amount with respect to the time. When float rises to maximum limit i.e. touches the top of float chamber, the collected water in float chamber is drained automatically through a syphoning arrangement. And float takes its initial position *i.e.* reaches at bottom of the chamber. Again, if rain is continued, the float rises up and recording work is continued, accordingly. Plotting of rainfall *i.e.* mass curve is shown in Fig. 3.2, in which vertical line indicates the syphoning of water from float chamber, while horizontal line indicates no rain fall.

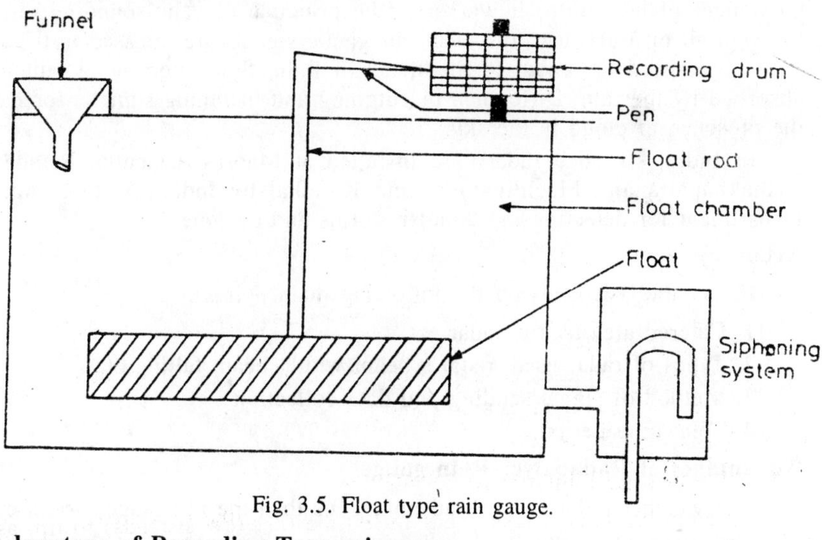

Fig. 3.5. Float type rain gauge.

Advantage of Recording Type raingauge

1. It provides a detail information about rainfall, such as rainfall depth with respect to time (*i.e.* rainfall intensity) etc.

2. As it automatically records the rainfall amount with respect to time, so there is no need to engage any attendant for recording the measurement.

3. Error in the rainfall data due to man mistakes is completely eliminated.

4. Recording type raingauge is the only means to record the rainfall data in remote areas.

5. It provides the informations on start and cessation of rainfall.

6. It records the rainfall measurement in form of graph, which can be used as permanent source for analysis of storm.

7. Measuring capacity of recording type rain gauge is comparitively more to that of the non-recording rain gauge.

8. Duration of rainfall is also recorded.

9. Provides more authentic measurement as compared to the non-recording type rain gauge.

Disadvantage

Apart from several advantages, it also has some disadvantages :

1. Its cost is very high to that of the non-recording type gauge.

2. It requires a regular servicing for its proper working.

3. Its maintanance cost is comparitively high.

4. More precautions are required to operate this gauge.

5. Recording of the rainfall may be interrupted due to mechanical faults incurred in the gauge.

3.2. Rainfall Measurement by Weather Radar

Radar is used for assessing the magnitude, areal extent, orientation and movement of the storm. It works on the principle of echo-sounding effect. For rainfall measurement, the electromagnetic signals are released in the sky with high speed i.e. equal to the speed of light. Some portion of which is absorbed by the rain. Difference in outgoing and incoming signals, forecasts the presence of cloud in the sky.

In India, six such radars are installed at Madras, Calcutta, Paradeep, Vishakhapattanam, Machlipatnam and Karaikal by Indian Meteorological Department for detecting the thunder storms and cyclones.

Accuracy

Its accuracy depends on the following main points :

1. Catered area by the radar.

2. Types of radar used, radar's beam width, beam falling etc.

3. Method of signal sending and data collection

4. Total time period.

Advantages of Radar over Rain gauge

The weather radar is more advantageous than the raingauge, because :

1. It gives 24-h rainfall intensity, which is not possible by the rain gauge.

2. It is adopted for taking rainfall measurements for large and inaccessible catchment areas. Generally, one radar is capable for collecting the

informations up to 100 km distance, while for covering such large area about 100 raingauges would be required.

3. Radar provides instantaneous precipitation map for the area.

4. It gives spatial and temporal rainfall measurement.

5. Obtained data from radars are more accurate to that of the rain gauge.

Disadvantages : These are as follows :

1. It is very-very costly set up.

2. Like rain gauge, the network of radars can not be developed.

3. Well trained engineering staffs are required to operate it.

4. Its repair and maintenance cost is very high as compared to other conventional instruments.

3.3. Automatic Radio-Reporting Raingauge

It is a special type raingauge, which forecasts the rainfall informations through radio- transmitter at pre known time instant. This rain gauge was developed by Indian Meteorological Department, Pune (India). It is used for measurement of rainfall from remote and inaccessible catchment areas. It can cover about 100 km distance at a time.

This method involves, the collection of rainfall by tipping bucket type raingauge. The specific feature of the tipping bucket is that, it actuates electrical pule due to tipping action, which is stored in the system by a data register. The electrical pulse data is converted in the form of 'message code' with the help of coding unit. These codes are impressed on the transmitter at the time of broadcasting. There is a programming unit, in the system, which governs the operating sequence at the time of broadcasting. In brief, this rain gauge collects the rainfall data in the form of 'code message' at the beginning, which is converted into rainfall depth.

Advantages

Specific advantages are given as under :

1. Beside, providing the informations on rainfall, it is also used for flood forcasting at the control centres.

2. It is single instrument, which records the rainfall data from inhibited hilly regions.

3. It is also usefull to record the temperature, humidity, wind velocity etc. of the area.

4. It provides instantancous rainfall data.

5. It gives more authentic information as compared to the conventional raingauges.

3.4. Rainfall Measurement By Satellite

The space satellites do not measure the rainfall directly, because they do not response the liquid or ice drops. They detect the presence of clouds in the sky, which is correlated with the precipitation, measured by the raingauges. The main advantage of this technique is that, it covers a large spatial domain for rainfall measurement.

3.5. Installation of Rain gauge

The rainfall catch is mainly affected by the surrounding exposures of the rain gauge. The effect of exposure on rainfall measurement within the limit can be maintained by proper installation of raingauge. The following points should be kept in view for installation of raingauge :

1. The ground surface must be level. Generally, the places such as slopy ground, terrace wall or roof are avoided for locating the raingauge.
2. Site should be such that it can represent the entire watershed.
3. Wind affected areas should be avoided.
4. The site should be open.
5. In hilly areas, the raingauge must be shield by fencing atleast $5.5 \times 5.5\ m^2$ area around it. Fencing controls the wind effect on precipitation catch.
6. In forest areas, the raingauge should be installed at the distance of twice the height of tallest tree (2*h*) from the forest. The guage's upper point should make the angle ranging from 20 to 30° from the upper point of the tree. In extreme case, the angle can be upto 45°. It is shown in Fig. 3.6.

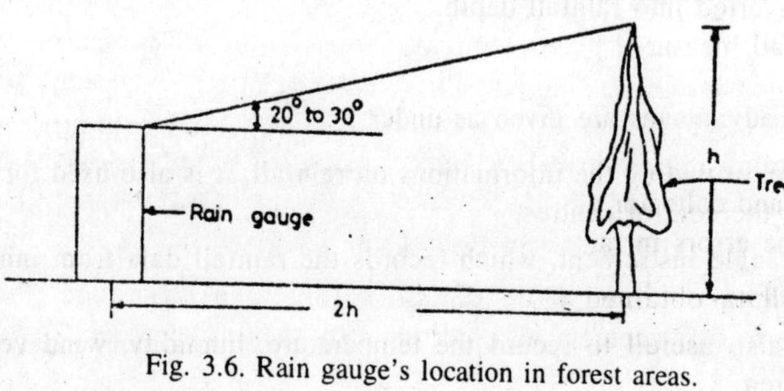

Fig. 3.6. Rain gauge's location in forest areas.

7. Location of raingauge should be avoided in the valley or at the ridge point of the area.
8. The surface over which the rain gauge is to be installed should be such that the receiver's height is about 75 cm above the ground surface.

9. Raingauge should be installed in vertical position.

10. Location of raingauge should be in easily accessible area.

Figure 3.7 shows the installation of raingauge.

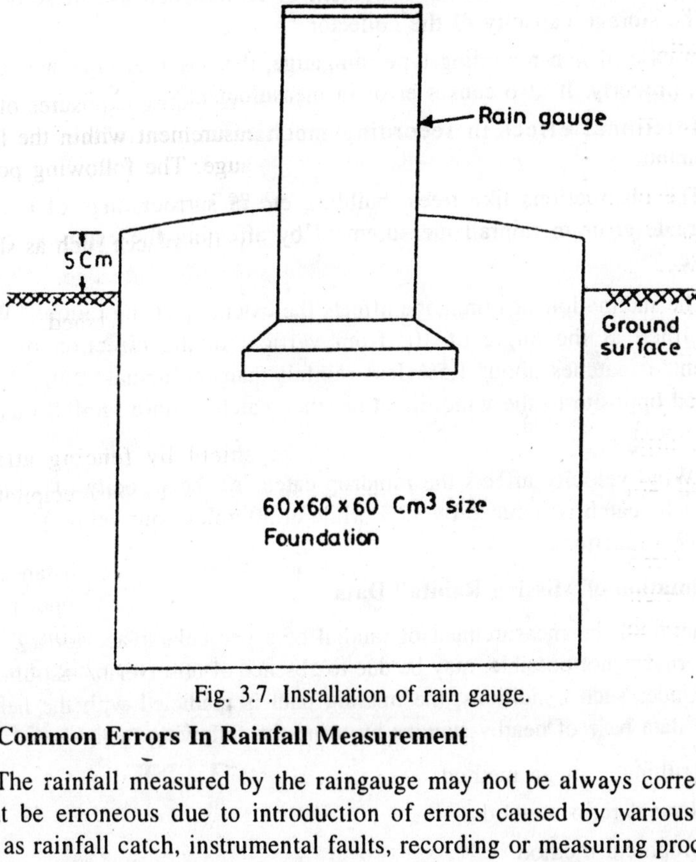

Fig. 3.7. Installation of rain gauge.

3.6. Common Errors In Rainfall Measurement

The rainfall measured by the raingauge may not be always correct. This might be erroneous due to introduction of errors caused by various factors such as rainfall catch, instrumental faults, recording or measuring procedures, splashing of rainwater from the collector, wetting of initially dried surfaces of the funnel and collector etc. However, the points which are responsible for introducing the errors in rainfall measurement are given below :

1. The data obtained from non-recording type raingauge may be erroneous due to displacement of water level by measuring scale. This error ranges up to 2%.

2. Few volume of water is lost in wetting of initially dried surfaces of the measuring gauge, which depends on the roughness and dryness of the surface. About 0.25 mm depth of rainfall is lost for satisfying this kind of water loss during measurement.

3. A high temperature also yields error by increasing the evaporation loss during rainfall measurement. This varies up to 2%.

4. Splashing of water from the funnel yields error.

5. In case of Symon type raingauge, the existing of bends and dents in the collector make inaccurate measurement of rainfall because these defects reduce the storage capacity of the collector.

6. In case of non-recording type raingauge, the observer does not record the data, properly. It also causes error in measurement.

7. Frictional effect in recording mechanism, introduces error in measurement.

8. The obstructions like trees, building etc in surroundings of the rain gauge create error in rainfall measurement by affecting the exposure of the raingauge.

9. The inclination of raingauge affects the catching of the rainfall. When it is inclined at the angle of 10° from vertical in the direction of wind movement, it catches about 1.5% less rainfall than the actual. But, when it is inclined opposite to the wind direction, then catches more rainfall than the actual amount.

10. Wind velocity affects the raindrop catch. At the velocity of 10 miles per hour, the catch is reduced by 17% while at 30 miles/hour velocity, it goes up to 60% reduction.

3.7. Estimation of Missing Rainfall Data

Sometimes, the measurement of rainfall of a particular place for a certain day or period is not possible, may be due to absence of observer or instrumental failure. Under such conditions, the missing data is predicted with the help of available data base of nearby stations by using the following methods :

1. Arithmatic mean method
2. Normal ratio method
3. Graphical method
4. Long term mean rainfall of new station method

Arithmetic mean method

For use of this method, the following points must be satisfied :

1. There should be available the rainfall records of atleast three adjoining stations.

2. All stations should be uniformly spaced around the station of which data is missed.

3. Variation in normal annual rainfall of the missing station and surrounding stations should be within 10%.

In arithmatic mean method, the value of missing rainfall is calculated by taking the mean of the station's record. Let, P_1, P_2 and P_3 are the annual precipitation at the stations 1, 2, and 3, respectively. And it is required to determine the missing rainfall amount (P_x) of station x. It can be obtained by computing the mean of precipitation of the three stations *i.e.*

$$P_x = \frac{1}{3}(P_1 + P_2 + P_3) \qquad ...(3.1)$$

Example 3.1. *In a watershed A, B, C and D are the rain gauge stations, installed for taking the rainfall measurements. If the annual rainfall recorded at stations A, B and C is 150, 75 and 153 cm, respectively, calculate the value of missing rainfall data of station D.*

Solution. Using arithmatic mean method.

$$P_x = \frac{1}{3}(P_1 + P_2 + P_3)$$

$$= \frac{1}{3}(150 + 75 + 153)$$

$$= \mathbf{126\ cm} \quad \textbf{Ans.}$$

Normal Ratio Method

This method is used, when

1. normal annual precipitation at index stations differs by more than 10% from the station which rainfall data is missed.
2. three adjoining station's rainfall data is available.
3. all stations are uniformly spaced.

In this method, the missing rainfall is determined by weighing the normal annual precipitation of each index station. Let, N_a, N_b and N_c are the normal annual precipitation of index stations A, B and C, respectively, N_x is the normal annual precipitation of station x which rainfall data (P_x) is missed and P_a, P_b and P_c are the rainfall of A, B and C stations. This method employs the following formula for estimating the P_x.

$$P_x = \frac{1}{3}\left[\frac{N_x}{N_a}\cdot P_a + \frac{N_x}{N_b}\cdot P_b + \frac{N_x}{N_c}\cdot P_c\right]$$

or

$$P_x = \frac{N_x}{3}\left[\frac{P_a}{N_a} + \frac{P_b}{N_b} + \frac{P_c}{N_c}\right] \qquad ...(3.2)$$

Example 3.2. *Calculate the value of missing rainfall of station x, based on the following rainfall data recorded at the neighbouring stations :*

Station	*X*	*M*	*N*	*O*
Storm rainfall (cm)	—	*10.5*	*14.0*	*15.5*
Normal annual rainfall (cm)	*105.0*	*120.0*	*150.0*	*155.0*

Solution. Since variation in normal annual rainfall at stations M, N, O and missing data station is more than 10 percent. Therefore, in this example normal-ratio method is used for computing the missing rainfall of station x.

Thus, by using the equation 3.2, we have

$$P_x = \frac{N_x}{3}\left(\frac{P_a}{N_a} + \frac{P_b}{N_b} + \frac{P_c}{N_c}\right)$$

in which, $N_x = 105$ cm $\quad P_a = 10.5$ cm

$N_a = 120$ cm $\quad P_b = 14.0$ cm

$N_b = 150$ cm $\quad P_c = 15.5$ cm

$N_c = 155$ cm

Therefore,
$$P_x = \frac{105}{3}\left[\frac{10.5}{120} + \frac{14.0}{150} + \frac{15.5}{155}\right]$$

$$= \mathbf{9.83\ cm} \quad \textbf{Ans.}$$

Example 3.3. *The normal annual rainfall of stations A, B, C and D is 106, 123, 96 and 103 cm, respectively. Amongst these stations, the station 'C' could not record the rainfall due to its failure in a particular year. Calculate the missing annual rainfall of station 'C' if the annual rainfall of stations A, B and D is 91, 98 and 83 cm, respectively.*

Solution. The rainfall data are summarized in following table.

Rain gauge station	*A*	*B*	*C*	*D*
Normal annual rainfall (cm)	106	123	96	103
Annual rainfall (cm)	91	98	x	83

Using the normal-ratio method, we have

$$P_x = \frac{N_x}{3}\left[\frac{P_a}{N_a} + \frac{P_b}{N_b} + \frac{P_c}{N_c}\right]$$

$$= \frac{96}{3}\left[\frac{91}{106} + \frac{98}{123} + \frac{83}{103}\right]$$

$$= \mathbf{78.75\ cm} \quad \textbf{Ans.}$$

Graphical Method

In this method, computation of missing rainfall is based on the record of only two adjoining stations. Rainfall data of both the stations are plotted on a graph paper, keeping one station's record on ordinate and other station's record on abassica. A straight line is drawn by passing through middle of the plotted points. And with the help of straight line, the missing rainfall corresponding to the known rainfall amount of index station is predicted. Estimation procedure is shown in example 3.4.

Example 3.4. *Compute the value of annual missing rainfall of station 'N' for the year 1986 by using the following data.*

Year	Annual rainfall (mm),	
	M	N
1981	1389	1505
1982	1459	1547
1983	1469	1590
1984	1323	1474
1985	1262	1450
1986	1538	—

Solution. The following steps are followed :

Step (1). Plot the annual rainfall data of stations *M* and *N* by keeping them on *x*- and *y*-axis, respectively.

Step (2). Draw a straight line by passing through the middle of the plotted points, as shown in Fig. 3.8.

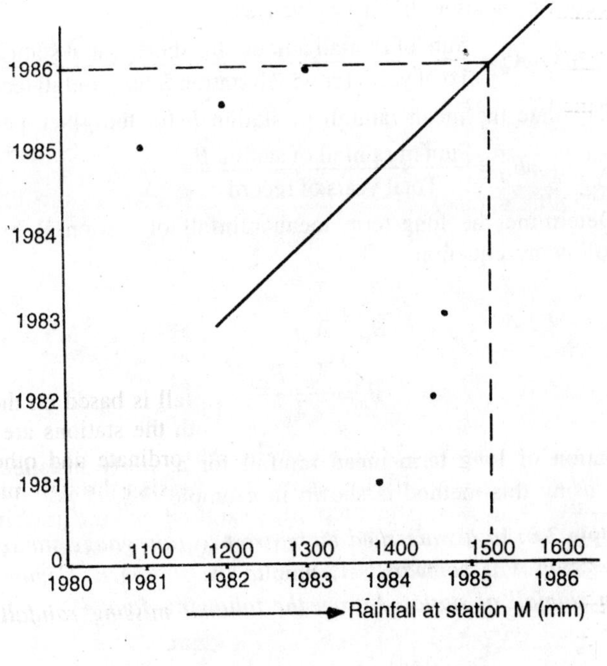

Fig. 3.8

Step (3). Draw ordinate against the rainfall amount i.e. 1538 mm of station M for the year 1986 and determine the value of rainfall of station N for the missing year (*i.e.* 1986) by drawing a horizontal line from the intersection point. It is obtained about 1525 mm.

Long-term Mean Rainfall for a New Station

Estimation of long term mean rainfall for a newly established station which has only few years record, is done by comparing the long term rainfall data of index stations (adjacent stations). This method assumes that, both the stations i.e. index stations and station of missed data are identical and fall in the same hydrological conditions.

Let, A and B are the two raingauge stations who have identical hydrological conditions to each other. The station A has long term rainfall record while B has few years record. For computing the long-term mean rainfall of station B, the following steps are followed :

1. Calculate the mean value of rainfall of station A for the given length of record. It is given by,

$$\bar{A}_{lt} = \frac{\text{Sum of rainfall amount during '}t\text{' years}}{\text{Total years '}t\text{'}}$$

2. Find out the mean value of rainfall of station A for the period of the record of station 'B'. It is given as,

$$A_{st} = \frac{\text{Sum of rainfall amount for short year at station } A}{\text{Total years for which station } B \text{ has rainfall record}}$$

3. Calculate the mean rainfall of station B for the given period (*i.e.*)

$$B_{st} = \frac{\text{Sum of rainfall of station } B}{\text{Total years of record}}$$

4. Determine the long-term mean rainfall of station B by using the following equation.

$$\frac{B_{lt}}{B_{st}} = \frac{\bar{A}_{lt}}{A_{st}} \qquad ...(3.3)$$

or

$$B_{lt} = \frac{\bar{A}_{lt} \cdot B_{st}}{\bar{A}_{st}} \qquad ...(3.4)$$

Estimation of long term mean rainfall for a newly installed raingauge station by using this method is shown in example. 3.5.

Example 3.5. I*n a watershed there are two rain gauge stations* A and B, *in which station A is comparitively new to the station B. Compute the long term mean rainfall of station A from the following data.*

Year	*1950*	*1951*	*1952*	*1953*	*1954*	*1955*	*1956*	*1957*
Rainfall of station A (cm)	—	—	—	—	—	—	—	*75*
Rainfall of station B (cm)	*75*	*120*	*105*	*130*	*50*	*75*	*85*	*90*
Year	*1958*	*1959*	*1960*	*1961*	*1962*	*1963*	*1964*	*1965*
Rainfall of Station A (cm)	*105*	*120*	*75*	*85*	*70*	*100*	*130*	*145*
Rainfall of station B (cm)	*75*	*65*	*85*	*105*	*135*	*65*	*100*	*105*

Solution. Computation is shown in following table.

Year	*Rainfall of station A (cm)*	*Rainfall of station B (cm)*	
1950		75	
1951		120	
1952		105	
1953		130	
1954		50	
1955		75	
1956		85	
1957	75	90	
1958	105	75	
1959	120	65	
1960	75	85	
1961	85	105	825
1962	70	135	
1963	100	65	
1964	130	100	
1965	145	105	
Total	905	1465	

Long-term mean rainfall of station A is computed by using the equation 3.6 *i.e.*

$$\frac{\overline{B}_{lt}}{\overline{B}_{st}} = \frac{\overline{A}_{lt}}{\overline{A}_{st}}$$

in which,

$$\overline{A}_{st} = \frac{905}{9} = 100.6 \text{ cm}$$

$$\overline{A}_{lt} = ?$$

$$\overline{B}_{lt} = \frac{1465}{16} = 91.60 \text{ cm}$$

$$\overline{B}_{st} = \frac{825}{9} = 91.67 \text{ cm}$$

$$\therefore \quad \overline{A}_{lt} = \frac{100.6}{91.67} \times 91.60 = \mathbf{100.53\ cm} \quad \textbf{Ans.}$$

Presentation of Rainfall Data

The commonly used techniques for presentation of rainfall data, suitable for interpretation and analysis in different aspects are given as under :

1. Mass curve 2. Hyetograph 3. Point rainfall.

Mass curve : It is the plot of cumulative rainfall (after arranging in chronological order) against time. The rainfall measurement by float type and weighing type rain gauges is in terms of mass-curve, while symon type raingauge records the data in terms of depth, only. The rainfall data recorded by non-recording type raingauge is processed (*i.e.* in form of cumulative w.r.t. time) to prepare the mass-curve. Mass curves are very useful tool to extract the following informations about the rainfall of the given place.

1. It furnishes the informations on duration of occurring rainfall and its magnitude.

2. It provides the information on starting and end times of the given rainfall.

3. Of a given storm, it enables to determine the rainfall intensity at different time intervals. The intensity of rainfall is the slope of mass curve. A mass curve is shown in figure 3.2.

Hyetograph : It is the plot of rainfall intensity and time interval(Fig. 3.9). For development of hyetograph, the intensity data of rainfall is extracted

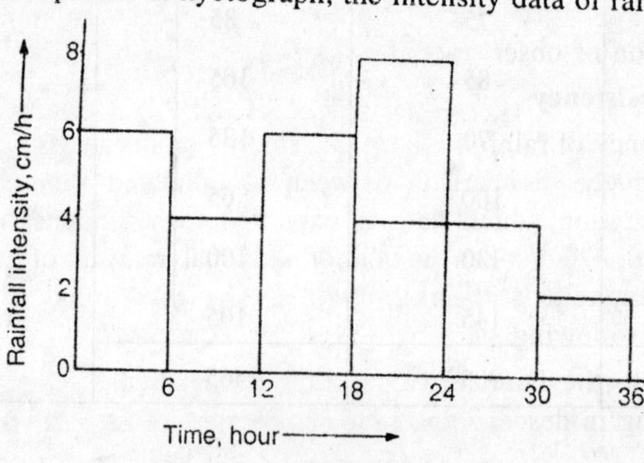

Fig. 3.9. Hyetograph.

from the mass curve. The presentation of hyetograph is in the form of bar digramm. The range of time interval of hyetograph depends on the purpose. Normally, for urban drainage problems, a small duration is used whereas for computation of flood-flows in large catchments, the 6-h time intervral is commonly used. A hyetograph furnishes following informations about the rainfall :

1. Total depth of rainfall, which is determined by computing the area of hyetograph.
2. Effective rainfall depth, which is computed by converting the hyetograph into effective rainfall hyetograph. The ERH is derived by deducting average loss of rain water during rainfall (*i.e.* ϕ-index)
3. Predicts the extreme floods by determining the design storm.
4. A hyetograph also provides the information on duration and depth of effective rainfall, both.

Point rainfall : It is also known as station rainfall. The rainfall measured at a given gauging station is the point rainfall. It is expressed in terms of daily, weekly, monthly, seasonal or annual, depending on the requirement. Point rainfalls are also plotted in form of bar digramm (*i.e.* magnitude Vs chronological time). This kind of presentation of point rainfall is not correct because there is considerable variations in the point rainfall during the selected time interval of bar digramm. However, this variation can be rectified by developing the moving average plot, in which mean precipitations of 3 or 5 consecutive time intervals are plotted through mid points of the selected time intervals.

3.8. Consistency of Rainfall Record

Consistency is determined for testing and adjusting the available rainfall data, especially when conditions relevant to the raingauge station have gone significantly change and thus, causing the data inconsistant. Generally, the following reasons are responsible for making the rainfall data, inconsistant.

1. Due to change in location of the rain gauge station.

2. When neighbourhoods of station have gone significantly changed due to construction of new buildings, development of forest or occurrence of land slides in hilly regions etc.

3. Repeatation of observational error from a certain period.

Test of Consistency

The consistency of rainfall record is tested by double-mass curve method, which deals with the comparison between accumulated annual or seasonal rainfall of the station which data is expected to be inconsistent and the concurrent accumulated mean annual or seasonal rainfall of the group of surrounding raingauge stations known as 'base stations'. Procedure is described under following steps :

1. Calculate the cumulative rainfall of the inconsistant station after arranging in descending order *i.e.* greatest at first and so on.

2. Calculate the cumulative of mean rainfall of the base station after arranging in descending order.
3. Prepare double mass-curve by plotting the cumulative of mean rainfall of the base station on ordinate and the cumulative rainfall of inconsistant station on abassica. It is shown in Fig. 3.10

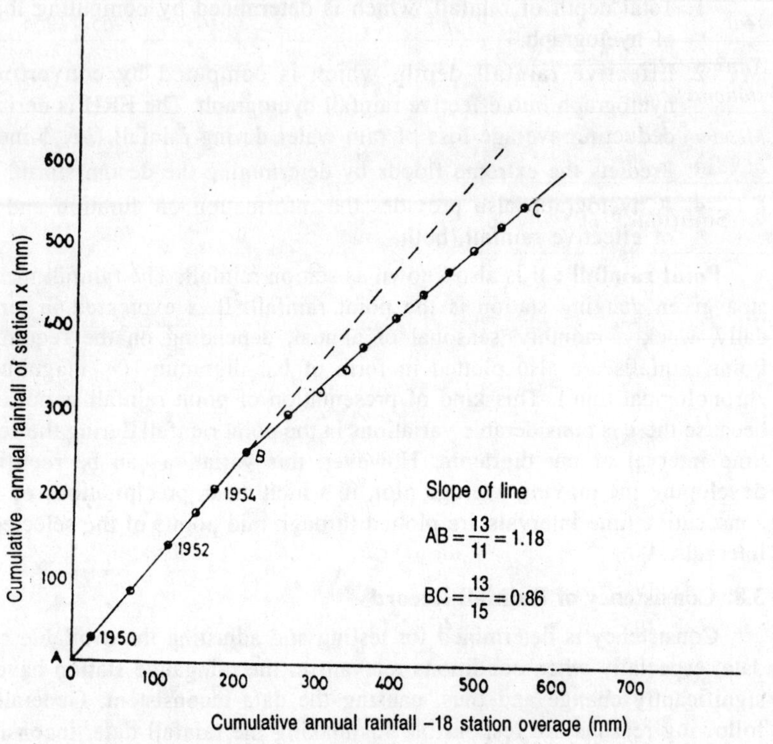

Fig. 3.10. Double mass curve.

4. Find out the regime, which is under inconsistency. It is demarcated by getting the change in slope of the double mass curve. Data related to this regime are needed for correction, which is done by multiplying a factor known as "correction factor". The correction factor is the ratio of slope of straight line of consistant and inconsistant data regime *i.e.*

$$f_c = S_b / S_a \qquad ...(3.5)$$

where, f_c = correction factor, dimension less

S_b = slope of straight line of consistant data regime

S_a = slope of straight line of inconsistant data regime

A sample computation is illustrated in example 3.6.

Example 3.6. *The mean annual rainfall of 18 rain gauge stations and annual rainfall of inconsistent station X are given below. Check the consistency of record of station X. Also indicate the regime of inconsistency.*

Year	*1950*	*1951*	*1952*	*1953*	*1954*	*1955*	*1956*	*1957*	*1958*
Annual rainfall of station x (cm)	*31.5*	*39.9*	*44.7*	*33.2*	*28.4*	*33.2*	*50.3*	*29.4*	*25.6*
Mean annual rainfall of 18 stn (cm)	*23.8*	*36.0*	*31.2*	*28.4*	*26.2*	*29.2*	*37.1*	*29.4*	*26.1*
Year	*1959*	*1960*	*1961*	*1962*	*1963*	*1964*	*1965*	*1966*	*1967*
Annual rainfall at station x (cm)	*22.8*	*29.2*	*18.3*	*23.3*	*29.4*	*25.1*	*27.9*	*21.6*	*30.5*
Mean annual rainfall of 18 stn (cm)	*24.6*	*34.3*	*24.4*	*37.0*	*32.2*	*24.1*	*24..4*	*24.1*	*34.2*

Solution.

Year	*Cumulative annual rainfall amount (cm)*	
	Station X	*18-stations (average)*
1950	31.5	23.8
1951	71.4	59.8
1952	116.1	91.0
1953	149.3	119.4
1954	177.7	145.6
1955	210.7	174.8
1956	261.0	211.9
1957	290.4	241.3
1958	316.0	267.4
1959	338.8	292.0
1960	368.0	326.3
1961	386.3	350.7
1962	409.6	387.7
1963	432.9	419.9
1964	458.0	444.0
1965	485.9	468.4
1966	507.5	492.5
1967	538.0	526.7

Cumulative annual rainfall of station *X* and cumulative mean annual rainfall of 18-station are plotted (Figure 3.10). Which showed that at point *B*, the straight line gets deflected, i.e. inconistancy in rainfall was happened onward from point *B*. For correction of inconsistant data, the correction factor (f_c) is obtained as 1.37 (approx).

3.9. Raingauge Distribution

Distribution of raingauge in a catchment depends on several factors, such as purpose of rainfall data to be used, catchment size, topography, meteorological conditions of the area etc. Adequate number of rain gauge stations provides a reliable picture on rainfall distribution. The following recommendations have been made about raingauge distribution.

WMO Recomendations

1. For flat regions of temperate, mediterranean and tropical zones

   Ideal – 1 station for 600 to 900 km^2 area

   Acceptable – 1 station for 900 to 3000 km^2 area

2. For mountaneous regions of temperate, mediterranean and tropical zones

   Ideal – 1 station for 100 to 250 km^2 area

   Acceptable – 1 station for 250 to 1000 km^2 area

3. In arid and polar zones - 1 raingauge station for 1500 to 10,000 km^2 area of catchment, depending on feasibility.

Generally, 10 percent of the total rain gauge stations are installed as the recording-type rain gauge for collecting the rainfall intensity data.

IMD Recommendations

1. In plain regions : 1 raingauge station should be installed for 520 sq km area of catchment

2. In regions of average elevation : 1 station should be for the area ranging from 260 to 360 km^2.

3. In predominently hilly areas with heavy rain fall : 1 station should be for the area of 130 km^2.

3.10. Adequacy of Rain gauge

Evaluation of adequate number of raingauge station in the catchment is very important for estimating the quantitative averages and extremes of rainfall events with greater accuracy. In addition, when mean areal precipitation is required to compute by using arithmatic mean method, the presence of optimum number of raingauge station in the catchment is also very essential for better result.

McCulloch (1961) has developed a relationship for determining the adequacy of raingauge. The formula is given as:

$$N = \left(\frac{C_v}{\varepsilon}\right)^2 \quad ...(3.6)$$

where, N = adequate number of raingauge station

C_v = coefficient of variation

ε = percent allowable error, generally taken as 10%

Equation 3.9 assumes that the rain gauges are uniformly distributed throughout the catchment. The computation procedure is described below :

1. Calculate, the mean value of annual rainfall of the existing rain gauge stations by using the following formula :

$$\overline{P} = \frac{\sum_{i=1}^{n} P_i}{n} = \frac{P_1 + P_2 + P_3 + P_4 + \ldots P_n}{n} \quad \ldots(3.7)$$

in which, $\overline{P}$ is the mean of annual rainfall, n is the total number of rain gauge stations and $P_1, P_2, P_3, P_4 \ldots P_n$ are the annual rainfall of stations 1 to n, respectively.

2. Compute standard deviation (σ) of the annual rainfall data. The formula is given as :

$$\sigma = \sqrt{\frac{p^2 - (\Sigma p)^2/n}{n-1}} \quad \ldots(3.8)$$

3. Find out the coefficient of variation C_v by the relationship as :

$$C_v = \frac{\sigma}{\overline{P}} \times 100 \quad \ldots(3.9)$$

4. Compute the optimum number of rain gauge station by using the following formula

$$N = \left(\frac{C_v}{\varepsilon}\right)^2$$

Example 3.7. *Determine the optimum number of raingauge station required to install in the watershed of 500 sq km area, if the normal annual rainfall of different stations of watershed are as*

Station	*A*	*B*	*C*	*D*	*E*	*F*
Annual rainfall(cm)	800	1040	780	450	650	350

(Assume the allowable error as 10%)

Solution.

Station	*Annual rainfall (P) mm*	$(P - \overline{P})$	$(P - \overline{P})^2$
A	800	121.67	14803.59
B	1040	361.67	130805.19
C	780	101.67	10336.79
D	450	– 228.33	52134.59
E	650	– 28.33	802.59
F	350	– 328.33	107800.59

$$\overline{P} = \frac{\Sigma P}{n} = \frac{4070}{6} = \mathbf{678.33\ mm}$$

$$\sigma = \sqrt{\frac{\Sigma (P - \bar{P})^2}{n-1}} = \sqrt{\frac{316683.34}{5}} = \mathbf{251.67}$$

$$C_v = \frac{\sigma}{\bar{P}} = \frac{251.67}{678.33} \times 100 = \mathbf{37.10\%}$$

∴ Optimum number of raingauge stations

$$N = \left(\frac{C_v}{\varepsilon}\right)^2 = \left(\frac{37.1}{10}\right)^2 = 13.76$$

$$= \mathbf{14 \text{ rain gauge stations}} \quad \mathbf{Ans.}$$

Example 3.8. *Determine the additional number of raingauge stations required to install in a watershed if,*

1. Number of raingauges already present in the area = 25

2. Allowable percentage error = 10%

3. Mean of annual rainfall = 275 cm

4. Standard deviation of the annual rainfall = 155

Solution. As per equation 3.9, the optimum number of rain gauge station is given by

$$N = \left(\frac{C_v}{\varepsilon}\right)^2 \qquad C_v = \frac{\sigma}{\bar{P}}$$

$$= \left(\frac{56.4}{10}\right)^2 \qquad = \frac{155}{275} \times 100$$

$$= 31.8 \qquad = \mathbf{56.4\%}$$

$$\approx \mathbf{32 \text{ rain gauges}}$$

∴ Additional number of raingauge stations = 32 – 25

$$= \mathbf{7 \text{ rain gauges}} \quad \mathbf{Ans.}$$

3.11. Point Precipitation

Precipitation occurring at a particular point *i.e.* raingauge is called point precipitation. It is essential for determining the weekly, monthly, seasonal or annual precipitation of the watershed.

Use of Point Precipitation

Point precipitation is used for the following purposes :

1. For deriving the intensity-duration and frequency relationship for different storm events.

2. For analysing the areal variability of the precipitation.

Normal Rainfall : It is the long-term average value of rainfall. It may be in the respect of a particular date, month or year. Generally, 30 years rainfall data is considered for determining the normal rainfall. For authenticity, the 30 years normal rainfall values are verified at every 10 years interval. The normal rainfall of a place may be in the form of normal annual rainfall, normal seasonal rainfall, normal monthly rainfall or normal weekly rainfall.

Normal rainfall is essential to determine the variations in trend of rainfall of a given watershed and also for evaluating the missed rainfall data.

3.12. Mean Areal Precipitation

The precipitation measured by raingauge, represents the depth of rainfall that has been occurred at a particular point (i.e. point precipitation); not the areal rainfall. For determining the mean areal precipitation of a given watershed, the rainfall data of various raingauge stations are collected and analysed. The mean areal precipitation is required for computing the runoff of catchment area. Generally, the authenticity of rainfall data for computing the mean areal precipitation depends on the following points.

1. Areal distance between rain gauge stations and centre of the representative area.
2. Topographical characteristics of the area.
3. Size of the watershed.
4. Characteristics of the storm-pattern and
5. Nature of the rainfall.

The following methods are employed for computing the mean areal precipitation :

1. Arithmatic mean method
2. Theissen polygone method, and
3. Isohyetal method

Arithmatic Mean Method

It is the simplest method for computing the mean areal precipitation. It consists of computing the mean value of measured rainfall of various raingauge stations of the watershed. This method computes better, when :

1. Raingauges are uniformly distributed throughout the catchment.
2. Rainfall does not differ very much among the rainfall of various raingauge stations.
3. Topography of watershed is nearly flat.

If $P_1, P_2, P_3 \ldots P_n$ are the rainfall depths measured at uniformly distributed raingauge stations 1, 2, 3 ... N, respectively in the catchment, then mean areal precipitation ($\overline{P}$) is determined by computing the mean of them, given as :

$$\overline{P} = \frac{P_1 + P_2 + P_3 + \ldots P_n}{N} \qquad \ldots(3.10)$$

or

$$\overline{P} = \frac{\sum_{i=1}^{n} P_i}{N} \qquad \ldots(3.11)$$

Limitations

1. This method computes inaccurate value of mean aeral precipitation, when raingauges are not uniformly distributed in the catchment area.

2. When there is considerable difference in topographical features of the catchment, then it also does not provide accurate estimation.

Example 3.9. *A catchment is equipped with 5 rain gauges. During rainy season, the magnitudes of rainfall measured by these gauges are 25, 35, 45, 10 and 75 cm, respectively. Calculate the mean areal rainfall by using arithmatic mean method.*

Solution. The arithmatic mean method computes the M.A.R. by the formula,

$$\text{Mean aerial rainfall } (\bar{P}) = \sum_{i=1}^{n} P_i/N$$

$$= \frac{25+35+45+10+75}{5}$$

$$= \mathbf{38\ cm} \quad \textbf{Ans.}$$

Theissen Polygen Method

In this method, the mean aeral precipitation is computed by weighing the rainfall depth with the area of polygone of the respective raingauge station. Due to this reason, sometimes this method is also known as weighed mean method. Theissen method estimates more accurate value of mean aeral precipitation, when :

1. Size of watershed is between 500 and 5000 km^2 area.
2. Topography is flat.
3. There is uniformity in distribution of rainfall measuring stations.
4. There is small variation in rainfall at different rain gauge stations in the catchment area.

Computation procedure is accomplished under following steps :

1. Plot the locations of raingauge stations on the base map of the catchment.

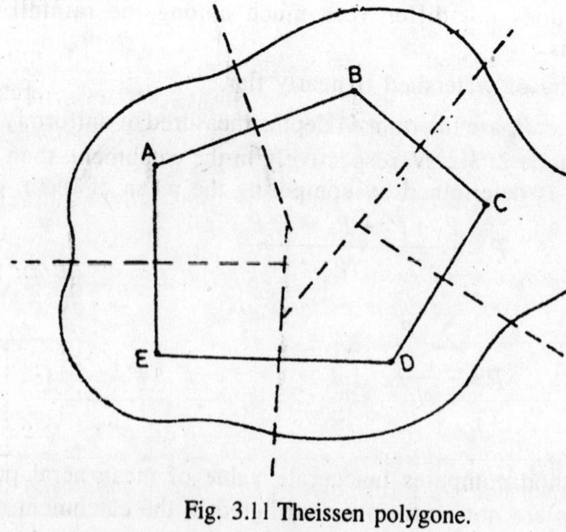

Fig. 3.11 Theissen polygone.

2. Join all the raingauge stations by straight line.
3. Draw perpendicular bisectors of each line joining the raingauge stations in such a way that, they form polygon containing one raingauge station. This polygon is known as "Theissen polygon". It is shown in Fig. 3.11.
4. Calculate the area of each polygon with the help of planimeter or any suitable method.
5. Determine the product of rainfall and enclosed area of respective polygone (*i.e.* $P \, . \, a$).
6. Calculate the mean areal precipitation by dividing the sum of all $P \, . \, a$ with the total area of catchment $\left(i.e. \sum_{i=1}^{m} P_i \, a_i \right)$

If $P_1, P_2, P_3 \ldots P_m$ are the rainfall depths recorded at 1, 2, 3 ...*m* stations and $a_1, a_2, a_3 \ldots a_m$ are the polygon's area enclosed by them, respectively, then mean areal precipitation is given by :

$$\bar{P} = \frac{P_1 \, a_1 + P_2 \, a_2 + P_3 a_3 + \ldots P_m \, a_m}{a_1 + a_2 + a_3 + \ldots \, a_m}$$

or

$$\bar{P} = \frac{\sum_{i=1}^{m} P_i \, a_i}{A} \qquad \ldots(3.12)$$

in which, $\bar{P}$ is the mean areal precipitation and *A* is the total area of the catchment.

Limitations : These are as follows :

1. If position of raingauge is changed in the watershed, then boundary of polygon also changes, hence it requires to sketch new polygones. In this condition fresh computation of mean areal precipitation is required.

2. This method is not suitable for computing the mean areal rainfall of mountaneous watersheds, because of orographic effect there is large variation in the rainfall measurement.

3. The influence of barriers, atmospheric pressures, wind velocity etc on the rainfall distribution is not taken into consideration.

Example 3.10. *Compute the value of mean areal rainfall of following data by using Theissen polygone method.*

Station	*A*	*B*	*C*	*D*	*E*	*F*	*G*	*H*	*I*
Rainfall (cm).	*10*	*25*	*35*	*22.5*	*16.2*	*13.5*	*25.0*	*30.0*	*45.0*
Polygone area (km^2)	*175*	*300*	*100*	*250*	*150*	*320*	*400*	*280*	*450*

Solution.

Station	*Rainfall (cm) (P)*	*Polygone area (km^2) (A)*	*P.A*	*Mean areal rainfall (P)*
A	10.0	175	1750	
B	25.0	300	7500	
C	35.0	100	3500	$P = \frac{\sum_{i=i}^{m} P_i A_i}{A}$
D	22.5	250	5625	
E	16.2	150	2430	
F	13.5	320	4320	$= \frac{63775}{2425}$
G	25.0	400	10,000	= **26.30 cm** **Ans.**
H	30.0	280	8400	
I	45.0	450	20250	

Example 3.11. *Compute the mean areal rainfall from the rainfall values shown in Figure 3.12.*

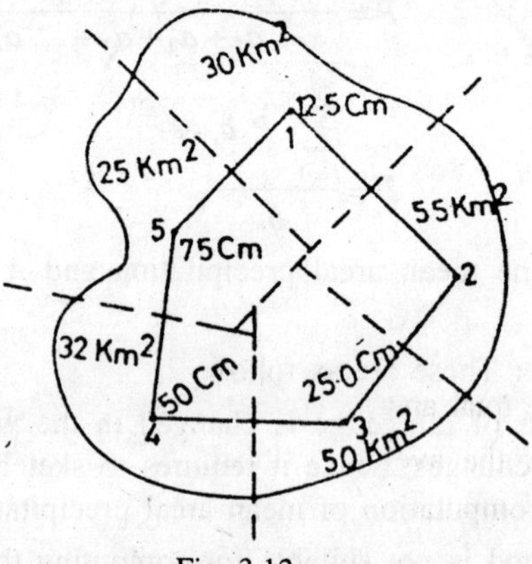

Fig. 3.12

Solution. Referring the Fig. 3.12, we have

Station	*Rainfall (cm) (P)*	*Polygones area (km^2) (A)*	*P.A.*	*P (cm)*
1	12.5	30	375.0	$P = \frac{\sum_{i=1}^{n} P_i A_i}{A}$
2	20.5	55	1127.5	
3	25.0	50	1250.0	$= \frac{6227.5}{192}$
4	50	32	1600.0	
5	75	25	1875.0	= **32.43 cm** **Ans.**

$\Sigma A = 192 \text{ km}^2$ and $\Sigma PA = 6227.5 \text{ cm·km}^2$

Isohyetal Method

It gives more reliable estimate of mean areal rainfall as compared to the other two methods, described above. In this method, isohytes are drawn by joining the points of equal rainfall depths on base map of the catchment. Usually, the isohyets are drawn at 1 cm interval. Accuracy of this method depends on isohyet map and skill of the analyst. Computation procedure is described under following steps :

1. Draw isohyetal map of the catchment.
2. Calculate the area between adjacent isohyets for entire map. If the isohyet goes out of the catchment boundary, then boundary of the catchment should be taken as the isohyet line (Fig. 3.13).

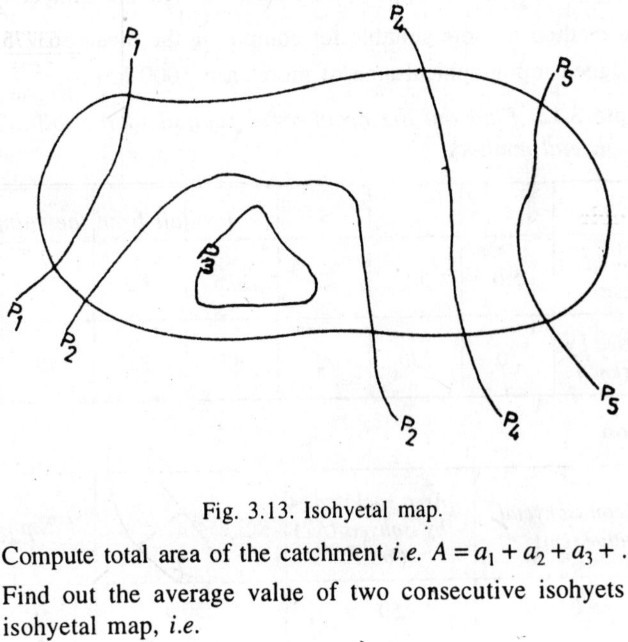

Fig. 3.13. Isohyetal map.

3. Compute total area of the catchment *i.e.* $A = a_1 + a_2 + a_3 + \ldots + a_n$.
4. Find out the average value of two consecutive isohyets for entire isohyetal map, *i.e.*

$$\left.\begin{aligned} P_{1-2} &= \frac{P_1 + p_2}{2} \\ P_{2-3} &= \frac{P_2 + P_3}{2} \\ P_{3-4} &= \frac{P_3 + P_4}{2} \\ p_{n-1-n} &= \frac{P_{n-1} + P_n}{2} \end{aligned}\right\} \qquad \ldots(3.13)$$

5. Determine the value of mean areal precipitation by the following formula,

$$P = \frac{\frac{(P_1+P_2)}{2} \cdot a_1 + \frac{(P_2+P_3)}{2} \cdot a_2 + \frac{(P_3+P_4)}{2} \cdot a_3}{A} + \ldots \qquad \ldots(3.14)$$

Special Features of Isohyetal Method

1. This method requires more number of raingauge stations in the catchment for preparing the isohyet map.

2. It provides more accurate estimate as compared to the other methods.

3. It needs skilled and experienced staff to sketch the isohyet map.

4. This method is more suitable for computing the mean areal rainfall of hilly and rugged topographical area of more than 5000 km^2.

Example 3.12. *Find out the mean areal rainfall of the following data, by using Isohyetal method.*

Zone	*1*	*2*	*3*	*4*	*5*	*6*	*7*
Mean isohyetal value (cm)	*5.0*	*3.5*	*7.5*	*10.5*	*3.0*	*5.0*	*11.5*
Area enclosed by isohyets (km^2)	*50*	*130*	*75*	*45*	*72*	*40*	*85*

Solution.

Zone	*Mean isohyetal value (cm) (P)*	*Area enclosed by isohyets (A) (km^2)*	*P.A*	*P (cm)*
1	5.0	50	250.0	
2	3.5	130	455.0	
3	7.5	75	562.5	$P = \frac{3133.5}{497}$
4	10.5	45	472.5	
5	3.0	72	216.0	**= 6.30 cm Ans.**
6	5.0	40	200.0	
7	11.5	85	977.5	
	Total	497 km^2	3133.5 cm.km^2	

Example 3.13. *Calculate the mean areal rainfall by using isohyetal method. Take the data from Fig. 3.14.*

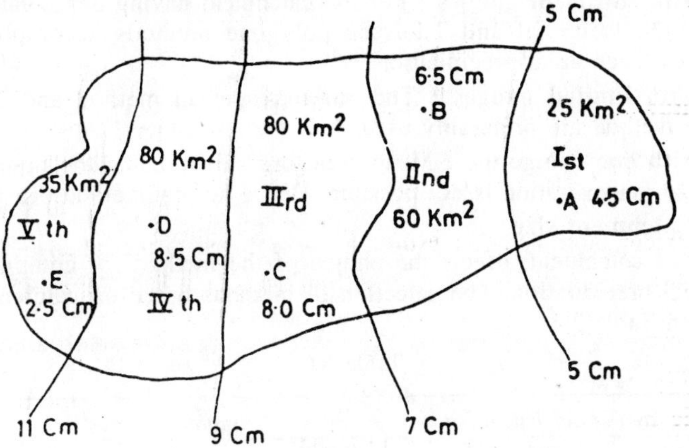

Fig. 3.14

Solution. Referring the Fig. 3.14, we have

Zone	*Isohyet (cm)*	*Mean isohyet (cm)*	*Area enclosed between isohyets (km²)*	*P.A*
I	< 5.0	Say 4.5	25.0	112.5
II	5—7	6.0	60.0	360.0
III	7—9	8.0	80.0	640.0
IV	9—11	10.0	80.0	800.0
V	> 11	Say 9.5	35.0	332.5
	Total		280 km^2	2245.0 cm km^2

$\therefore$ Mean areal rainfall $P = \dfrac{2245.5}{280} = \mathbf{8.02\ cm}$ **Ans.**

3.13. Selection of Suitable Methods for Computing the Mean Areal Precipitation

The selection of suitable method among arithmatic mean method, Theissen polygone method and isohyetal method for computing the mean aeral precipitation depends on the following three main factors :

1. Raingauge network of the catchment
2. Catchment size, and
3. Topographical features of the catchment

These are discussed below :

(1) Raingauge network

Raingauge network represents the total number of raingauge stations in the catchment area. For selecting suitable method, the raingauge network is categorized in two groups, in which one is with sufficient number of stations and other with limited number of stations. The choice on accurate method for estimating the mean areal rainfall based raingauge network, is given below :

1. With sufficient gauges : For the catchment having dense rain gauge network, the isohyetal and Theissen polygone methods accomplish best estimate of mean areal precipitation.

2. With limited gauges : The arithmatic mean method and Theissen polygone method are preferably used.

3. With one raingauge : Mean areal rainfall by using the rainfall data of one rain gauge station is not possible. Hence no any method can be used.

(2) Catchment size

Size of catchment affects the choice of the method for computing the mean areal precipitation. The selection of methods based on catchment size is given in Table 3.1.

Table 3.1

Area of catchment (sq.km)	*Suitable method*
Less than 500	Arithmetic mean method
500 - 5,000	Theissen polygone method
More than 5,000	Isohyetal method

(3) Topography of the Area : Selection of suitable method for computing the mean areal precipitation based on topographical feature of the area is given below :

1. Mountain – Theissen polygone method
2. Plain land – arithmatic mean method
3. Hilly and rugged terrain-isohyetal method

Precipitation Enveloping Curve : It is developed by plotting the rainfall depth against time data. Generally, the trend of curve is found in non-linear form. Few equations of enveloping curve are given below :

$$P = 38.36\, D^{0.486} \quad \text{... (3.15)}$$

Paulhus developed

$$P = 42.16\, D^{.475} \quad \text{... (3.16)}$$

Blesdale developed the following equation

$$P = 29.47\, D^{0.5} \quad \text{... (3.17)}$$

in which, P is the precipitation (cm) and D is the rainfall duration (hour)

Example 3.14. *Present the following rainfall data in following forms :*

1. Point form *2. Bar diagram*

3. Ordinate form.

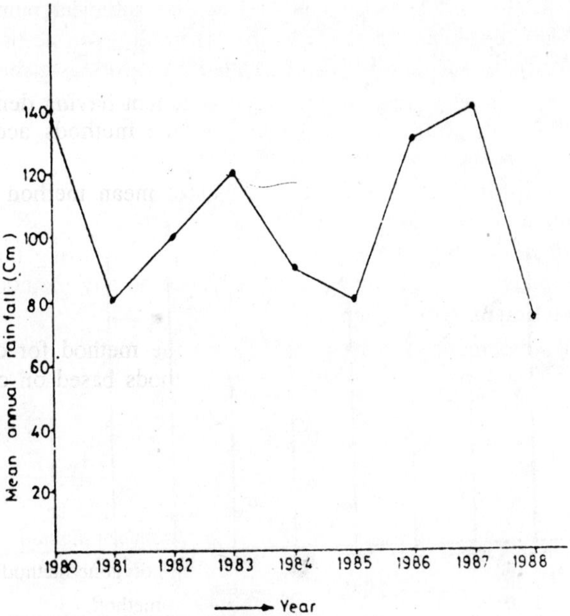

Fig. 13.15. Point Form.

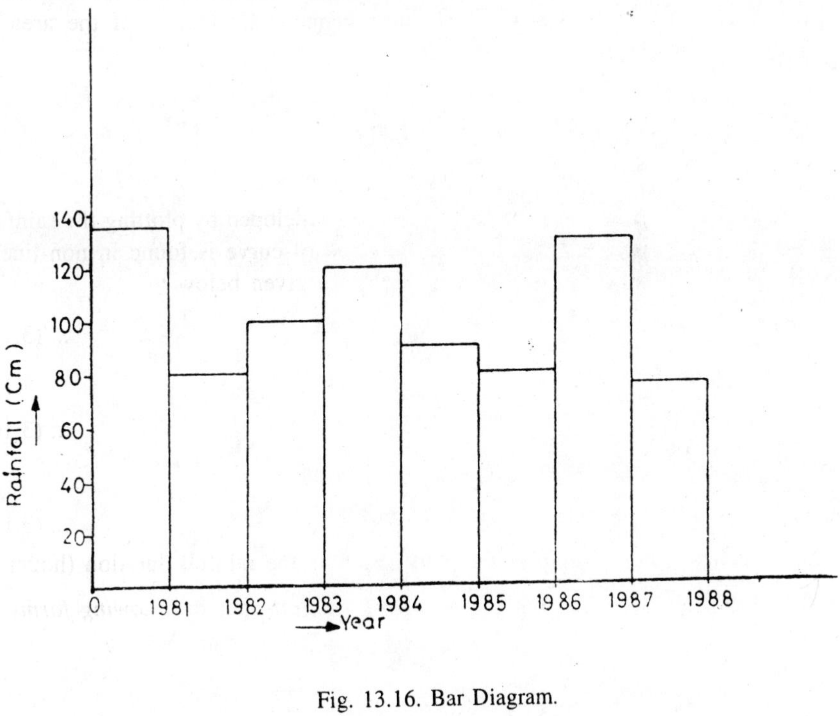

Fig. 13.16. Bar Diagram.

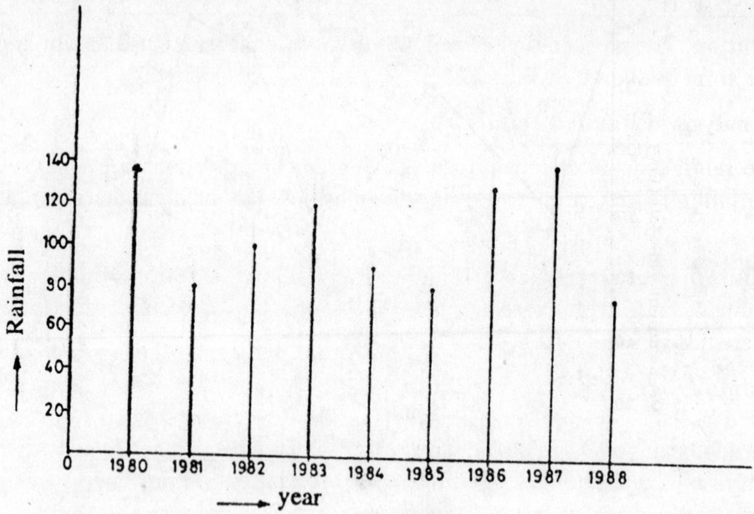

Fig. 13.17. Oridinate Form.

Year	*1980*	*1981*	*1982*	*1983*	*1984*	*1985*	*1986*	*1987*	*1988*
Rainfall(cm)	135	80	100	120	90	80	130	140	75

Solution. The presentation of rainfall data in point form, bar diagram and ordinate form is shown in Fig. 3.15, 3.16 and 3.17, respectively.

3.14. Analysis of Rainfall Data

The rainfall data collected from various raingauge stations are analysed for determining different hydrological relationships, few of them are given as under :

Rainfall characteristics : It includes intensity, duration, frequency, maximum & minimum rainfall etc. The methods to determine all these characteristics of rainfall are described below.

Rainfall intensity : It is defined as the rate of fall of precipitation expressed as cm/h or mm/h. The non-recording type raingauge records the rainfall depth only but incase of recording type raingauge, the duration and depth of rainfall are recorded simultaneously in the form of mass curve. Using mass-curve, the rainfall intensity for any desired time interval can be obtained, which is equal to the tan θ (*i.e.* slope of the mass curve) at given time. The rainfall intensity, in case of non-recording type raingauge is obtained by dividing the total rainfall depth with its duration *i.e.*

$$I = \frac{P}{t} \qquad ...(3.18)$$

in which, I is the rainfall intensity, P is the total rainfall depth and t is the duration of rainfall. Rainfall intensity is classified into following three groups :

1. Light intensity - 2.5 mm/h
2. Moderate intensity - 2.5 to 7.5 mm/h
3. Heavy intensity - more than 7.5 mm/h

Rainfall intensity is very important hydrological parameter for deriving the flood hydrograph of probable or possible flood/runoff to design different hydraulic structures viz spillways, flood control structures etc.

Intensity-Duration Relationship

Rainfall intensity is the inverse function of rainfall duration *i.e.* for longer storm duration, the rainfall intensity is less and vice-versa. It is general phenomena, that the rainfall intensity is not same throughout the storm period but varies time to time. For a shorter time, its value can be much higher than the mean rainfall intensity of the storm. For finding the rainfall intensity at any time 't' during the storm, Richard (1944) developed a relationship between intensity and duration of rainfall, given as under :

$$\frac{i}{I} = \frac{T+K}{t+K} \qquad ...(3.19)$$

in which, i and I are the rainfall intensity for any time t and T, respectively. T is the storm duration and K is the constant. The value of K is generally taken as 1, except for extreme events. Thus, after substituting the value of 'K' in the equation 3.19, we have,

$$\frac{i}{I} = \frac{T+1}{t+1}$$

or
$$i = I\left(\frac{T+1}{t+1}\right)$$

or
$$i = \frac{P}{T}\left(\frac{T+1}{t+1}\right) \qquad ...(3.20)$$

This equation can be used for computing the rainfall intensity for any time during rainfall, if storm duration and mean rainfall intensity of the given storm are known.

Tejwani et. al. (1975) developed graphical relationship between one hour rainfall intensity and other durations rainfall intensities, as shown in Fig. 3.18.

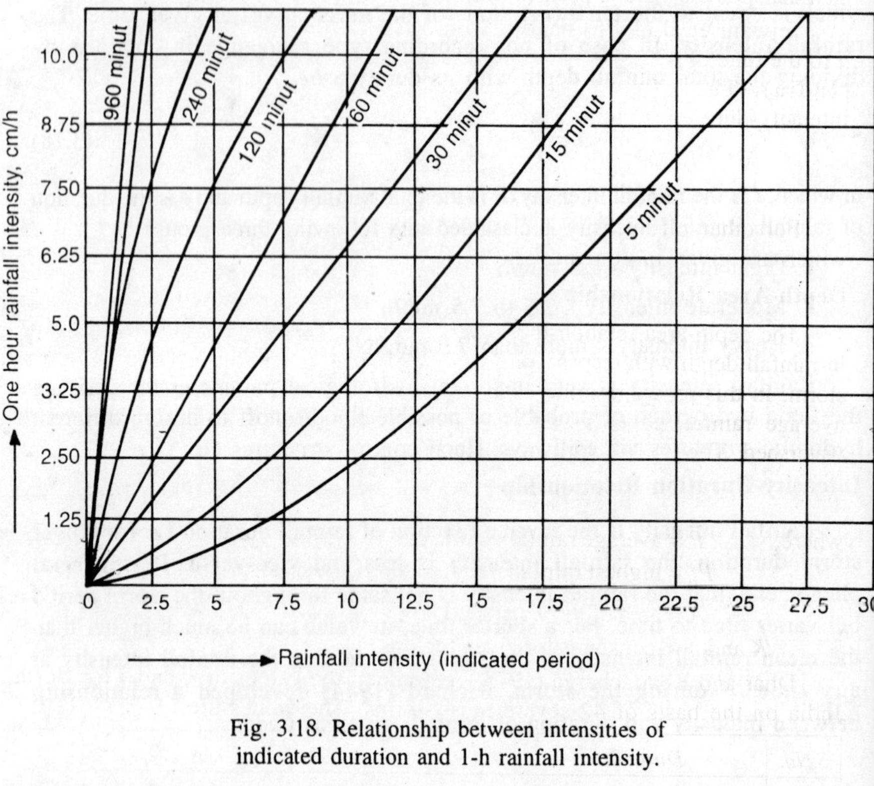

Fig. 3.18. Relationship between intensities of indicated duration and 1-h rainfall intensity.

Intensity-Duration-Frequency Relationship

It is general characteristics of the rainfall that as the rainfall duration increases, the intensity decreases and vice-versa. On contrast, the rainfall intensity increases with increase in return period and vice-versa. The relationship amongst intensity, duration and frequency of rainfall is given as under.

$$i = \frac{KT^a}{(t+b)^d} \quad ...(3.21)$$

where, i = average rainfall intensity, cm/h
t = duration of rainfall, hour
T = recurrence interval, years.
K, a, b and d = constants, depend on the geographical locations of the area.

The value of recurrence interval can be computed by using the following formula

$$T = 1/p \quad ...(3.22)$$

in which, p is the plotting position of the observed rainfall, expressed in present.

Tejwani et al (1975) have determined the values of constants K, a, b and d to the tune of 43.26, 0.17, 4 and 0.6857, respectively for Octacamund region (India). Thus, after substituting these values in eq. (3.21), the intensity-duration-frequency relationship for the said region is given by

$$i = \frac{43.26\, T^{0.17}}{(t+4)^{0.6857}} \quad ...(3.23)$$

For other places, they have also determined the values of K, a, b and d; which are given in Appendix I.

Depth-Area Relationship

The depth-area relationship is very important for determining the variations in rainfall depth with respect to the variation in area of watershed during a given storm. In this regard, Horton developed a mathematical model for prediting the average rainfall depth, based on the highest amount of rainfall and area of watershed. The model is given as under :

$$\overline{P} = P_o e^{-KA^n} \quad ...(3.24)$$

where, $\overline{P}$ = average rainfall depth, cm
P_o = highest rainfall depth occured at the storm centre, cm
A = area of the watershed, km^2
K and n = constants for given region.

Dhar and Bhattacharya (1975) determined the values of K and n for North India on the basis of 42 severe most storms. The values are:

S.No.	Duration	K	n
1.	One day	8.256×10^{-4}	6.614×10^{-1}
2.	Two days	9.877×10^{-4}	6.306×10^{-1}
3.	Three days	1.745×10^{-3}	5.961×10^{-1}

Depth-Area-Duration Relationship

For determining the rainfall depth within storm duration over the watershed due to any storm, the depth-area-duration relationship is very essential. Derivation of this relationship is carried out by plotting the progressively decreasing average rainfall depth over progressively increasing watershed area from the centre of the storm leading to its boundary. In other words, the depth-area-duration curve is derived by plotting the average depth of rainfall against corresponding area up to encompassing isohyets. Derivation procedure is described as under :

1. Find out 1-day, 2-days. 3-days upto 5 consecuting days maximum average ruinfall.

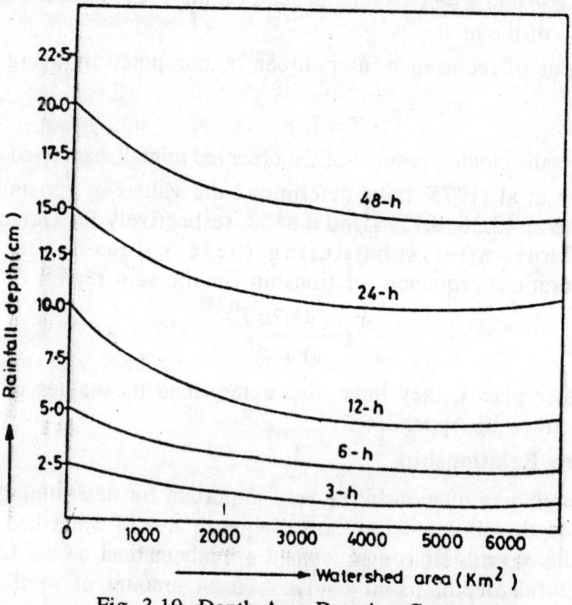

Fig. 3.19. Depth-Area-Duration Curve.

2. Prepare the isohyetal map of maximum average rainfall for 1- to 5-days rainfall durations, separately for each day.

3. Divide each isohyetal map into different zones, representing the centre of main storm.

4. Determine the enclosed area by each isohyet. It is determined by using the planimeter or any suitable method. Measurement of area is started from centre of the storm of each zone.

5. Calculate the rainfall volume between two isohyets. It is determined by multiplying the enclosed area between them and mean of the two adjacent isohyet value.

6. Compute the total rainfall volume by adding the incremental volume to the previous accumulated rainfall volume.

7. Find out the average rainfall depth over the area, which is obtained by dividing the total rainfall volume computed in step (6) with the total area of isohyetal map.

8. Determine the average rainfall depth for each zone by repeating the procedure upto step 7 and then combine the enclosed area by the common isohyets.

9. Plot the values of highest average rainfall depth and corresponding area and join all the points by smooth curve. The obtained curve is the depth-area-duration curve for maximum rainfall of a particular period. It is shown in Fig. 3.19. Procedure is also explained in example 3.15.

Example 3.15. *Develop the depth-area-duration curve by using the isohyetal pattern of a storm of 3-consecutive days, as shown in Fig. 3.20.*

Solution. From the Fig. 3.20, the values of different isohyets and enclosed area between isohyets are extracted and are shown in table (at page 80).

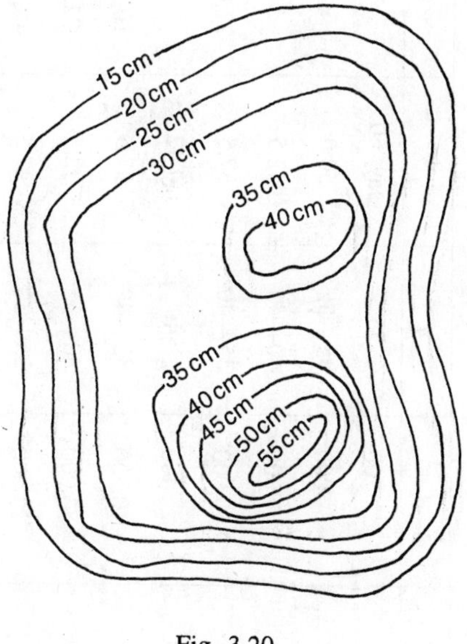

Fig. 3.20

The depth-area-duration curve is derived by plotting the values of average rainfall depths (i.e. column 9) and corresponding enclosed area (column 3) of the isohyets, on a graph paper by keeping the rainfall depth on y-axis and area on x- axis. It is shown in Fig. 3.21.

Storm centre	Isohyetal value (cm)	Area enclosed (km^2)	Range of isohyets (cm)	Mean isohyet value (cm)	Area between isohyets (km^2)	Incremental value ($cm.km^2$)(5 × 6)	Cumulative value ($cm.km^2$)	Average rainfall depth (cm) (8 ÷ 3)
1	2	3	4	5	6	7	8	9
A	55	700	55	say 60	700	42,000	42,000	60.0
	45	5000	45—55	50.0	4300	215,000	257,000	51.4
	40	8000	40—45	42.5	3000	127,500	384,500	48.06
	35	30,000	35—40	37.5	22,000	825,000	120,9500	40.32
B	40	400	>40	say 42.5	400	17,000	17,000	42.50
	35	10,500	35—40	37.5	10,100	378,750	395,750	37.70
A	30	83,000	30—35	32.5	72.,500	235,6250	235,6250	28.39
		123,000	25—30	27.5	40,000	110,000	345,6250	28.10
	20	157,000	20—25	22.5	34,000	765,000	422,1250	26.89
		237,000	15—20	17.5	80,000	140,0000	562,1250	23.72

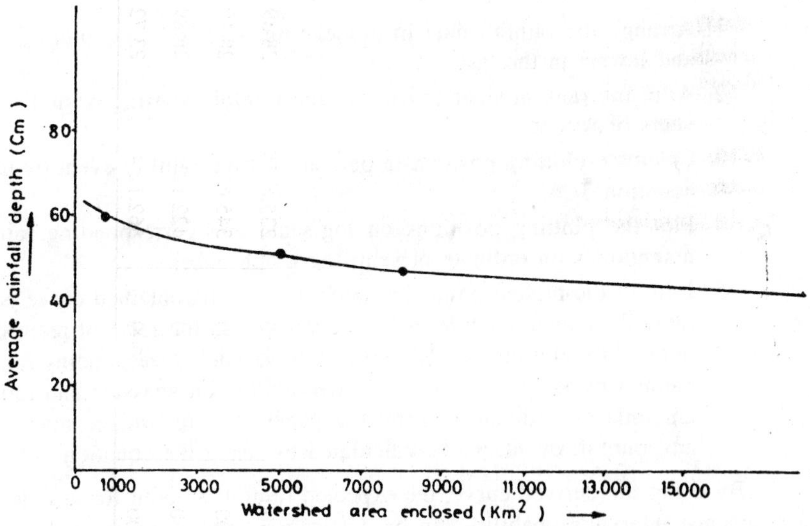

Fig. 3.21

Rainfall Frequency

The design of hydraulic structures, such as flood control structures, soil conservation structures, sewage systems, drains and culverts is based on the probability of occurrence of extreme rainfall events and resulting runoff, thereby. In addition, it is also useful for crop planning in agriculture by computing the expected rainfall amounts at different probability levels.

Frequency of rainfall event of a specified period is expressed in terms of recurrence interval, which is defined as the value that is equal to or greater than the specified magnitude, occured once in T years. The formula for computing T is given as under :

$$T = \frac{1}{p} \quad ...(3.25)$$

where, T = recurrence interval, years

p = plotting position of the event

If the rainfall data of any watershed for few years is available, then plotting positions of different years can be computed by using the following formula :

$$p(\%) = \frac{m}{n+1} \times 100 \quad ...(3.26)$$

in which, m is the rank number of the event after arranging in descending order by their magnitude and 'n' is the total number of years of record. This formula is referred as Weibull's formula. The procedure for determining the maximum expected rainfall for a specified recurrence interval or probability is described under following steps :

1. Arrange the rainfall data in descending order *i.e.* maximum at first and lowest in the last.
2. Allot the rank number to each of the rainfall, starting from 1 to the years of record.
3. Calculate plotting position in percent of each rainfall event by using equation 3.26.
4. Plot the plotting positions on log-scale and corresponding rainfall magnitudes on ordinate of semi-log graph paper.
5. Join all the plotted points by smooth line. The obtained curve is the rainfall frequency curve. It is also derived in the form of recurrence interval by plotting the recurrence interval and corresponding rainfall amount by keeping recurrence intervals (T) on abassica and rainfall amounts on ordinate of semi-log paper. The recurrence interval of any rainfall event can be calculated by using the equation 3.25.

By using the derived curve, the expected rainfall amount for any desired recurrence interval/probability can be determined. Procedure is explained in example 3.16.

Example 3.16. *Using the following rainfall data, prepare the rainfall frequency curve and determine the followings :*

1. Rainfall for 10, 20, 30 and 40 years recurrence interval

2. Rainfall at 50, 40, 20 and 10% probability levels.

Year	*1970*	*1971*	*1972*	*1973*	*1974*	*1975*	*1976*	*1977*	*1978*	*1979*
Annual rainfall (mm)	780.5	1495.7	749.1	1202.2	2077.7	1014.3	1829.2	1129.6	1152.5	1344.9
Year	*1980*	*1981*	*1982*	*1983*	*1984*	*1985*	*1986*	*1987*	*1988*	*1989*
Annual rainfall (mm)	1265.0	1770.0	732.8	1080.25	1153.69	1298.2	756.6	1954.1	1166.4	1416.1

Solution. Computation is given on next page.

Rainfall (mm)	*Rank number*	*Plotting position (%)* $p = \frac{m}{n+1} \times 100$	*Recurrence interval* $\left(T = \frac{1}{p}\right)$
2077.70	1	4.8	21.0
1954.10	2	9.5	10.5
1829.20	3	14.3	7.0
1770.00	4	19.0	5.3
1495.70	5	23.8	4.2
1416.10	6	28.6	3.5
1344.90	7	33.3	3.0
1298.20	8	38.1	2.6
1265.0	9	42.9	2.3
1202..2	10	47.6	2.1
1166.4	11	52.4	1.9
1153.69	12	57.1	1.8
1152.5	13	61.9	1.6
1129.6	14	66.7	1.5
1080.25	15	71.4	1.4
1014.30	16	76.2	1.3
780.50	17	81.0	1.2
756.60	18	85.7	1.1
749.10	19	90.5	1.1
732.80	20	95.2	1.0

The rainfall frequency curve is prepared by plotting the annual rainfall amounts and corresponding plotting positions on semi-log or probability graph paper, as shown in Fig. 3.22. By using the curve, the values of rainfall at desired recurrence intervals and probabilities are determined which are summarised as under :

Recurrence interval (T) year.	*Rainfall (mm)*	*Probability %*	*Rainfall (mm)*
10	1900	50	1280
20	2075	40	1400
30	2225	20	1675
40	2300	10	1875

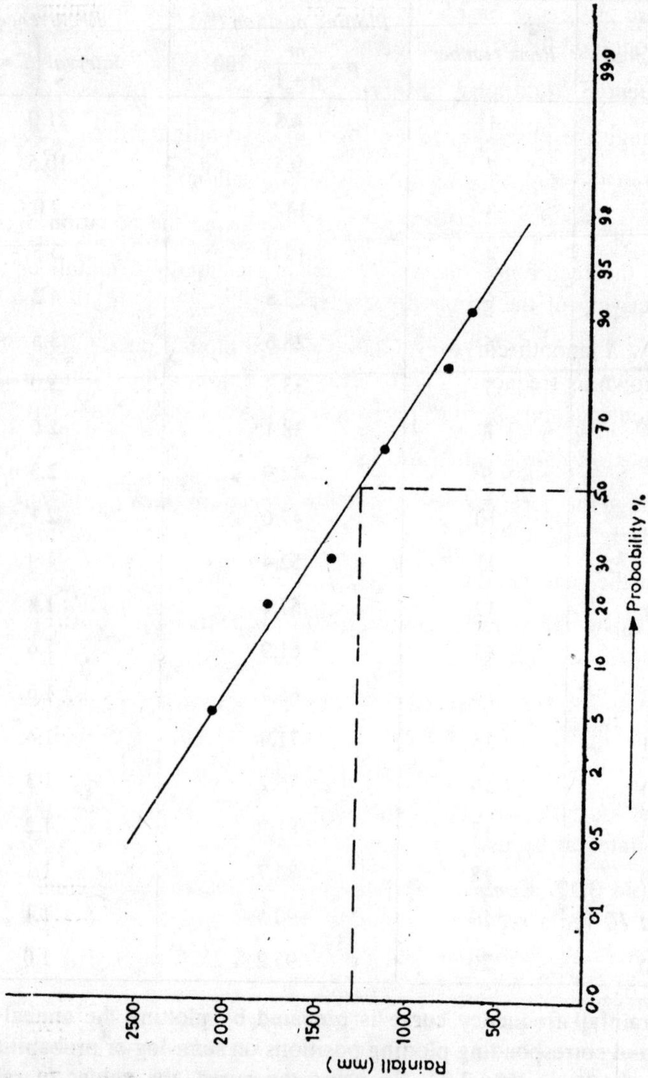

Fig. 3.22

Expected Maximum and Minimum Rainfall

Prediction of expected maximum and minimum rainfall magnitudes for a specified period is done by using the frequency formula, which is as follows:

$$T = \frac{n}{(m - 1/2)} \quad \text{(Hazen formula)} \qquad ...(3.27)$$

where, T = recurrence interval for which the rainfall is either equal to or greater than the specified amount.

m = rank number of the event after arranging in descending order

Stepwise procedure for computation of maximum and minimum expected rainfall amounts is described as under :

A. **Expected Maximum Rainfall**

1. Arrange the observed rainfall data in descending order.

2. Assign the rank number to each rainfall amount.

3. Calculate the recurrence interval (T) by using the equation 3.27.

4. Plot the recurrence interval (T) and corresponding rainfall on x and y axis, respectively of the probability paper.

5. Draw a smooth curve by joining all the plotted points. The obtained curve is known as frequency curve. Using this curve, the expected maximum rainfall amount against desired recurrence interval can be predicted.

B. **Expected Minimum Rainfall**

1. Arrange the observed rainfall data in ascending order *i.e.* lowest rainfall at first and highest in last.

2. Alot the rank number to each rainfall amount.

3. Calculate the recurrence interval (T) by using the equation 3.27 for each rainfall data.

4. Prepare the rainfall frequency curve by plotting the recurrence interval and corresponding rainfall amount on x and y axis, respectively of probability paper.

5. Find out the expected minimum rainfall amount for any desired recurrence interval by using the derived curve.

Example 3.17. *Compute the expected maximum and minimum rainfall amounts at 10 years recurrence interval from the following observed rainfall data recorded at a particular rain gauge station.*

Year	*1975*	*1976*	*1977*	*1978*	*1979*	*1980*	*1981*	*1982*	*1983*
Rainfall(cm)	*85.0*	*66.0*	*105.0*	*35.0*	*50.0*	*40.0*	*65.0*	*70.0*	*100*
Year	*1984*	*1985*	*1986*	*1987*	*1988*	*1989*	*1990*	*1991*	*1992*
Rainfall (cm)	*55.0*	*75.0*	*102.0*	*45.0*	*86.0*	*90.0*	*115.0*	*112.0*	*82.0*

Solution. 1. Computation of expected maximum rainfall

Rainfall (cm)	*Rank number*	*Recurrence interval* $T = \frac{n}{m - \frac{1}{2}}$
115.0	1	36
112.0	2	12
105.0	3	7.2
102.0	4	5.1
100.0	5	4.0
90.0	6	3.3
86.0	7	2.8
85.0	8	2.4
82.0	9	2.1
75.0	10	1.9
70.0	11	1.7
66.0	12	1.6
65.0	13	1.4
55.0	14	1.3
50.0	15	1.2
45.0	16	1.1
40.0	17	1.1
35.0	18	1.0

Plot the rainfall and corresponding recurrence interval on probability graph paper by keeping the recurrence interval on *x*-axis and rainfall on *y*-axis and draw a smooth curve through them. The obtained curve is called depth-frequency curve, shown in Fig. 3.23. From this curve, the expected maximum rainfall amount at 10-years recurrence is obtained as 109 cm.

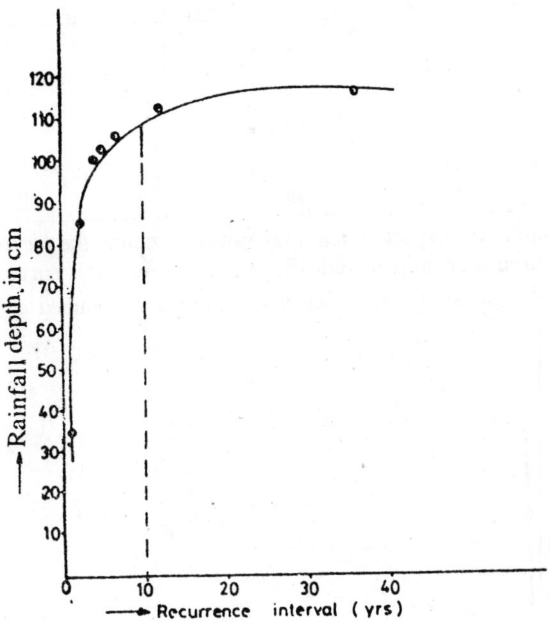

Fig. 3.23

2. Computation of expected minimum rainfall

Rainfall (cm)	*Rank number*	*Recurrence interval* $T = \frac{n}{m - \frac{1}{2}}$
35.0	1	36
40.0	2	12
45.0	3	7.2
50.0	4	5.1
55.0	5	4.0
65.0	6	3.3
66.0	7	2.8
70.0	8	2.4
75.0	9	2.1
82.0	10	1.9
85.0	11	1.7
86.0	12	1.6
90.0	13	1.4

Contd.

Rainfall (cm)	*Rank number*	*Recurrence interval* $T = \frac{n}{m - \frac{1}{2}}$
100.0	14	1.3
102.0	15	1.2
105.0	16	1.1
112.0	17	1.1
115.0	18	1.0

For determining the expected minimum rainfall amount, the recurrence interval (*T*) V_s rainfall curve is again prepared (Fig. 3.24) and from this curve, the expected minimum rainfall against 10 years recurrence interval is obtained as 43 cm.

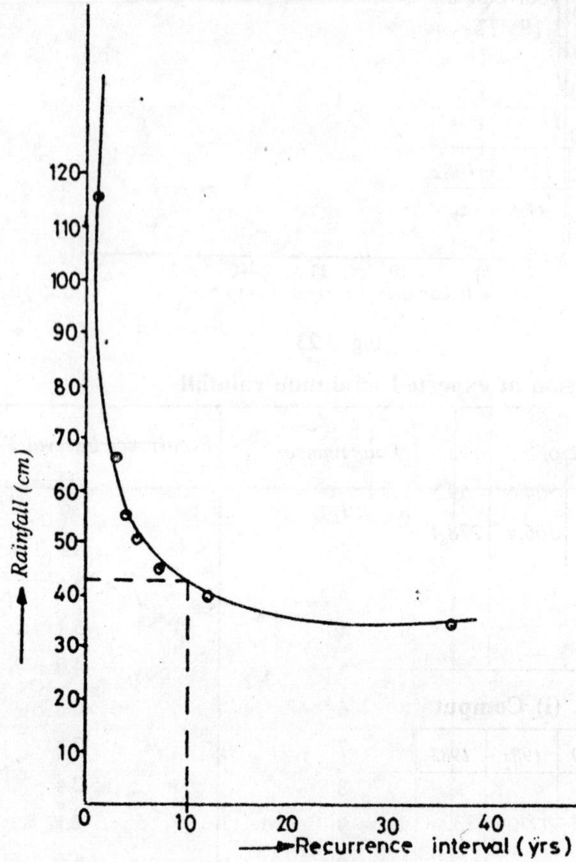

Fig. 3.24

Mean Monthly Rainfall

If a watershed is equipped with a number of rain gauge stations for recording the rainfall data, then from the daily rainfall records the mean weekly, monthly, seasonal or yearly rainfall values can be determined. Monthly rainfall is determined by adding the daily rainfall of the whole month and mean monthly rainfall is computed by taking the mean of the total rainfall of 12 months of the year.

Estimation of mean monthly rainfall is required for determining the rainfall variation within the months during a particular year. Similarly, the rainfall distribution during different months of the year is also dealt with the mean monthly rainfall. Inaddition, it is also helpful for assessing the quantity of water available for irrigation and hydropower generation from the given river basin. Computation procedure of mean monthly rainfall is explained in example- 3.18.

With the help of mean monthly rainfall, the normal, abnormal and drought months of the year can also be predicted.

Example 3.18. *The monthly rainfall data from 1980 to 1989 of 'Pusa farm' is given below. Compute the value of mean monthly rainfall of each year.*

Month	*Rainfall (mm)*									
	1980	*1981*	*1982*	*1983*	*1984*	*1985*	*1986*	*1987*	*1988*	*1989*
Jan	*4.0*	*31.6*	—	*14.0*	*21.54*	*12.0*	*0.5*	—	—	*1.5*
Feb	—	—	*3.2*	*0.5*	*23.0*	—	*7.0*	—	*15.0*	*15.4*
March	*27.2*	*10.0*	*20.8*	*1.0*	—	—		*4.0*	*11.0*	*6.4*
April	—	*34.6*	*13.8*	*43.5*	*0.5*	*9.0*	*4.0*	*77.5*	*28.6*	—
May	*80.8*	*76.2*	*14.0*	*121.25*	*70.0*	*52.6*	*125.5*	*18.5*	*22.4*	*124.3*
June	*94.8*	*81.2*	*139.8*	*142.0*	*317.0*	*139.6*	*74.5*	*138.7*	*189.4*	*115.6*
July	*481.2*	*658.3*	*192.0*	*324.0*	*310.2*	*352.6*	*271.2*	*298.5*	*315.6*	*811.6*
Aug	*398.9*	*564.6*	*59.5*	*220.5*	*160.25*	*227.8*	*115.7*	*744.2*	*259.8*	*102.8*
Sept	*157.5*	*306.4*	*278.4*	*129.5*	*244.2*	*291.0*	*103.5*	*66.4*	*268.7*	*198.4*
Octo	*19.6*	—	*9.8*	*71.5*	*7.0*	*211.6*	*42.7*	*0.30*	*35.8*	—
Nov	—	*7.2*	—	—	—	*0.10*	—	*0.3*	—	*19.6*
Dec	*1.0*	—	*1.5*	*12.5*	—	*2.0*	*12.0*	*8.1*	*20.1*	*20.5*

Solution. (i) Computation of yearwise mean monthly rainfall

Year	*1980*	*1981*	*1982*	*1983*	*1984*	*1985*	*1986*	*1987*	*1988*	*1989*
Total rainfall (mm)	1265	1770.1	732.8	1080.25	1153.69	1298.30	756.6	1356.5	1166.4	1400.7
*M.M.R. * (mm)*	105.42	147.51	61.06	90.02	96.14	108.19	63.05	113.04	97.2	116.72

$$* \text{ Mean Monthly Rainfall (M.M.R)} = \frac{\text{Total rainfall in the year}}{12}$$

(*ii*) **Computation of mean monthly rainfall for the given length of record.**

Year	Monthly rainfall (mm)											
	Jan	Feb	March	April	May	Jun	July	Aug	Sep	Oct	Nov	Dec
1980	4.0	—	27.2	-	80.8	94.8	481.2	398.9	157.5	19.6	—	1.0
1981	31.6	—	10.2	34.6	76.2	81.2	658.3	564.16	306.4	—	7.2	1.5
1982	—	3.7	20.8	13.8	14.0	139.8	192.0	59.5	278.4	9.8	—	12.5
1983	14.0	0.5	1.0	43.5	121.25	142.0	324.0	220.5	129.5	71.5	—	2.0
1984	21.54	23.0	—	0.50	70.0	317.0	310.2	160.25	244.2	7.0	—	12.0
1985	12.0	—	—	9.0	52.6	139.6	352.6	227.8	291.0	211.6	0.10	8.1
1986	0.5	7.0	—	4.0	125.5	74.5	271.2	115.7	103.5	42.7	-	20.1
1987	—	—	4.0	77.5	18.5	138.7	298.5	744.2	66.4	0.3	0.30	20.5
1988	—	15.0	11.0	28.6	22.4	189.4	315.6	259.8	268.7	35.8	—	—
1989	1.5	15.4	6.4	-	124.3	115.6	811.6	102.8	198.4	—	19.6	—
Total	851.14	64.10	80.60	211.50	705.55	1432.60	4015.2	2854.1	2044.0	398.3	27.2	77.7
M.M.R.(mm)	7.10	5.34	6.782	17.63	58.80	119.38	334.60	237.84	170.33	33.19	2.27	6.48

Mean Annual Rainfall

It is commonly used to express the rainfall of place. Sometimes, it is also referred as normal rainfall. The mean annual rainfall is computed by taking the mean of the total rainfall amount of some consecutive years. Usually, 30 years rainfall data is considered for the purpose. However, greater the number of years of data, the more accurate value of mean annual rainfall is obtained.

The mean annual rainfall is used for determining the normal, abnormal or deficit rainfall values of the place. It is described as under :

Normal year : Any year receiving the rainfall between $\bar{x} \pm S{\cdot}D$ is called normal year in which $\bar{x}$ is the mean rainfall and S.D. is the standard deviation. The S.D. of given rainfall data can be calculated by using the following equation :

$$\text{S.D.} = \frac{1}{n}(x_i - \bar{x})^2 \qquad ...(3.28)$$

where, n = total number of rainfall data

x_i = ith rainfall data

$\bar{x}$ = mean rainfall

The year, which receives the rainfall greater than the normal rainfall value is considered as good year.

Abnormal year : The year, which receives the rainfall more than or equal to $\bar{x}$ + S.D. is called abnormal year. The $\bar{x}$ and S.D. are the same as in equation 3.28.

Abnormal years are also referred as wet years. The abnormal years have also been defined by other ways, such as according to Bland Ford- a year is said to be the wet year when it receive the rainfall from 1.24 to 2.54 times the mean annual rainfall, *i.e.*

$$\text{Wet year} = (1.24 \text{ to } 2.54)\,\bar{x} \qquad ...(3.29)$$

Similarly, Alexander Binnie defined the wet year as the year receiving the rainfall equal to 1.51 times the mean annual rainfall, *i.e.*

$$\text{Wet year} = 1.51\,\bar{x} \qquad ...(3.30)$$

Drought year : A year with total rainfall less than $\bar{x}$–S.D is called drought year or deficit year. The rainfall deficiency can be classified into following three classes :

(*i*) **Large deficiency :** The rainfall ranging from 35 to 45% less than the normal rainfall is considered under large deficiency.

(*ii*) **Serious deficiency :** It includes the rainfall from 45 to 60% less than the normal rainfall.

(*iii*) **Disastrous deficiency :** It includes the rainfall more than 60% below the normal rainfall.

1. **Normal month :** A month which receives the rainfall between 50 and 200% of the mean monthly rainfall is termed as normal month.

2. **Abnormal month :** The month receiving the rainfall more than twice of the mean monthly rainfall is known as abnormal month.

3. **Drought month :** The month receiving the rainfall less than 50% of the mean monthly rainfall is called drought month. Computation of normal, abnormal and drought months is shown in Example 3.19.

Example 3.19. *Using the data cited in example 3.18, compute the followings :*

1. Normal month

2. Abnormal month, and

3. Drought month for each year

Solution.

Computation of Normal, Abnormal and Drought months

As per criteria of the normal, abnormal and drought months, the ranges of rainfall for them are given in following table.

Table

Month	*Rainfall (mm)*		
	Normal month	*Abnormal month*	*Drought month*
Jan	3.55—14.40	more than 14.40	less than 3.55
Feb	2.67—1068	" 10.68	" 2.67
March	3.36—13.44	" 13.44	" 3.36
April	8.82—35.26	" 35.26	" 8.22
May	29.4—117.6	" 117.6	" 29.4
June	59.69—238.76	" 238.76	" 59.69
July	167.3—669.2	" 669.2	" 167.3
Aug.	118.92—475.68	" 475.68	" 118.92
Sept.	85.17—340.66	" 340.66	" 85.17
Oct.	16.60—66.38	" 66.38	" 16.60
Nov.	1.14—4.54	" 4.54	" 1.14
Dec.	3.24—12.96	" 12.29	" 3.24

On the basis of above range of rainfall values the normal (*N*), abnormal (*A*) and drought months (*D*) are tabulated as under.

Year	*Jan*	*Feb*	*March*	*April*	*May*	*June*	*July*	*Aug.*	*Sept.*	*Oct.*	*Nov.*	*Dec.*
1980	N	D	A	D	N	N	N	N	N	N	D	D
1981	A	D	N	N	N	N	N	A	N	D	D	D
1982	D	N	A	N	D	N	N	D	N	D	D	D
1983	N	D	D	A	A	N	N	N	N	A	D	N
1984	A	A	D	D	N	A	N	N	N	D	D	D
1985	N	D	D	N	N	N	N	N	N	A	D	D
1986	D	N	D	D	A	N	N	N	N	N	D	N
1987	D	D	N	A	D	N	N	A	D	D	D	N
1988	D	A	N	N	D	N	N	N	N	N	D	A
1989	D	A	N	D	A	N	A	D	N	D	A	A

Importance of Analysis of Rainfall Data

1. It provides an estimate about future trend of rainfall.

2. The occurrence of floods, their severness and time span can be determined.

3. Adjustment of rainfall data can be done.

4. Seasonal and annual rainfall variations of any place can be determined.

5. Facilitates to design and construction of hydraulic structures on the basis of extreme rainfall events.

6. Rainfall distribution at different probability levels/return periods can be evaluated.

7. The normal, abnormal and drought months/years can be predicted and crop planning based on the same can also be done.

8. The relationship between rainfall and runoff for a given watershed can be developed.

9. Missing rainfall data of any raingauge station can be predicted by using the rainfall record of nearby stations, provided that they are meteorologically and hydrologically identical.

10. The maximum and minimum rainfall events of any watershed can also be determined and based on them, the project formulation for construction of hydraulic structures etc can be done.

SOLVED PROBLEMS

Problem 3.1. What would be the intensity of rainfall, if durng a given time interval the mass curve of the storm is indined at 30° with the horizontal. Assume the depth of rainfall in cm and time in second.

Soltion. Given that the inclination of mass curve is 30° with the horizontal.

Therefore, intensity of rainfall = tan θ

$$= \tan 30°$$

$$= \mathbf{0.577\ cm/s} \quad \textbf{Ans.}$$

Problem 3.2. Determine the ideal and acceptable number of raingauge stations for a mountaneous catchment of temperate climate with 1.5×10^3 sq km area.

Solution. (*i*) *As per W.M.O. recommendation*

For mountaneous regions, the ideal number of raingauge station is considered as 1 station for 100 to 250 sq km area. And acceptable number of raingauge station is at the rate of 1 station for 250 to 1000 sq km area. According to this norm, the ideal number of rain gauge stations will be

$$\frac{1.5 \times 10^3}{\left(\dfrac{100+250}{2}\right)} = 8.57 \approx \mathbf{9\ stations} \quad \textbf{Ans.}$$

Similarly, acceptable number of raingauge stations will be

$$\frac{1.5 \times 10^3}{\left(\dfrac{250+1000}{2}\right)} = 2.30 \approx \mathbf{2.00} \quad \textbf{Ans.}$$

(*ii*) *As per IMD recommendation*

The ideal number of raingauge stations will be

$$\frac{1.5 \times 10^3}{130} = 11.54 \approx \mathbf{12\ stations} \quad \textbf{Ans.}$$

Problem 3.3. Determine the ideal and acceptable number of raingauge stations for a catchment of flat region of temperate climate with 1.12×10^3 sq. km area.

Solution. (*i*) *As per WMO recommendation*

Ideal number of raingauge stations

$$= \frac{1.12 \times 10^3}{\left(\dfrac{600+900}{2}\right)} = 1.49 \approx \mathbf{2\ raingauges} \quad \textbf{Ans.}$$

Acceptable number of raingauge stations

$$= \frac{1.12 \times 10^3}{\left(\dfrac{900+3000}{2}\right)} = 0.57 \approx \mathbf{1\ station} \quad \textbf{Ans.}$$

(*ii*) *As per IMD recommendation*

Ideal number of rain gauge stations

$$\frac{1.12 \times 10^3}{520} = 2.15 = \mathbf{2.00\ stations} \quad \textbf{Ans.}$$

Problem 3.4. Determine the adequate number of raingauge stations for a given watershed, if the coefficient of variation of the annual rainfall data of the watershed is 30.12%. Assume, the percent allowable error as 9%.

Solution. Using the formula

$$N = \left(\frac{Cv}{\varepsilon}\right)^2 = \left(\frac{30.12}{9}\right)^2$$

$$= 11.20 \approx \textbf{11 stations} \quad \textbf{Ans.}$$

Problem 3.5. Determine the consistent value of precipitation of a given station if inconsistant precipitation is 500 mm. And slopes of the double mass curve of consistant and inconsistant data are 1.1 and 0.9, respectively.

Solution. Using the formula

Consistent value of precipitation = correction factor × precipitation

$$= \frac{1.1}{0.9} \times 500 \text{ mm} = \textbf{611.11 mm} \quad \textbf{Ans.}$$

Problem 3.6. Determine the value of correction factor for converting the rainfall data into consistant, if the slope of double mass curve of consistant and inconsistant rainfall data is 1.2 and 0.75, respectively.

Solution.

$$\text{Correction factor} = \frac{\text{Slope of double mass curve of consistant data}}{\text{Slope of the dounle mass curve of inconsistant data}}$$

$$= \frac{1.2}{0.75} = \textbf{1.6} \quad \textbf{Ans.}$$

Problem 3.7. Determine the consistant rainfall value, if the correction factor used to make the data consistant is 1.5 and value of inconsistant rainfall is 1050 mm.

Solution. It is given by

$$\text{Consistant rainfall} = f \times \text{inconsistant rainfall}$$

$$= 1.5 \times 1050$$

or $$= 1575 \text{ mm} \quad \textbf{Ans.}$$

Problem 3.8. If the mean areal rainfall of a watershed is 1050 mm and sum of rainfall of all rain gauge stations installed in the watershed is 3150 mm, then determine the total number of rain gauge stations installed there.

Solution. Using the formula

$$\overline{P} = \frac{\sum_{i=1}^{n} Pi}{N}$$

$$1050 = \frac{3150}{N}$$

or $$N = \frac{3150}{1050} = \textbf{3} \quad \textbf{Ans.}$$

Problem 3.9. Compute the mean areal precipitation of the watershed, if sum of product of polygone area and respective precipitation for entire watershed is 42550 sq km. cm and total area of watershed is 2500 sq km.

Solution. Using the formula,

$$\overline{P} = \frac{\sum_{i=1}^{n} P_i a_i}{A}$$

$$= \frac{42550 \text{ km}^2 \cdot \text{cm}}{2500 \text{ km}^2} = \mathbf{17.02 \text{ cm}} \quad \textbf{Ans.}$$

Problem 3.10. Determine the area of watershed if its mean areal precipitation is 700 mm and sum of the product of polygone area and respective precipitation for entire watershed is 42500 sq km. cm.

Solution. Using the formula

$$\overline{P} = \frac{\sum_{i=1}^{n} P_i a_i}{A}$$

$$70 \text{ cm} = \frac{42500}{A} \text{ sq km} \cdot \text{cm}$$

$$\therefore \quad A = \frac{42500}{70} \text{ sq km} = \mathbf{607.142 \text{ sq km}} \quad \textbf{Ans.}$$

Problem 3.11. Compute the value of mean areal precipitation of the watershed, if

(*a*) total area of watershed is 500 sq km

(*b*) sum of the product of inter-isohyetal area and average precipitation of two consecutive isohyet for entire watershed is 50250 km^2. cm.

Solution. It is given by the formula

$$\overline{P} = \frac{\sum_{i=1}^{n} \frac{(P_i + P_{i+1})}{2} \cdot a_i}{A}$$

$$= \frac{50250 \text{ km}^2 \cdot \text{cm}}{500 \text{ km}^2} = \mathbf{100.5 \text{ cm}} \quad \textbf{Ans.}$$

Problem 3.12. Determine the mean precipitation of the enclosed area between two isohyets if the two isohyets are of the values of 10.5 and 9.2 cm and area between them is 100 sq km.

Solution. Using the formula, we have

$$\overline{P} = \frac{\left(\frac{P_1 + P_2}{2}\right) a}{a}$$

$$= \frac{\left(\frac{10.5 + 9.2}{2}\right) 100}{100} = \mathbf{9.85\ cm} \quad \textbf{Ans.}$$

Problem 3.13. Determine the value of rainfall intensity, if

(*a*) area of hyetograph is 10 (cm/h).h

(*b*) storm duration is 15 h

Solution. It is given by the formula

$$\text{Rainfall intensity} = \frac{\text{Area of hyetograph}}{\text{Storm duration}}$$

$$= \frac{10 \frac{\text{cm}}{\text{h}} \cdot h}{15 \cdot h} = \mathbf{0.667\ cm/h} \quad \textbf{Ans.}$$

Problem 3.14. Compute the depth of rainfall due to a given storm of 10 h duration with intensity of 0.75 cm/h.

Solution. Using the formula

$$\text{Intensity of rainfall} = \frac{\text{Rainfall depth}}{\text{Storm duration}}$$

$$0.75 \text{ cm/h} = \frac{\text{Rainfall depth}}{10 \text{ h}}$$

or $\quad$ Rainfall depth $= 0.75 \times 10 \text{ cm} = \mathbf{7.5\ cm}$ **Ans.**

Problem 3.15. Determine the value of average rainfall depth of the watershed by using depth-area relationship. Consider,

(*a*) highest rainfall depth = 10 cm

(*b*) $K = 1.75 \times 10^{-3}$ and 9.0×10^{-4} for 3- and 2-days duration, respectively.

(*c*) $n = 0.5961$ and 0.6306 for 3- and 2-days duration, respectively.

(*d*) area of watershed = 500 sq km.

Solution. Using the formula of depth-area relationship

$$\overline{P} = P_0 \exp(-KA^n)$$

(*i*) *For 3-days duration*

$$\overline{P} = 10 \exp(-1.75 \times 10^{-3} \times 500^{0.5961}) = \mathbf{9.31\ cm} \quad \textbf{Ans.}$$

(*ii*) For 2-days duration

$$\overline{P} = 10 \exp(-9 \times 10^{-4} \times 500^{0.6306}) = \mathbf{9.56\ cm} \quad \textbf{ans.}$$

Problem 3.16. Compute rainfall intensity for 25-years return period due to a storm occurring for the duration of 1.5 h. Assume $K = 6.93$, $b = 0.53$, $a = 0.13$ and $d = 0.872$.

Solution. Using the formula, we have

$$i_{25\,y} = \frac{KT^a}{(t+b)^d}$$

$$i_{25\,y} = \frac{6.93\,(25)^{0.13}}{(1.5+0.53)^{0.872}} \text{ cm/h}$$

$$= \frac{10.5309}{1.8541} = \mathbf{5.68\ cm/h} \quad \textbf{Ans.}$$

Problem 3.17. Determine the storm duration, if

(*a*) 25-years return period rainfall intensity of the storm is 5.0 cm/h

(*b*) $K = 5.12$, $b = 1.25$, $a = 0.156$ and $d = 0.75$

Solution. Using the formula,

$$i_T = \frac{KT^a}{(t+b)^d}$$

$$5 = \frac{5.12\,(25)^{0.156}}{(t+1.25)^{0.75}}$$

or $$(t+1.25)^{0.75} = 1.6819$$

$$(t+1.25) = (1.6819)^{1/0.75} = 2.0160$$

$$t = 2.0160 - 1.25 = \mathbf{0.766\ hour} \quad \textbf{Ans.}$$

Problem 3.18. What would be the return period (year) of rainfall event if its plotting position is 50%.

Solution. Using the formula

$$T = \frac{1}{p} = \frac{1}{0.50} = \mathbf{2\text{–}years} \quad \textbf{Ans.}$$

Problem 3.19. Compute the plotting position and return period of the rainfall event if its rank number is 10 during 30-years record.

Solution. Using the formula

$$P_{(\%)} = \frac{m}{n+1} \times 100$$

$$= \frac{10}{30+1} \times 100 = \mathbf{32.258\%} \quad \textbf{Ans}$$

and $$T = \frac{1}{p} = \frac{1}{\frac{32.258}{100}} \text{ years}$$

$$= \mathbf{3.10\ years} \quad \textbf{Ans.}$$

Problem 3.20. Determine the rank number of the rainfall event if its return period is 20-years and length of rainfall record is 39 years.

Solution. Using the formula

$$T = \frac{1}{P}$$

or $$P = \frac{1}{T} = \frac{1}{20} \times 100 = 5\%$$

Therefore $$P_{\%} = \frac{m}{n+1} \times 100$$

$$\frac{5}{100} = \frac{m}{39+1}$$

or $$m = \frac{200}{100} = 2 \quad \textbf{Ans.}$$

IMPORTANT POINTS

1. Raingauge is also known as pluviometer, ombrometer and hyetometer.
2. The diameter of circular collecting area of non-recording raingauge is 12.7 cm or 5".
3. The recording time of rainfall is 8:30 AM (IST).
4. Tipping bucket type raingauge is 30.5 cm size rain gauge.
5. One compartment of tipping bucket type raingauge measures the rainfall of 0.25 mm depth.
6. The Siphon type rain gauge is considered as standard recording type rain gauge in India.
7. A radar can sense the rainfall for the areal exlent of as much as 10^5 sq km.
8. For sensing heavy rains, the wavelength of radar should be 10-cm.
9. For sensing the light rains and snow fall, the suitable radars are of 5-cm wavelength.
10. In catchment the number of recording type raingauge is used as 10% of the total rain gauge.
11. Mass curve is the plot of cumulative rainfall depth and time.
12. Hyetograph is the plot of rainfall intensity and time.
13. The checking of consistency of rainfall record is done by double-mass curve.
14. Mass curve and hyetograph are the forms of presentation of rainfall data.
15. Slope of mass curve at any time is the rainfall intensity.
16. The area of hyetograph represents the total depth of precipitation.
17. Point precipitation is measured by raingauge.
18. Contour of precipitation is called isohyet.
19. The isohyet method is superior than the other methods, especially when there is large number of raingauge stations in the watershed.
20. Areal distribution of rainfall can be evaluated by the depth-area relationship.
21. The depth-area-duration relationship is expressed as DAD.
22. Rainfall intensity (storm intensity) decreases with increase in storm duration
23. A storm of given duration will have high intensity for higher return period.

24. The line joining equal depths of rainfall is called iso-pluvial.
25. The world's greatest observed rainfall is expressed by the relationship as $P_m = 42.16\, D^{0.75}$, in which D is the duration of rainfall (h).
26. The PMP of north-Indian plains varies from 37 to 100 cm for 1-day rainfall.
27. In India, the measurement of rainfall was began in the 18th century.
28. The first recorded rainfall data was obtained in Calcutta in the year 1784.
29. The Indian Meterological Department was established in the year 1930.
30. At present there are more than 5472 raingauge stations in India.
31. In India, the overall rain gauge density is about 1/600 sqkm.
32. In India, there are more than 522 recording type raingauge stations.
33. Return period is the recoprocal of plotting position (%).
34. Hazen formula computes return period of the rainfall event.
35. A year receiving the rainfall of $\bar{x} \pm S.D.$ is called normal year ($\bar{x}$ is the mean rainfall and S.D. is standard deviation of rainfall).
36. A year receiving the rainfall more than or equal to $\bar{x}$ + S.D. is called abnormal-year.
37. A year receiving the rainfall from 1.24 to 2.54 times of the mean annual rainfall, is called wet year.
38. A year receiving the rainfall less than $\bar{x}$ - S.D. is called drought year.
39. A rainfall will be under large deficiency, if it is 35 to 45% less as compared to the normal rainfall.
40. A rainfall will be under serious deficiency, if it is 45 to 60% below the normal rainfall.
41. A rainfall will be under disastrous deficiency, if it is more than 60% less than the normal rainfall.
42. The months receiving the rainfall between 50 and 200% of the mean monthly rainfall are called normal months.
43. A month, which receives the rainfall greater than twice of the mean monthly rainfall is called abnormal month.
44. A month, which receives the rainfall less than 50% of the mean monthly rainfall is called drought month.
45. Recurrence interval is also known as return period.

RETERENCE

1. Chow V.T. Handbook of Applied Hydrology, McGraw-Hill, New York, 1964.
2. Das G, Hydrology and Soil Conservation, Prentice-Hall (India), 2000.
3. Kohler, M.A., Double-mass analysis for testing the consistency of records and for making required adjustments, Am. Meteorol. Soc. Bull, Vol. 30, 1949.
4. Kohlèr M.A. Design of Hydrological networks, World Meteorol. Organisation Tech, Note, 25, Geneva, 1958.

5. Dhar O.N. and Bhattacharya B.K. "A study of depth-area-duration statistics of the severe most storms over different meteorological divisons of North, India, Prosc. Nat, Symp. on Hydorlogy, Roorkee (India), 1975.

6. Tejwani K.G., Gupta S.K. and Mohan H.N. Soil & Water conservation Research. (1957 to 71), ICAR, New Delhi, 1975.

7. Richard, the flood estimation and control, Chapman and Hall, Ltd. London, 1944.

8. McCulloch J.S.G. Statistical Assesment of Rainfall, COTA Pub. No. 66 Inter-African conf. on Hydrology, Nairobi, 1961.

9. World Meterological Organisation, Manual for depth-area-duration analysis of storm precipitation, WMO No 237, T.P. 129, Genewa, 1969.

10. Inglis C.C., Technical paper No. 30, PWD, Bombay, 1940.

11. Horton R.E., U.S. Monthly Weather Reveiw, Vol No. 47, 1919.

12. Linsley R.K. Kohler M.A. and Pauhus J.L.H. Hydrology for Engineers, McGraw Hill Book Co. Ltd. New York, 1950.

13. Mutreja K.N. Applied Hydrology, Tata McGraw-Hill Co. Ltd., New Delhi, 1985.

14. Linsley R.K., Kohler M.A. and Paulhus J.L.H., Applied Hydrology, McGraw Hill-Book Co. Ltd. New York, 1949.

15. Sharma R.K., Hydrology and Water Resources Engineering, Dhanpat Rai and Sons, Delhi, 1987.

16. Battan. L.J. Radar Meteorology, University of Chicago Press, Chicago, 1959.

DESCRIPTIVE TYPE QUESTIONS

1. Explain various methods of rainfall measurement.

2. Define rain gauge and differentiate the recording and non-recording types rain gauge.

3. Explain rainfall measurement procedure of tipping bucket type rain gauge.

4. List various advantages and disadvantages of recording types rain gauges.

5. Explain the methodology of rain gauge installation.

6. List common errors occurring during rainfall measurement.

7. Write various recommendations on raingauge distribution and explain the adequacy of rain gauge.

8. Explain normal ratio method of estimating the missing rainfall data.

9. Calculate the missing rainfall data of station *A* installed in the watershed area of 500 km^2. If there are three more raingauge stations *B*, *C* and *D* with annual rainfall of 150 cm, 75 cm and 158 cm, respectively.

10. What is consistency of rainfall record. Explain the procedure to test the consistency.

11. Determine the number of rain gauges required to install in a watershed of 500 km^2 area, if normal annual rainrall at different stations are as under.

Station	A	B	C	D	E	F
Rainfall (mm)	500	1000	750	650	450	300

(Assume allowable error as 10%).

12. Define mean areal precipitation. Describe Theissen polygon method for its computation.

13. Compare different methods of computing the mean areal precipitation and state which is more authentic and why.

14. Determine the mean areal precipitation of the following data by using Thessen polygone method.

Station	A	B	C	D	E	F
Rainfall (cm)	5.0	15.0	7.5	8.0	25.0	12.5
Polygon area (sq km.)	175	300	100	250	300	400

15. Calculate the mean areal precipitation, using isohyctal method of following data

Zone	I	II	III	IV	V
Mean isohyctal value (cm)	5.0	3.5	7.5	8.0	15.0
Area enclosed by isohyets (km^2)	30	130	45	130	250

16. Define mass curve and write its various uses.

17. Explain the rainfall intensity-duration relationship.

18. Write the procedure to compute the rainfall intensity by using Intensity-Duration-Frequency relationship.

19. Explain the procedure to develop depth-area-duration relationship.

20. Define rainfall frequency and explain Weibull's method of frequency analysis.

21. By using the Hazen formula, compute the maximum and minimum rainfall amounts for 25 and 50% probability levels of following data

Year	1980	1981	1982	1983	1984
Rainfall (mm)	105.00	175.00	500.00	1750.00	1000.00
Year	1985	1986	1987	1988	1989
Rainfall (mm)	545.00	750.00	600	1300.00	1200.00

OBJECTIVE TYPE QUESTIONS

1. Rain gauge measures the rainfall in terms of
(*a*) depth or intensity (*b*) volume
(*c*) discharge (*d*) sp. volume

2. Recording type raingauge records the rainfall in terms of
(*a*) depth (*b*) depth and time
(*c*) volume (*d*) sp. weight

3. Non recording type rain gauge measures the rainfall in terms of
(*a*) intensity (*b*) depth, only
(*c*) sp. weight (*d*) None of above

4. The capacity of individual compartment of tipping bucket type rain gauge is
(*a*) 0.50 mm (*b*) 0.25 mm
(*c*) 1.00 mm (*d*) 0.15 cm

5. For rainfall intensity ranging from 1.25 to 1.5 cm/h, the tipping action is completed at
(*a*) 6 to 7 seconds (*b*) 10 seconds
(*c*) 0.2 second (*d*) 2 seconds

6. Tipping type rain gauge is unable to measure the
(*a*) sleet (*b*) rainfall
(*c*) snow (*d*) both *a* and *c*

7. Radar is capable to collect the rainfall information upto the distance of
(*a*) 100 km (*b*) 500 km
(*c*) 250 km (*d*) 1000 km

8. The location of raingauge should be avoided on
(*a*) valley and ridge points (*b*) plan land
(*c*) arid points (*d*) none of above

9. The receiver height of raingauge should be
(*a*) 75 cm above the ground
(*b*) 50 cm above the ground
(*c*) 15 cm above the ground
(*d*) 1.25 m above the ground

10. In windy storms, the rain gauge catches
(*a*) less rainfall (*b*) more rainfall
(*c*) ice crystal depending on wind direction
(*d*) 1.25 cm ranfall, only

11. Arithmatic mean method for computing the mean areal rainfall is used when
(*a*) rainfall does not differ much from the mean rainfall of different rain gauge stations
(*b*) there are atleast five rain gauge stations
(*c*) there is only one rangauge station
(*d*) none of above

12. The normal ratio method estimates accurately, when
(*a*) normal annual precipitation of index stations differs by more than 10% of the missing rainfall value.
(*b*) snow fall is there (*c*) drizzle is there
(*d*) there are 3 raingauge stations

13. As per WMO recommendation, the ideal number of rain gauge stations in flat regions should be as

(*a*) 1 station for 600 to 900 km^2 area

(b) 1 station for 900 to 3000 km^2 area

(*c*) 1 station for 130 km^2.

(*d*) 1 station for 75 km^2

14. In watershed, the proportion of recording and non-recording type rain gauge stations should be

(*a*) 1 : 9 (*b*) 2 : 8

(*c*) 3 : 7 (*d*) 3 : 2

15. For computing the adequate number of rain gauge stations, the value of allowable error (ε) is generally taken as

(*a*) 10% (*b*) 5.5%

(*c*) 7.5% (*d*) 25%

16. The Thessin polygon method provides a good estimation, when

(*a*) there is linear variation in the values of rainfall at different rain gauge stations

(b) irregular topography of the area.

(*c*) there is only one raingauge station.

(*d*) none of above..

17. For the watershed area more than 5000 km^2, which is most suitable method for computing the mean areal precipitation.

(*a*) Theissien polygon method

(*b*) Isohyctal method

(*c*) Arithmatic mean method

(*d*) Rader method

18. A rainfall is said to be heavy, when its intensity is

(*a*) 2.5 to 7.5 cm/h (*b*) more than 7.5 cm/h

(*c*) less than 2.5 cm/h (*d*) less than 10 cm/h

19. Weibul's method computes

(*a*) rainfall intensity (*b*) plotting position

(*c*) drop size (*d*) terminal velocity

20. The return period of rainfall, whose plotting position is 50%, will be

(*a*) 2 years (*b*) 5 years

(*c*) 50 years (*d*) 75 years

21. For the rainfall of 250 mm depth what would be its recurrence interval, if its plotting position is 100%.

(*a*) 100 years (*b*) 1 year

(*c*) 250 years (*d*) 75 years

22. Amongst five years of rainfall record *i.e.* 250 mm, 50 mm, 750 mm, 1000 mm and 150 mm, what would be the rank number of 750 mm rainfall.

(*a*) 1 (*b*) 2

(*c*) 3 (*d*) 5

23. A year is said to be normal, when its rainfall varies as

(*a*) $\bar{x} \pm 2D$ (*b*) $\bar{x} + c_v$

(*c*) $\bar{x} - 1.5D$ (*d*) None of above

24. A year is said to be wet year, when its rainfall varies
(*a*) (1.24 to 2.54) $\bar{x}$ (*b*) (1.24 to 3.54) $\bar{x}$
(*c*) (2.54 to 7.24) $\bar{x}$ (*d*) 159 mm

25. At greater temperature, the infiltration rate will be
(*a*) less (*b*) high
(*c*) 10 mm/h (*d*) none of these.

26. For rainfall analysis, there should be atleast
(*a*) 30 years data (*b*) 25 years data
(*c*) 10 years data. (*d*) 7 years data

27. Normal rainfall of any place is evaluated on the basis of
(*a*) 30 years data (*b*) 100 years data
(*c*) 15 years data (*d*) 50 years data

28. Consistency of rainfall is determined by
(*a*) mass-curve (*b*) hyetograph
(*c*) flow-duration curve (*d*) double-mass curve

29. Diameter of water droplets in drizzle is
(*a*) 0.5 mm (*b*) 1.0 mm
(*c*) 1.5 mm (*d*) 2.0 mm

30. Return period is expressed in the unit of
(*a*) hour (*b*) year
(*c*) minute (*d*) second.

Answer (Objective Type Question)

1.	(*a*)	**2.**	(*b*)	**3.**	(*b*)	**4.**	(*b*)	**5.**	(*a*)	**6.**	(*d*)	**7.**	(*b*)	**8.**	(*a*)
9.	(*a*)	**10.**	(*a*)	**11.**	(*a*)	**12.**	(*a*)	**13.**	(*a*)	**14.**	(*a*)	**15.**	(*a*)	**16.**	(*b*)
17.	(*b*)	**18.**	(*b*)	**19.**	(*b*)	**20.**	(*a*)	**21.**	(*b*)	**22.**	(*b*)	**23.**	(*a*)	**24.**	(*a*)
25.	(*b*)	**26.**	(*a*)	**27.**	(*a*)	**28.**	(*d*)	**29.**	(*a*)	**30.**	(*b*)				

4

Losses of Precipitation

During occurrence of precipitation over the land surface, a part of it is either retained on the vegetative foliage, initially dried building surfaces etc or absorbed by the soil itself. In addition, in the mean time a portion of precipitation is also returned back to the atmosphere by evaporation and transpiration process. And at last, the remaining rainfall flows over the land surface as overland flow. Amount of precipiration, which does not appear as overland flow or runoff is considered as loss of precipitation. The runoff refers to the flow of precipitated water into channel. The definition of water loss is governed on the need of specific concern, *e.g.* for hydrologists, the water loss is the difference of total precipitation amexnating from the cloud and total runoff amount. It may be expressed as :

Total rainfall – total water lost = runoff

or Water loss = total rainfall – runoff.

4.1. Water Loss

Various water losses, which could occur during or after the rainfall are given as under :

1. Interception loss
2. Evaporation loss
3. Transpiration loss
4. Evaportranspiration or consumptive use
5. Infiltration loss, and
6. Watershed leakage.

All these are described as under :

Interception

It is that part of precipitation, which is intercepted by the vegetative foliage, buildings and other objects lying over the ground surface and is returned back to the atmosphere by evaporation. Intercepted water does not reach to the ground surface.

Physical aspect of interception is described as : when precipitation starts to fall over the ground surface, it first strikes the vegetative foliage or some other objects lying the ground. At this time, few part of the precipitation is intercepted and retained by these objects in form of thin layer, which is subsequently evaporated and returned back to the atmosphere. After sometime, if rainfall is still continued, then there comes a situation when retention capacity of vegetative foliage gets staurated. After this, if rainfall takes place, then that directly falls over the land surface.

There have been made several studies on evaluation of interception loss under different kinds of forest cover. Table 4.1 indicates few findings on interception loss reported by few researchers in India.

Table 4.1. Interception loss by different kinds of forest cover

Forest cover (Tree species)	*Tree density (Trees/ha)*	*Interception (mm)*	*Through fall (mm)*	*Stem flow (mm)*
Shorea robusta (Sal)	668	38.2	54.6	7.2
Alstonia scholaris	1675	26.0	57.0	17.0
Pinus roxburhii (Chir)	1156	22.1	74.3	3.6
Tectona grandis (Teak)	472	20.8	74.3	6.0
Acacia catechu (Khair)	574	28.5	67.3	4.2
Eucalyptus hybrid	1658	11.6	60.8	7.6
Cedrus deodard (Deodar)	515	25.3	71.8	2.9

Interception Loss : It is that part of precipitation which is intercepted by the surface objects and returned back to the atmosphere through evaporation. At saturation stage, the interception loss is equal to the evaporation loss.

Interception storage : That amount of precipitated water, which wets the initially dried surfaces of the objects lying over the ground surface is called interception storage.

4.1.1. Factors Affecting Interception

Factors which affect the interception are as below :

1. Storm factor
2. Plant factor
3. Season of the year, and
4. Prevailing wind

Storm factor

Storm affects the interception by several ways, such as by its nature, duration etc. A precipitaion in the form of drizzle is completely absorbed by

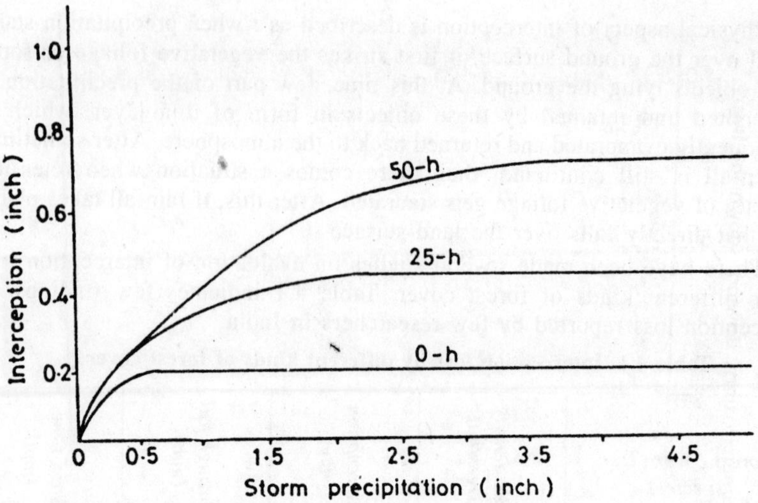

Fig. 4.1. Relationship between interception, precipitation and duration.

the vegetative foliage as interception. From field studies, it has been found that, if precipitation is less than 0.254 mm depth then it is completely intercepted and if it is more than 1.02 mm, then interception varies from 10 to 40% of the total precipitation. However, the percentage rainwater lost through interception is reduced with increase in duration and intensity of rainfall. The relationship amongst storm precipitation, duration and interception is shown in Fig. 4.1.

Plant Factor

Plant affects the interception loss by its phenological characteristics *i.e.* canopy size, canopy density and leaf characteristis. A plant with wide canopy causes greater interception loss. Also, from a dense canopy, the interception is always more. Leaf with rough surface absorbs more water *i.e.* greater interception loss. Variations in interception with the type of vegetal cover is shown in Fig. 4.2 and the variations in interception under different types of plant is also shown in table 4.2.

Table 4.2. Variations in interception under different vegetal covers

Vegetation	*Total rainfall mm*	*Amount of rain falling over ground surface, mm*	*Interception, mm*
Oak	73.6	12.8	21.8
Maple	71.5	6.0	22.5
Beech	65.4	12.8	21.8

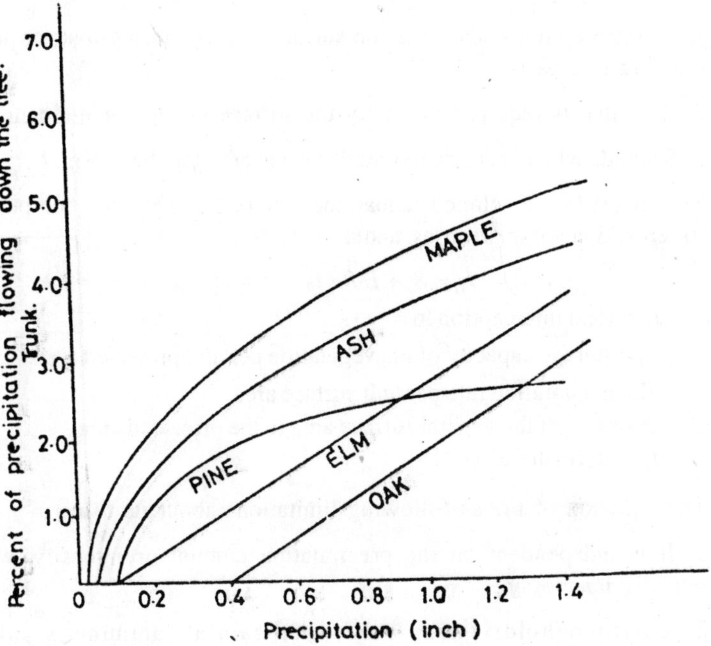

Fig. 4.2. Variations in interception with the types of vegetal cover.

Season of the year

It affects the interception loss by affecting the vegetative growth and phenological features of the crop. Vegetative growth refers to increase in surface-area of the crop canopy. Interception increases with increase in vegetative growth. Inaddition, the season also affects the amount and forms of precipitation. For example - rainly season receives majority of precipitation in the form of rainfall, while winter and summer season receive in the form of rainfall, hails etc. The forms of precipitation affect the interception *e.g.* a rainfall causes greater interception than the snowfall or hails.

Prevailing wind

It affects the interception by following two ways :

1. By reducing the storage capacity of vegetative foliage.
2. By increasing the evaporation rate from the storage build up on the canopy.

Case 1 : In steady rainfall with no wind condition the interception rate is relatively more and it is continued until the storage capacity of canopy is completly filled ; and then it starts decreasing at slower rate.

Case II : At the condition of rainfall occurrence along with wind, the interception rate is very less, because wind blows out the precipitating water away from the vegetative cover during precipitation. Wind also affects the interception by increasing the evaporation loss from the water storage made on the canopy.

4.2. Total Interception

Total interception made over the surface objects during a storm, consists of following two parts :

1. One, that is required to satisfy the surface storage of the canopy; and
2. Second, which gets evaporated during or after the storm.

Horton (1919) developed a mathmetical relationship for computing the total interception loss, given as under :

$$I_{ri} = S_v + E{\cdot}R \cdot t_R \qquad ...(4.1)$$

where, I_{ri} = total interception loss

S_v = storage capacity of the vegetation per unit projected area.

E = evaporation rate per unit surface area

R = ratio of the vegetal surface area to the projected area

t_R = storm duration

The equation (4.1) has following limitations about its use :

1. It is independent on the precipitation amount or intensity, which is theoretically not possibe.

2. Equation holds good, only when rainfall amount is sufficient throughout the storm period to satisfy the retention capacity.

Linsley (1949) also developed the following equation for computing the total interception loss :

$$I_{ri} = S_v\,(1 - e^{-p/S_v}) + K{\cdot}p \qquad ...(4.2)$$

where, p = precipitation, expressed in inch

$$K = \frac{E \cdot R \cdot t_R}{p}$$

If the value of p is more, then equation 4.2 is reduced to :

$$I_{ri} = S_v + K{\cdot}p \qquad ...(4.3)$$

Storage capacity of vegetation (S_v) can be determined by using the following equation :

$$S_v = A\,(B + C{\cdot}p)\,H \qquad ...(4.4)$$

where, A = factor, which depends on the vegetative cover

B = factor, depends on the storage capacity of vegetation

C = factor associated to the evaporation loss from the vegetal surface area

p = depth of precipitation, inch

H = crop height

The values of *A B* and *C* are given in Table 4.3

Table 4.3. Values of *A*, *B* and *C* for different types of crops

Crop	*A*	*B*	*C*
Oats	1.0	0.007	0.07
Maize	H*10	0.005	0.005
Grass	5/6	0.005	0.08
Wheat, Barley	1.0	0.005	0.05
Potato, Cabbage and Beans	H/4	0.02	0.15

*Plant height

Secondary Interception

The interception from more than one levels of vegetal surface, i.e. the vegetal surface formed by the combinations of trees of different heights or trees + grasses is called secondary interception. This type of interception is very common in forest areas. It is always greater than the primary interception loss because of following reasons :

1. Due to greater evaporation.
2. Due to enlarged surface area of the vegetation.

From forest areas, the interception loss can be determined by using the following formula :

$$I_s = P_g (T_f + S_f) + I'_{gs} \qquad ...(4.5)$$

where, I_s = secondary interception

P_g = gross precipitation

T_f = through fall

S_f = stem flow

I'_s = primary interception

4.3. Measurement of Interception

Interception is measured by an instrument called 'interceptometer'. The instrument is placed on the ground surface under canopy to collect the falling rain water. The collected rain-water by the interceptometer is compared with the rain water caught by the raingauge installed in the open area. The difference in the amount of rainfall collected by interceptometer and raingauge is considered as interception.

In order to determine the secondary interception, the measurements on stem flow and through fall are also required. Measurement procedures of stem flow and through fall are described as under :

Measurement of Stem Flow : Falling of rainwater along the stem is called stem flow. It depends on the roughness of stem bark. A stem, which is smooth has relatively more amount of stem flow than a rough stem, because smooth stem offers less resistance to flow as compared to the rough bark. From studies, it has been reported that in the case of rough bark stem, the stem flow varies from 0.02 to 0.03 of the precipitation, while in smooth bark stem, it is from 0.01 to 0.15 of precipitation.

The stem flow measurement is done by tieying a metal ring around the stem in such a way that the flowing water could not pass below the ring. At a convenient point, a pipe is equipped in the ring, through which the stem flow is collected into a container. Measurement procedure is shown in Fig. 4.3.

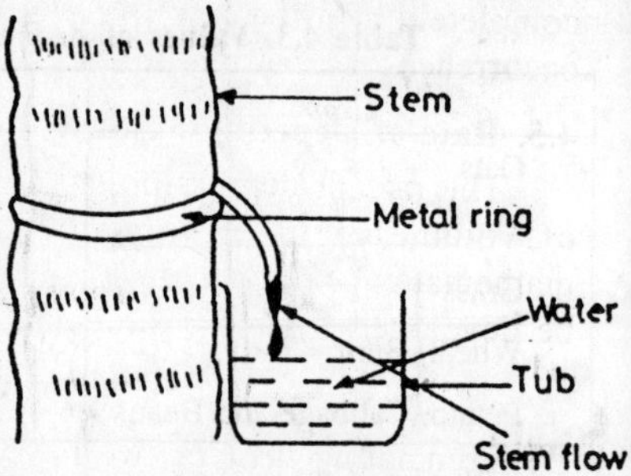

Fig. 4.3. Measurement of stem flow.

Measurement of Through fall : That part of precipitation, which reaches to the ground surface by passing through vegetal cover, inter space of crop canopy and falling of water-drops from the leaves, branches etc is known as through fall.

Measurement of through fall is carried out by putting a tub under tree canopy. The amount of water collected in the tub during precipitation is denoted as through fall. Precaution should be maintained that, the water collected in the tub should not be splashed during measurement and the tub should also not be touched with the stem.

4.4. Depression Storage

Depression storage is the volume of water retained in the puddles, ditches or some other depressions existing on the land surface. The size of depression may vary from micro to large capacity.

Physical aspect of depression storage may be described as, when precipitation takes place with the rate greater than the infiltration rate of the soil, then excess rainwater begins to collect in the surface depressions and then overland flow starts which also fills the bigger size depressions, existing in its path.

Depression storage affects the initial loss and thus to runoff, also.

4.4.1. Volume of Water Stored in the Depression

The volume of water stored in the surface depression during storm is approximated with the help of excess rainfall. The following relationship can be used for computing the depression storage :

$$V_s = S_d \{1 - \exp.(-K P_e)\} \quad ...(4.6)$$

where, V_s = volume of water stored in the surface depression

S_d = total depression storage-storage capacity of the basin

K = constant

P_e = rainfall excess

The equation 4.6 is derived by assuming that, initially the rainfall is completely absorbed by the depression. This equation does not consider the occurrence of evaporation loss from the depression storage during storm.

4.5. Rate of Depression Storage

The rate of depression storage builds up from the rainfall is the function of volume of water formed by the excess rainwater during storm. The mathematical relationship for determining the rate of depression storage can be developed by using the equation (4.6)

i.e. $$V_s = S_d(1 - e^{-KP_e}) \qquad \text{...(4.7)}$$

Defferenciating w.r.t P_e, we have

$$\frac{dV_s}{dP_e} = S_d e^{-KP_e} K$$

when $$P_e = 0, \frac{dV_s}{dP_e} = 1 = Sd \cdot K$$

or $$K = \frac{1}{S_d} \qquad \text{...(4.8)}$$

Rate of change of depression storage

$$V = \frac{dV_s}{dt} \qquad \text{...(4.9)}$$

Let, the overland flow rate $= \sigma$

rainfall intensity $= i$

infiltration rate $= I$

Then, overland flow + depression storage $= i - I$

or $$\sigma + V = i - I$$

$$\sigma = i - I - V$$

$$\frac{\sigma}{i - I} = \frac{i - I - V}{i - I} \qquad \text{...(4.10)}$$

We know that, $$V_s = S_d(1 - e^{-KP_e})$$

$$V = \frac{dV_s}{dt} = \frac{d}{dt}\left\{S_d(1 - e^{-KP_e})\right\}$$

$$= S_d \cdot K \cdot e^{-KP_e} \frac{dP_e}{dt}$$

$$= e^{-K \cdot P_e} S \frac{1}{S} \frac{dP_e}{dt}$$

$$V = e^{-KP_e} \frac{dP_e}{dt} \qquad \text{...(4.11)}$$

Rainfall excess $$(P_e) = i - I \qquad \text{...(4.12)}$$

Differentiating the equation 4.12 w.r.t. t, we have

$$\frac{dP_e}{dt} = i - I$$

Substituting the value of $\frac{d\,P_e}{dt}$ in equation 4.11, we have,

$$V = e^{-K \cdot P_e}(i - I) \qquad \text{...(4.13)}$$

Now, substituting the value of V in equation 4.10

$$\frac{\sigma}{i - I} = \frac{(i - I) - e^{-KP_e}(i - I)}{(i - I)}$$

or

$$\frac{\sigma}{i - I} \frac{(i - I)\,1 - e^{-KP_e}}{(i - I)}$$

$$\frac{\sigma}{i - I} = 1 - e^{-KP_e}$$

or

$$\frac{\sigma}{i - l} = 1 - \exp.\frac{1}{S_d}(P - F) \qquad \text{...(4.14)}$$

This is the desired expression for computing the rate of depression storage. In this equation P is denoted as total amount of precipitation and F as the accumutated infiltration.

4.6. Evaporation

Conversion of water into vapour form due to effect of temperature is called evaporation. In hydro-meteorological studies, the evaporation from free water surface and soil is only considered.

4.6.1. Evaporation from Water Surface

Liquids (mainly water) are continuously lost due to evaporation. The laws governing the evaporation process are not clearly understood. However, the basic theory on which, it depends, is given below :

Like other bodies, the water is also constituted by a number of molecules, which are constantly moving in different directions with different velocities. The average velocity of water molecules developes a fixed temperatures. At the temperature of zero degree absolute, the velocity of molecules is supposed to be zero. The molecules are also attracted by gravitational force, which is directly proportional to the product of their mass and inversely proportional to the intermolecular space. In this way, the water molecules which are close to the top of the water surface, will have greater force of attraction towards downward than the upward direction. Therefore, molecules of this zone are more liable to detach from the water surface, provided that their own velocity is sufficient to overcome the resisting force.

The water molecules continuously leave the water surface and other molecules take their position. The number of leaving molecules is not equal to the number of arriving molecules. If the number of leaving molecules is greater than the incoming molecules, then there is evaporation. On the other hand, if number of leaving molecules is lesser than the incoming molecules then there is 'condensation'.

Dalton's Law of Evaporation

It states that the evaporation rate is directly proportional to the difference of vapour pressure of the water surface and the atmosphere, expressed as :

$$E = K\,(e_w - e_a) \qquad ...(4.15)$$

where,

E = evaporation rate, cm/day

K = constant; its value depends on the atmospheric pressure, wind velocity, humidity etc.

e_w = saturated vapour pressure or maximum vapour pressure of the layer adjacent to the water surface.

e_a = actual vapour pressure of the air at 2 m height from the ground surface.

The equation 4.15 can be generalized by considering the wind velocity, given as :

$$E = K\,(e_w - e_a)\,(a + b \cdot v) \qquad ...(4.16)$$

in which, E, e_w, and e_a are the same as in equation (4.15). a, b & K are the constant and v is the wind velocity.

4.6.2. Factors Affecting Evaporation Rate

The factors affecting evaporation rate are listed below:

1. Surface area of the water body.
2. Depth of water in the reservoir.
3. Nature of the rainfall.
4. Humidity.
5. Wind velocity.
6. Temperature of water and atmosphere, and
7. Salinity of water.

All these factors are described as under :

1. **Exposed surface area of the water :** Amount of water lost through evaporation from any water body is directly affected by the exposed surface area. If exposed surface area is large, then evaporation loss will be more and vice-versa.

2. **Depth of water in the reservoir :** Depth of water available in the reservoir, greatly affects the evaporation loss. At greater water depth, the summer evaporation is less while winter evaporation is more.

3. **Nature of the rainfall :** The nature of rainfall, such as intensity, frequency and its duration affects the evaporation, considerably. For example- if duration of rainfall is more, then evaporation from intercepting objects like vegetative foliage, buildings etc will be continued for longer time and vice-versa.

4. **Humidity :** Higher the humidity, smaller will be the evaporation. The reason of it may be described as : during evaporation the water molecules move from higher moisture regime to lower moisture regime. Rate of this movement is governed by the difference of moisture content or moisture gradient of the air. Hence, if the air humidity is more, then moisture gradient will be less and accordingly the evaporation will be less and vice-versa.

5. **Wind velocity :** It affects the evaporation loss to a great extent. If wind velocity is more, then evaporation will be more, because the air containing water vapour tends to move faster, causing rapid diffusion and dispersion of vapour, which results fast evaporation.

6. **Temperature :** Evaporation loss is greatly affected by the temperature. If temperature is more, the saturated vapour pressure will be more and accordingly evaporation rate will be high. Due to this reason, evaporation loss is comparitively greater in summer season than the winter season.

7. **Salinity of the water :** Dissolved salts in the water reduce the evaporation loss.

4.6.3. Estimation of Evaporation from Water Surface

The evaporation loss from large water surface, such as rivers, ponds, reservoirs etc can be estimated by using the following methods :

1. Storage - equation method
2. Pan - measurement method
3. Energy - budget method
4. Penman equation method, and
5. Empirical formulae

1. Storage equation method. Storage equation is based on the concept that, there is balance between the amount of water lost and incoming water to the storage body. The form of storage-equation is given as under.

$$P + I \pm Q_g = E + O \pm S \qquad ...(4.17)$$

where,

P = amount of water added by the precipitation.

I = quantity of surface inflow.

Q_g = amount of ground water flow; the +ve sign is used for inflow and –ve sign is for the outflow.

E = evaporation rate from the water surface

O = out flow

S = change in storage, the +ve and –ve signs are used for increasing and decreasing of the storage, respectively.

Equation 4.17 can be rearranged as under :

$$E = (P + I \pm Q_g) - (O \pm S) \qquad ...(4.18)$$

In this equation, all parameters are converted in terms of 'depth' and by substituting them the evaporation loss from free water surface can be calculated. This method is not very much in use, as it involves combersome calculations for determining the values of different parameters associated to the equation.

Example 4.1. *Calculate the amount of water lost by evaporation, if:*

1. *amount of precipitation = 12 mm*
2. *quantity of surface inflow = 120 mm*
3. *ground water flow = 75 mm*
4. *surface outflow = 13 mm*
5. *decreased storage = 5 mm*

Solution. Using equation 4.18, the evaporation loss is given by

$$E = (P + I - Q_g) - (O - S)$$
$$= (12 + 120 - 75) - (13 - 5)$$
$$= \mathbf{49\ mm} \quad \textbf{Ans.}$$

2. Pan-measurement method. This method consists of standard size pan, in which water is filled to a fixed depth, for evaporation. The depth of water lost during a given time period is directly measured by the scale provided to the pan. The evaporation rate is calculated by dividing the depth of water lost with time. This evaporation rate is called pan evaporation which does not represent the areal evaporation. The evaporation rate varies with the areal extent of water body. From a lage water body, the evaporation rate will be different from a limited water body. That is why, a factor known as 'pan coefficient' is multiplied to the pan evaporation rate for getting the correct value.

Various types of pans have been designed for measuring the evaporation few of them are described below :

U.S. Weather Bureau Class-A Pan

It is made of G.I sheet. The diameter of pan is 1.22 m and depth 25.5 cm. It is kept over the wood griliage at the height of 15 cm from the ground surface for circulation of air below the pan. Pan also consists of several accessories, such as stilling well, vernier point gauge, thermometer etc. The whole pan assembly is covered with the wire screen. For measurement of evaporation, the depth of water in the pan is kept between 5 and 7.5 cm below the top of the pan.

The depth of water lost is measured by the vernier point gauge, at the interval of 8 hours, daily. Similarly, the air temperature is also measured by the dry bulb thermometer, located in the same enclosure. Wind velocity is recorded by using the anemometer. The pan coefficient ranging from 0.6 to 0.8 is multiplied to the measured evaporation for getting correct value.

Colorado Sunken Pan : The cross-sectional area of this pan is 92 sq cm and depth varies from 46 to 92 cm. It is sunk in the ground in such a way that only 5 to 15 cm pan height is projected above the ground surface. Water level is maintained within 2.5 cm depth from the ground level. Depth of water lost is measured directly by using the point gauge, provided to the pan. For determining the correct evaporation rate, a pan coefficient ranging from 0.75 to 0.86 is also multiplied to the observed evaporation rate.

Floating Pan : This pan is also known as U.S. Geological Survey floating pan. It is made of G.I sheet. The dimension of floating pan is 90 sq. cm as the cross-sectional area with 45 cm depth. Pan is kept on a rotating raft in the water. The water level in the pan is maintained to the height of water level in the water body. The volume of water lost due to evaporation is measured interms of volume of water added to maintain the original water level in the pan, daily. The measured evaporation from pan is multiplied by the pan coefficient to get the correct value. In floating pan method, the value of pan coefficient is generally taken as 0.8.

Pan Coefficient : The evaporation data obtained from different kinds of pan are not correct. Therefore, before using these data for analysis purposes, they are adjusted for the climatological and physical factors involved to affect the evaporation rate. For example- if we compare the pan evaporation, with the evaporation from a big water body whose surface area and depth is too large then there must be incorporation of some additional factors to compensate the variation in evaporation.

Since the pan contains very little volume of water as compared to the big water body, therefore the evaporation from it will be more. Because a small water column has greater effect of solar radiation, wind velocity, temperature etc on evaporation. In this way, the evaporation measured by pan evaporimeter is not correct. It is corrected by multiplying a coefficient known as 'pan coefficient'.

The pan coefficient is defined as the ratio of lake evaporation to the pan evaporation. It is given by,

$$P_c = \frac{E_L}{E_p} \qquad \text{...(4.19)}$$

where, P_c = pan coefficient (dimensionless)

E_L = lake evaporation

E_p = pan evaporation

Example 4.2. *Compute the value of pan coefficient, if lake and pan evaporations are 25 and 30 mm, respectively.*

Solution. Given that, the

lake evaporation $(E_L) = 25$ mm

pan evaporation $(E_p) = 30$ mm

$\therefore$ Pan coefficient $(P_c) = \frac{E_L}{E_p}$

$= \frac{25}{30} = \mathbf{0.83}$ **Ans.**

3. **Computation of Evaporation by Empirical Formulae :** There have been developed several empirical formulae for computing the evaporation rate on the basis of weather parameters, such as temperature, solar radiation, saturation vapour pressure, wind velocity etc. Few of them are described as under :

Rohwer's formula : It is given by the following equation :

$$E = 0.771\,(1.465 - 0.00732\,p)\,(0.44 - 0.00737\,V)\,(e_s - e_a) \qquad ...(4.20)$$

where,

$E =$ evaporation rate, cm/day

$p =$ mean barometric pressure at 0°C (cm)

$e_s =$ saturation vapour pressure at mean water temperature (cm of mercurry)

$e_a =$ average vapour pressure of the air (cm of mercurry)

$V =$ wind velocity (km/h) at the height of 60 cm from the ground surface. The following formula can be used for computing the wind velocity at any height :

$$V_z = V_1\,(1 + \log_{10} z) \qquad ...(4.21)$$

where, $V_Z =$ wind velocity at the height z from the ground surface.

$V_1 =$ wind velocity at 1 feet height from the ground surface.

4. **Energy Budget Method :** It estimates the evaporation on the principle of "conservation of heat energy. This method is theoretically sound, but requires large numbers of hydro-meteorological data which are not commonly available. In India, this method is not generally used for determining the evaporation. Various energy based-formulae are as follows :

1. Penman formula (1948)

$$E = 0.89\,(1 - 0.15\,U_2)\,(e_s - e_a) \qquad ...(4.22)$$

2. Meyer formula :

$$E = C\left(1 + \frac{U_8}{16}\right)(e_s - e_a) \qquad ...(4.23)$$

3. USSR formula $\quad E = 4.57\,T + 43.3 \qquad ...(4.24)$

4. Harbeck formula (1954)

$$E = 0.1156\, U_4\, (e_s - e_2) \qquad ...(4.25)$$

5. Shahtin formula $E = 0.35\, (e_s - e_a)\, (1 + 0.15\, U_2)$ ...(4.26)

Various notations used in above formulae are named as under :

E = evaporation (cm/day)

e_s = saturation vapour pressure at water surface temperature ,(mb)

e_a = saturation vapour pressure of air, (mb)

U_2 = wind velocity at 2 m height, (cm/s)

U_8 = wind velocity at 8 m height, (cm/s)

T = mean annual temperature °C

U_4 = wind velocity at 4 m height, (cm/s)

e_2 = vapour pressure at 2 m height, (mb)

C = coefficient ; it is taken as 0.36 for large deep lakes and 0.50 for small shallow lakes

Energy budget equation can be presented in the following form

$$H_i + H_r + H_{rl} + H_{le} + H_e + H_h + H_w = H_s + H_a + H_v \qquad ...(4.27)$$

or

$$H_i = (H_s + H_a + H_v) - H_r + H_{rl} + H_{le} + H_e + H_h + H_w) \qquad ...(4.28)$$

where, H_i = increase in energy stored by the water

H_s = solar radiation at water surface

H_a = incoming long wave radiation on the water surface

H_v = net advected energy into the water

H_r = reflected solar radiation

H_{rl} = reflected long–wave radiation

H_{le} = long–wave radiation emitted from the water surface.

H_e = energy consumed in evaporation

H_n = conducted energy from the water as sensible heat

H_w = advected energy by evaporated water.

Limitation : Energy budget method has following limitations :

1. This method is suitable for computation of evaporation from shallow lakes, because flowing of heat from bottom of the lake is not accounted.

2. Accuracy in computation depends on the accurate measurement of various components involved in the equation.

3. This method does not consider the effect of air stability, radiative diffusivity etc.

4.7. Soil Evaporation

It is the evaporation taking place from wet soil surface or loss of water from the soil surface when water-table is 1 m below the ground surface. Soil evaporation is also expressed by the term "evaporation opportunity", which is given as under :

$$\text{E.O.} = \frac{\text{Actual evaporation from land surface at a given time}}{\text{Equivalent evaporation from free water surface}} \times 100$$

The soil evaporation mainly depends on the water-table depth, soil types, nature of the soil and meteorological condition of the area.

4.7.1. Factors Affecting Soil Evaporation

There are various factors which affect the soil evaporation, given as under :

1. Moisture content of the soil
2. Soil cover
3. Barreness of the soil
4. Temperature
5. Humidity etc.

Soil evaporation is directly proportional to the moisture content and inversely proportional to the time *i.e.*

$$E \propto \frac{m{\cdot}c}{t}$$

or

$$E = k\frac{m{\cdot}c}{t} \qquad \text{...(4.29)}$$

where, E = evaporation

$m{\cdot}c$ = moisture content of the soil

k = constant

t = time

Soil cover greatly affects the evaporation by reducing the effect of wind velocity, solar radiation etc on the soil surface. If soil is under barren condition, then all the factors responsible for evaporation become very active and accelerate the evaporation rate. A soil which has less moisture holding capacity, involves greater evaporation and vice-versa. In sandy soil which has less moisture holding capacity than the clay soil, the evaporation rate is more as compared to the clay soil. But when both the soils are at saturation stage, then evaporation rate becomes same. Similarly, change in atmospheric condition, such as temperature, humidity etc also affects the soil evaporation to a large extent.

4.8. Transpiration

It is the process, in which water is lost through the living plants (especially from the leaves) during respiration process. In a living plant, there is continuous movement of water from the soil to the roots, from roots to the stem, from stem to the leaves and lastly from leaves to the atmosphere. Based on the study, it has been found that the velocity of flowing water through plant body varies from 25 to 175 cm/h. This could be increased, depending on the temperature, wind velocity etc. Major portion of water lost due to transpiration is during day hours, ranging from 90 to 95%, while a little portion to the night hours, ranging from 5 to 10%. Transpiration rate, gets increase with the advancement of clock time *i.e.* it is minimum in the early morning and reaches to the maximum at noon of the day. Again, it declines to the minimum in the evening. The relationship amongst *ET*, *T* and *E* is shown in Fig. 4.4

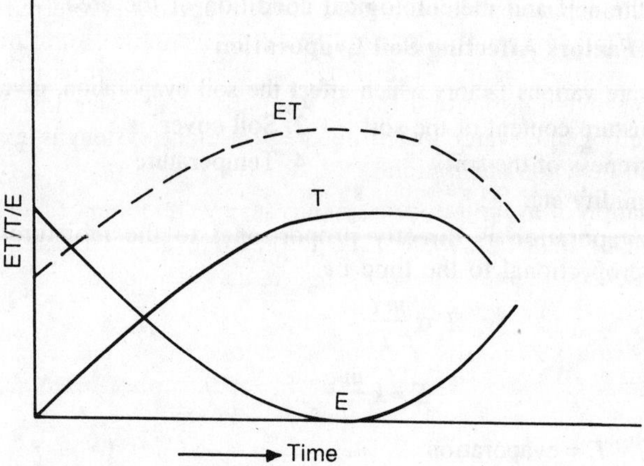

Fig. 4.4

4.8.1. Measurement of Transpiration

There have been developed various methods for measuring the transpiration. A common method *i.e.* Phytometer method is described below.

"Phytometer" consists of a closed tank, filled with sufficient soil. Plants are transplanted inside the tank in the soil. Tank is so constructed, that only plant is exposed to the atmosphere. The water is applied to the plant manually. For determining transpiration loss, the following observations are recorded :

1. Initial weight of the phytometer *i.e.* W_1
2. Water applied for the plant growth *i.e.* W_2
3. Final weight of the phytometer *i.e.* W_3

Let, the amount of water consumed by the plant (*i.e.* transpired) is W_e, then

$$W_e = (W_1 + W_2) - W_3 \quad \text{...(4.30)}$$

The obtained value of transpiration is multiplied by a coefficient for getting its correct value.

Sometimes, transpiration loss is also determined in terms of transpiration ratio (T.R.), which is defined as the ratio of the weight of absorbed water by the root system of plant during respiration process throughout growing season to the weight of dry matter produced exclusive of roots. It is expressed as :

$$\text{T.R.} = \frac{\text{Weight of transpired water (Wt)}}{\text{Weight of dry matter (Wd)}}$$

The value of transpiration ratio for different crops is generally found in the range of 300 to 800. For paddy crop, it is about 700.

4.9. Evaportranspiration

It is combine term of evaporation and transpiration, defined as the total loss of water through evaporation and transpiration from the soil-plant system. The term "transpiration" is associated to the plant and is referred for the water lost through plant during respiration process. Evaportranspiration occurs only from the cropped land. Practically, it is not possible to separate the evaporation and transpiration losses from the total water lost from cropped land, therefore, the water lost from the soil-plant system is expressed by a single term "evapotranspiration".

Estimation of evapotranspiration has several importance, such as planning and design of irrigation systems, determination of crop water requirement, irrigation scheduling etc. However, hydrology is concerned, its importance is for determining the hydrologic losses.

In agricultural fields, the evaporation loss is counted from the period of land preparation to the sowing of seeds. When seeds are germinated and seedlings bear the leaves, the transpiration loss begins to happen. Transpiration loss increases with increase in the vegetative growth of the plant. In the mean time, a position arrives, when vegetative growth covers the soil surface to maximum level, then evaporation loss becomes minmum, while transpiration loss reaches at its maximum limit. If the soil surface is fully covered by the vegetative foliage of the crop and water is non limiting then evapotranspiration becomes independent of the soil & plant but depends on the atmospheric conditions.

As the time passes, the crop gets matured and leaves are fall down on the soil surface, resulting into more exposure of soil surface to the sun light. Under this condition, transpiration loss is reduced to its minimum level, while evaporation loss reaches to the maximum.

4.9.1. Factors Affecting Evapotranspiration

On the basis of different phases of water movement, *i.e.* starting from absorption of water from the soil, transmitting the same into the stems, leaves and finally exhausting into the atmosphere through plants, the factors affecting evapotranspiration can be grouped into following four main categories :

1. Soil factor	2. Plant factor
3. Atmospheric factor; and	4. Cultural factor.

All these factors are described as under :

Soil Factor : Soil plays a significant role in evapotranspiration process. It controls the evaporation by following ways :

1. Supplying limited water for evaporation.
2. Altering absorption of radient energy.
3. Altering the heat or vapour transmission for evaporation.

A barren soil is more affected by the evaporation loss, because of the lack of vegetative covers. In these soils, evaporation loss is directly proportional to the available soil moisture. Evaporation generally takes place from the soil depth of 10 to 15 cm. The soil colour, slope, surface condition and moisture content also affect the evaporation loss. A dark colour soil involves comparitively greater evaporation loss, because it absorbs more radient energy. Similarly, the soils having low moisture content or moisture holding capacity and low colloidal content, are also succeptible to fast evaporation rate.

Plant Factor : A plant affects the evapotranspiration by its species, rooting characteristics, leaf geometry, density, growth stage etc. Plants with shorter height and dense vegetative cover involve comparitively high evapotranspirtaion. The effect on evapotranspiration by the crop types is due to variations in their cultivation times, rooting depth etc. If all the conditions remain same, then a dense root crop causes maximum ET for longer time by extracting more water from the soil and transmitting the same into various parts of the plant. The crop height also affects the evapotranspiration. If height is more ET will be more and vise-versa, because a tall crop receives greater direct beam of solar radiation than the short height crop. Amount of intercepted solar radiation by the crop, can be computed by using the following formula :

$$\frac{r}{R} = 1 + \frac{h}{W} \cdot \tan Z \qquad ...(4.31)$$

where, r = intercepted radiation by the plant

R = received radiation at the horizontal surface

h = height of the crop above soil surface

W = width of vegetation in the direction of solar azimuth

Z = solar azimuth angle

Atmosopheric Factor : The temperature, wind velocity, humidity, solar radiation etc are the main atmospheric factors affecting the evapotranspiration rate. Temperature increases the evapotranspiration, while humidity decreases the same. At higher solar radiation and temperature, the evapotranspiration increases because of lowering of humidity.

Cultural Practices Factor : The practices, such as irrigation and its method, irrigation time interval, mulching, shading etc. affect the evapotranspiration. If irrigation interval is more and soil surface is dried, then ET is reduced. It is comparitively more in flooding method of irrigation as compared to the furrow or sprinkler methods. Mulch, such as rice straw, wheat straw, sugarcane trash, maize stalks and polythene spreadings over the ground surface, reduces the ET. Similarly, the shading either done by manually or naturally, always reduces the ET, because of reduction in absorption of radiation energy by the soil surface.

Evaporation-Index : It is given as under :

$$ET = k \cdot E_p$$

or $$k = \frac{ET}{E_p}$$ ...(4.32)

where, k = coefficient, is the ratio of evapotranspiration and pan evaporation. Its value changes with the growth stages of the crop.

ET = evapotranspiration

E_p = pan evaporation

Example 4.3. *Find out the value of daily ET of wheat crop for the month of January, if pan evaporation for this month is 8.5 mm. Take the value of coefficient as 0.52.*

Solution. Using the formula

$$ET = k \cdot E_p$$

Here, $k = 0.52$

$E_p = 85$

$\therefore$ $ET = 0.52 \times 8.5 = 4.42$ mm

Daily ET $= \frac{4.42}{31} = \mathbf{0.142\ mm}$ **Ans.**

Consumptive Use : The consumptive use is equivalent to the evaportranspiration. It is used to denote the cumulative loss of water *i.e.* consumption of water by the plants including metabolic consumption; and evaporation from the bare land & water surfaces existing in the area, covered by the crops. In brief, consumptive use is the loss of water through ET and metabolic action of the plant. Plant consumes the water in its metabolic action less than 1% of ET, which is very less in comparison to ET, therefore, ET is generally considered equivalent to the consumptive use.

Seasonal Consumptive Use : It is total amount of water consumed by the cropped area during growing season of the crop. Seasonal consumptive use is generally expressed in terms of depth or volume of water. The knowledge of seasonal consumptive use is very important for evaluating the seasonal crop water requirement.

Peak Period Consumptive Use : It is the highest consumptive use during crop season. It is used for planning and design of irrigation methods.

4.9.2. Measurement of Evapotranspiration

Measurement of evapotranspiration is labour consuming, costly and time taking job. The following methods are commonly used for measuring the evapotranspiration :

1. Lysimeter method
2. Field experiment method
3. Soil moisture depletion method, and

4. Water balance approach.

Lysimeter Method

Lysimeter is a device used for measuring the ET. It consists of few volume of soil, planted with vegetations in a container, which is hydrologically isolated from its surroundings. In other words"it is a device, which involves growing of the crop in a big size container and measuring the amount of water lost *i.e.* evapotranspiration from the crop grown soil.

Types of Lysimeter : Following two types of lysimeters are mostly used for measuring the ET :

1. Weighing type and
2. Non-weighing type

Weighing Type Lysimeter : This type of lysimeter results comparitively more accurate measurement of ET than the others. During measurement, the data on volume of water added to the container or wăter retained in the soil and amount of water lost due to evaporation, transpiration & deep percolation, are recorded in terms of weight, which are taken by floating the lysimeter in the water or in some heavy liquids. Change in liquid displacement is determined against water lost from the tank, which is considered equivalent to the total water lost from the field.

During experiment, the water-level in the tank is maintained to a specific depth by connecting the water supply tank. Supply tank is equiped with a float mechanism, which has arrangement for supplying the net volume of water that is required for maintaining the water - level to a fixed depth in the lysimeter's tank. An equal amount of water is also added to the crop, grown in the neighbouring field. The deep percolation or outflow, if taking place from the lysimeter, they are also measured properly. And lastly, on the basis of these measured data, the ET is computed by using the following relationship :

$$ET = \text{change in weight} + \text{amount of water added} - \text{deep percolation.}$$

Limitations : Following limitations are observed in the lysimeteric technique for measuring the *ET* :

1. It is not possible to create the same physical condition of the soil filled in the lysimeter tank, such as temperature, water - table, soil texture, density of the soil etc. as already existing in the surrounding soil (*i.e.* undisturbed soil).

2. Proper drainage similar to the surrounding field, is not possible to maintain under this method. To overcome this problem, there must be provided an isolated soil column at the base of the container, at the same depth as in the undisturbed soil.

3. Sometimes, temperature of the soil in lysimeter is raised to such extent that, it becomes necessary to provide air condition for reducing the temperature, which is not practically possible.

Non-Weighing Type Lysimeter : This type of lysimeter is inferior to the weighing type lysimeter for measuring the evapotranspiration.

Use of lysimeter : 1. The lysimeter can be used to study the change in chemical composition of percolating water.

2. It determines the natural ground water recharge and crop's effect on it.

3. It studies the interactions amongst types of soil, ground water depth, evapotranspiration and crop yield.

4. Amount of moisture added by dew and condensation of atmospheric water to the soil rather than manual method, can also be determined by using the weighing type lysimeter.

Field Experimental Plot Method

This method determines the consumptive use in terms of seasonal water requirement of the crop on the basis of total irrigation water supplied to the field, effective seasonal rainfall amount, presence of moisture content at beginning and end of the season, depth of root zone etc. Accuracy of this method depends on the accurate measurement of the water supplied to the field. The following formula is used for computing the seasonal water requirement :

$$W_r = IW + R_e + \sum_{i=1}^{n} \left(\frac{mc_{bi} - mc_{ei}}{100} \right) Ai \cdot Di \qquad ...(4.33)$$

where, W_r = seasonal water requirement of the crop

IW = total amount of irrigation water supplied to the field.

R_e = effective seasonal rainfall amount

mc_{bi} = moisture content at begining of the season in the i th layer of the soil

mc_{ei} = moisture content at end of the season in the ith layer of the soil

n = number of soil layers in the root zone depth D

A_i = apparent specific gravity of the i th soil layer

Limitation : The main draw back of this method is that, it does not provide the informations about the level of intermediate moisture content in the soil, short term use, profile use, deep percolation loss and peak water use rate of the crop.

Example 4.4. *Determine the seasonal water requirement of a particular crop from the following data, recorded by conducting the field experiment.*

Soil depth (mm)	*Moisture content at the begining of season (%)*	*Moisture content at the end of season (%)*	*Apparent sp. gravity (g/cc)*
0—150	*32.2*	*16.2*	*2.65*
150—300	*34.2*	*16.5*	*2.70*
300—450	*33.4*	*23.4*	*2.75*
450—600	*33.8*	*33.8*	*2.80*

Assume, the values of effective rainfall and amount of irrigation water supplied to the field are 8.5 and 75.0 mm, respectively.

Solution.

Soil depth	mc_{bi} *(%)*	mc_{ei} *(%)*	A_i *(g/cc)*	$\frac{mc_{bi} - mc_{ei}}{100}$	$A_i D_i$	*Col (5) × Col (6)*
1	*2*	*3*	*4*	*5*	*6*	*7*
0—150	32.2	16.2	2.62	0.16	397.5	63.60
150—300	34.2	16.5	2.70	0.18	405.0	72.90
300—450	33.4	23.4	2.75	0.10	412.5	41.25
450—600	33.8	33.8	2.80	0.0	420.0	0.00
Total						177.75 mm

$$\therefore \quad W_r = IW + R_e + \sum_{i=1}^{n} \frac{mc_{bi} - mc_{ei}}{100} Ai\, Di$$

$$= 75 + 8.5 + 177.75$$

$$= \mathbf{26.13\ cm} \quad \textbf{Ans.}$$

Soil-Moisture Depletion Method

In this method, soil samples are collected from successive depths throughout the crop period for finding the change in moisture content. The following formula is used for calculating the consumptive use of the crop, based on the determined status of soil moisture content in successive soil depths.

$$U = \sum_{i=1}^{n} \left(\frac{mc_{1i} - mc_{2i}}{100} \right) Ai \cdot Di \qquad \text{...(4.34)}$$

where,

U = amount of water consumed from the root zone during one irrigation cycle

mc_{1i} = soil moisture during Ist sampling in the *i*th soil layer

mc_{2i} = soil moisture during 2nd sampling in the *i*th soil layer

Ai, n and Di are the same, as denoted in equation (4.33).

After determining the value of 'U' of different soil samples collected from different depths, the consumptive use 'Cu' is computed by adding them together *i.e.*

$$C_u = U_1 + U_2 + U_3 + ...U_n$$

or

$$C_u = \sum_{i=1}^{n} U_i \quad ...(4.35)$$

Limitation : This method is not suitable for determining the consumptive use of the crops, grown in non-uniform soils.

Example 4.5. *Calculate the consumptive use of wheat crop from the following data. Use soil moisture depletion technique for computation.*

Soil depth (cm)	*Soil moisture before 2 days of Ist irrigation (%)*	*Soil moisture after 2 day of Ist irrigation %*	*Apparent sp. gravity of the soil (g/cc)*
0—15	*16.2*	*32.2*	*2.65*
15—30	*16.5*	*34.4*	*2.70*
30—45	*23.4*	*33.4*	*2.75*
45—60	*33.8*	*33.8*	*2.80*

Solution. Calculation is shown in following table.

Soil depth (cm)	mc_{1i} *(%)*	mc_{2i} *(%)*	$\frac{mc_{1i} - mc_{2i}}{100}$	$A_i D_i$	$U = \frac{mc_{1i} - mc_{2i}}{100} A_i D_i$
1	2	*3*	*4*		
0—15	32.2	16.2	0.16	39.75	6.36
15—30	34.4	16.5	0.18	40.50	7.29
30—45	33.4	23.4	0.10	41.25	4.13
45—60	33.8	33.8	0.00	42.00	0.00
		$C_u =$			**17.78 cm Ans.**

Water-Balance Method

This method is based on the principle that, the amount of water inflow into the field is equal to the outflow of water from the same. Sometimes, water balance method is also known as inflow-outflow method. The parameters, which are essential for computing the ET under this method, are given as under :

Inflow parameters : These are,

1. Precipitation (P)
2. Moisture content in the root zone (M)
3. Amount of irrigation water supplied to the field (I)

Outflow parameters : It includes the following,

1. Change in soil moisture (m)
2. Evapotranspiration (ET)

3. Seepage loss (S)
4. Deep percolation loss (D)
5. Surface runoff (R)

Equating the inflow and outflow parameters, we have

$$P + M + I = m + ET + S + D + R$$

or

$$ET = (P + M + I) - (m + S + S + D + R) \quad \text{... (4.36)}$$

In this equation, if all the parameters are known, then ET can be determined simply by substituting the values and solving them.

This method is suitable for larger areas (*i.e.* watershed) and for long term evaluation of ET. For various agricultural operations, the water balance in terms of weekly, monthly, seasonal or annual can also be determined by using this technique.

Example 4.6. *Using the following data base, compute the ET*

1. Amount of rainfall = 8.5 mm
2 Moisture content in the root zone = 4.5 mm
3. Water supplied during irrigation = 75 mm
4 Seepage loss = 3.5 mm
5. Deep percolation = 4.5 mm
6. Surface runoff = 6.5 mm
7. Change in soil moisture = 3 mm

Solution. Given that, the

Inflow components $P = 8.5$ mm
$M = 4.5$ mm
$I = 75$ mm

Outflow components $\Delta m = 3$ mm
$S = 3.5$ mm
$R = 6.5$ mm
$D = 4.5$ mm

Substituting above values in equation 4.36, we have

$$ET = (P + M + I) - (\Delta M + S + D + R)$$
$$= (8.5 + 4.5 + 75) - (3 + 3.5 + 4.5 + 6.5)$$
$$= 88 - 17.5 = \mathbf{70.5\ mm} \quad \textbf{Ans.}$$

4.9.3. Computation of Evapotranspiration from Climatological Data

Climatological data based computations of evapotranspiration are dealt under following methods :

1. Blaney-Criddle Method
2. Thornthwait Method
3. Penman Method

4. Christiansen Method
5. Radiation Method
6. Jensen-Haise Method
7. Hargreaves Equation
8. Modified Penman Formula.

Blaney-Criddle Method

Blaney and Cridle (1950) developed the formula for computing the consumptive use of the crop, on the basis of temperature and day-time sun -shine hours data. Formula is given as under :

$$U = 25.4\, k \cdot f \qquad \text{...(4.37)}$$

where, U = consumptive use of the crop for given period of time, mm

k = crop consumptive use coefficient

f = sum of the monthly consumptive use factor for the entire growing season of the crop. It is calculated by multiplying the mean temperature and percent of day-time sun-shine hours of the year, *i.e.*

$$f = \frac{t \cdot p}{100} \qquad \text{...(4.38)}$$

After substituting the value of '*f*' in equation 4.37, we have

$$U = 25.4\, k \sum \frac{t \cdot p}{100} \qquad \text{...(4.39)}$$

This is the desired equation for computing the consumptive use of the crop for a given time period. For computing the monthly consumptive use, the above equation can be written as

$$U = 25.4\, k \cdot \frac{t \cdot p}{100} \qquad \text{...(4.40)}$$

where, U = monthly consumptive use, mm

k = monthly crop coefficient

t = mean monthly temperature

p = monthly day –time sun shine hours % (Appendix–2)

Example 4.7. *Determine the evapotranspiration by using Blanney-Criddle method for a specified crop at the location of* 60° *latitude. The mean monthly temperature of the place is given as under :*

Month	*Oct*	*Nov*	*Dec*	*Jan*	*Feb*
Mean monthly temperature (°C)	20	15	15	21	22

(Assume the value of crop coefficient k = 0.80)

Solution. Computation is shown in following table

Month	*Mean monthly temp. (°C)*	*Monthly day-time sun-shine hours * (%)*	$f = \frac{t \cdot p}{100}$	$U = 25.4\, k\, \Sigma \frac{t \cdot p}{100}$
1	2	*3*	*4*	*5*
Oct	20	6.98	1.39	
Nov.	15	4.31	0.65	
Dec.	15	4.22	0.63	$U = 25.4 \times 0.8 \times 4.89$
Jan	21	4.67	0.98	**= 99.36 mm Ans.**
Feb	22	5.65	1.24	
Total			4.89	

*The value of monthly day-time sun-shine hours for each month is taken from Appendix 2 against given latitude of the place.

Limitations : The Blaney-Criddle method includes following limitations :

1. This method does not compute the consumptive use for the period less than one month.

2. For the regions, where temperature remains fairly constant and other parameters, such as humidity, wind velocity etc. are varied, this method does not compute satisfactory consumptive use.

3. For the areas having large variations in the sunshine hours during transition months of the year, this method does not compute accurate Cu.

4. For computation of consumptive use of islands, where temperature is affected by surrounding sea climate, this method is not suitable.

5. At higher altitudes, where day-time radiation is independent on night temperature, application of this method is not suitable.

Thornthwaite Method

Thornthwaite (1948) developed a relationship for computing the consumptive use of the crop on the basis of mean daily temperature, latitude of the place and month of the year. He assumed that there is a good correlation between the mean termperature and the variables such as moisture, wind velocity and solar radiation. Relationship is given as under :

$$e' = 1.6 \left(\frac{10\, t_m}{I} \right)^a \qquad \text{...(4.41)}$$

where, e' = unadjusted potential evapotranspiration for the month of 30 days with 12 hours day time period, each day.

t_m = mean air temperature, °C

I = annual or seasonal heat index, calculated by using the following formula :

$$I = \sum_{i=1}^{12} i_i \qquad ...(4.42)$$

where, i is the monthly heat index, given as :

$$i = \left(\frac{t_m}{5}\right)^{1.514}$$

a= empirical exponent, can be calculated by following formula :

$$a = 6.75 \times 10^{-7} I^3 - 7.71 \times 10^{-5} I^2 + 1.792 \times 10^{-2} I + 0.49239 \qquad ...(4.43)$$

The unadjusted potential evapotranspiration is adjusted for the number of days of the month and day light hours. For this purpose, a correction factor (f) is used. The values of correction factor and monthly values of i are given in Appendix–3 and –4, respectively. Thus, adjusted PET is

$$e = e' \cdot f \qquad ...(4.44)$$

This method results accurate estimate of ET for the temperate and continental climates of north - America, where temperature and radiation are strongly correlated with each other.

Demerits of Thornthwaite Method : Chang (1968) has enumerated following drawbacks of this method :

1. This method considers only temperature as an indicator for availability of energy to cause the evapotranspiration.

2. Air temperature is not considered.

3. This method does not take care the effect of cold and warm airs on the temperature.

4. Wind is also an important factor to cause ET, but this method does not consider it.

5. Thornthwaite formula indicates that, if mean temperature is below 0°C, then value of PET will be zero, which is not true.

Example 4.8. *Calculate the PET of Alfalfa crop grown at* 50° N *latitude. The mean monthly temperature of the place is given as under :*

Month	*May*	*June*	*July*	*Aug*	*Sep*	*Oct*
Mean monthly temp. (t_m), °C	*12.0*	*21.0*	*20.5*	*22.0*	*10.0*	*5.0*

Solution. Computation procedure is shown in following table.

Month	*Mean monthly temp.* (t_m) °C	$i = \left(\frac{t_m}{5}\right)^{1.51}$	e'*	*Day-light factor* ** (f)	*Adjusted PET* $e = e' \cdot f$
May	12.0	3.75	5.92	1.33	7.87
June	21.0	8.71	10.60	1.36	14.42
July	20.5	8.42	10.33	1.37	14.15
Aug.	22.0	9.37	11.12	1.25	13.90
Sept.	10.0	2.85	4.90	1.06	5.19
Oct.	5.0	1.0	2.38	0.92	2.19
		$I = \Sigma i = 34.10$			

$$*e' = 1.6\left(\frac{10\, t_m}{I}\right)^a$$

$$a = 6.75 \times 10^{-7} I^3 - 7.71 \times 10^{-5} I^2 + 1.792 \times 10^{-2} I + 0.49239$$

$$= 6.75 \times 10^{-7} (34.1)^3 - 7.71 \times 10^{-5} (34.1)^2 + 1.792 \times 10^{-2} (34.1) + 0.49239$$

$$= 1.04$$

$$\therefore \quad e' = 1.6\left(\frac{10 \times 12}{34.1}\right)^{1.04}$$

$$= \mathbf{5.92}$$

**The values of '*f*' for respective months are taken from Appendix-3 against given latitude.

Jensen-Haise Method

This method follows following formula for computing the ET :

$$Et_p = C_t\,(t - t_1)\, R_s \qquad ...(4.45)$$

where, Et_p = potential evapotranspiration

C_t = coefficient, depends on the temperature of the area

t = temperature °C

t_1 = intercepted temperature on temperature axis

R_s = incident solar radiation (langlay/day)

Value of C_t is generally taken as 0.025. However, the following formula can also be used for computing the C_t

$$C_t = \left(\frac{1}{C_1} + C_2 \cdot C_H\right) \qquad ...(4.46)$$

in which, $$C_H = \left(\frac{50}{e_2 - e_1}\right) \text{mbar} \quad \text{...(4.47)}$$

$$C_1 = 38 - \left(\frac{2°\text{C} \cdot EL}{305}\right) \quad \text{...(4.48)}$$

$$C_2 = 7.6°\text{C}$$

e_1 and e_2 = saturation vapour pressure of water at maximum and minimum temperatures, respectively for warmest month of the year of the given place.

The value of t_1 is taken as -3. However, its value can also be determined by using the following formula :

$$t_1 = -2.5 - 0.14\,(e_2 - e_1)°\text{C/mbar} - EL/550 \quad \text{...(4.49)}$$

After determining the value of Et_p, the crop consumptive use is calculated by using the following equation :

$$E_t = K_{co} \cdot Et_p \quad \text{...(4.50)}$$

where, E_t = crop consumptive use

K_{co} = crop coefficient, given in Appendix–5.

Inaddition, computed value of crop consumptive is also adjusted for the existing soil water condition *i.e.* when soil water drops to the level of plant stress.

Use of Jensen-Haise Method

This method is widely used in semi-arid and arid zones for computing the *ET* on day to day basis. It gives realistic estimation for the periods ranging from 5 to 7 days, provided that the fluctuations in wind and humidity are mild.

Lowry-Johnson Method

It computes satisfactory value of ET and is widely used in western arid zones of United States. This method is based on the concept that, there is an indication of water loss through evaporation and transpiration by the plant due to temperature just above the freezing temperature during growing period. It follows following formula for estimating the consumptive use :

$$C_u = 0.244 + 0.026\, I_f \quad \text{...(451)}$$

where, C_u = consumptive use, ha. m/day

I_f = effective heat in thousands of day, °C

Hargreave Equation

Hargreave developed a relationship for determining the crop water requirement on the basis of data collected from grass lysimeter. Relationship is given as

$$Et_g = 0.0135\,(t + 17.78)\,R_s \qquad ...(4.52)$$

where, Et_g = reference crop potential consumptive use

t = mean daily temperature, °C

R_s = incident solar radiation, langlay/day. It can be calculated by using the following formula

$$R_s = 0.10\,R_{so}\,(S)^{1/2} \qquad ...(4.53)$$

in which, S is the percent possible sun-shine hour and R_{so} is the clear day solar radiation in langlay/day. This method does not require fruther adjustment in computed PET for any specific conditions.

Hargreave also mentioned that, the reference crop alfalfa has 20% greater consumptive use than the other local grasses. Thus, for alfalfa crop the equation 4.53 can be written as,

$$Et_p = 1.2\,[0.0135\,(t + 17.78)\,R_s] \qquad ...(4.54)$$

Radiation Method

In the areas, where data on air temperature, sunshine hours or cloudness radiation are available, this method can suitabily be used for computing the crop evapotranspiration. This method employs following formula :

$$Et_o = a + b{\cdot}w{\cdot}R_s \qquad ...(4.55)$$

where, Et_o = crop evapotranspiration, mm/day

a, b = coefficients

w = weighing factor; depends on the temperature and altitude of the place.

R_s = solar radiation. Its value can be computed by using the following formula,

$$R_s = 0.25 + 0.50\,\frac{n}{N}\,R_a \qquad ...(4.56)$$

in which, $\frac{n}{N}$ is the ratio of actual and possible bright sunshine hours. Values of N for different latitudes & months are given in Table 4.4 and R_a in Appendix-6.

Christiansen Method

This method computes potential evapotranspiration by correlating the pan evaporation with the climatological data. Formula is given by

Table 4.4. Values of 'N' for different latitudes and months

Latitudes (North or south)	*Jan. & July*	*Feb & Aug.*	*March & Sept.*	*April & October*	*May & Nov.*	*June & Dec.*	*July. & Jan.*	*August & Feb.*	*Sept. & March*	*Oct. & April*	*Nov. & May*	*Dec. & June*
0	12.1	12.1	12.0	12.1	12.1	12.1	12.1	12.1	12.1	12.1	12.1	12.1
0	11.8	11.9	12.0	12.2	12.3	12.4	12.3	12.3	12.1	12.0	11.9	11.8
5	11.6	11.8	12.0	12.3	12.6	12.7	12.6	12.4	12.1	11.8	11.6	11.5
15	11.3	11.6	12.0	12.5	12.8	13.0	12.9	12.6	12.2	11.8	11.4	11.2
20	11.0	11.5	12.0	12.6	13.1	13.3	13.2	12.8	12.3	11.7	11.2	10.9
25	10.7	11.3	12.0	12.7	13.3	13.7	13.5	13.0	12.3	11.6	10.9	10.6
30	10.4	11.1	12.0	12.9	13.6	14.0	13.9	13.2	12.4	11.5	10.6	10.2
35	10.1	11.0	11.9	13.1	14.0	14.5	14.3	13.5	12.4	11.3	10.3	9.8
40	9.6	10.7	11.9	13.3	14.4	15.0	14.7	13.7	12.5	11.2	10.0	9.3
42	9.4	10.6	11.9	13.4	14.6	15.2	14.9	13.9	12.6	11.1	9.8	9.1
44	9.3	10.5	11.9	13.4	14.7	15.4	15.2	14.0	12.6	11.0	9.7	8.9
46	9.1	10..4	11.9	13.5	14.9	15.7	15.4	14.2	12.6	10.9	9.5	8.7
48	8.8	10.2	11.8	13.6	15.2	16.0	15.6	14.3	12.6	10.9	9.3	8.3
50	8.5	10.1	11.8	13.8	15.4	16.3	15.9	14.5	12.7	10.8	9.1	8.1

$$\text{PET} = 0.473\,CH \qquad \text{... (4.57)}$$

where, PET = potential evapotranspiration

C = coefficient

H = solar radiation at the top of canopy, causing evaporation.

The value of coefficient 'C' can be computed by using the following formula :

$$C = C_h \cdot C_t \cdot C_u \cdot C_s \cdot C_e \cdot C_m \qquad \text{...(4.58)}$$

where,
$$C_h = 1.25 + 0.348\left(\frac{H_n}{40}\right) + 0.12\left(\frac{H_n}{40}\right)^2 - 0.022\left(\frac{H_n}{40}\right)^4$$

inwhich, H_n is the mean relative humidity at noon.

$$C_t = 0.393 + 0.559\left(\frac{T_c}{20}\right) + 0.047\left(\frac{T_c}{20}\right)^2$$

where, T_c is the mean daily air temperature (°C)

$$C_u = 0.708 + 0.327\left(\frac{u}{96.56}\right) - 0.036\left(\frac{u}{96.56}\right)^2$$

where, u is the daily wind movement, km/day

$$C_s = 0.542 + 0.64\left(\frac{S}{80}\right) - 0.499\left(\frac{S}{80}\right)^2 + 0.317\left(\frac{S}{80}\right)^3$$

where, $S = n/N$ percent of sunshine

$$C_e = 0.97 + 0.03\left(\frac{E}{304.88}\right)$$

where, E = elevation of the place, m

C_m = vegetative coefficient (monthly) given in Table 4.5

Table 4.5. Value of monthly vegetative coefficient (cm) (for Indiana)

S.No.	*Month*	*Cm*
1.	January	1.08
2.	Febuary	1.00
3.	March	0.93
4.	April	0.89
5.	May	0.88
6.	June	0.87
7.	July	0.88
8.	August	0.91
9.	September	0.99
10.	October	1.07
11.	November	1.13
12.	December	1.16

Penman Method

Penman (1948) developed the formula for determining the evaporation from an open water body, on the basis of combination of energy balance and sink strength theory, which was fruther modified for computing the ET. Penman formula of evaporation is given by

$$E_o = \frac{\Delta\, Q_n + r \cdot E_a}{\Delta + r} \qquad \text{...(4.59)}$$

where, E_o = evaporation rate from the open water body, mm/day

Δ = slope of curve, drawn between saturation vapour pressure and temperature (*i.e.*the mean air temperature T_a) is expressed in mm Hg per °C. It is given as :

$$\frac{d}{dT_a} e_a$$

e_a = saturation vapour pressure of evaporating surface, expressed in mm Hg at mean air temperature, given in Table 4.6.

T_a = mean air temperature, K (*i.e.* $K = 273 + °C$)

Q_n = net radiation, mm of water. Value of Q_n can be calculated by using the following formula :

$$Q_n = Q_A\,(1 - x)\left(0.18 + 0.55\,\frac{n}{N}\right) - \sigma \cdot T_a^4$$

$$(0.55 - 0.92\,\sqrt{e_d})\left(0.10 + 0.90\,\frac{n}{N}\right) \qquad \text{...(4.60)}$$

Q_A = mean monthly extra–terristiral radiation known as Agot value. It is expressed in terms of mm of water/day.

x = reflection coefficient (0.06) of open evaporating surface.

$\frac{n}{N}$ = ratio of actual to possible bright sunshine hours

(Value of N is given in Table 4.4)

σ = Boltzman constant

e_d = saturation vapour pressure at dew point temperature, mm Hg

r = ratio of specific heat of air to the latent heat of water, also known as psychrometric constant.

$\sigma\, T_a^4$ is given in Table 4.7.

Table 4.6. Saturation vapour pressure (e_a) as the function of T_m

Mean air temp (°C)	e_a *(mbar)*	*Mean air temp (°C)*	e_a *(mbar)*
0	6.1	15	17.0
1	6.6	16	18.2
2	7.1	17	19.4
3	7.6	18	20.6
4	8.1	19	22.0
5	8.7	20	23.4
6	9.4	21	24.9
7	10.0	22	26.4
8.	10.7	23	28.1
9.	11.5	24	29.8
10.	12.3	25	31.7
11.	13.1	26	33.6
12.	14.0	27	35.7
13.	15.0	28	37.8
14.	16.1	29	40.1
		30	42.2

Table 4.7. Values of 'σT_a^4' for use in Penman (1948) method of PET computation.

Temperature (K)	σT_a^4 *(mm H_2O/day)*	*Temperature °F*	σT_a^4*(mm H_2O/day)*
270	10.73	35	11.48
275	11.51	40	11.96
280	12.40	45	12.45
285	13.20	50	12..94
290	14.26	55	13.45
295	15.30	60	13.96
300	16.34	65	14.52
305	17.46	70	15.10
310	18.60	75	15.65
315	19.85	80	16.25
320	21.15	85	16.85
325	22.5	90	17.46
		100	18.80

$$E_a = 0.35\,(e_a - e_d)\,(1 + 0.0098\,U_2) \qquad ...(4.61)$$

in which, U_2 is wind speed at 2 meter height, miles/day

$$= U_1 \left(\log \frac{6.6}{\log h} \right)$$

U_1 = wind speed at any height 'h' in feet. Value of correction factor for converting the wind velocity at 2 m hight is given in Table 4.8

After determining the value of evaporation rate by using eqn. 4.59, the evapotranspiration (*ET*) is computed by multiplying the crop coefficient to E_o,

i.e.

$$ET = K \cdot E_o \qquad ...(4.62)$$

where, K = crop coefficient

E_o = pan evaporation, computed by the the equation 4.59

Values of '*K*' for short grasses are given in Table - 4.9.

Table 4.8. Values of correction factor for converting the wind velocity at 2 m height

Height (m)	*Correction factor*
0.5	1.35
1.0	1.15
1.5	1.06
2.0	1.00
3.0	0.93
4.0	0.88
5.0	0.85
6.0	0.83
10.0	0.77

Table 4.9. Value of '*K*' for short grasses

S.No.	*Period*	*K*
1	November to December	0.6
2	March, April, September	0.7
3	May to August	0.8

Penman (1948) formula can also be used for computing the potential evapotranspiration (PET) by introducing reflection coefficient. For most of the crops, the value of reflection coefficient is taken as 0.25.

This method results satisfactory estimate of ET or PET for humid and arid zones, under calm weather condition.

Modified Penman Equation

Dorenbos and Pruitt (1975) have modified the Penman equation (1948), on the basis of climatic data and measured values of grass evapotranspiration from various locations throughout the world and developed a new formula which is known as modified Penman equation. The modified formula is the combination of radiation and aerodynamic terms, given as under :

$$Et_c = \underbrace{W \cdot R_n}_{\text{Radiation term}} + \underbrace{(1 - W) \cdot f(u)\,(e_a - e_d)}_{\text{Aerodynamic term}} \qquad \text{...(4.63)}$$

where, Et_c = unadjusted reference crop evapotranspiration, mm/day

W = weighing factor for the effect of radiation on ET_c. It depends on temperature and elevation of the area, given in Table 4.10

$(1 - W)$ = weighing factor, depends on temperature and elevation. It incroporates the effect of wind and humidity on Et_c Values of $(1 - W)$ are given in Table 4.11.

R_n = net radiation given as

$$= R_{ns} - R_{nl} \qquad \text{... (4.64)}$$

R_{ns} = net incoming short wave solar radiation, computed by the following formula

$$= R_A\,(1 - \alpha)\left(0.25 + 0.50\,\frac{n}{N}\right) \qquad \text{...(4.65)}$$

in which, R_A is the extra - terrestrial radiation (mm/day), α is the reflection coefficient and $\frac{n}{N}$ is the same as in equation (4.59). Values of R_A and N are given in Appendix-6.

R_{nl} = net long wave radiation, computed by using the following formula :

$$= f(t) \cdot f(e_d) \cdot f\left(\frac{n}{N}\right) \qquad \text{...(4.66)}$$

Values of the factors $f(t), f(e_d)$ and $f(n/N)$ are given in the Tables. 4.12, 4.13 and 4.14, respectively.

$f(u)$ = wind function, can be obtained from Table 4.15

e_d = mean actual vapour pressure of the air (mbar), given as

$$= \frac{e_a\, R_H\%\ (\text{mean})}{100}$$

The value of Et_c (*i.e.* estimated by equation 4.63) is multiplied to the correction factor. Correction factor depends on the day-night time, and wind and humidity levels of the location, given in Appendix-8.

Table 4.10 : Values of weighing factor (*W*) for use in modified Penman equation

Temperature (°C)	*'W' at altitude (m) of*					
	0	*500*	*1,000*	*2,000*	*3,000*	*4,000*
2	0.43	0.44	0.46	0.49	0.52	0.54
4	0.46	0.48	0.49	0.52	0.55	0.58
6	0.49	0.51	0.52	0.55	0.58	0.61
8	0.52	0.54	0.55	0.58	0.61	0.64
10	0.55	0.57	0.58	0.61	0.64	0.66
12	0.58	0.60	0.61	0.64	0.66	0.69
14	0.61	0.62	0.64	0.66	0.69	0.71
16	0.64	0.65	0.66	0.69	0.71	0.73
18	0.66	0.67	0.69	0.71	0.73	0.75
20	0.68	0.70	0.71	0.73	0.75	0.77
22	0.71	0.72	0.73	0.75	0.77	0.79
24	0.73	0.74	0.75	0.77	0.79	0.81
26	0.75	0.76	0.77	0.79	0.81	0.81
28	0.77	0.78	0.79	0.81	0.82	0.84
30	0.78	0.79	0.80	0.82	0.84	0.85
32	0.80	0.81	0.82	0.84	0.85	0.86
34	0.82	0.82	0.83	0.85	0.86	0.87
36	0.83	0.84	0.85	0.86	0.87	0.88
38	0.84	0.85	0.86	0.87	0.88	0.90
40	0.85	0.86	0.87	0.88	0.89	0.90

Table 4.11 : Values of weighing factor (1–W) for use in modified Penman Equation

Temperature(°C)	*(1-W) at altitude (m) of*					
	0	*500*	*1,000*	*2,000*	*3,000*	*4,000*
2	0.57	0.56	0.54	0.51	0.48	0.46
4	0.54	0.52	0.51	0.48	0.45	0.42
6	0.51	0.49	0.48	0.45	0.42	0.39
8	0.48	0.46	0.45	0.42	0.39	0.36
10	0.45	0.43	0.42	0.39	0.36	0.34
12	0.42	0.40	0.39	0.36	0.34	0.31
14	0.39	0.38	0.36	0.34	0.31	0.29
16	0.36	0.35	0.34	0.31	0.29	0.27
18	0.34	0.33	0.31	0.29	0.27	0.25
20	0.32	0.30	0.29	0.27	0.27	0.23
22	0.29	0.28	0.27	0.25	0.25	0.21
24	0.27	0.26	0.25	0.23	0.23	0.19
26	0.25	0.24	0.23	0.21	0.19	0.18
28	0.23	0.22	0.21	0.19	0.18	0.16
30	0.22	0.21	0.20	0.18	0.16	0.15
32	0.20	0.19	0.18	0.16	0.15	0.14
34	0.19	0.18	0.17	0.15	0.14	0.13
36	0.17	0.16	0.15	0.15	0.13	0.12
38	0.16	0.14	0.14	0.13	0.12	0.11
40	0.15	0.14	0.13	0.12	0.11	0.10

Table 4.12 : Correction factor for temperature [*i.e f*(*t*)]

Temperature (°C)	*f*(*t*)	*Temperature* (°C)	*f*(*t*)
0	11.0	20	14.6
2	11.4	22	15.0
6	11.7	24	15.4
8	12.0	26	15.9
10	12.4	28	16.3
14	12.7	30	16.7
16	13.1	32	17.2
18	13.5	34	17.7
		36	18.1

Table 4.13 : Correction factor for vapour pressure [*i.e* $f(e_d) = 0.34 - 0.444\, e_d$]

Vapour pressure (e_d), *mbar*	$f(e_d)$	*Vapour pressure* (e_d), *mbar*	$f(e_d)$
6	0.23	24	0.12
8	0.22	26	0.12
10	0.20	28	0.11
12	0.19	30	0.10
14	0.18	32	0.09
16	0.16	34	0.08
18	0.15	36	0.08
20	0.14	38	0.07
22	0.13	40	0.06

Table 4.14 : Correction factor for $\frac{n}{N}$ $\left(\textit{i.e.}\ \frac{n}{N} = 0.1 + 0.9\,\frac{n}{N}\right)$

$\frac{n}{N}$	$f\left(\frac{n}{N}\right)$	$\frac{n}{N}$	$f\left(\frac{n}{N}\right)$
0	0.10	0.55	0.60
0.05	0.15	0.60	0.64
0.10	0.19	0.65	0.69
0.15	0.24	0.70	0.73
0.20	0.28	0.75	0.78
0.25	0.33	0.80	0.82
0.30	0.37	0.85	0.87
0.35	0.42	0.90	0.91
0.40	0.46	0.95	0.96
0.45	0.51	1.00	1.0
0.50	0.55		

Table 4.15 : Values of $f(u) = 0.27\left(\frac{1+U_2}{100}\right)$ for use in modified Penman equation

Wind velocity (km/h)	*0*	*10*	*20*	*30*	*40*	*50*	*60*	*70*	*80*	*90*
		0.30	0.32	0.35	0.38	0.41	0.43	0.46	0.49	0.51
100	0.54	0.57	0.59	0.62	0.65	0.67	0.70	0.73	0.76	0.78
200	0.81	0.84	0.86	0.89	0.92	0.94	0.97	1.00	1.03	1.05
300	1.08	1.11	1.13	1.16	1.19	1.21	1.24	1.27	1.30	1.32
400	1.36	1.38	1.40	1.43	1.46	1.49	1.51	1.54	1.57	1.59
500	1.62	1.65	1.67	1.70	1.73	1.76	1.78	1.81	1.84	1.90
600	1.89	1.92	1.94	1.97	2.00	2.02	2.05	2.08	2.11	2.15
700	2.16	2.19	2.21	2.24	2.27	2.29	2.32	2.35	2.38	2.40
800	2.43	2.46	2.48	2.51	2.54	2.56	2.59	2.62	2.64	2.65
900	2.70	—	—	—	—	—	—	—	—	—

Example 4.9. *Using modified Penman formula, compute the reference ET from the following data :*

1. *Mean air temperature = 16°C*
2. *Mean relative humidity = 70%*
3. *Mean sun-shine hour (n) = 5.75 hours/day*
4. *Wind speed at 3m height (U) = 130 km/day*
5. *Reflection coefficient (α) = 0.30*
6. *Month = December*
7. *Elevation = 30°N and 283.89 m altitude*

Solution. Modified Penman equation is given by

$$ET_c = W \cdot R_n + (1 - W) \cdot f(u) \cdot (e_a - e_d)$$

(A) ***Computation of Radiation term i.e.***

$$W \cdot R_n = W\,(R_{ns} - R_{nl})$$

in which, $W = 0.65$ (from Table 4.10)

(*i*) $R_{ns} = R_A\,(1 - \alpha)\left(0.25 + 0.5\,\frac{n}{N}\right)$

$R_A = 8.3$ (from Appendix–6)

$N = 10.2$ (from Appendix–6)

$\alpha = 0.30$

$n = 5.75$

$\therefore \quad R_{ns} = 8.3\,(1 - 0.30)\left(0.25 + 0.5\dfrac{5.75}{10.2}\right) = 3.09$

(*ii*) $\quad R_{nl} = f(t) \cdot f(ed) \cdot f\left(\dfrac{n}{N}\right)$

in which, $\quad f(t) = 13.8$ (from Table 4.12)

$f(e_d) = 0.19$ (from Table 4.13 against e_d)

$$\left(e_d = \frac{18.2 \times 70}{100} = 12.74 \text{ mbar}\right)$$

$$f\left(\frac{n}{N}\right) = f\left(\frac{5.75}{10.2}\right) = f(0.56)$$

$= 0.6$ (from Table4.14)

$\therefore \quad R_{nl} = 13.8 \times 0.19 \times 0.60 = 1.6$

$\therefore \quad W \cdot R_n = 0.65\,(3.09 - 1.6) = 0.97$

(B) ***Computation of Aerodynamic term***

$$(1 - W) f(u) \cdot (e_a - e_d)$$

In which, (*i*) $(1 - W) = 0.35$ (from Table 4.11 against given temp and altitude)

(*ii*) $f(u) = 0.85$ (from Table 4.15 against given wind velocity and U_2)

(*iii*) $(e_a - e_d) = (18.2 - 12.74) = 5.46$

$\therefore \quad (1 - W) f(u) \cdot (e_a - e_d)$

$= 0.35 \times 0.85 \times 5.46 = 1.62$

(*c*) Unadjusted $\quad ET_c = 0.97 + 1.62$

$= \mathbf{2.59}$ **mm/day**

(*d*) Adjusted $\quad ET = ET_c \times C^*$

$= 2.59 \times 0.92$

$= \mathbf{2.38}$ **mm/day** **Ans.**

*Value of crop coefficient (C) is obtained from Table 4.5 as 0.92.

4.10. Infiltration

In hydrology, the infiltration of rain water is counted as one of the hydrologic lossess. It plays an important role for generating the runoff from rainfall. "Infiltration" term was firstly used by Horton (1935) to describe the phenomena of soaking of water by the soil. Generally, it is defined as the entry of water into the soil through top surface layer.

4.10.1. Mechanics of Infiltration

Infiltration mechanism can be explained by the physiology of soil mass. The soil consists of a network of macro pores extending laterally in all the directions and forms a continuous path, known as gravity water channel. Through gravity channels, water moves downward under influence of gravity force following least-resistance path.

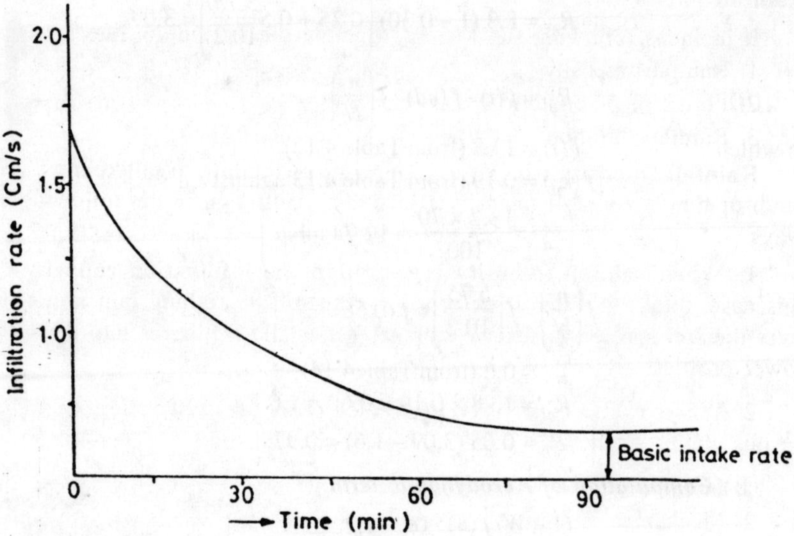

Fig. 4.5. Infiltration curve.

In addition to the macro-pores, the soil is also permeated by small size capillary pore-spaces, which have comparitively greater affinity with water than the air. Besides, the capillary pore spaces also have greater capillary force in all directions than the gravity force. Thus, when water comes in contact with the soil surface, it tends to enter the soil profile downward through gravity channels and capillary pore spaces. The capillary water always has tendency to move from wet zone to the dry zone, but its movement speed decreases on increment of soil wetness due to decrease in capillary potential. This is the reason that, the infiltration rate declines with advancement of time or increase in the level of moisture content. In gravity channels, the flow of water is always continued which meets to the water-table known as percolation. When water flowing through capillary pores attains steady state condition, then infiltration rate becomes equal to the percolation rate. The steady infiltration rate is termed as basic intake rate. Trend of infiltration rate for any soil is shown in Fig. 4.5.

4.10.2. Factors Affecting Infiltration Rate

Infiltration rate of soil is affected by following factors :

1. Rainfall factor
2. Soil factor
3. Surface cover factor
4. Climatic factor
5. Other factors

Rainfall Factor

It includes following sub factors affecting the infiltration rate :

1. Rainfall intensity
2. Forms of precipitation; and
3. Rainfall duration

Rainfall Intensity : It is the falling rate of rainfall, usually expressed as cm/h or mm/h. Rainfall intensity affects the infiltration in the following two ways :

1. **When rainfall intensity is less than the infiltration capacity :** In this case, total rainwater is absorbed by the soil *i.e.* falling rain is not held over the soil surface as surface storage, but totally infiltrates into the soil in lower profiles.

2. **When rainfall intensity is greater than the infiltration capacity :** In this condition, infiltration rate decreases due to following reasons :

1. Increment in supply of moisture to the soil
2. Mechanical effects
3. Inwashing of the soil particles.

Addition of moisture to the soil, results into reduction of infiltration rate due to decrease in intake capacity of the capillary pore spaces. In addition, this phenomena also increases the frictional resistance in path of the gravity flow and thus slow down the infiltration rate.

A heavy intensity storm is composed of bigger size raindrops. When such rain drops strike the soil surface, the soil particles are compressed, as result the top soil surface becomes compact. A compact soil has lesser infiltration rate than the loose soil. In this way, the infiltration rate gets reduced.

Heavy intensity storm also causes inwashing effect. During occurrence of intense storm, when a bigger drop falls over the ground surface, the coarser soil particles are broken into finer particles, which enter into the pore spaces and thus seal them. In this way, infiltration rate of the soil also gets reduced.

Soil Factor

Soil types and their surface characteristics, such as compaction, depth of water storage, sun cracks, slopes, cultivation practices etc, mainly affect the infiltration rate. These are described as under :

Soil Types : It is related to the textural and structural properties of the soil. A light texture soil has fast rate of infiltration than the heavy texture soil, because in light texture soil, the particle size is big, causing formation of large size pore spaces in the soil mass, which increases the infiltration rate. While in heavy textured soil, a reverse effect is found. The best example of this fact is that, a sandy soil has greater infiltration rate than the clay soil.

Surface Characteristics

Compaction : Compaction of soil may be either due to absence of vegetation over the soil surface, heaves of grazing animals in pasture/grassland or sometimes due to passing of vehicles over the soil. The soil compaction poses noticeable effect on reduction of infiltration rate.

Depth of Surface Storage. Infiltration rate is affected by the depth of water storage. On this aspect, Phillip (1964) conducted an experiment and concluded that, the initial infiltration rate increases maximum of about 2% for each centimeter of water depth.

Sun Cracks : The sun cracks are generally found in the heavy textured soils *i.e.* in clay soil. Development of sun cracks is due to removal of moisture from the surface layer of the soil, under the effect of sun heat. A soil having sun cracks, includes high infiltration rate, as the water gets direct path to go down into the soil.

Soil slope : There is inverse relationship between slope of the soil surface and infiltration rate. For example, on steep slope, the velocity of flowing water is more, causing availability of very little time to water for going down into the soil *i.e.* there is reduction in infiltration rate, while on gentle or flat soil surface, the water either moves very slowly or gets ponded over the surface, as result there is high infiltration rate.

Cultivation practices : The effect of cultivation practices on infiltration rate is described by the following points :

1. The close-growing vegetal cover protects the soil against compaction by dissipating the effect of kinetic energy of falling rain drops on soil surface.

2. Vegetation checks the lossening of soil particles because the root system binds the soil particles very tightly. This effect causes reduction of inwashing of finer soil particles and thus to affect the infiltration rate.

3. The cultural practices, such as tillage operations make the soil rough, causing high infiltration rate, because runoff gets greater time to go into the soil.

4. During cultivation operations, the soil structure gets disturbed, which also resulted into high infiltration rate.

Soil Moisture : Infiltration rate also varies with the degree of soil moisture content, particularly in the early of rainfall. The moisture affects the infiltration rate in following three ways :

1. High degree of moisture content reduces the infiltration rate of the soil, because a large percent of available pore spaces are filled with water.

2. Soil moisture also affects the infiltration rate by the virtue of colloidal swelling.

3. When rain water wets the dry soil surface, a strong capillary force is created, which tends to suck the water rapidly, causing a high infiltration rate.

Surface Cover Factor

1. **Vegetation type :** Vegetative cover always increases the infiltration rate. This effect is due to development of retarding effect on the water flow. The surface retardance causes greater time to the water for entering into the soil profile. In addition, the vegetation effect is also on reduction of the soil compaction, causing to increase the infiltration rate.

2. **Types of crops :** Types of crop also affect the infiltration rate. A pasture land, which consists of close-growing grasses, involves high infiltration rate, while widely spaced row-cropped land has less infiltration rate as compared to the pasture land. Musgrave (1955) evaluated the infiltration rate for two different types of crop grown in the same soil, shown in Fig. 4.6, which indicates that, the soil has high infiltration rate, when it was under pasture, while it was less, when soil was under corn crop.

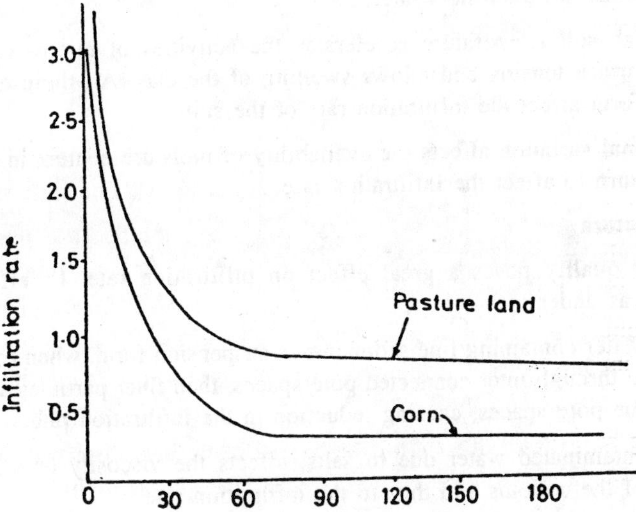

Fig. 4.6

3. **Litter :** Penman (1963) mentioned that, the presence of litter layer on the ground surface affects the infiltration rate to an appreciable extent as compared to the vegetative cover. Litter acts in two ways : first it dissipates the impact of kinetic energy of falling raindrops over the ground surface; and

second it filters the water trickling through it. These two actions in combine form protect the pore spaces against chocking from the finer soil particles. And thus, enchancing the infiltration rate.

4. **Snow cover :** It affects the infiltration rate in the same way, as litters in the forest area. The reason is that, the ground surface is less likely to freeze under snow cover, which encourages the infiltration of melted water and rainwater, too. However, the occurrence of rainfall is not common in the areas covered with the snow, therefore, infiltration of rain water is not, there.

Urban area. These areas are covered under buildings and paved surfaces, which significantly reduce the infiltration rate of the soil. Under intense storms, these areas are likely to be affected by flood occurence because of this phenomena.

Climatic Factor

Infiltration rate of the soil is also affected by the climatic factors, such as temperature, seasonal change etc. The effect of temperature on infiltration is described as under :

1. Temperature reduces the water viscosity, causing water enters very rapidly into the soil. Due to this fact, infiltration rate of soil becomes greater in summer season than the winter.

2. High soil temperature accelerates the activities of micro- organism, reduces surface tension and allows swelling of the clay. All these effects in combine form affect the infiltration rate of the soil.

Seasonal variation affects the availability of moisture content in the soil, which in turn to affect the infiltration rate.

Other Factors

Water quality poses a great effect on infiltration rate. Its effects are explained as under :

1. A water containing fine sediments in suspension form, when enters the soil profile through inter connected pore spaces, then finer particles are settle down in the pore spaces, causing reduction in the infiltration rate.

2. Contaminated water due to salts, affects the viscosity of water and swelling of the colloids and thus to the infiltration rate.

4.10.3. Infiltration Equations

Kostiakov's equation : Kostiakov (1932) developed following equation for computing the infiltration rate.

$$I = kt^n \ (0 < n < 1) \qquad ...(4.67)$$

where, I = infiltration rate

k and n = constants

t = time

Total depth of infiltration can be determined by integrating the equation 4.62 with respect to time, *i.e.*

$$Y = \int_0^t kt^n \cdot dt$$

or
$$Y = \frac{k}{n+1} t^{n+1} \qquad ...(4.68)$$

This equation computes the value of infiltration as zero for larger time period which is not correct. However, it computes accurate value of infiltration depth for the time, which is generally used in irrigation practice.

Lewis and Milne Equation : This equation is also known as Horton equation, gives as :

$$y = at + b\,(1 - e^{-rt}) \qquad ...(4.69)$$

where, y = total infiltration depth

t = time

a, b, r = constants

Infiltration rate (I) can be obtained by differentiating the equation 4.69, *i.e.*

$$I = \frac{d}{dt}(y)$$

$$= a + br\,e^{-rt} \qquad ...(4.70)$$

This equation holds good for small as well as large time periods, both.

Phillip's Equation : It is used for computing the cumulative infiltration depth, given below,

$$y = S \cdot t^{1/2} + A \cdot t \qquad ...(4.71)$$

where, y = cumulative infiltration

S = soil property, known as sorptivity. It can be computed by using the following formula

$$S = \frac{y}{t^{1/2}} \qquad ...(4.72)$$

The dimension of sorptivity is L/T or LT^{-1}

t = time

A = constant

By differenciating the equation 4.66, the infiltration rate can also be determined. It is given by

$$I = \frac{d}{dt}(y)$$

$$= \frac{S}{2} t^{-1/2} + A \qquad ...(4.73)$$

In equation 4.71, the first term is accounted for capillary force which is significant, when time is small. While second term for gravity force, which dominantes when time is large. The equation 4.71 can be fitted by least square method for determining the values of A and S for a specified condition.

In addition to the various formulae described sofar, the following formula is also used for determining the infiltration rate.

$$y = at^{\alpha} + b \quad ...(4.74)$$

in which, y is the cumulative infiltration, t is the time and α, a, and b are the constant. The values of a, b and α vary from 0 to 1. Michael et al (1972) suggested that, this formula computes the cumulative infiltration better than the Kostiakovs equation. Infiltration rate can be obtained by differenciating the equation *i.e.*

$$I = \frac{dy}{dt} = a\,\alpha\,t^{\alpha-1} \quad ...(4.75)$$

Values of a, b and α can be determined by using the following steps :

1. Plot the cumulative infiltration (y) and time (t) data on linear graph paper by keeping on y- and x-axis, respectively and draw curve passing through the plotted points.
2. Select two points *i.e.* (y_1, t_1) and (y_2, t_2) on the curve
3. Determine the value of t_3, as :

$$t_3 = \sqrt{t_1 \cdot t_2} \quad ...(4.76)$$

4. Find out the value of y_3 against t_3 from the curve.
5. Calcutate the value of constant 'b' by using the following formula :

$$b = \frac{y_1\, y_2 - y_3^2}{y_1 + y_2 - 2y_3} \quad ...(4.77)$$

6. Take the log of equation 4.68 on both sides *i.e.*

$$\log(y - b) = \log a + \alpha \log t \quad ...(4.78)$$

7. Substitute the values of b, y and t in equation 4.78 for all sets of observations and solve for α and t.

Example 4.10. *Compute the characteristics constants a, α and b of the infiltration equation $y = at^{\alpha} + b$, based on the following data base.*

Elapsed time (minute)	*1*	2	3	4	5	10	15	20	30	45	60	80	100	120
Accumulated infiltration(cm)	0.500	0.750	0.950	1.050	1.100	1.435	1.500	1.695	1.830	2.100	2.380	2.700	3.000	3.100

Solution. The following steps are followed :

Step 1. Plot the cumulative infiltration (y) and corresponding elapsed time (t) data on linear graph paper and draw curve passing through the plotted points.

Step 2. Select two arbitrary points 'a' and 'b' on the curve and find their co-ordinates. Points should be selected on or near the extremites of the smooth curve. Let, the ordinates at points a & b are,

at point $a\ (t_1, y_1) = (4, 1.055)$

at point $b\ (t_2, y_2) = (100, 3.005)$

Step 3. Calculate 't'$_3$ by using the formula

$$t_3 = \sqrt{t_1 \cdot t_2}$$
$$= \sqrt{4 \times 100} = \mathbf{20\ minutes}$$

Step 4. Find out the value of y_3 corresponding to t_3 from the derived curve in step (1). Let, it is 1.630 cm.

Step 5. Calculate the value of 'b' by using the equation 4.77, for all sets of observations.

Step (6). Compute 'a' and 'α'

Considering the equation $y = at^{\alpha} + b$ ...(4.79)

or $y - b = at^{\alpha}$

Taking the log on both sides of the equation, we have

$$\log(y - b) = \log a + \alpha \log t \qquad ...(4.80)$$

Substituting the values of b, 'y' and 't' in equation 4.80 for all sets of observation, we have

$$-0.958 = \log a + 0.3010\ \alpha \qquad ...(4.81)$$
$$-0.508 = \log a + 0.4771\ \alpha \qquad ...(4.82)$$
$$-0.387 = \log a + 0.6020\ \alpha \qquad ...(4.83)$$
$$-0.337 = \log a + 0.6989\ \alpha \qquad ...(4.84)$$
$$-0.099 = \log a + \alpha \qquad ...(4.85)$$
$$-0.065 = \log a + 1.1760\ \alpha \qquad ...(4.86)$$
$$-0.002 = \log a + 1.3010\ \alpha \qquad ...(4.87)$$
$$0.075 = \log a + 1.4771\ \alpha \qquad ...(4.88)$$
$$0.164 = \log a + 1.6532\ \alpha \qquad ...(4.89)$$
$$0.240 = \log a + 1.7781\ \alpha \qquad ...(4.90)$$
$$0.313 = \log a + 1.9030\ \alpha \qquad ...(4.91)$$
$$0.372 = \log a + 2\ \alpha \qquad ...(4.92)$$
$$0.390 = \log a + 2.0791 \qquad ...(4.93)$$

Adding first 7 equations in one and remaining 6 equations in one *i.e.*

$$-2.356 = 7 \log a + 5.5560\ \alpha \qquad ...(4.94)$$
$$1.559 = 6 \log a + 10.8905\ \alpha \qquad ...(4.95)$$

Solving the equations 4.89 and 4.90 for 'a' and 'α', we have

$$a = 0.0737$$

$$\alpha = 0.58$$

Thus, the infiltration equation becomes as

$$y = 0.0737\, t^{0.58} + 0.64 \quad \textbf{Ans.}$$

Horton's Equation

Horton (1939) developed the following equation for computing the infiltration rate at any time period.

$$f = f_c + (f_o - f_c)\, e^{-kt} \qquad ...(4.96)$$

where, f = infiltration rate at any time.
f_c = constant infiltration rate
f_o = initial infiltration rate
k = constant, depends on the soil and vegetation
e = base of the Napierian logarithism
t = time from beginning of the storm

Value of k can be determined by using the equation, given as:

$$k = \frac{f_o - f_c}{F_c} \qquad ...(4.97)$$

in which, F_c is the shaded area, as shown in the Fig. 4.7.

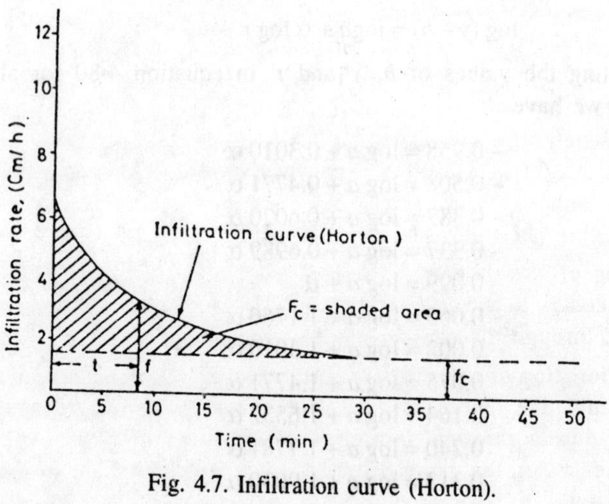

Fig. 4.7. Infiltration curve (Horton).

Equation 4.97 states that when rainfall intensity is equal to or greater than f_o (*i.e.* $i \geq f_o$), then infiltration takes place at its capacity level, but when $i < f_o$, then actual infiltration rate is being approximately equal to the rainfall intensity.

Limitations of Horton's Equation : Using this equation, it is very difficult to find the variation in the parameters f_o, f_c and k based on soil characteristics and antecedent moisture content.

Green and Ampt (1911) Eqution

This was the first equation for computing the infiltration rate, given as under :

$$I = k\left(\frac{h_w + Z - h_{we}}{Z}\right) \quad ...(4.98)$$

This equation follows the Darcy law of fluid flow. Different parameters associated to this equation are named as under.

k = hydraulic conductivity of the soil
h_w = depth of water over the soil surface
Z = depth of wetted front
h_{we} = pressure or capillary head

4.11. Components of Infiltration Process

Ifiltration process is completed under three independent sub processes, namely : entry of water into the soil, water storage within the soil profile and water transmission through soil. Increase or decrease in infiltration rate is due to effect of above three sub-processes, which are also considered as the components of infiltration process, are described as under :

Water-Intake : It is the process of entry of water in the soil, depends on the soil wetness, soil type, soil compactness, surface characteristics etc. A soil in dry condition has high infiltration rate and vice-versa. Initially, infiltration rate is high, but after sometime decreases monotonically and approaches asymptotically at constant rate, called final infiltration rate, basic intake rate or steady state infiltrability. This happening is invariabily true for all soil types, either they are sandy, clayey or any other. The water - intake is mainly affected by the following factors :

1. Filling of finer pores with the water : At this condition capillary force is reduced, which causes reduction in the hydraulic gradient, as result, water- intake through the soil surface gets reduced.

2. Deterioration of the soil structure : Deterioration of the soil structure happens, mainly due to breaking or detachment of soil aggregates by rain drop impact during rainfall, splashing or migration of fines over the soil surface and entry of the same into the pore spaces. All these impede the water-intake rate.

3. Compression and swelling of soil : Due to compaction, the soil is compressed, causing reduction in the size of voids. Reduced voids affect the water entry into the soil. In clay soil, the infiltration r[illegible] is reduced due to swelling of the soil particles, because as the soil becomes wet, the particles are swelled, by which the net size of voids ge[illegible] reduce.

Soil Moisture Storage : It represents the amount of water absorbed by the soil at ovane dry condition, and is expressed as the volume of water present in a unit volume of bulk soil. Basically, adhesion and cohesion are the two forces, which attract and retain the moisture in the soil mass. Energy of water in the soil depends on the soil surface, soil structure and solute contents. The disolved salts tend to reduce the energy of water ; and in this condition water is held by the osmotic force. When moisture content is reached at saturation stage, then soil moisture tension almost becomes zero and water is held freely in the voids of the soil. At this stage, the water present in the larger pores tends to drain out due to gravitational effect. On the contrast, in micro pores, the water is retained under capillary and osmotic forces, which is not drained due to gravitational effect. Amount of moisture left after drainage of the gravitational water is termed as "field capacity" of the soil, expressed as percent of volume. The field capacity of soil acts as upper limit of available moisture; it varies soil to soil, as shown in Table 4.16. The soil moisture tension at field capacity varies from 0.1 to 0.3 atmosphere.

The gravitational drainage can be slow, but never stop at field capacity. By this virtue, moisture is continously depleted from the soil. Regarding moisture loss from the soil is concerned, the evapotranspiration is one of the most dominant factors. The abstraction of soil moisture through root system and evaporation, accelerately reduces the moisture content of soil below field capacity. As moisture content decreases, the plant abstracts the water by applying greater suction and after some time a situation arises, when plants are no longer to abstract the sufficient moisture to meet their evapotranspirational requirement. Ultimately, the plants are likely to wilt, unless some additional water is added to the soil. This stage of soil moisture is termed as "permanent wilting point". In other words, the "permanent wilting point is that level of moisture, at which the plants are unable to abstract the water from the soil for their survival. At this stage, the water in soil is held so forcly, that the root system is being unable to extract rapidly, causing wilting of the plant leaves etc. Table 4.16 shows the range of F.C, PWP and available water for different soils. The soil moisture tension at permanent wilting point is from 7 to 32 atmosphere, depending on the soil texture, amount of solute contents, type & condition of the plants and to some extent on climatic condition, also. The range of PWP for different soils is different e.g. the fine textured soils have wide difference between field capacity and permanent wilting point, while in coarse textured soils, it lies in a narrow range might be due to presence of large size pores.

When soil moisture is reached at permanent wilting point and if further depletion of soil moisture takes place, then plants are not able to recover themselves even on supplying the irrigation water. This stage is called "ultimate wilting point." The soil moisture tension at this stage is as high as 60 atmosphere.

The permanent wilting point and field capacity are the two soil moisture levels, based on which the magnitude of available moisture in the soil, able to get utilized by the plants for their growth, can be determined. The range of F.C., P.W.P. and available soil moisture (cm/meter depth of soil) is given in Table 4.16.

Table 4.16. Range of F.C. PWP and available water for different soils

Soil type	*F.C. (%) by weight*	*PWP (%) by weight*	*Available water (cm/m soil depth)*
Sandy	5—10	2—6	5—10
Sandy loam	10—18	4—10	9—16
Loam	18—25	8—14	14—22
Clay loam	24—32	11—16	17—25
Clay	32—40	15—22	20—28

Source : Rai & Hukkeri (1979).

Soil Drainage

Drainage of soil is an important activity to keep the soil in proper order for providing better environment to the crop. Development of water logged lands, marshy lands etc. is the result of poor soil drainage. In India about 6.0 mha lands are affected by the problem of water logging. Soil drainage is mainly affected by the texture. A fine textured soil is usually poorly drained soil, while coarser soil falls under the category of good drained soil. Drainage ability of soil is closely related to the infiltration rate of that particular soil. A soil containing high infiltration rate, has greater drainage ability, because percolation of water to the water-table is higher in such soil.

4.12. Measurement of Infiltration

The purpose and types of irrigation method to be used, decide the method for measuring the infiltration rate of the soil e.g. for large areas infiltration rate is determined based on the soil properties and condition of vegetal cover, whereas for small areas when detail informations are required to design the land management practices etc., infiltration rate is directly assessed on the basis of runoff rate, assuming that few percentage of runoff is entered into the soil by infiltration phenomena. However, following methods are most common for determining the infiltration rate :

1. Cylinder infiltrometer method
    a) Single cylinder method
    b) Double cylinder method

2. Tube infiltrometer method
3. Sprinkling type infiltrometer method
4. Furrow infiltrometer method
   a) Blocking type furrow infiltrometer
   b) By-pass type furrow infiltrometer

Cylinder Infiltrometer Method

Haice etal (1956) used first the cylinder infiltrometer to determine the intake characteristics (*i.e.* infiltration) of the irrigated soils. It measures the infiltration rate, better for smaller area. Cylinder infiltrometers are found in following two types :

1. Single Cylinder Infiltrometer : This type of infiltrometer consists of single metal ring to flood the water on soil surface for measuring the infiltration rate. The diameter of metal ring is 30 cm and 45 to 60 cm as the length, is made of 0.31 cm thick M.S. sheet. It is shown in Fig. 4.8. Metal ring is driven into the soil, approximately for 10 cm depth with the help of falling hammer weight and driving unit. Water is flooded into the projected part of ring to the depth, ranging from 25 to 50 cm, depending on the existing vegetation and humus on the soil surface. Volume of water added in the ring is noted carefuly. Initially, the time interval for measurement should be kept shorter, because infiltration increases very rapidly at the initial of experiment. Normally, 2 to 3 hours duration is required to attain constant infiltration rate.

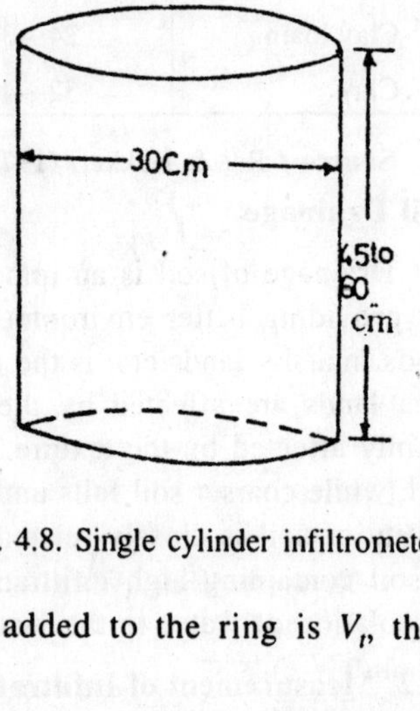

Fig. 4.8. Single cylinder infiltrometer.

If after time '*t*', the volume of water added to the ring is V_t, then infiltration rate is given by :

$$I = \frac{V_t}{a \cdot t}$$

in which, *I* is the infiltration rate and '*a*' is the cross- sectional area of cylinder. Example 4.11 shows the procedure for computing the infiltration rate under cylinder infiltrometer method.

Example 4.11. *For determining infiltration rate, a concentric- ring infiltrometer was installed in the field plot of 5000* cm^2 *size. During experiment the following data were recorded :*

Elapsed time (minute)	*0*	*1*	*2*	*5*	*10*	*15*	*30*	*60*	*90*	*120*
Volume of water added since start (c.c)	*0*	*50*	*100*	*241*	*420*	*541*	*820*	*1000*	*1150*	*1355*

(i) Diameter of concentric ring = 30cm

(ii) Constant depth of water in the ring = 1.5 cm

Calculate, infiltration rate and basic intake rate of the soil.

Solution. Computation of infiltration rate is shown in following table.

Elapsed time (min)	*Volume of water added (c.c)*	*Accumulated depth*	*ΔF** (cm)*	*Infiltration capacity (f)*	
				cm/minute	*cm/h*
0	0	0	0	0	0
1	50	0.1000	0.100	0.10	6.00
2	100	0.200	0.100	0.05	3.00
5	241	0.4820	0.282	0.094	5.64
10	420	0.8400	0.358	0.072	4.32
15	541	1.0820	0.242	0.048	2.88
30	820	1.6400	0.558	0.037	2.22
60	1000	2.0000	0.360	0.012	0.72
90	1150	2.3000	0.300	0.010	0.60
120	1335	2.7100	0.410	0.014	0.84

Basic intake rate = 0.84 cm/h otherwise, if infiltration rate becomes constant at this value; measurement should be carriedout for few more hours.

Limitations : The single cylinder infiltrometer method involves following limitations :

1. When cylinder is driven into the soil, the structure of adjoining soil gets disturbed, causing the measured infiltration rate by this method is not absolutely correct.

2. In this method, if soil surface is not protected by the vegetations or humas, then structure of soil is likely to be altered due to destruction of soil aggregates caused by impact of water pouring. In this situation measured infiltration rate is not correct.

3. The impact of water pouring is not simulated.

4. Development of lateral pressure during driving of cylinder into the soil also causes significant effect on infiltration rate of the soil.

5. The uncontrolled lateral movement of water from the bottom of ring, introduces errors in measurement of infiltration rate.

Double Cylinder Infiltrometer

It is also known as concentric-ring infiltrometer. In this infiltrometer, the lateral movement of water into surrounding soil is checked by driving an additional ring, outside the single cylinder infiltrometer. The outer ring acts as a buffer boundary for inner cylinder and ensures downward movement of water in the soil. In this way, it provides a reliable measurement of infiltration rate. However, measured infiltration rate by this technique can also be affected by the factors, like diameter & thickness of cylinder, method used for driving the cylinder into soil and the depth up to which the cylinder has been driven. The recommended specification of concentric-cylinder is given as under :

1. Thickness = 5 mm
2. Internal diameter of inner cylinder = 200 to 300 mm
3. Internal diameter of outer cylinder = 400 to 500 mm
4. Length of inner and outer cylinders = 450 mm

Lower edge of both cylinders is sharpend by grinding, to provide 45° shamper on outside.

Measurement of infiltration : For measurement of infiltration rate, the concentric infiltrometer is installed in the soil, as shown in Fig. 4.9. Care should be taken that, an annular buffer strip of 10 cm must be left around the inner cylinder, throughout. Water is filled in both the compartments for same depth; usually 6 to 12 cm depth is preferred. Measurements are recorded only from the inner cylinder, by maintaining a constant water level. The measurement includes, volume of water poured into the inner compartment to maintain the constant water level and corresponding elapsed time. Computation procedure of infiltration rate is the same, as shown in example 4.11.

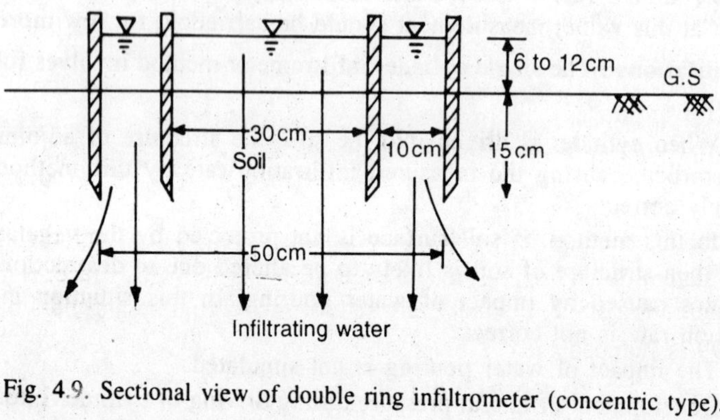

Fig. 4.9. Sectional view of double ring infiltrometer (concentric type).

Although, the cylinder infiltrometer is cheap, simple in construction and installation, but provides only relative rate of infiltration. This method can not be used to determine the effect of various factors such as, land use, vegetations, land slope etc on the infiltration rate. Field studies revealed that, the infiltration rate measured by this technique is 2 to 10 times greater than the infiltration rate measured under natural rainfall condition.

Tube Infiltrometer Method

It consists of a metal tube of about 22.5 cm internal diameter and 45 to 60 cm length. For infiltration measurement, the tube is driven into the soil, atleast for the depth up to which, it is expected to penetrate the water into the soil during experiment. It normally varies from 37.5 to 52.5 cm. Water is filled in the tube to a certain level, which is maintained by adding the water throughout the experiment period. The rate, at which water is added in the tube, corresponds the infiltration rate.

Sprinkling Type Infiltrometer Method

It is also known as "Rainfall Simulator". It rectifies all the deficiencies observed in cylinder infiltrometer method. United State Department of Soil Conservation Services has introduced two types of sprinkling infiltrometers, given as under :

1. F-type infiltrometer and
2. FA-type infiltrometer

Constructional feature of these two sprinkling infiltrometers is the same, but difference is in respect of size of the experimental plot, used for them. F- type sprinkling system is normally used on the plot of $1.83 \times 3.66\ m^2$ size, while F.A. Type on $30 \times 76\ m^2$ size plot.

Sprinkling system consists of a set of nozzles equipped on the lateral, to sprinkle the water on the field plot. Nozzles are designed to simulate the size and falling velocity of water droplets similar to the natural rainfall. Water is supplied to the laterals from the water source at constant rate, which fall down through nozzles inform of droplets over the plot. For determining infiltration rate, the following observations are recorded during experiment :

1. Depth of water sprinkled over the plot (P), cm
2. Depth of surface runoff generated from the plot (SRO), cm

Based on above two informations, the following formula can be used for calculating the depth of infiltrated water in the soil :

$$F = P - (SRO + D_a + S_d) \qquad ...(4.99)$$

in which, F is the depth of water infiltrated, and D_a & S_d are the depth of surface detention and depression storage made on the soil surface, respectively. At saturation stage, D_a and S_d are reduced to negligible and thus the equation 4.99 is reduced to:

$$F = P - SRO \qquad ... (4.100)$$

Furrow Infiltrometer Method

The cylinder infiltrometer provides accurate measurement of infiltration rate from level surface of the soil. In corrugated condition (i.e. furrow) it does not measure so accurate, because of the variations in soil compaction at the sides and bottom of the furrow. To overcome this kind of effect, the infiltrometer owing to the furrow shape, is designed and constructed called furrow infiltrometer. This infiltrometer is of two types i.e. blocking type and by-pass type.

Blocking Type Furrow Infiltrometer : It was designed by Bordurant in the year 1957 for measuring the infiltration rate of the soil, corrugated by furrow system. It consists of two metal plates, which are placed in the furrow section to confine a certain length of the furrow. Water is filled into the confined part of furrow from a supply tank. A constant water-level is maintained in the furrow, throughout the experiment. The lowering of water level in the supply tank is measured at fixed time interval. If 'h' is the initial height of water level in the supply tank and after elapsed time 't' water attains the height h_t in the tank, then cumulative infiltration depth (f) is given as :

$$f = (h - h_t)\,K \qquad \text{...(4.101)}$$

in which, K is the multiplying factor, which is the ratio of cross-sectional area of supply tank to the area of furrow section, *i.e.*

$$K = \frac{A}{a} \qquad \text{...(4.102)}$$

where, A = cross-sectional area of supply tank
$= \pi r^2$ (assuming the cross-section of tank as circular)
r = radius of tank
a = area of furrow section
$= (b + 2D{\cdot}Z) \cdot S$
(assuming the cross-section of furrow as trapezoidal)
b = bottom width
D = depth of furrow
$Z = \frac{e}{d}$ (as shown in Fig. 4.10)
S = spacing of plates.

Equation (4.101) assumes that, the infiltration rate within the furrow infiltrometer remains constant in isolated furrow cross-section. Example 4.12 describes the computation procedure of infiltration rate under this technique.

Example. 4.12. *Calculate the cumulative infiltration depth by using following informations, recorded from blocking type furrow infiltrometer,*

Elapsed time (minute)	*0*	*5*	*10*	*20*	*40*	*60*	*120*
Water level in supply tank (cm)	*30.0*	*28.75*	*26.25*	*25.00*	*21.00*	*19.00*	*15.00*

if

1. Furrow cross-section is trapezoidal with the bottom width as 20 cm and side slope 4 : 3 (H:V)

2. Spacing of plate = 60 cm

3. Constant depth of water in the furrow = 5 cm

4. Internal diameter of supply tank = 30 cm

Solution. Referring Fig. 4.10

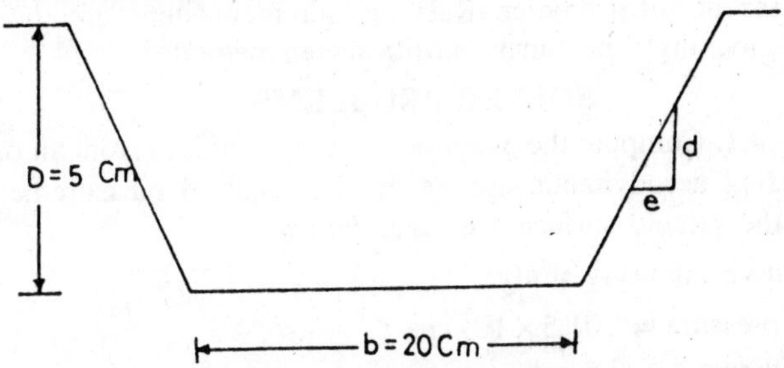

Fig. 4.10. A view of trapezoidal shaped furrow section.

Top width of furrow section $(T) = b + 2\,D{\cdot}Z$

$$= 20 + 2 \times 5 \cdot \frac{4}{3} = 33.33 \text{ cm}$$

Area of top of the water surface

$$= 33.33 \times 60 = 1999.8 \text{ cm}^2$$

Cross-sectional area of the supply tank $(A) = \pi r^2$

$$= \pi \times (15)^2 = 706.85 \text{ cm}^2$$

$$\therefore \qquad K = \frac{A}{a} = \frac{706.85}{1999.80} = 0.35$$

Computation of Accumulated Infiltration Depth : It is shown in following table.

Elapsed time (minute)	*Water level in the supply tank (cm)*	*Decrease in water level of the tank (cm)*	*Accumulated infilatration depth (cm)**
1	*2*	*3*	*4*
0	30.00	0	0.00
5	28.75	1.25	0.44
10	26.25	3.75	1.31
20	25.00	5.00	1.75
40	21.00	9.00	3.15
60	19.00	11.00	3.85
120	15.00	15.00	5.25

*Accumulated infiltration depth

$$= \text{Col (3)} \times K$$

$$= \text{Col (3)} \times 0.35$$

By Pass-Type Furrow Infiltrometer Method

By-passs type furrow infiltrometer was developed by Shull in the year 1961. This infiltrometer simulates similar condition in the furrow section, as generally occurs during irrigation. For infiltration measurement, a small segment of furrow is isolated by the infiltrometer; and in remaining furrow length, water is directed to flow. By this happening, the water does not flow in the encloser of infiltrometer. Rest measurement steps are the same, as described in blocking type furrow infiltrometer method.

SOLVED PROBLEMS

Problem 4.1. Compute the evaporation rate (mm/day) from an open water surface by using aerodynamic approach. The required measurements at 2m height from the ground surface are given below :

1. Relative humidity = 40%
2. Air pressure = 101.5×10^3 kpa
3. Wind speed = 2.5 m/s
4. Density of air = 1.19 kg/m^3
5. Density of water = 1000 kg/m^3
6. Ambient vapour pressure and vapour pressure at the soil surface are 1230 and 3000 Pa, respectively.
7. Roughness height = 0.035 cm

Solution : Using the formula

Evaporation rate (mm/day) = $K\,(e_{as} - e_a)$

in which, $$K = \frac{0.622\,k^2 \cdot P_a\,U_2}{p \cdot P_w \left[\ln\left(\frac{z_2}{z_n}\right)\right]^2}$$

$$= \frac{0.622 \times (0.4)^2 \times 1.19 \times 2.5}{101.5 \times 1000 \times 1000 \left[\ln\left(\frac{2}{0.035/100}\right)\right]^2} \quad \text{(taking } k = 0.4\text{)}$$

$$= \frac{0.296072}{10.15 \times 10^7\,[\text{In}\,(5714.285714)]^2}$$

$$= \mathbf{3.9 \times 10^{-11}\ m/Pa.s}$$

Therefore, evaporation rate

$$E_a = K\,(e_{as} - e_a)$$

$$= 3.9 \times 10^{-11}\,(3000 - 1230) = 6.903 \times 10^{-8}\ \text{m/s}$$

$$= 6.903 \times 10^{-8} \times 1000 \times 3600 \times 24 = \mathbf{5.96\ mm/day} \quad \textbf{Ans.}$$

Problem 4.2. Determine the evaporation rate (mm/day) from an open water surface by using energy balance method, if the net radiation is 150 W/m^2 and air temperature is 25°C. Also, consider that there is no sensible heat or ground heat flux.

Solution : Using the formula

Latent heat of vaporization (l_v) = $2.501 \times 10^6 - 2370\,T$ (J/kg)

$$= 2.501 \times 10^6 - 2370 \times 25 = 2441750\ \text{J/kg}$$

$$= \mathbf{2441.75 \times 10^3\ J/kg}$$

Therefore, evaporation $= \dfrac{R_n}{l_v \cdot \rho_w}$

$$= \frac{150}{2441.75 \times 10^3 \times 1000} \text{ m/s} \quad (\rho_w = 1000 \text{ kg/m}^3$$

$$= 6.143 \times 10^{-8} \text{ m/s} = \mathbf{5.31\ mm/day} \qquad \textbf{Ans.}$$

Problem 4.3. Calculate the shear velocity of wind, if wind velocities at 2 and 5.0 m heights from the ground surface are 1.5 and 3.0 m/s, respectively.

Solution. Using the formula

$$U^* = \frac{k\,(U_2 - U_1)}{In\left(\dfrac{z_2}{z_1}\right)} \qquad \text{(taking } k = 0.40)$$

$$U^* = \frac{0.40\,(3 - 1.5)}{In\left(\dfrac{5}{2}\right)} = \frac{0.60}{0.91629} = \mathbf{0.65\ m/s} \quad \textbf{Ans.}$$

Problem 4.4. Determine the wind velocity at 7.5 m height from the ground surface, if

(*a*) Shear velocity of wind is 0.60 m/s

(*b*) Ronghness height is 0.025 cm

Take the Von Karman constant (*k*) as 0.4.

Solution : Using the formula

$$\frac{U}{U^*} = \frac{1}{k}\, In\left(\frac{z}{z_0}\right)$$

$$\frac{U}{0.6} = \frac{1}{0.4}\, In\left(\frac{7.5}{0.025/100}\right)$$

$$\frac{U}{0.6} = 25.7724$$

$$\therefore \qquad U = \mathbf{15.46\ m/s} \quad \textbf{Ans.}$$

Problem 4.5. Compute the Von Karman constant (*k*) if wind velocities at 2 and 5.0 m heights from the ground surface are 1.5 and 4.0 m/s, respectively and shear velocity is 0.75 m/s.

Solution : Using the formula

$$U^* = \frac{k\,(U_2 - U_1)}{In\left(\dfrac{z_2}{z_1}\right)}$$

$$0.75 = \frac{k\,(4 - 1.5)}{In\left(\dfrac{5}{2}\right)}$$

$$0.75\, In\,(2.5) = 2.5\, k = \frac{0.75}{2.5}\, In\,(2.5) = \mathbf{0.274} \quad \textbf{Ans.}$$

Problem 4.6. Determine the psychrometric constant (γ) if specific heat at constant pressure is 1001 J/kg; air pressure is 101.3×10^3; latent heat of vaporization is 2500×10^3 J/kg and K_h/K_w is 1.

Solution : Using the formula

$$\text{Psychrometric constant } (\gamma) = \frac{c_p \cdot K_h \cdot p}{0.622\, l_v \cdot K_w}$$

$$= \frac{1001 \times 1 \times 101.3 \times 10^3}{0.622 \times 2500 \times 10^3} = \mathbf{65.21\ Pa/°C} \quad \textbf{Ans.}$$

Problem 4.7. Compute the value of saturated vapour pressure gradient (Δ) at 30°C temperature, when saturated vapour pressur is 2550 Pa at the same temperature.

Solution : Using the formula

$$\Delta = \frac{4098\, e_s}{(237.3 + T)^2}$$

$$= \frac{4098 \times 2550}{(237.3 + 30)^2} \text{ Pa/°C} = \mathbf{146.26\ Pa/°C} \quad \textbf{Ans.}$$

Problem 4.8. Calculate evaporation rate (mm/day), if

(*a*) Evaporation rate at net radiation of 220 W/m^2 is 7.0 mm/day.

(*b*) Evaporation rate from open water surface is 7.75 mm/day

(*c*) Psychrometric constant is 60 Pa/°C

(*d*) Saturated vapour pressure gradient is 100 Pa/°C.

Solution : Using the formula

$$E_{(mm/day)} = \frac{\Delta}{\Delta + \gamma} E_r + \frac{\gamma}{\Delta + \gamma} E_a$$

$$= \frac{100}{100 + 60} \times 7.0 + \frac{60}{100 + 60} \times 7.75$$

$$= 4.375 + 2.90625 = \mathbf{7.28\ mm/day} \quad \textbf{Ans.}$$

Problem 4.9. Calculate evaporation rate (mm/day), if the net radiation of a given place is 250 W/m^2.

Solution : Using the formula

$$E_r = 3.53 \times 10^{-2} R_n \text{ (mm/day)}$$

$$= 3.53 \times 10^{-2} \times 250 = \mathbf{8.825\ mm/day} \quad \textbf{Ans.}$$

Problem 4.10. Compute saturated vapour pressure at the ground surface, if air temperature is 30°C.

Solution : Using the formula

$$e_{as} = 611 \exp\left(\frac{17.27\, T}{237.3 + T}\right) Pa$$

$$= 611 \exp\left(\frac{17.27 \times 30}{237.3 + 30}\right)$$

$$= 611 \exp(1.93827) = \mathbf{4244.45\ Pa} \quad \textbf{Ans.}$$

Problem 4.11. Calculate the value of saturated vapour pressure, if vapour pressure at the ground surface is 4000 Pa and ıelative humidity is 70%.

Solution : Using the formula

$$e_a = R_h \cdot e_{as}$$

$$0.7 \times 4000 \text{ Pa} = \mathbf{2800\ Pa} \quad \textbf{Ans.}$$

Problem 4.12. Calculate pan coefficient, if the lake and pan evaporations are 25 and 30 mm/day, respectively.

Solution : Using the formula

Lake evaporation = C_p . pan evaporation

or
$$C_p = \frac{\text{Lake evaporation}}{\text{Pan evaporation}}$$

$$= \frac{25}{30} = \mathbf{0.833} \quad \textbf{Ans.}$$

Problem 4.13. Compute the volume of water lost from the reservoir due to evaporation during a month of 30-days, if surface area of reservoir is 1525 m^2; pan evaporation is 20 mm/day and pan coefficient is 0.65.

Solution : Using the formula

$$V_E = A \cdot Ep_m \cdot C_p$$

$$= 1525 \times \frac{20}{1000} \times 30 \times 0.65 \text{ m}^3$$

$$= \mathbf{594.75\ m^3} \quad \textbf{Ans}$$

Problem 4.14. Calculate saturation vapour pressure (mm of Hg) at the mean air temperature of 25°C.

Solution : Using the formula

$$e_a = 4.584 \exp\left(\frac{17.27\,T}{237.3 + T}\right) \text{mm of Hg}$$

$$= 4.584 \exp\left(\frac{17.27 \times 25}{237.3 + 25}\right)$$

$$= 4.584 \exp(1.646) = \mathbf{23.77\ mm\ of\ Hg} \quad \textbf{Ans.}$$

Problem 4.15. A small hollow cylindrical tube of 45 cm^2 cross-sectional area is filled with soil and laid horizontally, and open end of it is saturated. After 15 minutes about 75 cm^3 of water was allowed to infiltrate into the tube. Determine how much infiltration was took place in 45 minutes duration, if the soil column had initially been placed upwright with its upper surface saturated. (Assume the saturated hydraulic conductivity of the soil is 0.35 cm/h)

Solution : Given that,

Cumulative volume of infiltration = 75 cm^3

or Cumulative depth of infiltration $= \frac{75}{40}$ cm = **1.875 cm**

In case of horizontal infiltration, the cumulative infiltration is the function of soil suction, therefore infiltration rate after 15 minutes or (1/4) *h*, is given as

$$F(t) = St^{1/2}$$

$$1.875 = S(1/4)^{1/2}$$

or

$$S = \frac{1.875}{(1/4)^{0.5}} \text{ cm}/h^{0.5} = \mathbf{3.75\ cm \cdot h^{-1/2}}$$

Infiltration through vertical column after 45 minutes is given by

$$F(t) = St^{1/2} + Kt$$

$$= 3.75 \times (0.75)^{1/2} + 0.35 \times 0.75$$

$$= \mathbf{3.51\ cm} \quad \textbf{Ans.}$$

Problem 4.16. Determine the ponding time and depth of water ponding in silt loam soil of 30% initial effective saturation, for the following rainfall intensities

(*a*) 1.5 cm/h (*b*) 5.5 cm/h

Solution : Using the formula for ponding time

$$t_p = \frac{k\psi \cdot \Delta Q}{i(i-k)}$$

where, k = hydraulic conductivity of soil

ψ = wetting front capillary pressure head

ΔQ = difference of initial and final moisture contents of the soil. It is given as $(1 - s_e)\,\theta_e$

i = rainfall intensity

The value of ψ for silt loam soil is generally taken as 16.7 cm; hydraulic conductivity as 0.65 cm/h and θ_e as 0.486. In question, the value of s_e is given 0.30. Using these values, we have,

$$\Delta Q = (1 - 0.30)\, 0.486 = 0.3402$$

(*a*) For i = 1.5 cm/h

$$t_p = \frac{0.65 \times 16.7 \times 0.3402}{1.5\,(1.5 - 0.65)} = \mathbf{2.896\ h} \quad \textbf{Ans.}$$

and depth of ponding $= i \cdot t_p$

$$= 1.5 \times 2.89 \text{ cm} = \mathbf{4.335\ cm} \quad \textbf{Ans.}$$

(*b*) For $i = 5.5$ cm/h

$$t_p = \frac{0.65 \times 16.7 \times 0.3402}{5.5\,(5.5 - 0.65)}\; h = \mathbf{0.138}\, h \quad \textbf{Ans.}$$

and depth of ponding $= 5.5 \times 0.138$ cm $=$ **0.7859 cm** **Ans.**

Problem 4.17. Determine the cumulative infiltration after 1.5 hours of the rainfall, if rain fall intensity is 3.5 cm/h on silty loam soil having initial effective saturation as 25%.

Solution : For silty loam soil, the values are

$$\psi = 16.7 \text{ cm}$$
$$k = 0.65 \text{ cm/h}$$
$$\theta_e = 0.486$$

Therefore, $\Delta Q = (1 - 0.25) \times 0.486 = \mathbf{0.3645}$

$$\therefore \quad t_p = \frac{0.65 \times 16.7 \times 0.3645}{3.5\,(3.5 - 0.65)} \text{ h} = \mathbf{0.397\ h}$$

and depth of ponding $(F_p) = i \cdot t_p$

$$= 3.5 \times 0.397 \text{ cm} = \mathbf{1.3895\ cm}$$

Cumulative infiltration is given by the following formula

$$F - F_p - \psi\,\Delta Q \ln\left[\frac{\psi\,\Delta Q + F}{\psi\,\Delta Q + F_p}\right] = K\,(t - t_p)$$

(in which F is the cumulative infiltration)

Therefore, on substitution of the values of different parameters, we have

$$F - 1.3895 - 16.7 \times 0.3645 \cdot \ln\left[\frac{16.7 \times .3645 + F}{16.7 \times .3645 + 1.3895}\right]$$

$$= 0.65\,(1 - 0.397) = 0.39$$

or

$$F - 7.48 \ln\left[\frac{6.09 + F}{7.48}\right] = 0.39$$

This equation can be solved by hit and trial method.

Important Points

1. In hydrology, the evaporation and transpiration phases are treated as 'loss'.
2. The precipitation, which is not effective for resulting the runoff is called initial loss.
3. In terms of groundwater development, infiltration of water is treated as 'gain'.
4. Evaporation is likely to continue till the saturation vapour pressure at the water temperature (e_w) and actual vapour pressure (e_a) are equilibrated.
5. If saturation vapour pressure at the water temperature (e_w) is greater than the actual vapour pressure, then there is condensation to take place.
6. The latent heat of vaporization is about 585 cal/g of evaporated water.

7. Evaporation rate increases with increase in wind velocity upto a critical velocity, beyond which there is no effect on evaporation due to any further increase in wind velocity.
8. At high altitudes, the decrease in barometric pressure causes increase in evaporation rate.
9. Dissolved salts reduce vapour pressure of the water.
10. Dissolved salts reduce the evaporation rate.
11. The percent reduction in evaporation corresponds the percent increase in specific gravity of the solution.
12. Under identical conditions, the evaporation from sea water is about 2 to 3% less as compared to the fresh water.
13. Deep water bodies contain greater heat storage than the shallow water bodies.
14. A deep lake involves less evaporation in summer and more evaporation in winter as compared to the shallow lake, because deep lake stores radiant energy during summer season and releases in winter.
15. Class A evaporation pan is considered as the standard pan. It has 1210 mm diameter and 255 mm depth.
16. In class A evaporation pan, the depth of water is maintained between 5 and 7.5 cm.
17. Cross-sectional area of Colorado sunken pan is 92 sq. cm.
18. The ISI standard pan is made of copper sheet of 0.9 mm thick.
19. The cross-section of U.S. floating pan is square with 900 mm side and 450 mm deep.
20. A pan of 1.0 m diameter measures 20% greater evaporation than the 3-m dia pan.
21. Lake evaporation is equal to the product of pan coefficient (C_p) and pan evaporation.
22. The average pan coefficient of class-A pan is generally taken as 0.70.
23. The average pan coefficient of ISI pan is taken as 0.80.
24. The average pan coefficient of Colorado sunken pan is 0.78.
25. The average pan coefficient of US floating pan is 0.80.
26. As per WMO recommendations, the density of evaporation station for arid zones should be 1/30,000 sq km.
27. As per WMO recommendations, the density of evaporation measuring stations for humid temperate climates should be 1/50,000 sq km.
28. As per WMO recommendations, the density of evaporation measuring stations for cold regions should be 1/100,000 sq km.
29. In India, the total number of pan evaporimeters is more than 200.
30. In the lower atmosphere *i.e.* upto the height of about 500 m above the ground surface, the wind velocity follows the **1/7 th power law**, which is given by $u_h = ch^{1/7}$ where u_h is the wind velocity at height h above the ground surface and c is the constant.

31. The transfer of sensible heat from water surface to the air (H_a) can be estimated by using the Bowen's ratio (β), which is given by $\frac{H_a}{\rho \cdot L \cdot E_L}$ in which ρ is the density of water; L is latent heat of evaporation, and E_L is the evaporation.

32. In India, the annual evaporation loss from the water body is about 160 cm.

33. Lysimeter measures the evapotranspiration.

34. Albedo of close growing crops is from 0.15 to 0.25.

35. Albedo of bare land is from 0.05 to 0.45.

36. Albedo of water surface is 0.05.

37. Albedo of snow cover is from 0.45 to 0.95.

38. At 0°C temperature, the saturation vapour pressure (e_w) is 4.58 mm Hg.

39. The relationship between e_w and temperature (T°C) is given by

$$e_w = 4.584 \exp\left(\frac{17.27\,T}{237.3 + T}\right) \text{mm Hg}$$

40. The 'isopleth' is the contour of ET.

41. In India, the highest annual PET is of Rajkot, equal to 214.5 cm.

42. The 'initial loss' refers to the loss of precipitation due to interception and depression storage, together.

43. Interception loss is solely due to evaporation. It does not include the losses due to transpiration, throughfall or stem flow.

44. From an area, during plant-growing season the interception loss varies from 10 to 20% of the total rainfall.

45. Interception is zero at saturation stage.

46. Interception loss is more from a small storm.

47. Interception storage varies from 0.25 to 1.25 mm.

48. In sandy soils, the depression storage loss during intense storm is more than 0.50 cm.

49. In loamy soils, the depression storage loss during intense storm can be as 0.40 cm.

50. In clay soils, the depression storage loss during intense storm can be as 0.25 cm.

51. Infiltration activates the ground water recharge.

52. The maximum rate of infiltration by which the soil can absorb water is called infiltration capacity.

53. When soil occurs in layers, then transmission capacity of the layers determines the overall infiltration rate.

54. A soil with good drainage contains high infiltration capacity.

55. Water contamination reduces the infiltration rate.

56. Turbidity of water reduces the infiltration rate.

57. Measurement of infiltration should be continued till steady state condition.

58. The infiltration capacity of bare sandy soil is about 1.2 cm/h.

59. ϕ-index is the average rate of water loss, above which the volume of rainfall is equal to the volume of runoff.

60. ϕ-index is evaluated from the hyetograph by considering the constant infiltration rate as the initial loss.

61. The rainfall amount in excess of ϕ-index is called rainfall excess.

62. The ϕ- and *W*-indices vary storm to storm.

63. Generally, to estimate the maximum floods for design purposes (in absence of any other data), the value of ϕ-index is considered as 0.10 cm/h.

64. Central Water Commission developed the relationship for ϕ-index of flood producing storms as $\phi = \frac{I - R}{24}$ in which, I is the rainfall intensity (cm/day) and R is the runoff in cm.

References

1. Horton R.E. U.S. Monthly Weather Reveiw, Vol. No. 47, 1919.
2. Linsley R.K., Kohler M.A. and Paulhus J.L.H., Applied Hydrology, McGraw Hill-Book Co. Ltd., New York, 1949.
3. Linsley R.K., Kohler M.A. and Paulhus J.L.H., Hydrology for Engineers, McGraw Hill-Book Co. Ltd., New York, 1950.
4. Penman H.L., Natural Evaporation from open water, Bare soil and Grass, Prosc. Roy. Soc. London, Vol. 193, 1948.
5. Blaney H.F. and Criddle W.D., Determining Water Requirements in Irrigated Areas from Climatological and Irrigation data, U.S.D.A. SCS-TP-96, 1950.
6. Thornthwait C.W. An approach towards a rational classification of climate, Geographical Reveiw, 38, 1948.
7. Doorenbos J. and Pruitt W.C., Guidelines for predicting crop water requirements, Irrigation and Drainage paper-24, FAO, Rome, 1975.
8. Horton R.E., An approach towards a physical interpretation of infiltration capacity, Soil Sci Soc. Am Prosc, 5, 1935.
9. Penman H.L., Vegetation and Hydrology, Farnham Royal, Common Wealth Agricultural Bureaux, 1963.
10. Musgrave G.W. "How much of the rain enters the soil" in "Water", USDA Year book, 1955.
11. Michael A.M., Mohan S and Swaminathan K.R., Design and evaluation of irrigation methods, IARI Monograph No. 1, WTC (IARI), New Delhi, 1972.
12. Horton R.E. Analysis of runoff-plot experimants with varying infiltration - capacity, Trans., Am. Geophysics Union, Vol. 20, 1939.
13. Green W.H. and Ampt G.A. Studies on soil physics, Part-1, The flow of air and water through soils, J. Agric, Sci, Vol 4 (1), 1911.
14. Hillel D. Applications of Soil Physics, Academic Press, Orlando, 1980.
15. Phillip J.R. The Theory of infiltration : 1. The infiltration equation and its solution, Soil Sci. Vol 83(5), 1957.

16. Chow V.T. Handbook of Applied Hydrology, McGraw-Hill, New York, 1964.

17. Weisner, C.J. Hydrometeorology, Chapman and Hall, Ltd., London, 1970.

DESCRIPTIVE TYPE QUESTIONS

1. (*a*) Define water loss regarding hydrological aspect and list its various forms.

(*b*) Differentiate interception loss and interception storage.

(*c*) Describe various factors affecting interception.

2. Define total interception and describe the formula for estimating it.

3. What is the secondary interception. Is it greater than the normal interception, if so, why.

4. Define depression storage and explain the method to determine the volume of water stored in the depression.

5. Define evaporation and explain various factors affecting it.

6. Write difference between evaporation and condensation.

7. Lists various methods for computing the evaporation loss and describe storage-equation method.

8. Define pan coefficient and explain why it is needed to determine.

9. Write the difference between the mechanism of evaporation from water and soil surface. If we have water evaporation data, then how we get the value of soil evaporation.

10. Define evapotranspiration and describe lysimetric technique for determining it.

11. List various methods for computing the evapotranspiration based on climatological data. And describe modified Penman equation.

12. Explain the procedure to compute ET by using Blanney-Criddle method.

13. Define infiltration and describe the factors affecting infiltration rate.

14. Explain different components of infiltration and describe infiltration measurement by using double ring infiltrometer.

15. Define various infiltration indices and write the procedure for computing the water loss.

OBJECTIVE TYPE QUESTIONS

(Multiple Choice)

1. If total rainfall depth and runoff are 15 and 10 cm, respectively at a particular watershed, then what would be the water loss.

(*a*) 25 cm (*b*) 10 cm

(*c*) 5 cm. (*d*) 7.5 cm

2. In forest areas, during rainfall the major water loss is due to

(*a*) interception (*b*) evapotranspiration

(*c*) infiltration (*d*) stemflow

3. That part of intercepted water, which is returned back to the atmosphere through evaporation is called

(*a*) interception loss (*b*) interception storage

(*c*) through fall (*d*) stem flow

4. Interception is more in case of
(*a*) drizzle (*b*) heavy rainfall
(*c*) low rainfall (*d*) sleet

5. Initially, interception is
(*a*) less (*b*) more
(*c*) zero (*d*) about 10% of the total rainfall

6. Secondary interception takes place from
(*a*) uniform vegetation height
(*b*) non-uniform vegetation levels
(*c*) both *a* and *b*
(*d*) grass land

7. At high humidity, evaporation is
(*a*) less (*b*) more
(*c*) moderate (*d*) 80%

8. Barren soils are more affected by evaporation, because of
(*a*) lack of vegetation (*b*) greater compaction
(*c*) *a* and *b* (*d*) less humidity

9. If coefficient K is 0.5 and pan evaporation is 5.0 cm, then ET will be
(*a*) 5.5 cm (*b*) 2.5 cm
(*c*) 1.25 cm (*d*) none of above

10. If crop consumptive use is E_t and k_{co} is the crop coefficient, then potential ET would be
(*a*) $\frac{E_t}{k_{co}}$ (*b*) $k_{co} \cdot E_t$
(*c*) $\frac{k_{co}}{E_t}$ (*d*) $\frac{K_c}{T_{mean}}$

11. The unit of solar radiation is
(*a*) langly/day (*b*) hertz
(*c*) m/s (*d*) watt

12. Movement of any thing within the same medium is called
(*a*) infiltration (*b*) percolation
(*c*) both *a* & *b* (*d*) seepage

13. Entry of any thing from one medium to another medium is called
(*a*) infiltration (*b*) percolation
(*c*) both *a* & *b* (*d*) seepage

14. During intense storm, infiltration loss is
(*a*) less as compared to the mild rainfall.
(*b*) more as compared to the mild storm
(*c*) not affected
(*d*) about 1.5 cm

15. A cropped land involves
(*a*) high infiltration rate (*b*) low infiltration rate
(*c*) less initial loss (*d*) none of above

16. Infiltration rate is more in case of
(*a*) barren soil (*b*) vegetated soil
(*c*) rocky land (*d*) waterlogged land

17. A slopy land involves
(*a*) less infiltration (*b*) more infiltration
(*c*) moderate infiltration (*d*) 1.25 cm/h as percolation rate

18. Clay soil includes less infiltration rate because of
(*a*) less percentage of macro pores
(*b*) less porosity
(*c*) greater entraped air
(*d*) none of above.

19. If soil *A*, *B* and *C* have water depth 15, 20 and 10 cm, respecticely, then infiltration rate will be more in soil
(*a*) *A* (*b*) *B*
(*c*) *C* (*d*) both *A* & *C*

20. Soil *A* contains 35% m.c, soil *B* 40% and soil *C* 55%. In which soil infiltration will be less
(*a*) *A* (*b*) B
(*c*) C (*d*) both *B* & *C*

21. A dry soil has high infiltration rate, because of
(*a*) less m.c (*b*) less compaction
(*c*) greater porosity (*d*) higher entrapped air

22. Blocking type furrow infiltrometer is suitable for measuring the infiltration rate in
(*a*) flat lands (*b*) furrow
(*c*) both '*a*' & '*b*' (*d*) borders

23. Dissolve salts in water
(*a*) reduce the infiltration rate
(*b*) increase the infiltration rate
(*c*) increase the seepage
(*d*) result no effect on infiltration rate

24. Paved surface involves high runoff, because of
(*a*) less infiltration (*b*) greater temperature
(*c*) less time of concentration (*d*) less seepage loss

25. The dissolve salts affect the infiltration rate, because of
(*a*) increase in water viscosity (*b*) swelling of colloids
(*c*) both '*a*' & '*b*'. (*d*) less temperature

26. Lysimeter is used to measure
(*a*) evaporation (*b*) evapotranspiration
(*c*) infiltration (*d*) rainfall intensity

27. Evpotranspiration takes place only in
(*a*) day time (*b*) night-time
(*c*) land surface (*d*) forest areas

28. Interception loss includes
(*a*) evaporation, stemflow and through fall
(*b*) only evaporation
(*c*) only stem flow
(*d*) only depression storage

29. Interception loss is greater in

(*a*) forest (*b*) agricultural land

(*c*) grass land (*d*) residential area

30. Infiltration loss will be more in

(*a*) shallow sandy soil (*b*) very deep heavy soil

(*c*) very deep loam soil (*d*) very deep sandy loam soil

31. Reflection coefficient is generally taken as

(*a*) 0.25 (*b*) 1.0

(*c*) 0.50 (*d*) 0.75

32. Kostiakov equation estimates

(*a*) infiltration rate (*b*) cumulative seepage

(*c*) percolation capacity (*d*) basic intake rate

33. Infiltration rate is greater during

(*a*) initial of measurement (*b*) end of experiment

(*c*) mid of observation (*d*) none of above

Answer (Objective Type Question)

1. (*c*)	**2.** (*a*)	**3.** (*a*)	**4.** (*c*)	**5.** (*b*)	**6.** (*b*)	**7.** (*a*)	**8.** (*c*)
9. (*b*)	**10.** (*a*)	**11.** (*a*)	**12.** (*b*)	**13.** (*a*)	**14.** (*a*)	**15.** (*a*)	**16.** (*b*)
17. (*a*)	**18.** (*a*)	**19.** (*c*)	**20.** (*a*)	**21.** (*a*)	**22.** (*b*)	**23.** (*a*)	**24.** (*a*)
25. (*c*)	**26.** (*b*)	**27.** (*a*)	**28.** (*a*)	**29.** (*a*)	**30.** (*d*)	**31.** (*a*)	**32.** (*a*)
33. (*a*)							

5

Runoff and its Computation

Rainfall is the source of water for runoff generation in the channel. During occurrence of rainfall, a part of it is intercepted by the vegetations, buildings and several other objects lying over the ground surface, which does not reach the land surface. Few portion of rainfall also infiltrates into the soil, and lastly the rest amount of rain fall makes some depth of water over the ground surface, which tends to move from one place to another under effect of land gradient is called overland flow, which ultimately meets to the streams, channels etc. is known as runoff.

Thus, runoff may be defined as that portion of rainfall which flows through the rivers, streams, nala etc.

Steps for conversion of precipitation to Runoff

The conversion of precipitation into the runoff over the watershed involves several processes which are shown as under (Chow, 1964)

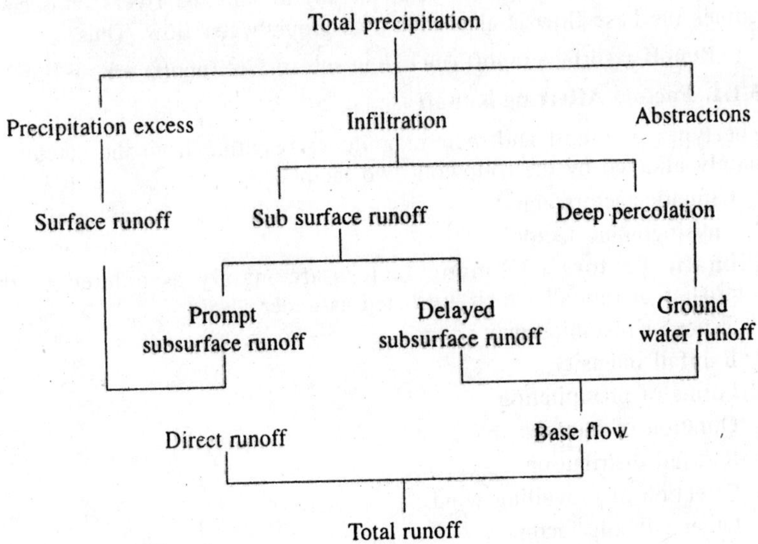

5.1. Types of Runoff

Runoff is broadly classified into following three types :

1. Surface runoff
2. Sub-surface runoff and
3. Base flow.

Surface Runoff : It is that part of rainfall, which enters the streams, channels etc. immediately after occurring the rainfall. The process may be described as, when all losses *i.e.* interception, depression storage, infiltration etc. are satisfied and if the rain is still continued with the rate greater than infiltration rate, then excess water makes a head over the soil surface, which tends to move due to land slope, is known as overland flow. After laps of few time, the overland flow joins the stream, channel or nala etc., is called surface runoff. Sometimes, the surface runoff is also termed as prompt runoff as it takes very little time to join the streams etc.

Sub-Surface Runoff : It is that amount of rainfall, which first goes into the soil and then starts flowing laterally towards nearby streams, rivers etc. without joining the water-table. Sometimes, sub-surface runoff is also treated as the surface runoff due to the fact that, it takes very little time to reach the rivers, like surface flow.

Base Flow : It is the delayed flow, defined as that part of rainfall which after falling over the ground surface, percolates into the soil and meets to the water-table/ground water and finally joining to the streams, oceans etc. In other words, the flow of ground water towards streams, channels etc. is known as base flow.

Movement of water in this type of runoff is very slow. It takes a long time (*i.e.* from a month to few years or so) to join the rivers or oceans. Sometimes the base flow is also known as groundwater flow. Thus,

Runoff = surface runoff (including sub-surface runoff) + base flow

5.1.1. Factors Affecting Runoff

The types of runoff and their magnitudes resulting from the catchment are mainly affected by the following two factors :

1. Climatic factors and
2. Physiographic factors

Climatic Factors : Climatic factors are mainly associated to the characteristics of rainfall which are listed as under :

1. Types of precipitation
2. Rainfall intensity
3. Forms of precipitation
4. Duration of rainfall
5. Rainfall distribution
6. Direction of prevailing wind
7. Other climatic factors

Effect of these factors on runoff are described as under :

Types of Precipitation : The types of precipitation have great effect on runoff. For example : a precipitation which occurs in the form of rainfall, starts moving immediately in the form of overland flow/runoff depending on intensity and duration of the precipitation. While another precipitation, which takes place in the form of snow or hails, the flow of water on the ground surface will not take place immediately, but after melting of the same. During this time lag, a large amount of melted water is absorbed by the soil, resulting into very less runoff generation.

Rainfall Intensity : Intensity of rainfall has dominating effect on the runoff yield from the calchment. If rainfall intensity is greater than the infiltration rate of the soil, then surface runoff is generated very quickly, while in case of low intensity rainfall the generation of runoff is certain only when it is more than the infiltration, otherwise there is no runoff. For a given time a high intensity rainfall causes high runoff and vice-versa.

Duration of Rainfall : Rainfall duration directly affects the runoff volume because infiltration capacity of the soil goes on decreasing with the advancement of time, as result a mild rainfall occurring for longer duration can produce the runoff from catchment.

Rainfall Distribution : Runoff from a catchment also depends on the rainfall distribution patterm. The effect of rainfall distribution on runoff can be presented by a term known as "distribution coefficient", which is the ratio of maximum rainfall to the mean rainfall of the catchment. *i.e.*

$$C_d = \frac{\text{Maximum rainfall}}{\text{Mean rainfall}} \quad ...(5.1)$$

For a given total rainfall, if all the conditions are the same, then greater the coefficient of distribution, higher will be the runoff and vice-versa. However, for the same distribution coefficient, the peak runoff would be very shortly from the storm falling on the lower part of the catchment (*i.e.* near to the outlet) than the storm occurring on the upper part of the catchment.

Direction of Prevailing Wind : The direction of prevailing wind affects the runoff, greatly. If the direction of wind is towards the runoff flow in the drainage system of the catchment, then the resulting runoff will be more at short interval, while duration of surface runoff will be less and vice-versa. Due to this reason, a storm moving in the direction of stream flow results high peak very shortly as compared to the storm moving in opposite direction.

Other Climatic Factors : It includes temperature, wind velocity, relative humidity, annual rainfall etc. All these factors also affect the runoff producing characteristics of the watershed to some extent. Normally, these factors affect the runoff by increasing the initial losses from the precipitation.

Physiographic Factors

These factors are associated to the physiographic characteristics of the watershed and channel both, which affect the runoff yield from the area. Various factors related to watershed characteristics are given as under :

1. Size of watershed
2. Shape of watershed
3. Slope of watershed
4. Watershed orientation
5. Land use
6. Soil moisture
7. Soil type
8. Topographic characteristics

Size of Watershed : If the climatic factors, such as depth and intensity of rainfall are same, then two watersheds irrespective of their size will produce the same runoff. However, a large watershed takes longer time for delivering the runoff to the outlet and hence the peak flow rate becomes smaller and vice-versa. Also, a small watershed is dominated by overland flow, while large watershed by runoff.

Shape of Watershed : The watersheds are generally found in following two shapes :

1. Fan shape and
2. Fern shape

In case of fan shaped watersheds the axial length and width are approximately equal. While in fern shaped watersheds, axial length is greater than the width. Fan shaped watersheds produce high peak rate of runoff in shorter duration than the fern shape watershed because in former case all parts of the watershed contribute the runoff to the outlet immediately during rainfall.

Generally, the shape of watershed is expressed by two factors i.e. form factor and compactness factor, described as under :

Form factor : It is defined as the ratio of average width to the axial length of watershed, expressed as :

$$\text{From factor} = \frac{\text{Average width of watershed}}{\text{Axial length of watershed}}$$

$$F_f = \frac{B}{L} \quad \text{...(5.2)}$$

Axial length of watershed is the distance between outlet and remotest point of the area. Width is determined by dividing the area of watershed (A) with the axial length. Thus,

$$F_f = \frac{B}{L}$$

$$F_f = \frac{A/L}{L} = \frac{A}{L^2} \quad \text{...(5.3)}$$

Compactness factor : It is the ratio of perimeter of watershed to the circumference of a circle whose area is equal to the area of watershed, i.e

$$\text{Compactness factor} = \frac{\text{Perimeter of watershed}}{\text{Circumference of circle whose area is equal to the area of watershed}}$$

$$= \frac{P}{2\,\pi A} \qquad \text{...(5.4)}$$

where, P = perimeter of watershed

A = area of the watershed

$\pi = 3.14$

Slope of Watershed : Slope of watershed poses an important effect on runoff likely to be generated from the watershed. It reduces the time of concentration and thus, peak runoff occurs relatively at shorter duration. In other words, incase of slopy land, the runoff velocity is more and infiltration loss is less resulting into high peak runoff immediately and vice-versa.

Orientation of Watershed : This factor affects the evaporation and transpiration losses by affecting the amount of heat received from the sun. The north or south orientation of watershed affects the melting time of snow and accordingly to the runoff, also. Similarly, in mountaneous watersheds, the windward side of mountain receives greater rainfall than the leeward side due to orientation effect.

Land Use : The land use pattern and land management practices followed in the watershed have great effect on runoff. For example - an area which is under forest cover in which a thick layer of mulch of leaves and grasses is accumulated, the generation of surface runoff becomes too less because a huge rainfall amount is absorbed by the soil due to high infiltration rate and resistance in the flow path of water over the ground surface, while in barren lands a reverse trend is found.

Soil Moisture : The runoff likely to be generated from the catchment also depends on the level of moisture present in the soil at the time of rainfall. If rain occurs over the land with more soil moisture, then water absorbing capacity of the soil becomes too less and thus resulting into generation of more runoff. Similarly, if rain occurs after a long dry spell, then soil becomes to dry and total rain water may be absorbed by the soil, causing no extra water to be available for making the runoff. In this condition, even intense storm becomes unable to produce the runoff in appreciable amount. On the other hand, if rain occurs frequently, a reverse effect on runoff yield is obtained.

Soil Types : The surface runoff also depends on the types of soil of the catchment because absorption of rain water varies from soil to soil. For example - a light soil (*i.e* sandy soil) which consists of coarser particles and large pore spaces, involves rapid absorption of water and thus it has less runoff generating potential. In heavy textured soil (*i.e.* clay soil), the particles are finer and size of pore spaces is too small, causing little absorption of rain water and formation of huge runoff.

Topographic characteristics

It refers to the surface features of the watershed. Unduiate land yields less runoff to that of the flat land, because the overland flow gets obstruction to flow towards the outlet due to undulation effect, if unduations are across the watershed slope.

Regarding channel characteristics, the cross-section, roughness, storage, channel density etc. are considered as the factors affecting runoff.

Drainage Density : It is defined as the ratio of total channel length existing in the watershed to the total area of watershed expressed as m/ha. Drainage density is given as :

$$\text{Drainage density} = \frac{\text{Total channel length}}{\text{Total area of watershed}}$$

or
$$D_d = L/A \qquad ...(5.5)$$

At greater drainage density, the runoff yield at the outlet is more, because rain water enters the drainage channels, immediately and reaches to the outlet.

5.2. Runoff Computation

Computation of accurate runoff rate or volume due to any storm from the watershed is a difficult task, because it depends on several factors related to the watershed and atmosphere; prediction of whom is not so easy. However, the commonly used methods are given below :

1. Rational method
2. Cook's method
3. Curve number method
4. Hydrograph method
5. Infiltration indices method
6. Empirical formulae.

All these methods are described as under :

5.2.1. Rational Method

It is a common method for computing the peak runoff rate from small catchments. The peak runoff refers to the discharge rate used for design of hydraulic structures, that must carry the runoff. Rational method involves following formula for computing the peak runoff :

$$Q_{peak} = \frac{CIA}{360} \qquad ...(5.6)$$

where, Q_{peak} = peak runoff rate, m^3/s

C = runoff coefficient

I = rainfall intensity (mm/h) for the duration equal to the time of concentration

A = area of watershed, hectare.

Computation of peak runoff is performed under following steps.

Step-1. Calculate the runoff coefficient

Runoff coefficient is the ratio of peak runoff rate to the rainfall intensity. It is a dimensionless term, varies from 0 to 1. depending on land use and soil types (Table 5.1). When watershed is under different types of land use systems and soils, then weighted value of runoff coefficient is determined. An example for computing the weighted runoff coefficient is shown as under :

Let, watershed is divided into five sub-parts based on soil types and land use practices followed on them, having the area a_1, a_2, a_3, a_4 & a_5 and their runoff coefficients are C_1, C_2, C_3, C_4 and C_5, respectively, then the value of weighted runoff coefficient (C_w) of the watershed is given by :

$$C_w = \frac{C_1 a_1 + C_2 a_2 + C_3 a_3 + C_4 a_4 + C_5 a_5}{a_1 + a_2 + a_3 + a_4 + a_5}$$

or $$C_w = \frac{\sum_{i=1}^{n} C_i a_i}{A} \qquad ...(5.7)$$

in which, A is the total area of watershed.

Example 5.1. *Compute the value of weighted runoff coefficient of the watershed from the following data.*

Land use and topography	*Cultivated land (flat, soil is sandy)*	*Pasture land (rolling, sandy soil)*	*Populated with flat topography and tight clay soil*
Area (ha)	*100*	*30*	*75*

Solution. Using equation 5.7, the weighted runoff coefficient is given by

$$C_w = \frac{C_1 a_1 + C_2 a_2 + C_3 \cdot a_3}{a_1 + a_2 + a_3}$$

in which, the values of C_1, C_2 and C_3 are obtained from the table 5.1 for given land use and topographical features of the watershed. Calculation is shown in following table :

Land use/topography	*Area (ha)*	*Runoff coefficient (C)*	*Computation*
Cultivated land + flat topography + sandy soil	100	0.30	$C_w = \frac{C_1a_1 + C_2a_2 + C_3a_3}{a_1 + a_2 + a_3}$
Pasture land + rolling topography + sandy soil	30	0.16	
Populated lnad + flat topography + tight clay soil	75	0.40	$= \frac{100 \times .3 + 30 \times .16 + 75 \times .40}{205}$
			$= \mathbf{0.32}$ **Ans.**

Table 5.1. Values of runoff coefficient (*C*) for use in Rational method

S.No.	*Land use and topography*	*Soil type*		
		Sandy loam	*Clay and silt loam*	*Tight clay*
1.	Cultivated land			
	(i) Flat	0.30	0.50	0.60
	(ii) Rolling	0.40	0.60	0.70
	(iii) Hilling	0.52	0.70	0.82
2.	Pasture land			
	(i) Flat	0.10	0.30	0.40
	(ii) Rolling	0.16	0.36	0.55
	(iii) Hilling	0.22	0.42	0.60
3.	Forest land			
	(i) Flat	0.10	0.30	0.40
	(ii) Hilling	0.30	0.50	0.60
4.	Populated land			
	(i) Flat	0.40	0.55	0.65
	(ii) Rolling	0.50	0.65	0.80

Step (2) : Compute rainfall intensity for the duration equal to time of concentration of the watershed.

Time of Concentration : The time required to reach the surface runoff from remotest point of the watershed to its outlet is known as time of concentration (T_c).

When rainfall duration approaches to the time of concentration, then all parts of watershed start to generate the flow to the outlet, simultaneously. At this stage, the resulting discharge at the outlet is maximum which is referred as peak discharge/runoff.

Computation of Time of Concentration : There have been developed several empirical relationships for computing the time of concentration. However, the formula developed by Kirpich (1940) is very common, which is based on the channel length and its average slope, given as under :

$$T_c = 0.02\, L^{0.77} \cdot S^{-0.385} \qquad ...(5.8)$$

where, T_c = time of concentration, min

L = length of channel reach, m

S = average channel slope, m/m

Example 5.2. *Calculate the time of concentration of 300 ha size watershed. The maximum length of drainage course is 350 m and average slope of it is 4 m/100 m.*

Solution. Given that,

$$L = 350 \text{ m}$$

$$S = 4/100$$

∴ Time of concentration $(T_c) = 0.02L^{0.77} \cdot S^{-.385}$

$$= 0.02\,(350)^{0.77} \times \left(\frac{4}{100}\right)^{-.385}$$

$$= \mathbf{6.28\ minutes.} \quad \textbf{Ans.}$$

Haan et al (1982) reported that the Kirpich (1940) relationship (*i.e.* eq. 5.8) does not provide accurate estimation of time of concentration for small watersheds i.e. less than 5 sq. km area. He justified that, the small watersheds are mainly dominated by overland flow rather than channel flow. Incorporating this effect, he developed the following equation for computing the time of concentration, which is the addition of overland flow component in equation 5.8.

$$T_c = 0.02\,L^{0.77} \cdot S^{-.385} + \left[\frac{2L_o\sqrt{n}}{S_o}\right]^{0.467} \quad ...(5.9)$$

where, L_o = length of overland flow, m

n = Manning's roughness coefficient (Table–5.2)

S_o = slope of the flow path, m/m

In equation 5.9, the second term is accounted for overland flow. From studies, it has been found that, the overland flow can vary for the length of 100 to 150 m in the watershed. On contrast, the channel length increases with increase in the size of watershed, and time of concentration increases, accordingly. This equation is valid for all size of watersheds for estimating the T_c.

Table 5.2. Value of Mannings roughness coefficient(n)

S.No.	*Surface condition*	*Value of 'n'*
1.	Smooth and impervious surface	0.02
2.	Smooth and bare surface	0.10
3.	Cultivated row crops	0.20
4.	Pasture or average grassed surface	0.40
5.	Forest area with dense grass cover	0.80

California Culverts Practice (1942) developed the relationship for computing the time of concentration for small mountaneous basins of California. It is given as

$$T_c = 60\left(\frac{11.9\,L^3}{H}\right)^{0.385} \quad ...(5.10)$$

in which L is the length of longest water course (mile) and H is the elevation difference between watershed divide and the outlet (ft)

Federal Aviation Administration (1970) developed the formula for T_c with the help of air field drainage database assembled by Corps of Engineers. This formula is widely used for computing the overland flow in urban basins. Formula is given as under :

$$T_c = \frac{1.8\,(1.1 - C)\,L^{0.50}}{S^{0.333}} \quad ...(5.11)$$

where, C is the runoff coefficient of rational formula, L is the length of overland flow (*ft*) and S is the surface slope (%).

Kinematic Wave Formula : Morgali & Linsley (1965) and Aron & Erborge (1973) developed the following formula for time of concentration.

$$T_c = \frac{0.94\, L^{0.6} \cdot n^{0.6}}{(i^{0.4}\, S^{0.3})} \qquad ...(5.12)$$

where, L is the length of overland flow (*f*), n is the Manning's roughness coefficient, i is the rainfall intensity (inch/h) and S is the average slope of soil surface (*ft/ft*).

SCS Lag equation (1973) : It is in following form

$$T_c = \frac{100\, L^{0.8} \left[\left(\frac{1000}{CN} \right) - 9 \right]^{0.7}}{1900\, S^{0.5}} \qquad ...(5.13)$$

in which L is the hydraulic length of watershed (*i.e.* longest flow path), *ft*, CN is the SCS curve number and S is the average slope of watershed (%). This formula was developed by SCS based on agricultural watershed database. Its applicability is limited to the small urban basins less than 2000 acre size. It generally results good estimation where area is completely paved. For heterogeneous soil surface, it overestimates. For impervious areas, an adjustment factor is introduced to get the T_c *i.e.*

$$T_c = 1.67 \times \text{basin lag} \qquad ...(5.14)$$

SCS average velocity chart (1975 & 1986) follows the following formula for T_c

$$T_c = \frac{1}{60} \sum \frac{L}{V} \qquad ...(5.15)$$

where L is the length of flow path (*ft*) and V is the average flow velocity (*ft/s*). The flow velocity is the function of the slope of water course and surface cover.

The following formula can also be used for predicting the time of concentration for a small plot, in which flow occurs in form of overland flow.

$$T_c = \frac{111 \cdot b\, (L_o)^{1/3}}{(K_p)^{2/3}} \qquad ...(5.16)$$

where, b = coefficient

K_p = runoff coefficient

L_o = length of overland flow

The value of '*b*' can be determined by using the following equation:

$$b = \frac{2.75 \times 10^{-4} \cdot p + Cr}{(S_o)^{1/3}} \quad \text{...(5.17)}$$

in which, p is the rainfall intensity and Cr is the retardance coefficient, which depends on the roughness of soil surface. Its values are given in Table 5.3.

Table 5.3. Values of retardance coefficient

S.No	*Types of surface*	*Value of Cr*
1.	Dense blue grass	0.060
2.	Closely clipped soil	0.046
3.	Concrete pitched surface	0.012
4.	Tar and gravel pitched surface	0.017

Linsely et.al. (1979) have also developed the following formula for computing the time of concentration for small area :

$$T_c = t_p = C_t \left(\frac{L \cdot L_{ca}}{S} \right)^n \quad \text{...(5.18)}$$

where, C_t and n = basin constants

S = slope of the basin

L_{ca} = distance from gauging point (*i.e.* outlet) to the point opposite to the centre of watershed.

L = basin length, measured along the main water course from the basin divide to the gauging point.

This formula assumes that the time of concentration is approximately to the lag time.

Assumptions of Rational Method : The rational formula assumes following assumptions :

1. Rainfall has been occured with uniform intensity for the duration atleast equal to the time of concentration of the catchment area.

2. The rainfall intensity is uniform throughout the catchment.

If above two assumptions are satisfied for any storm, then relationship between rainfall and runoff produced by the catchment may be represented by the curve as shown in Fig. 5.1, which indicates that any storm with uniform intensity, if occurrs for the duration greater than the time of concentration, the rate of runoff will be less than the peak value, because rainfall intensity is reduced for longer storm duration. Similarly, a storm occurring for the duration less than the time of concentration, the resulting runoff would also be less than the peak value, as in this condition all parts of watershed are not able to contribute the discharge to the outlet, simultaneously.

Limitations of Rational Method : The following limitations are found in case of rational method :

1. Rational method assumes that the rainfall intensity is uniform throughout the watershed, but it is never satisfied.

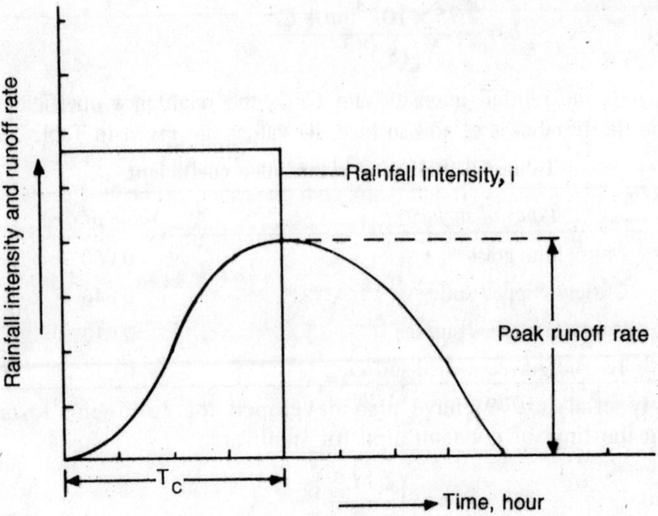

Fig. 5.1. Relationship between rainfall and runoff.

2. This method does not take care of the effect of initial losses, such as interception, depression storage, initial infiltration, channel storage etc. on the runoff.

3. The runoff coefficient is computed only on the basis of watershed characteristics, which do not provide correct estimate. The value of runoff coefficient is also dependent on the atmospheric charcteristics, like season, rainfall etc.

Example 5.3. *Calculate the peak runoff rate for 10 years return period from a watershed of 175 ha area. The whole area is divided into three sub-parts based on the land use and soil texture. In which, first part of 100 ha land with 1% slope is kept under cultivation ; the second part of 45 ha has 7% slope is engauged under pasture farming and remaining land with 12% slope is covered under forest. The other informations are given as under :*

1. Max. length of channel reach =2500 m

2. Average channel slope = 5%

3. Rainfall depth = 3.58 cm

Solution. The following steps are followed :

1. *Computation of runoff coefficient 'C'*

Area (ha)	*Land use*	*Slope*	*Runoff coefficient (C)*	*Weighted runoff coefficient*
100	Cultivation	1%	0.50	$C_w = \frac{100 \times .50 + 45 \times .36 + 30 \times .50}{175}$
45	Pasture	7%	0.36	$= \mathbf{0.46}$
30	Forest	12%	0.50	

2. *Computation of time of concentration* (T_c)

$$T_c = 0.02\, L^{0.77} \cdot S^{-.385}$$

$$= (0.02)\,(2500)^{0.77} \cdot \left(\frac{5}{100}\right)^{-.385} = \mathbf{26.20\ minutes.}$$

3. *Computation of rainfall intensity for the duration of* T_c *as 26.20 minutes* : It is determined by dividing the rainfall depth with T_c, which is obtained as 8.2 cm/h

4. *Computation of peak runoff*

$$Q_{peak} = \frac{CIA}{36} = \frac{1}{36} \times 0.46 \times 8.2 \times 175 = \mathbf{8.34\ m^3/s\ \ Ans.}$$

Modified Rational Method (Craig and Rankl, 1978, Donahue, McCuen and Bondelid, 1981)

It is extension of rational method for the rainfalls lasting for the duration longer than the time of concentration. This method was developed to derive the hydrograph for storage design rather than peak discharge computation. It can be used for preliminary design of detention storage for the watershed area ranging from 20 to 30 acres. The modified formula is given by

1. $$Q_p = CA\left(\frac{a}{T_d + b}\right) \qquad ...(5.19)$$

in which C is the runoff coefficient of rational method, A is the area of basin, T_d is the duration of rainfall and a & b are the constant.

2. Duration of rainfall or critical duration (T_d) refers to one that is required to form maximum detention storage in the watershed. It is given by the following formula :

$$T_d = \left(\frac{b \cdot C \cdot A \cdot a}{Q_A - \dfrac{Q_A^2\, T_p}{2C \cdot A \cdot a}}\right) \qquad ...(5.20)$$

where, Q_A is the allowable discharge i.e. the peak discharge and T_p is the time to peak or time of concentration of the detention basin.

3. Volume of storage in detention basin (V_s) : It is given by

$$V_s = T_d \cdot Q_p - Q_A \cdot T_d - Q_A \cdot T_p + \frac{\gamma \cdot Q_A\, T_P}{2} + \frac{Q_A^2\, T_P}{2QP} \qquad ...(5.21)$$

in which γ is the ratio of time to peak of the two hydrographs or the ratio of time of concentration of the developed to undeveloped condition of watershed.

4. Volume of runoff after development (V_r) : It is given by

$$V_r = Q_p \cdot T_d \qquad ...(5.22)$$

5.2.2. Cook's Method

This method is named after Cook (1946). It computes the runoff based on four characteristics of watershed i.e relief, infiltration rate, vegetal cover and surface depression, which are the main parameters affecting the runoff from the watershed. Numerical values to each of the above four characteristics are assigned on the basis of comparison with the similar condition of other watershed. The range of numerical values for above four characteristics are given in Table 5.4. Computation procedure is described under following steps :

Step 1. Evaluate the degree of watershed characteristics *i.e.* relief, infiltration rate, vegetal cover and surface depression by comparing them with the similar conditions of other watershed.

Step 2. Assign numerical value (W) to each of the four characteristics with the help of table 5.4.

Table 5.4

S. No.	*Range*	*Numerical values for runoff producing watershed's characteristics*			
		Relief	*Soil infiltration*	*Vegetal cover*	*Surface storage*
		(20 to 10)	(10)	Forest or equivalent, (10)	(10)
1.	Normal	Land is in rolling shape and slope ranges from 5 to 10%	Infiltration rate varies from 0.75 to 2 cm/h; soil is normal and deep permeable in nature.	About 50% of total area is under good grass cover or any other equivalent cover	Considerable depression storage, lakes, ponds and marshes are less than 2% of entire drainage system.
2.	High	(30 to 20)	(15)	(15)	(15)
		Lands are hilly in nature, average slope ranges from 10 to 30%.	Infiltration rate ranges from .25 to 0.75 cm/h, soil is relatively hard such as clay soil.	Vegetal cover varies from poor to fair; less than 10% of total area is under grass cover.	Surface depression is very low. Area is well drained.
3.	Extreme	(40 to30)	(20)	(20)	(10)
		Lands are steep and rugged terrain; slope ranges upto 30%.	Infiltration rate is less	Land is bare, no effective grass cover.	Surface depression is negligible ; drainage of land is very well. No ponds or tanks are available.

Step 3. Find out the sum of numerical values (ΣW) assigned to each four characteristics of the watershed.

i.e. $$\Sigma W = R + I + V + D \qquad ...(5.23)$$

where, ΣW = total numerical value of all four characteristics

R = marks given to the relief characteristics

I = marks given to the initial infiltration

V = marks assigned to the vegetal cover

D = marks given to the surface depression

Step 4. Determine the runoff rate against ΣW by using the runoff curve, as shown in Fig. 5.2. Obtained runoff is valid for a specified geographical location of the watershed and 10 years of recurrence interval. Computed runoff rate is again modified for the desired location of watershed and recurrence interval.

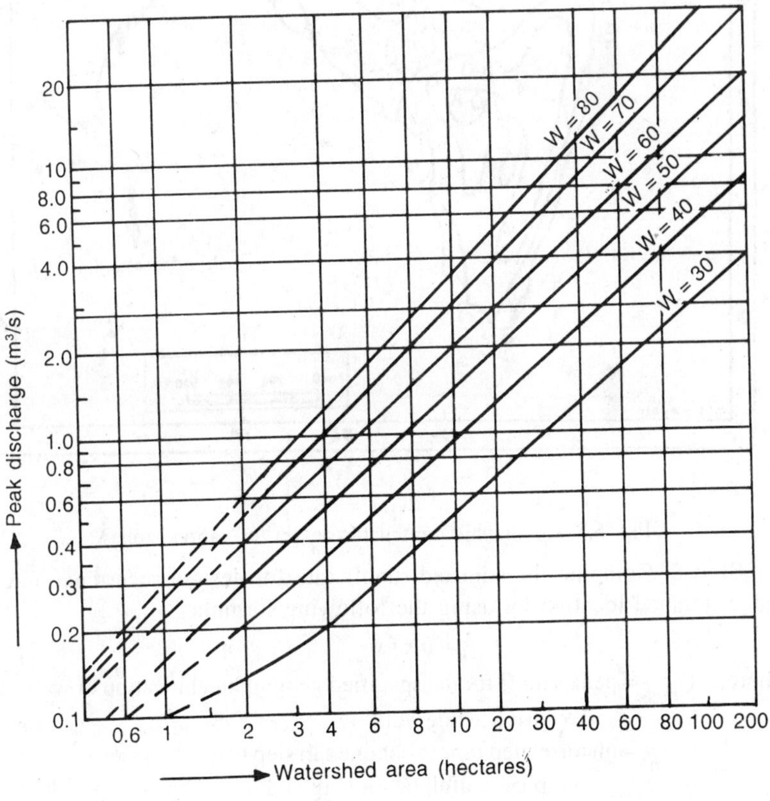

Fig. 5.2. Computation of runoff under Cook's method.

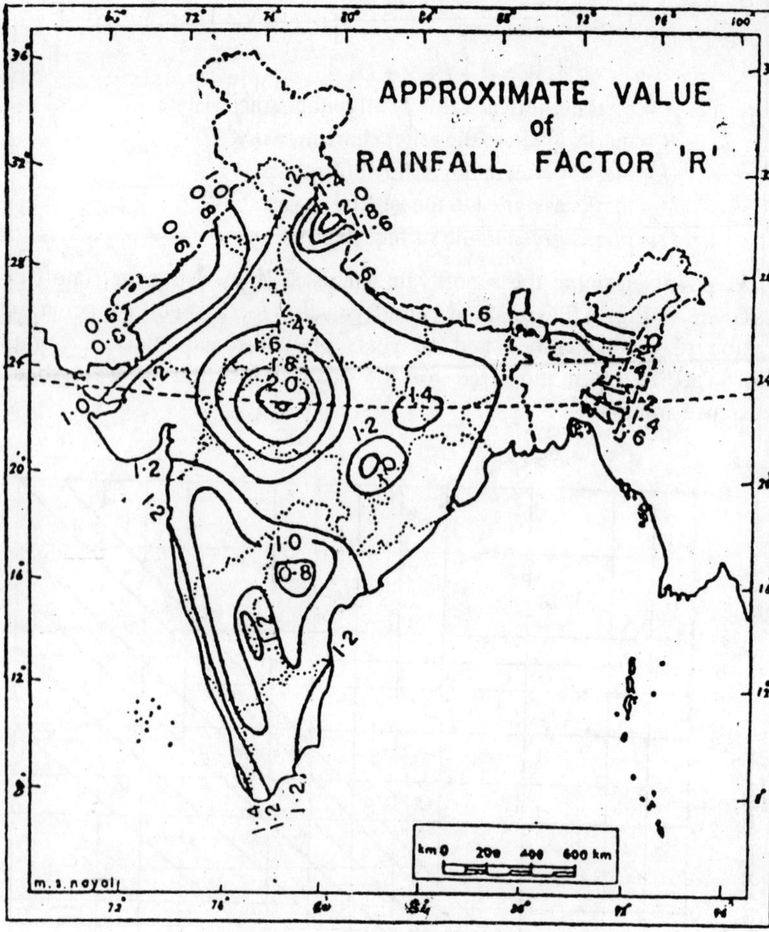

Fig. 5.3. Geographic rainfall factor, (*r*) for various zones.

Step 5. Compute the adjusted runoff rate for desired recurrence interval and watershed location by using the following formula :

$$Q_{peak} = p \cdot r \cdot f \cdot s \qquad \text{...(5.24)}$$

where, Q_{peak} = peak runoff for the specified geographical location of watershed and recurrence interval

p = uncorrelated runoff obtained in step (4)

r = geographic rainfall factor (Fig. 5.3)

f = recurrence interval factor (Fig. 5.4)

s = shape factor, given in table 5.5

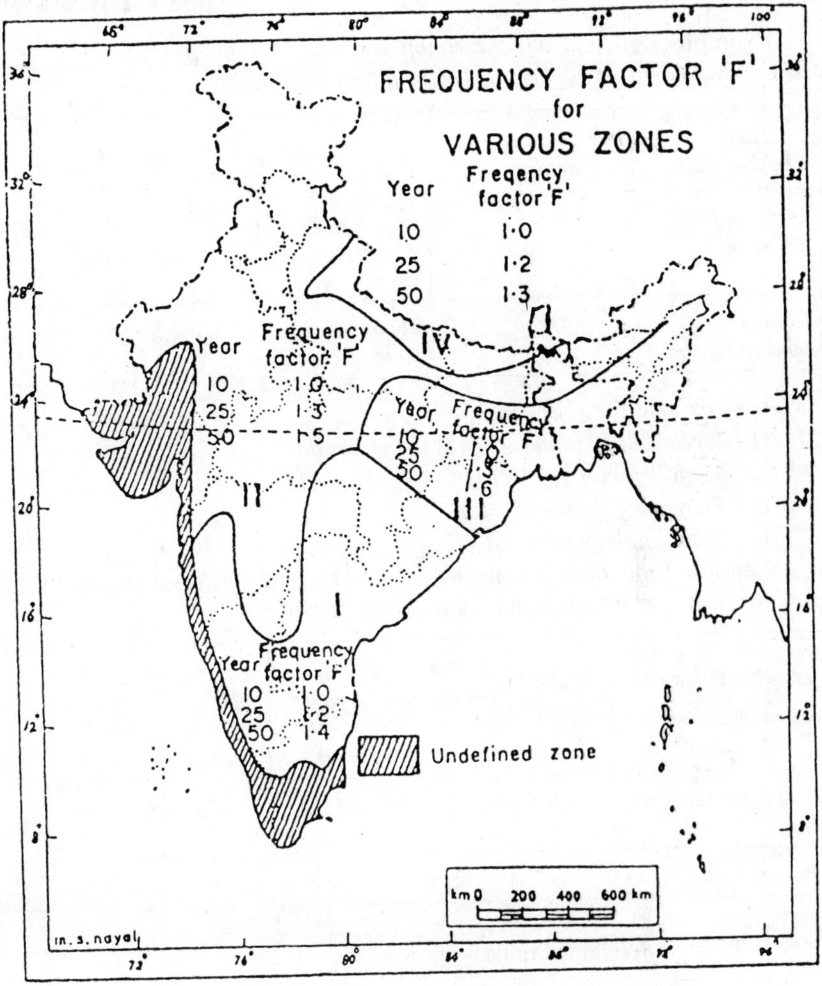

Fig. 5.4. Recurrence interval or frequency factor, F

Table 5.5. Shape factor for use in Cook's method

Length/Width	Area of watershed (ha)				
	20	40	80	200	240
1	1.00	1.00	1.00	1.00	1.00
1 – 1– 1$\frac{1}{2}$	0.92	0.92	0.91	0.90	0.90
2	0.88	0.87	0.86	0.84	0.83
2 – 2 – $\frac{1}{2}$	0.85	0.84	0.82	0.80	0.78
3	0.81	0.80	0.78	0.76	0.74
4	0.76	0.72	0.70	0.68	0.66
5	0.74	0.70	0.68	0.66	0.64
6	0.72	0.68	0.66	0.64	0.62
7	0.68	0.66	0.64	0.61	0.59

Example 5.4. *Find out the runoff rate for 25-years recurrence interval from a watershed of 40 hectares with following details :*

Land use/area (ha)	*Slope (%)*	*Infiltration capacity (cm/h)*	*Vegetal cover*	*Surface storage*
Cultivated 25 ha	*1*	*0.75*	*Less than 10% area is under good grass cover*	*Ponds are less than 2% of drainage ways*
Pasture land 15 ha	*5*	*1.00*	*About 90% area is under grass cover*	*Negligible*

Also, assume the followings

(i) Length and breadth ratio of the watershed = 3

(ii) Rainfall factor (r) = 1.0

(iii) Frequency factor (f) = 1.3

(iv) Shape factor (s) = 0.8.

Solution. From table 5.4, the numerical values for different characteristics of watershed are obtained and summarised as under :

Land Use/area (ha)	*Relief*	*Soil infilatration*	*Vegetal cover*	*Surface storage*	*Total (ΣW) = 2 + 3 + 4 + 5*
1	2	*3*	*4*	*5*	*6*
Cultivated land (25 ha)	2.0	15.0	15.0	10.0	42.0
Pasture land (15 ha)	10.0	3.0	5.0	15.0	33.0

$$\text{Weighted value} = \frac{42 \times 25 + 33 \times 15}{25 + 15}$$

$$= 38.62 \approx 39$$

The uncorrelated peak runoff rate is determined from the Fig. 5.2 against ΣW as 39, which is obtained as 2.05 m^3/s.

$$\therefore \text{ Correlated peak runoff rate} = \text{p.r.f.s}$$

$$= 2.05 \times 1 \times 1.3 \times 0.8$$

$$= \mathbf{2.13\ m^3/s.} \quad \textbf{Ans}$$

5.2.3. Curve Number Method

This method computes the runoff on the basis of relention capacity of the soil, which is predicted by knowing the wetness status (*i.e.* antecedent moisture condition) and physical features of the watershed. CN method computes the direct runoff, stormwise.

Let,

I_a = initial abstraction, such as interception, infiltration and depression storage made in the watershed during rainfall

Q = direct runoff

P = rainfall depth

S = retention capacity of the soil

This method assumes that before runoff generation from the area, the initial losses are satisfied ; and ratio of direct runoff to the rainfall depth minus initial losses (*i.e.* $P - I_a$) is equal to the $\frac{P - Q - I_a}{S}$, *i.e.*

$$\frac{Q}{P - I_a} = \frac{P - Q - I_a}{S} \quad ...(5.25)$$

In this equation, the value of I_a is taken as 0.2 S, thus,

$$\frac{Q}{P - 0.2S} = \frac{P - Q - 0.2S}{S}$$

$$\frac{Q}{P - 0.2S} = \frac{(P - 0.2S)}{S} - \frac{Q}{S}$$

or
$$\frac{Q}{(P - 0.2S)} + \frac{Q}{S} = \frac{(P - 0.2S)}{s}$$

or
$$\frac{Q \cdot S + (P - 0.2S)\, Q}{S\,(P - 0.2S)} = \frac{(P - 0.2S)}{S}$$

or
$$Q \cdot S^2 + Q \cdot S\,(P - 0.2S) = S\,(P - 0.2S)^2$$

or
$$Q \cdot S + Q\,(P - 0.2S) = (P - 0.2S)^2$$

$$Q\,(S + P - 0.2S) = (P - 0.2S)^2$$

$$Q\,(P + 0.8S) = (P - 0.2S)^2$$

$$\therefore \quad Q = \frac{(P - 0.2S)^2}{(P + 0.8S)} \quad ...(5.26)$$

This is the expression of direct runoff, which consists of S as unknown variable. The retention capacity of soil (i.e. S)is determined by using the curve number, developed by U.S. Soil Conservation Service (1972), given as under

$$CN = \frac{2540}{25.4 + S} \quad ...(5.27)$$

in which, CN is the curve number which depends on landuse pattern, treatments, hydrologic condition and hydrologic soil group of watershed. The curve numbers for different land use conditions and hydrologic soil groups are given in table 5.6. This equation computes the value of S in C.G.S. unit.

Computing Steps

Various steps for computing the direct runoff by using curve number method are as follows :

1. Find out the value of curve number for the given land use condition and hydrologic soil group of the watershed from Table 5.6
2. Using equation 5.27, determine the value of retention capacity of the watershed.
3. Collect the rainfall data for the given storm.
4. Substitute the value of retention capacity (S) and rainfall depth (P) in equation 5.26 and solve for runoff.

Table 5.6. Curve number for different hydrologic soil groups and hydrologic conditions

Land use pattern	*Treatment/practice adopted*	*Hydrologic condition*	*Hydrologic soil group*			
			A	*B*	*C*	*D*
Fallow-row crops	Straight row	—	77	86	91	94
		Poor	72	81	88	91
		Good	67	78	85	89
	Contoured + terraced condition	Poor	70	79	84	88
Small grain	Straight row	Poor	65	76	84	88
		Good	63	75	83	87
	Contoured condition	Poor	63	74	82	85
		Good	63	75	83	87
	Contoured + terraced condition	Poor	61	72	79	82
		Good	59	70	78	81
Seeded	Straight row	Poor	66	77	85	89
Legumed		Good	55	69	78	83
Pasture land	Contoured condition	Poor	47	67	81	88
		Fair	25	59	75	83
		Good	6	35	70	79
Farm		Poor	45	66	77	83
Woodland		Fair	36	60	73	79
		Good	25	55	70	77
Hard surface			74	84	90	92
Farm steads			59	74	82	86
Meadow			330	58	71	78

Computed runoff by using equation 5.20 is valid for A.M.C. II condition. For getting the runoff of other AMCs (*i.e.* I or III), a correction factor is multiplied to the estimated runoff. The values of correction factor are given in table 5.7.

Table 5.7. Factors for converting AMC II to AMC I or AMC III

Curve number for AMC II	*Converson factor*	
	AMCI	*AMC III*
10	0.40	2.22
20	0.45	1.85
30	0.50	1.67
40	0.55	1.50
50	0.62	1.40
60	0.67	1.30
70	0.73	1.21
80	0.79	1.14
90	0.87	1.07
100	1.00	1.00

Antecedent Moisture Content (A.M.C.) : It is wetness status of the watershed. There are following three levels of A.M.C.

AMC-I : If refers to the lowest runoff generating potential of the watershed because of dryness of the soil

AMC-II : Average moisture status regarding runoff generating potential.

AMC-III : It refers highest runoff generating potential of the watershed, because of saturation of soil from antecident rains.

Grouping of different A.M.Cs based on antecedent rainfall amounts is shown in table 5.8.

Table 5.8. Classification of AMCs as per antecedent rainfall (inch)

AMC group	*5-day antecedent rainfall (inch)*	
	Dormant season	*Growingseason*
I	less than 0.5	less than 1.4
II	05 to 1.1	1.4 to 2.1
III	more than 1.1	more than 2.1

(Source : SCS 1972)

Hydrologic Soil Group : Based on the hydrologic characteristics, the soils are classified into following four groups :

Soil (A) : It is characterized by low runoff generating potential. This group of soils are mainly constituted by sands or gravel particles. These soils involve high infiltration rate.

Soil (B) : Soils of this group have moderate infiltration rate, even if they are thoroughly wetted. Soils are composed of moderately fine to moderately coarse particles.

Soil (C) : This group of soil contains low infiltration rate. The soil may be composed of a thin hard layer which impedes the downward movement of water. Soils are generally constituted with moderately fine to fine particles.

Soil (D) : This group of soils are characterized by high runoff potential due to very low infiltration rate. Clay soil is the example of this group.

Example 5.5. *Calculate the runoff for 50-years recurrence interval from a watershed for AMC-III, if the total area of watershed is 50 hectare in which 40 hectares land is under row crop on terraced land and remaining 10 hectares land is under poor grass cover. Assume, maximum rainfall depth as 15 cm is occurred during 6-h duration at 50-years recurrence interval and hydrologic soil group is 'C'.*

Solution. The curve number technique is followed for computing the runoff, described as under :

1. Determination of curve number : The curve numbers for different land use practices, followed in the watershed are obtained from table 5.6, for the given hydrologic soil group 'C', which are as

Land use practice	*Curve number*
1. Row crop on terraced land	80
2. Pasture land	86

$$\text{Weighted curve number} = \frac{40 \times 80 + 10 \times 86}{40 + 10} = 81.2$$

As per method's assumption that, the value of curve number (*i.e.* 81.2) obtained so is valid for AMC-II condition. Hence, in order to modify this value for AMC-III, a multiplying factor equal to 1.14 is obtained from table 5.7, and multiplied to the weighted curve number *i.e.*

$$= 8.12 \times 1.14 = 93 \text{ (approx.)}$$

2. Computation of retention capacity (S) of the watershed : Using the equation 5.21, we have

$$CN = \frac{2540}{25.40 + S}$$

$$93 = \frac{2540}{25.40 + S}$$

$$\therefore \quad \mathbf{S = 1.91\ cm}$$

3. Computation of peak runoff rate : It is as under :

$$Q_{peak} = \frac{(P - 0.2S)^2}{P + 0.8S}$$

$$= \frac{(15 - 0.2 \times 1.91)^2}{(15 + 0.8 \times 1.91)}$$

$$= \mathbf{12.93\ cm} \quad \textbf{Ans.}$$

5.2.4. Hydrograph Method

Hydrograph is the graphical presentation of instantaneous runoff rate against time. It is used for computing the runoff from the watershed. The unit hydrograph is mainly used for the purpose. The hydrograph has been described in detail in Chapter 6.

5.2.5. Infiltration Indices Method

Infiltration is defined as the entry of water into the soil. The capacity of any soil to absorb the rain water falling continiously at an excessive rate, goes on decreasing with time until a minimum infiltration rate is attained. The trend of infiltration is shown in Fig. 5.5. When rainfall (*i.e.* intensity) and infiltration rate are plotted on the same axis, then the area between rainfall and infiltration curve is the excess rainfall which is responsible for generating the runoff. While, the area below the infiltration curve, represents the loss of rainfall due to infiltration as shown in Figure 5.5. This loss of water varies greately in the early of the rainfall and subsequently decreases with the advancement of rainfall duration.

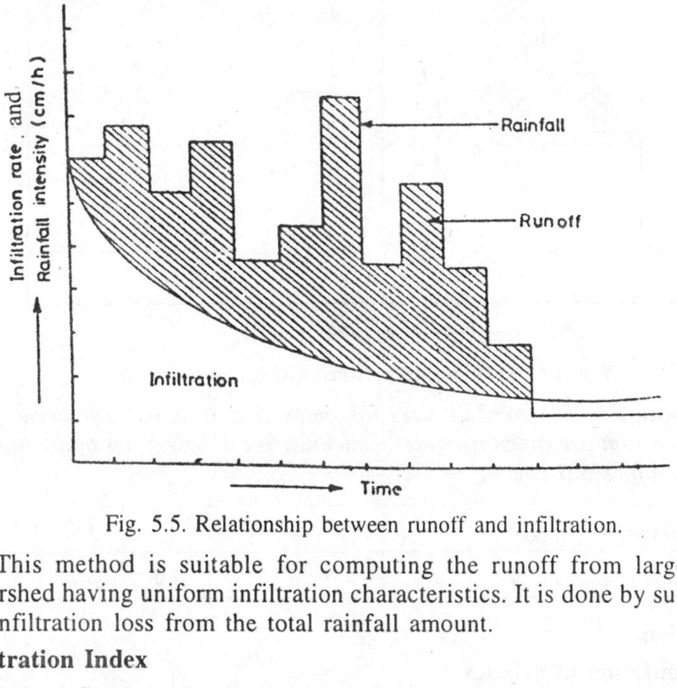

Fig. 5.5. Relationship between runoff and infiltration.

This method is suitable for computing the runoff from large area of watershed having uniform infiltration characteristics. It is done by substracting the infiltration loss from the total rainfall amount.

Infiltration Index

It is defined as the rate of loss of rain water such that the volume of rainfall excess is equal to the direct runoff. Infiltration indices are of following two types :

1. ϕ-index ; and
2. W-index

ϕ-Index

It is the rate of loss of rain water above which the volume of rainfall is equal to the volume of runoff, as shown in Fig. 5.6. ϕ-index is given as :

$$\phi\text{-index} = \frac{\text{Total basin recharge}}{\text{Rainfall discharge}} \quad ...(5.28)$$

This formula is suitable when rainfall intensity is in excess of ϕ-index, continuously. It assumes that, at the beginning of storm a less runoff is generated and more at the end of storm due to the fact that the rate of surface retention and infiltration are decreased with the time. The ϕ-index is also known as retention rate rather than infiltration index. A sample calculation for computing the ϕ-index is shown in example 5.6.

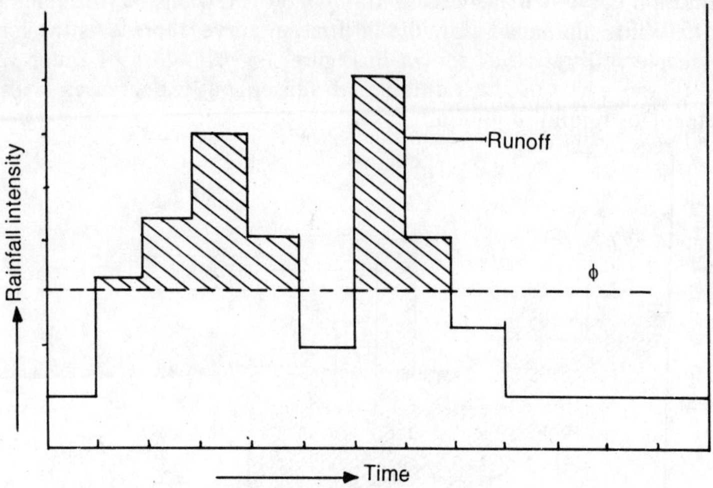

Fig. 5.6. Relationship between ϕ-index and runoff.

Example 5.6. *The rainfall rates for successive 30-minutes interval up to 3-hours duration are given as under. Calculate the ϕ-index, assuming that the surface runoff is 3.6 cm.*

Time (minute)	*0*	*30*	*60*	*90*	*120*	*150*	*180*
Rainfall rate (cm/s)	*0*	*1.6*	*3.6*	*5.0*	*2.8*	*2.2*	*1.0*

Solution.

Computation of ϕ-index

Let, if 'I' is the rainfall intensity, then surface runoff $= (I - \phi)\cdot t$ and total runoff $= \Sigma\,(I - \phi)\,t$

Substituting the value of 'I' and 't', we have,

$$3.6 = \frac{30}{60}\left[(1.6 - \phi) + (3.6 - \phi) + (5 - \phi) + (2.8 - \phi) + (2.2 - \phi) + (1 - \phi)\right]$$

or $$7.2 = [(1.6 + 3.6 + 5 + 2.8 + 2.2 + 1) - 6\,\phi] = [16.2 - 6\,\phi]$$

$$6\,\phi = 9.0$$

∴ $\boldsymbol{\phi = 1.5}$ **cm/h Ans.**

W-index : It is defined as the average water loss during storm, when rainfall intensity exceeds the infiltration capacity (*i.e.* maximum infiltration rate). It is given as

$$W_{index} = \frac{F}{t_r} \quad ...(5.29)$$

$$= \frac{P - Q - S}{t_r} \quad ...(5.30)$$

where, F = total amount of water lost through infiltration

t_r = time, during which rainfall intensity exceeds the infiltration capacity

P = total rainfall amount occurred during t_r

Q = amount of surface runoff and

S = amount of water retained through surface retention.

In the condition, when infiltration rate of the soil becomes equal to the infiltration capacity and surface retention is at minimum level, then values of W and ϕ-indices become same. In this condition, W-index is known as W_{min}-index.

5.2.6. Empirical Formulae

Empirical relationships are normally used for computing the runoff when sufficient hydrologic informations are not available. Such relationships have demerit that, they can not be used for all the places, because they are developed based on the data base of a specified zone and condition.

There have been developed several empirical relationships for different zones of the country, few of them are described as under.

Run off Coefficient Method : The runoff coefficient is the fraction of rainfall converted into runoff. This method estimates the runoff by multiplying the runoff coefficient to the rainfall depth of the area. It is given by

$$R = k \cdot P \quad ...(5.31)$$

where, R = runoff, cm

k = runoff coefficient, and

P = rainfall depth, cm

Values of runoff coefficient for different land use systems are given in table 5.9.

Table 5.9. Values of runoff coefficient (*k*)

S.No.	*Area*	*k*
1.	Urban area covered by,	
	(i) buildings	0.3
	(ii) garden apartments	0.5
2.	Commercial and industrial areas	0.9
3.	Forest areas	0.5 to 0.2

Regression formula : Chow (1964) listed several regression equations for predicting the runoff on the basis of area of drainage basin. The form of equation is given as under :

$$Q = CA^n \quad \text{...(5.32)}$$

where, Q = runoff rate, ((m^3/s)

n, C = constants,

A = drainage area, (km^2)

Dicken formula : It is a regression model for computing the runoff. Originally, it was developed for evaluating the capacity of waterway for design of bridge. The equation is given as

$$Q = CA^{3/4} \quad \text{...(5.33)}$$

This formula holds goods for central and northern parts of India. The value of constant C varies from 2.80 to 5.6 for plain lands and 14 to 28 for mountaneous regions.

Ryve's formula : It is modified form of Dicken's formula, is suitable for computing the runoff for south Indian parts *i.e.* the coastal areas lying within the periphery of 25 km from the sea. Formula is given as under :

$$Q = CA^{2/3} \quad \text{...(5.34)}$$

In this formula, the value of constant 'C' for flat tracts is taken as 6.8, while for western ghat areas, it is about 42.40.

Inglis formula : C.C. Inglis (1940) developed the following empirical formulae for two different areas, given as

1. For ghat areas $R = 0.85\,P - 30.5$ ...(5.35)

2. For non-ghat areas $R = \dfrac{P - 17.8}{254}$ ...(5.36)

In above equations R stands for runoff depth (cm) and P for rainfall depth (cm).

Khosla's formula : This formula was developed by considering the temperature, inaddition to precipitation. It is given as :

$$R = P - \frac{T - 32}{3.74} \quad \text{...(5.37)}$$

in which, R & P are the same as denoted in Inglis formula and T is the average temperature of the area in °F.

Mayer's (1926) formula : It is popular in United States of America for predicting the runoff. This formula has limitation that the area should be more than 10 km^2. Formula is given as under

$$Q = 177.05\,A^{0.50} \quad \text{...(5.38)}$$

Coutagne formula : This formula was developed for the catchments of France. It is given as :

$$Q = 150\, A^{0.5} \qquad \text{... (5.39)}$$

Validity of this formula is for the catchments of the area ranging from 400 to 3000 sq km.

Ali Nawaz Jung Bahadur's formula : It is given as under :

$$Q = C\,(0.3906\, A)\,\frac{0.925 - 1}{14 \log 0.3906\, A} \qquad \text{...(5.40)}$$

Value of C is taken as 49 for south and north Indian catchments.

5.3. Water Year

The time duration from start of rainfall to the end of rainfall during year is called "water year". In India it is from Ist June to 31st May.

5.4. Classification of Streams

Based on the flow duration, the streams are classified into following three categories :

1. Perrineal streams
2. Intermittent streams and
3. Ephemeral streams

5.4.1. Perrineal Streams

Streams, carrying the flow throughout the year are called perrineal streams. The discharge V_s time graph (*i.e.* hydrograph) for such streams is shown in Fig. 5.7. In such streams there is appreciable ground water contribution throughout the year and water-level remains above the stream bed. The streams found in humid zones are normally perrineal.

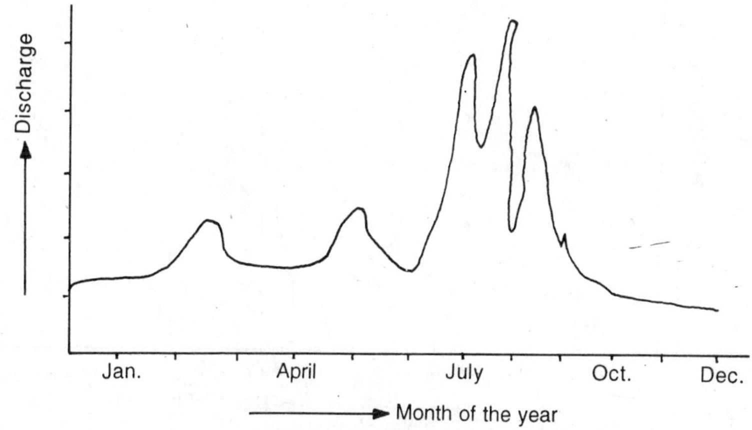

Fig. 5.7. Hydrograph of Perrineal Stream.

5.4.2. Intermittent Streams

These streams have limited contribution of ground water. In rainy seasons, groundwater-table rises above the stream bed, causing base flow to these streams. While in dry season (*i.e.* summer season) the water-table goes down below the stream bed and streams get dry. The annual hydrograph of intermittent streams is illustrated in Fig. 5.8.

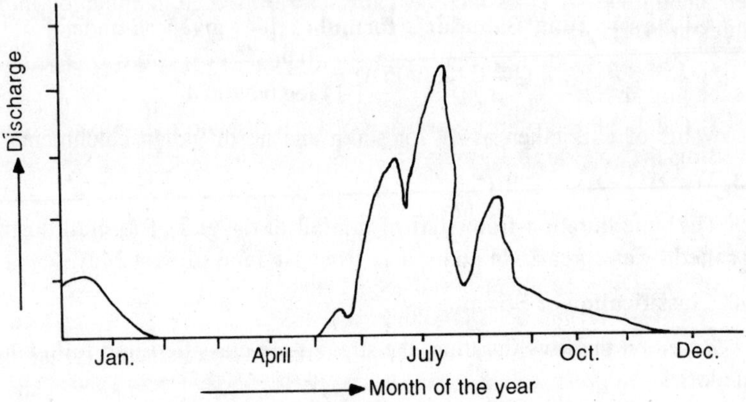

Fig. 5.8. Annual hydrograph of Intermittent stream.

5.4.3. Ephemeral Streams

Ephemeral streams are found in arid zones. These streams carry the flow due to rainwater, only. In other words, if there happens rainfall in the watershed, then water comes into the stream and flow takes place which is continued as long as the rain is in occurrence. Streams become dry soon after end of the rainfall. This types of stream do not have base flow contribution. Annual hydrograph of ephemeral stream is shown in Fig. 5.9.

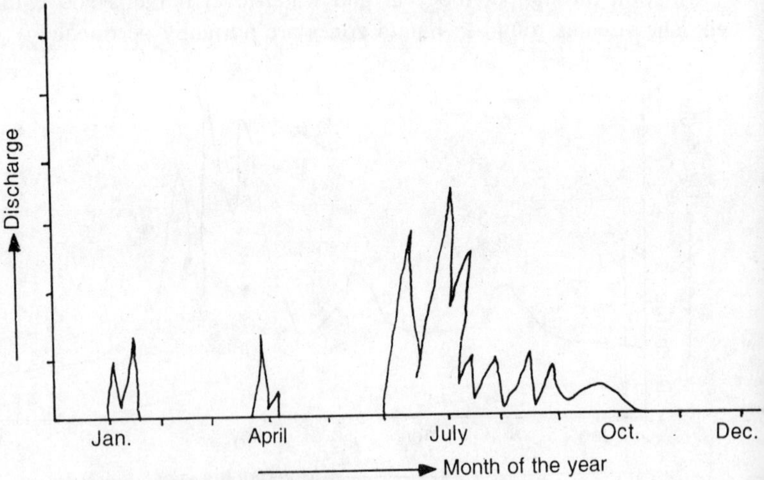

Fig. 5.9. Hydrograph of ephemeral stream.

5.5. Flow-Duration Curve

To characterize the variability of stream flow during the water year, the derivation of flow duration curve is required.

It is derived by plotting the discharge against plotting position. Derivation procedure is explained as under :

1. Arrange the stream flow data (*i.e.* discharge) in descending order of their magnitude. A class-interval can also be used, if number of individual values are large.

2. Assign rank number to each discharge data after arranging in descending order.

3. Calculate the plotting position of each discharge data or class interval by using the following formula

$$p(\%) = \frac{m}{n+1} \times 100 \qquad ...(5.41)$$

where, p = plotting position
m = rank number of the discharge event
n = total number of discharge events

4. Plot the plotting positions (p) and their corresponding discharge; and draw curve by joining the plotted points. Obtained curve is the flow-duration curve. Using this curve, the expected runoff for any desired probability level can be predicted. The flow-duration curve can be derived for daily, weekly, monthly or annual discharge series.

The flow-duration curve, which is the cumulative frequency distribution curve can also be used for representing the variations in stream flow during an average year. The predicted discharge for a desired probability level is called dependent flow. Generally, the Q_{100} *i.e.* 100% dependent flow is considered as the finite value for perrineal streams, while for intermittent and ephemeral streams, the dependent flow is zero for a finite part of the water year. The flow-duration curves of perrineal, intermittent and ephemeral streams are shown in Fig. 5.10.

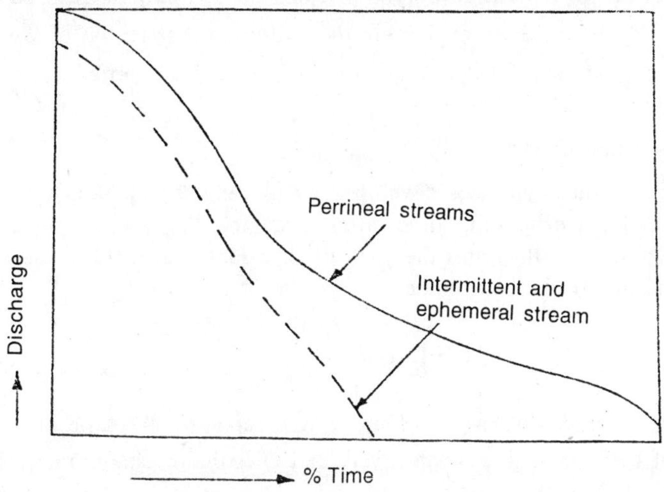

Fig. 5.10. Flow-duration curves of perrineal, intermittent and ephemeral streams.

Characteristics of Flow-duration Curve

A flow-duration curve includes following characteristics of interest :

Curve characteristics : It is divided into following four parts.

1. **Steep slope :** It indicates the highly variable flow.

2. **Flat slope :** This segment shows that there is little variation in the stream flow.

3. **Flat portion at top of the curve :** This revealed that, the stream has large flood plain and there is no rainfall during winter season.

4. **Flat portion at lower end of the curve :** Indicates about considerable base flow.

In addition to the above characteristics, the flow-duration curve also includes following other features

1. Slope of curve depends on the interval selected for arranging the data. A flow duration curve derived from daily flow data has steep slope, while there is flat slope incase of flow duration curve derived from monthly flow data, because of smooth small peaks.

2. The virigin-flow duration curve gets change due to presence of reservoirs and nature of the flow regulation method, used.

3. A flow-duration curve, when prepared by plotting the discharge against percent probability on the log probability paper, follows a flat trend at the central part of the curve.

Utility of Flow-Duration Curve : It has following uses :

1. For planning of water-resources project.

2. It is helpful in design of drainage systems.

3. Useful for deciding the type of flood control structures to be used.

4. It can be used for evaluating the hydropower potential of the river.

5. It is also used for determining the sediment load carried by the stream flow.

5.6. Flow-Mass Curve

The flow-mass curve is developed by plotting the cumulative discharge volume and corresponding time, after arranging the data in chronological order. Figure 5.11 illustrates the view of flow-mass curve. Ordinate of curve represents the discharge volume at any time. It is given by :

$$V = \int_{t_0}^{t_1} Q \cdot dt \qquad ...(5.42)$$

in which, V is the discharge volume, t_0 & t_1 represent the time of beginning & end of the mass-curve, respectively and Q is the discharge rate. The flow

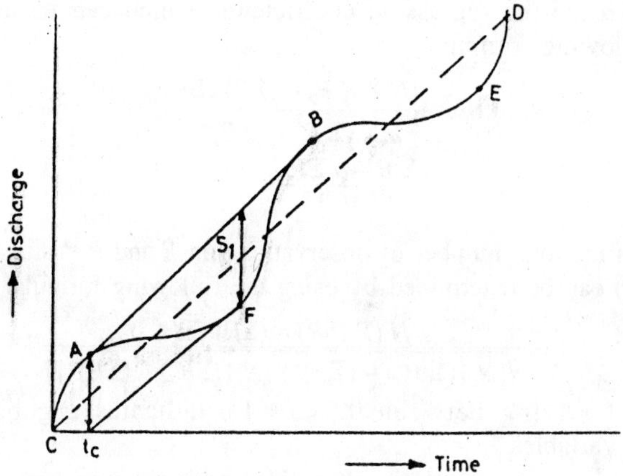

Fig. 5.11. Flow-mass curve.

mass curve is an integral or summation curve of the hydrogrpah. Some times, it is also known as Rippl mass-curve, after the name of Rippl (1982), who firstly suggested its use.

Slope of flow-mass curve represents the discharge rate $\left(i.e. \dfrac{dv}{dt} = Q\right)$. Knowning the discharge at starting and end points of the curve and joining them by a straight line, the average discharge for entire period of flow-mass curve can be predicted.

5.7. Rainfall-Runoff Correlation

Runoff is affected by several factors related to the watershed and atmospheric characteristics. Behaviour of these factors on runoff is very complex, causing the relationship between rainfall and runoff is uncertain. The development of relationship between rainfall and runoff is important to overcome the problem of paucity of data. There are two types of relationships *i.e.* linear and non-linear. The linear relationship between rainfall and runoff is found for small watersheds, while non-linear relationships for large watersheds. The non-linear relationships may be in power, logarithmic or exponential form.

Relationship is developed by plotting the rainfall (P) and corresponding runoff (R) data and drawing a best fit curve. However, it gives an approximation. More authentic method is drawing the best fit "linear regression line" between runoff and rainfall, which gives accurate estimate when correlation coefficient between them is 1. The form of linear regression equation between R and P is given as,

$$R = aP + b \qquad \text{... (5.43)}$$

where, a and b are the regression coefficients, which can be determined by using the following formula :

$$a = \frac{(N \Sigma R{\cdot}P) - (\Sigma R)(\Sigma P)}{N (\Sigma P^2 - (\Sigma P)^2}$$

$$b = \frac{\Sigma R - a \Sigma P}{N} \qquad ...(5.44)$$

in which N is the total number of observations on R and P. Value of correlation coefficient (r) can be determined by using the following formula :

$$r = \frac{N (\Sigma P{\cdot}R) - (\Sigma R)(\Sigma P)}{\sqrt{[N \{(\Sigma P^2) - (\Sigma P)^2\} [N \{(\Sigma R^2) - (\Sigma R)^2\}]}} \qquad ...(5.45)$$

Value of r lying between $0.6 < r < 1.0$ indicates a good correlation between the variables.

The linear regression relationship did not give the accurate prediction of runoff for given rainfall from large watersheds, but exponential relationship is found more accurate. The from of exponential relationship between rainfall and runoff is given as

$$R = CP^m \qquad ...(5.46)$$

in which, C and m are constant, which can be determined in the same way as a and b for linear regression line.

A non-linear equation (*i.e.* eq 5.46) can be linearise by taking the log *i.e.*

$$\log R = \log C + m \log P \qquad ...(5.47)$$

This is in the form of linear equation.

Annual Yield of Stream

Total volume of water likely to be generated from the given stream during a year is called 'annual yield' of the stream. It is calculated on yearly basis. It is used to determine the mean annual runoff volume of the stream. The yield of watershed reflects the richness of water resource potential of the area. For assessment of water resource potential, the estimation of annual yield is essentially required. The followings are the methods, which are commonly used for computation :

1. Rainfall-runoff correlation method
2. Empirical formulae and
3. Simulation techniques.

5.8. Hydrologic Water-Budget

It is also termed as watershed simulation method. Under this method, runoff is computed for a specified time period. The hydrologic water-budget equation can be as under

$$R = R_s + G_o \qquad ... (5.48)$$

where, R = total runoff flow or stream flow

R_s = surface runoff

G_o = net ground water flow

This equation can also be written in following form

$$R = P - ET - S \quad \text{... (5.49)}$$

where, P = precipitation amount

ET = evapotranspiration

S = change in soil moisture storage.

In equation 5.49 by substituting the values of ET, P and S, the runoff can be estimated. This method provides erroneous estimate, if involved parameters are not determined, accurately.

SOLVED PROBLEMS

Problem 5.1. Axial length and average width of a watershed are 1.521 and 0.753 km, respectively. Determine form factor of the watershed.

Solution. Using the formula

$$\text{Form factor} = \frac{\text{Average width}}{\text{Axial length}} = \frac{0.753}{1.521} = \mathbf{0.495} \quad \textbf{Ans.}$$

Problem 5.2. Compute compactness factor of the watershed, if

(*a*) diameter of watershed (circular shape) is 1.10 km

(*b*) circumference of the circle whose area is equal to the area of watershed is 6.250 km.

Solution. Using the formula

Compactness factor

$$= \frac{\text{Perimeter of watershed}}{\text{Circumference of circle whose area is equal to the watershed}}$$

$$= \frac{2\pi \times 0.55}{6.250} = \mathbf{0.5529} \quad \textbf{Ans.}$$

Problem 5.3. Total length of stream network of a watershed is 6.350 km. Calculate its drainage density, if the area of watershed is 7.5 sq. km.

Solution. Using the formula

$$D_d = \frac{\text{Total length of stream network}}{\text{Total area of the watershed}}$$

$$= \frac{6.350}{7.50} = \mathbf{0.8467\ km^{-1}} \quad \textbf{Ans.}$$

Problem 5.4. Determine the values of drainage density of different sub watersheds. The requisite database are as follows :

Sub watershed	*A*	*B*	*C*	*D*	*E*
Total channel length (km)	1.5	0.85	1.125	0.35	0.75
Sub area (km^2)	5.0	1.75	3.70	0.90	1.35

Also determine the drainage density of entire watershed.

Solution. Using the formula

$$D_d = \frac{\text{Total length of stream network}}{\text{Total area of the watershed}}$$

$$D_d \text{ of sub-watershed } A = \frac{1.5}{5.0} = \mathbf{0.3\ km^{-1}} \quad \textbf{Ans.}$$

$$D_d \text{ of sub-watershed } B = \frac{0.85}{1.75} = \mathbf{0.4857\ km^{-1}} \quad \textbf{Ans.}$$

$$D_d \text{ of sub-watershed } C = \frac{1.125}{3.70} = \mathbf{0.304\ km^{-1}} \quad \textbf{Ans.}$$

$$D_d \text{ of sub-watershed } D = \frac{0.35}{0.90} = \mathbf{0.3889\ km^{-1}} \quad \textbf{Ans.}$$

$$D_d \text{ of sub-watershed } E = \frac{0.75}{1.35} = \mathbf{0.556\ km^{-1}} \quad \textbf{Ans.}$$

Drainage density of entire watershed

$$= \frac{1.5 + 0.85 + 1.125 + 0.35 + 0.75}{5.0 + 1.75 + 3.70 + 0.90 + 1.35} = \frac{4.575}{12.7} = \mathbf{0.3602\ km^{-1}} \quad \textbf{Ans.}$$

Problem 5.5. Determine the runoff coefficient of the watershed, if total annual rainfall and runoff of the watershed are 1050 and 670 mm, respectively.

Solution. Using the formula

$$\text{Runoff coefficient} = \frac{\text{Runoff}}{\text{Total rainfall}} = \frac{670}{1050} = \mathbf{0.6381} \quad \textbf{Ans.}$$

Problem 5.6. Compute the runoff coefficient of watershed using the following data on rainfall and their corresponding runoff values

Rainfall (cm)	5.25	0.387	1.75	2.30	4.30	5.00
Runoff (cm)	3.15	0.105	0.70	1.25	2.77	3.05

Solution. $\text{Runoff coefficient} = \frac{11.025\text{ cm}}{18.987\text{ cm}} = \mathbf{0.5806}$ **Ans.**

Problem 5.7. Determine the runoff coefficient of the watershed, if

(*a*) area of hyetograph = 15 cm

(*b*) area of effective hyetograph = 0.75 cm

Solution. Using the formula,

$$C = \frac{\text{Total runoff depth}}{\text{Total rainfall depth}}$$

In this case, area of ERH represents the total effective rainfall depth or direct runoff depth and area of hyetograph to the total rainfall depth, therefore

$$C = \frac{0.75}{15.00} = \mathbf{0.05} \quad \textbf{Ans.}$$

Problem 5.8. Determine the runoff coefficient of the watershed based on following database :

Sub watershed	*A*	*B*	*C*	*D*	*E*
Runoff coefficient	0.35	0.70	0.57	0.75	0.60
Area (*ha*)	50	75	12.5	21.70	1.5

Solution. Since this problem shows heterogeneity in the watershed features/characteristics, therefore, weighted runoff coefficient of the watershed is required to determine. The weighted runoff coefficient is given by

$$C_w = \frac{C_1a_1 + C_2a_2 + C_3a_3 + C_4a_4 + ...}{a_1 + a_2 + a_3 + a_4 + ...}$$

$$= \frac{(0.35 \times 50) + (0.7 \times 75) + (0.57 \times 12.5) + (0.75 \times 21.5) + (0.6 \times 1.5)}{50 + 75 + 12.5 + 21.70 + 1.5}$$

$$= \frac{17.5 + 52.5 + 7.125 + 16.275 + 0.9}{160.7} = \frac{94.3}{160.7} = \mathbf{0.5868} \text{ Ans.}$$

Problem 5.9. Calculate retention capacity of the watershed, if initial loss is 5.0 mm.

Solution. Using the formula

$$I_a = 0.2\,S$$

$$5 = 0.2\,S$$

$$\therefore \quad S = \frac{5}{0.2} \text{ mm} = \mathbf{25\ mm} \text{ Ans.}$$

Problem 5.10. Calculate initial loss of the watershed, if its retention capacity is 15 mm.

Solution. Using the formula

$$I_a = 0.2\,S = 0.2 \times 15 \text{ mm}$$

$$= \mathbf{3\ mm} \text{ Ans.}$$

Problem 5.11. Determine the initial loss and retention capacity of the watershed, if curve number of watershed is 75.

Solution. Using the formula

$$CN = \frac{2540}{25.4 + S}$$

$$75 = \frac{2540}{25.4 + S}$$

$$75\,(25.4 + S) = 2540$$

or

$$S = \frac{2540}{75} - 25.4 = \mathbf{8.47\ cm} \text{ Ans.}$$

and,

$$I_a = 0.2\,S = 0.2 \times 8.47 = \mathbf{1.694\ cm} \text{ Ans.}$$

Problem 5.12. Calculate the rainfall intensity for the duration of time of concentration to compute the peak runoff rate for 25 years return period, if

(*a*) Maximum length of drainage course from watershed divide to the outlet is 1.570 km

(*b*) Weighted slope of drainage course is 0.4%

(*c*) Values of coefficient i.e. $K = 4.68$, $a = 0.189$, $b = 0.50$ and $d = 0.75$

Solution. Time of concentration (T_c)

$$= 0.01947\, L^{0.77} \cdot S^{-.385}$$
$$= 0.01947 \times (1570)^{.77} \times (.4)^{-.385}$$
$$= 8.01 \text{ minutes} = \mathbf{0.133\ h}$$

Therefore, rainfall intensity for the duration of time of concentration and 25-years return period,

$$i_{tc,\,p} = \frac{KT^a}{(t_c + b)^d} = \frac{4.68 \times (25)^{0.189}}{(0.133 + 0.5)^{0.75}} \text{ cm/h}$$
$$= \frac{8.5992}{0.70966} = \mathbf{12.12\ cm/h} \quad \textbf{Ans.}$$

Problem 5.13. Compute the curve number and initial loss of the watershed, if its retention capacity is 7.0 cm.

Solution. Using the formula

$$CN = \frac{2540}{25.4 + S} = \frac{2540}{25.4 + 7.0}$$
$$= 78.39 \approx \mathbf{78} \quad \textbf{Ans.}$$

and Initial loss $(I_a) = 0.2\, S = 0.2 \times 7 = \mathbf{1.4\ cm}$ **Ans.**

Problem 5.14. Determine the retention capacity (mm) of watershed, if CN is 80 for AMC-I condition.

Solution. Taking average condition *i.e.* AMC-II

Modified CN for AMC-II is $80 \times 0.79 = 63.2$

Using the formula, $CN = \dfrac{25400}{254 + S}$

$$63.2 = \frac{25400}{254 + S}$$
$$S = \frac{25400}{63.2} - 254 = \mathbf{147.9\ mm} \quad \textbf{Ans.}$$

Problem 5.15. What is the retention capacity (S) of paved surface of the watershed.

Solution. Using the formula

$$CN = \frac{2540}{25.4 + S}$$

For paved surface, CN = 0, therefore

$$0 = \frac{2540}{25.4 + S}$$
$$S = \mathbf{0} \quad \textbf{Ans.}$$

Problem 5.16. Calculate retention capacity of the soil with zero runoff generating potential.

Solution. Using the formula $CN = \frac{2540}{25.4 + S}$

For such soils the CN is taken as 100, therefore

$$100 = \frac{2540}{25.4 + S}$$

or

$$S = \frac{2540}{100} - 25.4 = \mathbf{0} \quad \textbf{Ans.}$$

Problem 5.17. Calculate the retention capacity of paved surface for AMC-I and III conditions

Solution. Using the formula

$$CN = \frac{2540}{25.4 + S}$$

For AMC-II, the CN for paved surface is 100, which is modified for AMC-I and III by multiplying correction factors, i.e.

CN for AMC-I $= 100 \times 1 = 100$

CN for AMC-III $= 100 \times 1 = 100$

Therefore,

$$\left.\begin{aligned} S \text{ for AMC-I} &= 0 \\ \text{and} \quad S \text{ for AMC-III} &= 0 \end{aligned}\right\} \textbf{Ans.}$$

Problem 5.18. Compute the peak runoff rate (m^3/s) of the watershed, if

(*a*) Area of watershed is 500 ha

(*b*) Runoff depth is 5.0 cm

(*c*) Time of concentration is 0.75 h

Solution. Using the formula for peak runoff rate,

$$Q_p = \frac{0.0208\, A \cdot Q}{T_p}$$

in which Q_p is in m^3/s, A is in *ha*, Q is in depth (cm) and T_p in hour. The time to peak (T_p) can be computed by using the following formula

$$T_p = 0.6\, T_c + \sqrt{T_c}$$

$$= 0.6 \times 0.75 + \sqrt{0.75} = \mathbf{1.32\ hour}$$

Substituting the values of A, Q, and T_p, we have

$$Q_p = \frac{0.0208 \times 500 \times 5}{1.32}\ m^3/s$$

$$= \mathbf{39.4\ m^3/s} \quad \textbf{Ans.}$$

Problem 5.19. Determine the peak runoff likely to be generated from the watershed, if

(*a*) CN of watershed is 70

(*b*) Rainfall depth due to given storm is 10 cm

(*c*) Area of watershed is 250 ha

(*d*) Maximum length and average slope of water course is 1500 m and 0.4, respectively.

Solution. Using the formula

$$Q_p = \frac{0.0208\, A \cdot Q}{T_p} \text{ m}^3/\text{s}$$

Q (runoff depth) from SCS method, we have

$$CN = \frac{2540}{25.4 + S}$$

$$70 = \frac{2540}{25.4 + S}$$

$$S = \frac{2540}{70} - 25.4 = \mathbf{10.89\ cm}$$

$$\therefore \quad Q = \frac{(P - 0.25)^2}{(P + 0.85)}$$

$$= \frac{(10 - 0.2 \times 10.89)^2}{10 + 0.8 \times 10.89} \text{ cm} = \mathbf{3.27\ cm}$$

$$\text{Time of concentration } (T_c) = 0.01947\, L^{0.77} \cdot S^{-.385}$$

$$= 0.01947\, (1500)^{.77} \times (.4)^{-.385} = 7.73 \text{ minutes}$$

or $$T_c = 0.13 \text{ h}$$

$$\therefore \text{ Time to peak } (T_p) = 0.6\, T_c + \sqrt{T_c}$$

$$= 0.6 \times 0.13 + \sqrt{0.13} = \mathbf{0.44\ hour}$$

Substituting the values of T_p, A and Q in the equation, we have

$$Q_p = \frac{0.0208 \times 250 \times 3.27}{0.44} \text{ m}^3/\text{s}$$

$$Q_p = \mathbf{38.65\ m^3/s} \quad \textbf{Ans.}$$

Problem 5.20. Determine the time of concentration of watershed, if

(*a*) Longest length of watercourse is 1500 m

(*b*) CN of watershed is 75

(*c*) Average slope of watershed is 0.4 m/m

Solution. The formula for computation of T_c under SCS method is given by Schwab et. al. (1993), as,

$$T_c = \frac{L^{0.8}\left[\left(\frac{1000}{CN}\right) - 9\right]^{0.7}}{4407\, (S_g)^{0.5}} \text{ hour}$$

in which L is the longest length of water course (m) and S_g is the average slope of watershed. Substituting these values in the equation, we have

$$= \frac{(1500)^{0.8}\left[\left(\frac{1000}{70}\right)-9\right]^{0.7}}{4407\,(.4)^{0.5}} \text{ hour}$$

$$= \mathbf{0.40\ hour\quad Ans.}$$

Problem 5.21. Calculate the time of concentration of watershed, if maximum length of water course is 1700 m and elevation difference between remotest point and the outlet is 5 m.

Solution. Using the formula for T_c,

$$T_c = 0.01947\,(K)^{0.77}$$

in which $K = \sqrt{\frac{L^3}{H}}$

where, L is the longest length of watercourse (m) and H is the elevation difference between remotest point and the outlet (m), thus

$$K = \sqrt{\frac{(1700)^3}{5}} = 31346.45$$

$$\therefore \quad T_c = 0.01947\,(31346.45)^{0.77} = \mathbf{56.42\ minutes\quad Ans.}$$

Problem 5.22. Using Dicken's formula, calculate peak discharge of the watershed, if area of watershed is 150 sq km. Assume Dicken's coefficient as 15.

Solution. Using the Dicken's formula

$$Q_p = C_d \cdot A^{0.75}$$

$$= 15 \times (150)^{0.75}\ \text{m}^3/\text{s}$$

$$= \mathbf{642.92\ m^3/s\quad Ans.}$$

Problem 5.23. Determine ϕ-index, if a storm of 12 cm generated 7.0 cm runoff. Assume the duration of excess rainfall as 8h.

Solution. Given that,

Total rainfall = 12 cm
Runoff = 7 cm
Duration of excess rainfall = 8h
$\therefore$ Infiltration loss = 12 − 7 = 5 cm

$$\therefore \quad \phi \text{ index} = \frac{5}{8} = \mathbf{0.625\ cm/h\quad Ans.}$$

Problem 5.24. Calculate ϕ-index, if a given storm of 15.0 cm resulted 6.0 cm runoff. The distribution of rainfall during storm is given below :

Time of start (h)	*1*	*2*	*3*	*4*	*5*	*6*	*7*	*8*
Incremental rainfall in each hour	0.5	1.2	2.0	3.0	1.5	1.0	2.5	3.3

Solution. Given that

Total rainfall depth = 15 cm

Runoff depth = 6.0 cm

$\therefore$ Infiltration depth = 15 – 6 = **9.0 cm**

Taking the storm duration as 8 hours (as given in Table)

$$\therefore \quad \phi\text{-index} = \frac{9}{8} = \mathbf{1.125\ cm/h}$$

The computed value of ϕ-index *i.e.* 1.125 cm/h makes the first and sixth hour's rainfall *i.e.* 0.5 and 1.0 cm ineffective, because these values are less than the determined ϕ-index. Therefore, taking the effective duration of storm equal to 6 h (*i.e.* 8 – 2) for second trial.

$$\phi\text{-index} = \frac{(15 - 0.5 - 1.0 - 6.0)}{6} = \frac{7.5}{6} = \mathbf{1.25\ cm/h}$$

This value of ϕ-index makes the second hour rainfall to be ineffective. Thus,

$$\phi\text{-index} = \frac{(15 - 0.5 - 1.0 - 6.0 - 1.2)}{5} = \frac{6.3}{5} = \mathbf{1.26\ cm/h}$$

Check : It should be made to verify the amount of direct runoff, which is done by subtracting the ϕ- index (cm) from respective incremental rainfall depth. It is given in following table.

Time from start (h)	*1*	*2*	*3*	*4*	*5*	*6*	*7*	*8*
Rainfall excess (cm)	0.00	0.00	0.74	1.74	0.24	0.00	1.24	2.04

Total rainfall excess = 0.74 + 1.74 + 0.24 + 124 + 2.04 cm

= **6.0 cm = Total runoff depth**

The computed value of ϕ-index *i.e.* 1.26 cm/h is thus correct.

Problem 5.25. Calculate the value of W-index, if

(*a*) Storm precipitation is 15 cm

(*b*) Total runoff is 7.5 cm

(*c*) Effective duration of rainfall excess is 6h

(*d*) Initial loss is 1.125 cm

Solution. Using the formula

$$W\text{index} = \frac{P - R - I_a}{t_e}$$

$$= \frac{15 - 7.5 - 1.125}{6} \text{ cm/h} = \mathbf{1.0625\ cm/h} \quad \textbf{Ans.}$$

Problem 5.26. Determine the duration of effective rainfall of the following rainfall measurements, if ϕ-index is 1.125 cm/h. Also, calculate the depth of direct runoff.

Time from start (h)	*1*	2	3	4	5	6	7	8	9
Incremental rainfall (cm)	0.5	0.75	1.0	1.127	2.5	3.0	1.5	1.55	2.0

Solution.

1. From the table value of incremental rainfall depth, it is observed that the rainfall depths of 1st, 2nd and 3rd hours are ineffective to generate the rainfall excess. Thus, the duration of effective rainfall is $9 - 3 = \mathbf{6h}$ **Ans.**
2. Direct runoff depth

$$= [(1.127 - 1.125) + (2.5 - 1.125) + (3 - 1.125) + (1.5 - 1.125) + (1.55 - 1.125) + (2 - 1.125)]$$

$$= (0.002 + 1.375 + 1.875 + 0.375 + 0.425 + 0.875) \text{ cm}$$

$$= \mathbf{4.927\ cm} \quad \textbf{Ans.}$$

Problem 5.27. Determine total loss of rain water due to infiltration from the watershed, if ϕ index is 1.5 cm/h and duration of storm to cause effective rainfall is 8h.

Solution. Using the formula,

$$\phi\text{-index} = \frac{\text{Total infiltration depth}}{\text{Effective duration of rainfall excess}}$$

or $$\text{Total infiltration depth (cm)} = \phi\text{-index} \times \text{duration of ER}$$

$$= 1.5 \times 8 = \mathbf{12\ cm} \quad \textbf{Ans.}$$

Problem 5.28. Calculate the duration of effective rainfall, if ϕ-index is 1.3 cm/h and total depth of water lost during storm is 7.5 cm.

Solution. Using the formula, i.e.

$$\phi\text{-index} = \frac{\text{Total infiltration depth}}{\text{Effective duration of ER}}$$

or $$\text{Effective duration of ER} = \frac{\text{Total infiltration depth}}{\phi\text{-index}}$$

$$= \frac{7.5}{1.3} \text{ h} = \mathbf{1.153\ h} \quad \textbf{Ans.}$$

Important Points

1. Runoff is the output of watershed due to rainfall.
2. Movement of excess rain water over the ground surface to reach the smaller channels is called overland flow.
3. The overland flow is generally under laminar flow regime.
4. The rain water flow at the outlet of watershed is runoff.
5. The interflow, through flow, storm seepage, subsurface storm flow or quick return flow are the synonymous terms.
6. Interflow is of two types, i.e. (1) prompt interflow (2) delayed interflow.
7. Interflow with least time lag between infiltration and outflow is called prompt interflow.
8. Interflow with longer time lag between infiltration and outflow is called delayed interflow.
9. The ground water flow facilitates the dry-weather flow in perennial rivers.
10. The ground water flow is also called ground water runoff.
11. The time lag of ground water runoff is being in the order of months or years.
12. The runoff generated immediately after precipitation is called direct runoff.
13. Direct runoff includes the surface runoff, prompt interflow and channel precipitation.
14. The direct storm runoff and storm runoff are the direct runoff.
15. The delayed flow that reaches the stream as ground water flow is called base flow.
16. Some times delayed interflow is included under base flow.
17. A true runoff is the stream flow in the natural condition.
18. The stream flow which is unaffected by man made storage structures and diversons in the stream is called virgin flow.
19. The stream flow/runoff affected by storage structures or diversons is not the true runoff.
20. The true runoff is the virgin flow.
21. In India, the Ist June is considered as the begining of water year.
22. In a water year, the water budget contains a least amount of carry over.
23. In a water year the cycle of climate is likely to complete.
24. A perennial river always carries flow.
25. In intermittent stream, the ground water flow is only during wet season.
26. An ephemeral stream does not carry the base flow.
27. In arid zones, the streams are normally ephemeral type.
28. Annual runoff volume of the river is called yield of river.
29. The antecedent rainfall affects the initial loss and thus the infiltration rate at the begining of storm.
30. Antecedent precipitation index is used to calculate the annual runoff from the annual rainfall series.

31. Empirical relationships are applicable only to that regions for which they are developed.
32. The Binnie's percentage tables were developed for small catechments of Nagpur regions.
33. Binnie's percentages are used to compute runoff from the watershed.
34. Barlow's tables were developed by the first chief Engineer of the Hydro-Electric Surrey of India in the year 1915.
35. Barlow's tables are used for computation of runoff from the watershed.
36. The Stranger's tables are used to determine the runoff of the watersheds of Maharashtra and Karnatka States.
37. Inglis and Do Souza formula computes the runoff for ghat regions of western India and Decan plateau.
38. The Khosla formula of runoff prediction is based on the water-balance approach and mean monthly temperature of the watershed.
39. The Stanford Watershed Model (SWM) is the watershed simulation model.
40. A flow-duration curve determines the stream flow variability during the water-year.
41. A flow-duration curve is the plot of discharge Vs plotting position of the flow data.
42. A flow-duration curve is also known as discharge-frequency curve.
43. A flow-mass curve is the plot of cumulative discharge volume and time in chronological order.
44. Flow-mass curve is the integral or summation curve of the hydrograph.
45. The flow-mass curve is also known as Rippl's curve. Rippl suggested its use, firstly in the year 1882.
46. Slope of flow-mass curve at any point is the rate of flow.
47. Rational method computes the peak runoff rate from the smaller watersheds.
48. Runoff coefficient is the ratio of runoff to rainfall. It ranges from 0 to 1.
49. In Rational method, the rain fall intensity should be for the duration of time of concentration of the watershed.
50. The runoff coefficient represents the integral effect of watershed on runoff.
51. The Rational formula computes the peak runoff rate accurately for the small watersheds ranging upto 50 sq km area.
52. The word "rational" of Rational formula signifies the consideration of time of concentration and runoff coefficient in a subjective manner.
53. Time of concentration is the function of watershed features *i.e.* length of longest channel and its weighted slope.
54. The curve number method is also known as S.C.S. method.
55. S.C.S. method computes the direct runoff, storm-wise.
56. In S.C.S. method, the intial abstraction (I_a) is taken as 0.2 S, in which S is the retention capacity of the soil.
57. In S.C.S. method, the value of I_a for Indian watersheds is taken as 0.3 S.

58. The retention capacity (*S*) in S.C.S. method of runoff computation is the function of curve number (CN).

59. The curve number (CN) depends on the landuse pattern, treatments, hydrologic condition of the soil and hydrologic soil group.

60. The value of curve number (CN) is maximum for hydrologic soil group D.

61. The value of curve number (CN) is lowest for the hydrologic soil group A.

62. SCS method estimates the runoff, directly for AMC-II.

63. AMC-II indicates the average wetness of watershed.

64. Hydrologic-soil group-A involves low runoff potential because of greater infiltration loss.

65. Hydrologic-soil group-B involves high runoff potential because of very less infiltration loss.

References

1. Betson R.P. "What is watershed runoff", J. Geophysics Res, Vol. 69 (8), 1964.

2. Chow V.T. Handbook of Applied Hydrology, McGraw-Hill, New York, 1964.

3. Cook H.L., The infiltration approach to the calculation of surface runoff, Trans. Arn. Geophys Union, 25, 1946.

4. Garg S.K. Hydrology and Water Resources Engineering, Khanna Publishers Distributors, Delhi, 1985.

5. Greg D.M. Principles of Hydrology, Water Information centre, New York, 1971.

6. Haan C.T., Jhonson H.P. and Brakensiek D.L., Hydrologic modelling of small watershed, ASAE Monograph No-5, 1982.

7. Inglis C.C., Technical paper No-30, PWD. Bombay, 1940.

8. Kirpich P.Z., Time of concentration of small Agril. Watersheds, Civil Engineering, New York, 1940.

9. Linsley R.K., Kohler M.A. and Paulhus J.L.H., Applied Hydrology, Tata McGraw-Hill, New Delhi, 1979.

10. Linsley, R.K., Kohler M.A. and Paulhus J.L.H. Hydrology for Engineers. McGraw Hill Book Co. Singapore, 1988.

11. Mayer L.D., Transaction ASCE, Vol., 89, 985, 1926.

12. Raghunath M.M. Hydrology, Wiley Eastern Pvt., Ltd., Delhi, 1985.

13. Ramser C.E., Runoff from small agricultural areas, J. Agr. Res., Vol., 34 (9) pp 797-823, 1927.

14. Singh J. Irrational use of Rational formula, paper presented at 3rd Annual meeting of ISAE, Allahabad (India), 1964.

15. Soil Conservation Service, National Engineering Handbook, Section-4, Hydrology, USDA, 1972.

16. Soil Conservation Service, Urban Hydrology for small watersheds, Tech, bull. no. 55, USDA, Washington D.C., 1975.

17. Subramanya K. Engineering Hydrology. Tata McGraw-Hill Publishing Co. Ltd., New Delhi, 2000.

DESCRIPTIVE TYPE QUESTIONS

1. (*a*) Define runoff and explain its mechanism.

(*b*) Describe various factors affecting runoff.

2. (*a*) Classify the runoff and differentiate each other.

(*b*) Define drainage density and explain 'how it affects the runoff'

3. (*a* Define peak runoff and list the factors affecting peak runoff.

(*b*) Explain Rational formula for computing the peak runoff.

4. (*a* Describe Rational formula and its limitations.

(*b*) Write the necesity of peak runoff computation.

5. (*a*) Explain, why small watersheds are dominated by overland flow.

(*b*) Distinguish overland flow and runoff.

6. (*a*) Explain Cook's method to compute the runoff rate.

(*b*) Write applicability of Cook's method.

7. (*a*) Explain curve number method for determining the runoff.

(*b*) Amongst various runoff computing methods, recommend the most suitable method alongwith justification.

8. (*a*) Define infiltration index.

(*b*) Explain *W* and ϕ-indices

9. (*a*) Write importance of flow-duration curve.

(*b*) Explain the derivation procedure of flow-duration curve.

(*c*) Explain various characteristics of flow-duration curve.

OBJECTIVE TYPE QUESTIONS

1. Runoff takes place after

(*a*) satisfying the losses (*b*) satisfying the infiltration

(*c*) satisfying the interception (*d*) 30 minutes

2. Direct runoff is the

(*a*) surface runoff (*b*) interflow only

(*c*) interflow and base flow (*d*) delayed runoff

3. Interflow is the part of

(*a*) surface runoff (*b*) ground water

(*c*) base flow (*d*) indirect runoff

4. Base flow is

(*a*) delayed flow (*b*) ground water

(*c*) both '*a*' and '*b*' (*d*) direct runoff

5. Total runoff represents the sum of

(*a*) surface runoff and interflow

(*b*) direct runoff and base flow

(*c*) both '*a*' and '*b*'

(*d*) stem flow and base flaw

6. For a given watershed, if one storm occurs as rainfall and other as snow fall for the same duration, which storm will result high peak runoff.
   (*a*) that occurs as rainfall.
   (*b*) that occurs as snow fall.
   (*c*) '*a*' and '*b*'
   (*d*) sleet
7. A high intensity rainfall causes greater peak runoff, because of
   (*a*) greater rainfall amount
   (*b*) less rainfall loss
   (*c*) decrease in interception loss
   (*d*) less stem flow
8. Storm *A* has rainfall intensity of 7.5 cm/h and *B* 2.5 cm/h, which storm will result high peak runoff, if duration of rainfall is the same
   (*a*) storm *A*
   (*b*) storm *B*
   (*c*) both will result equal peak runoff rate
9. A rainfall with greater 'distribution coefficient' causes
   (*a*) greater runoff
   (*b*) lower peak runoff
   (*c*) no effect
   (*d*) zero direct runoff
10. Two watersheds *A* and *B* have the same area, but *A* has greater stream density than the *B*, which watershed will produce high peak runoff.
    (*a*) *A*
    (*b*) B
    (*c*) both storm will generate same peak runoff
11. Greater relative humidity
    (*a*) increases the runoff (*b*) decreases the runoff
    (*c*) no effect on the runoff (*d*) reduces interception
12. Fan shaped watershed results high peak runoff as compared to the fern shaped watershed, because of
    (*a*) greater watershed area.
    (*b*) greater time of concentration.
    (*c*) less time of concentration.
    (*d*) less intercaption less.
13. Small watersheds are dominated by
    (*a*) surface runoff (*b*) overland flow
    (*c*) both '*a*' and '*b*' (*d*) snow fall
14. Wind velocity towards stream slope causes
    (*a*) greater runoff (*b*) greater water loss
    (*c*) both '*a*' and '*b*' (*d*) less runoff
15. Watershed *A* and *B* have same total area but *A* has a large area under rock and *B* has plain land. In which case runoff will be more, if rainfall duration and other characteristics are the same.
    (*a*) *A*
    (*b*) *B*
    (*c*) same in both '*A*' and '*B*'.

16. Watershed shape is evaluated by
(*a*) form factor and compactness factor
(*b*) form factor
(*c*) compactness factor.
(*d*) stream density

17. In mountaneous watersheds, the wind ward side receives greater rainfall than the leeward side, because of
(*a*) orientation effect (*b*) less wind velocity
(*c*) greater area (*d*) high humidity

18. In Rational formula *i.e.* $Q_p = \frac{CIA}{360}$, the value of rainfall intensity (I) is expressed as
(*a*) cm/h (*b*) mm/h
(*c*) m/h (*d*) mm/s

19. The runoff coefficient (C) of Rational formula is defined as the ratio of
(*a*) peak runoff rate to the rainfall intensity.
(*b*) watershed area to the peak runoff rate.
(*c*) $P/\overline{P}$
(*d*) W_{50} and W_{25}

20. The unit of runoff coefficient (C) of Rational formula is
(*a*) dimensionless (*b*) cm
(*c*) mm (*d*) km

21. The value of runoff coefficient C for cultivated flat sandy loam soil is generally
(*a*) 0.30 (*b*) 0.50
(*c*) 0.40 (*d*) 1.10

22. The Kirpich (1940) formula for time of concentration (T_c) (i.e. $T_c = 0.02\, L^{0.77} \cdot S^{-385}$) computes the T_c in the unit of
(*a*) minute (*b*) second
(*c*) hour (*d*) day

23. For a 350 m long water course having slope as 4%, the value of T_c will be
(*a*) 6.28 minutes (*b*) 7.5 minutes
(*c*) 400 seconds (*d*) 15 minutes

24. A small size watershed is dominated by
(*a*) surface runoff (*b*) sub surface runoff
(*c*) overland flow (*d*) indirect runoff

25. For predicting peak runoff by Cook's method, the numerical value of 'relief' for normal condition is taken between
(*a*) 30 and 20 (*b*) 20 and 10
(*c*) 40 and 30 (*d*) 10 and 15

26. The 'shape factor' for the watershed having equal length-width ratio is taken as
(*a*) 0.50 (*b*) 1.0
(*c*) 1.5 (*d*) 2.3

27. The curve number method directly computes the runoff for
(*a*) AMC I (*b*) AMC II
(*c*) AMC III (*d*) both AMC-I & III

28. The hydrologic soil group includes
(*a*) four classes *i.e.* *A*, *B*, *C* and *D*
(b) three classes *i.e.* *A*, *B*, and *C*
(*c*) four classes *i.e.* I, II, III, and IV.
(*d*) two classes *i.e.* *A* & *B*.

29. The soil of hydrologic soil group – *C* involves
(*a*) low infiltration rate
(*b*) moderate infiltration rate
(*c*) less runoff potential
(*d*) 1.25 cm/h as deep percolation rate

30. The *W* and ϕ-indices become same, when
(*a*) infiltration rate approaches infiltration capacity
(b) infiltration rate is greater than the infiltration capacity
(*c*) rainfall intensity is 1.25 cm/h
(*d*) none of the above.

31. Dicken formula is suitable for computing the runoff of watersheds located in
(*a*) central India
(*b*) northern India
(*c*) both '*a*' and '*b*'
(*d*) southern India

32. The value of '*C*' in Dicken formula for mountaneous regions varies from
(*a*) 2.8 to 5.6 (*b*) 14.0 to 28.0
(*c*) 5 to 10 (*d*) 7 to 8.5

33. Ryve's formula is suitable for computing the runoff of the watersheds located in
(*a*) south India (*b*) eastern India
(*c*) north India (*d*) none of above

34. Khosla's formula for computation of runoff, is the function of
(*a*) precipitation and temperature
(*b*) precipitation and watershed area
(*c*) both '*a*' and '*b*'
(*d*) rainfall, area and time

35. In India, the water year is from
(*a*) Ist June to 31st May
(*b*) Ist July to 31st July
(*c*) Ist Jan to 31st Dec.
(*d*) None of above

36. A stream, in which flow is continued throughout the year is called
(*a*) ephemeral stream (*b*) perineal stream
(*c*) intermittent stream (*d*) springs

37. Streams of humid zones are generally
(*a*) perineal (*b*) intermittent
(*c*) ephemereal (*d*) springs

38. Ephemeral streams are found in
(*a*) arid zones (*b*) humid zones
(*c*) semi-arid zones (*d*) polor zones

39. A flow-duration curve is the plot of
   (*a*) discharge and percent of time
   (*b*) discharge and percent probability
   (*c*) both '*a*' and '*b*'
   (*d*) intensity and time

40. Steep portion of flow-duration curve indicates
   (*a*) highly variable flow (*b*) little variable flow
   (*c*) zero flow (*d*) discrete flow

41. A flow-mass curve is the plot of
   (*a*) cumulative discharge volume and time.
   (*b*) discharge and probability.
   (*c*) discharge and time.
   (*d*) intensity and time.

Answer (Multiple Choice Questions)

1. (*a*)	**2.** (*a*)	**3.** (*a*)	**4.** (*c*)	**5.** (*b*)	**6.** (*a*)	**7.** (*a*)	**8.** (*a*)
9. (*a*)	**10.** (*a*)	**11.** (*a*)	**12.** (*c*)	**13.** (*b*)	**14.** (*a*)	**15.** (*a*)	**16.** (*a*)
17. (*a*)	**18.** (*a*)	**19.** (*a*)	**20.** (*a*)	**21.** (*a*)	**22.** (*a*)	**23.** (*a*)	**24.** (*c*)
25. (*b*)	**26.** (*a*)	**27.** (*b*)	**28.** (*a*)	**29.** (*a*)	**30.** (*a*)	**31.** (*c*)	**32.** (*b*)
33. (*a*)	**34.** (*a*)	**35.** (*a*)	**36.** (*b*)	**37.** (*a*)	**38.** (*a*)	**39.** (*c*)	**40.** (*a*)
41. (*a*)							

6

Hydrograph

The hydrograph is the plot of instantaneous discharge rate against time. Sometimes, it is also known as storm hydrograph or flood hydrograph. The hydrograph shows the distribution of total runoff at the gauging point of the watershed. A hydrograph consists of three regions, namely : rising limb, crest segment and falling limb, are shown in Fig. 6.1.

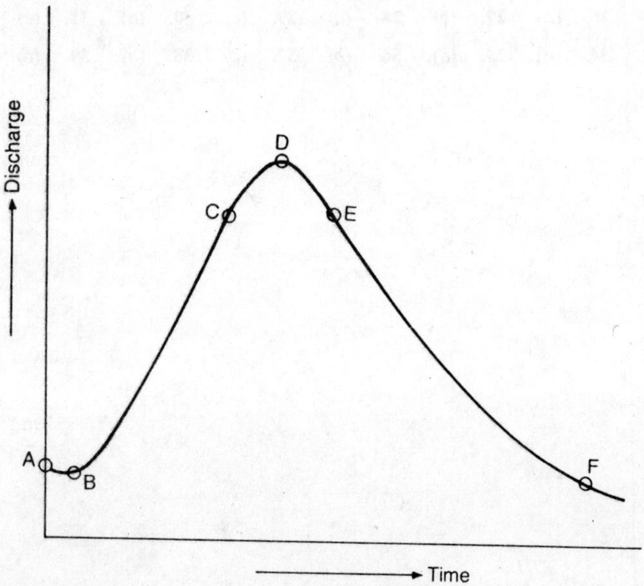

Fig. 6.1. Hydrograph

The nature of hydrograph depends on the characteristics of rainfall and watershed, both. An isolated storm results single peak hydrograph, while complex storm yields multiple peak hydrograph, which is known as complex hydrograph. For hydrological analysis, generally single peak hydrographs are preferred.

Stream flow Hydrograph

It is also known as discharge hydrograph, which shows the flow rate as the function of time at a given gauging point of the stream. In effect, a hydrograph represents the integral expression of physiographic and climatic characteristics that govern the rainfall-runoff relationship of the watershed.

Annual Hydrograph

The annual hydrograph is plotted between stream flow and time over a year. This hydrograph shows the long term balance of precipitation, evaporation and streamflow in the watershed. The forms of annual hydrograph for perennial, ephemeral and snow- fed rivers are shown in Figure 6.2. The

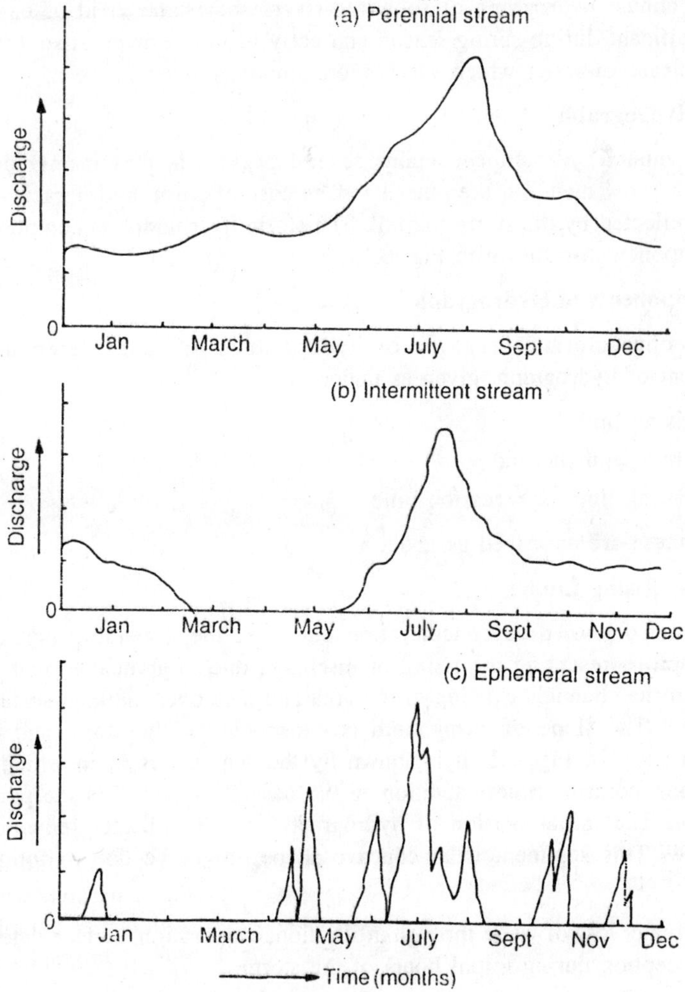

Fig. 6.2

total volume of flow under annual hydrograph is known as basin yield. In case of perennial rivers, the most of the basin yield is contributed by base flow, which advocates that a large proportion of rainfall is absorbed (infiltration) by the soil which ultimately reaches to the river as the sub-surface flow. In annual hydrograph (Figure 6.2), the spikes show the quick flow, while slowly varying flow during rainless period indicates to the base flow.

In case of annual hydrograph of ephemeral stream, there is long period of dry spell causing no flow through the river. Only intense rainfall generates the direct runoff. Basin yield is only due to direct runoff from large storms and there is no contribution of base flow.

The annual hydrograph of snow-fed rivers shows the yield of basin as very significant during spring season and early of the summer. Also, there is steady release of water which varies more smoothly over the year.

Storm Hydrograph

The annual hydrograph contains several peaks which is mainly due to rainfall or snow melt. On the other hand, in case of storm hydrograph single peak is reflected by the storm rainfall. The storm hydrograph is composed of four components as shown in Fig. 6.1.

6.1. Components of Hydrograph

The characteristic regions of hydrographs are considered as the component of hydrograph, given as under :

1. Rising limb
2. Crest segment, and
3. Falling limb or recession limb

All these are described as under :

6.1.1. Rising Limb

It is also known as concentration curve, is the ascending portion of hydrograph representing the rising of discharge due to gradual formation of storage in the channels existing in the area and also over the land surface of watershed. The slope of rising limb is dependent on the storm and basin characteristics. In Fig. 6.1, it is shown by the segment *B C,* in which *B* is the starting point of runoff addition to the base flow and *C* is the point of inflection. The initial portion of hydrograph *i.e. AB* indicates reduction in base flow. This segiment is in concave shape, might be due to following reasons :

1. Greater loss of water through infiltration, evaporation, surface detention and interception during initial hours of the storm.

2. Greater contributing area between isochrones at middle and upper parts of the watershed.

In a simple hydrograph, the rising limb is comparitively shorter than the falling limb ; accordingly the area below the rising limb is less to that of the falling limb of the hydrograph.

6.1.2. Crest Segment

It is extended from the point of inflection on the rising limb to a similar inflection point on the falling limb. Crest segment is one of the most important components of the hydrograph, because it indicates the peak flow rate. Generally when all parts of watershed start to yield the runoff simultaneously to the outlet, the peak flow occurs. In large watersheds, it occurs after end of rainfall. It is controlled by the storm and watershed characteristics, as these two affect the time interval between the centre of mass of rainfall and the peak of the hydrograph. Sometimes, hydrographs also have more than one peak. Such hydrographs are known as multiple peak hydrograph. The appearance of more than one peak is due to occurrence of two or more storms of different intensities in a close interval. In figure 6.1, the crest segment is shown by the points *C D E*.

6.1.3. Falling Limb

It is descending portion of the hydrograph, is also known as recession limb. It is extended from the point of inflection at the end of crest segment to the commencement of natural ground water flow or base flow in the channel. The inflection point on recession limb represents the time, at which the occurrence of rainfall is stopped. The shape of falling limb is independent of the storm characteristics, but completely dependent on the watershed characteristics. A hydrograph, which is resulted from a large watershed in which rainfall has occurred only in a part of the watershed, the trend of falling limb is different. The nature of falling limb varies from storm to storm, depending on characteristics of the watershed. Generally, the falling limb is convex in nature due to continuous decrease in runoff rate. Variations in rainfall distribution on the watershed also affect the shape of falling limb, but minutely. In figure 6.1, it is shown by the segment *EF*, in which *E* is the point of inflection and *F* is the point at which surface runoff is finished and commencement of base flow in the stream.

6.2. Recession Constants

For determining the characteristics of surface runoff by using hydrograph, the most difficult problem is to separate the base flow, precisely from the hydrograph. For the purpose, several methods have been introduced, based on the ground water recession or depletion curves. Barnes (1940) developed the following formula for determining the recession constant :

$$Q_t = Q_o K_r^{\,t} \qquad \text{...(6.1)}$$

where, Q_t = discharge at any time interval 't'

Q_o = initial discharge rate

K_r = recession constant

The value of recession constant is less than 1. Basically, there are three types of basin storages, *i.e.* surface storage, interflow storage and base flow storage. Accordingly, the recession constant (K_r) is divided into following three components, as

1. Recession constant for surface storage (K_{rs})
2. Recession constant for interflow storage (K_{ri})
3. Recession constant for baseflow storage (K_{rb}).

The values of above three recession constants are given as under.

$$K_{rs} = 0.05 \text{ to } 0.20$$

$$K_{ri} = 0.50 \text{ to } 0.85$$

$$K_{rb} = 0.85 \text{ to } 0.99$$

If the contribution of interflow storage is not significant, then the value of K_{ri} is assumed to be unity.

6.2.1. Determination of Recession Constants

Considering the equation 6.1, *i.e.*

$$Q_t = Q_o K_r^{-t}$$

Taking the log on both side of this equation, we have

$$\log Q_t = \log Q_o - t \log K_r \qquad \text{...(6.2)}$$

It is in the form of straight line equation (*i.e.* $y = mx + c$), in which

$$y = \log Q_t$$

$$m = \log K_r,\ c = \log Q_o \text{ and}$$

$$x = t$$

If Q_t V_s t data are plotted on the semi-log paper, then a straight line is obtained. The K_r is determined by selecting the point in such a way that there is little or no direct runoff contribution. Since the value of K_r is not constant therefore it is essential to predict its value at different points of recession curve, within a given flow range. Usually for this purpose, the recession curve is divided into a series of time segment in such a way that, the segment should not be exactly straight line, but in the form of curve having gradual decreasing slope.

Barnes (1940) suggested the following steps for computing different components of recession constant.

Step (1). Plot the discharge and time data on semi - log paper by keeping the discharge on y- axis and time on x- axis, and prepare the hydrograph.

Step (2). Separate the surface runoff by extending the tail end of hydrograph backward upto the point below the point of inflection on recession limb. Generally, tail end of hydrograph is in straight line trend. In Fig. 6.3

it is shown by the line *DE*. The straight line *DE* is known as ground water recession curve.

Step (3). Find out the value of recession constant for base flow storage (K_{rb}), which is the slope of straight line at the tail end of hydrograph.

Step (4). Deduct the ground water flow form the total runoff hydrograph and plot the new ordinates V_s time data on the same graph, in the same way as in step (1).

Step (5). Extend the tail end of new hydrograph, backward upto the point below the point of inflection on falling limb for seperating the interflow from the new hydrograph (*i.e.* in step 4). In Figure 6.3, it is shown by the line G.L. and L.F.

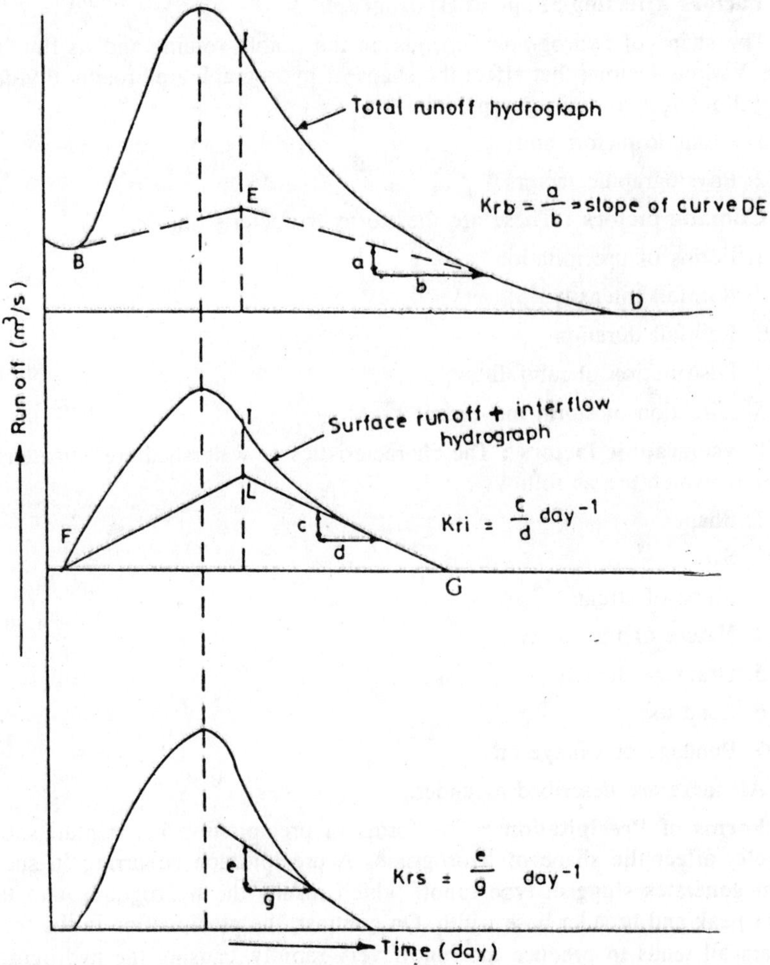

Fig. 6.3. Determination of recession constant.

Step (6). Findout the value of recession constant for interflow storage (K_{ri}), which is the slope of straight line at tail end of the new hydrograph.

Step (7). Determine the ordinates of surface runoff by deducting the inter flow from the new hydrograph (*i.e.* in step 6) and plot the ordinates against time data and draw the hydrograph. This hydrograph is known as surface flow hydrograph.

Step (8). Extend the tail end of surface flow hydrograph, backward and calculate its slope, which is the value of recession constant for surface storage (K_{rs}).

In this way, the values of different components of recession constant are determined.

6.3. Factors Affecting Shape of Hydrograph

The shape of hydrograph depends on the runoff volume and its time to peak. Various factors, that affect the shape of hydrograph are broadly divided into following two main groups :

1. Climatic factors and
2. Physiographic factors

Climatic factors : These are the storm characteristics, *i.e.*

1. Forms of precipitation
2. Rainfall intensity
3. Rainfall duration
4. Distribution of rainfall
5. Direction of storm movement

Physiographic factors : The characteristics of watershed are considered under it, which are as follows :

1. Shape
2. Size
3. Slope of stream
4. Nature of the valley
5. Drainage density
6. Land use
7. Pondage or storage etc.

All these are described as under.

Forms of Precipitation : The forms of precipitation i.e. rainfall snow fall etc. affect the shape of hydrograph. A precipitation occurring in snow form, generates sluggish type runoff which results the hydrograph with the lower peak and broader base width. On contrast, the precipitation in the form of rainfall tends to produce the runoff very rapidly, causing the hydrograph with high peak and narrow base width.

Rainfall Intensity : The rainfall intensity directly affects the amount runoff volume, occurrence of peak flow and duration of surface runoff. If rainfall intensity is high then peak flow occurs immediately, as result the shape of hydrograph becomes conical, while incase of less rainfall intensity, a reverse shape is obtained.

Duration of Rainfall : Its effect is disimilar to the rainfall intensity. For a given rainfall intensity, the amount of runoff is directly proportional to the duration of rainfall *i.e.* if duration of rainfall is longer then resulting runoff will be more. However, in real practice it is not so; because an intense storm (*i.e.* heavy intensity storm) does not occur for longer duration. A storm with longer duration involves less intensity and runoff is generated at very slow rate. The peak runoff is resulted after longer time. In this case, the resulting hydrograph will be flater with broader base.

Distribution of Rainfall : Its effect on shape of hydrograph can be described under following two cases :

(*i*) **When heavy rainfall is occurred near the outlet :** In this case, the peak flow occurs very shortly at the outlet, which results the hydrograph with sharp peak and rapid recession limb, as shown in Fig. 6.4 (*a*).

(*ii*) **When heavy rainfall is occurred in upper reaches of watershed :** In this condition, the peak flow occurs after few hours because the time to reach the runoff at the outlet is comparitively more, thus the resulting hydrograph includes lower peak and broad base width, as shown in Fig. 6.4 (*b*).

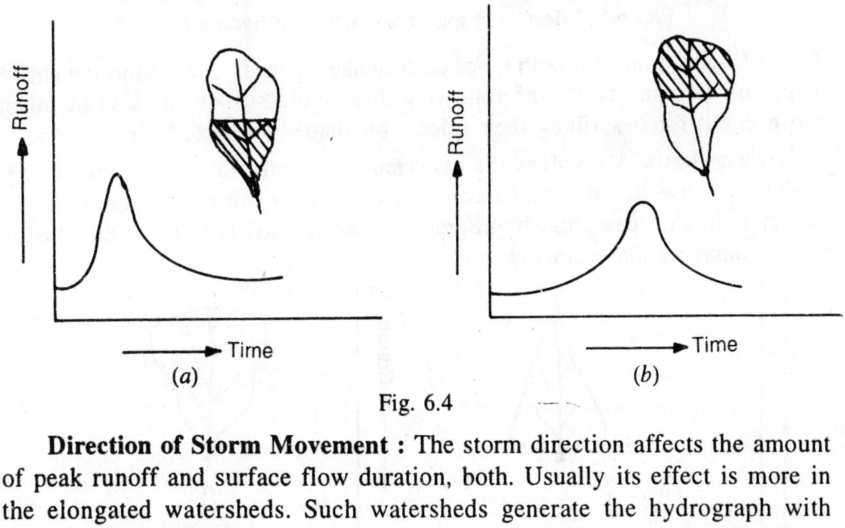

Fig. 6.4

Direction of Storm Movement : The storm direction affects the amount of peak runoff and surface flow duration, both. Usually its effect is more in the elongated watersheds. Such watersheds generate the hydrograph with lower peak and broader base when storm moves towards upstream side. While storm moving downstream side results the hydrograph with sharp peak and narrow base width from the elongated watershed.

Shape of Basin : It affects the shape of hydrograph by affecting the time of concentration of flowing runoff. Generally, the following two shapes of basin are considered for the purpose :

1. Fan shape and
2. Fern shape

In fan shaped drainage basin, the peak flow occurs very soon because of less time of concentration, as result the shape of hydrograph becomes narrow with high peak.

The fern shape drainage basin yields the peak flow at longer time interval, because of greater time of concentration. The resulting hydrograph for such drainage basin contains broad base and lower peak. Figure 6.5 illustrates the

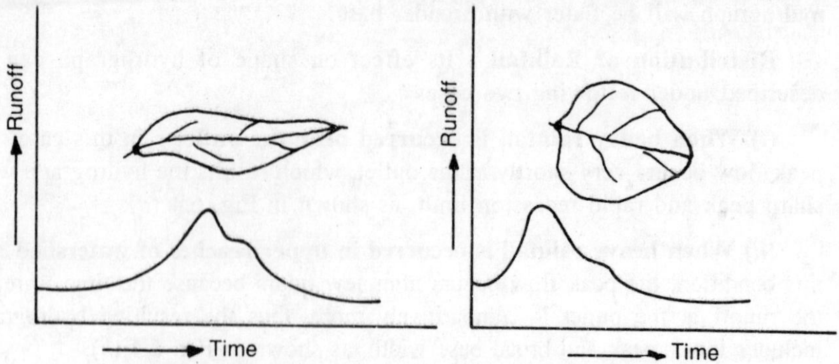

Fig. 6.5. Effect of shape of watershed on hydrograph.

shape of hydrograph for both types of drainage basin. In addition to the above shapes of drainage basin, the following three more shapes can also be taken into account for describing their effects on shape of hydrograph :

(*i*) The basin *A* involves the occurrence of peak flow at the outlet very shortly, because the shape of basin is skewed opposite to the outlet (*i.e.* to the left). In this case, the hydrograph is skewed towards left side causing narrow base, as shown in Fig. 6.6.

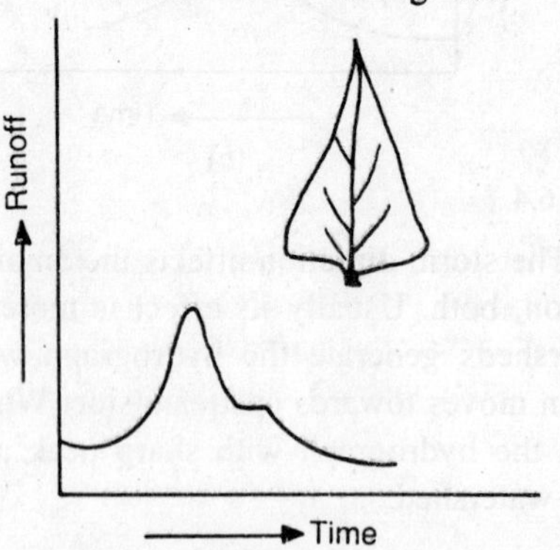

Fig. 6.6

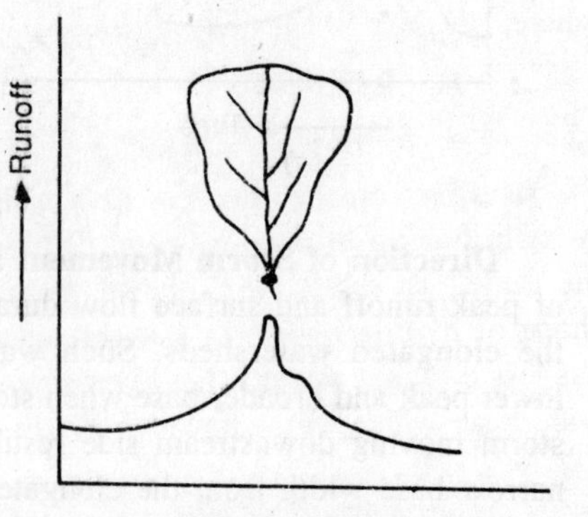

Fig. 6.7

(*ii*) The basin *B* which is skewed towards outlet, generates the peak flow relatively after longer time. In this case, the hydrograph is skewed right side *i.e.* with broad base, as shown in 6.7.

Size of Basin : Basin size affects the shape of hydrograph by changing the discharge rate with respect to time. A small basin is mainly dominated by overland flow which joins the channel very shortly, as result the peak flow occurrs relatively sooner and the shape of hydrograph is with narrow base and high peak.

In large drainage basins, the channel flow is more pronounced as compared to the overland flow. Generally, the peak flow is found to vary in the form of 'A^n', in which *A* is the basin area and n is an exponent which value is less than unity, usually taken as 0.5. Also, in large basin, the duration of surface runoff from time of peak is found to vary as A^m', where *A* is the area of basin and *m* is an exponent, which value is less than unity, usually taken as 0.2. The hydrograph resulting from large size basin contains broader base and low peak.

Stream Slope : It affects the shape of recession limb by affecting the withdrawal of water from the storage made in the basin. A greater stream slope, increases the slope of recession limb and reduces the base width of hydrograph. While small stream slope makes the recession limb flatter, causing the base width of hydrograph to be wider.

Nature of Valley : The nature of valley refers to the slope of bed and side of the valley. If affects the shape of hydrograph in the same way as the stream slope *i.e.* greater valley slope increases the slope of recession limb and decreases the time element of hydrograph.

Drainage Density : It is defined as the ratio of total length of existing channels in the basin to the total area of basin, *i.e.*

$$D_d = \frac{L_c}{A} \quad \text{...(6.3)}$$

where, D_d = drainage density, km/ha

L_c = total channel length, km

A = total area of the basin, ha

Its effect on the shape of hydrograph is similar to the slope of channel. A basin having greater drainage density, disposes the runoff very quickly at the outlet, as result the slope of recession limb becomes steep causing the shape of hydrograph to be narrow with high peak. For another basin, which has less drainage density, the hydrograph has slow moving rising limb causing wide base width. It is shown in Fig. 6.8.

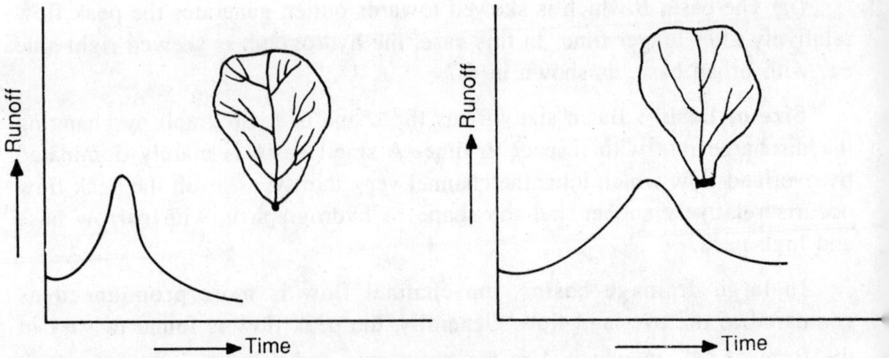

Fig. 6.8

Land Use : The land use directly affects the runoff yield from the watershed, because vegetations increase the loss of water by enhancing the interception loss, infiltration rate and evapotranspiration, simultaneously. It is more effective in small size watersheds i.e. less than 150 sq km area.

If two watersheds have same characteristics, except vegetal cover, the one which has high vegetation density will produce less peak flow as compared to the other having less vegetation density. Accordingly, the shape of hydrograph gets affected.

Surface Depression : The presence of surface depressions, such as ponds, rills etc. in the watershed, affects the occurrence of peak flow by delaying and modifying the flow pattern of runoff. However, the surface storage decreases the peak flow and resulting hydrograph involves low peak and wide base width.

6.4. Base Flow Separation

6.4.1. Single Peak Hydrograph

A hydrograph represents the total runoff against time of a given storm. The total runoff is the sum of surface runoff, interflow and base flow, inwhich the interflow is included under surface runoff or direct runoff. The surface runoff hydrograph is derived by separating the base flow from runoff hydrograph. The base flow separation is performed by the following methods :

(*i*) **Straight line method :** This method consists of separating the base flow by joining the starting and end points of the surface runoff by a straight line. In Fig. 6.9, it is shown by the line *AB*, in which *A* is the starting point and *B* is the end point of surface runoff. The point *B* is obtained after $N = 0.83\,A^{0.2}$ days from peak of the hydrograph (Linesly, 1949), in which 'A' is the area of watershed in sq km. The area of hydrograph below the line AB represents the base flow and area above the line is as surface runoff.

(*ii*) **Base flow-recession curve method :** In this method, the base flow is separated by extending the base flow-recession curve backward, till it intersects the perpendicular line drawn from the inflection point of the

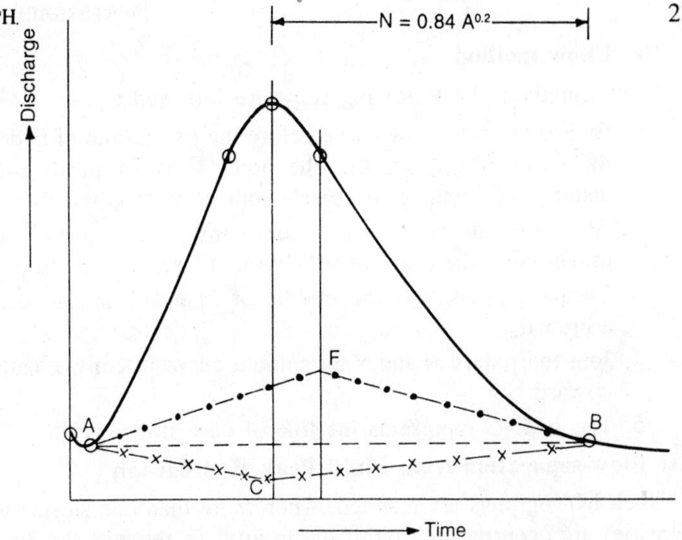

Fig. 6.9. Base flow separation of single peak hydrograph.

recession limb. The tail end of hydrograph is generally found in the form of straight line is extended as recession curve. In Fig. 6.9, it is shown by the line *BF* and *FA*. This method provides a relastic base flow separation especially when ground water contribution to the stream is significant.

(*iii*) Extending the base flow separation curve before rising limb to the peak and joining to the point *B*. The point *B* is at $N = 0.83\,A^{0.2}$ days from the peak. In Fig. 6.9 the separation of baseflow unde this method is illustrated by the lines AC and CB.

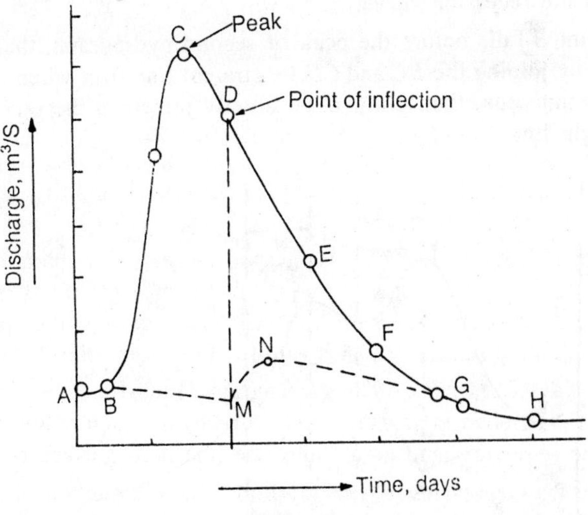

Fig. 6.10

(*iv*) Chow method

In this method, the following steps are followed :

1. Extend the base flow curve before the rising limb of hydrograph upto the point *M* (Fig. 6.10). The point *M* is arbitrarily located at the distance of 1⁄10th of the base width of hydrograph from the peak.
2. Also, extend the recession curve inward to intersect the ordinate drawn from the point of inflection (E) at the recession limb.
3. Locate a point *N* at the middle of *M* and *G* on the recession limb, arbitrarily.
4. Join the points *M* and *N* by smooth curve in convex nature shooting upward.
5. The BMNG represents the line of base flow.

Base Flow-separation from Multi Peak Hydrograph

Such hydrographs are resulted, when more than one storms with varying intensities are occurred in a close succession. To separate the base flow from complex hydrographs, the knowledge of effect of rainfall event on base flow is most essential instead of separating the base flow from the total runoff.

In Fig. 6.11, a two peaked hydrograph is shown, from which it is required to separate the base flow. The following steps are followed :

1. Demarcate the points *B* and *D* after *N* days from peak (1) and (2), respectively.

2. Extend the initial curve of hydrograph forward to cut the perpendicular line drawn from peak (1). It is shown by the line *FE*.

3. Join the point *A* on recession limb of peak (1) to the point (*B*) by using composite recession curve.

4. If point *B* falls before the peak of second hydrograph, then base flow is separated by joining the *BC* and *CD* by straight line. But when point *B* falls after the second peak, then point *D* is directly joined to the recession curve *AB* by straight line.

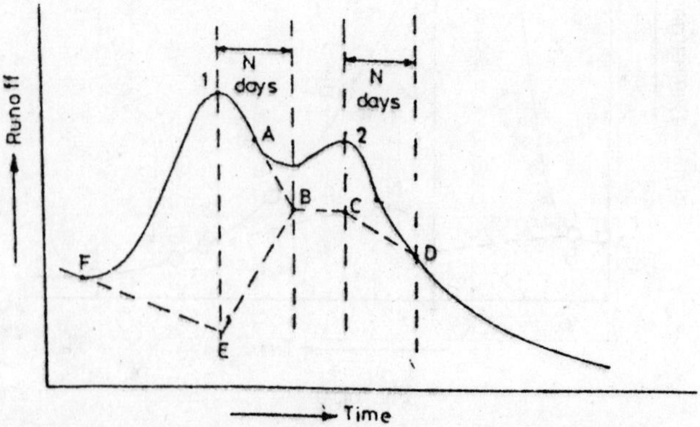

Fig. 6.11. Separation of base flow from complex hydrograph.

Precipitation Excess, Rainfall Excess and Effective Rainfall

During occurrence of runoff producing storm, the total precipitation is the sum of precipitation excess and abstractions, in which that part of total precipitation which generates surface runoff is called rainfall excess, when precipitation is in the form of rainfall. The part of precipitation that entirely contributes to the formation of direct runoff is called effective precipitation or effective rainfall if only rainfall is involved. The effective rainfall consists of rainfall excess and that part of precipitation which becomes prompt surface runoff.

Hyetograph

It is the plot of rainfall intensity verses time data. The mass curve of the storm generated by recording type rain gauge is used as the mother source to develop the hyetograph. The form of presentation of hyetograph is bar diagram, of which the time interval is decided on the basis of rainfall duration and convenience. Basically, the hyetograph is another form of mass curve. The area enclosed by the hyetograph represents the total rainfall depth. A view of hyetograph is shown in Fig. 3.3.

Effective Rainfall Hyetograph

It is abbreviated as ERH, also called supra rainfall. It is the hyetograph minus abstractions (*i.e.* initial loss). The abstractions are referred by a single term *i.e.* ϕ-index. An ERH provides the following informations about the storm :

1. Effective rainfall depth and its duration
2. Direct runoff volume
3. Amount of initial losses

The view of ERH is shown in Fig. 6.12.

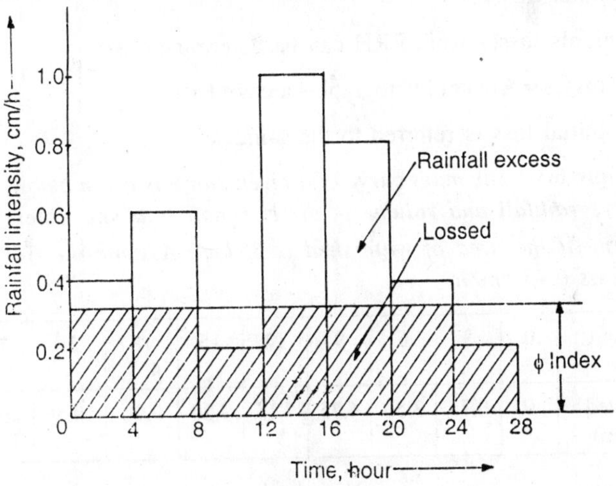

Fig. 6.12

From a given effective rainfall hyetograph, the depth of effective rainfall is determined by computing its enclosed area *i.e.*

$$ER = \sum_{i=1}^{n} I_i \cdot \Delta t \qquad ...(6.4)$$

where ER = effective rainfall depth

I_i = rainfall intensity, at any instant i

Δt = time interval of bar diagrame

The volume of direct runoff by the ERH can be determined by using the following formula :

Volume of direct runoff = Area of ERH × area of watershed

$$= \left(\sum_{i=1}^{n} I_i \, \Delta t \right) \times A \qquad ...(6.5)$$

If I is in cm/h, Δt in h and area of watershed is in *ha*, then

$$\text{Volume of direct runoff } (m^3) = A \cdot \sum_{i=1}^{n} I_i \, \Delta t \times \frac{1}{100} \times 10^4$$

$$= 100 \, A \sum_{i=1}^{n} I_i \, \Delta t \qquad ...(6.6)$$

This equation represents the relationship between direct runoff and effective rainfall for a given watershed.

The duration of effective rainfall from ERH is determined as its base width (*i.e.* total time).

The initials losses from ERH can be determined as :

Initial losses = Area of hyetograph − area of ERH

Here, initial loss is referred to the ϕ-index.

Example 6.1 : *The mass curve of a given storm is given below. Determine the effective rainfall and volume of direct runoff from the watershed due to given storm, if the area of watershed is 35 km^2. Assume the ϕ-index of the watershed as 0.45 cm/h.*

Time of start of storm h	0	3	6	9	12	15	18	21	24	27
Accumulated rainfall (cm)	0	0.75	3.50	4.75	7.15	9.20	9.90	10.50	11.75	13.0

Solution : Computation is shown in following table.

Time since start of storm (h)	*Time interval, Δt (h)*	*Accumulated rainfall (cm)*	*Actual rainfall in time Δt (cm)*	*Amount of water lost in time Δt cm*	*Rainfall excess (ER), (cm)*	*Infensity of ER (cm/h)*
(1)	*(2)*	*(3)*	*(4)*	*(5)**	*(6)***	*(7)****
0	—	0.0	—	—	—	0.000
3	3.0	0.75	0.75	1.35	0.00	0.000
6	3.0	3.50	2.75	1.35	1.40	0.466
9	3.0	4.75	1.25	1.35	0.00	0.00
12	3.0	7.15	2.40	1.35	1.05	0.350
15	3.0	9.20	2.05	1.35	0.70	0.233
18	3.0	9.90	0.70	1.35	0.00	0.000
21	3.0	10.50	0.60	1.35	0.00	0.000
24	3.0	11.75	1.25	1.35	0.00	0.0000
27	3.0	13.00	1.25	1.35	0.00	0.000

* ϕ-index × Δt
** col (4) – col (5)
*** col (6)/Δt

(*i*) Effective rainfall = Area of ERH

$$= (0.466 + 0.350 + 0.233) \times 3 \text{ cm}$$

$$= \mathbf{1.049 \text{ cm}} \quad \textbf{Ans.}$$

(*ii*) Volume of direct runoff = ER × area of watershed

$$= \frac{1.049}{100} \times 35 \times 10^6 \text{ m}^3$$

$$= \mathbf{367.15 \times 10^3 \text{ m}^3} \textbf{ Ans}$$

Example 6.2 *Using the data of example 6.1 compute the duration of effective rainfall.*

Solution : The duration of ER is the sum of time intervals (Δt) during which there is ER. In present case, it is $3 + 3 + 3$ hours $= 9h$ **Ans**

Example 6.3 *Compute the ER due to following storm. Take the ϕ-index for the watershed as 0.35* cm/*h*

Time since start of rainfall (*h*)	0	3	6	9	12
Accumilated rainfall (cm)	0	4.0	11	15	17

Solution : The ER is determined by subtrating the storm loss (ϕ index × rainfall duration) from the rainfall. Computation is shown in following table

Time interval (Δt)	0-3	3-6	6-9	9-12
Strom loss (cm)	1.05	1.05	1.05	1.05
ER (cm)	2.95	5.95	2.95	0.95

Triangular Hyetograph

It is the plot of rainfall intensity and time, similar to the general hyetograph, but plotting shape is in triangle form (Fig. 6.13). A triangle is the simple shape for construction of hyetograph, because by having the precipitation depth and its duration, the base length and height of the triangle can easily be determined. Referring the Fig. 6.13, if the

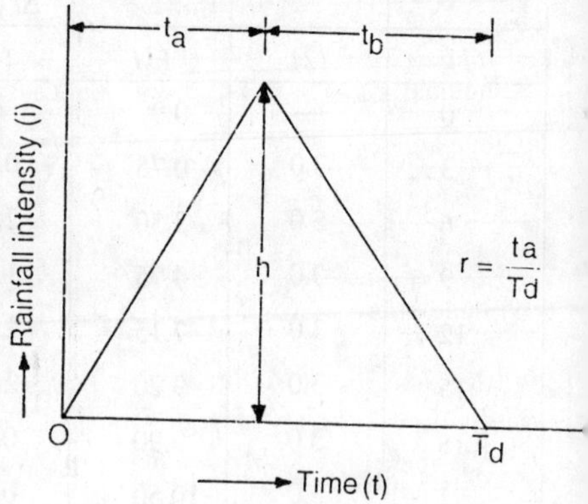

Fig. 6.13

(*i*) base length $= T_d$
(*ii*) height $= h$
(*iii*) total depth of precipitation $= P$

Then, (*a*) Total precipitation, $P = \frac{1}{2} T_d \cdot h$ ...(6.7)

or

$$h = \frac{2P}{T_d} \quad ...(6.8)$$

(*b*) Recession time

$$T_b = T_d - t_a \quad ...(6.9)$$

in which t_a is equal to the product of storm advancement coefficient (r) and base length of triangular hyetograph, *i.e.*

$$t_a = r \cdot T_d \quad ...(6.10)$$

Substituting the value of t_a in equation 6.9, we have

$$T_b = T_d - r \cdot T_d$$
$$= T_d (1 - r) \quad ...(6.11)$$

The storm advancement coefficient (r) is defined as the ratio of time before the peak (t_a) to the total duration *i.e.* base length (T_d). The values of r for various locations in the world are given in Table 6.1. A value of r as 0.5 refers to the occurrence of peak of rainfall in the middle of the storm *i.e.* $t_a = 0.5\ T_d$

Table 6.1 : Values of storm advancement coefficient (r)

Location	r	*Reference*
Baltimore	0.399	McPherson (1958)
Chicago	0.294	McPherson (1958)
Cincinnati	0.325	Prowl and Papadakis (1973)
Cleveland	0.375	Havens and Emerson (1968)
Guahati (India)	0.416	Bandyopadhyay (1972)
Ontario	0.480	Marsalek (1972)
Philadelphia	0.414	Mc Pherson (1958)

while less than 0.5 shows the peak to occur earlier and r greater than 0.5 to occur the peak after the middle of storm. As per values of 'r' shown in Table. 6.1, it is found that the peak intensity generally takes place sooner than the mid of the storm.

Direct Runoff Hydrograph

It is simply denoted as DRH, which is the plot of direct runoff (m^3/h) and time (t) data. Its presentation is in the form of hydrograph; not in the from of bar diagrame. The area of DRH represents the volume of direct runoff, which is the response of effective rainfall in the watershed system. A direct runoff hydrograph is always originate from origin of the quadrant. It has its fixed region and no inclusion of base flow.

Relation between DRH and ERH

The DRH and ERH represent the same total quantity of direct runoff but in different units. An ERH is the plot of rainfall intensity and time data which area multiplied by the area of watershed results into the total volume of direct runoff. In case of DRH, its area itself is the volume of direct runoff. The relation between DRH and ERH can be shown as,

Area of ERH × area of watershed = area of DRH

$$A_{erh} \cdot A_w = A_{DRH}$$

$$A_{erh} = \frac{A_{DRH}}{A_w}$$

or

$$ER = \frac{A_{DRH}}{A_w} \qquad ...(6.12)$$

in which A_{erh} is the area of ERH, A_w is the area of watershed and A_{DRH} is the area of DRH.

Example 6.4 *On a watershed of area* 35 km^2, *two storms of magnitude 2.5 and 2.0 cm occuring consecutively at 3.0 hour durations. The produced hydrograph at the outlet of watershed is given below. Determine, the rainfall excess and* ϕ*-index.*

Time (*h*)	– 3	0	3	6	9	12	15	18	21	24	27	30	33
Discharge (m^3/s)	4.5	4.5	11.0	23.0	16.0	14.5	11.5	7.0	6.5	5.0	4.5	4.5	4.5

Solution : Stepwise computation procedure is given below :

Step (1) : Separate the base flow: From the given data it is seen that there is the base flow component in hydrograph. For separating the base flow, the straight line method is used in this example. The base flow of 4.5 m^3/s is uniformly deducted from the ordinates of hydrograph.

Step (2): Compute the volume of direct runoff : It is computed by deriving the DRH and determining its area. The ODRH are given as under:

Time (h)	– 3	0	3	6	9	12	15	18	21	24	27	30	33
ODRH (m^3/s)	0	0	6.5	18.5	11.5	10.0	7.0	2.5	2.0	0.5	0.0	0.0	0.0

Area of DRH = volume of direct runoff

$$= (3 \times 60 \times 60) \times \left[\frac{1}{2}(0+6.5) + \frac{1}{2}(6.5+18.5) + \frac{1}{2}(18.5+11.5) + \frac{1}{2}(11.5+10) + \frac{1}{2}(10+7) + \frac{1}{2}(7+2.5) + \frac{1}{2}(2.5+2) + \frac{1}{2}(2+0.5) + \frac{1}{2}(0.5+0) \right]$$

$$= 6.318 \times 10^5 \text{ m}^3$$

Step (3): Compute runoff depth : it is given as under

$$\text{Runoff depth} = \frac{\text{Volume of direct runoff}}{\text{Area of watershed}}$$

$$= \frac{6.318 \times 10^5}{35 \times 10^6} \text{ m}$$

$$= 0.018 \text{ m} = 1.8 \text{ cm}$$

The runoff depth (*i.e.* direct runoff) is the rainfall excess Thus, rainfall excess = 1.8 cm **Ans**

Step (4): Compute ϕ-index : It is given by the following relationship.

$$\phi\text{–index} = \frac{\text{Total rainfall} - \text{rainfall excess}}{\text{Rainfall duration}}$$

$$= \frac{(2.5+2.0) - 1.8}{6} \text{ cm/h}$$

$$= 0.45 \text{ cm/h } \textbf{Ans}$$

Example. 6.5 *The followings are the ordindates of 3 – h unit hydrograph of a given watershed. Determine the ordinates of DRH due to ER of 3.0 cm.*

These (*h*)	0	3	6	9	12	15	18	21	24	27	30	33	36	39	42	45
OUGH (m^3/s)	0	30	70	105	150	180	205	170	100	85	60	50	35	25	25	15

Solution: The ordinates of DRH are determined by using the principle of linear response *i.e.* $ODRH = ER \times OUHG$. The computation is given in following table.

Time (h)	*Ordinate of UHG (m^3/s)*	*Ordinate of DRH due to 3.0 cm ER (m^3/s)*
0	0	0
3	30	90
6	70	210
9	105	315
12	150	450
15	180	540
18	205	615
21	170	510
24	100	300
27	85	255
30	60	180
33	50	150
36	35	105
39	25	75
42	15	45
45	0	0

Example 6.6 : *At the outlet of a given watershed the following hydrograph was produced by a storm of 4.2 cm. Compute the ordinates of DRH and total volume of surface runoff. Assume the constant base flow as 3.0 m^3/s.*

Time (hour)	0	3	6	9	12	15	18	21	24
Ordinate of hydrograph (m^3/s)	3.0	4.5	7.0	2.0	10.5	7.0	5.0	4.0	3.0

Solution : The ordinates of DRH are computed by substracting the base flow from the ordinates of hydgraph. It is given in following table.

Time (hour)	*Ordinate of hydrograph* (m^3/s)	*Ordinate of DRH (m^3/s)*
0	3.0	0.0
3	4.5	1.5
6	7.0	4.0
9	12.0	9.0
12	10.5	7.5
15	7.0	4.0
18	5.0	1.0
21	4.0	1.0
24	3.0	0.0

Volume of direct runoff = Area of DRH

$$= 3 \times 60 \times 60 \left[\frac{1}{2}(0+1.5) + \frac{1}{2}(1.5+4) + \frac{1}{2}(4+9) + \frac{1}{2}(9+7.5) + \frac{1}{2}(7.5+4) + \frac{1}{2}(4+2) + \frac{1}{2}(2+1) + \frac{1}{2}(1+0) \right]$$

$$= 31.32 \times 10^4 \text{ m}^3 \textbf{ Ans}$$

Example 6.7 *Compute the ordinates of DRH due to two successive storms of 3–h duration having their rainfall excess as 2.5 and 3.0 cm, respectively. The ordinates of unit hydrograph of 3–h duration are the same as given in example 6.5.*

Solution : In this case the ordinates of resultant DRH are computed by using the principle of superposition. Since, 3 cm ER is after 2.5 cm ER, therefore the DRH due to 3 cm ER is lagged by 3h from the DRH due to 2.5 cm ER. The ordinates of resultant DRH are determined by adding the ordinates of DRH due to 3 cm and 2 cm ER. Computation is shown in following table.

Time *h*	*Ordinates of 3 – h UHG* (m^3/s)	*Ordinates of DRH due to 2.5 cm ER* (m^3/s)	*Ordinates of DRH due to 3 cm lagged by 3 – h* (m^3/s)	*Ordinates of DRH due to 5 cm ER* (m^3/s)
0	0	0.0	0.0	0.0
3	30	75.0	0.0	75.0
6	70	175	90.0	265.0
9	105	262.5	210.0	472.5
12	150	375.0	315.0	690.0
15	180	450.0	450.0	900.0
18	205	512.5	540.0	1052.5
21	170	425.0	615.0	1040.0
24	100	250.0	510.0	760.0
27	85	212.5	300.0	512.5
30	60	150.0	255.0	4050.0
33	50	125.0	180.0	305.0
36	35	87.5	150.0	237.5
39	25	62.5	105.0	167.2
42	15	37.5	75.0	112.0
45	0	0.0	45.0	45.0
			0.0	0.0

Example 6.8 *Compute the ordinates of hydrograph of 5 cm ER, from the given unit hydrograph in example 6.5. Consider the constant base flow as* $10m^3/s$.

Solution : The computation is shown in following table.

Time h	*Ordinates of unit hydrograph (m^3/s)*	*DRH due to 5 cm ER (m^3/s)*	*Base flow (m^3/s)*	*Ordinates of hydrograph (m^3/s)**
(1)	*(2)*	*(3)*	*(4)*	*(5)*
0	0	0	10	10
3	30	150	10	160
6	70	350	10	360
9	105	525	10	535
12	150	750	10	760
15	180	900	10	910
18	205	1025	10	1035
21	170	850	10	860
24	100	500	10	510
27	85	425	10	435
30	60	300	10	310
33	50	250	10	260
36	35	175	10	185
39	25	125	10	135
42	15	75	10	85
45	0	0	10	10

* col (3) + col (4)

Example 6.9 *Derive the flood hydrograph of the watershed due to following storms. The average rate of storm loss is 0.3 cm/h*

Time since start of storm (*h*)	0	3	6	9
Accumulated rainfall (cm)	0	3.0	10.0	15.0

Consider the same unit hydrograph for the wateshed, as given in example 6.5. The base flow at the rate of $25 m^3/s$.

Solution : Computions are shown in following steps.

Step (1) : Determine the ER : In this example, the ER is determined separately for each time interval of the storm. The time interval (Δt) is 3 – *h*. Computation is given below :

Time interval (Δt), *h*	0 – 3	3 – 6	6 – 9
Storm loss @ 0.30 cm/h for 3 hours	0.90	0.90	0.90
Rainfall depth (cm)	3.0	7.0	5.0
Effective rainfall (cm)	2.10	6.10	4.10

Step (2) : Compute the ordinates of DRH due to the ER of 2.10 cm, 6.10 cm and 4.10 cm by using the super position principle.

Step (3) : Compute the ordinates of flood hydrograph. It is the sum of base flow and the ordinate of DRH during a given time interval. The detail compution is shown in following table.

Time (h)	*Ordinates of UHG (m^3/s)*	*DRH due to 2.10 cm ER*	*DRH due to 6.1 cm ER advanced by 3hour*	*DRH due to 4.1 cm ER advanced by 6 hour*	*Ordinates (m^3/s)*	*Base flow (m^3/s)*	*Ordinates of hydrograph (m^3/s)*
(1)	*(2)*	*(3)*	*(4)*	*(5)*	*(6)**	*(7)*	*(8)***
0	0	0	0	0	25 m^3/s	↕ 25 m^3/s	25.0
3	30	63.0	0	0	63.0		88.0
6	70	147.0	183.0	0	330.0		355.0
9	105	220.5	427.0	123.0	770.6		795.5
12	150	315.0	640.5	287.0	1242.5		1267.5
15	180	378.0	915.0	426.4	2961.9		2986.9
18	205	430.5	1098.0	615.0	2143.5		2168.5
21	170	357.0	1250.5	738.0	2345.5		2370.5
24	100	210.0	1037.0	840.5	2087.5		2112.5
27	85	178.5	610.0	697.0	1485.5		1510.5
30	60	126.0	518.5	410.0	1054.5		1079.5
33	50	105.0	366.0	348.5	819.5		844.5
36	35	73.5	305.0	246.0	624.5		649.5
39	25	52.5	213.5	205.0	471.0		496.0
42	15	31.5	152.5	143.5	327.5		352.5
45	0	0	9.5	102.5	194.0		219.0
48			0	61.5	61.5		86.5
51				0	0		25.0

* col (3) + col (4) + col (5)

** col (7) + col (6)

History of unit hydrograph

The relationship between rainfall and runoff of a given storm over the watershed system was studied in the early 1929 by False (1929) who also presented the concept of base flow separation alongwith reduction in rainfall due to various losses. By having all these developments, three years latter

Shereman proposed the successive ordinates of 24-h unit hydrograph. Two years latter, the Boston Society of Civil Engineers (1930) reported that the flood hydrographs afford the best basis for study of drainage basins and also concluded that the base of the flood hydrograph is generally constant for different floods while the peak flows directly vary with the volume of runoff generated by the flood. In the year 1932, Sherman fruther proposed the theory of unit hydrograph. Initially he named the unit hydrograph as the unit-graph, which was defined as the hydrograph of direct runoff resulting from 1 inch of effective rainfall uniformly generated over the basin at a uniform rate during a specified period of time or duration. Originally, he used the term "unit" to denote the specific time period or unit time of the effective rainfall. At that time, Sherman classified the runoff into surface runoff and ground water runoff only ; the recognition of subsurface runoff was not made during his time. Due to this reason, the unit hydrograph was related to the surface runoff only. Later, the concept was fruther applied to derive the runoff hydrograh for any effective rainfall amount.

Modern Unit Hydrograph

It is the unit hydrograph which was developed by Sherman (1932) but in metric system, defined as the hydrograph of direct runoff resulting from unit depth (*i.e.* 1 cm) of excess rainfall occurring uniformly over the basin and at a uniform rate for a specified duration ($D - h$). In this definition the term 'unit' refers to the unit depth of rainfall excess which is usually taken as 1 cm; however it can also be 1 inch or 1 mm. Duration of unit hydrograph is very important parameter, used to denote the unit hydrograph of a specified duration. The ordinate of unit hydrograph is expressed as $u(T, t)$ in which T denotes the duration of effective rainfall producing the direct runoff and t is the any time instant. Based on the duration of effective rainfall (*i.e.* T) the unit hydrograph is specified. For example, the UHG of $6 - h$ duration of rainfall excess is specified as $6 - h$ unit hydrograph; similarly, UHG of 12-h duration of ER is referred as 12-h unit hydrograph. Apart from all these, there are few more important points about the unit hydrograph :

1. Unit hydrograph relates the rainfall excess to the direct runoff, only.
2. Area of unit hydrograph represents the volume of direct runoff resulted by unit depth of rainfall excess over the watershed.
3. Area enclosed by unit hydrograph is equal to unit depth of ER.
4. The rainfall intensity of the storm is equal to $1/D$ for the storm of $D -$ hour duration.
5. The distribution of storm should be uniform, spatially and temporally.

Assumptions of Unit Hydrograph

The following two are the main assumptions for development of unit hydrograph :

1. Time invariance, and
2. Linear response

Time Invariance

It states that the direct runoff due to the rainfall excess over the watershed is time-invariant. In other words, the DRH of given effective rainfall in the watershed is always same; the time of rainfall occurrence has no effect.

Linear Response

This assumption is also known as principle of linearity, principle of super position and principle of proportionality. According to this assumption, the relation between direct runoff and rainfall excess is linear, *i.e.* the direct runoff is directly proportional to the effective rainfall. In other way, it can be expressed as if a given ER of x cm generates y m^3 direct runoff, then $3x$ cm ER will generate $3y$ m^3 direct runoff. The assumption of linear response also states that the ordinates of direct-runoff hydrograph (DRH) of a common base time are directly proportional to the amount of direct runoff represented by the hydrograph. The theory of unit hydrograph based on this assumption is especially known as linear unit-hydrograph theory.

The assumption of linear response is affected under following situations :

1. Occurrence of precipitation in the form of snow fall.
2. Existing of big depressions on the surface of watershed.
3. Larger size of watershed.
4. Non-uniformity in occurrence of precipitation.
5. Significant variations in the watershed characteristics.

Apart from above two assumptions, the followings are also counted as the assumptions of unit hydrograph theory :

1. The effective rainfall is uniformly distributed within its duration.
2. The effective rainfall is uniformly distributed throughout the watershed.
3. The base of direct runoff hydrograph due to effective rainfall of unit duration is constant.

Derivation of Unit Hydrograph

It is accomplished under following steps :

Step (1) : Selection of Hydrograph

Several isolated storm hydrographs resulted from short spells of rainfall excess for the duration ranging from 0.9 to 1.1 D hour are selected for development of unit hydrograph. In case of flood hydrograph to be considered for derivation of unit hydrograph, the following points are essentially taken into consideration :

1. Isolated storms occurring individually, should be preferred.
2. There should be temporal and spatial uniformity in the rainfall.
3. Rainfall duration should be from 1/5 to 1/3 of the basin lag of the watershed.
4. A high rainfall excess producing storm should be preferred.

Normally preferable depth of ER varies from 1 to 4.0 cm.

Step (2) : Separation of Base flow

The base flow separation is performed to determine the volume of direct runoff produced by the selected storm in the watershed. In case of perennial rivers, the base flow is generally off-season flow *i.e.* in summer or winter seasons. On the other hand, in ephemeral or intermittent rivers, there is no appearance of base flow. In such case, the measured runoff data at gauging point of the watershed is considered as the direct runoff, due to the given storm.

There are several methodologies have been developed for base flow separation (section 6.4); any suitable method can be used for it.

Step (3) : Determination of volume of direct runoff

It is determined for computation of rainfall excess of the selected storm. The volume of direct runoff is the leftout runoff after separation of base flow from the storm hydrograph. In other words, it is the enclosed area of the hydrograph above the line of base flow. The formula for computation of volume of direct runoff from the hydrograph is given as,

$$\text{Volume of direct runoff} = 60 \times 60 \times \Delta t \times \text{sum of ordinates of DRH (m}^3/\text{s)}$$

where, Δt = time interval of DRH (hour)

DRH = direct runoff hydrograph.

The DRH is the remaining hydrograph after separating the base flow. The features of DRH are given below :

(*i*) It has its well demarcated boundary *i.e.* start and end point.

(*ii*) It starts from origin (*i.e.* 0, 0 coordinate) and ends somewhere at (*x*, 0) coordinate.

(*iii*) It has no base flow.

(*iv*) It is equivalent to the ER of the given storm.

(*v*) Its area is the volume of direct runoff produced by the storm.

Step (4) : Determination of ER

The ER of selected storm is computed for determining the ordinates of DRH per unit ER or OUHG (*i.e.* ordinate of unit hydrograph), and thus to develop the UHG. The effective rainfall or rainfall excess is given by

$$ER = \frac{\text{Volume of direct runoff}}{\text{Area of watershed}} \qquad \text{...(6.13)}$$

The determined ER should preferably be either in the unit of cm or mm.

Step (5) : Determination of OUHG

It is given by the following formula :

$$\text{OUHG} = \frac{\text{Ordinate of DRH}}{\text{ER}} \qquad \text{...(6.14)}$$

If the computed ER appears to be as 1 cm or 1 mm, then OUHG is the ordinate of DRH as such. The above formula is used, when $ER \neq 1$ cm or 1 mm.

Step (6) : Sketching of UHG

The determined ordinates of OUHG at different time intervals are plotted on linear graph paper, keeping the time intervals on *X*- axis and OUHGs at

Y-axis. The plotted points are joined by smooth line. A precaution should always be kept in mind that the area enclosed by the sketched UHG should represent unit depth of ER. It can be verified by dividing the enclosed area of UHG (*i.e.* volume of direct runoff) with the area of watershed, which should be come to 1. However, if it is not obtained as the unit depth of ER, then some adjustments in sketched UHG is required.

Step (7) : Averaging of unit hydrograph

The unit hydrographs of a given watershed are not identical because of temporal and spatial variations in rainfall. In this situation, it is suggested to average the unit hydrograph. The averaging of UHG is carried out by computing the following components of the graph :

1. Average peak flow (q_{apeak})
2. Average time to peak (q_{atpk})
3. Average base length (b_a)

After determining the average values of peak flow, time to peak and base length, a mean curve of best fit by eye judgment is drawn by passing through the point of average peak and closed on the average base length. A precaution is also taken that the area enclosed by the average unit hydrograph should represent unit depth of rainfall excess, otherwise sketching of curve should be adjusted, accordingly. At the same time, the average ERH is also determined and is drawn in the plot of unit hydrograph to indicate the type and duration of rainfall, considered for developing the unit hydrograph.

Example 6.10 *Derive the ordinates of 3 – h unit hydrograph for a watershed. The measured dischare rates at the outlet of watershed are given below. The area of watershed is 500 sq km.*

Time (h)	– 3	0	3	6	9	12	15	18	21	24	27	30
Discharge (m^3/s)	10	10	10	37.0	50	75	115	110	101	79	65	61
Time (h)	33	36	39	42	45	48	51	54	57	60	63	66
Discharge (m^3/s)	57	50	47	45	40	33	30	25	17	15	10	10

Solution : The steps-wise computations are given below :

Step (1): Compute the ordinates of DRH — It is done by determining the base flow and then separting it from the ordinates of given hydrograph. In this example, the base flow is $10m^3/s$.

Step (2) : Determine the ER — The depth of ER is computed by dividing the total volume of direct runoff with the area of watershed. It is given as under :

$$\text{ER(cm)} = \frac{3 \times 60\,(\sum \text{ of ordinates of DRH})}{\text{Area of watershed}}$$

$$= \frac{3 \times 60 \times 60 \times 282}{500 \times (10)^6}\ \text{m} = 0.0186 \text{ or } 1.86 \text{ cm}$$

Step (3) : Compute the ordinates of UHG — It is computed by dividing the ODRH with ER.

The detail computations are shown in following table.

Time h	*Ordinate of hydrograph* (m^2/s)	*Base flow* (m^3/s)	*Ordinate of DRH* (m^3/s)	*Ordinate of 3 – h unit hydrograph* (m^3/s)
(1)	(2)	*(3)*	*(4)*	*(5)**
– 3	10		0	0
0	10		0	0
3	10	↑	0	0
6	37		27	14.52
9	50		40	21.51
12	75		65	34.95
15	115		105	56.95
18	110		100	53.76
21	101	10 m^3/s	91	48.92
24	79		69	37.10
27	65		55	29.57
30	61		51	27.42
33	57		47	25.27
36	50		40	21.51
39	47		37	19.89
42	45	↓	35	18.82
45	40		30	16.13
48	33		23	12.37
51	30		20	10.75
54	25		15	8.06
57	17		7	3.76
60	15		5	2.69
63	10		0	0
66	10		0	0

* col (4) ÷ 1.86

Example 6.11 *Drive a 9– h unit hydrograph from the ordinates of 3 – h unit hydrograph given in example 6.5*

Solution : Computation are shown in following table.

Time h	*Ordinate of U.G.H. (m^3/s)*	*Ordinate of 3 – h UHG Lagged by*		*Ordinate of DRH due to 3 cm ER in 9 – h (m^3/s)*	*Ordinate of 9 – h UHG (m^3/s)*
		3 – h	6 – h		
(1)	*(2)*	*(3)*	*(4)*	*(5)*	*(6)*
0	0	0	0	0	0
3	30	0	0	30	10
6	70	30	0	100	33.33
9	105	70	30	205	68.33
12	150	105	70	325	108.33
15	180	150	105	435	145.00
18	205	180	150	535	178.33
21	170	205	180	555	185.00
24	100	170	205	475	158.33
27	85	100	170	355	118.33
30	60	85	100	245	81.67
33	50	60	85	195	65.00
36	35	50	60	145	48.33
39	25	35	50	110	36.67
42	15	25	35	75	25.00
45	0	15	25	40	13.33
48		0	15	15	5.00
51			0	0	0

Development of Unit Hydrograph from Complex Storm

The derivation of unit hydrograph from a simple hydrograph is easy. But when suitable and simple hydrograph is not available, then the runoff data of complex storm is used to develop the unit hydrograph. The method of successive approximation (Collin, 1939) is used for this purpose. The general formula for the ordinate of unit hydrograph from complex storm is given as under :

$$Q_n = \sum_{m=1}^{n \leq M} R_m \, U_{n-m+1} \qquad ...(6.15)$$

where, m = numbers of successive rainfall excesses

n = numbers of runoff observations

R = rainfall excess

U = ordinate of unit hydrograph

Q = ordinate of composite/complex DRH

The set of equations for different time periods can be written as :

$$\begin{aligned} Q_1 &= R_1u_1 \\ Q_2 &= R_1u_2 + R_2u_1 \\ Q_3 &= R_1u_3 + R_2u_2 + R_3u_1 \\ Q_4 &= R_1u_4 + R_2u_3 + R_3u_2 + R_4u_1 \\ Q_5 &= R_1u_5 + R_2u_4 + R_3u_3 + R_4u_2 + R_5u_1 \end{aligned} \quad ...(6.16)$$

By solving the above equations (i.e. 6.16), the values of ordinates of unit hydrograph for successive time intervals can be determinined. In this method, the derived unit hydrograph can show the erratic variation and even can have negative values, also. This kind of variation is mainly due to non-linearity in the effective rainfall-direct runoff relationship in the watershed.

Computation of OUHG by Matrix Method

Various sub-equations shown in equation 6.16 can also be solved by the method of matrix, described as under :

$$\begin{bmatrix} R_1 & 0 & 0 & \ldots & 0 & 0 & \ldots & 0 & 0 \\ R_2 & R_1 & 0 & \ldots & 0 & 0 & \ldots & 0 & 0 \\ R_3 & R_2 & R_1 & \ldots & 0 & 0 & \ldots & 0 & 0 \\ \cdot & & & & \cdot & & & \cdot & \\ \cdot & & & & \cdot & & & \cdot & \\ R_m & R_{m-1} & R_{m-2} & \ldots & R_1 & 0 & \ldots & 0 & 0 \\ 0 & R_m & R_{m-1} & \ldots & R_2 & R_1 & \ldots & 0 & 0 \\ \cdot & & & & \cdot & & & \cdot & \\ \cdot & & & & \cdot & & & \cdot & \\ \cdot & & & & \cdot & & & & \\ 0 & 0 & 0 & \ldots & 0 & 0 & \ldots & R_m & R_{m-1} \\ 0 & 0 & 0 & \ldots & 0 & 0 & \ldots & 0 & R_m \end{bmatrix} \begin{bmatrix} u_1 \\ u_2 \\ u_3 \\ \cdot \\ \cdot \\ \cdot \\ u_{n-m+1} \end{bmatrix} = \begin{bmatrix} Q_1 \\ Q_2 \\ Q_3 \\ \cdot \\ \cdot \\ Q_m \\ Q_{m+1} \\ \cdot \\ \cdot \\ \cdot \\ Q_{n-1} \\ Q_n \end{bmatrix}$$

or

$$[R] \cdot [u] = [Q] \quad ...(6.17)$$

For the given values of rainfall excess (R) and discharge (Q), the solution of above equation is given as under :

$$[R]\,[\underline{u}] = [\overline{Q}] \quad ...(6.18)$$

or

$$\overline{Q}_n = R_nu_1 + R_{n-1}u_2 + R_{n-2}\,u_3 + ... R_{n-m+1}\,u_m \quad ...(6.19)$$

$$(n = 1 \ldots N)$$

Derivation of Unit Hydrograph for different Durations

The derivation of unit hydrograph for different durations of effective rainfall is performed as per requirement, for which gauged data is essential. However, if there is no adequate database, then from the unit hydrograph of any isolated storm hydrograph, it can be derived by using the following two methods :

1. Method of superposition and
2. S-curve method

Superposition Method

This method is used, when a unit hydrograph for the duration as multiple of the duration of given unit hydrograph is required to develop. In other words if a $D-h$ unit hydrograph is available for the given watershed and it is required to develop $nD-h$ unit hydrograph, where n is the integer multiple *i.e.* $n = 1, 2, 3, 4$ ..., then it is carried out by using the method of superposition. The following steps are followed :

1. Take the $D-h$ unit hydrograph of the watershed, suppose it is of $3-h$ duration.
2. Decide the multiple duration (n) for which the new unit hydrograph is required to develop. Let it is $9h$ *i.e.* $n = 3$.
3. Lag the given unit hydrograph at the interval of 3 hours, two times. Or, draw the given unit hydrograph two times lagged by 3 hours. Number of lag is equal to $n - 1$. Therefore, in this case, it is 2.
4. Add the ordinates of all three unit hydrographs. The obtained ordinates are the ordinates of direct runoff hydrograph for 3 cm rainfall excess of 9 hour duration.
5. Calculate the ordinates of unit hydrograph of $9-h$ duration by dividing the ordinates of DRH of 3 cm rainfall excess obtained in step (4) with 3.
6. Plot the ordinates of UHG, determined in step (5) on linear graph paper. Care should always be taken that the area enclosed by the unit hydrograph should represent unit depth of rainfall excess.

Example 6.11 explains the procedure.

S-curve Method

The demerit of superposition method is that, it can not compute the unit hydrograph for the fraction of duration of rainfall excess of given unit hydrograph. The *S*-curve method is used for deriving such unit hydrograph. The *S*-curve is also known as summation curve or simply *S*- hydrograph. Over the watershed, this kind of hydrograph is produced by continuous occurrence of effective rainfall at constant rate for an infinite period. Analytically, it is derived by summation of an infinite series of $D-h$ unit hydrographs lagged by $D-h$ duration. The ordinate of *S*- curve at any given time is the sum of all the ordinates of different $D-h$ unit hydrographs occuring at that time. The plotting of the ordinates on a linear graph paper results the *S*- curve (Fig. 6.14). A *S*- curve reveals the following points :

(*i*) It is the sum of a series of $D-h$ unit hydrographs.

(*ii*) It has initial steep portion, which attains maximum equilibrium discharge at the time equal to base width (*i.e.* time base) of the first unit hydrograph.

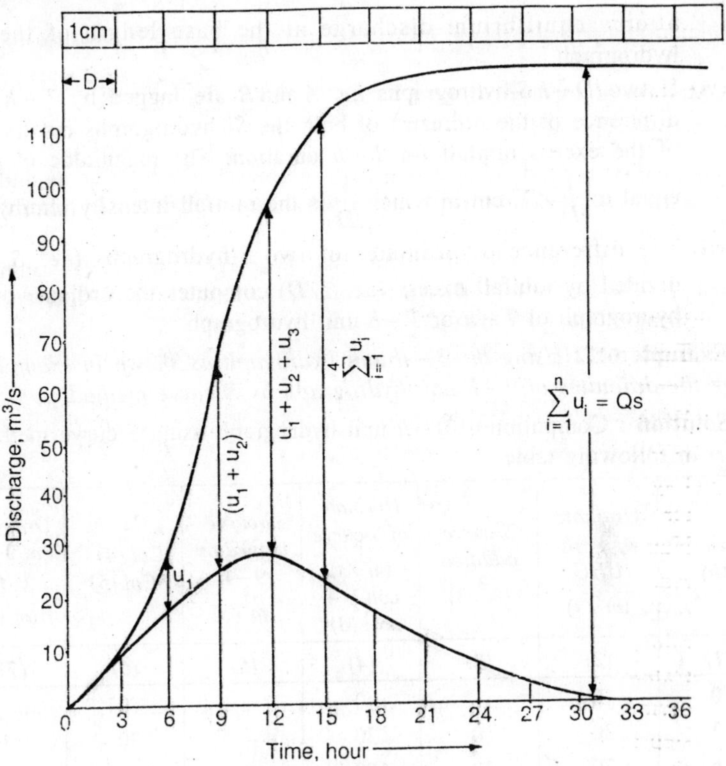

Fig. 6.14

(*iii*) The average intensity of effective rainfall of *S*-curve is given by

$$I_{aer} = \frac{1}{D} \text{ cm/h} \quad ...(6.20)$$

(*iv*) The equilibrium discharge of *S*-curve is equal to

$$Q_{eq} = \left(\frac{A}{D} \times 10^4\right) \text{m}^3/\text{h} \quad ...(6.21)$$

or

$$2.778 \times \frac{A}{D} \text{ m}^3/\text{h}$$

where,

Q_{eq} = equilibrium discharge, m^3/h; it represents the maximum rate of discharge at the rainfall intensity of $1/D$ cm/h

A = area of the watershed, km^2

D = duration of effective rainfall of the given unit hydrograph, hours

(*v*) The *S*-curve is found in oscillating nature at the top around the equilibrium value, which is mainly due to magnification and accumulation of errors in the hydrograph. To rectify this nature of *S*-curve, an average smooth curve is drawn in such a way that it attains equilibrium discharge at the base length of the unit hydrograph.

(*vi*) If two $D-h$ *S*-hydrographs *i.e.* *A* and *B* are lagged by $T-h$, then difference of the ordinates of both the *S*- hydrographs results DRH of the excess rainfall for $T-h$ duration. The magnitude of *ER* is equal to $\frac{1}{D} \times T$, cm in which $\frac{1}{D}$ is the rainfall intensity (cm/h).

(*vii*) The difference of ordinates of two *S*-hydrographs (*i.e.* $S_A - S_B$) divided by rainfall excess (*i.e.* T/D) computes the ordinate of unit hydrograph of $T-h$ or $T-h$ unit hydrograph.

Example 6.12 *Using the 3 – h unit hydrogaph as shown in example 6.5 derive the ordinates of 9 – h unit hydrograph by S curve method.*

Solution : Compution of 9 – *h* unit hydrograph using *S* curve method is shown in following table.

Time (h)	*Ordinate of 3 – h UHG (m^3/s)*	*S-curve addition (m^3/s)*	*Ordinate of S-curve (m^3/s) col(2) + col (3)*	*S-curve lagged by 9 – h (m^3/s)*	*Col (4) - Col (5)*	*Ordinates of 9 – h UHG (m^3/s)*
(1)	*(2)*	*(3)*	*(4)*	*(5)*	*(6)*	*(7)**
0	0	—	0	—	0	0
3	30	0	30	—	30	10
6	70	30	100	—	100	33.33
9	105	100	205	0	205	68.33
12	150	205	355	30	325	108.33
15	180	355	535	100	435	145.0
18	205	535	740	205	535	178.33
21	170	740	910	355	555	185.0
24	100	910	1010	535	475	158.33
27	85	1010	1095	740	355	118.33
30	60	1095	1105	910	195	65.00
33	50	1155	1205	1010	195	65.00
36	35	1205	1240	1095	145	48.33
39	25	1240	1265	1105	160	53.33
42	15	1265	1280	1205	75	26.00
45	0	1280	1280	1240	40	13.00
48		0	1280	1280	1265	15
51				1280	0	0
54				1280	0	0

* col (6)/9/3

Duration of Unit Hydrograph

As per assumption of unit hydrograph, the rainfall excess is occrued uniformly over the entire watershed during unit hydrograph duration (*D*). Keeping this in view, the ideal duration for a unit hydrograph is that during which there is very small fluctuation in the rainfall intensity and also there is insignificant effect on the resulting runoff. The watershed tends to develop damping effect on the fluctuation of rainfall intensity to generate the runoff. This effect can be minimized by adopting a shorter duration of unit hydrograph for smaller watersheds and vice-versa. Generally, the duration of unit hydrograph ranges from 1/5 to 1/3 of the basin lag. The 6-hour duration is found satisfactory for the watershed of the area 250 sq. km and for the watershed area more than 1200 km^2, $12 - h$ duration is preferred.

The choice of unit hydrograph duration also depends on the length of available rainfall record. However, the choice is not much on the daily rainfall record. An approximation about duration of unit hydrograph can be made based on the following parameters :

(*i*) time of rise

(*ii*) basin lag and

(*iii*) time of concentration.

The duration of unit hydrograph should not exceed the atleast value of above parameters. The duration of UHG equal to 1/4 of the basin lag is the best.

Limitations of Unit Hydrograph

Various limitations of unit hydrograph are grouped in two parts *i.e.*

1. **Limitations Regarding Assumptions of U.H.G. :** These are as follows :

(*a*) The unit hydrograph assumes that the rainfall excess should be uniformly distributed over the watershed in addition to constant intensity of rainfall excess within its duration. This assumption is never satisfied in the watershed during any storm. In this way, it poses a limitation. However, non-uniformity in areal distribution of rainfall and variations in rainfall intensity within storm duration are very common. With all these limitations the unit hydrograph can still be developed, provided that the areal distribution of rainfall must be consistent amongst different storm events.

(*b*) Unit hydrograph also involves the limitation about the size of watershed. In a very large size watershed, the centre of storm is likely to vary from storm to storm, causing variations in DRHs. It poses the errors in development of unit hydrograph. The watershed ranging from 200 ha to 5000 sq km is found satisfactory for development of unit hydrograph. In large watersheds, the total area is divided into different sub-watersheds and individual DRH is developed for each of them. These DRHs are again routed through their respective channels to result a composite DRH at the outlet.

2. **Other Limitations**

(*a*) The precipitation should always be in the form of rainfall. Snow or other solid forms of precipitation do not result satisfactory unit hydrograph.

(*b*) The watershed should not consist of large size storages *i.e.* tanks, ponds etc. because these affect the linearity assumption of the unit hydrograph.

(*c*) A decidedly non-uniform precipitation results inaccurate unit hydrograph.

Variation in base of hydrograph to the tune of ± 20% and ± 10% in the discharge is generally considered as the acceptable range for the unit hydrograph.

Uses of Unit Hydrograph

The unit hydrograph shows the relationship between effective rainfall hyetograph (ERH) and direct runoff hydrograph (DRH) for a given watershed. This relationship is very useful for approximation of amount of direct runoff likely to be generated due to rain storm from the watershed. Besides, it is also useful for following purposes :

1. Development of flood hydrographs for extreme rainfall events, which can be used for design and construction of hydraulic structures, such as culverts, bridges etc.
2. It is useful for extension of flood-flow records based on the available rainfall database.
3. Flood forecasting and development of warning system about occurrence of floods in the watershed can also be done by using the unit hydrograph as a tool.

Distribution Graph

This graph was introduced by Bernard in the year 1935 which is the conversion of composite unit hydrograph. It is treated as a special type of unit hydrograph, in which ordinates are in the form of percentage of total runoff in successive periods of equal time intervals of $D-h$ (Fig. 6.15). The ordinates of distribution graph represent the volume per unit storm period rather the rate of discharge, resulting into stepped form of this graph. The successive percentages are applied in turn to the volumes of rainfall excess in each unit storm period, resulting into an equal number of overlapping hydrographs. The direct runoff hydrograph (DRH) is obtained by adding the coinciding ordinates of the distribution graph, *i.e.* in the same way as unit hydrograph.

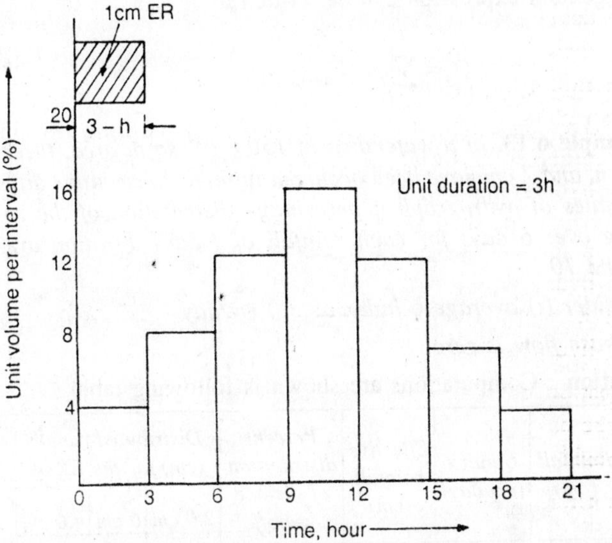

Fig. 6.15

Let, $P_1, P_2 \ldots$ are the volumes of rainfall excess in the successive unit storm periods and $u_1, u_2 \ldots$ are the percentage of the distribution graph, then discharge volumes $Q_1, Q_2 \ldots$ of each unit storm are given as :

P_1	P_2	P_3	P_4	P_5	P_6	P_7	P_8
$u_1 P_1$	$u_2 P_1$	$u_3 P_1$	$u_4 P_1$	$u_5 P_1$		,	
	$u_1 P_2$	$u_2 P_2$	$u_3 P_2$	$u_4 P_2$	$u_5 P_2$	,	
		$u_1 P_3$	$u_2 P_3$	$u_3 P_3$	$u_4 P_3$	$u_5 P_3$,	
			$u_1 P_4$	$u_2 P_4$	$u_3 P_4$	$u_4 P_4$	$u_5 P_4$
				$u_1 P_5$	$u_2 P_5$	$u_3 P_5$	$u_4 P_5$
					$u_1 P_6$	$u_2 P_6$	$u_3 P_6$
Q_1	Q_2	Q_3	Q_4	Q_5	Q_6	Q_7	Q_8

The discharge values for successive unit time intervals are as follows :

$$Q_1 = u_1 P_1$$
$$Q_2 = u_2 P_1 + u_1 P_2$$
$$Q_3 = u_3 P_1 + u_2 P_2 + u_1 P_3$$
$$Q_4 = u_4 P_1 + u_3 P_2 + u_2 P_3 + u_1 P_4$$
$$Q_5 = u_5 P_1 + u_4 P_2 + u_3 P_3 + u_2 P_4 + u_1 P_5$$
$$Q_6 = 0 + u_5 P_2 + u_4 P_3 + u_3 P_4 + u_2 P_5 + u_1 P_6$$
$$Q_7 = 0 + 0 + u_5 P_3 + u_4 P_4 + u_3 P_5 + u_2 P_6$$
$$Q_8 = 0 + 0 + 0 + u_5 P_4 + u_4 P_5 + u_3 P_6$$

The general expression can be written as

$$Q_n = \sum_{i=1}^{n} u_i \, P_{n-(i-1)} \qquad ...(6.22)$$

Example 6.13. *In a watershed of 150×10^4 sq m area, three rainfalls of 5 cm, 3 cm and 7 cm have been occurred in three consecutive days. Determine the ordinates of hydrograph if percentage distribution of the surface runoff extending over 6 days for each rainfall of 1-days duration are 10, 25, 45, 30, 15 and 10.*

Consider (i) average φ index as 3.0 cm/day

(ii) base flow is zero.

Solution : Computations are shown is following table.

Time interval (days)	*Rainfall (cm)*	*φ-index (cm/day)*	*Effective rainfall (cm)*	*Percent distribution of surface runoff*	*Distributed runoff (cm) for the ER of*			*Runoff*	
					2.0 cm	*0 cm*	*4.0 cm*	*cm*	*m^3/s**
0 – 1	5.0	3.0	2.0	10	0.2	0	0	0.20	3.472
1 – 2	3.0	3.0	0.0	25	0.5	0	0	0.50	8.680
2 – 3	7.0	3.0	4.0	45	0.9	0	0.4	1.30	22.569
3 – 4				30	0.6	0	1.0	1.60	27.777
4 – 5				15	0.3	0	1.8	2.10	36.548
5 – 6				10	0.2	0	1.2	1.40	24.305
6 – 7				0	0	0	0.6	0.60	10.416
7 – 8							0.4	0.40	6.944
8 – 9									0

* $1\text{cm runoff} = \dfrac{150 \times 10^4 \times 1}{24 \times 3600 \times 100} = 0.17361 \text{ m}^3/\text{s} \times 10^{-2}$

Specific features of Distribution Hydrograph

These are as follows :

1. It is a $D-h$ unit hydrograph, which discharge values are in dimensionless form *i.e.* percent of the total runoff volume.
2. This hydrograph is free from the limitations of size of watershed.
3. When unit hydrographs of different sizes of watershed with identical physiographic characteristics are compared, then their peak discharges vary; although total runoff volume is the same (*i.e.* 1 cm) over the watershed. Also, the base length increases with increase in the area of watershed, because runoff takes longer time to reach at the outlet in larger size watershed.

4. When discharge rates are converted into dimensionless form, the magnitude of peak discharge gets increase which is due to the reason that the discharge rate becomes free from the effects of size of the watershed.
5. The unit hydrographs of two watersheds of different sizes can be compared in the form of their distribution graph.

S-Hydrograph of Distribution Graph

A *S*-hydrograph of distribution graph is the plot of cumulative percentage of total runoff volume verses time by keeping on ordinate and abssica, respectively. This hydrograph is used for determination of basin lag or lag time of the watershed for a given flood. The basin lag refers to the time taken by the flood to get drained from the watershed. Sometimes, it is also taken as the time difference between centroid of ERH and hydrograph of surface runoff. From summation hydrograph, it is computed as the time form beginning of the surface runoff to the time of 50% cumulative runoff. It shown in Fig. 6.16.

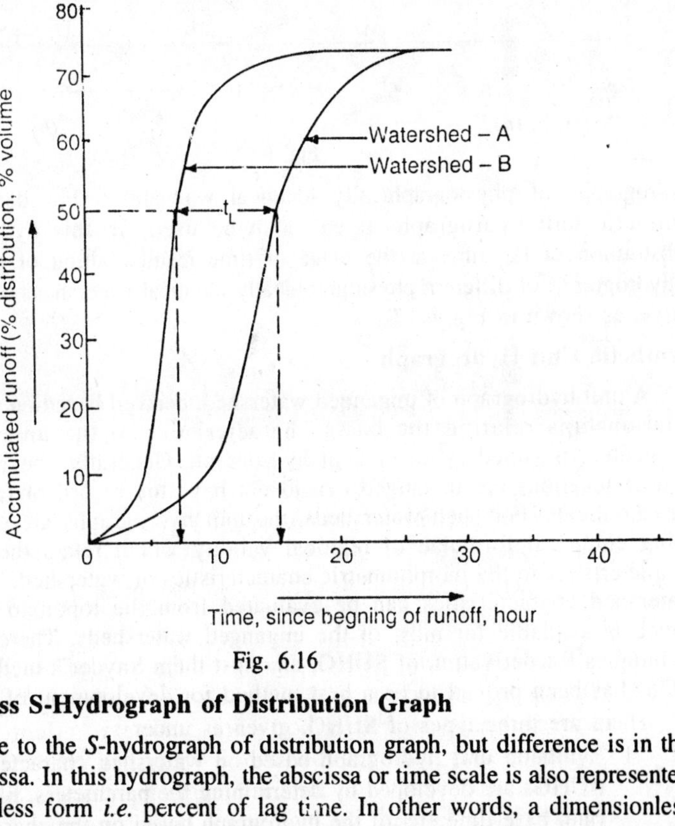

Fig. 6.16

Dimensionless S-Hydrograph of Distribution Graph

It is same to the *S*-hydrograph of distribution graph, but difference is in the scale of abscissa. In this hydrograph, the abscissa or time scale is also represented in dimensionless form *i.e.* percent of lag ti me. In other words, a dimensionless *S*-hydrograph is the plot of accumilated runoff volume on ordinate and percent of lag time on abscissa. This hydrograph is used for comparison of unit

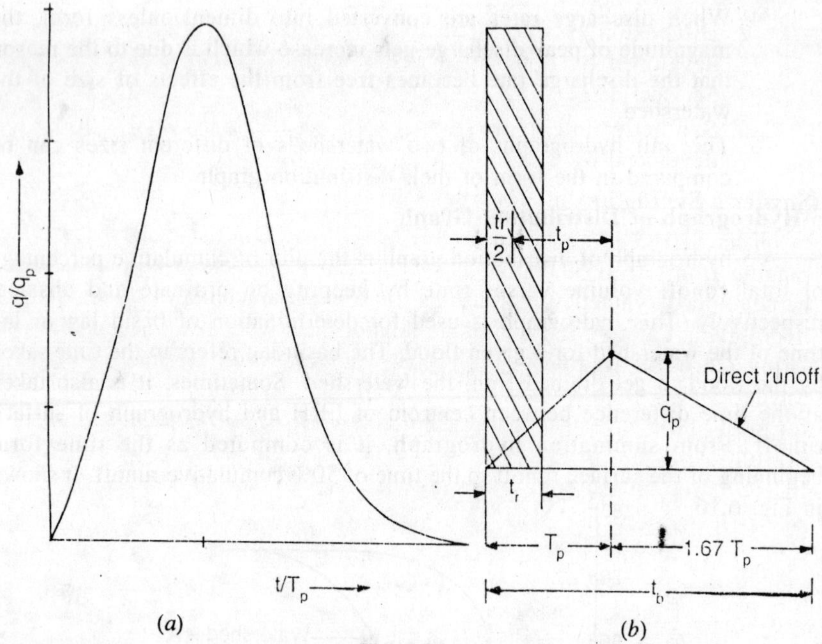

Fig. 6.17

hydrographs of physiographically identical watersheds. For development of synthetic unit hydrographs it can also be used. In this hydrograph, the substitution of lag time at the place of time results falling of dimensionless *S*-hydrographs of different physiographically identical watersheds over the single curve, as shown in Fig. 6.17.

Synthetic Unit Hydrcgraph

A unit hydrograph of ungauqed watershed, derived based on the empirical relationships relating the basin characteristics to the unit hydrograph parameters is called synthetic unit hydrograph. Generally, the watersheds at remote locations are ungauged *i.e.* do not have the record of rainfall-runoff measurements. For such watersheds, the unit hydrographs are developed by using empirical formulae of regional validity which relate the hydrograph characteristics to the morphometric characteristics of watershed. The requisite watershed characteristics can be evaluated from the topomap of the area, which is available for most of the unganged watersheds. There are various techniques for derivation of SUHG, amongst them Snyder's method (Snyder, 1938) has been proved to be a best method for development of SUHG.

There are three types of SUHG, given as under :

1. Synthetic unit hydrograph based on watershed characteristics. Such SUHGs are developed by determining the parameters, like peak flow rate, base time etc. of the hydrograph based on the characteristics of the watershed. The methodology suggested by Snyder (1938) and Gray (1961) falls under this category of SUHG.

2. Dimensionless Synthetic unit hydrograph. This hydrograph was developed by the United States Department of Soil Conservation Service (1972).
3. Synthetic unit hydrograph based on the watershed storage, was developed by Clark (1943).

Snyder's Synthetic Unit Hydrograph

This SUHG is named after Snyder (1938). For the watersheds of size ranging from 30 to 30,000 sq km located in Appalachian highlands (USA), he developed synthetic relationships for some characteristics of standard unit hydrograph. Lateron, few additional relationships were also developed by U.S. Army Corps of Engineers (1964). By incorporating all the relations, the Snyder SUHG took a latest form of SUHG, which validity has been found for most of the watersheds, throughout the world. The Snyder method consists of following sets of relationships for computing different components of SUHG based on morphometric characteristics of the watershed :

1. **Basin Lag (t_p)** : It is the time interval (hour) between the mid-point of unit rainfall excess and the peak of the unit hydrograph. The lag time is also called basin lag. It is an important characteristics of the watershed affecting the hydrograph due to a given storm. The t_p is determined based on the physical characteristics of the watershed, such as size, length, stream density and status of vegetations. The formula for its computation is given as under :

$$t_p = C_t \, (L \cdot L_{ca})^{0.30} \qquad ...(6.23)$$

where, t_p = basin lag (hour)

C_t = regional constant. It is the function of slope of watershed and storage.

The value of C_t is determined for gauged watershed and is applied for derivation of SUHG for ungauged watershed which is meteorologically and morphometrically identical to the gauged watershed. The C_t values, determined by different researchers/watersheds are given as under :

1. 1.35 to 1.65 (according to Snyder)
2. 0.30 to 6.0 (reported by Sokolov, 1976)
3. 0.65 (Himalayan catchments of Ramganga river)

L = length of main water course (km), measured from the outlet to the watershed divide.

L_{ca} = distance (km) from the outlet to a point on the stream opposite to the centroid of watershed.

2. **Standard duration of effective rainfall (t_r)** : It is required to determine the peak flow rate for derivation of SUHG. Snyder adopted following formula for its computation :

$$t_r = \frac{t_p}{5.5} \qquad ...(6.24)$$

3. **Peak discharge** (Q_{ps}) : The formula for computation of peak discharge for standard duration (t_r) is given as under :

$$Q_{ps} = \frac{2.78\ C_p \cdot A}{t_p} \qquad \text{...(6.25)}$$

where, C_p = regional constant, depends on the retention and storage capacities of the watershed. The values reported by different investigators/or for different catchments are as follows :

(*a*) 0.56 to 0.69 (reported by Snyder)

(*b*) 0.31 to 0.93 (reported by others)

(*c*) 0.94 (for Himalayan catchments of India)

A = area of the watershed (km^2)

4. **Non-standard duration of effective rainfall :** It is the duration of effective rainfall other than standard duration. The non-standard duration of effective rainfall can be computed by using the following formula :

$$t_{pr} = t_p\left(\frac{t_R - t_r}{4}\right)$$

$$= \frac{21}{22} t_p + \frac{t_R}{4} \qquad \text{...(6.26)}$$

where, t_{pr} = modified basin lag for non–standard duration of effective rainfall

t_R = non–standard duration of effective rainfall ; it can be any time instead of standard duration (t_r).

It is basically the modified formula of basin lag.

At non-standard duration of effective rainfall, the peak discharge gets change. Accordingly the modified formula for new peak discharge is given by

$$Q_{pr} = \frac{2.78\ C_p \cdot A}{t_{pr}}$$

in which, Q_{pr} is the rate of peak discharge (m^3/s) for non-standard duration of ER.

5. **Time base** (T_b) : It represents the duration of direct runoff flow. Snyder suggested following formula for computation of time base :

(*i*) $t_b = 3 + \frac{t_p}{8}$ (*days*) (for standard-duration) ...(6.27)

$72 + 3t_p$ (hour)

(*ii*) $t_b = 3 + \frac{t_{pr}}{8}$ (days) (for non-standard duration) ...(6.28)

$= 72 + 3t_{pr}$ (hour)

The above formulae estimate a reasonable value of time base (t_b) for large watersheds while for small watershed they estimate quite high value of T_b.

Taylor and Schwartz Butler S.C., (1957) have also reported the following formula for computation of time base of SUHG :

$$t_b = 5\left(t_{PR} + \frac{t_R}{2}\right) \text{hours} \quad \text{...(6.29)}$$

For small Indian watersheds, Mutreja (1986) suggested the following formula for T_b

$$t_b = (t_{peak})\ (3 \text{ to } 5) \quad \text{...(6.30)}$$

6. **Unit hydrograph shape :** After determining the values of basin lag (t_p), standard or non-standard duration of effective rainfall (t_r or t_{pr}), peak discharge for standard or non-standard duration of effective rainfall (Q_p or Q_{pr}) and time base (t_b), the sketching of SUHG can be done, but there is possibilities of investment of time for adjusting the shape of SUHG to represent the enclosed area of graph equivalent to unit depth of effective rainfall. To avoid this happening and for giving a proper shape of SUHG, the U.S. Corps of Engineers has developed following sets of formulae for determining the widths of SUHG at 50 and 75% of the peak discharge rate.

(*i*) Width of SUHG at 50% peak flow rate (W_{50})

$$W_{50} = \frac{5.87}{q^{1.08}} \quad \text{...(6.31)}$$

(*ii*) Width of SUHG at 75% peak flow rate (W_{75})

$$W_{75} = \frac{W_{50}}{1.75} \quad \text{...(6.32)}$$

in which q is the peak discharge per unit area of the watershed ($m^3/s/sq\ km$)

The Snyder's SUHG is shown in Fig. 6.18.

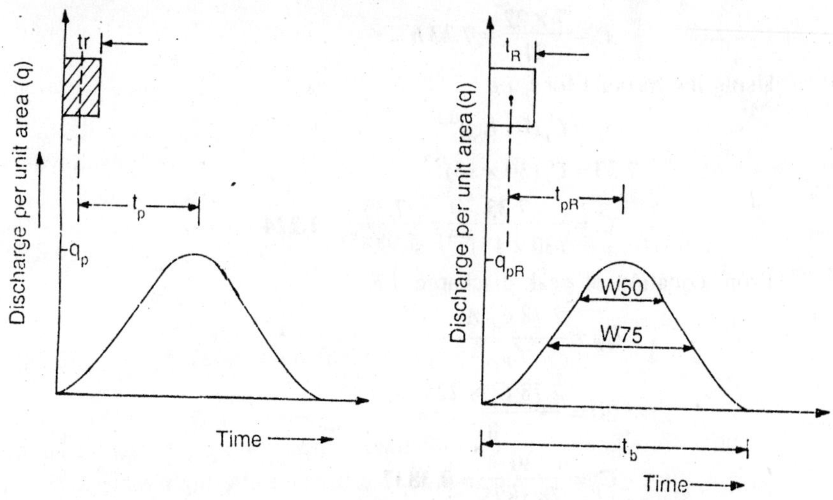

Fig. 6.18

Example 6.14. *Drive the S.U.H.G. of watershed A, if peak discharge of 4–h unit hydrograph of watershed B is 30 m^3/s; and its time to peak is 10 hour. The other details of watersheds are as follows :*

Watershed–A	*Watershed–B*
$L = 35$ km	$L = 30$ km
$L_{ca} = 18$ km	$L_{ca} = 13$ km
$A = 300$ km^2	$A = 225$ km^2

Solution : The SUHG is derived by using Snyder's method. Essential computations are as follows :

(1) **Computation of constants C_p and C_t** : These two are determined with the help of available hydrological data of gauged watershed (*i.e.* watershed–B), *i.e.*

$$t_R = 4 \text{ hour}$$

Time to peak from begining of ER $= \frac{t_R}{2} + t'_p$

$$\therefore \quad 10 = \frac{4}{2} + t'_p$$

$$\text{or} \quad t'_P = 8 \text{ hour}$$

t'_p is also equal to

$$\frac{21}{22} t_p + \frac{t_R}{4}$$

Thus, $$8 = \frac{21}{22} t_p + \frac{4}{4}$$

$$\therefore \quad t_p = \frac{7 \times 22}{21} = \mathbf{7.33}\ \boldsymbol{h}$$

Using the formula for t_p *i.e.*

$$t_p = C_t (L \,.\, L_{ca})^{0.3}$$

$$7.33 = C_t (30 \times 13)^{0.3}$$

$$\therefore \quad C_t = \frac{7.33}{(30 \times 13)^{0.3}} = \frac{7.33}{5.9885} = \mathbf{1.224}$$

From equation of peak discharge, *i.e.*

$$Q_P = \frac{2.78\, C_P\, A}{t'_P}$$

$$30 = \frac{2.78\, C_p \times 225}{8}$$

$$\therefore \quad C_p = \frac{30}{78.1875} = \mathbf{0.3837}$$

(2) **Computation of S U H G parameters of watershed—A :**

(*a*) Time to peak $(t_P) = C_t (L \, . \, L_{ca})^{0.3}$

$$= 1.224\,(35 \times 18)^{0.3}$$

$$= \mathbf{8.464\ hour}$$

(*b*) Duration of ER $(t_r) = \dfrac{t_p}{5.5}$

$$= \frac{8.464}{5.5}$$

$$= \mathbf{1.54\ hour}$$

Considering $t_R = 4h$, *i.e.* for $4 - h$ unit hydrograph,

$$t'_P = t_P \frac{21}{22} + \frac{t_R}{4}$$

or

$$8.464 \frac{21}{22} + \frac{4}{4}$$

$\therefore$

$$t'_P = 9.08\ h$$

(*c*) Peak discharge $(Q_P) = \dfrac{2.78 \times 0.3837 \times 300}{9.08}$

$$= 35.243\ \text{m}^3/\text{s}$$

(*d*) W_{50} and W_{75} : $W_{50} = \dfrac{5.87}{\left(\dfrac{35.243}{300}\right)^{1.08}}$ hour

$$= \frac{5.87}{0.09898} = \mathbf{59.30\ hours}$$

$$W_{75} = \frac{W_{50}}{1.75}$$

$$= \frac{59.30}{1.75} = \mathbf{33.89\ hours}$$

(*e*) Time base of hydrograph

$$t_b = 72 + 3\,t'_P$$

$$= 72 + 3 \times 9.08 = \mathbf{99.24\ hours}$$

or

$$t_b = 5\left(t'_P + \frac{t_R}{2}\right)$$

$$= 5\left(9.08 + \frac{4}{2}\right) = \mathbf{55.4\ hours}$$

(*f*) sketching of SIUHG : It is done by considering the computed parameters of SUHG in such way that the area enclosed by the curve should represent unit depth of ER.

Espey, Altman and Graves SUHG

Espey, Altman and Graves (1977) developed a set of generalized equations for development of 10-minute SUHG based on the study of 41 watersheds with the area ranging from 0.014 to 15 sq. miles. The equations are given as under :

1. **Time of rise to the peak of the SUHG** (T_P). It is given by the following formula :

$$T_P = 3.1\, L^{0.23}\, S^{-0.25}\, I^{-0.18}\, \phi^{1.57} \quad ...(6.33)$$

where, L = distance (feet) along the main channel, measured from outlet to the upstream boundary of watershed

S = channel slope (feet per feet); it is given by

$= H/0.8\, L$

H = elevation difference between A and B, in which A is the point on the channel bottom at the distance of 0.2 L downstream from the u/s watershed boundary and B is the point on the channel bottom at the d/s point being taken into consideration.

I = percent impervious area in the watershed, generally taken as 5% of the area of undeveloped watershed.

ϕ = watershed conveyance factor (dimensionless) which is the function of percent impervious area and roughness.

The above formula estimates the T_P in minute.

2. **Peak flow** (Q_P) **:** It is given by the following formula :

$$Q_P = 31.62 \times 10^3\, A^{0.96} \cdot T_P^{-1.07} \quad ...(6.34)$$

in which, A is the area of watershed (sq miles). This formula estimates the value of peak flow in cfs/inch.

3. **Time base** (T_B) **:** It can be computed by using the following formula :

$$T_B = 125.89 \times 10^3\, A \cdot Q_P^{-0.95} \quad ...(6.35)$$

It computes the value of time base in minute.

4. **Width of graph :** The widths of unit hydrograph at 50 and 75% of Q_p are given as under :

(*a*) $W_{50} = 16.22 \times 10^3\, A^{0.93} \cdot Q_P^{-0.92}$ ...(6.36)

(*b*) $W_{75} = 3.24 \times 10^3\, A^{0.79} \cdot Q_P^{-0.78}$ ...(6.37)

Above two equations compute the values of width of graph in minute.

Indian Practices for Development of SUHG

The Central Water Commission (India), 1973 recommended the following sets of formulae for development of synthetic unit hydrograph based on the study of large numbers of Indian catchments of varying sizes ranging from 25 to 500 sq km.

1. **Peak discharge (Q_{pd}) :** The peak discharge for $D-h$ unit hydrograph is given by

$$Q_{pd} = 4.44\, A^{0.75} \quad \text{for } S_m > 0.0028 \qquad \text{...(6.38)}$$

and

$$Q_{pd} = 222\, A^{0.75} \cdot S_m^{0.666} \text{ for } S_m < 0.0028 \qquad \text{...(6.39)}$$

where, A = area of watershed(sq km)

S_m = weighted mean slope. It can be computed as

$$S_m = \left[\frac{L_{ca}}{\frac{L_1}{\sqrt{S_1}} + \frac{L_2}{\sqrt{S_2}} + \frac{L_3}{\sqrt{S_3}} + ... \frac{L_n}{\sqrt{S_n}}} \right]^2 \qquad \text{...(6.40)}$$

L_{ca} = distance along the main water course (river) from the gauging point to a point in the river opposite to the c.g. of watershed.

$L_1, L_2, L_3 \ldots L_n$ = length of channels 1 to n, respectively.

$S_1, S_2, S_3 \ldots S_n$ = slope of the channels 1 to n, respectively.

The channel lengths and their slopes are determined from the topomap of the watershed. The equations 6.38 and 6.39 compute the value of peak discharge (Q_{pd}) in the unit of m^3/s.

2. **Lag time (t_{pl}) :** The time from mid of the rainfall excess to the peak of the unit hydrograph is called lag time. It is given as under :

$$t_{pl} = \frac{3.95}{\left(\frac{Q_{pd}}{A}\right)^{0.9}} \qquad \text{...(6.41)}$$

This formula computes the value of t_{pl} in hours.

3. **Duration of excess rainfall (D) :** It is given as

$$D = 1.1\, t_{pl} \qquad \text{...(6.42)}$$

4. The time to peak can be computed by using the Snyder's formula of basin lag (t_{pl}).

For development of synthetic unit hydrograph for ungauged Indian catchments, Mutreja, (1982) has also reported following sets of formulae :

1. Basin lag $(t_p) = 1.13 \dfrac{(L \cdot L_{ca})^{0.2769}}{S^{0.5}}$ ...(6.43)

2. Peak discharge $(Q_{ps}) = 0.315\, A^{0.93}\, S^{0.53}$ ...(6.44)

3. Time base $(t_b) = 4.3 \dfrac{(L \cdot L_{ca})^{0.28}}{S^{0.5}}$ ...(6.45)

4. Width of SUHG at 50% peak $(W_{50}) = 2.18\left(\frac{Q_{peak}}{A}\right)^{-1.12}$ ...(6.46)

5. Width of SUHG at 75% peak $(W_{75}) = 0.81\, W_{50}^{0.72}$ ...(6.47)

6. Width of rising side of SUHG at 50% peak $(W_{R-50}) = 0.69\,(W_{50})^{0.69}$ ...(6.48)

7. Width of rising side of SUHG at 75% peak

$$(W_{R-75}) = 0.605\,(W_{R-50})^{0.95} \qquad \text{...(6.49)}$$

Finalization of S.U.H.G.

It is performed under following steps :

1. Based on the computed values of t_r, Q_{pr}, W_{50}, W_{75} and t_b, sketch the tentative SUHG.
2. Develop *S*-hydrograph and plot it. The *S*-hydrograph obtained so, has clinks, which are smoothened.
3. Again derive the *S*-hydrograph, logically.
4. Determine back the t_r (*h*) of SUHG by using the *S*- hydrograph in step (3).
5. Check the enclosed area of the SUHG, which should represent unit depth of effective rainfall. If it does not represent unit depth of ER, then repeat the procedure of adjustment, described in the steps from 2 to 4.

Apart from above, it should also be noted that amongst various parameters estimated for development of S.U.H.G., the time base (t_b) is the least accurate, which can be changed to meet the requirement.

SCS Dimensionless Unit Hydrograph

It is also a kind of synthetic unit hydrograph, developed by U.S. Soil Conservation Services in the year 1972. The ordinate of this unit hydrograph is expressed as the ratio of discharge to the peak discharge (Q/Q_P) and abscissa in the ratio of time (t) to the time to peak (t/t_{pk}). The ordinates of SCS dimensionless unit hydrograph are shown in Table 6.2. A dimensionless unit hydrograph reveals the following points :

1. For the given peak discharge and lag time, a unit hydrograph can be developed from the synthetic dimensionless unit hydrograph for any watershed.
2. For development of unit hydrograph by using dimensionless unit hydrograph, the requisite equations are as follows :

$$t_r = 1.33\, t_c \qquad \text{...(6.50)}$$

and

$$Q_{ps} = \frac{5.36\, A}{t_{peak}} \qquad \text{...(6.51)}$$

in which, t_{peak} is given by

$$t_{peak} = \left(t_{pR} + \frac{t_R}{2}\right) \qquad \text{...(6.52)}$$

3. By definition the

$$Q/Q_P = 1 \text{ when } t/t_{pr} = 1. \quad ...(6.53)$$

4. The .coordinates of SCS synthetic dimensionless unit hydrograph (Table 6.2) can be used for development of SUHG at the place of Snyder's equations.

The coordinates of USSCS average dimensionless unit hydrograph reported by Mockus (1957) are given in Table 6.2.

Table 6.2. Average dimènsionless unit hydrograph.

t/t_{peak}	Q/Q_{ps}	t/t_{peak}	Q_t/Q_{ps}
0.0	0.00	2.75	0.105
0.25	0.12	3.00	0.075
0.50	0.43	3.25	0.053
0.75	0.83	3.50	0.036
1.00	1.00	3.75	0.026
1.25	0.88	4.00	0.018
1.50	0.66	4.25	0.012
1.75	0.45	4.50	0.009
2.00	0.32	4.75	0.006
2.25	0.22	5.00	0.004
2.50	0.15		

Triangular Hydrograph

This hydrograph was developed by Mockus in the year 1957. It is used for conversion of dimensionless values of t and Q of dimensionless unit hydrograph to the real values. The area of triangular hydrograph represents the runoff volume. Accordingly, if Q_v is the runoff volume, height of triangle is Q_p and width of triangle is $(t_{peak} + t_b)$, then

$$Q_v = \frac{1}{2}(t_{peak} + t_b)\, Q_p \quad ...(6.54)$$

or

$$Q_p = \frac{2Q_v}{(t_{peak} + t_b)} \quad ...(6.55)$$

The value of t_{peak} from dimensionless unit hydrograph is given by

$$t_{peak} = 0.7\, T_C$$

or

$$= \frac{\text{effective rainfall duration}}{2} + 0.6\, T_c \quad ...(6.56)$$

and

$$t_b = 1.67\, t_{peak}$$

$$= 1.67 \times 0.7\, T_C = 1.169\, T_C$$

Thus $$Q_p = \frac{2Q_v}{(0.7\, T_C + 1.169\, T_C)} = \frac{2\, Q_v}{1.869\, T_C} \quad ...(6.57)$$

or $$\frac{2\, Q_v}{(t_{peak} + 1.67\, t_{peak})} = \frac{2\, Q_v}{2.67\, t_{peak}}$$

or $$Q_p = \frac{0.75\, Q_v}{t_{peak}} \quad ...(6.58)$$

If discharge Q_v in m^3 and area in sq km, then

$$Q_p = 0.75 \frac{0.278\, A \cdot Q_v}{t_{peak}}$$

$$= 0.208 \frac{A \cdot Q_v}{t_{peak}} \quad ...(6.59)$$

Instantaneous Unit Hydrograph (IUH)

A unit hydrograph is also presented as $D - h$ unit hydrograph, in which D is the duration of effective rainfall. The coordinate of unit hydrograph is expressed as $u(T, t)$ or $u\,(D, t)$. The duration D significantly affects the shape of unit hydrograph, because of the reason that the intensity of rainfall excess gets increase as D reduces and vice-versa. When D approaches zero, then resulting unit hydrograph is finite, which is limiting case of unit hydrograph called instantaneous unit hydrograph. In other words, it may be defined as the unit hydrograph resulting from infinitesimally small duration of effective rainfall. Its coordinate is expressed as $u\,(0, t)\, u\,(t)$ in which 0 refers to the duration of effective rainfall as 0 and t to the any time.

The IUH is a fictitious/conceptual unit hydrograph representing the direct runoff hydrograph resulting from an instantaneous precipitation of 1 cm effective rainfall of infinitesimally small duration in the watershed. It is single peak with a finite base width.

Properties of IUH

The IUH has following main properties :

1. $0 \le u\,(t) \le$ a positive peak value for $t > 0$
2. $u\,(t) = 0$ for $t \le 0$
3. $u(t) \longrightarrow 0$ for $t \to \infty$
4. $\int_0^\infty u\,(t)\, dt =$ unit depth over the catchment ...(6.60)
5. $\int_0^\infty u\,(t)\, dt =$ lag time of the IUH ...(6.61)
6. $u\,(t - t_0) = 1$, when $t = t_0$ ...(6.62)
7. $u\,(t - t_0) = 0$, when $t \ne t_0$ ...(6.63)
8. $\int_0^\infty u\,(t - t_0)\, dt = 1$ ...(6.64)

or $$\int_{t_1}^{t_2} u\,(t - t_0)\, dt = 1, \text{ when } t_1 < t_0 < t_2 \quad ...(6.65)$$

9. $$\int_0^{\infty} f(t) \cdot u\,(t - t_0)\, dt = f(t_0) \quad ...(6.66)$$

10. Time to peak < time to the centroid of the curve.

IUH in System Modelling

In terms of system modelling, the IUH is the impulse response of watershed. In other words, it is output from the watershed due to instantaneous impulse input of unit rainfall excess. The IUH is the response of watershed only. It is independent of the duration of effective rainfall which is practically not possible. It is basically an imaginary situation.

If $I(\tau)$ is the effective rainfall of duration t_0, is applied to the watershed (Figure 6.19), then each infinitesimal element of this effective rainfall will produce the direct runoff at the rate of

$$Q(t) = \int_0^{t'} u\,(t - \tau)\, I(\tau)\, d\tau \quad ...(6.67)$$

where $t' = t$ when $t < t_0$

and $t' = t_0$ when $t \geq t_0$

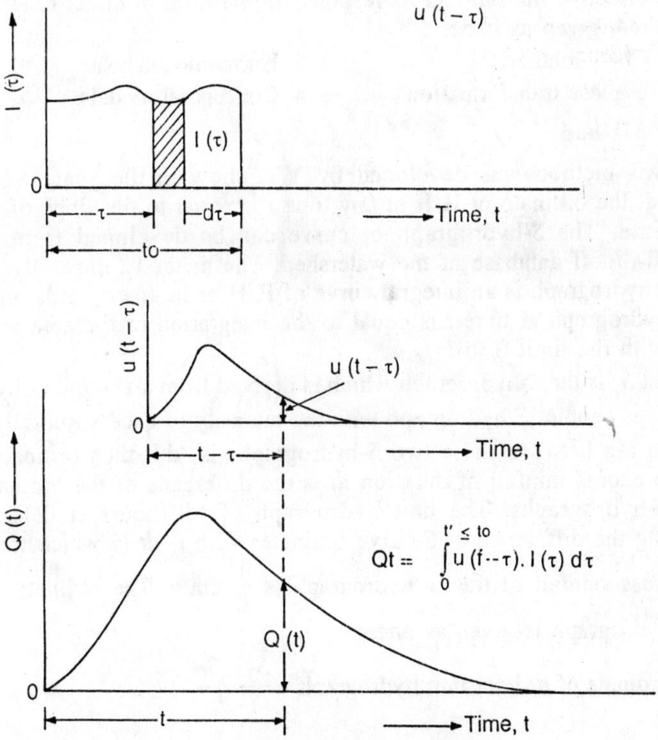

Fig. 6.19

The above relationship (eq. 6.67) is called convolution integral or Duhamel integral, in which $u(t-\tau)$ is the Corneal function, $I(\tau)$ is input with boundary condition, $t' = t$ for $t \le t_0$ and $t' = t_0$ for $t > t_0$.

The convolution integral (equation 6.67) can also be expressed in the following form

$$Q(t) = \int_0^t u(\tau)\, I(t-\tau)\, d\tau \quad ...(6.68)$$

or

$$Q(t) = u(t) \times I(t) \quad ...(6.69)$$

The graphical presentation of equation 6.68 is shown in Figure ____.

Advantage of IUH

It has following advantages :

1. The IUH is independent of the duration of effective rainfall and thus it has one parameter less than the $D-h$ unit hydrograph.
2. It is eminently suitable for theoretical analysis of excess rainfall-runoff (direct runoff) relationship for the watershed.
3. It is also useful for analysing the storage characteristics of the watershed, as IUH is independent of the rainfall characteristics.

Development of IUH

There have been developed various methods for derivation of IUH based on the effective rainfall and its response in the form of direct runoff from the watershed, given as under :

1. Chow method
2. Harmonic analysis
3. Laplace transformation
4. Conceptual models

Chow Method

This method was developed by V.T. chow in the year 1962. In this method, the ordinate of IUH at any time t is equal to the slope of S-curve at that time. The S-hydrograph or curve can be developed from the given rainfall-runoff database of the watershed. The method follows the basis that the S- hydrograph is an integral curve of IUH or in other words, the ordinate of S-hydrograph at time t is equal to the integration of the area enclosed by IUH with the limit 0 to t.

Let S_1 is the S-hydrograph which is derived from a $D-h$ unit hydrograph. And S_2 is another S-hydrograph with the intensity of excess rainfall as i cm/h. If time lag between these two S-hydrographs is 'dt', then ordinate of DRH due to excess rainfall of duration dt is the difference of the ordinates of the two S-hydrographs. The unit hydrograph of 'dt'-hours is determined by dividing the difference of S-curve ordinates with $i \cdot dt$ in which the intensity of excess rainfall of the S- hydrograph is $\frac{1}{D}$ cm/h. The ordinate of dt-hour unit hydrograph is given as under :

$$\text{Ordinate of } dt\text{-hour unit hydrograph} = \frac{S_2 - S_1}{i \cdot dt} \quad ...(6.70)$$

In this relationship, if dt is kept very small approaching zero *i.e.* $dt \to 0$, then resulting ordinate is the ordinate of IUH. In brief, the ordinate of IUH at any time 't' is given by

$$u(t) = \lim_{dt \to 0} \left(\frac{S_2 - S_1}{i \cdot dt} \right)$$

$$= \frac{1}{i} \frac{dS}{dt} \qquad \text{...(6.71)}$$

If intensity of excess rainfall (i) is equal to 1 cm/h then above equation is reduced to

$$u(t) = \frac{dS'}{dt} \qquad \text{...(6.72)}$$

in which S' is the S-hydrograph with intensity of excess rainfall as 1 cm/h.

In this way, the ordinate of instantaneous unit hydrograph is the

(*a*) slope of the S-hydrograph/curve with excess rainfall intensity as 1 cm/h.

(*b*) S-hydrograph derived from a unit hydrograph of 1- h duration.

Harmonic Analysis for IUH derivation

This method was proposed by O' Donnell in the year 1960. In this method, the ERH, DRH and resulting IUH are presented by three harmonic series. Harmonic coefficients for IUH are determined from ERH and DRH, based on which the ordinates of IUH are computed. For more details readers may refer the reference 0'. Donnell (1960).

Laplace Transformation Method

It is a theoretical procedure for deriving IUH, which was firstly suggested by Pointer (1952), and lateron also reported by Amoroche and Orlob in 1961. Diskin in the year 1964 used this method to analyse the non-linear properties of hydrograph. Under laplace transformation method, the ordinate of IUH is expressed by the following relation

$$\bar{u}(p) = \int_0^{\infty} e^{-pt} \cdot u(t)\, dt \qquad \text{...(6.73)}$$

in which p is the variable of laplace transform in the unit of $time^{-1}$. In this equation, since $u(t)$ is a bounded function of exponential order, therefore $\bar{u}(p)$ is finite for all positive values of 'p'. The $\bar{u}(p)$ is non-negative because $u(t)$ and e^{-pt} are positive functions. $\bar{u}(p)$ approaches zero when p increases. At $p = 0$, the $\bar{u}(p) = 1$; at $p = 1$, the $d\bar{u}(p)/dt = -t_L$ (as per equation 6.73). The $d\bar{u}(p)/dt$ is always negative and tends to zero when p approaches infinity.

The laplace transform of convolution integral, given by the equation $Q(t) = \int_0^{t'} u(t-0)\, I(0)\, d\tau$ is equal to the product of laplace transform of two functions involved in the integral *i.e.*

$$\bar{Q}(p) = \bar{u}(p) \cdot \bar{I}(p) \qquad \text{...(6.74)}$$

In which $\overline{Q}(p)$ and $\overline{I}(p)$ are the functions of laplace transform of DRH $Q(t)$ and ERH $I(t)$, respectively. The above equation can also be written in integral form, as

$$\overline{Q}(p) = \int_0^{\infty} e^{-pt} \cdot \overline{Q}(t)\, dt \qquad ...(6.75)$$

and

$$\overline{I}(p) = \int_0^{\infty} e^{-pt} \cdot I(t)\, dt \qquad ...(6.76)$$

The laplace transform of IUH (from equation 6.76) can be given as

$$\overline{u}(p) = \frac{\overline{Q}(p)}{\overline{I}(p)} \qquad ...(6.77)$$

Conceptual Models for IUH

Conceptual models are also known as parametric models. These are either deterministic or stochastic models. Or either physical analogies or simulation models. In field of hydrology, the parametric or conceptual models consist of simulated components *i.e.* linear reservoirs and linear channels, which are explained as under :

Linear reservoirs

It is a fictitious or imaginary reservoir, inwhich storage volume is directly proportional to the rate of outflow. The relationship between storage volume and outflow for the linear reservoir is given as under :

$$S = KQ \qquad ...(6.78)$$

where, S = storage volume of the reservoir
Q = outflow rate
K = reservoir constant ; also called storage coefficient

The rate of change of storage is also equal to the difference of the rates of inflow and outflow, *i.e.*

$$\frac{ds}{dt} = I - Q \qquad ...(6.79)$$

in which I is the inflow rate to the reservoir.

From equation 6.78, the $\frac{ds}{dt}$ is equal to $K\frac{dQ}{dt}$. Substituting this value in equation 6.79, we have

$$I - Q = K\frac{dQ}{dt}$$

or

$$I = K\frac{dQ}{dt} + Q \qquad ...(6.80)$$

Now, applying the conditions, *i.e.*

1. When time is just before the beginning of outflow from the reservoir or in other words when time $t = 0$, the outflow from the reservoir is zero (*i.e.* $Q = 0$). For this case, the equation 6.80 can be written as

$$I = K\frac{dQ}{dt} + Q$$

$$I - Q = K\frac{dQ}{dt}$$

or
$$\frac{dQ}{I - Q} = \frac{dt}{K} \quad ...(6.81)$$

Integrating the equation 6.81, we have

$$\int \frac{dQ}{I - Q} = \int \frac{dt}{K}$$

or
$$In\,(1 - Q) + C_1 = \frac{t}{K}$$

or
$$(Q - I) = C_1\, e^{-t/k} \quad ...(6.82)$$

where C_1 is the constant

Applying the condition *i.e.* at $t = 0$, the $Q = 0$, we have

$$C_1 = -I \quad ...(6.83)$$

Substituting the value of C_1 as $-I$ in the equation 6.82

$$(Q - I) = -I\, e^{-t/k}$$

or
$$Q = I - Ie^{-t/k}$$

$$= I\,(1 - e^{-t/k}) \quad ...(6.84)$$

2. When $t = \infty$ or outflow has been occured for a very long period of time, then equation 6.83 is reduced to

$$Q = I$$

This states that, at the operation of reservoir for infinite time, the inflow and outflow becomes equal to each other or inflow and outflow reached at equilibrium state.

3. When inflow is terminated just at the time when outflow from reservoir begins. For this case, the inflow (I) to the reservoir is zero and discharge at the time t_0 is Q_0. The inflow-outflow relationship is given as

$$I - Q = K\frac{dQ}{dt}$$

or
$$-Q = K\frac{dQ}{dt}$$

or
$$-\frac{dQ}{Q} = \frac{dt}{K} \quad ...(6.85)$$

Integrating the equation 6.84, we have

$$\int_{Q_0}^{Q} \frac{dQ}{Q} = \int_{t_0}^{t} \frac{dt}{K}$$

On solving, we have

$$Q = Q_0 \, e^{-(t - t_0)/k}$$

$$Q = Q_0 \, e^{-\tau/k} \qquad ...(6.86)$$

where $(t - t_0) = \tau$

4. When there is instantaneous inflow to the reservoir in time $t_0 = 0$. For this case, by replacing the outflow Q as Q_0 and storage S as S_0, the equation 6.78 can be written as

$$S_0 = K \, Q_0$$

or

$$Q_0 = \frac{S_0}{K} \qquad ...(6.87)$$

On substitution of Q_0 as $\frac{S_0}{K}$ in equation 6.85, we have

$$Q = \frac{S_0}{K} \, e^{-\tau/k} \qquad ...(6.88)$$

or

$$Q = I \cdot e^{-\tau/K} \qquad ...(6.89)$$

Equation of IUH

Let for a linear reservoir, the storage (S) at time t_0 is S_0 due to unit depth of excess rainfall. For this case, the t and I are 0. Accordingly, we have

$$I - Q = K \frac{dQ}{dt}$$

or

$$-Q = K \frac{dQ}{dt}$$

or

$$\frac{dQ}{Q} = -\frac{dt}{K} \qquad ...(6.90)$$

Integrating equation 6.89, we have

$$\int \frac{dQ}{Q} = -\int \frac{dt}{K}$$

$$In \, Q = -\frac{t}{K} + C$$

or

$$Q = C_1 \, e^{-t/K} \qquad ...(6.91)$$

where C_1 is the constant. Applying boundary conditions *i.e.* $t = 0$ and $S = 1$, we have

$$S = KQ$$

$$1 = KQ$$

or

$$Q = \frac{1}{K} \qquad ...(6.92)$$

Substituting the value of $Q = \frac{1}{K}$ in equation 6.91, we have

$$\frac{1}{K} = C_1 \cdot e^{-t/k} \qquad ...(6.93)$$

Since time $t_0 = 0$, therefore equation 6.93 is reduced to

$$\frac{1}{K} = C_1$$

Again substituting the value of C_1 as $\frac{1}{K}$ in equation 6.91, we have

$$Q = \frac{1}{K} e^{-t/k} \qquad ...(6.94)$$

This equation represents the ordinate of IUH for linear reservoir (single). The term $e^{-t/k}$ is known as exponential decay function.

Linear Channel

It is a fictitious channel in which the time required to translate the discharge of any magnitude through a fixed channel reach is constant. When an inflow hydrograph is routed through the linear channel, the shape of hydrograph will not change.

For example, if inflow rate at a given channel reach is I which is the function of time 't' *i.e.* $I = f(t)$, then its outflow will also be the function of t except that the change in time is equal to the translation time (T), *i.e.* $Q = f(t - T)$. Similarly, the velocity of flow also remains unchange for all discharge values at any section of fixed length of the linear channel, but for different sections it may vary. For linear channel, the relation between flow area (*i.e.* wetted area) A and the flowing discharge Q is found to be linear, given as under :

$$A \alpha Q$$

or

$$A = CQ \qquad ...(6.95)$$

in which C is the translation coefficient which is the function of translation time (T) *i.e.* $C = f(T)$. The value of C remains constant for a given section of channel.

Routing of Hydrograph through a linear channel

Referring the figure 6.20, if,

(*i*) duration of inflow segment = Δt

(*ii*) volume of routed flow = S

Then, the outflow through the linear channel is given by

$$Q = S\,\delta\,(t, \Delta t) \qquad ...(6.96)$$

where

$$\delta\,(t, \Delta t) = \frac{1}{\Delta t}$$

For $0 \le \tau \le \Delta t$ and $t = \tau + T$, it is zero otherwise. Here τ is the time measured from the beginning of segment. Equation 6.96 is the pulse response function, which is converted into impulse function *i.e.* $\delta(t)$ when the value of Δt approaches zero. The impulse function is also called 'Direct-delta function', which represents the instantaneous unit hydrograph (IUH) for the linear channel.

A drainage basin is analogous to the linear channel with spatially varied flow, as shown in figure 6.20. Let, total area of the drainage basin is 'a', which is subdivided into 'n' sub-areas of size Δa_j by the isochrones, inwhich $J = 1, 2, 3 .... n$. denotes the sequence of isochrones/sub areas from the outlet of the drainage basin. The iso-chrone may be defined as the contour of travel time Δt. If the effective rainfall i_J is supplied to the sub area a_J, then outflow from the sub-area will be equal to

$$Q_J = i_J \cdot \Delta a_J \qquad ...(6.97)$$

And flow at the outlet will be

$$Q = i_J\, \Delta a_J\, \delta\,(t - T, \Delta t) \qquad ...(6.98)$$

in which $T = (J - 1)\, \Delta t.$

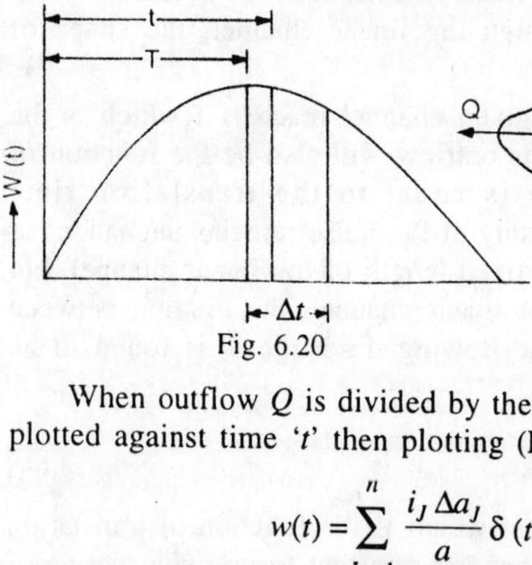

Fig. 6.20

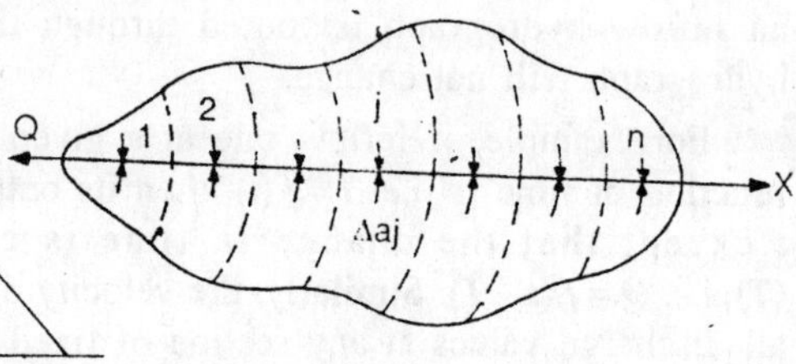

Fig. 6.21

When outflow Q is divided by the total area of drainage basin (a) and is plotted against time 't' then plotting (Figure 6.21) can be expressed as

$$w(t) = \sum_{J=1}^{n} \frac{i_J\, \Delta a_J}{a}\, \delta\,(t - T, \Delta t) \qquad ...(6.99)$$

In this equation, when t approaches zero and i_J is kept constant, then plotting is represented by a curve which ordinate is directly proportional to the size of drainage basin projected on the channel. This plotting is called time- area or time-area-concentration diagrame.

IUH Models

Based on the analogy of linear reservoirs and linear channels, there have been developed several models for instantaneous unit hydrograph. Zoch (1934 to 37) developed the rainfall-runoff relationship by applying the concept of linear reservoir. Turner and Burdoin (1941) derived the runoff hydrograph as the product of routing time-area diagram through the reservoir and linear storage coefficient, determined from the recession curve of the hydrograph. In the year 1945 the Clerk and 0′ Kelly in 1955 developed the IUH by considering the concept of linear reservoir. Similarly, Sugawara and Maruyama (1956) introduced the conceptual application of mechanism of linear reservoirs as analogous model to analyse the runoff flowing through the river system. Nash (1957) also developed the IUH model by considering the drainage basin as *n*-identical linear reservoirs in series.

In present description of IUH models, the Clark and Nash models are described as under :

Clark Model of IUH

This IUH model is also known as Time-area- histogram Under this model, it is assumed that the rainfall excess is subject to following two functions :

(*i*) Translation of rainfall excess and

(*ii*) Attenuation in rainfall excess due to storage properties of the watershed.

The rainfall excess first goes for translation and then attenuation. The translation of rainfall excess is performed by time-area histogram (TAH) and attenuation is determined by routing the translated rainfall excess through a linear reservoir at the watershed outlet. The routing of rainfall excess is done by using the Muskingum routing method.

Principle

The basis of development of IUH is the distribution of arrival time of the volume of rainfall excess or surface runoff at the outlet of watershed. The arrival time of runoff at the outlet of watershed is the time of concentration. This time duration is considered as the maximum translation time of the surface runoff because it is the time required to move the unit volume of rainfall excess from remotest point of the watershed to its outlet. In this model, the rainfall excess is the input, watershed as the system and output is the unit hydrograph. The unit hydrograph follows the assumption that there is uniform distribution of unit rainfall excess over the entire watershed. The time distribution of rainfall excess results the time-area histogram, which is considered as the inflow hydrograph to a hypothetical storage reservoir at the outlet of watershed.

Methodology

It is accomplished under following two steps :

1. **Development of time-area histogram**

In TAH, the time refers to the time of concentration (t_c) and area to the total area of watershed. The t_c is the time required for a unit volume of water to move from the remotest point of the watershed to the outlet. For gauged watersheds, the t_c is determined as the time interval between the end of rainfall excess and point of inflection of the surface runoff, as shown in Figure 6.22. On the other hand for ungauged watersheds, the empirical formulae such as Kirpich (1940) etc. are used for determining the time of concentration.

The TAH is prepared by using the following steps :

(*i*) Locate several points on the topo map of watershed and compute their travel time (let *t*). The computed time (*t*) is being less than t_c.

(*ii*) Draw isochrones by joining the points of equal travel time. The isochrones divide the entire watershed into different segments having equal travel time. For drawing isochrones, the surface profile of longest water course is plotted interms of elevation Vs distance curve (Figure 6.22), which is started from the outlet of the watershed. The total length of longest watercourse is divided into *N* parts and their respective elevations are determined, and are transferred on the map of the watershed.

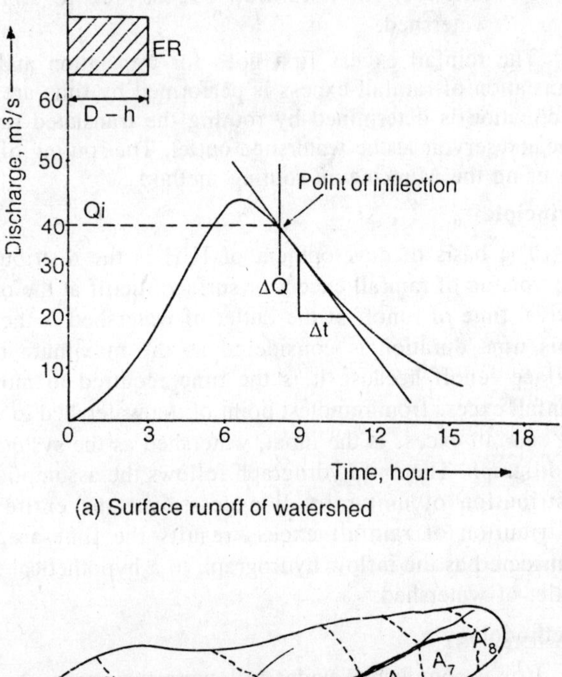

(a) Surface runoff of watershed

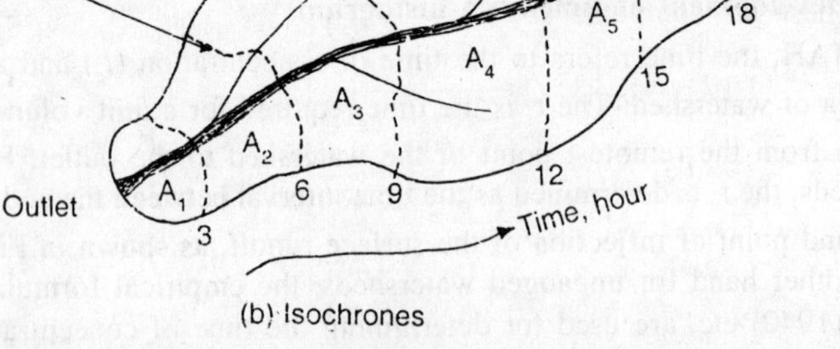

(b) Isochrones

Fig. 6.22

(*iii*) Determine the inter-isochrone areas, which is carried out by using the planimeter.

(*iv*) Construct the TAH by plotting the inter-isochrone areas V_s time interval in form of bar diagram or histogram (Figure 6.23).

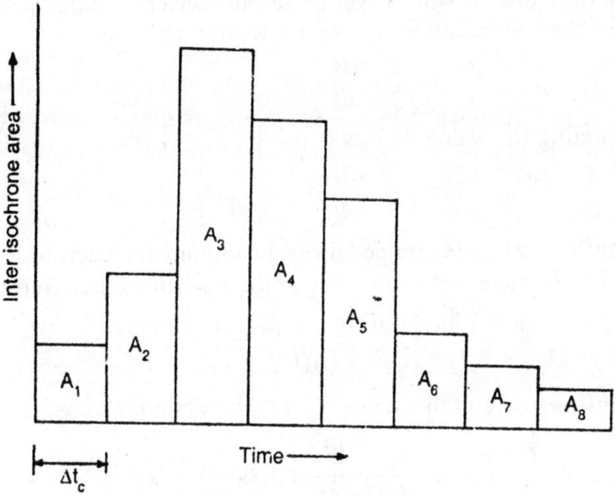

Fig. 6.23

The TAH represents the volume of unit rainfall excess over the watershed. If unit depth of rainfall excess (1 cm) is occurred uniformly over the watershed, then TAH will produce the volume of runoff in the unit of ha.cm or sq. km. cm, in which *ha* or sq km is the area of watershed. TAH can also be derived as the unit hydrograph in discrete unit through translation process.

2. **Routing of TAH**

It is done to determine the IUH. The Muskingum equation is used for this purpose, which is given by

$$Q_2 = C_0 I_2 + C_1 I_1 + C_2 Q_1 \qquad ...(6.100)$$

where, Q_2 = ordinate of IUH

C_0, C_1 and C_2 = constants.

These are computed as follows :

$$\left.\begin{aligned} C_0 &= \frac{0.5\,\Delta t_c}{K + 0.5\,\Delta t_c} \\ C_1 &= \frac{0.5\,\Delta t_c}{K + 0.5\,\Delta t_c} \\ C_2 &= \frac{K - 0.5\,\Delta t_c}{K + 0.5\,\Delta t_c} \end{aligned}\right\} \qquad ...(6.101)$$

$$C_0 + C_1 + C_2 = 1 \qquad ...(6.102)$$

or $$2C_1 + C_2 = 1 \qquad \text{...(6.103)}$$
$$(C_0 = C_1)$$

The value of K is determined by considering the point of inflection at the runoff hydrograph of the watershed. The inflection point indicates the situation when inflow into channel has been ceased and out flow from the channel is only due to withdrawal of storage water. For this point/condition, the inflow- outflow relationship can be written as

$$I - Q = \frac{ds}{dt}$$

Substituting the value of I as 0

$$-Q = \frac{ds}{dt}$$

The inflow rates determined from histogram for each time interval are equal *i.e.* $I_1 = I_2$. Here inflow denotes to the rainfall excess. Substituting these values in equation 6.100, we have

$$Q_2 = 2C_1 I_1 + C_2 Q_1 \qquad \text{...(6.104)}$$

The inflow or rainfall excess (I_1) can be determined as

$$= \frac{A_n \times 10^4}{3600 \times \Delta t_c} = 2.78 \frac{A_n}{\Delta t_c} \text{ m}^3\text{/s}$$

in which, A_n is the inter isochrone area (sq km) and Δt_c in second.

Routing the TAH by using equation 6.104, the ordinates of IUH can be determined *i.e.*

$$K \frac{dQ}{dt}$$

Therefore, $$K = -\frac{Q_i}{(dQ/dt)_i} \qquad \text{...(6.105)}$$

By using equation 6.105, the value of K can be determined. In this equation, the suffix i denotes the point of inflection.

Example 6.15. *A watershed has following characteristics*

(*i*) *Area* = 100 *sq km*;

(*ii*) *Time of concentration* = *21 hours* ;

(*iii*) *Storage constant* = *15 hours* ; *and*

(*iv*) *Inter-isochrone area distribution are as below* :

Travel time (h)	0–3	3–6	6–9	9–12	12–15	15–18	18–21
Inter isochrone area (sq. km)	2.5	5.0	15.0	11.0	8.0	5.0	3.0

Drive IUH, by using Clark model. (Assume necessary data, if required).

Solution. Given that $K = 15$

$$t_c = 21 \text{ hour}$$
$$\Delta t_c = 3 \text{ hour.}$$

Computations of required IUH parameters.

(*a*) Coefficients C_1 and C_2

$$C_1 = \frac{0.5\,\Delta t_c}{K + 0.5\,\Delta t_c} = \frac{0.5 \times 3}{15 + 0.5 \times 3} = 0.09$$

$$C_2 = \frac{K - 0.5\,\Delta t_c}{K + 0.5\,\Delta t_c} = \frac{15 - 0.5 \times 3}{15 + 0.5 \times 3} = 0.82$$

Substituting the values of C_1 and C_2 in IUH equation

$$Q_2 = 2C_1 I_1 + C_2 Q_1$$
$$= 2 \times 0.09\, I_1 + 0.82\, Q_1$$
$$Q_2 = 0.18\, I_1 + 0.82\, Q_1$$

(*b*) Computation of ordinates of IUH : It is shown in following table.

Time (h)	*Inter-iso-chrone area (km^2)*	*Inflow* I (m^3/s)*	*0.18 I_1*	*0.82 Q_1*	*ordinate of I U H, i.e. $Q_2 = 0.18\,I_1 + 0.82\,Q_1$ (m^3/s)*
0	0.0	0.00	0.00	0.00	0.00
3	2.5	2.32	0.42	0.00	0.42
6	5.0	4.63	0.83	0.34	1.17
9	15.0	13.90	2.50	0.96	3.46
12	11.0	10.19	1.83	2.84	4.67
15	8.0	7.41	1.33	3.83	5.16
18	5.0	4.63	0.83	4.23	5.06
21	3.0	2.78	0.50	4.15	4.65
			0.00	3.81	3.81
			0.00	3.12	3.12
				2.56	2.56

* Inflow $(I) = \dfrac{2.78\,Ar}{\Delta t_c}\ \text{m}^3/\text{s}$

Nash Model

It is also a conceptual model, used for development of instantaneous unit hydrograph for the watershed. This model was developed by Nash in the year 1957. In this model, the watershed is assumed to be segmented into a series of identical linear reservoirs having the same storage constant (K), as shown in Fig. 6.24. In this case, the outflow of any reservoir is the input to the next reservoir. Amongst all the linear reservoirs, the first reservoir receives a unit volume *i.e.* 1 cm effective rainfall in instantaneous way. This inflow of unn

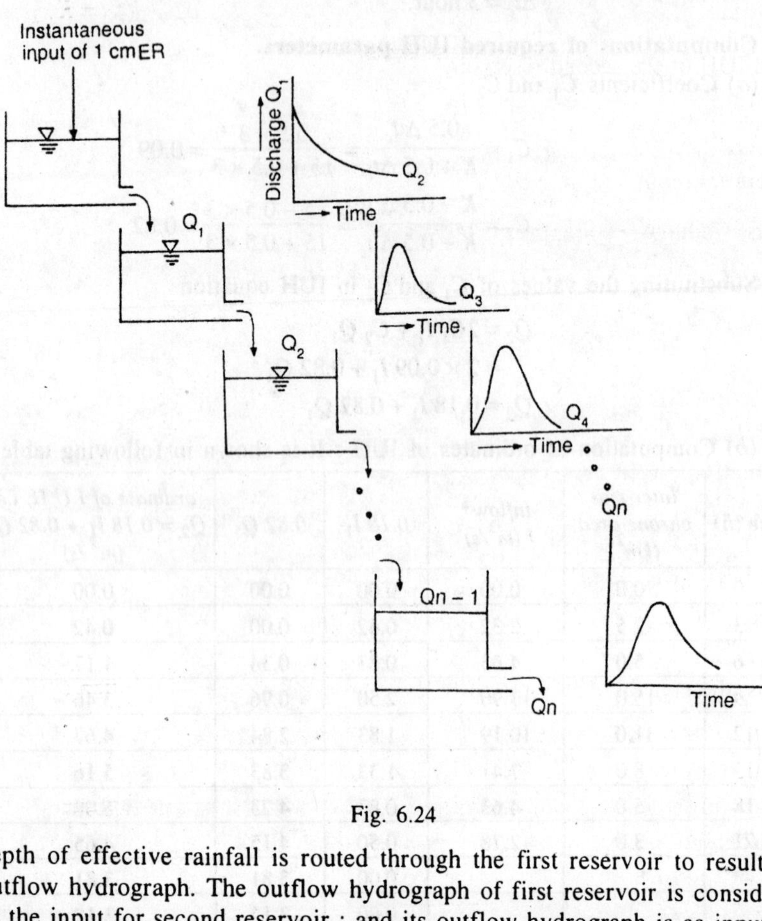

Fig. 6.24

depth of effective rainfall is routed through the first reservoir to result the outflow hydrograph. The outflow hydrograph of first reservoir is considered as the input for second reservoir ; and its outflow hydrograph is as input for the third reservoir and so on for all the reservoirs in series.

The outflow hydrograph is determined by the process of convolution of the system function, represented by the following equation

$$Q = \frac{1}{K} e^{-t/k}$$

where K is the storage constant. The outflow (Q) hydrograph is the IUH for the reservoir.

Accordingly, if

IUH of Ist reservoir is

$$Q_1 = \frac{1}{K_1} e^{-t/K_1}$$

Then input of 2nd reservoir is given by

$$\frac{1}{K_2} e^{-t/K_2} \text{ or } \frac{1}{K} e^{-t/K} \qquad (K_1 = K_2 = \dots K)$$

And IUH of the second reservoir

$$Q_2 = \frac{1}{K} e^{-t/k} \cdot \int e^{t/K} \cdot I \cdot dt$$

where $I = \text{input} = Q_1 = \frac{1}{K} e^{-t/k}$.

Thus, we have

$$Q_2 = \frac{1}{K} e^{-\frac{t}{K}} \cdot \int e^{t/K} \cdot \frac{1}{K} e^{-t/K} \cdot dt$$

$$= \frac{1}{K^2} t\, e^{-t/K} \quad \text{...(6.106)}$$

$$= \frac{t}{K^2} e^{-t/K} \quad \text{...(6.107)}$$

Similarly, for third reservoir

$$\text{Input } (I) = Q_2 = \frac{t}{K^2} e^{-t/K}$$

and IUH of third reservoir *i.e.* Q_3 will be equal to

$$Q_3 = \frac{1}{2} \cdot \frac{t^2}{K^3} e^{-t/k} \quad \text{...(6.108)}$$

Thus, the general expression of IUH for *n*th reservoir can be written as

$$Q_n = \frac{1}{(n-1)!} \frac{t^{n-1}}{K^n} e^{-t/K} \quad \text{...(6.109)}$$

Replacing the Q_n by the notation of the ordinate of instantaneous unit hydrograph as $u(t)$, we have

$$u(t) = \frac{1}{(n-1)!} \frac{t^{n-1}}{K^n} e^{-t/k} \quad \text{...(6.110)}$$

In this equation, $u(t)$ is in cm/h 't' is in hours, and K and n are constants. The equation 6.110 is valid for 'n' as integer; not for fractional numbers. To make its validity, both for n as integer numbers and fractional numbers, the term $(n-1)!$ is replaced by Γn.

Accordingly, the above equation is reduced to

$$u(t) \frac{1}{K\Gamma n} \left(\frac{t}{K}\right)^{n-1} \cdot e^{-t/K} \quad \text{...(6.111)}$$

For this equation, when 'n' is an integer, then $\Gamma n = (n-1)!$, which can be easily determined. But when 'n' is not integer number *i.e.* fractional number, then value of Γn is determined from Gamma Table, given in Table 6.3.

Table 6.3. Gamma Function Γ(*n*)

n	Γ(*n*)	*n*	Γ(*n*)	*n*	Γ(*n*)
1.00	1.000000	1.34	0.892216	1.68	0.905001
1.02	0.988844	1.36	0.890185	1.70	0.908639
1.04	0.978438	1.38	0.888537	1.72	0.912581
1.06	0.968744	1.40	0.887264	1.74	0.916826
1.08	0.959725	1.42	0.886356	1.76	0.921375
1.10	0.951351	1.44	0.885805	1.78	0.926227
1.12	0.943590	1.46	0.885604	1.80	0.931384
1.14	0.936416	1.48	0.885747	1.82	0.936845
1.16	0.929803	1.50	0.886227	1.84	0.942612
1.18	0.923728	1.52	0.887039	1.86	0.948687
1.20	0.918169	1.54	0.888178	1.88	0.955071
1.22	0.913106	1.56	0.889639	1.90	0.961766
1.24	0.908521	1.58	0.891420	1.92	0.968774
1.26	0.904397	1.60	0.893515	1.94	0.976099
1.28	0.900718	1.62	0.895924	1.96	0.983743
1.30	0.897471	1.64	0.898642	1.98	0.991708
1.32	0.894640	1.66	0.901668	2.00	1.000000

Nash model of IUH

Input data

The following data are required :

1. Effective rainfall hyetograph
2. Direct runoff hydrograph ; and
3. Area of watershed.

Determination of Nash Parameters i.e. n and K

These are computed by taking the moments about origin *i.e.* $t = 0$, which are given as under :

1. First moment (M_1) about origin

$$M_1 = n \cdot K \quad \text{...(6.112)}$$

2. Second moment (M_2) about origin

$$M_2 = n\,(n+1)\,K^2 \quad \text{...(6.113)}$$

Based on above two equations, the values of Nash parameters (*n* and *K*) for the given watershed can be determined, provided that the effective rainfall hyetograph (ERH) and corresponding direct runoff hydrograph (DRH) are available. The following formulae can be used :

$$MQ_1 - MI_1 = nK.$$

$$MQ_2 - MI_2 = n\,(n+1)\,K^2 + 2n\,KMI_1 \qquad ...(6.114)$$

where, MQ_1 and MQ_2 = first and second moments of the DRH about origin divided by total direct runoff, respectively

MI_1 and MI_2 = first and second moments of ERH about origin divided by the total effective rainfall, respectively

The computation procedures of MQ_1, MQ_2, MI_1 and MI_2 and n & K are shown in example 6.16.

Computation of Ordinates of IUH

After determining the values of Nash parameters n and K, the ordinates of instantaneous unit hydrograph $u\,(t)$ is computed by using the equation 6.110 *i.e.*

$$u\,(t) = \frac{1}{K\,\overline{|(n)}} \cdot \left(\frac{1}{K}\right)^{n-1} \cdot e^{(-t/K)}$$

In this equation, the values of K, n and t are known. The t is the time interval of ordinates of IUH. If the value of K and t is in hour, then $u\,(t)$ is obtained in the unit of cm/h, which is converted into m^3/s by using the following relationship

$$u\,(t)_{m^3/s} = u\,(t)_{cm/h} \times 2.78\,A \qquad ...(6.115)$$

in which, A is the area of watershed in sq km.

Example 6.16 shows the procedure to calculate the ordinates of IUH by using Nash model.

Derivation of Unit Hydrograph (D-hour) from IUH

Considering the equation

$$u\,(t) = \frac{dS'}{dt} \qquad \text{(for } i = 1\text{)}$$

the

$$dS' = u\,(t)\,dt \qquad ...(6.116)$$

Integrating equation 6.115 we have

$$\int_{S_1'}^{S_2'} dS' = \int_{t_1}^{t_2} u\,(t)\,dt$$

$$[S']_{S_1'}^{S_2'} = \int_{t_1}^{t_2} u\,(t)\,dt$$

$$S_2' - S_1' = \int_{t_1}^{t_2} u\,(t)\,dt \qquad ...(6.117)$$

If $u(t)$ is linear within the limit t_1 and t_2, then for small value of $\Delta t = (t_2 - t_1)$ the ordinate $u(t)$ can be taken as

$$u(t) = \bar{u}(t) = \frac{1}{2}[u(t_1) + u(t_2)]$$

Therefore $$S_2' - S_1' = \frac{1}{2}[u(t_1) + u(t_2)]\,\Delta t$$

$$= \frac{1}{2}[u(t_1) + u(t_2)]\,(t_2 - t_1)$$

or $$\frac{S_2' - S_1'}{(t_2 - t_1)} = \frac{1}{2}[u(t_1) + u(t_2)]$$

But $\frac{S_2' - S_1'}{(t_2 - t_1)}$ is equal to the ordinate of unit hydrograph of duration D_1 (*i.e.* $t_2 - t_1$). Accordingly, the general relationship between IUH and $D - h$ unit hydrograph can be written as

$$(D_1 - \text{hour UHG})_t = \frac{1}{2}\left[(\text{IUH})_t + (\text{IUH})_{t - D_1}\right] \quad ...(6.118)$$

This equation revealed that, if two IUHs are lagged by D_1-hour duration then sum of their corresponding ordinates of IUH divided by 2, results the ordinate of $D_1 - h$ unit hydrograph.

The computed ordinates of $D_1 - h$ unit hydrograph are then converted for any $D - h$ unit hydrograph ordinate by using super position/*S*-curve method.

Example 6.16. *In a watershed (100 sq km area) of DVC Hazaribag (Jharkhand), the effective rainfall from an isolated storm was analysed as under :*

Time (*h*)	0 – 3	3 – 6
Effective rainfall intensity cm/h	4.5	3.0

In response of this storm, the ordinates of direct runoff hydrograph are given as below ;

Time, *h*	0	3	6	9	12	15	18
O.DRH m^3/s	0.0	15.0	45.0	60.0	24.0	5.0	0.0

Compute the followings:

(1) n and k

(2) ordinates of IUH by using Nash model

Solution:

(1) Computation of *n* and *K*: The following steps are followed :

(*a*) Evaluation of $M1_1$ and $M1_2$: It is given in following table.

Time, (h)	*Incremental rainfall excess rate (cm/h)*	*Time interval Δt(h)*	*Incremental rainfall excess (cm)*	*Moment arm (h)*	*First moment (4)×(5)(cm – h)*	Second moment		
						Incremental vol. × (moment arm)^2 (4) × (5)^2	*1/22.5 × (3)^3 × (4)*	*Total (7) + (8)*
(1)	*(2)*	*(3)*	*(4)*	*(5)*	*(6)*	*(7)*	*(8)*	*(9)*
0	0.0	0	0	0	0	0	0	0
3	4.5	3	13.5	1.5	20.25	30.375	16.20	46.575
6	3.0	3	9.0	4.5	40.50	182.25	10.80	193.05
	Total		22.50		60.75	212.625	27.0	239.625

Therefore, $$M1_1 = \frac{\sum \text{column.(6)}}{\sum \text{column (4)}} = \frac{60.75}{22.50} = \mathbf{2.70}$$

and $$M1_2 = \frac{\sum \text{column (9)}}{\sum \text{column (4)}} = \frac{239.625}{22.50} = \mathbf{10.65}$$

Evaluation of MQ_1 and MQ_2 : It is given in following table.

Time (h)	Ordinates of DRH (m^3/s)	Average rate of direct runoff in time $\Delta t(m^3/s)$	Interval (Δt)(h)	Incremental vol. of runoff (i.e. area of histogram) col (3) × (col 4)	Moment arm (h)	First moment col (5) × col (6)	Col (5) × col $(6)^2$	1/ 22.5 × (col) $(4)^3$ × col (5)	Second moment col (8) + col (9)
(1)	(2)	(3)	(4)	(5)	(6)	(7)	(8)	(9)	(10)
0	0	0.0	0	0.0	0.0	0.00	0.000	0.00	0.00
3	15	7.5	3	22.5	1.5	33.75	50.625	27.00	77.63
6	45	30.0	3	90.0	4.5	405.00	1822.50	108.00	1930.50
9	60	52.5	3	157.5	7.5	1181.25	8859.375	189.00	9048.38
12	24	42.0	3	126.0	10.5	1323.00	13891.50	151.20	14042.70
15	5	14.5	3	43.5	13.5	587.25	7927.875	52.20	7980.10
18	0	2.5	3	7.50	16.5	123.75	2041.875	9.00	2050.90
Total				447.0		3654.0			35130.21

Therefore, $$MQ_1 = \frac{\sum \text{col (7)}}{\sum \text{col(5)}} = \frac{3654}{447} = \mathbf{8.1745}$$

and, $$MQ_2 = \frac{\sum \text{col (10)}}{\sum \text{col (5)}} = \frac{35130.21}{447} = \mathbf{78.59}$$

Now, using the formula,

$$MQ_1 - M1_1 = nk$$

$$8.1745 - 2.70 = nk$$

or $$nk = 5.475 \qquad \ldots(a)$$

and $$MQ_2 - M1_2 = n(n+1)K^2 + 2nK\,M1_1$$

$$78.59 - 10.65 = n^2K^2 + nK^2 + 2nK \times 2.70$$

$$67.94 = (5.475)^2 + 5.475K + 2 \times 5.475 \times 2.70$$

$$= 29.98 + 5.475\,K + 29.57$$

$$= 59.55 + 5.475\text{ K}$$

or $$5.475\,K = 8.39$$

$\therefore$ $$\mathbf{K = 1.53\ hours}$$

and form equation (*a*),

$$nk = 5.475$$

$$1.53\, n = 5.475$$

$$\therefore \quad n = \mathbf{3.58} \approx 3.6$$

(2) **Computation of ordinates of IUH :** It is carried out by using Nash formula for I.UH., *i.e.*

$$u(t) = \frac{1}{K\Gamma(n)}\left(\frac{t}{K}\right)^{n-1} . e^{-(t/k)} \text{ cm/h} \qquad \ldots(b)$$

In which, the values of *n* and *K* have been determined as 3.60 and 1.53 hours, respectively. The value of $\Gamma(n)$ *i.e.* (3.6) is determined, as below:

$$\Gamma(3.6) = 2.6\,\Gamma(2.6)$$
$$= 2.6 \times 1.6\,\Gamma(1.6)$$
$$= 2.6 \times 1.6 \times 0.893515 = \mathbf{3.717}$$

Substituting the values of *n*, *k* and 3.6 in equation (*b*)

$$u(t) = \frac{1}{1.53 \times 3.717}\left(\frac{t}{1.50}\right)^{3.6-1} . e^{-\left(\frac{t}{1.53}\right)}$$

or

$$u(t) = 0.176\left(\frac{t}{1.53}\right)^{2.6} . e^{-\left(\frac{t}{1.53}\right)}$$

The ordinates of 3 – *h* IUH for different values of *t*, are calculated, as shown in following table :

Time (h)	$\left(\frac{t}{1.53}\right)$	$\left(\frac{t}{1.53}\right)^{2.6}$	$e^{-(t/1.53)}$	*u*(t) = *0.176 × col(3) × col (4)* *cm /*λ	3 – *h unit hydrograph* *u(t) = 2.78 × 100 × col (5) (m³/s)*	*u(t) lagged by 3 – h (m³/s)*	*Unit hydrograph (col (6) + col (7)) ÷ 2 (m³/s)*
(1)	(2)	(3)	(4)	(5)	(6)	(7)	(8)
0	0	0	0	0	0	0	0
3	1.9607	5.7579	0.14075	0.14263	39.6511	0	19.8255
6	3.9215	34.9120	0.01981	0.12172	33.8381	39.6511	36.7446
9	5.8823	100.1895	0.00278	0.04902	13.6275	33.8381	23.7328
12	7.8431	211.6743	0.00039	0.01452	4.0365	13.6275	8.8320
15	9.8039	378.1264	5.52 E–05	0.00367	1.0202	4.0365	2.5283
18	11.7647	607.4495	7.77 E–06	0.00083	0.2307	1.0202	0.6254
21	13.7254	906.9117	1.09 E–06	0.00017	0.0472	0.2307	0.1389
24	15.6862	1283.3530	1.54 E–07	0.00003	0.0083	0.0472	0.0277
27	17.6470	1743.1883	2.16 E–08	0.000006	0.0016	0.0083	0.0049

Geomorphological Instantaneous Unit Hydrograph (GIUH)

It is the instantaneous unit hydrograph, derived on the basis of geomorphological parameters of the watershed. The concept of GIUH was firstly introduced by Rodriguez and Valde in the year 1979. The hypothesis of GIUH is based on the distribution of arrival time of unit instantaneous impulse injected throughout the channel network, which is affected by the morphological and hydrological characteristics of the channel.

Development of GIUH

Input data

Contour map of the watershed is required as input data for development of GIUH.

Methodology

It is accomplished under following steps :

1. **Determination of geomorphological parameters of the watershed :** The stream orders, stream length, contributing drainage area of each order streams, bifercation ratio, stream length ratio and stream area ratio are the geomorphological parameters of the watershed. These parameters are determined by using the procedure suggested by Strahler (1957) with the help of contour map of the watershed.

2. **Determination of flow velocity :** The flow velocity is considered as the dynamic property of the watershed, which can be computed by using the formula given by Sorman (1955)

(*i*) For $t_e \geq t_c$

$$V_{peak} = \alpha_{\Omega}^{0.6} \cdot A_{\Omega} (I_c)^{0.4} \quad \text{...(6.119)}$$

(*ii*) For $t_e < t_c$

$$V_{peak} = \alpha_{\Omega} (t_c \cdot i_e)^{2/3} \left(\frac{A_{\Omega}}{L_{\Omega}} \right)^{2/3} \quad \text{...(6.120)}$$

in which

$$\alpha_{\Omega} = \frac{S_{\Omega}^{0.50}}{n \cdot b_{\Omega}^{2/3}} \quad \text{...(6.121)}$$

where, t_e = duration of excess rainfall (s)

t_c = time of concentration (s)

α_{Ω} = kinematic wave parameter $\left(m^{-1/2} \cdot s^{1/2} \right)$

A_{Ω} = area of watershed (m^2)

i_e = intensity of rainfall excess (m/s)

L_{Ω} = length of main stream (km)

S_{Ω} = slope of main stream (m/m)

n = Manning's roughness coefficient

b_{Ω} = width of main stream (m)

Subramaniyam and Kumar (1990) have also suggested the following formula for computing the value of flow velocity.

$$V = 0.665\, \alpha_{\Omega}^{0.6}\, (i_r \cdot A_{\Omega})^{0.4} \qquad ...(6.122)$$

in which i_r is the rainfall intensity (cm/h) and A_{Ω} is the area of watershed (sq km).

Subramaniyan and Kumar (1989) and Rosso (1984) also suggested following formula for flow velocity.

$$t_L = 2.303 \left(\frac{R_B}{R_A}\right)^{0.30} \cdot \left(\frac{1}{R_L^{0.41}}\right) \cdot \frac{L_{\Omega}}{V} \qquad ...(6.123)$$

in which t_L is the lagtime of watershed, which is the function of area of watershed, rainfall intensity and duration of rainfall excess, given as

$$t_L = f(A_{\Omega}, i_e, t_e) \qquad ...(6.124)$$

Singh (1983) developed the relationship between t_L and area of the watershed (A), given as under :

$$t_L = 0.823\, A^{0.38} \qquad ...(6.125)$$

In equation 6.123, if t_L, R_B, R_A, R_L and L_{Ω} are known for the given watershed, then V can be determined. In which R_B is the bifercation ratio, R_A is the stream area ratio, R_L is the stream length ratio and L_{Ω} is the length of main stream. All these parameters are determined from the contour map of the watershed.

3. **Computation of Nash parameters (n and K)**

Nash parameters are determined on the basis of geomorphological parameters of the watershed, such as bifercation ratio (R_B), stream length ratio (R_L), stream area ratio (R_A) and flow velocity (V). Computation of n and K is given as under :

1. **Computation of n :** For this, the following formula (Subramaniyan and Kumar, 1989) can be used :

$$n = 3.29 \left(\frac{R_B}{R_A}\right)^{0.78} \cdot R_L^{0.07} \qquad ...(6.126)$$

2. **Computation of K :** It can be computed by using the following formula :

$$K = 0.70 \frac{(R_A)^{0.48}}{R_B \cdot R_L} \cdot \frac{L_{\Omega}}{V} \qquad ...(6.127)$$

4. **Computation of Peak runoff (q_p) and Time to peak (t_p)**

The q_p and t_p are the most important characteristics of the GIUH. As long as these are correct, the exact form of GIUH is not very important ; triangular approximation is quite satisfactory (Hinderson, 1963). For computation of q_p and t_p, the following formula (Rodriques - Iturbe, 1980) can be used :

1. Peak discharge (q_p)

$$q_p = \frac{1.31}{L_\Omega} \cdot R_L^{0.43} \qquad ...(6.128)$$

2. Time to peak (t_p)

$$t_p = \frac{0.44\, L_\Omega}{V} \left(\frac{R_B}{R_A} \right)^{0.55} R_L^{-0.38} \qquad ...(6.129)$$

For triangular IUH, Hinderson (1963) suggested the following relationship

$$\frac{Q_p}{Q_e} = \frac{2 \cdot t_e}{t_b} \left(1 - \frac{t_e}{2\, t_b} \right) \qquad ...(6.130)$$

where, Q_p = peak discharge produced by an effective rainfall of constant intensity and duration 't_e'

Q_e = equilibrium discharge, equal to $i_e \cdot A_\Omega$.

t_e = duration of effective rainfall

t_b = base time of IUH or concentration time of watershed.

Since $q_p \times t_b = 2$, therefore equation 6.130 can be reduced to

$$\frac{Q_p}{Q_e} = t_e \cdot q_p \left(1 - \frac{t_e \cdot q_p}{4} \right) \qquad ...(6.131)$$

Time to peak for triangular IUH is given by

$$T_p = t_p + 0.75\, t_e \qquad ...(6.132)$$

Computation procedure of GIUH is shown in example 6.17.

Example 6.17. *The followings are the morphological characteristics of a watershed of D.V.C. Hazaribagh (Jharkhand):*

(i) *Bifercation ratio* (R_b) = *4.5*

(ii) *Stream length ratio* (R_l) = *1.28*

(iii) *Stream area ratio* (R_a) = *3.72*

(iv) *Length of main stream* (L_Ω) = 1446.72 *m*

(v) Average breadth of main stream (b_Ω) = *19 m*

(vi) *Average slope of main stream* (S_Ω) = 1.75×10^{-4}

(vii) Area of watershed (A_Ω) = 29.93×10^6 sq m

(viii) *Time of concentration* (t_c) = *149.77 minutes*

Compute the ordinates of G.I.U.H., if

(i) *Effective rainfall intensity* (i_e) = 1.441×10^{-6} *m/s*

(ii) *Effective rainfall duration* (t_e) = *3600* sec

(*iii*) *Rainfall excess = 1.36 mm*

(*iv*) *Kinematic wave parameter* $(\alpha_\Omega) = 0.0464.$

(*v*) *Manning's roughness coefficient* (n) = *0.04*

Solution The computation of ordinates of G.I.U.H is accomplished under following steps :

Step (1) : Computation of flow velocity (V_{peak}) : It is done by using following formula:

$$V_{peak} = \alpha_\Omega \left(t_e \, . \, i_e \right)^{2/3} . \left(\frac{A_\Omega}{L_\Omega} \right)^{2/3}$$

$$= 0.0464\,(3600 \times 1.441 \times 10^{-6})^{2/3} . \left(\frac{27.93 \times 10^6}{1446.72} \right)^{2/3}$$

$$= 1.39052 \times 10^{-3} \times 719.60757 = 1.0 \text{ m/s}$$

Step (2) : Computation of Nash parameters : It is given below:

(*i*) Shape parameter $\quad (n) = 3.29 \left(\frac{R_b}{R_a} \right)^{0.78} . R_l^{0.07}$

$$= 3.29 \left(\frac{4.5}{3.72} \right)^{0.78} . (1.28)^{0.07} = 3.88$$

(*ii*) Scale parameter $\quad (K) = \frac{0.70\,(R_a)^{0.48}}{(R_b \, . \, R_l)} \times \left(\frac{L_\Omega}{V_{peak}} \right)$

$$K = \frac{0.70\,(3.72)^{0.48}}{(4.5 \times 1.28)} \times \left(\frac{1.44672}{1} \right) = 0.33$$

Step (3) : Computation of ordinates of G.I.U.H: It is carried out by using the following formula :

$$u(t) = \frac{1}{K\Gamma(n)} \left(\frac{t}{K} \right)^{n-1} . e^{-\left(\frac{t}{K}\right)}$$

$$= \frac{1}{0.33\Gamma 3.9} \left(\frac{t}{0.33} \right)^{2.90} e^{-(t/0.33)}$$

The value of $\Gamma 3.9$

$$= 2.9\Gamma 2.9$$
$$= 2.9 \times 1.9\Gamma 1.9$$
$$= 2.9 \times 1.9 \times 0.961766 = 5.2933$$

Thus,

$$u(t) = \frac{1}{0.33 \times 5.2933} \left(\frac{t}{0.33} \right)^{2.9} . e^{-\left(\frac{t}{0.33}\right)}$$

$$= \frac{\mathbf{1}}{\mathbf{1.748}} \left(\frac{t}{\mathbf{0.33}} \right)^{\mathbf{2.9}} . e^{-(t/0.33)}$$

The computation of ordinates of GIUH of 1 – *h*, for different values of *t* is shown in following table:

Time (h)	$\left(\frac{t}{0.33}\right)$	$\left(\frac{t}{0.33}\right)^{2.9}$	$e^{-(t/0.33)}$	$u(t) = \frac{1}{1.748} \times col(3) \times col(4)$ (cm/h)	$u(t) = 278 \times col(5)$ (m^3/s)	1 – h unit hydrograph: $u(t)$ lagged by $1-h$ (m^3/s)	1 – h unit hydrograph: Unit hydrograph $\frac{col(6)+col(7)}{2}$ (m^3/s)
(1)	(2)	(3)	(4)	(5)	(6)	(7)	(8)
0	0	0	0	0	0	0	0
1	3.0303	24.9062	0.04830	0.6880	191.2640	0	95.6320
2	6.0606	185.9068	0.00233	0.2465	68.5270	191.2640	129.8955
3	9.0909	602.5040	0.00011	0.0379	10.5362	68.5270	39.5316
4	12.1212	1387.6575	5.442 E – 06	0.0043	1.1954	10.5362	5.8658
5	15.1515	2650.4604	2.628 E – 07	0.00039	0.10842	1.1954	0.6519
6	18.1818	4497.2490	1.269 E – 08	0.000033	0.00917	0.10842	0.0587
7	21.2121	7032.2229	6.133 E – 10	2.466 E – 06	0.00068	0.00917	0.0049
8	24.2424	10357.8418	2.962 E – 11	1.755 E – 07	0.00004	0.00068	0.0003
9	27.2727	14575.1016	1.430 E – 12	1.192 E – 08	0.000003	0.00004	0.00002
10	30.3030	19783.7363	6.911 E – 14	7.82 E – 10	2.17 E – 07	0.000003	1.60 E – 06
11	33.3333	26082.3730	3.338 E – 15	4.98 E – 11	1.38 E – 08	2.17 E – 07	1.15 E – 07
12	36.3636	33568.6540	1.612 E – 16	5.41 E – 12	1.50 E – 09	1.38 E – 08	7.65 E – 09

SOLVED PROBLEMS

Problem 6.1. Determine the direct runoff generated from the watershed, if area of hydrograph due to a given storm is 4500 m^3 and total base flow in the stream is 1200 m^3.

Solution. Area of hydrograph represents the total volume of runoff due to rainfall. In this way the volume of direct runoff is equal to

$$= 4500 - 1200 = \mathbf{3300\ m^3} \quad \textbf{Ans.}$$

Problem 6.2. Determine the baseflow in stream, if total runoff volume due to a given storm is 2500 m^3 and volume of direct runoff is 1500 m^3.

Solution. The base flow is the difference of total runoff volume and direct runoff, therefore it is equal to

$$= 2500 - 1500 = \mathbf{1000\ m^3} \quad \textbf{Ans}$$

Problem 6.3. Compute the end time of direct runoff flow from the peak of hydrograph if the area of watershed is 170 sq km.

Solution. The time from peak runoff to the end of direct runoff flow from the watershed is given by the following formula :

$$N\,(days) = 0.83\,A^{0.2}$$

$$= 0.83\,(170)^{0.2} = \mathbf{2.32\ days} \quad \textbf{Ans.}$$

Problem 6.4. Calculate the recession constant, if initial discharge and discharge after 2 days are 6.5 and 4.0 m^3/s, respectively.

Solution. Given that

$$Q_t = 4.0\ m^3/s$$

$$Q_s = 6.5\ m^3/s$$

$$t = 2\ days$$

Using the formula

$$Q_t = Q_s\,K_r^t$$

$$4 = 6.5\,K_r^2$$

or

$$K_r^2 = \frac{4}{6.5} = 0.62$$

Taking the log both sides, we have

$$2 \log K_r = \log 0.62$$

$$\log K_r = \frac{1}{2} \log (0.62)$$

$$K_r = \mathbf{0.787} \quad \textbf{Ans.}$$

Problem 6.5. Determine the recession constant for surface storage (K_{rs}), if

(*i*) $K_r = 0.79$

(*ii*) $K_{ri} = 0.85$

(*iii*) $K_{rb} = 0.99$

Solution. Using the formula,

$$\text{fvb}K_r = K_{rs} \cdot K_{ri} \cdot K_{rb}$$

$$0.79 = K_{rs} \times 0.85 \times 0.99$$

$$\therefore \quad K_{rs} = \mathbf{0.94} \quad \textbf{Ans.}$$

Problem 6.6. Determine the discharge at the outlet of watershed after 2 days from the rainfall, if recession constant is 0.79 and initial discharge is 7.0 m^3/s.

Solution. Given that,

$$t = 2 \text{ days}$$

$$Q_s = 7.0 \text{ m}^3/\text{s}$$

$$K_r = 0.79$$

Using the formula, $Q_r = Q_s K_r^t$

$$= 7\,(0.79)^2 = \mathbf{4.37\ m^3/s} \quad \textbf{Ans.}$$

Problem 6.7. Determine the initial discharge at the outlet of watershed, if recession constant is 0.79 and discharge after 2 days from rainfall is 4.37 m^3/s.

Solution. Given that

$$K_r = 0.79$$

$$t = 2 \text{ days}$$

$$Q_t = 4.37 \text{ m}^3/\text{s}$$

Using the formula, $Q_t = Q_s\,(K_r)^t$

$$4.37 = Q_s\,(0.79)^2 = 0.6241\,Q_s$$

$$\therefore \quad Q_s = \frac{4.37}{0.6241} = \mathbf{7.0\ m^3/s} \quad \textbf{Ans.}$$

Problem 6.8. If at the outlet of watershed, the initial discharge and discharge after few days from the rainfall are measured as 7.0 and 4.37 m^3/s respectively, calculate the time interval between two discharge. Assume K_r as 0.79.

Solution. Given that

$$Q_s = 7 \text{ m}^3/\text{s}$$
$$Q_t = 4.37 \text{ m}^3/\text{s}$$
$$K_r = 0.79$$
$$t = ?$$

Using the formula $Q_t = Q_s (K_r)^t$

or
$$(K_r)^t = \frac{Q_t}{Q_s} = \frac{4.37}{7} = 0.6243$$

Taking the log both side

$$t \log K_r = \log 0.6243$$
$$t = \frac{\log 0.6243}{\log 0.79} \text{ days}$$
$$= 1.998 \backslash \mathbf{2\ days} \quad \textbf{Ans.}$$

Problem 6.9. From the following hyetograph

Time interval (*h*)	0 – 1	1 – 2	2 – 3	3 – 4	4 – 5	5 – 6	6 – 7	7 – 8
Rainfall intensity (cm/h)	5	7.5	3.0	1.5	2.0	1.0	0.50	1.0

Compute the total depth of rainfall, effective rainfall, total infiltration loss and duration of effective rainfall if ϕ-index is 1.125 cm/h

Solution.

1. Total depth of rainfall is the area of hyetograph, given as under

$$= 1 \times (5 + 7.5 + 3.0 + 1.5 + 2.0 + 1.0 + 0.50 + 1.0) \text{ cm}$$
$$= \mathbf{21.5\ cm} \quad \textbf{Ans.}$$

2. Effective rainfall is computed as

Time interval (*h*)	0 – 1	1 – 2	2 – 3	3 – 4	4 – 5	5 – 6	6 – 7	7 – 8
Effective rainfall intensity*	3.875	6.375	1.875	0.375	0.875	—	—	—

* It is difference of rainfall intensity and ϕ-index.

Therefore, total $ER = 1 \times (3.875 + 6.375 + 1.875 + 0.375 + 0.875)$ cm

$$= \mathbf{13.375\ cm} \quad \textbf{Ans.}$$

2. Total infiltration loss $= 21.5 - 13.375 =$ **8.125 cm** **Ans.**

3. Duration of ER = **5h** **Ans.**

Problem 6.10. Determine the ϕ-index, if the total direct runoff volume due to a given rainfall is 1.40×10^6 m^3 at the outlet. The area of watershed is 27×10^6 m^2. Take rainfall depth as 7 cm and its duration as 7 h.

Solution. Given that

Volume of direct runoff $= 1.4 \times 10^6$ m^3

Area of watershed $= 27 \times 10^6$ m^2

Rainfall depth $= 7$ cm

Storm duration $= 7$ h

Therefore, runoff depth (*i.e.* ER) $= \dfrac{1.4 \times 10^6}{27 \times 10^6}$ m

$= 0.0519$ m $= 5.19$ *cm*

$$\phi\text{–index} = \frac{\text{total loss of rain water}}{\text{duration of rainfall}}$$

$= \dfrac{7 - 5.19}{7}$ cm/h $=$ **0.259 cm/h** **Ans.**

Problem 6.11. Area of DRH due to a given storm is 1.50×10^6 m^3. Determine the value of ER, if area of the watershed is 15×10^6 m^2.

Solution. Using the formula

$$ER = \frac{\text{area of DRH}}{\text{area of watershed}}$$

$= \dfrac{1.50 \times 10^6}{15 \times 10^6}$ m

$= 0.10$ m $=$ **10 cm** **Ans.**

Problem 6.12. Determine the direct runoff (m^3) or area of DRH due to an effective rainfall of 5 cm over the watershed of 15×10^6 m^2 area.

Solution. Using the formula

$$ER = \frac{\text{Area of DRH or volume of direct runoff}}{\text{Area of watershed}}$$

$\therefore$ Volume of direct runoff $= \dfrac{5}{100} \times 15 \times 10^6$ m^3

$=$ **7.5×10^5 m^3** **Ans.**

Problem 6.13. The mass curve of a given storm is given as under :

Time from start of storm (h)	0	1.5	3.0	4.5	6.0	7.5	9.0	10.5
Cumulative rainfall (cm)	0	0.60	2.50	6.25	6.75	8.00	9.50	10.00

Determine (1) the ordinates of ERH, (2) ER, (3) duration of ER and (4) volume of direct runoff from the watershed, if

(*a*) area of watershed is 7.5 sq km

(*b*) ϕ-index is 0.45 cm/h

Solution.

1. **Computation of ordinate of ERH :** It is shown in following table

Time from start of storm (h)	*Time interval Δt (h)*	*Cumulative rainfall in Δt time (cm)*	*Rain fall depth in Δt time (cm)*	*Amount of rain water lost Δt · φ (cm)**	*ER** (cm)*	*Intensity of ER (cm/h)****
0	1.5	0.0	—	—	—	—
1.5	1.5	0.60	0.60	0.675	—	—
3.0	1.5	2.50	1.90	0.675	1.225	0.82
4.5	1.5	6.25	3.75	0.675	3.075	2.05
6.0	1.5	6.75	0.50	0.675	—	—
7.5	1.5	8.00	1.25	0.675	0.575	0.38
9.0	1.5	9.50	1.50	0.675	0.825	0.55
10.5	1.5	10.00	0.50	0.675	—	—

* The amount of water lost is determined as the product of φ-index and time interval (Δ*t*).

** The depth of ER is computed by subtracting the loss of water (*i.e.* φ index × Δ*t*) from the total rainfall depth in time Δ*t*.

*** The intensity of effective rainfall is determined by dividing the depth of ER with Δ*t*

2. **Total depth of ER :** It is determined by adding the ER during different time intervals, *i.e.*

$$= 1.225 + 3.075 + 0.575 + 0.825 \text{ cm}$$
$$= \mathbf{5.70 \text{ cm}} \quad \textbf{Ans.}$$

3. **Duration of ER :** It is the total time during which ER is generated, *i.e.*

$$= (1.5 + 1.5 + 1.5 + 1.5) \text{ hours}$$
$$= \mathbf{6.0 \text{ hours}} \quad \textbf{Ans.}$$

4. **Volume of direct runoff :** It is computed by multiplying the total depth of ER to the area of watershed, given as under :

$$= ER \times \text{area of watershed}$$
$$= \frac{5.7}{100} \times 7.5 \times (1000)^2 \text{ m}^3$$
$$= \mathbf{4.275 \times 10^5 \text{ m}^3} \quad \textbf{Ans.}$$

Problem 6.14. Due to a given storm over the watershed, the generated hyetograph is given as under :

Time from start of storm (h)	0	2	4	6	8	10	12	14
Intensity of rainfall (cm/h)	0	0.5	2.5	4.7	7.5	10.0	12.5	15.0

Compute, (a) ordinates of ERH (b) ER (c) duration of ER (d) volume of direct runoff. If the area of watershed is 5×10^6 m^2 and ϕ-index is 1.25 cm/h

Solution

(*a*) **Ordinate of ERH :** Its computation is shown in following table.

Time from start of rainfall (h)	*Intensity of rainfall (cm/h)*	*ϕ-index (cm/h)*	*Intensity of ER (cm/h)*	*ER (cm)***
0	0.0	1.25	—	—
2	0.50	1.25	—	—
4	2.50	1.25	1.25	2.50
6	4.70	1.25	3.45	6.90
8	7.50	1.25	6.25	12.50
10	10.00	1.25	8.75	17.50
12	12.50	1.25	11.25	22.50
14	15.00	1.25	13.75	27.50

* The intensity of ER is computed by subtracting the ϕ-index from intensity of rainfall.

** The ER is calculated by multiplying the intensity of ER with the time interval (*i.e*, $\Delta t = 2h$)

(*b*) Total depth of ER = (2.50+ 6.9+ 12.50+ 17.50+ 22.50+ 27.50) cm

= 89.4 cm Ans

(*c*) Duration of ER = $6 \times 2h$ = **$12h$ Ans**

(*d*) Volume of direct runoff = ER× area of watershed

$$= \frac{89.4}{100} \times 5 \times 10^6 \text{ m}^3 = 4.47 \times 10^6 \text{ m}^3 \textbf{ Ans.}$$

Problem 6.15. If the area of unit hydrograph due to a given rainstorm is 13×10^6 m^3, then determine the volume of direct runoff for 3cm ER.

Solution. The area of unit hydrograph represents the volume of direct runoff due to 1cm ER. Accordingly, the volume of direct runoff for 3 cm ER will be equal to

$$= 3 \times 13 \times 10^6 \text{ m}^3$$

$$= 39 \times 10^6 \text{ m}^3 \textbf{ Ans.}$$

Problem 6.16. Compute the ordinate of unit hydrograph, if the direct runoff due to 2.5 cm ER is 39×10^2 m^3/s.

Solution. It is computed by using the following formula

$$OUHG = \frac{\text{Ordinate of DRH or direct runoff rate}}{\text{ER}}$$

$$= \frac{39 \times 10^2}{2.5} = \textbf{1560 m}^3\textbf{/s Ans}$$

Problem 6.17. If the ordinate of unit hydrograph is 2500 m^3/s, then calculate the ordinate of DRH for 3.5 cmER.

Solution. Using the linearity assumption of unit hydrograph, we have

Ordinate of DRH = $ER \times$ ordinate of unit hydrograph

$= 3.5 \times 2500 = \mathbf{8750\ m^3}$ **Ans.**

Problem 6.18. The ordinates of 3-*h* unit hydrograph due to a given storm are given as under. Compute the ordinates of DRH for 2.75 cm effective rainfall. Also compute the volume of direct runoff.

Time (h)	0	3	6	9	12	15	18	21	24	27
OUHG(m^3/s)	0	25	150	175	225	185	120	75	30	0

Solution. Computation of DRH of 2.75 cm ER is shown in following table.

Time (h)	*O.U.H.G.(m^3/s)*	*ODRH (m^3/s) for 2.75 cm ER (column 2 × 2.75)*
(1)	*(2)*	*(3)*
0	0	0
3	25	68.75
6	150	412.5
9	175	481.25
12	225	618.75
15	185	508.75
18	120	330.00
21	75	206.25
24	30	82.50
27	0	0.0

The volume of direct runoff is determined as the product of ordinate of DRH and time interval ($\Delta t = 3h$). It is given as under :

$= 3 \times 3600\ [\ 68.75 + 412.5 + 481.25 + 618.75 + 508.75 + 330 + 206.25 + 82.50\ ]\ m^3$

$= 3 \times 3600\ [\ 2708.75\ ]\ m^3$

$= \mathbf{2.925 \times 10^7\ m^3}$ **Ans**

Problem 6.19. The ordinates of DRH due to 2.5 cm ER over the watershed are given as under. Compute the ordinates of unit hydrograph. Also determine the area of watershed.

Time (h)	0	2	4	6	8	10	12	14	16	18
Ordinates of DRH (m^3/s)	0	25	75	175	225	150	80	55	15	0

Solution. The computation of OUHG is shown in following table.

Time (h)	*Ordinate of DRH* (m^3/s)	*Ordinate of UHG* (m^3/s)
(1)	*(2)*	*(3)*
0	0	0.0
2	25	10.0
4	75	30.0
6	175	70.0
8	225	90.0
10	150	60.0
12	80	32.0
14	55	22.0
16	15	6.0
18	0	0.0

Area of watershed can be determined by using the formula.

$$ER = \frac{\text{Total volume of direct runoff}}{\text{Area of watershed}}$$

In this case, total ordinates of unit hydrograph represent the total volume of direct runoff due to 1 cm ER. Accordingly, we have

$$\text{Area of watershed} = \frac{\text{total volume of direct runoff}}{1}$$

$$= \frac{2 \times 3600 \times (10 + 30 + 70 + 90 + 60 + 32 + 22 + 6) \times 100}{1}$$

$$= 2.304 \times 10^8 \text{ m}^2$$

$$= \mathbf{230.4 \text{ sq km Ans}}$$

The area of watershed can also be determined by considering the ordinates of DRH, *i.e.*

Area of watershed

$$= \frac{2 \times 3600 \times 100\,(25 + 75 + 175 + 225 + 150 + 80 + 55 + 15)}{2.5}$$

$$= \frac{2 \times 3600 \times 100 \times 800}{2.5} \text{ m}^2$$

$$= 230.4 \times 10^6 \text{ m}^2 = \mathbf{230.4 \text{ sq km}} \quad \textbf{Ans.}$$

Problem 6.20. A 3-h unit hydrograph due to a given storm is given as under. Calculate the DRH, if two successive storms of 3-h with rainfall excess of 2.5 and 4.0 cm, respectively took place in the watershed. The 4.0 cm excess rainfall was occurred after 3 hour from 2.5 cm ER.

Time (h)	0	3	6	9	12	15	18	21	24	27	30
OUHG (m^3/s)	0	15	20	35	60	75	50	35	20	10	0

Solution. Computation of DRH is shown in following table.

Time (h)	Ordinate of UHG (m^3/s)	Ordinate of 2.5 cm DRH (m^3/s)	Ordinate of 4 cm DRH (lagged by 3-h), m^3/s	Ordinate of 6.5 cm DRH (col (3) + col (4) (m^3/s)
(1)	(2)	(3)	(4)	(5)
0	0	0.0	0.0	0.0
3	15	37.5	0.0	37.5
6	20	50.0	60	110.0
9	35	87.5	80	167.5
12	60	150.0	140	290.0
15	75	187.50	240	427.50
18	50	125.0	300	425.00
21	35	87.50	200	287.50
24	20	50.0	140	190.0
27	10	25.0	80	105.0
30	0	0.0	40	40.0
			0.0	0.0

Problem 6.21. Determine the total direct runoff and ER from the following rainfall and stream flow data. If area of watershed is 5.0 sq km, base flow 60 m^3/s and abstraction 0.70 cm/h.

Date	Time (Clock hour)	Rainfall (cm)	Stream flow (m^3/s)
15 August	8:30 PM	0.4	60
	9:00	0.65	74
	9:30	3.40	85
	10:00	5.60	250
	10:30	5.30	697
	11:00	0.50	1710
	11:30	0.23	2860
16 August	12:00 AM		3308
	12:30		2470
	1:00		1296
	1:30		674
	2:00		541
	2:30		370
	3:00		214
	3:30		118
	4:00		106
	4:30		91

Solution. The excess rainfall is determined by subtracting the abstraction from rainfall depth ; and direct runoff is computed by subtracting the baseflow from observed stream flow data. Computations are shown in following table.

Time (clock hour)	*Time (hour)*	*Ramfall depth (cm)*	*Ramfall excess (cm)*	*Direct runoff* (m^3/s)
8:30	0	—	—	—
9:00	0.5	0.40	0.05	14
9:30	1.0	0.65	0.30	25
10:00	1.5	3.40	3.05	190
10:30	2.0	5.60	5.25	637
11:00	2.5	5.30	4.95	1650
11:30	3.0	0.50	0.15	2800
12:00	3.5	0.23	—	3248
12:30	4.0			2410
1:00	4.5			1236
1:30	5.0			614
2:00	5.5			481
2:30	6.0			310
3:00	6.5			154
3:30	7.0			58
4:00	7.5			46
4:30	8.0			31
		Total	**13.75 cm**	**13904**

Problem 6.22. Determine the peak intensity of triangular hyetograph of a given storm for the depth of rainfall as 5 cm during 30 minutes duration.

Solution. Using the formula for peak intensity of triangular hyetograph

$$= \frac{2P}{T_d}$$

$$= \frac{2 \times 5 \times 60}{30} \text{ cm/h}$$

$$= \mathbf{20 \text{ cm/h}} \quad \textbf{Ans.}$$

Problem 6.23. Calculate the time to peak intensity of triangular hyetograph of the storm occurring 30 minutes duration. Take the storm advancement coefficient (r) as 0.38.

Solution. Using the formula

Time to peak intensity $(t_a) = r \cdot T_d$

$$= 0.38 \times \frac{30}{60} \text{ h} = \mathbf{0.19 \text{ h}} \quad \textbf{Ans.}$$

Problem 6.24. Compute the value of recession time and base length of triangular hyetograph of the storm occurring for the duration of 35 minutes. Assume the storm advancement coefficient (r) as 0.41.

Solution. Using the formula

$$t_b = (1 - r)\, T_d = (1 - 0.41) \times \frac{35}{60} = \mathbf{0.344\ h} \quad \textbf{Ans.}$$

and $$t_a = r \cdot T_d = 0.41 \times \frac{35}{60} = \mathbf{0.24\ h}$$

Base length $= 0.344\,h + 0.24\,h = \mathbf{0.584\ h}$ **Ans.**

Problem 6.25. Determine the triangular hyetograph of the storm occurring for 15 minutes duration. The depth of rainfall was measured as 3.25 cm. Assume the value of storm advancement coefficient(r) as 0.30.

Solution. Given that the

duration of storm = 15 minutes or 0.25 h

depth of rainfall = 3.25 cm

storm advancement coefficient (r) = 0.3

Using the formulae, we have

(*i*) Peak intensity (h) $= \frac{2P}{T_d} = \frac{2 \times 3.25}{0.25} = \mathbf{26\ cm/h}$

(*ii*) Time to peak intensity $(t_a) = r \cdot T_d$

$= 0.3 \times 0.25 = 0.075\,h = \mathbf{4.5\ minutes}$

(*iii*) Recession time $(t_b) = T_d - t_a$

$= 0.25 - 0.075 = 0.175\,h = \mathbf{10.5\ minutes}$

(*iv*) Base length $= t_a + t_b = 4.5 + 10.5 = \mathbf{15\ minutes}$

Problem 6.26. Compute the ordinates of 3-h unit hydrograph for the following data recorded at the outlet of watershed. Area of watershed is 400 sq km .

Time from start of storm (h)	-3	0	3	6	9	12	15	18	21
Discharge (m^3/s)	20	20	60	150	230	205	160	140	110
Time from start of storm (h)	24	27	30	33	36	39	42	45	48
Discharge (m^3/s)	85	78	60	50	40	35	30	25	20

(Assume the constant base flow as 20 m^3/s)

Solution. Computation of unit hydrograph is shown in following table

Time (h)	*Discharge* (m^3/s)	*Base flow* (m^3/s)	*Ordinate of DRH* (m^3/s)	*Ordinate of 3-h unit hydrograph* (m^3/s)
– 3	20	20	—	—
0	20	20	—	—
3	60	20	40	12.78
6	150	20	130	41.53
9	230	20	210	67.10
12	205	20	185	59.10
15	160	20	140	44.73
18	140	20	120	38.34
21	110	20	90	28.75
24	85	20	65	20.77
27	78	20	58	18.53
30	60	20	40	12.78
33	50	20	30	9.58
36	40	20	20	6.39
39	35	20	15	4.80
42	30	20	10	3.20
45	25	20	5	1.60
48	20	20	—	—
		Total	1158	

Computation of ER : It is given as under

$$ER = \frac{\text{Total volume of direct runoff (m}^3)}{\text{Area of watershed}}$$

$$= \frac{3 \times 3600 \times 1158}{400 \times 10^6} \text{ m}$$

$$= 0.0313 \text{ m} = \mathbf{3.13 \text{ cm}}$$

Computation of OUHG : It is done by dividing the ordinate of DRH with ER as 3.13 cm.

Problem 6.27. Determine the base width of triangular unit hydrograph of 3h duration ; if

1. peak flow due to a storm of 3 – *h* duration is 210 m^3/s.
2. total rainfall is 6.0 cm.
3. area of watershed is 550 km^2
4. average infiltration loss is 0.25 cm/h.
5. constant base flow is 25 m^3/s.

Solution. Since the shape of unit hydrograph is triangle (let it is right angles triangle). Therefore, area of unit hydrograph

$$= \frac{1}{2} \text{ base} \times \text{perpendicular height}$$

In this case, base and height of triangle denotes the base width and peak of the unit hydrograph. Also, the area of tiangular unit hydrograph is equal to the product of area of watershed and 1 cm ER. Thus, by equating

$$\frac{1}{2} \text{ base} \times \text{perpendicular height of } \Delta \text{ UHG} = \frac{1}{100} \times 550 \times 10^6 \text{ m}^3$$

The computations of other parameters of UHG are given as under :

Given that the

Duration of storm	$= 3h$
Total rainfall depth	$= 6.0$ cm
Infiltration loss	$= 0.25 \times 3 = 0.75$ cm
∴ Rainfall excess	$= 6.0 - 0.75 = 5.25$ cm
Peak of hydrograph	$= 210 \text{ m}^3/\text{s}$
Base flow	$= 25 \text{ m}^3/\text{s}$
Peak direct runoff flow	$= 210 - 25 = 185 \text{ m}^3/\text{s}$
∴ Peak flow of 3-h unit hydrograph	$= \frac{185}{5.25} \text{ m}^3/\text{s}$
	$= \mathbf{35.24 \text{ m}^3/\text{s}}$

Now, considering the value of peak flow of 3-h unit hydrograph as the height of triangular unit hydrograph, we have

$$\frac{1}{2} \times \text{base width} \times 35.24 \times 3600 = 550 \times 10^6 \times \frac{1}{100}$$

63432 base width	$= 550 \times 10^4$
∴ Base width	$= 86.71$ hours
	$\approx$ **87 hours Ans.**

Problem 6.28. Followings are the ordinates of 3-h unit hydrograph due to a given storm. Calculate the ordinates of 12-h unit hydrograph.

Time (h)	*0*	*3*	*6*	*9*	*12*	*15*	*18*	*21*
OUHG of 3-h (m^3/s)	0	5	7.5	12.0	20.5	40.0	55.0	50.0
Time (h)	24	27	30	33	36	39	42	45
OUGH of 3-h (m^3/s)	48.0	35.0	30	25	22.0	10	7	0

Solution. The 9-h unit hydrograph is derived by using the principle of superposition. Computation is shown in following table.

Time (h)	*3-h OUHG (m^3/s)*	*Ordinates lagged by* 3-h	6-h	*DRH of 12-h for 3 cm (Col 2 + 3 + 4)*	*12-h OUHG m^3/s**
(1)	*(2)*	*(3)*	*(4)*	*(5)*	*(6)*
0	0.0	—		0.0	0.0
3	5	0.0	—	5.0	1.67
6	7.5	5.0	0.0	12.5	4.17
9	12.0	7.5	5.0	24.5	8.17
12	20.5	12.0	7.5	40.0	13.33
15	40.0	20.5	12.0	72.5	24.17
18	55.0	40.0	20.5	115.	38.50
21	50.0	55.0	40.0	145.0	48.33
24	48.0	50.0	55.0	153.0	51.0
27	35.0	48.0	50.0	133.0	44.33
30	30.0	35.0	48.0	113.0	37.67
33	25.0	30.0	35.0	90.0	30.0
36	22.0	25.0	30.0	77.0	25.67
39	10.0	22.0	25.0	57.0	19.0
42	7.0	10.0	22.0	39.0	13.0
45	0.0	7.0	10.0	17.0	5.67
		0.0	7.0 7.0	2.3,	
			0.0	0	0.00

* column (5)/3

Problem 6.29. The ordinates of 9-h unit hydrograph are given below. Compute the ordinates of 18-h unit hydrograph

Time (h)	*0*	*9*	*18*	*27*	*36*	*45*	*54*	*63*
9-h UHG (m^3/s)	0	1.67	4.17	8.17	13.33	24.17	38.50	48.33
Time (h)	72	81	90	99	10.8	117	126	135
9-h UHG (m^3/s)	51.0	44.33	37.67	30.0	25.67	19.0	13.0	5.67
Time (h)	144	153						
9-h UHG (m^3/s)	2.33	0.0						

Solution. Computation of 18-h unit-hydrograph is done by using S-curve method, which is given as below :

Time (h)	*Ordinate of 9-h UHG (m^3/s)*	*S-curve addition (m^3/s)*		*S-curve lagged by 18-h*	*Difference of S-curve addition and lagged S-curve*	*18- h UHG m^3/s*
0	0	—	0		0.0	*0*
9	1.67	0	1.67		1.67	0.835
18	4.17	1.67	5.84	0	5.84	2.92
27	8.17	5.84	14.01	1.67	12.34	6.17
36	13.33	14.01	27.34	5.84	21.50	10.75
45	24.17	27.34	51.51	14.01	37.5	18.75
54	38.5	51.51	90.01	27.34	62.67	31.34
63	48.33	90.01	138.34	51.51	86.83	43.42
72	51.0	138.34	189.34	90.01	99.33	49.67
81	44.33	189.34	233.67	138.34	95.33	47.67
90	37.67	233.67	271.34	189.34	82.00	41.00
99	30.0	271.34	301.34	233.67	67.67	33.84
108	25.67	301.34	327.01	271.34	55.67	27.84
117	19.0	327.01	346.01	301.34	44.67	22.34
126	13.0	346.01	359.01	327.01	32.0	16.00
135	5.67	359.01	364.68	346.01	18.67	9.34
144	2.33	364.68	367.01	359.01	8.0	4.00
153	0.00	367.01	367.01	364.68	2.33	1.17
		367.01	367.01	367.01	0.0	0.0
			367.01	367.01	0.0	0.0

Problem 6.30. Compute the ordinates of 3-h unit hydrograph from 6-h unit hydrograph given as below :

Time (h)	*0*	*6*	*12*	*18*	*24*	*30*	*36*	*42*	*48*
6-h UHG (m^3/s)	0	5	12.0	21.0	35	50	75	90	75
Time (h)	54	60	66	72	78	84	90	96	102
6-h UHG (m^3/s)	65	60	50	45	37	25	15	8	0

Solution. The ordinates of 3-h unit hydrograph from 6-h U.H.G. are determined by using the S-curve method. Computations are given as under :

Table : Computation of 3-h unit hydrograph from 6-h unit hydrograph

Time	*6-h unit hydrograph (m^3/s)*	*S-curve addition*	*S- curve ordinate (Col 2 + col 3)*	*S-curve lagged by 3-h*	*Col 4 - Col 5*
(1)	*(2)*	*(3)*	*(4)*	*(5)*	*(6)*
0	0	—	0		0
3	3.0	0	3.0	0	3.0
6	5.0	0	5.0	3.0	2.0
9	9.0	3.0	12.0	5.0	7.0
12	12.0	5.0	17.0	12.0	5.0
15	18.0	12.0	30.0	17.0	13.0
18	21.0	17.0	38.0	30.0	8.0
21	30.0	20.0	50.0	38.0	12.0
24	35.0	38.0	73.0	50.0	23.0
27	42.0	50.0	92.0	73.0	19.0
30	50.0	73.0	123.0	92.0	31.0
33	61.0	92.0	153.0	123.0	30.0
36	75.0	123.0	198.0	153.0	45.0
39	84.0	153.0	237.0	198.0	39.0
42	90.0	198.0	288.0	237.0	51.0
45	85.0	237.0	322.0	288.0	34.0
48	75.0	288.0	363.0	322.0	41.0
51	70.0	322.0	392.0	363.0	29.0
54	65.0	363.0	428.0	392.0	36.0
57	63.0	392.0	455.0	428.0	27.0
60	60.0	428.0	488.0	455.0	33.0
63	53.0	455.0	508.0	488.0	20.0
66	50.0	488.0	538.0	508.0	30.0
69	43.0	508.0	551.0	538.0, ,	
72	45.0	538.0	583.0	551.0, ,	
75	41.0	551.0	592.0	583.0, ,	
78	37.0	583.0	620.0	592.0, ,	
81	33.0	592.0	625.0	620.0, ,	
84	25.0	620.0	645.0	625.0, ,	
87	21.0	625.0	648.0	645.0, ,	
90	15.0	645.0	660.0	648.0, ,	
93	13.0	646.0	659.0	660.0, ,	
96	8.0	660.0	668.0	659.0, ,	
99	5.0	659.0	664.0	668.0, ,	
102	0	668.0	668.0	664.0, ,	

Problem 6.31. Compute the ordinates of unit hydrograph by using distribution graph for a watershed of 3 sq km area which received three rainfall of 10, 3.5 and 7.5 cm in three successive days. The percentage of surface runoff distribution graph for every rainfall of 1-day duration is 5, 15, 40, 20, 15 and 5. Also assume, the average ϕ-index as 2.5 cm/day and base flow as negligible.

Solution. The computation of unit hydrograph by using distribution graph method is shown in following table

Time interval (days)	*Rainfall (cm)*	*ϕ-index cm/ day*	*ER (cm)*	*Percentage of runoff of distribution graph*	*Runoff distribution for rainfall excess of OUHG*				
					7.5 cm	1.0 cm	5 cm	cm	m^3/s*
0-1	10.0	2.5	7.5	5	0.375	—	—	0.375	0.130
1-2	3.5	2.5	1.0	15	1.125	0.05	—	1.175	0.41
2-3	7.5	2.5	5.0	40	3.00	0.15	0.25	3.40	1.18
3-4				20	1.50	0.40	0.75	2.65	0.92
4-5				15	1.125	0.20	2.00	3.325	1.15
5-6				5	0.375	0.15	1.00	1.525	0.53
6-7				0	0.0	0.05	0.75	0.80	0.28
7-8					0.0	0.00	0.25	0.25	0.09
								0.00	0.0

$$\text{*Runoff } (m^3/s) = \frac{\text{Area (sq km)} \times \text{runoff depth (cm)}}{24 \times 3600 \times 100} = \frac{3 \times 10^6 \text{ runoff depth (cm)}}{86400 \times 100}$$

$$= \mathbf{0.347 \times runoff\ depth\ (cm)\ m^3/s}$$

Problem 6.32. Compute the ordinates of 9-h unit hydrograph by using S-curve method for the given data in example 6.28.

Solution. The computation of 9-h unit hydrograph by using S-curve method is shown in following table.

Time (h)	Ordinate of 3-h UHG (m^3/s)	S-curve addition * (m^3/s)	S-curve ordinate (m^3/s)**	S- curve lagged by 9-h (m^3/s) ***	Col (4) - col (5)	9-h OUHG $\frac{\text{col (6)}}{9/3}$
(1)	(2)	(3)	(4)	(5)	(6)	(7)
0	0.0	—	0.0	—	0	0
3	5.0	0	5.0	—	5.0	1.67
6	7.5	5.0	12.5	—	12.5	4.17
9	12.0	12.5	24.5	0	24.5	8.17
12	20.5	24.5	45.0	5.0	40.0	13.33
15	40.0	45.0	85.0	12.5	72.5	24.17
18	55.0	85.0	140.0	24.5	115.5	38.50
21	50.0	140.0	190.0	45.0	145.0	48.33
24	48.0	190.0	238.0	85.0	153.0	51.0
27	35.0	238.0	273.0	140.0	133.0	44.33
30	30.0	273.0	303.0	190.0	113.0	37.67
33	25.0	303.0	328.0	238.0	90.0	30.00
36	22.0	328.0	350.0	273.0	77.0	25.67
39	10.0	350.0	360.0	303.0	57.0	19.00
42	7.0	360.0	367.0	328.0	39.0	13.00
45	0.0	367.0	367.0	350.0	17.0	5.67
		367.0	367.0	360.0	7.0	2.33
			367.0	367.0	0.0	0.00

* The S-curve addition is performed by calculating the successive cumulative values and arranging them in their respective order.

** The S-curve ordinates are computed by adding the ordinates of col (2) and col (3).

*** Since 9-h unit hydrograph is required to determine, therefore at a time, the ordinates of S-curve (*i.e.* values of col 4) are lagged by 9-h.

Problem 6.33. Compute the equilibrium discharge of S-curve, if area of the watershed is 5 sq km and ER as 6h.

Solution. Using the formula for equilibrium discharge

$$Q_s = 2.778 \frac{A}{D} \text{ m}^3/\text{s}$$

in which A is in sq km and D is in hour.

$$Q = 2.778 \frac{5}{6} = \mathbf{2.315\ m^3/s} \quad \textbf{Ans.}$$

Problem 6.34. Determine the duration of ER in the watershed of area $4 \times 10^6\ m^2$. The equilibrium discharge is $1.75 \times 10^6\ m^3/s$.

Solution. Given that the

Area of watershed $= 4 \times 10^6\ m^2 = 4$ sq km

Equilibrium discharge $= 4.75\ \text{m}^3/\text{s}$

Using the formula, $$Q_s = \frac{2.778\,A}{D}$$

$$4.75 = \frac{2.778 \times 4}{D}$$

$\therefore$ $$D = \mathbf{2.34\ h} \quad \textbf{Ans.}$$

Problem 6.35. Calculate the value of basin lag (hour) for derivation of synthetic unit hydrograph of the watershed having longest length of watercourse as 15 km and distance along the main watercourse from watershed divide to the point opposite to the centroid of watershed as 7 km. Assume the value of regional constant (C_t) as 1.25.

Solution. Given that,

$$L = 15\ \text{km}$$
$$L_{ca} = 7\ \text{km}$$
$$C_t = 1.25$$

Using the formula for basin lag *i.e.*

$$t_p = C_t\,(L \cdot L_{ca})^{0.3}$$
$$= 1.25\,(15 \times 7)^{0.3}\ \text{hours} = \mathbf{5.05\ hours} \quad \textbf{Ans.}$$

Problem 6.36. Calculate the value of basin lag of watershed, if

(*i*) basin constant (C_{tL}) $= 1.25$

(*ii*) longest length of watercourse (L) $= 17$ km

(*iii*) L_{ca} $= 8.0$ km

(*iv*) basin slope (S) $= 0.5$ m/m

(*v*) constant n $= 0.25$

Solution. Using the formula for basin lag

$$t_p = C_{tL}\left(\frac{L \cdot L_{ca}}{\sqrt{S}}\right)^n$$

$$= 1.25\left(\frac{17 \times 8}{\sqrt{0.5}}\right)^{0.25}\ \text{hours} = \mathbf{4.66\ hours} \quad \textbf{Ans.}$$

Problem 6.37. Determine the standard duration of effective rainfall to derive the synthetic unit hydrograph, if time to peak of the hydrograph is 14.67 hours.

Solution. Using the formula,

$$t_r = \frac{t_p}{5.5} = \frac{14.67}{5.5} \text{ hours} = \mathbf{2.67 \text{ hours}} \quad \textbf{Ans.}$$

Problem 6.38. Compute the value of non-standard duration of effective rainfall for derivation of synthetic unit hydrograph, if basin lag is 13.75 hours and standard duration of effective rainfall is 2.50 hours. Take the basin lag (t_p') for effective duration of non-standard time as 14 hours.

Solution. Given that,

$$t_r = 2.5 \text{ hours}$$
$$t_p = 13.75 \text{ hours}$$
$$t_p' = 14 \text{ hours}$$

Using the formula, $t_p' = \frac{21}{22} t_p + \frac{t_R}{4}$

$$14 = \frac{21}{22} \times 13.75 + \frac{t_R}{4}$$

or

$$\frac{t_R}{4} = 13 - \frac{21}{22} \times 13.75$$

$$t_R = 4\left(14 - \frac{21}{22} \times 13{,}75\right) = \mathbf{3.5 \text{ hours}} \quad \textbf{Ans.}$$

Problem 6.39. Calculate the standard duration of ER and peak discharge to derive the synthetic unit hydrograph for an ungauged watershed having the area as 50 sq km. The basin lag of watershed is 14 hours. Take the value of regional constant (C_p) as 0.35.

Solution. Given that,

$$A = 50 \text{ sq km}$$
$$C_p = 0.35$$
$$t_p = 14 \text{ hours}$$

1. Standard duration of effective rainfall (t_r)

$$= \frac{t_p}{5.5} = \frac{14}{5.5} = \mathbf{2.55 \text{ hours}} \quad \textbf{Ans.}$$

2. Peak discharge (Q_p) $= \dfrac{2.78 \times C_p \cdot A}{t_p} \text{ m}^3/\text{s}$

$$= \frac{2.78 \times 0.35 \times 50}{14} = \mathbf{3.48 \text{ m}^3/\text{s}} \quad \textbf{Ans.}$$

Problem 6.40. Calculate the peak discharge for non-standard duration of effective rainfall to derive the synthetic unit hydrograph, if the area of watershed is 500 sq km, basin lag (t_p) is 13.0 hours and non-standard duration of effective rainfall is 14.75 hours. Assume the value of C_p as 0.37.

Solution. Given that,

$$A = 500 \text{ sq km}$$
$$t_p = 13 \text{ hours}$$
$$t_R = 14.75 \text{ hours}$$
$$C_p = 0.37$$

$$\text{Non-standard time to peak } (t_p') = \frac{21}{22} t_p + \frac{t_R}{4}$$
$$= \frac{21}{22} \times 13 + \frac{14.75}{4}$$
$$= 12.41 + 3.69 = \mathbf{16.1 \text{ hours}}$$

Therefore, peak discharge for non-standard duration of time to peak (t_p') is

$$Q_p = \frac{2.78\, C_p \cdot A}{t_p'}$$
$$= \frac{2.78 \times 0.37 \times 500}{16.1} \text{ m}^3/\text{s}$$
$$= \mathbf{31.94 \text{ m}^3/\text{s}} \quad \textbf{Ans.}$$

Problem 6.41. Determine the base time of synthetic unit hydrograh, if basin lag and non standard duration of effective rainfall are 14 and 15 hours, respectively.

Solution. Given that

$$t_p = 14 \text{ hours}$$
$$t_R = 15 \text{ hours}$$

Therefore,

$$t_p' = \frac{21}{22} t_p + \frac{t_R}{4}$$
$$= \frac{21}{22} \times 14 + \frac{15}{4} = 17.11 \text{ hours}$$

Using the formula for base time of SUHG

$$t_b = (72 + 3t_p') \text{ hours}$$
$$= 72 + 3 \times 17.11 = \mathbf{123.33 \text{ hours}} \quad \textbf{Ans.}$$

Problem 6.42. Determine the widths of synthetic unit hydrograph at 50 and 75% peak discharge, if the

(*a*) area of watershed = 150 sq km

(*b*) basin lag = 12.5 hours

(*c*) regional constant (C_p) = 0.35

Solution. Using the formula for peak discharge

$$Q_p = \frac{2.78\ C_p \cdot A}{t_p}\ \text{m}^3/\text{s}$$

$$= \frac{2.78 \times 0.35 \times 150}{12.5}\ \text{m}^3/\text{s} = \mathbf{11.67\ m^3/s}$$

or $$q = \frac{Q}{A} = \frac{11.67}{150} = 0.078\ \text{m}^3/\text{s/sqkm}$$

Widths of synthetic unit hydrograph,

$$W_{50} = \frac{5.87}{q^{1.08}}$$

$$= \frac{5.87}{(0.078)^{1.08}}\ \text{hours} = \mathbf{92.3\ hours} \quad \textbf{Ans.}$$

$$W_{75} = \frac{W_{50}}{1.75}$$

$$= \frac{92.3}{1.75}\ \text{hours} = \mathbf{52.74\ hours} \quad \textbf{Ans.}$$

Problem 6.43. Determine the basin lag of the watershed of area 150 sq km. The width of S.U.H.G. at 50% peak discharge is 92.3 hours. Take the regional constant (C_p) as 0.35.

Solution. Given that,

Area of watershed = 150 sq km

W_{50} = 92.3 hours

C_p = 0.35

Using the formula

$$W_{50} = \frac{5.87}{(q)^{1.08}}$$

$$92.3 = \frac{5.87}{(q)^{1.08}}$$

or $$q^{1.08} = \frac{5.87}{92.3}$$

$$q = \left(\frac{5.87}{92.3}\right)^{1/1.08}$$

$$= (0.0636)^{0.926} = 0.078\ \text{m}^3/\text{s/sqkm}$$

or $$Q_p = .078 \times 150\ \text{m}^3/\text{s} = 11.70\ \text{m}^3/\text{s}$$

∴ Therefore, basin lag by using the formula

$$Q_p = \frac{2.78\ C_p \cdot A}{t_p}$$

$$11.70 = \frac{2.78 \times 0.35 \times 150}{t_p}$$

or $$t_p = \frac{2.78 \times 0.35 \times 150}{11.70} \text{ hours}$$
$$= \mathbf{12.47 \text{ hours}} \quad \textbf{Ans.}$$

Problem 6.44. Followings are the characteristics of two meteorologically identical watersheds. Watershed (B) is ungaged.

Parameters	*Watershed (A)*	*Watershed (B)*
(*i*) L	35 km	40 km
(*ii*) L_{ca}	20 cm	30 km
(*iii*) A 300 sqkm	300 sqkm	350 sq km
(*iv*) Peak discharge of 2-h unit hydrograph	60 m^3/s	—
(*v*) Time to peak	9h	—

Develop the synthetic unit hydrograph for watershed *B* by using Snyder's method.

Solution. Derivation of SUHG is accomplished under following steps :

Step (1). Compute the value of regional constants C_t and C_p

These two constants are determined for the gauged watershed and are applied to the ungauged watershed for development of SUHG. Computation is done as follows :

(*a*) Using the formula of basin lag, *i.e.*

$$t_p = C_t (L \cdot L_{ca})^{0.3} \quad \text{...}(A)$$

in which, t_p is determined by using the formula

$$t_p' = \frac{21}{22} t_p + \frac{t_R}{4} \quad \text{...}(B)$$

In this formula, t_p' is unknown which is calculated as under

$$\frac{t_R}{2} + t_p' = 9h$$

or $$t_p' = 9 - \frac{2}{2}$$

$$t_p' = 8 \text{ hours}$$

Now, substituting the value of t_p' as 8h in equation (*B*), we have

$$8 = \frac{21}{22} t_p + \frac{2}{4}$$

or $$\frac{21}{22} t_p = 8 - 0.5$$

$$t_p = (7.5) \times \frac{22}{21} \text{ hours}$$
$$= \mathbf{7.857 \text{ hours}}$$

By substituting the t_p as 7.857 hours in equation (*A*), the value of C_t is obtained as

$$7.857 = C_t (35 \times 20)^{0.3}$$

$$1.10 = C_t$$

or $$C_t = \mathbf{1.10}$$

And C_p from the formula

$$Q_p = \frac{2.78\, C_p \cdot A}{t_p}$$

$$60 = \frac{2.78\, C_p \times 300}{7.857}$$

$\therefore$ $$C_p = \mathbf{0.57}$$

Step (2). Compute the parameters of SUHG for watershed B

The constants C_t and C_p are required for computation of different parameters of SUHG. Computation is as follows :

1. Basin lag $(t_p) = C_t (L \cdot L_{ca})^{0.3}$

$$= 1.1\,(40 \times 30)^{0.3} = \mathbf{9.23\ hours}$$

2. Standard duration of ER $(t_r) = \dfrac{t_p}{5.5}$ hour

$$= \frac{9.23}{5.5} = \mathbf{1.68\ hours}$$

3. Considering the non-standard duration of ER *i.e.* t_R as $2h$ the t_p' is given by

$$t_p' = \frac{21}{22}\, t_p + \frac{t_R}{4}$$

$$= \frac{21}{22} \times 9.23 + \frac{2}{4} = \mathbf{9.31\ hours}$$

4. Peak discharge $(Q_p) = \dfrac{2.78\, C_p \cdot A}{t_p'}\ \text{m}^3/\text{s}$

$$= \frac{2.78 \times 0.57 \times 350}{9.31}\ \text{m}^3/\text{s}$$

$$= \mathbf{59.57\ m^3/s}$$

5. Widths of SUHG at 50 and 75% peak discharge

$$W_{50} = \frac{5.87}{\left(\dfrac{59.57}{350}\right)^{1.08}}\ \text{hour} = \mathbf{39.74\ hours}$$

and $$W_{75} = \frac{W_{50}}{1.75}$$

$$= \frac{39.74}{1.75}\ \text{hour} = \mathbf{22.71\ hours}$$

6. Base time $(t_b) = (72 + 3t_p')$

$$= 72 + 3 \times 9.31 = \mathbf{99.93\ hours}$$

Step (3) Sketching of SUHG

With the help of computed values of time to peak (t_p'), peak discharge, base time and widths at 50% and 75% of peak discharge for watershed B, the synthetic unit hydrograph is drawn, by keeping the view that the area enclosed by the sketched SUHG should represent 1 cm ER. Otherwise, shape is modified to represent the unit depth of ER. The shape of hydrograph may be triangular also.

Problem 6.45. Derive the synthetic unit hydrograph by using the Indian methodology, for an ungauged watershed which morphometric characteristics are as follows :

(*a*) Length of longest water course from watershed divide to the outlet is 20 km

(*b*) Length of main watercourse from outlet to the point opposite to the centroid of watershed is 13 km.

(*c*) Average slope of water course is 0.50 m/m

(*d*) Area of watershed is 375 sq km

Solution. Given that

$$L = 20 \text{ km}$$
$$L_{ca} = 13 \text{ km}$$
$$S = 0.50$$
$$A = 375 \text{ sq km}$$

Therefore,

1. Time to peak or lag time (t_p)

$$= \frac{1.13\,(L \cdot L_{ca})^{0.2269}}{\sqrt{S}}$$

$$= \frac{1.13\,(20 \times 13)^{0.2269}}{\sqrt{0.5}} = \mathbf{5.64\ hours}$$

2. Peak discharge $(Q_p) = 0.315\, A^{0.93} \cdot S^{0.53}$

$$= 0.315 \times (375)^{0.93} \cdot (0.5)^{0.53}\ \text{m}^3/\text{s}$$

$$= \mathbf{54.03\ m^3/s}$$

3. Widths of SUHG at 50% and 75% of peak discharge

$$W_{50} = \frac{2.18}{(q)^{1.12}}$$

$$= \frac{2.18}{\left(\dfrac{54.03}{375}\right)^{1.12}} \text{ hour} = \mathbf{19.10\ hours}$$

$$W_{75} = 0.81 \cdot W_{50}^{0.72}$$

$$= 0.81\,(19.10)^{0.72} = \mathbf{6.77\ hours}$$

4. Widths of rising side of SUHG at 50 and 75%

$$W_{R-50} = 0.69\,(W_{50})^{0.69}$$

$$= 0.69\,(19.10)^{0.69} \text{ hour} = \mathbf{5.28\ hours}$$

$$W_{R-75} = 0.605\,(W_{R-50})^{0.95}$$

$$= 0.605\,(5.28)^{0.95} = \mathbf{2.94\ hours}$$

5. Base time (t_b) $= 4.3 \dfrac{(L \cdot L_{ca})^{0.28}}{\sqrt{S}}$

$$= \frac{4.3 \times (20 \times 13)^{0.28}}{\sqrt{.5}} = \mathbf{28.85\ hours}$$

6. **Sketching of unit hydrograph :** It is drawn in such a way that the area enclosed by the graph should represent unit depth of effective rainfall.

Problem 6.46. Derive a unit hydrograph of 3-h duration for the watershed having 300 sq km area, by using USSCS method. Take the lag time of watershed as 8-h.

Solution. Here USSCS method refers to the dimensionless unit hydrograph. Computations are shown as under :

1. Time to peak

$$(t_{peak}) = t_p' + \frac{t_R}{2} = 8 + \frac{3}{2} = \mathbf{9.5\ hours}$$

2. Peak discharge (Q_p) $= \dfrac{5.36\,A}{t_{peak}}$

$$= \frac{5.36 \times 300}{9.5}\ \text{m}^3/\text{s} = \mathbf{169.26\ m^3/s}$$

We know that, at the peak discharge

$$\frac{t}{t_{peak}} = 1$$

or

$$t = t_{peak} = \mathbf{9.5\ hours}$$

Thus, at time $t = 9.5$ hours, the peak discharge is 169.26 m^3/s

3. Time base of unit hydrograph (t_b) $= 5 \times t_{peak} = 5 \times 9.5 = \mathbf{47.5\ hours}$

4. Now, by using the computed parameters, the discharge values for different $\dfrac{t}{peak}$ are determined with the help of Table 6.2. These are given as below :

4.1. At $\dfrac{t}{t_{peak}} = 0.5$, the value of $\dfrac{Q}{Q_p} = 0.43$ (from table 6.2)

It results $t = 0.5\, t_{peak} = 0.5 \times 9.5 = \mathbf{4.75\ hours}$

and $Q = 0.43\, Q_p = 0.43 \times 169.26 = \mathbf{72.78\ m^3/s}$

4.2. At $\dfrac{t}{t_{peak}} = 0.75$, the $\dfrac{Q}{Q_p} = 0.83$

It results $t = 0.75\, t_{peak} = 0.75 \times 9.5 = \mathbf{7.13\ hours}$

and $$Q = 0.83\, Q_p = 0.83 \times 169.26 = \mathbf{140.5\ m^3/s}$$

4.3. At $\dfrac{t}{t_{peak}} = 1$ the $\dfrac{Q}{Q_p} = 1$

It results $t = t_{peak} = \mathbf{9.5\ hours}$

and $$Q = Q_p = \mathbf{169.26\ m^3/s}$$

4.4 At $\dfrac{t}{t_{peak}} = 2$, the $\dfrac{Q}{Q_p} = 0.32$

It results $$t = 2\, t_{peak} = 2 \times 9.5 = \mathbf{19\ hours}$$

and $$Q = 0.32\, Q_p = 0.32 \times 169.26 = \mathbf{54.16\ m^3/s}$$

4.5. At $\dfrac{t}{t_{peak}} = 3$ the $\dfrac{Q}{Q_p} = 0.075$

It results $t = 3\, t_{peak} = 3 \times 9.5 = \mathbf{28.5\ hours}$

and $$Q = 0.075\, Q_p = 0.075 \times 169.26 = \mathbf{12.70\ m^3/s}$$

4.6. At $\dfrac{t}{t_{peak}} = 4$, the $\dfrac{Q}{Q_p} = 0.018$

It results $$t = 4\, t_{peak} = 4 \times 9.5 = \mathbf{38\ hours}$$

and $$Q = 0.018\, Q_p = 0.018 \times 169.26 = \mathbf{3.05\ m^3/s}$$

4.7. At $\dfrac{t}{t_{peak}} = 5$ the $\dfrac{Q}{Q_p} = 0.004$

It results $$t = 5\, t_{peak} = 5 \times 9.5 = \mathbf{47.5\ hours}$$

and $$Q = 0.004\, Q_p = 0.004 \times 169.26 = \mathbf{0.68\ m^3/s}$$

5. Sketching of unit hydrograph. From computed values of t and Q the coordinates (t, Q) are determined. Using different set of coordinates, the dimensionless unit hydrograph is sketched in such a way that the area enclosed by the graph should represent unit depth of ER.

Problem 6.47. Followings are the ordinates of 1-h instantaneous unit hydrograph of a watershed. Derive the DRH due to a storm of 6h duration producing 3 cm as effective rainfall.

Time (h)	0	1	2	3	4	5	6	7	8	9	10	11
IUH (m^3/s)	0	7.0	30	55	45	35	27	22	20	15	5	0

Solution. Computations are shown in following table

Time (h)	*IUH (m^3/s*	*IUH lagged by 1h*	*Ordinate of 1-h unit hydrograph (m^3/s)**	*S-curve addition (m^3/s)*	*Ordinates of S-curve ***	*S-curve lagged by 6-h*	*DRH of 6h for 6 cm ****	*Ordinate of 6-h unit hydrograph (m^3/s)*****	*DRH of 3 cm ER*
(1)	*(2)*	*(3)*	*(4)*	*(5)*	*(6)*	*(7)*	*(8)*	*(9)*	*(10)*
0	0	—	0	—	0	—	0	0	0
1	7	0	3.5	0	3.5	—	3.5	0.58	1.74
2	30	7	18.5	3.5	22.0	—	22.0	3.67	11.01
3	55	30	42.5	22.0	64.5	—	64.5	10.75	32.25
4	45	55	50.0	64.5	114.5	—	114.5	19.08	57.24
5	35	45	40.0	114.5	154.5	—	154.5	25.75	77.25
6	27	35	31.0	154.5	185.5	0	185.5	30.92	92.76
7	22	27	24.5	185.5	210.0	3.5	206.5	34.42	103.26
8	20	22	21.0	210.0	231.0	22.0	209.0	34.83	104.49
9	15	20	17.5	231.0	248.5	64.5	184.0	30.67	92.01
10	5	15	10.0	248.5	258.5	114.5	144.0	24.0	72.0
11	0	5	2.5	258.5	261.0	154.5	106.5	17.75	53.25
12		0	0.0	261.0	261.0	185.5	75.5	12.58	37.74
13			0.0	261.0	261.0	210.0	51.0	8.50	25.50
14				261.0	261.0	231.0	30.0	5.0	15.0
15				261.0	261.0	248.5	12.5	2.08	6.24
16				261.0	261.0	258.5	2.5	0.42	12.60
						261.0	0	0.0	0.0
						261.0	0	,	

* Ordinates of 1-h unit hydrograph are computed as the sum of col (2) and col (3) devided by 2 *i.e.*

$$\frac{col\,(2) + col\,(3)}{2}$$

** Ordinates of S-curve are determined as $col\,(4) + col\,(5)$

*** Ordinates of DRH due to 6 cm ER are computed as $col\,(6) - col\,(7)$

**** Ordinates of 6-h unit hydrograph are calculated as $col\,(8)/6$

***** Ordinates of DRH of 3 cm ER are determined as $col\,(9) \times 3$

Problem 6.48. Determine the storage volume of the linear reservoir, when outflow is 40 m^3/s. Take reservoir constant or storage coefficient as 0.35.

Solution. For linear reservoir, the relationship between storage and outflow is given by

$$S = KQ$$

In which $S = ?$, $K = 0.35$ and $Q = 40\ m^3/s$ are given.

Thus, $S = 0.35 \times 40\ m^3/s$

$= \mathbf{14\ m^3/s}$ **Ans.**

Problem 6.49. Compute the ordinates of instantaneous unit hydrograph by using Clark model for a given watershed with following data base :

(*a*) Area of watershed = 150 sq km

(*b*) Time of concentration = 20 h

(*c*) Storage constant = 14 h

The inter-isochrone areas with respect to travel time are as follows :

Travel time (h)	0-2	2-4	4-6	6-8	8-10	10-12	12-14	14-16	16-18	18-20
Inter iso-chrone area (sq km)	5	10	36	30	25	13	11	9	7	4

Solution. Given that

$$K = 14 \text{ hour}$$

$$t_c = 20 \text{ hour}$$

$$\Delta t_c = 2 \text{ hour}$$

$$A = 150 \text{ sq km}$$

Computations are shown under following steps.

Step 1 : Compute the C_1 and C_2 of formula

Q_2 (ordinate of IUH) $= 2C_1 I_1 + C_2 Q_1$.

in which
$$C_1 = \frac{0.5\,\Delta t_c}{K + 0.5\,\Delta t_c}$$

$$= \frac{0.5 \times 2}{14 + 0.5 \times 2} = \mathbf{0.067}$$

and
$$C_2 = \frac{K - 0.5\,\Delta t_c}{K + 0.5\,\Delta t_c}$$

$$= \frac{14 - 0.5 \times 2}{14 + 0.5 \times 2} = \mathbf{0.867}$$

Step 2 : Compute the ordinates of IUH *i.e.*

$$Q_2 = 2C_1 I_1 + C_2 Q_1$$

$$= 0.134\, I_1 + 0.866\, Q_1$$

Computations are shown in following table :

Time (h)	*Area (km^2) (Ar)*	*Inflow (m^3/s) (I)**	*0.134 I_1*	*0.866 Q_1 ***	*Ordinates of IUH (m^3/s)*
(1)	*(2)*	*(3)*	*(4)*	*(5)*	*(6)*
0	0	0	0	0	0
2	5	6.95	0.93	0	0.93
4	10	13.90	1.86	0.81	2.67
6	36	50.04	6.71	2.31	9.02
8	30	41.70	5.59	7.81	13.40
10	25	34.75	4.66	11.60	16.26
12	13	18.07	2.42	14.08	16.50
14	11	15.29	2.05	14.29	16.34
16	9	12.51	1.68	14.15	15.83
18	7	9.73	1.30	13.71	15.01
20	4	5.56	0.75	13.00	11.91
22			—	10.31	10.31
24			—	8.93	7.73
26				6.85	6.85
28				5.93	5.93
30				5.13	5.13
32				so on	so on

* The inflow (I) is determined by using the following formula

$$I = \frac{2.78\,A_r}{\Delta t_c}\ \text{m}^3/\text{s}$$

in which A_r is the isochrone area (km^2) and Δt_c is time interval *i.e.* 2h in present case

** The values of 0.866 Q_1 for different time intervals are computed by considering the Q_1 as the previous value of ordinate of IUH.

Problem 6.50. Determine the inflow rate (m^3/s) to an inter isochrone area of 50 sq km, if its travel time is 3 hour.

Solution. Given that the

Inter isochrone area $(A_r) = 50\text{km}^2$

Travel time $(\Delta t_c) = 3$ hour

Using the formula

$$\text{inflow} = \frac{2.78\, A_r}{\Delta t_c}$$

$$= \frac{2.78 \times 50}{3}\ \text{m}^3/\text{s}$$

$$= \mathbf{46.33\ m^3/s}\quad \textbf{Ans.}$$

Problem 6.51. Determine the ordinate of IUH for the inter-isochrone area of watershed as 50 sq km. Consider the formula of IUH as

$$Q_2 = 2C_1 I_1 + C_2 Q_1$$

Assume the value of K as 10 hour and Δt_c as 3 hour.

Solution. Using the formula for C_1 and C_2

$$C_1 = \frac{0.5\,\Delta t_c}{K + 0.5\,\Delta t_c} = \frac{0.5 \times 3}{10 + 0.5 \times 3} = \mathbf{0.130}$$

$$C_2 = \frac{K - 0.5 \times \Delta t_c}{K + 0.5\,\Delta t_c} = \frac{10 - 0.5 \times 3}{10 + 0.5 \times 3} = \mathbf{0.74}$$

Substituting the values of C_1 and C_2 in the given formula, we have

$$Q_2 = 0.26\, I_1 + 0.74\, Q_1$$

In this formula, the value of I_1 is determined as

$$I_1 = \frac{2.78\, A_r}{\Delta t_c} = \frac{2.78 \times 50}{3} = \mathbf{46.33\ m^3/s}$$

and Q_1 is taken as 0

Thus, the ordinate of IUH *i.e.* $Q_2 = 0.26\, I_1$

$$= 0.26 \times 46.33 = \mathbf{12.05\ m^3/s}\quad \textbf{Ans.}$$

IMPORTANT POINTS

1. Hydrograph is the plot of discharge and time data.
2. Hydrograph is also known as storm hydrograph or flood hydrograph.
3. A hydrograph resulted from an isolated storm has single peak.
4. The rising limb of hydrograph is also known as concentration curve.
5. The steepness of rising limb is dependent on the characteristics of climate and watershed in combine form.
6. The falling limb of hydrograph is dependent on the watershed characteristics, only.
7. The falling limb of hydrograph is also known as depletion curve.
8. The beginning point of falling limb of hydrograph is the point of inflection towards it.
9. Area of hydrograph represents the total rainfall volume due to a given storm.
10. Two different storms in a given watershed produce two different hydrographs.

11. The shape of hydrograph is affected by climatic and physiographic factors of the watershed.

12. Fan-shaped watersheds produce narrow hydrograph with high peak.

13. Elongated watersheds produce broader hydrograph with low-peak.

14. The size of watershed affects the time base of hydrograph.

15. The slope of main stream of the watershed significantly affects the recession limb of the hydrograph.

16. A large slope of main stream produces the hydrograph with small time base.

17. Drainage density is the ratio of total length of streams to the total area of watershed.

18. A high drainage density causes quick disposal of runoff from the watershed. The resulting hydrograph is in narrow shape.

19. A watershed with poor drainage density produces squat type hydrograph with slow right limb.

20. The runoff is directly proportional to the rainfall intensity.

21. The rainfall intensity affects the size of hydrograph.

22. The duration of storm affects the rising limb and peak of the hydrograph.

23. The rising limb of hydrograph represents the increase in discharge due to gradual building of storage in the channel and on the surface of watershed.

24. Generally, in large watersheds the peak flow occurs after cessation of rainfall.

25. The inflection point on falling limb represents the end of rainfall and maximum storage in the channel.

26. The water storages in the basin are the surface storage, interflow storage and ground water storage.

27. The surface storage in the watershed includes the surface detention and channel storage.

28. The recession constant for surface storage varies from 0.05 to 0.20.

29. The recession constant for interflow varies from 0.50 to 0.85.

30. The recession constant for base flow varies from 0.85 to 0.99.

31. The end of direct runoff from peak of the hydrograph can be demarcated by the formula $N = 0.83\, A^{0.2}$, in which N is in days and A is the area of watershed (sq km).

32. The surface runoff hydrograph is obtained by separating the base flow from the hydrograph. It is also called direct runoff hydrograph (DRH).

33. The effective rainfall hyetograph (ERH) is also known as "supra rainfall".

34. The area of ERH represents the depth of rainfall excess.

35. Product of area of ERH and area of watershed is the total volume of direct runoff.

36. Area of DRH is the total volume of direct runoff.

37. Area of DRH divided by area of watershed is equal to the ER.

38. A unit hydrograph is the DRH of unit depth of rainfall excess.

39. Unit depth of rainfall excess to derive the unit hydrograph may be 1 mm, 1 cm or 1 inch. However, 1 cm is commonly considered.

40. Unit hydrograph theory was introduced by Sherman in 1932.

41. The unit depth of rainfall excess used to derive the unit hydrograph should be uniformly distributed, both spatially and temporally in the watershed.

42. The ordinate of unit hydrograph is represented as $u(T, t)$.

43. In the ordinate of unit hydrograph $u(T, t)$, T refers to the duration of rainfall excess.

44. A unit hydrograph relates the direct runoff with the rainfall excess.

45. Area of unit hydrograph represents the volume of direct runoff due to unit depth of rainfall excess.

46. Ratio of area of unit hydrograph to the area of watershed is equal to the unit depth of rainfall excess.

47. The intensity of rainfall excess considered for unit hydrograph is equal to $1/D$ cm/h.

48. The "time invariance" assumption of unit hydrograph states that the DRH for a given ER is always same irrespective of time of occurence.

49. The "linear response" assumption of unit hydrograph states that if an input $x_1(t)$ causes $y_1(t)$ as output and input $x_2(t)$ causes $y_2(t)$ as output, then

(*a*) sum of inputs *i.e.* $x_1(t) + x_2(t)$ will result $y_1(t) + y_2(t)$ as output.

(*b*) similarly, if $x_2(t) = r \cdot x_1(t)$ then

$$y_2(t) = r\, y_1(t)$$

50. The assumption of linear response of unit hydrograph enables the method of superposition to derive the DRH.

51. The storm duration for derivation of unit hydrograph should be from 1/5 to 1/3 of basin lag.

52. The preferable range of depth of rainfall excess to derive the UHG is from 1 to 4 cm.

53. Duration of unit hydrograph should be between 1/5 and 1/3 of basin lag.

54. Generally, for the watersheds having the area greater than 250 km^2, the 6-h unit hydrograph is satisfactory.

55. The method of superposition is used to derive the unit hydrograph of $n \cdot D - h$ duration, where n is the multiple integer of D–h.

56. The method of *S*-curve is used to derive the unit hydrograph of $m \cdot D$–h duration, in which '*m* is any number including fractional number.

57. The average intensity of ER producing the S-curve is $1/D$ cm/h.

58. The equilibrium discharge (Q_s) of S-curve is given by

$$Q_s = \left(\frac{A}{D} \times 10^4 \right) \text{m}^3/\text{h}$$

in which A is the area of watershed (sq km) and D is the duration of ER (hour).

59. The upper limit of size of watershed to develop the unit hydrograph is 5000 sq km.

60. The lower limit of size of watershed to derive the unit hydrograph is 200 ha.

61. For development of unit hydrograph, the selected isolated storm should have rainfall, only. For snow-melt runoff, unit hydrograph is not satisfactory.

62. The surface features of watershed *i.e.* existing of large size depressions, tanks, ponds etc. affect the linearity assumption of unit hydrograph. For such watersheds the development of unit hydrograph is not satisfactory.

63. For development of unit hydrograph, the variations in base of hydrograph should be as much as ± 20% and in case of peak discharge, it should be ± 10%.

64. The duration of unit hydrograph should not exceed atleast the time of rise, basin lag and time of concentration of the watershed.

65. Normally, the duration of unit hydrograph as 1/4 of the basin lag is considered as the best duration.

66. Generally, for the watersheds with area more than 1200 sq km, the duration of unit hydrograph is considered as 12-h.

67. Distribution graph is introduced by Bernard in the year 1935.

68. Distribution graph is the plot of percentage of the surface runoff Vs duration.

69. The unit interval of distribution graph is taken as the duration of rainfall excess ($D - h$).

70. A 4-h distribution graph indicates the time interval or the duration of rainfall excess as 4-h.

71. The area of distribution graph represents the total runoff.

72. Distribution graphs are derived to compare the runoff producing characteristics of watershed.

73. The synthetic unit hydrograph is developed for ungauged watershed.

74. Snyder's method is used for development of synthetic unit hydrograph.

75. The 'basin lag' is considered as one of important characteristics of the watershed affecting the hydrograph.

76. Basin lag is also known as "lag time", which is the time difference between the centroid of rainfall excess and surface runoff.

77. The lag time physically represents the travel time of water particle from all parts of the watershed to its outlet during storm.

78. Snyder's basin lag (t_p) is the function of watershed characteristics *i.e.* $t_p = C_t (L \cdot L_{ca})^{0.3}$, in which C_t is the regional constant, L is the basin length measured along the main water course from devide line to the outlet and L_{ca} is the distance along the main water course, measured from gauging station to the point opposite to the centroid of watershed.

79. The area enclosed by synthetic unit hydrograph should represent unit depth of rainfall excess.

80. A dimensionless unit hydrograph is the plot of discharge ratio (Q/Q_p) and time ratio (t/t_{pk}).

81. In dimensionless unit hydrograph, the co-ordinate $\dfrac{Q}{Q_p} = 1$ at $\dfrac{t}{t_{pk}} = 1$.

82. A unit hydrograph of zero duration of rainfall excess is known as instantaneous unit hydrograph.

83. Instantaneous unit hydrograph is the conceptual unit hydrograph.

84. The ordinate of IUH is expressed as $u(t)$ or $u\,(0, t)$.

85. The IUH is single peak unit hydrograph with a finite base width.

86. IUH is independent of duration of ER.

87. The Nash model (1957) is used for development of IUH.

88. The Nash model (1957) follows the concept of linear reservoir.

89. A reservoir is said to be linear when storage is directly proportional to the outflow.

90. Clark's Model (1945) derives the IUH.

91. Clark model (1945) assumes that the rainfall excess first gets translated and then attenuated.

92. In clark method of IUH development, the translation of ER is determined by time-area-histogram (TAH) and attenutation by routing method.

93. Time-area-histogram is the plot of inter-isochrone area and time. It is in the form of bar diagram.

94. The contour of time of concentration is known as isochrone.

95. In clark method of IUH development, the flow routing is performed by using the Muskingum method.

REFERENCES

1. Bandopadhyay M. Synthetic storm pattern and runoff for Gauhati, India, J. Hyd. Div. Am. Soc., Civ. Eng, Vol 98, No HY-5, pp 845- 857, 1972.
2. Barnes B.S. Discussion on Analysis of runoff characteristics by O.H. Meyer, Trans, Am. Soc. Civil engrs, Vol 105, pp 104-106, 1940.
3. Bernard M.M. An approach to determine stream flow, Trans. Am. Civil Engrs, Vol. 100, pp 347-395, 1935.
4. Buller S.C. Engineering Hydrology, Prentice Hall Inc U.SA., 1957.
5. Central Water Commission, Estimation of Design Flood Peak, Report No 1, Flood Estimation Directorate, CWC, New Delhi (India), 1973.
6. Clark C.O. storage and the unit hydrograph, Trans. Am. Soc. Civil Engrs, Vol. 110, pp 1419-1446, 1945.
7. Chow V.T. Handbook of Applied Hydrology, McGraw-Hill, New York, 1964.
8. Das G. Hydrology and Soil Conservation, Prentice-Hall (India), 2000.
9. Gray D.M. Synthetic unit hydrographs for small watersheds, Prosc, Am. Soc, Civil. Engrs, J. Hydraulics Div. Vol 87, no Hy-4, pp. 33-53, 1961.
10. Gray, D.M. Principles of Hydrology, Water Information Centre, New York, 1970.
11. Gupta V.K, Waymire E, and Wang C.T., A representation of an Instantaneous unit Hydrograph from geomorphology, Water Resources Res. 16(5) 865, 1983.

12. Havns and Emerson Consulting Engineers, master plan for pollution abatement, Cleveland, Ohio, 1968.

13. Hinderson F.M., Some properties of the unit hydrograph, J. Geophysics Res 68(16)4785, 1963.

14. Horton R.E. Erosional development of streams and their drainage basin, Hydrophysical approach to quantative morphology, Geol. Soc. Am. Bull, 56, 275, 1945.

15. Linsley R.K., Kohler M.A. and Paulhus J.L.H., Applied Hydrology, McGraw-Hill Book Co. Inc, New York, 1940.

16. Marsalek J. Research on the design storm concept, Tech. mono. 33, Am. Soc, Civ. Eng, Urban Water Resource Res. Prog, New York, 1978.

17. Mc Pherson M.B., Discussion of synthetic storm pattern for drainage design, J. Hyd Div., Am. Soc, Civ. Eng, Vol 84, No HY1, pp 49-60, 1958.

18. Mocus V. Use of storm and watershed characteristics in synthetic unit hydrograph analysis and applications, USSCS, 1957.

19. Mutreja K.N. Applied Hydrology, Tata McGraw-Hill, New Delhi, 1986.

20. Nash J.E., A unit hydrograph study with particular reference to British catchments, Prosc, Inst. Civil Engineers (England) 17, 249, 1960.

21. O.' Donnel T. Instantaneous unit hydrograph derivation by harmonic analysis, Intern, Assoc Sci Hydrology, Pub 51, pp 546- 557, 1960.

22. Preul H.D. and Papadakis C.N., Development of design storm hyetographs for Cincinnati, Ohio, Water Resource Bull. Vol. 101, No 2 pp 81-95, 1975.

23. Raghunath H.M. Hydrology, Wiley Eastern Pvt. Ltd. Delhi, 1985.

24. Rodriquez-Iturbe I., Gonzates, Sanabaria, M.K. and Bras R.L., A geomorphormation theory of instantaneous unit hydrograph, Wat. Resources Res, 18(4), 877, 1982.

25. Rodriquez-Iturbe I, Sanabaria G.M. and Cammano, G., On the climatic dependence of the IUH : A rainfall runoff analysis of the Nash model and the geomorphoclimatic theory. Wat. Resources Res. 18(4) 887, 1982.

26. Rosso R. Nash Model relation to Horton order ratios, Wat. Resources Res 15(6) 1406, 1984.

27. Sherman L.K., Stream flow from rainfall by the unit-graph method, Eng-News-Rec, Vol 108, pp 501-505, 1932.

28. Snyder F.F. Synthetic unit-graphs, Trans. Am. Geophys. Union, Vol. 19, pp 447-454, 1938.

29. Sokolov. A.A. Flood Flow Computation, The UNESCO Press, Paris, 1976.

30. Strahler A.N., Quantitative geomorphology of drainage basins and channel networks, Handbook of Applied Hydrology (Ed. V.T. Chow), McGraw-Hill Book, Co. New York, 1964.

31. Subramanya K. Engineering Hydrology, Tata, McGraw-Hill Publishing. Co. Ltd., New Delhi, 2000.

32. Subramanyan S and Kumar A., Runoff model based on channel network Geomorphology, J. Soil & Water Conservation (India), Vol. 32 (3 & 4) p. 202, 1988.

33. Sugawara, Masami and Fumiyuki Maruyama, A method of rivison of the river discharge by means of a rainfall model, Symposia, Darcy, Intern, Assoc, Sd., Hydrology, Pub 42, Vol 3, pp 71-76, 1956.

34. Turner H.M. and Burdoin A.J. The Flood Hydrograph, J. Boston Soc. Civil Engrs, Vol. 28, 1944.

35. U.S. Army Corps of Engineers, Routing of floods through river channel, Engineering and Power Manual. EM 1110-2-1408, 1964.

36. Zoch R.T. On the relation between rainfall and stream flow, Monthly Weather Rev, Vol. 62, pp 315-322, 1934, Vol 64 pp 105- 121, 1936, Vol 65 pp 135-147, 1937.

DESCRIPTIVE TYPE QUESTIONS

1. (*a*) Define hydrograph and describe its different components.
   (*b*) Explain various factors affecting the shape of hydrograph.
2. (*a*) A hydrograph represents the total runoff, explain it.
   (*b*) Define recession constant and describe its different types.
3. (*a*) How drainage density affects the shape of hydrograph.
   (*b*) Define effective rainfall and explain its uses.
4. (*a*) Define unit hydrograph.
   (*b*) Describe the procedure for development of unit hydrograph.
5. (*a*) Define direct runoff and write the procedures/methods to compute it.
   (*b*) Explain different methods of separating the base flow.
6. (*a*) Describe various uses and limitations of U.H.G.
   (*b*) Derive the O.U.H.G by using the following data

Time (h).	0	5	10	15	20	25	30	35	40	45	50
Discharge (m^3/s)	0	15	30	40	50	35	30	25	20	15	15

   (Assume the base flow as 15 m^3/s).

7. (*a*) Write the procedure to derive U.H.G. from a complex hydrograph.
   (*b*) Derive a 4-h U.H.G. from the stream flow caused by three successive storms of 2.00, 4.00 and 3.00 cm in a specified watershed. The stream flow data is given as under :

Time (h)	0	3	6	9	12	15	18	21	24	27	30	33
Stream flow (m^3/s)	30	60	102	150	209	212	214	154	94.5	55.5	39	30

   Assume
   (i) base flow = 30 m^3/s
   (ii) average loss of rainfall = 0.20 cm
   (iii) area of watershed = 125.5 km^2

8. (*a*) What is average unit hydrograph.

(*b*) Compute the OUHG of 6-h duration from 3-h UHG given as under :

Time (h)	0	3	6	9	12	15	18	21	24	27
U.H.G. (m^3/s)	0	2.5	3.5	7.5	10.5	15.0	13.0	8.0	5.0	1.0

9. (*a*) Define *S*-curve and write its applications.

(*b*) Calculate the ordinates of 3-h unit hydrograph from the following 6-h U.H.G.

Time (h)	0	6	12	18	24	30	36	42	48	54
UHG (m^3/s)	0	30	105	165	195	175	115	35	6.5	0

10. (*a*) Define synthetic unit hydrograph and describe its derivation procedure, using Snyder's method.

(*b*) Compute the ordinates of 2-h U.H.G. of Ganga basin, if ordinates of 4-h UHG are as follows :

Time (h)	0	4	8	12	16	20	24	28	32	36	40
OUHG (m^3/s)	0	59	90	110	98	65	35	20	10	4	0

(Assume, the data which are not given)

11. (*a*) Define dimensionless unit hydrograph

(*b*) Describe the procedure to derive the dimensionless unit hydrograph.

12. (*a*) Define instantaneous unit hydrograph and explain its various properties.

(*b*) Describe the derivation procedure of IUH by using Clark and Nash methods.

OBJECTIVE TYPE QUESTIONS

1. A hydrograph is the plot of

(*a*) instantaneous discharge and time

(*b*) discharge and probability

(*c*) discharge and watershed area

(*d*) intensity and time

2. The shape of hydrograph depends on the characteristics of

(*a*) rainfall and watershed (*b*) rainfall, only

(*c*) watershed, only (*d*) none of above.

3. Single peak hydrograph is resulted from

(*a*) an isolated storm (*b*) rainfall of varying intensity

(*c*) both '*a*' and '*b*' (*d*) any storm

4. A complex storm produces

(*a*) single peak hydrograph

(*b*) multi peak hydrograph

(*c*) simple hydrograph

(*d*) IUH, only

5. Rising limb of hydrograph is affected by
(*a*) storm and basin's characteristics, both
(*b*) storm characteristics, only
(*c*) basin characteristics, only
(*d*) watershed temperature.

6. Rising limb of hydrograph is in
(*a*) convex shape (*b*) concave shape
(*c*) harmonic shape (*d*) none of the above

7. Falling limb of hydrograph is independent on
(*a*) storm characteristics (*b*) basin characteristics
(*c*) temperature only (*d*) none of the above

8. Falling limb of hydrograph is also known as
(*a*) recession limb (*b*) ascending limb
(*c*) both '*a*' and '*b*' (*d*) concentration curve.

9. The crest segment of hydrograph is extended from
(*a*) the point of inflection on rising limb to the similar point on falling limb
(*b*) rising limb to falling limb
(*c*) centre of mass of ERH to peak flow rate
(*d*) both '*a*' and '*b*'.

10. Crest segment of hydrograph is influenced by
(*a*) storm and basin characteristics
(*b*) storm characteristics, only
(*c*) basin characteristics, only
(*d*) temperature of watenshed.

11. The recession constant of surface storage (Krs) varies from
(*a*) 0.05 to 0.20 (*b*) 0.05 to 0.85
(*c*) 0.85 to 0.99 (*d*) 0.1 to 0.15

12. The recession constant of interflow varies from
(*a*) 0.50 to 0.85 (*b*) 0.05 to 0.20
(*c*) 0.85 to 0.99 (*d*) 0.1 to 0.15

13. The reession constant of base flow varies from
(*a*) 0.85 to 0.99 (*b*) 0.50 to 0.85
(*c*) 0.05 to 0.20 (*d*) 0.01 to 0.05

14. Snow fall results the hydrograph with
(*a*) lower peak (*b*) broader base width
(*c*) both '*a*' and '*b*' (*d*) small base width.

15. A hydrograph resulted form rainfall may involve
(*a*) high peak and narrow base width.
(*b*) low peak and narrow base width.
(*c*) high peak and broad base width.
(*d*) all above

16. For the given storm, a fan shape watershed results the hydrograph with
(*a*) high peak and narrow base width.
(*b*) low peak and broad base width.
(*c*) high peak and broadder base width.
(*d*) none of above.

17. The presence of surface depressions on the land surface, affects the shape of hydrograph, because of
(*a*) delay in occurrence of runoff.
(*b*) surface storage.
(*c*) time invriant.
(*d*) none of the above.

18. Separation of base flow is essential for derivation of
(*a*) hydrograph (*b*) flow-duration curve
(*c*) unit hydrograph (*d*) flood rowting

19. The unit hydrograph theory was introduced by
(*a*) C.E. Ramser (1940) (*b*) Sherman (1932)
(*c*) Linsley (1935) (*d*) Clark, 1954.

20. The plot of rainfall intensity and time is called
(*a*) hydrograph (*b*) hyetograph
(*c*) mass-curve (*d*) triangular hydrograph.

21. Area of hydrograph represents the
(*a*) rainfall depth (*b*) total runoff volume
(*c*) discharge rate (*d*) ER

22. The product of area of ERH and area of catchment results
(*a*) total direct runoff volume(*b*) total rainfall depth
(*c*) discharge rate (*d*) ER

23. The storm of unit duration regardless of its intensity is called as
(*a*) unit storm (*b*) isolated storm
(*c*) unit rainfall (*d*) none of above

24. The time period of unit storm is referred as
(*a*) unit period (*b*) base width
(*c*) recession time (*d*) rising time

25. The ordinate of direct runoff divided by the effective rainfall depth is called
(*a*) O.U.H.G. (*b*) O.D.R.H.G.
(*c*) both '*a*' and '*b*' (*d*) OIUH

26. The application of U.H.G. is suitable for the watershed area ranging from
(*a*) minimum 25 km^2 to maximum 5000 km^2.
(*b*) 25 to 5000 ha
(*c*) 500 to 5000 ha
(*d*) 10,000 ha.

27. Snyder's method is used to derive the
(*a*) unit hydrograph
(*b*) synthetic unit hydrograph
(*c*) dimensionless unit hydrograph
(*d*) distribution graph

28. Snyder's method is suitable to derive the S.U.H.G. for the watershed area ranging from
(*a*) 25 to 25000 km^2 (*b*) 30 to 30,000 km^2
(*c*) 25 to 250 km^2 (*d*) 10,000 ha

29. If the area of watershed is 2000 Km^2 and Q_p is 810 m^3/s, then the value of W_{50} and W_{75} will be as

(*a*) 14.86 h and 8.52 h (*b*) 14.86 h and 9.52 h
(*c*) 20.50 h and 10.25 h (*d*) 10 and 15h

30. The time interval between start of effective rainfall and the centre of mass of runoff is called as

(*a*) unit period
(*b*) base time
(*c*) lag + semi duration factor.
(*d*) lag + t_c

31. A plot of time (% of lag + semi-duration) and

$$\text{discharge} \times \frac{\text{lag plus + semi duration factor}}{\text{runoff}}$$ is called as

(*a*) S.U.H.G. (*b*) Dimensionless unit hydrograph
(*c*) I.U.H. (*d*) Distribution UHG

32. The I.U.H. theory was firstly proposed by

(*a*) C.E. Ramser (1940) (*b*) Clark (1945)
(*c*) Shermen (1932) (*d*) Phillip (1932)

33. The I.U.H. can be derived by using the method of

(*a*) S-curve (*b*) Convolution integral approach
(*c*) both '*a*' and '*b*' (*d*) Bernard method

34. A reservoir is said to be linear when

(*a*) storage ∝ outflow (*b*) storage ∝ inflow
(*c*) inflow ∝ outflow (*d*) $K \alpha T$

35. The I.U.H. is

(*a*) single peak (*b*) infinite base width
(*c*) both '*a*' and '*b*' (*d*) hydrograph with base flow

36. A unit hydrograph is for

(*a*) unit depth of rainfall excess
(*b*) unit rainfall duration
(*c*) T as zero
(*d*) both '*a*' and '*b*'.

37. The assumptions of unit hydrograph are

(*a*) linear response and time invariant
(*b*) non-linear response of time
(*c*) non-linear time variance, only.
(*d*) none of the above.

38. The clark model is associated to

(*a*) IUH (*b*) Distribution HHG
(*c*) SUHG (*d*) all above

39. Ordinate of UHG is expressed as

(*a*) $u(t)$ (*b*) $u(T)$
(*c*) $u(o, t)$ (*d*) $u(T, t)$

40. Ordinate of IUH is expressed as

(*a*) $u(o, t)$ (*b*) $u(T)$
(*c*) $u(t, T)$ (*d*) $u(\alpha, t)$

Answer (Objective Type Question)

1. (*a*)	**2.** (*a*)	**3.** (*a*)	**4.** (*b*)	**5.** (*a*)	**6.** (*a*)	**7.** (*a*)	**8.** (*c*)
9. (*a*)	**10.** (*a*)	**11.** (*a*)	**12.** (*a*)	**13.** (*a*)	**14.** (*c*)	**15.** (*d*)	**16.** (*a*)
17. (*a*)	**18.** (*c*)	**19.** (*b*)	**20.** (*b*)	**21.** (*b*)	**22.** (*a*)	**23.** (*a*)	**24.** (*a*)
25. (*a*)	**26.** (*a*)	**27.** (*b*)	**28.** (*b*)	**29.** (*a*)	**30.** (*a*)	**31.** (*b*)	**32.** (*b*)
33. (*c*)	**34.** (*a*)	**35.** (*c*)	**36.** (*d*)	**37.** (*a*)	**38.** (*a*)	**39.** (*d*)	**40.** (*a*)

7

Stream Gauging

Stream gauging is also known as stream flow measurement, which is the measurement of discharge/stream flow passing through the stream section in a unit time. It is expressed in terms of m^3/s or cubic meter per second. The knowledge of stream flow is very important for assesment of available water for planning of irrigation projects in the area. It also gives a guideline to establish the flood control works in the river basin etc. The importance of stream gauging are given below:

1. It is essential for assessment of the available water potential for irrigation planning and flood control works in the watershed.

2. Occurrence of flood can be forecasted.

3. Variations in seasonal and annual runoff of any stream can be determined.

4. Estimation of water loss at different reaches of stream, can be done.

5. A comprehensive and coordinated planning of rivers and their tributaries can be made for optimum utilisation of water flowing through them.

6. It is also helpful in design and construction of various multipurpose river valley development structures for facilitating the irrigation.

Before discussing the techniques of stream flow measurement, it is essential to know about the gauging site and its various features.

7.1. Gauging Site

The stream point, at which flow measurement is conducted is called gauging site. Some times, it is also known as gauge point, gauging station etc. For determining the location of gauging site, initially one or more stream points are tentatively selected and are studied to confirm, whether they fulfil the essential requirements of the flow measurement or not. A gauging site should satisfy the following points :

1. A site should be such that it acts as permanent control for stream flow measurement.

2. It should be clearly visible and easily assessible.

3. The stream point which is confluenced by the other streams, should be avoided because there is likelyhood of change in stream flow due to back water flow.

4. The gauging site should be capable to record the highest and lowest gauges corresponding to the highest and lowest flood peaks.

5. The site should enable to record the level of water surface for a given rate of stream flow.

6. The gauging site should be free from vigrous vegetal growth, boulders or other obstructions, such as bridge, piers etc.

7. It should be avoided from the influencing zone of back water flow form the dam etc.

8. The site should be firm and stable so that the cross-section of gauging station may not be changed due to silting or scouring during various stages of stream flow.

9. Straight and uniform reach of stream should be preferred for locating the gauging site.

10. The gauging site should also be well protected, so that the destruction caused by floating debris or ice can be overcome.

7.2. Measurement of Flow Stage

The flow stage refers to the water surface elevation, measured above a datum line which may be mean-sea level (MSL) or any other reference point. The stage measuring devices are called stage level recorder. These are classified according to the method by which they record the flow stage and the way by which they are used. The staff gauge, chain, tape, wire gauge, float gauge, electric tape gauge, pressure transmitter, etc are commonly used for measurement of flow stage in the river system. These are described as under :

Staff gauge : It is a graduated scale, made of durable material with low expansion coefficient. The gauge is placed in the river/stream by fastening with the pier, wall or other structures. The gauge height is read by observing the level of water surface contact with the gauge. Sometimes, fluctuation in water surface elevation is very large and it is not possible to read entire range of water surface elevation by single staff gauge. In such situations, several gauges are installed at various sections and at different locations of stream. These gauges are known as sectional gauge. During measurement, the gauge should be in vertical position. The staff gauge can also be used as a sloping scale over the stream bank. Important point regrading installation of staff gauge is that, it is either vertical or inclined whatever, but the graduation of scale should be clearly visible during measurement. One of the major problems in installation of staff gauge, is to protect it from boats, flood-transported debris etc. Therefore, its location should be such that, the disturbances across the gauge are minimum.

Chain, tape and wire gauge : The measurement of flow stage with these devices is performed by putting a weight to lower on the water surface. The chain gauge is read from a reference bead moving along the graduated scale, while the tape gauge is read by a pointer contact with the tape. The wire gauge is read by means of a mechanical counter attached to the reel, on which the wire is wound. The rotation of reel (wheel) is proportional to the length of released wire. The wire gauge is used to measure the water- surface elevation from some height above the water surface, such as from the bridge or similar structures. The measuring range of this gauge is about 25m.

Electric tape gauge : In case of different gauges described so far, the measurement of instant contact of gauge with water surface is not possible, causing introduction of errors in measurement. In such condition, the electrical tape gauge is more accurate. It consists of an electrical circuit, galvanometer etc. During measurement, the contact of water surface deflects the needle of galvanometer or produces a click. Electric tape gauge is used for precise measurement of water surface elevation.

Pressure transmitter gauge : In this gauge, measurement is obtained in terms of pressure with respect to the water stage. This gauge is equipped with a cylinder, through which water is allowed to a flexible diaphragm. Water suppress the diaphragm, which is transmitted to the dial via transmitter . At the dial, the reading of observation is indicated.

Crest-stage indicator : This instrument is used to delineate the peak stages of flood, which are essential for establishment of flood profiles and determination of their slopes for development of formulae to compute the flood flow through the river.

It consists of a pipe in vertical position with open and screened bottom and a vented top. A wooden staff gauge is also equipped in the pipe, which is held in place by a cap. Powdered cock in small amount is kept at top of the pipe and is washed to the bottom with water, where screen retains it. On passing of flood water through indicator, the cock is lifted up and at the crest, it clings to graduated staff. After taking the observation on flood stage, the instrument is returned to its original condition by pouring a little water for washing the cork, back down the pipe.

Automatic Stage Recorder

Although, the devices, such as staff gauge, chain tape & wire gauge, electrical gauge, crest-stage recorder etc. used for measurement of flow stage in the river/stream are simple, inexpensive and manually operated, but these require to take the observations at frequent interval, otherwise, there is likelihood of erroneous observation. To overcome such errors, the use of automatic stage recorders has been proved very efficient and accurate. The followings are the commonly used automatic stage recorder :

1. Float-gauge recorder
2. Bubble gauge
3. Tensiometric recorder

Float-gauge recorder : It is commonly used automatic stage recorder. It consists of a stilling well equipped with float operating system, recording mechanism, flush tank, staff gauge, intakes etc. The float operating system includes float and counter weight, mainly. The float is tied with string at one end and counter weight at the other end, and is kept over the pulley of the recorder. The position of float gets change with change in water level in the river/stilling well. The water enters the well through intakes. The counter weight keeps the string in proper tension and balance the float. The intake pipes connect the stream to the stilling well. The flush tank is used for removing the debris and sediments from the intake pipes.

The recording mechanism consists of angular movable pully, recorder and clockwise rotating drum. As the float gets displacement due to rising or lowering of the water-level, the pully gets angular movement. A chart is wrapped over the clock wise rotating drum, over which, the angular movement of pully is traced by the pen. When pen covers the full width of chart to trace the water stage, it is reversed back, automatically. In this way, the recording of water stage is done in linear scale. The clock mechanism can record the date for the day, week or fortnight period.

The recorder should be installed above the expected highest water level in the river to prevent inundation during recurrence of flood.

Bubble gauge : In this gauge, Nitrogen gas is bubbled slowly through a small tube which is discharged into a liquid through an orifice at a fixed elevation. A pressure gauge (mercury manometer) is provided to measure the gas pressure, inside the tube. The gas pressure corresponds the water column above the outlet (orifice). The change in water- surface elevation is indicated in terms of change in pressure at the pressure gauge. To adjust the pressure, a mechanism called 'servomotor' is equipped to the system. The servomotor brings the gas to bleed at the original rate at changed water-surface elevation. The servomoter also drives the pen on recording chart to trace the stage-hydrograph.

The bubble gauge offers several advantages over float-gauge recorder, which are as follows :

1. This gauges does not require the stilling well, which is very costly to construct.

2. The change in stage upto 30m or more can be measured.

3. There is a large gap (i.e. 300 m or more) between the recording mechanism and orifice, as result the measurement of gauge is relatively more accurate.

4. The likelihood of inlet chocking is very less, because of constant bleeding of gas.

Tensiometric Recorder : It is used for measuring the height of waves. It consists of diaphragm, flexible metal strip and air chamber. The diaphragm is attached to the flexible metal strip, which is mounted inside the air chamber. Wires are fastened on each side of the strip. The wires have the property of variable resistance with tension. Variations in pressure on the diaphragm change the tension in the wire, that inturn to produce voltage, which is read by whetstone *bridge.* The voltage variation is denoted in terms of stage fluctuation. This device is free form temperature effect.

Apart from aforesaid devices under automatic stage recorder, the followings are also used for the purpose :

1. Water-stage recorder
2. Automatic printer, and
3. Low-distance transmitter

Presentation of Stage Data

Stage data of river/stream flow is often presented in the form of stage hydrograph, which is the plot of stage against time.

Importance of Stage Data : Its various importance in hydrology are given as under :

1. It is very important for flood warning.
2. It is useful for design and construction of flood protection measures.
3. The long-term stage data of peak floods of any river system enables to estimate the design peak that is essential for design of hydraulic structures.
4. Measurement of flow stage is useful for renewal of valuable historic data.

Segmentation of Stream Cross-section

When stream flow is determined especially by using area- velocity method, the recording of observations on flow depth and velocity at various points in the stream cross-section becomes essential, for which segmentation of stream section is carried out. Segmentation is the division of entire flow section into some suitable number of segments (vertical section) of appropriate width. For each segment, the discharge is determined individually. The total stream flow is obtained by adding all the segmental discharge. The greater is the number of segments, more will be the accuracy in the stream flow measurement. However, the following points are kept in view, while segmenting the stream cross-section :

1. The segment size should be such that, the variation in discharge between any two adjacent segments, is not more than 4%.

2. The segments should be such that, the discharge passing through any segment is not more than 10% of the total discharge.

3. Mean velocity of flow in any segment should not be more than 20% of the lowest measured velocity.

4. The total number of segments should be such that, the observations can be recorded within $4\frac{1}{2}$ hours duration.

Indian standard has also made some recommendations on the segmentation, are given in Table 7.1.

Table 7.1. Segment size for different widths of stream section

S.No.	*Stream width (m)*	*No. of observation posts*	*Width of segment (m)*
1.	< 15	15	1.5
2.	15—90	15	6.0
3.	90—180	15	15.0
4.	> 180	25	Varies

7.3. Stream Gauging Methods

The common methods used for measurement of the stream flow are given as under :

1. Area-velocity method
2. Slope-area method
3. Hydraulic structures method
4. Stage-discharge curve
5. Other methods, such as tracer method, colour velocity method, radio-tracer method etc.

All these methods are described as under :

7.3.1. Area-Velocity Method

This method consists of determining the area of stream flow cross-section and mean velocity of flow and multiplying them together to obtain the stream flow *i.e.*

$$Q = A \cdot V \quad \text{...(7.1)}$$

in which, Q is the discharge, A is the cross- sectional area of the stream flow and V is the mean flow velocity.

The cross-sectional area of stream flow is obtained by measuring the flow depth át different segments. Generally, the measurement of depth and velocity of flow is conducted, simultaneously. The methods, used for measuring the depth and velocity of flow are described below :

7.3.1.1. Depth Measurement

It is performed by using the following devices :

1. Suspenson rod

2. Sounding rod and
3. Echo-sounder.

Suspenson rod : It is used when flow velocity is about 1 m/s and flow depth is very small, *i.e.* upto 1 m. The length of suspenson rods is 3 m. They are equipped with a base plate at their bottom. The purpose of base plate is to prevent the rod from sinking into the stream bed. The rods are graduated in the order of meter, decimeter and centimeter by using the enamel paint. Rods are also provided with an ellipitical or flat rod to keep in vertical position. The elliptical rod also minimizes the error due to obstruction in the flow, caused by the rod.

The flow depth is directly measured by placing the suspension rod into the stream flow over the bed.

Sounding rod : The sounding rod is suitable when suspenson rods are found difficult for measuring the stream flow depth. It measures the flow depth up to 6 m. These rods are also graduated in the order of meter, decimeter and centimeter with the help of enamel paint. Generally, white, red or black paints are used for graduation. The letter size is usually kept 2.5 cm. Based on the materials used for constructing the sounding rods, these are classified into following two types :

1. Wooden rod, and
2. Bamboo rod.

The wooden rods are made of strong and well seasoned wood. Their size ranges from 2 to 3 m length and $80 \times 20\ mm^2$ as cross-sectional area. For preventing to sink into the stream bed, a base plate is also provided at bottom of the rod. The plate is made of metal sheet in 150 mm diameter and 5 mm in thickness. A circular flange having 80 mm diameter opening is also provided to the rod for connecting the nipple of the same diameter (*i.e.* 80 mm). The wooden type sounding rods are generally used for the stream flow depth ranging from 2 to 3 m.

The bamboo type sounding rods are made of bomboo. These rods are more common to that of the wooden rods, as they are light in weight and uniform in diameter. The length varies from 3 to 6 m and diameter up to 38 mm. A metal base plate of 100 mm diameter along with flange is also provided at the base of the rod. Flange helps in holding the rod in proper position. The use of bamboo rod is found suitable for measuring the stream flow depth from 3 to 6 m.

Echo Sounder : It is used for getting accurate and rapid measurement of flow depth, particularly when stream flow depth is more and flow velocity is too high. It can also be used for measuring the small flow depth up to 0.30 m, but the measurement is not so accurate.

The working procedure consists of transmitting the pressure wave by a transmeter from water surface to the stream bed for a short duration. The transmitted wave is reflected back in the form of echo, which is received by the receiver. The time interval between transmitted pressure wave and receiving of echo sound is recorded in the form of graph. The measured time is calibrated in terms of flow depth automatically.

The echo sounder records single measurement for each depth of stream flow. The demerit of this instrument is that, it requires regular calibration.

7.3.1.2. Accuracy of Depth Measurement

The accuracy of depth measurement by using different divices, depends on the following points :

1. Stream flow depth.
2. Configuration of flow cross-section in the vicinity of gauging point.
3. Precautions used during meaurement.
4. Flow velocity.
5. Direction and strength of wind.

7.3.2. Measurement of Stream Flow Velocity

The rate of stream flow is determined by knowing the velocity and cross-sectional area of flow. Since cross section of stream flow varies with the depth of flow, therefore, it is essential to take the measurements at several depths in the stream cross-section for getting more accurate result. The mean velocity of stream flow is obtained by averaging them.

Various devices used for measuring the flow velocity, are given below :

1. Float —— | —Surface float
| —Sub-surface float

2. Velocity rods

3. Current meter —— | —Pigmy type current meter
| —Propeller type current meter
| —Price current meter

Surface float : It is generally used, when high degree of accuracy in flow velocity is not require and use of more expensive devices is also not feasible.

Surface float is very simple in construction. It consists of a wooden disc of 7 to 15 cm in diameter. For measurement of flow velocity, it is placed over the stream flow. The time (t) taken by the float to cover a certain distance (L) is recorded for several attempts and flow velocity (V_s) is calculated as

$$V_s = \frac{L}{t} \qquad ...(7.2)$$

The mean flow velocity (V_m) is determined by multiplying a correction factor *i.e.*

$$V_m = 0.85\ V_s \quad ...(7.3)$$

Precautions : The following precautions are taken during measurement of flow velocity under surface float method :

1. Stream section must be straight, uniform and least surface irregularities.

2. Floats are generally affected by the blowing winds, water waves, eddies etc. as result the measurement is not accurate. To overcome these effects, a metallic hollow cylindrical float is also attached to the float by means of a thin string.

Limitations : The use of surface float involves following limitations :

1. The measurement of flow velocity is suitable for the flow depth up to 4.5 m only. For greater flow depth, it is not suitable.

2. It involves more time for taking observations.

3. It requires more strength of observations crew.

4. A large number of observations are required for determination of correct flow velocity.

5. Control of float in stream flow, is very difficult.

6. It does not provide accurate measurement of flow velocity in the vicinity of stream bed (*i.e.* 0.94 d) because weed growth and bed irregularities affect the movement of float.

7. Surface floats are generally disturbed by the wind and water currents, causing erroneous measurement.

Sub-surface float : Sub-surface floats are found in following two types :

1. Double float and
2. Twin float.

Double float : Consists of two floats, in which one is kept over the water surface and other into the water. The float, submerged in the water is known as sub-surface float. The sub-surface float is made of hollow metal in the shape of sphere or cylinder, is suspended from the surface float by a thin cord of known length. The length of cord is decided on the basis of depth of flow. The sub-surface float should always be at 0.2 *d* above the stream bed (d is the flow depth) which can be maintained by adjusting the cord length. The purpose of sub-surface float is to keep the surface float in proper position against wind and water current. The use of double float for measurement of flow velocity is shown in the Fig. 7.1.

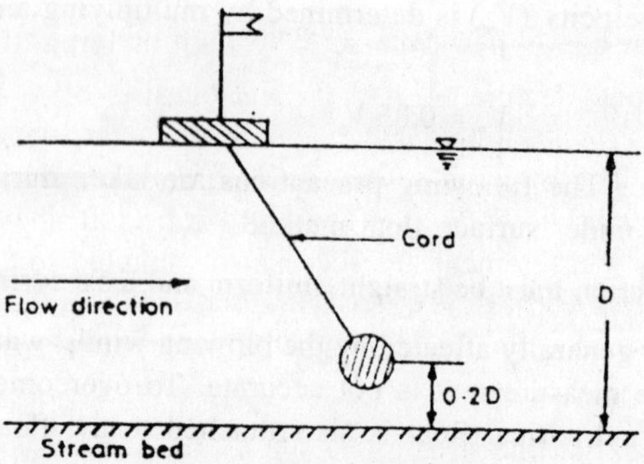

Fig. 7.1. Double float.

Twin float : It is another type of sub-surface float, which consists of two similar spherical floats made of hollow metal. Both the floats are connected with a thin cord, in such a way that, the upper one is floating over the water surface and other is suspended into the flow, to keep the surface float in vertical position. During measurement, the surface float is partially submerged in the flowing water, while lower float is completely submerged in the stream flow. At the time of measurement, the lower float is maintained at the depth of 0.6 *d* from the water surface by adjusting the cord length. The velocity measured by the twin float is considered as mean flow velocity. The velocity measurement by twin float is illustrated in Fig. 7.2.

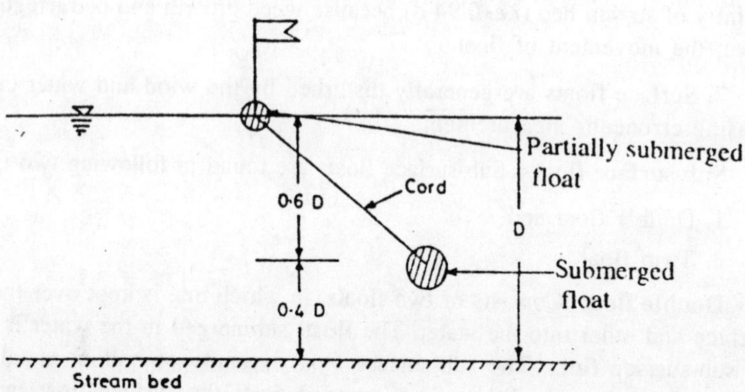

Fig. 7.2. Twin float.

Velocity rods : Use of velocity rods for measurement of flow velocity, is found suitable under following conditions :

1. When streams have uniform cross- section. Generally, artificial channels are preferred.

2 When flow depth is constant *i.e.* not exceeding 4.5 m.

3. When stream bed is free from weed growth or lying of stones etc.

The constructional feature of velocity rod consists of a wooden rod in square or circular cross-section; 3 to 5 cm in diameter, depending on the length of rod. The length of rod should be such that, it could not touch the bottom of stream and 3 to 5 cm gap should also be left above the bed. At the time of velocity measurement, the rod is also weighted so that it can float on the water surface in vertical position. In velocity rod method, the following observations are recorded for determining the (mean) flow velocity :

1. Velocity of the rod, (V)
2. Depth of water in the stream (D), and
3. Distance between lower end of the velocity rod and stream bed (d).

The following formula is used for computing the mean flow velocity (V_m),

$$V_m = V\left(1.02 - 0.0116\sqrt{\frac{d}{D}}\right) \qquad \text{...(7.4)}$$

Example 7.1. *Calculate the mean velocity of stream flow by using the following data, recorded by velocity rod*

1. Velocity of rod = 1.50 m/s

2. Depth of water in the stream = 4.5 m

3. Gap between lower end of the rod and stream bed = 0.5 m

Solution : The mean flow velocity (V_m) is given as

$$V_m = V\left(1.02 - 0.0116\sqrt{\frac{d}{D}}\right)$$

in which,

$$V = 1.5 \text{ m/s}$$
$$d = 0.5 \text{ m}$$
$$D = 4.5 \text{ m}$$

$$\therefore \quad V_m = 1.5\left(1.02 - 0.0116\sqrt{\frac{.5}{4.5}}\right)$$

$$= \mathbf{1.52\ m/s} \quad \textbf{Ans.}$$

The velocity rod provides more accurate measurement of stream flow velocity as compared to the current meter, at the flow depth of 0.6 D However, it takes more time.

Assumption : It approximates the mean flow velocity in a particular segment.

Limitations : Various limitations of velocity rod method are given as under:

1. Use of velocity rod is suitable only to those streams, which are throughout uniform.

2. For accurate measurement, the rod should always travel in middle of the segment, which is very difficult to maintain.

3. The observations must be recorded in large number of segments.

4. Some times, the rods travelling in different segments, are collide and thus make erroneous measurement.

5. Movement of rod is also affected by the wind, causing inaccurate measurement.

Current Meter

It is an instrument for measurement of the stream flow velocity. The current meter consists of a rotating device, which revolution corresponds the velocity of flow when placed on the flowing water surface. For measuring the flow velocity, the meter is mounted on a rod or tied with cable and is lowered to the stream water. The mounting rod is preferred for shallow streams; and cable for the deep stream flows.

Several observatons are taken at each segment of the stream section and corresponding flow velocities are determined with the help of rating curve, which is supplied to the current meter. The mean flow velocity is obtained by averaging them.

Types of Current meter : Various types of current meter are given as under:

1. Cup type
2. Pigmy current meter
3. Optical type, and
4. Curley type

Cup type current meter : This type of current meter is also known as rotating cup current meter. Working principle of it is the "flow velocity is directly proportional to the revolution of wheel". In this current meter, the number of revolutions are recorded by an electrical circuit. The circuit can be either closed or broken, intermittently.

For measurement of flow velocity, the current meter is placed in the stream flow at desired depth and observations on number of revolutions for some specified duration are taken. The mean flow velocity is determined by using the rating curve or table, provided to the meter.

Pigmy type current meter : It is also known by the name of miniature type current meter. Its design and construction is similar to the curley type current meter. This meter is found more suitable for measuring the flow velocity in following conditions :

1. When velocity and flow depths are less. Generally, the flow velocities in shallow streams, irrigation channels etc. are measured by this type of current meter.

2. When stream flow velocity is ranging up to 1 m/s.

Optical current meter : It is a stroboscopic device used for measuring the surface flow velocity without immersing into water, especially at the time of extreme floods. This current meter is equipped with light weight battery, low power telescope, rotating mirror, motor (variable speed drive) and tachometer. The meter is operated by the motor, powered by battery unit. Observation is taken, when angular velocity of motor increases gradually. The apparent velocity of stream flow is seen by the telescope attached to the meter. For taking observation, the meter is synchronized. At synchronized stage, the angular speed of mirror wheel and vertical distance between optical axis and the water surface is measured with the help of weighted tape. These two informations are used for computing the mean flow velocity of the stream.

Curely current meter : It is also known as price current meter, is one of the most common type current meters used for measuring the stream flow velocity. This current meter consists of following parts :

1. Head
2. Tail
3. Hanger
4. Recorder, and
5. Suspending device

Head : It includes a yoke, which consists of wheel of 12.7 cm diameter and 6 conical cups mounted on the horizontal frame. The wheel is rotated on a shaft in anti-clockwise direction. The revolutions made by the wheel are indicated by electric show in a box, known as "commentator box".

Tail : It has two vanes, which are mounted on the stem. In both of the two vanes, one is adjustable and other is rigidly fixed. The adjustable vane is attached to the weight, which can be increased or decreased as per requirement. The function of tail is to balance and keep the meter, parallel to the stream current.

Hanger : It is a thin steel rod, connected to the frame with a torped shaped weight at the bottom. The weight keeps the meter plumb, when it is hanged with the cable.

Recorder : The recording mechanism consists of telephone and a set of battery. The function of recording unit is to convey the message to the observer about the number of revolutions made by the meter.

Suspending device : It consists of lead and rack & pinion arrangement. The suspending device is used to lower the current meter to the stream water. The lead or cable is very common for suspending the meter from the bridge etc. In high flow velocity condition, the use of cable is avoided for lowering the meter, as it is deflected by the flowing water from the observation point. In rack & pinion arrangement the rack is in rigid condition and is attached with a toothed wheel. Rack is also graduated for indicating the flow depth ranging from 0.6D to 6 m.

Rating of Current Meter : Development of relationship between the number of revolutions and the stream flow velocity is known as rating of the current meter', which is in the form of equation called as rating equation'. Generally, the rating equation of current meter is supplied by the manufacturer. However, the given equation should be verified. The form of rating equation is given as under :

$$V = aN + b \quad \text{...(7.5)}$$

where, V = velocity of stream flow (m/s)

N = revolutions per second

a, b = constant

Example 7.2. *The measurement of stream flow velocity was conducted by using curely type current meter. If current meter makes 50 rps, then what would be the stream flow velocity. Assume the value of a and b as 0.3 and 0.05, respectively.*

Solution. Give that,

$$N = 50 \text{ rps}$$
$$a = 0.3$$
$$b = 0.05$$

$\therefore$ Flow velocity

$$V = aN + b$$
$$= 0.3 \times 50 + 0.05$$
$$= \mathbf{15.05\ m/s} \quad \textbf{Ans}$$

Rating Procedure

Rating of the current meter is performed in a masoonary tank of $90 \times 2.4 \times 2.1\ m^3$ size (approx.). Method involves the toweing of current meter in still water of the tank either by a trolley, pushed with the hand or by an electric motor. The trolley should be pushed in such a way that, it can move on the track at a constant speed. The track on which trolley is moved, is graduated in the order of meter and centimeter with enamel paint. A metromone is also kept on the trolley to produce the ticks at 2, 3, 4, 5, up to 10 seconds. The man, who is performing the work should be well trained, so that he can put his pace uniformly to synchronize the ticking of the metromone, very well, particularly when motor speed is required to adjust for getting different velocities. A cantilever beam is also fixed on the trolley in such a way that, the projecting end of the beam can fall at the centre of the rating tank. The current meter is hanged with the help of suspension rod. The current meter is lowered into the tank water for 1 m depth from the top of water surface. Now, for a fixed number of revolutions, the trolley is pushed and the time as well as distance coverd by it, are recorded. Generally, 10 to 100 revolutions are considered for the purpose. A set of such observations are recorded by repeating the procedure and a curve is prepared by plotting the pushing velocity and revolutions per second, on a simple graph paper. It is obtained in the form of straight line, as shown in Fig. 7.3. The values of constant a and b are shown in the figure.

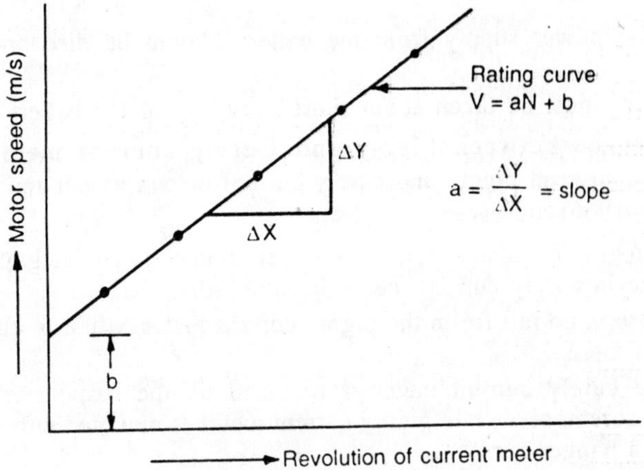

Fig. 7.3. Rating curve.

Precautions during use of current meter : The following precautions must be taken into consideration while operating the current meter :

1. Before putting the current meter into operation, the initial checking such as tightening of the screws etc. should be done properly.

2. In cup type current meter, the cups should be freely rotated. For this purpose, the raising should always be kept slack.

3. The cups should not be turned by the hand.

4. The current meter should always swivel freely on the rod, rack or chain, which ever is used.

5. During observation, if there is any inconsistency in the meter, that should be investigated very sincerely, without any delay.

6. For measuring flow velocity, the current meter should always be kept in horizontal position.

7. At the time of observation, the meter should not be overtopped from the water surface. This may be achieved by using the balance weight.

8. For measurement of flow velocity less than 0.15 m/s, the current meter should not be used, as it does not provide authentic measurement.

9. When current meter is suspended by cable in high wind velocity condition, balance weight must be added to it, so that the meter can be in vertical position in the stream water.

10. The cups should not be allowed to ride on the pivot, when meter is not in operation.

11. After completing the measurements, the water present in the meter should be drained properly and the pivot point should be lubricated very well.

12. The lock nut provided on the pivot point should always be in tight condition, so that the cups can rotat properly.

13. The power supply from the battery should be disconnected, when meter is not in use.

14. Care must be taken about short circuiting of the battery.

Difference between Pigmy and Curely current meters. Various differences between pigmy and curely current meters as per Indian Standard (IS : 3910–1966) are given as under :

1. In pigmy current meter, the contact chamer is an integral part of the yoke, while in curely current meter, it is not so.

2. There is no tail fin in the pigmy current meter, while in curely current meter, it is there.

3. The curely current meter is mounted on the suspension device for taking measurements, while pigmy current meter is mounted either on wading rod or on a hanger bar.

4. Pigmy current meter is used for single contact, while curely meter is for double contacts.

Essential Requirements for Use of Current Meter : On this matter, the Indian Standard has made following recommendations (IS : 3910 - 1966) :

1.The current meter should always response instantly and consistently to all the changes took place in the stream flow.

2. After completing the measurements, all parts of the current meter must be disengaged, cleaned and reassembled.

3. The meter should be capable of moving in sediment ladden water.

4. There should be some suitable means for raising or lowering the bucket wheel and separating the pivot and its bearing, especially when meter is transported to the other places.

5. At the time of measurement, the current meter should be in horizontal position in the flow. This may be done by using the counter weight to the meter.

6. The meter should be mounted on the cable or on the hanging bar for lowering to the stream flow.

Methods of Velocity Determination

Various methods used for determining the average flow velocity are described as under :

1. Velocity distribution method : This is an accurate method for velocity determination, but has limitation about involvement of more time for recording the observations at various points in each stream segment. In this method, the velocity of flow is determined, minimum at 6 points and preferably at 10 points by using the current meter. Generally, these points are 0.1, 0.2, 0.3,. up to 0.9 times the depth of flow from the top of the water surface at each segment. A graph is prepared by plotting the velocity and stream flow depth data on simple graph paper. The mean flow velocity is computed by dividing the enclosed area of the graph, with the total stream flow depth. The enclosed area of the graph is determined by means of area measuring device called "plainimeter".

2. One point method : It is also known as six-tenth point method. The measurement of flow velocity is taken at the depth of 0.6 times the stream flow depth, from the top of water surface. The velocity measured at this depth is considered as the average flow velocity at the stream segment. This method determines the accurate value of stream flow velocity in normal flow condition. It is widely used for measuring the mean velocity of river flow. Its accuracy ranges within ± 5 percent.

3. Two point method : Consists of taking the velocity measurements at two points in each segment. One is at 0.2 and other is at 0.8 time the depth of stream flow from the top of water surface. The velocities at these two points are averaged to get the mean flow velocity in the segment, *i.e.*

$$V_m = \frac{1}{2}(V_{0.2d} + V_{0.8d}) \quad \text{...(7.6)}$$

where, V_m = mean flow velocity

$V_{0.2d}$ = velocity at 0.2 time the depth of stream flow

$V_{0.8d}$ = velocity at 0.8 time the depth of stream flow

This method results more accurate measurement as compared to the one point method. Its accuracy varies within 2%. Limitation of this method is that, it is not suitable for measuring the flow velocity in the streams of less than 0.6 m width, because stream's boundary affects the observation.

Example 7.3. *Determine the mean flow velocity of stream flow, using two point method. The recorded data by using the current meter are given as under :*

Depth	*Revolutions*	*Time (second)*
0.2d	*35*	*50*
0.8d	*25*	*55*

Assume the value of a = 0.3 and b = 0.05

Solution. Using the equation 7.6

$$V_m = \frac{1}{2}(V_{0.2d} + V_{0.8d})$$

in which,

$$V_{0.2d} = 0.3 \times \frac{35}{50} + 0.05$$

$$= 0.26 \text{ m/s}$$

$$V_{0.8d} = 0.3 \times \frac{25}{55} + 0.05$$

$$= 0.19 \text{ m/s}$$

$$\therefore \quad V_m = \frac{1}{2}(0.26 + 0.19)$$

$$= \mathbf{0.23 \text{ m/s}} \quad \textbf{Ans.}$$

4. Three point method : In this method, the measurements of flow velocity are taken at three different points in the stream segments. In which, first is at 0.2d, second at 0.6d and third at 0.8d from the top of the water surface. The mean flow velocity is determined by averaging all three velocities *i.e.*

$$V_m = \frac{1}{3}(V_{0.2d} + V_{0.6d} + V_{0.8d}) \qquad ...(7.7)$$

This method is found accurate, particularly where flow velocities are non-uniform at different flow depths.

Example 7.4. *Find out the mean flow velocity, by using three point method. The following observations were recorded by using curely type current meter :*

Stream depth	*Revolutions*	*Time (second)*
0.2d	*40*	*58*
0.6d	*15*	*50*
0.8d	*30*	*54*

Assume, a = 0.4 and b = 0.06

Solution. Using equation 7.7

$$V_m = \frac{1}{3}(V_{0.2d} + V_{0.6d} + V_{0.8d})$$

in which,

$$V_{0.2d} = 0.4 \times \frac{40}{58} + 0.06$$

$$= 0.34 \text{ m/s}$$

$$V_{0.6d} = 0.4 \times \frac{15}{50} + 0.06$$

$$= 0.18 \text{ m/s}$$

and

$$V_{0.8d} = 0.4 \times \frac{30}{54} + 0.06$$

$$= 0.28 \text{ m/s}$$

$\therefore$

$$V_m = \frac{1}{3}(0.34 + 0.18 + 0.28)$$

$$= \mathbf{0.27 \text{ m/s}} \quad \textbf{Ans.}$$

5. Six point method : In this method, the observations of flow velocity are taken at six different points throughout the stream flow depth. These points are 0.1*d*, 0.2*d*, 0.4*d*, 0.6*d*, 0.8*d* and 0.9*d* at each segment. This method is found most accurate, when stream is badly clogged by weeds or some other objects such as ice deposits etc.

A graph is prepared by plotting the measured flow velocities and coresponding depths ; and enclosed area of plotted graph is determined with the help of plainimeter. The mean flow velocity is computed by dividing the enclosed area with the stream flow depth.

6. Integration method : In integration method, a continuous measurement is performed by lowering and raising the current meter into the stream flow. The raising and lowering should be done with a uniform speed, not more than 0.04 m/s. The observations on number of revolutions for a given time are noted at each segment. The mean flow velocity at each segment is calculated by multiplying the mean value of revolutions per second to the calibration coeffcient, given for the meter. In this method, if obtained velocities differ by more than 10 percent, then measurement should be repeated, again.

At the time of observation, if current meter is retained for sufficient period near or over the stream bed, it yields erroneous measurement. So it should not be allowed to retain the meter for longer time.

7. Two-tenth method : In two-tenth method, the measurement of flow velocity is done at the depth of 0.2 time the stream flow depth from the water surface at each segment; and mean flow velocity is computed by multiplying the number of revolutions per second made by the current meter to the calibration coefficient. The calibration coefficient can be determined on the basis of mean flow velocity at different flow stages by using six-tenth, two-tenth, eight-tenth or velocity-distribution techniques.

8. One-point continuous method : In this method, the measurements are taken in the same way, as in two-tenth method. However, it results less accurate measurement of flow velocity. Measurement is taken at any point between 0.3 to 0.6 time the flow depth from the top surface, in some selected segments. The measured flow velocities are averaged for 24 hours duration and multiplied with the factor, to determine the mean flow velocity.

9. Surface velocity method : This method consists of taking the measurement of flow velocity either by the current meter or by using the surface float. The mean flow velocity is computed by multiplying a reduction coefficient to the observed flow velocity. It can be expressed as

$$V_m = K \cdot V_o \quad ...(7.7)$$

where, V_m = mean flow velocity

K = reduction coefficient

V_o = observed flow velocity

The value of reduction coefficient varies from 0.85 to 0.95 depending on the depth of stream water, flow velocity, flow stage, characteristics of river bed etc. However, a value of 0.89 is generally used. After substituting the value of K, the equation 7.7 becomes

$$V_m = 0.89\ V_0 \quad ...(7.8)$$

Velocity measurement by Pitot tube : This is also an accurate method for measuring the flow velocity, but has limitation about its unsuitability for natural stream flows, as the pilot tube is liable to get clogged by fine silts. It is especially designed to use for laboratory purpose.

Pitot tube consists of 'L' shaped tube, of which lower end is bent at 90° angle and is fitted with a nozzle. For taking measurement, it is suspended in the channel, facing the nozzle end towards up stream face of the flow. The water starts to rise in the vertical tube to some height due to pressure exerted by the flowing water on its mouth. The rise of water level in the tube is recorded as observation; and the flow velocity is computed by using the following formula :

$$V = \sqrt{2gh} \qquad ...(7.9)$$

where, V = flow velocity

g = acceleration due to gravity

h = water height in the vertical tube, as shown in Fig. 7.4

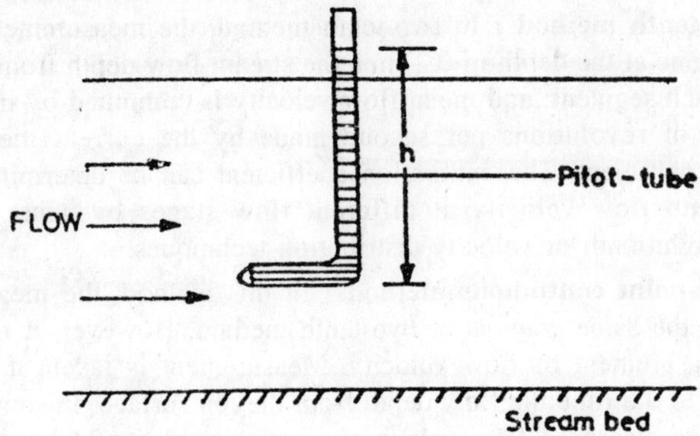

Fig. 7.4. Discharge measurement by Pitot tube.

Example 7.5. *Compute the discharge of a given stream by using the following methods :*

1. Two point method, and

2. Three point method

Use the following data of stream flow :

Distance from one end (m)		0	1	2	3	4	5	6	7
Depth (m)		0	1.4	3.3	5.0	9.0	5.4	3.8	1.8
Velocity (m/s) at	0.2d	0	0.40	0.60	0.84	0.90	0.80	0.62	0.54
	0.6d	0	0.25	0.35	0.60	0..70	0.65	0.50	0.36
	0.8d	0	0.20	0.30	0.50	0.62	0.55	0.40	0.30

Solution. (1) **Stream discharge by using two point method**

$$Q = A \cdot V_m$$

$$= (b \cdot d) \cdot V_m$$

$$= d \cdot V_m \qquad \text{(assuming unit width of stream flow)}$$

Distance (m)	0	1	2	3	4	5	6	7
Depth (m)	0	1.4	3.3	5.0	9.0	5.4	3.8	1.8
$V_m = \frac{0.2d + 0.8d}{2}$	0	0.30	0.45	0.67	0.76	0.68	0.51	0.42
$Q = d \cdot V_m$ (m³/s)	0	0.42	1.49	3.35	6.84	3.67	1.94	0.76

$\therefore$ Stream discharge $(Q_t) = \Sigma Q$

$= 0.42 + 1.49 + 3.35 + 6.84 + 3.67 + 1.94 + 0.76$

$=$ **18.47 m³/s** **Ans.**

2. **Stream discharge by using three point method**

$Q = d\,V_m$ (assuming unit width of flow)

Distance (m)	0	1	2	3	4	5	6	7
Depth (m)	0	1.4	3.3	5.0	9.0	5.4	3.8	1.8
$V_m = \frac{1}{3}(V_{0.2d} + V_{0.6d} + V_{0.8d})$	0	0.28	0.42	0.65	0.74	0.67	0.51	0.40
Discharge $Q = d \cdot V_m$	0	0.392	1.39	3.25	6.66	3.62	1.94	0.72

Stream discharge $(Q_t) = \Sigma Q$

$= 0.392 + 1.39 + 3.25 + 6.66 + 3.62 + 1.94 + 0.72$

$=$ **13.97 m³/s** **Ans.**

Example 7.6. *Calculate the stream flow rate from the following data :*

Distance from one end (m)		*0*	*0.5*	*1.0*	*1.5*	*2.0*	*2.5*	*3.0*	*3.5*
Depth (m)		*0*	*0.30*	*1.30*	*2.5*	*3.0*	*1.5*	*0.50*	*0*
Velocity (m/s) at	*0.2d*	*0*	*0.50*	*0.75*	*0.81*	*0.95*	*0.60*	*0.45*	*0*
	0.8d	*0*	*0.30*	*0.45*	*0.31*	*0.45*	*0.30*	*0.25*	*0*

Use 'two point method' and mean section method for computation.

Solution.

(1) Computation of stream flow rate by using 'Two point method'.

Computation is shown in following table :

Distance from one end (m)	Water depth (m)	Segment width (m)	Segment area (m^2)	Velocity at		V_m* (m/s)	Discharge (m^3/s)
				0.2d	0.8d		
0	0.0	0.0	0.00	0.00	0.00	0.00	0.00
0.5	0.30	0.50	0.15	0.50	0.30	0.40	0.06
1.0	1.30	0.50	0.65	0.75	0.45	0.60	0.39
1.5	2.50	0.50	1.25	0.81	0.30	0.56	0.70
2.0	3.00	0.50	1.50	0.95	0.45	0.70	1.05
2.5	1.50	0.50	0.75	0.60	0.30	0.45	0.34
3.0	0.50	0.50	0.25	0.45	0.25	0.33	0.08
3.5	0.0	0.50	0.00	0.00	0.00	0.00	0.00

$$*V_m = \frac{V_{0.2d} + V_{0.8d}}{2}$$

$\therefore$ Stream discharge $(Q_t) = \Sigma Q$

$= 0.06 + 0.39 + 0.70 + 1.05 + 0.34 + 0.08$

$= \mathbf{2.62\ m^3/s}$ **Ans.**

(2) Computation by using Mean Section Method : It is shown in following table

Distance from one end (m)	Water depth (m)	Avg water depth (m)	Velocity (m/s)		V_m (m/s)	Avg. velocity at two adjacent segments	Discharge at verticals (m^3/s)
			0.2d	0.8d			
0	0.0	0.0	0.0	0.0	0.00	0.00	0.00
.50	0.30	0.15	0.50	0.30	0.40	0.20	0.03
1.00	1.30	0.80	0.75	0.45	0.60	0.50	0.40
1.50	2.50	1.90	0.81	0.30	0.56	0.58	1.10
2.00	3.00	2.75	0.95	0.45	0.70	0.63	1.73
2.50	1.50	2.25	0.60	0.30	0.45	0.58	1.31
3.00	0.50	1.00	0.45	0.25	0.33	0.39	0.39
3.50	0.0	0.25	0.0	0.0	0.00	0.17	0.04
						Total	5.00

$\therefore$ Stream discharge $(Q_t) = 5.00 \times 0.5$

$= \mathbf{2.50\ m^3/s}$ **Ans.**

Slope-Area Method

This method is not so accurate as velocity - area method. It computes an approximate value of stream flow rate. It is especially used for determination of flood discharge, when velocity - area method is not possible to use for the purpose. In this method, the stream flow rate is calculated by multiplying the average cross-sectional area of the stream flow and flow velocity determined with the help of slope of water surface in the stream. The computation of stream flow rate is carried out under following steps :

Step (1) Computation of cross-sectional area of the stream flow :

It is carried out by selecting three different cross-sections throughout the stream length. In which, two are taken at the ends of the selected stream length and third is at the centre. The mean cross sectional area of the stream flow is computed by using the following formula

$$A = \frac{a_1 + 2a_2 + ...2a_{n-1} + a_n}{2(n-1)} \quad ...(7.10)$$

in which, A is the mean cross-sectional area of the stream flow and $a_1, a_2 ...a_n$ are the cross-sectional areas of the stream flow at the points 1, 2, ...n within the reach.

Step (2) Computation of wetted perimeter : The mean wetted perimeter of stream flow can be computed by using the following formula.

$$P = \frac{p_1 + 2p_2 + ... 2p_{n-1} + p_n}{2(n-1)} \quad ...(7.11)$$

in which P is the mean wetted perimeter of the stream flow and $p_, p_2 \cdots p_n$ are the wetted perimeters at the points, 1, 2 ... n within the selected stream length.

Step (3) Computation of slope of the water surface : It is performed by installation of the gauge, atleast at three cross-sections of the stream length. The installation of gauges should be such that, the top most graduation of each gauge should fall in the straight of zero mark of the next gauge, located on the upper side. The readings *i.e.* water levels at the respective gauge are recorded at the beginning and end of the flood, with reference to some permanent bench mark. The mean value of the water levels is used for computation of the slope of the water surface. However, if gauges are not possible to install due to some unforseen reasons, then slope of the water surface profile can also be computed from the flood marks made on either sides of the river bank.

Step (4) Computation of flow Velocity : In slope - area method, the velocity of stream flow is determined with the help of water surface slope, wetted perimeter and cross - sectional area of the flow. The following formulae can be used.

1. **Manning's formula**

$$V = \frac{1}{n}, R^{2/3} \cdot S^{1/2} \quad \text{...(7.12)}$$

2. **Chezy's formula**

$$V = C\sqrt{R \cdot S} \quad \text{...(7.13)}$$

where, V = mean flow velocity

n = Manning's roughness coefficient. Its values for different types of stream bed materials are given in table 7.2.

R = hydraulic mean radius

$= \frac{A}{P}$

A = cross–sectional area of the stream flow

P = wetted perimeter of the stream flow

S = slope of the water surface

C = Chezy's constant, depends on the shape and surface conditions of the channel.

Table 7.2. Manning's roughness coefficient (*n*)

S.No.	*Stream bed material*	*Value of 'n'*
1.	Earth with vegetation	0.025 to 0,.040
2.	Only earth material	0.020 to 0.030
3.	Smooth cement	0.010 to 0.014
4.	Brick masonary	0.012 to 0.020
5.	Concrete	0.011 to 0.013
6.	Gravel	0.022 to 0.035

Limitations of Area-Velocity Method : This method involves followin limitations :

1. It does not determine the accurate value of stream flow rate, becau the determined values of stream flow cross sectional area and mean flo velocity are not so accurate.

2. The computed flow rate can also be erroneous, if cross-sectional are of the flow at upper and lower ends of the reach are not approximately t same.

3. Determination of slope of water surface profile is a difficult job.

4. In this method, the cross-sectional area of the stream flow can not be measured during or just after recording the gauge readings, causing introduction of errors in discharge computation.

5. For determining the flow velocity by using Manning's formula, the selection of Manning's roughness coefficient (n) is difficult, as its value is likely to change with the variation in the flow stages of the stream.

Site Selection for Slope-Area Method : The site selection criterion for taking the measurements to calculate the discharge under slope-area method are given below :

1. There should be straight reach of the stream section for selecting the observation points.

2. The length of reach should be atleast 10 times of the stream width or 300 m, which ever is more.

3. The slope of water surface should be atleast 150 mm. However, it can be minimum 30 mm. The larger slope should always be preferred.

4. The stream bed and its banks should be firm and stable.

5. Site should preferably be slected at the point where wind effect is minimum.

6. The measurement site should not be at the point of confluence of the tributaries.

7. It should be free from back water effects.

8. Site should always be free from abrupt falls, sudden contractions or enlargements etc.

9. At the gauging site, the flow direction should be towards the direction of prevailing wind.

10. The selected site should be easily accessible at all the times.

Stage-Discharge Curve Method

In any flow measurement program, it is not possible to record the discharge data, day-to-day or even when desired, because of heavy expenditure of the money or some other factors. For example at high flood-condition, the measurement of discharge becomes impossible due to high flow velocity. Under this condition, the estimation of stream flow is carried out by using the already developed stage-discharge curve of the given strem/river system.

A stage-discharge curve is drawn by plotting the stream discharge and corresponding gauge height, on log-log paper. This curve is also known as the rating curve. With the help of stage-discharge curve, if the stage of stream flow is known, then discharge can be obtained directly. A such stage-discharge curve is shown in Fig. 7.5.

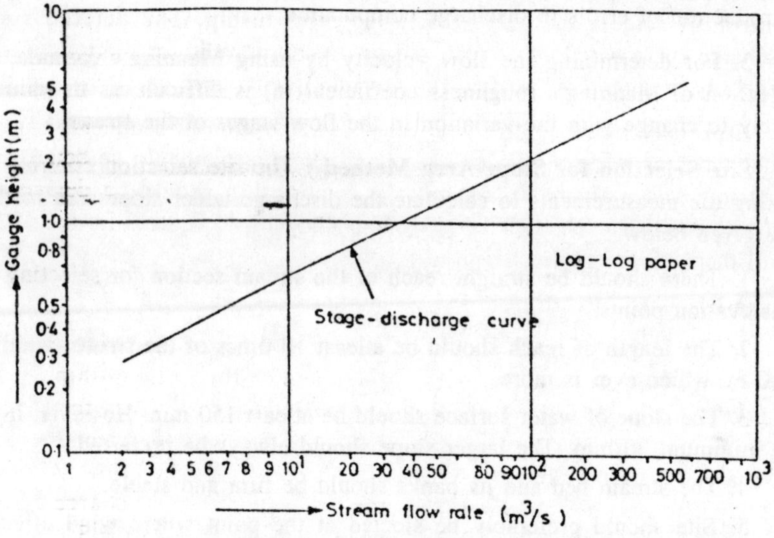

Fig. 7.5. Stage-discharge curve.

Use of stage-discharge curve requires following conditions :

1. The trend of flowing water at the gauging station should not be change much *i.e.* the flow pattern should be constant.

2. Alterations in the site condition should not be there.

3. There should not be the deposition of ice etc over the stream bed.

4. Hydraulic properties of stream cross-section should also be constant.

Terminology

1. Control : It is the stream section, at which the discharge against stage data are recorded for deriving the stage-discharge relationship. The control may be permanent or temporary and natural or artificial.

2. Permanent control : A control, which does not change with time and produces the same effect on the stream flow for all the stages of flow, is called permanent control. The permanent control is always preferred to collect the stage-discharge data for developing the stage-dischrage relationship, as it makes the validity of measurement or derived stage-discharge relationship for longer duration. In general, it is not possible to locate the absolute permanent control, because continuous stream flow and change in atmospheric conditions tend to disintegrate the stream bank materials. However, as far as possible, a control consisting of hard materials (rocks) should be preferred, as these materials keep the site unchange for longer duration.

Shifting Control : The control, which changes gradually or rapidly due to flow pattern or change in physical properties of the site, is called shifting control. It affects the stage-discharge relationship. The derived stage-discharge curve based on data of shifling control, is valid for shorter duration. Generally, it should be verified time to time for its use.

Especially, when control is affected by deposition of sediments or some other types of material, the rate of change in control should be determined, precisely and a fresh stage-discharge relationship should be derived for existing condition. The new $G-Q$ relationship should be used for the period, until there occurs some change at the control.

Stage-Discharge Relationship

It is also known as G-Q relationship, in which G is the stage of stream flow and Q is the discharge. Development of this relationship is very important for determination of discharge, directly for the given for stage, A G-Q relationship of a given river acts a reliable tool for computation of discharge based on flow stage. In other words, if stage of flow is known, then by using G-Q relationship, the corresponding discharge can be determined. The view of G-Q relationship is shown in Figure 7.5.

The stage-discharge curve of the given flow system represents the integral effect of all physical characteristics of gauging station and flow parameters. This integrated effect is known as 'control', which is either in the nature of permanent or temporary. A control is said to be permanent, when G-O relationship remains constant or does not change with time. Especially, in the non-alluvial areas, the rivers exhibit permanent type control, because stream sections/gauging stations are not likely to get eroded due to flow because of hard formations. The form of G-Q relationship for permanent type control is given by

$$Q = C_r (G - a)^{\beta} \qquad ...(7.14)$$

where Q = stream discharge

G = gauge height

a = constant *i.e.* the gauge reading corresponding to zero discharge

C_r and β = constants of rating curve.

The G-Q relationship represented by the equation 7.14 is in non- linear form, which can be linearize by taking the log at both the sides *i.e.*

$$\log Q = \beta \log (G - a) + \log C_r$$

or

$$Y = \beta \log X + b \qquad ...(7.15)$$

This is the straight line relationship with $Y = \log Q$ (discharge) as the dependent variable, $X = \log (G - a)$ as independent variable and β & b are the constant. The value of β and b can be determined by using the regression analysis. The formula is given by

$$\beta = \frac{N\,(\Sigma XY) - (\Sigma X)\,(\Sigma Y)}{N\,(\Sigma X^2) - (\Sigma Y^2)} \qquad ...(7.16)$$

$$b = \frac{\Sigma Y - \beta\,(\Sigma X)}{N} \qquad ...(7.17)$$

And correlation coefficient (r) is

$$r = \frac{N\,(\Sigma XY) - (\Sigma X)\,(\Sigma Y)}{\sqrt{N\,(\Sigma X^2) - (\Sigma X)^2}\;\sqrt{N\,(\Sigma Y^2) - (\Sigma Y)^2}}$$

Normally, the value of r lying between 0.6 and 1, is considered as the good correlation. The value of $r = 1$ refers to the perfect correlation. In this equation, r is positive, because, as the discharge (Q) increases with increase in $(G - a)$, the variables X and Y are positively correlated.

The $G - Q$ relationship *i.e.* equation 7.15 is in straight line form (Figure 7.5).

Example 7.7 : *For the following stage-discharge data of a given watershed, derive the stage-discharge relationship (i.e.* $Q = C_r\,(G - a)^{\beta}$*). Take the value of a as 7.15 m.*

Gauge reading (m)	7.25	7.30	7.50	7.60	7.85	8.15
Discharge (m^3/s)	35	65.0	85.0	95.0	145	165
Gauge reading (m)	8.25	8.40	8.65	8.75	8.85	9.00
Discharge (m^3/s)	235	285	400	470	535	615

Also, compute the discharge rate at 13.75 m gauge reading.

Solution.

The stage-discharge relationship is given by

$$Q = C_r\,(G - a)^{\beta}$$

Taking log on both side, we have

$$\log Q = \log C_r + \beta \log (G - a)$$

or $\quad y = mx + c$

in which, $\quad y = \log Q$

$$m = \beta$$

$$x = \log (G - a)$$

$$C = \log C_r$$

Essential computations for deriving the relationship are shown in following table

Gauge reading (m)	G – a (m)	Q (m^3/s)	x = log (G – a)	X^2	y = log Q	y^2	xy
7.25	0.10	35	–1.000	1.000	1.544	2.384	–1.544
7.30	0.15	65	–0.824	0.679	1.813	3.286	–1.494
7.50	0.35	85	–0.456	0.208	1.929	3.721	–0.879
7.60	0.45	95	–0.347	0.120	1.977	3.908	–0.686
7.85	0.70	145	–0.155	0.024	2.161	4.669	–0.335
8.15	1.00	165	0.000	0.000	2.217	4.915	0.000
8.25	1.10	235	0.041	0.001	2.371	5.621	0.097
8.40	1.25	285	0.097	0.009	2.455	6.027	0.238
8.65	1.50	400	0.176	0.031	2.602	6.770	0.458
8.75	1.60	470	0.204	0.042	2.672	7.139	0.545
8.85	1.70	535	0.230	0.053	2.728	7.442	0.627
9.00	1.85	615	0.267	0.071	2.789	4.778	0.745
			– 1.767	2.238	27.258	63.660	–2.230

Computations

(1)
$$\beta = \frac{N(\Sigma xy) - (\Sigma x)(\Sigma y)}{N(\Sigma x^2) - (\Sigma x)^2}$$

$$= \frac{12 \times (-2.30) - (-1.767)(27.258)}{12(2.238) - (-1.767)^2} = \mathbf{3.192}$$

(2)
$$C = \log C_r$$

$$= \frac{\Sigma y - \beta(\Sigma x)}{N}$$

$$= \frac{27.258 - 3.192(-1.767)}{12} = \mathbf{2.741}$$

$\log C_r = 2.741$

$\therefore \quad C_r = \text{Antilog}(2.741) = \mathbf{550.807}$

Substituting the values of β and C_r in stage-discharge relationship, *i.e.*

$Q = 505.807\,(G - a)^{3.192}$

Discharge at 13.75 gauge reading

$$Q = 550.807\,(13.75 - 7.15)^{3.192}\ \text{m}^3/\text{s}$$

$$= \mathbf{227.5 \times 10^3\ m^3/s\ Ans}$$

Determination of stage for zero discharge (a)

In stage-discharge relationsship *i.e.* $Q = C_r\,(G - a)^{\beta}$, inwhich Q and G are measured under stream gauging. The C_r and β are determined by using the eqn. 7.15 and 7.17, respectively, while the value of '*a*' which is the stage for zero discharge is unknown. It is basically a hypothetical parameter ; can not be measured under stream gauging. However, the following methods can be used for its determination.

Method—1 : It follows following steps :

(*i*) Draw a best fit curve by plotting the Q Vs G data on arithmatic graph paper.

(*ii*) Extrapolate the best fit curve by eye judgment and find the value of "a" corresponding to zero discharge.

(*iii*) Considering the determined value of '*a*' in step (*ii*), plot the curve between log Q and log $(G-a)$. If it is obtained straight line, then determined value of '*a*' in step (*ii*) is correct. Otherwise select another value of '*a*' in the neighbour of previous value and again plot the log Q Vs log $(G-a)$ till the straight line plotting is obtained.

Method—2 : The following step are followed :

(*i*) Plot Q Vs G data on arithmetic graph paper and draw smooth curve through the plotted points (Figure 7.6).

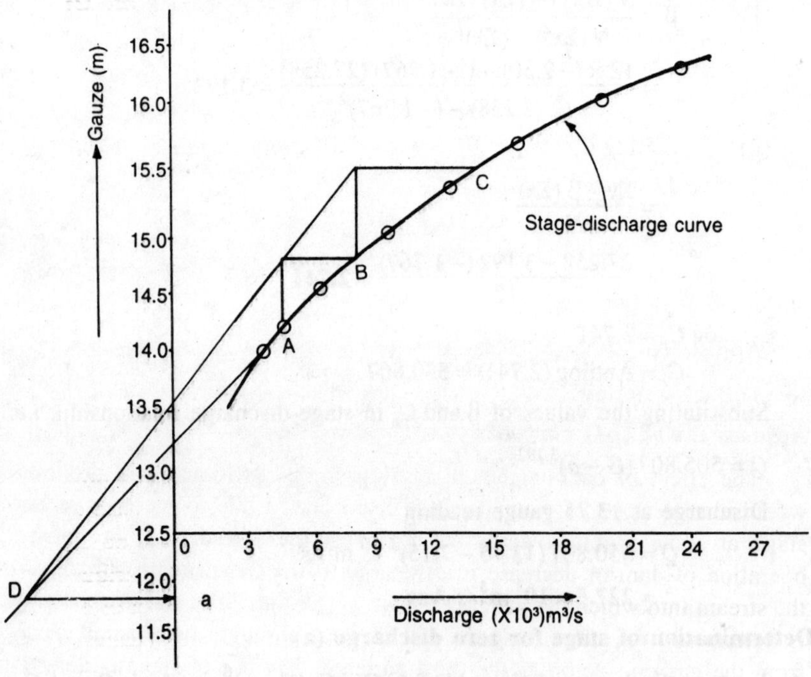

Fig. 7.6. Stage-discharge curve.

(*ii*) Select any three points A, B and C on the curve, in such a way that their discharge values are in geometric progression *i.e.*

$$\frac{Q_A}{Q_B}=\frac{Q_B}{Q_C} \qquad ...(7.18)$$

(*iii*) Draw vertical line from points *A* and *B* and also draw horizontal line from points *B* and *C* to get intersection with the verticals.

(*iv*) Draw straight line by joining E to D and extend forward.

(*v*) Also, draw straight line joining B to A and extend forward.

(*vi*) The two straight lines *i.e.* EF and BF where meet, represents the value of '*a*'.

(This method assumes that the lower segment of $G-Q$ curve is in parabolic shape).

Method—3 : It includes following steps :

(*i*) Plot Q Vs G data on arithmetic graph paper and draw a smooth curve.

(*ii*) Select three discharges *i.e.* Q_1, Q_2 and Q_3 in such a way that they are in geometric progression *i.e.*

$$\frac{Q_1}{Q_2}=\frac{Q_2}{Q_3} \qquad ...(7.19)$$

(*iii*) Read G_1, G_2 and G_3 values corresponding to Q_1, Q_2 and Q_3, respectively form the plotted curve.

(*iv*) Express the G_1, G_2 and G_3 in following form

$$\frac{(G_1-a)}{(G_2-a)}=\frac{(G_2-a)}{(G_3-a)} \qquad ...(7.20)$$

(*v*) Solve for '*a*' *i.e.*

$$a=\frac{G_1G_3-G_2^2}{(G_1+G_3)-2G_2} \qquad ...(7.21)$$

Adjustment of G-Q curve

Adjustment of stage-discharge curve is essential when there is

1. Back water effect. 2. Unsteady flow effect.

Adjustment of G-Q curve for back water effect

The effect of back water on stage-discharge relationship is pronounced, when normal slope of water surface is decreased due to increase in normal stage at some points towards downstream side, which may be caused by operation of dam or decrease in discharge to the downstream tributary or in the stream into which the gauging stream gets empty. The effect of back water is determined by introducing the fall of stage through the channel reach d/s from the gauging point, as the third variable. The fall of stage is determined by installing secondary or auxiliary gauge, which is installed at some distance towards downstream from the gauging point. The stage readings of both gauges are recorded. The difference of gauge reading of main and auxiliary gauges is the 'fall' of water surface within the reach. In the condition of back water effect, the discharge is the function of fall (F) or Q is the function of G and F. Adjustment of G–Q curve for constant fall rate is done in following way :

1. **Constant fall Rating :** Under this, the mean value of fall is taken into consideration. Let it is F_0, is also called normalized value of the fall, which is assumed as constant for all the stages. And F is the actual fall for the discharge Q. For adjusting the rating curve, all observed discharge data are adjusted for the condition of constant fall as given in the following equation :

$$\frac{Q}{Q_0} = \left(\frac{F}{F_0}\right)^p \qquad ...(7.22)$$

where, Q_0 = normalized discharge at the given stage, when fall is F_0

p = exponent, taken as 0.5

The following steps are followed

1. Plot the curve between $\frac{Q}{Q_0}$ and $\frac{F}{F_0}$ and draw the best fit curve. The obtained curve is called adjustment curve.

2. Find the adjusted value of $\frac{Q}{Q_0}$ for each given valus of $\frac{F}{F_0}$.

3. Calculate the adjusted value of Q_o by dividing the measured Q by $\frac{Q}{Q_0}$.

4. Plot Q_o Vs G data and draw the best fit curve.

This curve is called constant fall curve.

Limiting-fall Rating : Normally, stage-discharge relationships are not affected by the existing d/s conditions until a limiting or normal fall is created in the stream flow. If there is reduction in the fall, then back water effect is produced, which causes reduction in the discharge for the same stage. The limiting fall is dependent on the flow stage.

A relationship between the ratio of measured fall (F_m) to limiting fall (F_L) and measured discharge (Q_m) to back- water free discharge (Q_R) is developed (Figure 7.7). Each discharge measurent is adjusted according to this ratio, and a normal stage-discharge relationship is derived. The derived relationship is called limiting fall or normal fall rating.

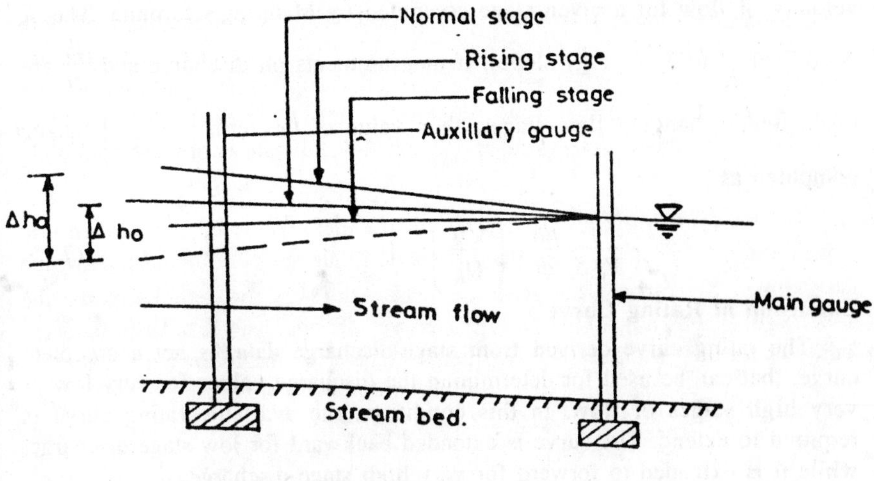

Fig. 7.7. Auxiliary gauge for flow measurement.

Adjustment for Unsteady flow effect

The unsteady flow effect is also called rapidly changing flow effect. If discharge changes rapidly during the measurement, then slope of water surface either becomes less or more than the constant stage, depending on whether the discharge is decreasing or increasing. Under this type of stream flow, the development of normal stage-discharge relationship is done based on the following formula :

$$\frac{Q_R}{Q_M} = \sqrt{\frac{S_e}{S_e + \left(\frac{1}{V_w}\right) \cdot \frac{dh}{dt}}} \qquad ...(7.23)$$

where, Q_R = adjusted discharge (normal discharge at the given stage under steady uniform flow)

Q_M = measured discharge (actual unsteady flow discharge)

S_e = slope of water surface at constant discharge

$\frac{dh}{dt}$ = rate of change of stage

V_w = velocity of flood wave.

This equation is also known as the Jones formula.

After inverting and simplifying the equation 7.23, it becomes

$$\frac{Q_M}{Q_R} = \sqrt{1 + \frac{1}{V_w S_e} \cdot \frac{dh}{dt}} \qquad ...(7.24)$$

In this equation, the term $\frac{1}{V_w \cdot S_e}$ is the function of flow stage. For natural channels (river), the V_w is generally taken as 1.4 V, in which V is the average velocity of flow for a given stage computed by Manning's formula. The S_e is equivalent to S_f. (energy slope). If measurements on discharge and $\frac{dh}{dt}$ are taken under changing flow stages, then value of the term $\left(\frac{1}{V_w S_e}\right)$ can be computed as

$$\frac{1}{V_w S_e} \frac{dh}{dt} = \left(\frac{Q_M}{Q_R}\right)^2 - 1 \qquad ...(7.25)$$

Extension of Rating Curve

The rating curve derived from stage-discharge data, is not a complete curve, that can be used for determining the discharge values for very low or very high stages of flow. In this condition, the available rating curve is required to extend. The curve is extended backward for low stage-discharge, while it is extended to forward for very high stage-discharge.

The common methods for extension of rating curve are given as under :

1. Logarithmic method
2. Steven's method, and
3. $\sqrt{S}/n$ method

All these methods are described below :

Logarithmic Method : This method is applied in that condition, when stream cross-section is uniform at the gauging site and where the segment of circle, parabola, rectangle or trapezoid can also be easily fitted. Considering the stage-discharge relationship *i.e.*

$$Q = C_r (G - a)^{\beta} \qquad ...(7.26)$$

where, Q = discharge rate (cumec)

C_r, β = constant for stream gauging point

G = height of gauge (m)

a = height of gauge at zero discharge (m)

Taking the log of the equation, we have,

$$\log Q = \log C_r + \beta \log (G - a) \qquad ...(7.27)$$

if $\log Q = y$

$$\log C_r = c$$

$$\beta = m$$

and $\log (G - a) = x$

Then equation 7.27 is reduced to

$$y = mc + x \qquad ...(7.28)$$

It is the straight line equation, with m as the slope and $C_r = Q$, when $(G-a) = 1$. In equation (7.27), the value of 'a' (*i.e.* gauge height at zero descharge) is unknown. To determine the value of a, a graph is plotted between $\log Q$ and $\log (G-a)$, keeping the $\log Q$ on ordinate and log $(G-a)$ on absicca, for various assumed values of 'a' except zero, until a straight line is obtained on plotting.The procedure for determining the value of a and extension of the rating curve is explained below :

Procedure : It follow the following steps :

1. Develope stage-discharge curve by plotting the discharge Q V_s gauge height 'G' data, in such a way that, the equal number of points should fall on both sides of the fitted curve.

2. Select few random points on the curve and find out their ordinates *i.e.* Q and G.

3. Assume some arbitary values of a and plot the curve between Q and $(G-a)$ on log-log paper until a straight line is obtained.

4. Determine the value of β and C_r in the following way

   (*i*) β is obtained by determining the slope of curve.

   (*ii*) C_r is determined by equating $(G-a) = 1$

   i.e. $C_r = Q$ when $(G-a) = 1$

5. Calculate the values of discharge for the lowest and higest gauge heights by using equation 7.26.

6. Extend the rating curve by joining the determined discharge values for lowest and highest gauge heights.

Steven's Method

This technique is suitable for wide and shallow streams. It uses the Chezy's formula for computing the discharge at given gauge heights for extending the stage-discharge curve. The chezy's formula is given as under :

$$Q = A \cdot C\sqrt{RS} \qquad \text{...(7.29)}$$

where, Q = discharge rate

A = cross–sectional area

C = roughness coefficient

R = hydraulic mean radius

$= \frac{A}{P}$

P = wetted perimeter

S = slope of the energy line.

The equation (7.27) can also be written as

$$Q = A \cdot C \sqrt{R}\,\sqrt{S}$$

$$Q = C \cdot A \sqrt{D} \cdot \sqrt{S} \qquad \text{...(7.30)}$$

in which D is the depth of stream flow. For shallow and wide streams if $C\sqrt{S}$ is constant, then equation 7.30 is reduced to

$$Q \,\alpha\, A\sqrt{D}$$

Thus,

$$Q = f(A\sqrt{D})$$

Since A and D are the function of gauge height, therefore a curve can be plotted between Q and $A\sqrt{D}$ based on the observations of discharge and stage which is found in the nature of straight line, provided that the value of $C\sqrt{S}$ is constant. By extending this curve in forward direction, the discharge for any value of $A\sqrt{D}$ during high flow stage can be obtained. Figure 7.8 shows the extension of rating curve, using Steven's method.

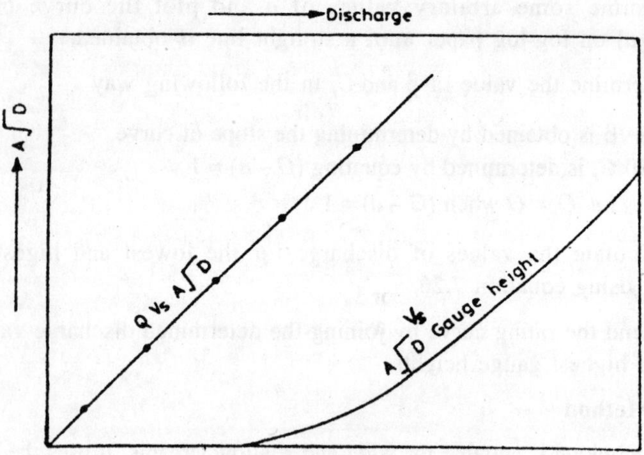

Fig. 7.8. Extension of Rating curve using $A\sqrt{D}$ method.

$S\sqrt{n}$ Method : This method is similar to the Steven's method, but in this method Manning's formula is used in place of Chezy's formula to compute the discharge values at lowest and highest flow stages. The discharge equation is given as :

$$Q = \frac{A\,R^{2/3}\,S^{1/2}}{n} \qquad \text{...(7.31)}$$

where, Q = discharge rate (cumec)

R = hydraulic mean radius (m)

A = cross–sectional area of the stream (m^2)

S = slope

n = Manning's roughness coefficient

In above equation $\frac{\sqrt{S}}{n}$ is about to constant for high flow stages. Accordingly, the equation 7.31 can be rewritten as

$$Q \propto A R^{2/3}$$

or $$Q = KAR^{2/3} \quad ...(7.32)$$

where, $$K = \frac{\sqrt{S}}{n}$$

The procedure for extending the rating curve under this method is described below :

1. Develop a best fit stage-discharge curve by plotting the discharge (Q) and gauge height (G) data, keeping in view that the equal number of points should fall on either sides of the curve.

2. Find out the values of $AR^{2/3}$ for different gauge heights and streamcross-sections.

3. Plot the gauge heights and corresponding $AR^{2/3}$ on simple graph by keeping the gauge height on ordinate and $AR^{2/3}$ on abscissa and draw a best fit curve.

4. Find out the value of $AR^{2/3}$ for the maximum observed discharge, using the derived curve in step (3).

5. Determine the $\sqrt{S}/n$ by substituting the value of $AR^{2/3}$ in equation (7.30) for known value of maximum observed discharge.

In this way, by knowing the value of $AR^{2/3}$ and $\sqrt{S}/n$, for lowest and highest gauge heights, the corresponding discharge flowing through the stream can be predicted and stage-discharge curve is extended beyond the range, accordingly.

Hydraulic Structures for flow Measurement

The hydrualic structures are constructed in the stream/channel's section for ensuring a fixed stage - discharge relationship and also to result more accurate discharge measurement, without aid of velocity data. In hydraulic structure method, the discharge rate is estimated by using formula or tables related to the stage of water flow. Generally, the following structures are commonly used for measuring the stream flow :

1. Weir
2. Flume, etc.

Weir : It is a notch of regular form. Weirs are generally made of wooden plank, metal sheet, concrete etc. There is an opening gate at the top edge of the weir to release the flow. For discharge measurement, the weirs are installed in the stream section, across the flow direction. The use of weir is suitable to the small size streams and canals for measuring the discharge. Different types of weir used for measurement of discharge are given as under :

1. Sharp crested weir, and
2. Broad crested weir

Sharp crested weir : This type of weir consists of a sharp edge on the upstream side of the crest. It is used for measuring the discharge free from silt and debris. Measurement of silt ladden flow is not suitable. The sharp crested weirs are again classified as :

(*i*) **Rectangular weir :** It has level crest and vertical sides as shown in Fig. 7.9 a.The equation used for computing the flow rate is given as :

$$Q = 0.0184\, L\, H^{3/2} \qquad ...(7.31)$$

in which, L is the crest length and H is the flow depth over the crest.

(*ii*) **Trapezoidal weir :** It is also known as Cippoleti weir; has level crest and slopping sides outward from the vertical, in the ratio of one horizontal to four vertical (*i.e.* 1:4). Cippoleti weir is shown in Figure-7.9 b. The following formula is used for calculating the discharge :

$$Q = 0.0186\, L\, H^{3/2} \qquad ...(7.34)$$

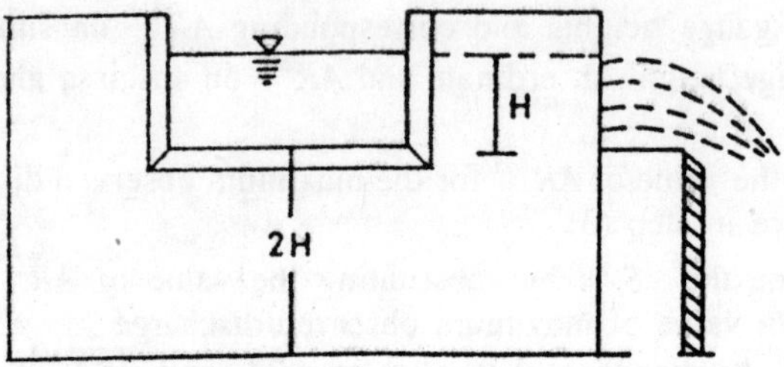

(a) Rectangular weir

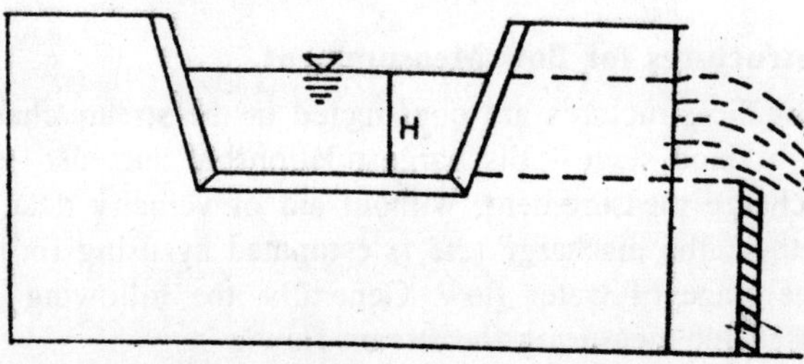

(b) Trapezoidal weir

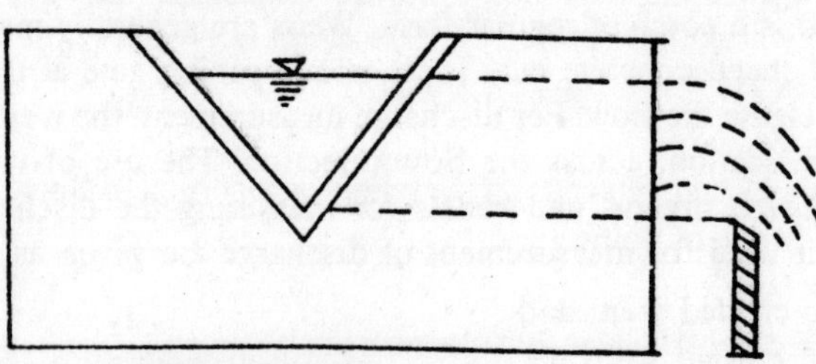

(c) Triangular weir

Fig. 7.9.Different types of weir.

(*iii*) **Triangular weir :** This type of weir is also called V-notch. In this weir the angle between two sides is kept 45°, 90° and 120°. However, among all these angles, the 90° is most common and widely used. The weirs having 90° angle are known as 90°-V-notch. A triangular weir is shown in Fig-7.9*c*. For this weir, the following formula is used for computing the discharge :

$$Q = 0.0138\, H^{2.48} \qquad ...(7.35)$$

Essential Requirements for Weir

The following points as rule are generally considered for installation of weirs

1. The stream reach should be straight and uniform.
2. The weirs should have sharp crest and sharp sides.
3. The effect of back water flow should be negligible.
4. The depth of flow over the weir should be measured at the distance of atleast 4 times the depth of flow from the weir towards upstream side.
5. Weir crest should be fixed at the height of 2 times the depth of flow from the channel bed.
6. The distance between notch end and the stream bank should not be less than 2 times the depth of flow over the weir.
7. The falling water from weir should have free flow.

Flume : It is constructed in the channel shape. The flow measurement by flume is based on the concept of specific energy and critical flow in the open channel. The specific energy at any section is the sum of all energies with reference to the stream bed. The energy equation is given as :

$$E = h + \frac{V^2}{2g} \qquad ...(7.36)$$

in which, E is the specific energy, h is the depth of flow, V is the flow velocity and g is the acceleration due to gravity.

The following types of flume are commonly used for measuring the discharge flowing through open channel :

1. Meter flume, and
2. Venturi flume

Meter flume : By this flume, the discharge is determined by measuring the depth of flow over the crest and using the relationship between discharge and specific energy at critical depth. The relationship is given by

$$Q = 1.7\, C.b.H^{3/2} \qquad ...(7.37)$$

where, Q = discharge

C = constant, depends on the relative proportion of flume dimension.

b = width of flume

$H = D_1 + ha$

D_1 = depth of water flow over the crest

ha = head due to velocity approach

Venturiflume : It is a kind of meter flume, consists of contracted throat which causes drop in the hydrualic gradient line. Discharge is determined by measuring the difference of water heads at entrance and throat points of the flume. The discharge formula is given as under :

$$Q = \frac{C\, a_1, a_2 \sqrt{2g\,(h_1 - h_2)}}{\sqrt{a_1, a_2}} \quad \text{...(7.35)}$$

where, Q = discharge

C = constant; its value depends on the relative proprtion of the dimension of flume.

a_1, a_2 = cross–sectional area at entrance and throat points of the flume, respectively.

h_1, h_2 = depth of flow at entrance and throat points of the flume, repectively.

Other methods : It includes following methods :

1. Salt concentration method
2. Salt-velocity method
3. Radio-tracer method
4. Ultrasonic signal method
5. Electro magnetic induction method etc.

Salt concentration method : This method is also known as dilution method, tracer method or chemical method. In this method, discharge is determined by injecting the chemical (normally common salts) in the stream flow at a known rate and determining the amount of chemical present in the flow at down stream point, which is located at sufficient distance from injecting point. The distance between injecting and measuring points should be sufficient, so that a thorough mixing of chemical in the flow can take place.

Let, if

1. Quantity of chemical injected into the flow is 'q' cc/s
2. Concentration of salt in dosing solution is C gm/cc
3. Concentration of salt already present in the flow is C_1 gm/cc
4. Concentration of salt in sampled water is C_2 gm/c.c

Then discharge passing through the stream is given by the following relationship :

$$Q = \frac{C - C_2}{C_2 - C} \cdot q \quad \text{...(7.39)}$$

This method is based on the assumption that the stream flow is in steady state. If flow is not in steady state condition, then error is expected to occur in measurements. The salt-concentration method is found suitable, when water flow is in turbulent nature because turbulence makes thorough mixing of chemicals in the flowing water, very easily. However, it is a costly method for measuring the discharge.

Types of Tracer : The following types of tracers are commonly used :

1. **Chemical :** It includes common salts and Sodium Dichromate. The common salts can be detected upto the concentration of 10 ppm and Sodium Dichromate upto 0.2 ppm concentration.

2. **Fluorescent dyes :** Rhodamine - W_T and Sulpho-Rhodamine-B extra are the typical Fluorescent, used as tracer for flow measurement. These tracers have advantage that, they can be detected upto the concentration of 10 nanogram per liter. Due to this reason, these are required in very small amount for injecting into the stream flow. However, these are more costly than the common salts.

3. **Radio-active tracer :** The commonly used radio-active tracers for measurement of discharge are the Bromine-82, Sodium-24 and Iodine-132. Radio-active tracers are more sensitive than the other tracers and can be detected upto the concentration of 10^{-14} gm/liter. This types of tracers are more expensive and require sophisticated instruments as well as trained staff for determining the stream flow.

Properties of Tracers : The tracers to be used for measurement of stream flow should have following properties :

1. The tracers should not be absorbed by the vegetations existing in the stream flow.

2. It should also not be absorbed by the sediments in the flow and boundaries of the channel.

3. The tracers should not be reacted with the sediments, vegetations and channel boundaries.

4. It should not be lost due to evaporation.

5. It should not contain toxic properties.

6. The tracers should also not be costly.

Advantages of Salt Concentration Method : It includes following advantages :

1. Discharge can be easily determined by knowing the concentration of salts in the stream flow.

2. It is suitable for turbulent streams, *i.e.* streams existing in the hilly areas.

3. This method can also be used for checking the consistency of stage-discharge relationship of the river flow.

Salt-velocity method : This method of discharge measurement is suitable for small streams having uniform cross-section. It is based on the principle that, the salt increases the electrical conductivity of the water. In this method, two stream cross-sections are selected at sufficient distance apart and insulated electrodes are installed, there. Electrodes are connected to the galvanometer

The system is energised by the electric current. The following observations are recorded during measurement :

1. Distance between two electrodes (L)
2. Travel time, second (T)
3. Cross - sectional areas of stream (A)

Based on above observations, the discharge can be computed by using the following formula :

$$Q = \frac{AL}{T} \quad ...(7.40)$$

Radio-tracer method : It is fast and accurate method for gauging the stream flow, which is performed by sophisticated instruments and trained staff. In this method, a known amount of radio-tracer is injected into the flow and mixed thoroughly. A Geiger counter is fixed at some distance apart towards downstream side in the stream flow for recording the total number of clicks made by the tracer during movement Concentration of tracer varies inversely with the discharge rate. The relationship between number of clicks recorded by the Geiger and stream discharge is given by the following formula :

$$N = \frac{A \cdot F}{Q} \quad ...(7.41)$$

or

$$Q = \frac{A \cdot F}{N} \quad ...(7.42)$$

where, Q = discharge flowing through the stream
A = amount of radio–tracer, used
F = constant, depends on the characteristics of radio–isotopes.
N = number of clicks recorded by the Geiger.

Ultrasonic Signals method : This method was introduced by Swingel in the year 1955. Since then it is being used for measuring the stream discharge. This method follows the concept of area - velocity method, in which flow velocity (mean) is measured by using the ultrasonic devices. For accurate measurement the following points are essentially required :

1. The stream cross - section should be throughout uniform.
2. Velocity of water should be constant and regular.

In this method, for mesurement of flow velocity, two transducers are installed at same level from the stream bed on either sides of the stream, as shown in Figure 7.10. These transducers emitt the ultrasonic signals to each other. The elapsed time between emitting and receiving of the signal by both trasducers, are recorded as observation for determining the flow velocity. Let, two ultrasonic transducers A and B are installed on either sides of the channel. The transducer-A emitts the signal, which is received by the transducer-B after time t_1 and transducer B emitts the signal to the transducer A, which is received by A after elapsed time t_2. If velocity of sound in water is C, then

$$t_1 = \frac{L}{(C + V_p)} \qquad \text{...(7.43)}$$

and
$$t_2 = \frac{L}{(C - V_p)} \qquad \text{...(7.44)}$$

in which, L is the length of travel path *i.e.* distance between both transducers and V_p is the velocity component along sounding path.

From the equations 7.43 and 7.44, we have

$$\frac{1}{t_1} - \frac{1}{t_2} = \frac{C + V_p}{L} - \frac{C - V_p}{L}$$

or
$$= \frac{2\,V_p}{L}$$

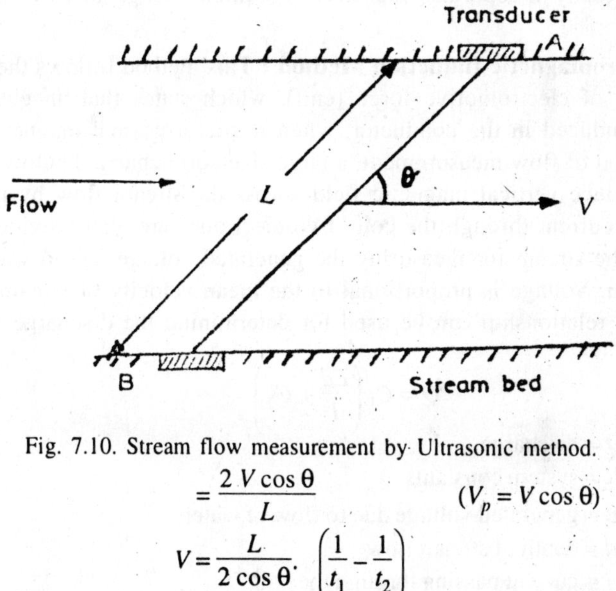

Fig. 7.10. Stream flow measurement by Ultrasonic method.

$$= \frac{2\,V \cos\theta}{L} \qquad (V_p = V\cos\theta)$$

$$V = \frac{L}{2\cos\theta} \cdot \left(\frac{1}{t_1} - \frac{1}{t_2}\right) \qquad \text{...(7.45)}$$

By using the equation 7.42 for a known value of θ, L and time t_1 & t_2, the stream flow velocity (V) can be computed. The obtained velocity is not the average flow velocity (V_a) of the stream flow. For determination of average velocity of flow, a calibration curve between $\frac{V}{V_a}$ and depth of flow (h) is derived for the given stream cross-section,

After knowing the mean flow velocity, the stream discharge can be computed by multiplying it to the cross-sectional area of the flow *i.e.*

$$Q = A \cdot V_a \qquad \text{...(7.46)}$$

in which, Q is the discharge, A and V_a are the cross - sectional area of the stream flow and mean velocity, respectively.

The following points affect the accuracy of this method :

1. Unstability of the stream cross-section.
2. Weed growth in the stream flow.
3. Entrainment of air.
4. Change in temperature and salinity level of the flowing water.
5. Presence of silt load in the flowing water.

Advantage : This method provides following advantages :

1. It is very quick and accurate method.
2. For automatic recording of flow velocity, it is more suitable.
3. Installation cost is independent of stream size.
4. It easily incoporates the effect of quick change in flow rate and its direction.

Electromagnetic Induction Method : This method follows the Faraday's principles of electromotive force (emf), which states that an electromotive force is induced in the conductor, when it cuts a normal magnetic field. In this method of flow measurement, a large size coil is burried below the stream bed to induce vertical magnetic field across the stream flow by passing the electrical current through the coil. Two electrodes are also provided at either sides of the stream for measuring the generated voltage due to water flow in the stream. Voltage is proportional to the mean velocity of stream flow. The following relationship can be used for determining the discharge rate :

$$Q = C_1\left(\frac{Ed}{I} + C_2\right)^n \qquad ...(7.47)$$

where, Q = discharge
n, C_1, C_2 = system constants
E = generated voltage due to flow of water
d = depth of stream flow
I = current passing through the coil

Use of this method is suitable for the stream widths ranging up to 70 m only and also for those streams, in which considerable changes take place in the characteristics of stream due to weed growth, sedimentation, debis, skew flow as well as variations in the flow stages.

Hydrometry Station

Hydrometry stations are meant for measurement of discharge flowing through the river system. On networking of hydrometry stations, the W.M.O. has given following recommendations :

1. For flat regions of temperate, mediterrean and tropical zones :
   (*a*) Minimum density — 1000 to 2500 Km^2/station.

(*b*) Tolerable density under difficult condition — 3000 to 10,000 Km^2/station

2. For mountaneous regions of temperate, mediterrean and tropical zones :

   (*a*) Minimum density — 300 to 1000 Km^2/station

   (*b*) Tolerable density under difficult condition — 1000 to 5,000 Km^2/station

3. For arid and polar zones

   (*a*) Minimum density — 5000 to 20,000 km^2/station.

To assess accurate water potential of the area, it is essential to install the hydrometry stations in adequate numbers in the catchment area of all major streams.In India upto 1984 about 542 hydrometry stations had been reported, which are under control of Central Water Commission. As per WMO recommendations, it should be 1700. Amongst 542 stations, 242 are for the measurement of flow stage and discharge. And rest 318 stations for the measurement of sediment load and water quality in addition to flow stage and discharge. State governments have also installed about 800 hydrometry stations for measurement of discharge. In addition, a large number of gauging stations have also been installed by NGOs for taking the measurements on water flow stage.

Stream Flow Characteristics

Stream flow characteristics are the function of following parameters :

1. **Rainfall characteristics** — Under it, the magnitude, intensity and distribution of rainfall within storm duration and space are the main parameters affecting the stream flow characteristics.

2. **Catchment characteristics** — The soil, vegetation, slope, geology, shape & size and drainage density are considered as the catchment characteristics to affect the stream flow.

3. **Climatic factors** — These are those which affect the ET of the area.

Apart from above, the followings are also counted as the factors affecting stream flow characteristics.

(*a*) The effect of seasonal rainfall on runoff is very significant. For example, during rainy season each and every stream carries runoff flow, while in off-seasons *i.e.* summer and winter it is not so. Also, during rainy season a high discharge occurs through stream, while during rest seasons only base flow (perennial streams) is there.

(*b*) Shape and size of hydrograph are controlled by the storm characteristics combined with watershed features.

(*c*) The rainfall and ET control the annual runoff of the stream.

IMPORTANT POINTS

1. Stream flow represents the runoff phase of hydrologic cycle.
2. Stream flow is the only part of hydrologic cycle, which can be measured accurately.
3. A channel which carries the runoff from watershed is called stream.
4. Rainfall depth, stream flow etc. are the historic data.
5. The stream flow is expressed in the unit of m^3/s.
6. The stage of river flow is expressed as the water-surface elevation, which is measured with refrence to a datum.
7. The staff gauge and wire gauge are used for measurement of flow stage.
8. The measurement of flow stage by wire gauge is upto 25 m.
9. The float-gauge recorder and bubble gauge are the automatic type stage recorder.
10. The bubble gauge can be used to measure the flow stage as much as 30 m.
11. Flow stage data can be presented in the form of stage hydrograph.
12. Current meter measures the velocity of stream flow.
13. The normal range of measurement of flow velocity by using vertical- axis current meter is from 0.15 to 4.0 m/s.
14. The range of velocity measurement by using horizontal-axis current meter is from 0.15 to 4.0 m/s.
15. The accuracy of measurement of flow velocity by vertical-axis current meter is about 1.5% at threshold value.
16. The accuracy of measurement of flow velocity by horizontal-axis current meter is about 1% at threshold value and 0.25% at or above 0.3 m/s.
17. The rating formula of current meter is in the form of $V = aN + b$, in which V is the flow velocity (m/s), N is the number of revolutions per second and a & b are constant.
18. The value of constants a & b of rating curve ($V = aN + b$) for standard size (12.5 cm cup diameter) current meter (cup type) is 0.65 and 0.03, respectively.
19. The value of constants a & b of rating curve ($V = aN + b$) for pigmy current meter (5 cm cup diameter) is o.30 and 0.003, respectively.
20. The nature of distribution of flow velocity in the stream, across vertical section is logarithmic.
21. In turbulent flow, the velocity distribution is presented by the relationship $V = 5.75\ V_* \log_{10}\left(\frac{30y}{K_s}\right)$, in which V is the velocity of flow at depth 'y' above the stream bed, V_* is the shear velocity and K_s is the equivalent sand- grain roughness.
22. In shallow streams upto 3m depth, the average velocity of flow is determined at the depth of 0.6d from top water surface. (d is the flow depth).
23. In moderately deep streams, the average velocity of flow is determined by measuring the velocities at 0.2d and 0.8d and taking their mean value.

24. In the ivers carrying flood flow, the flow velocity is measured within 0.5 m depth from the top water surface ; and average velocity is determined by multiplying a factor (0.85 to 0.95) to it.

25. The sounding weights are used to keep the current meter in proper position.

26. The minimum sounding_weight required for current meter, can be calculated by the formula $W = 50\,\bar{V} \cdot d$, in which W is the minimum sounding weight, $\bar{V}$ is the mean velocity of flow (m/s) and d is flow depth (m) at the vertical.

27. Width of stream segment for measurement of stream flow velocity/depth should be from 1/15 to 1/20 of the river/stream width.

28. The size of segment of flow width should be such that the discharge in each segment is less than 10% of the total discharge. And difference of velocities in adjacent segments should is not more than 20% of the mean value.

29. The tracers used under dilution technique of stream flow measurement are common salts and sodium dichromate fluorescent dye-Rhodamine-WT and Sulpho-Rhodamine B Extra ; radioactive materials-Bromine-82, Sodium-24 and Iodine- 132.

30. Under stream flow measurement by using dilution technique, the common salts can be detected upto the concentration of 10 ppm with an error of ± 1%, while Sodium dichromate can be detected upto 0.2 ppm concentration.

31. Dilution technique of stream flow measurement is also known as sudden injection method or integration method.

32. Dilution method is based on the assumption that the stream flow is steady. For unsteady flow condition, this method is not suitable.

33. Under dilution method, the distance between dosing and sampling points in mountaneous streams carrying the discharge of 1.0 m^3/s should be about 1 km while for the rivers carrying the discharge 300 m^3/s, it should be about 100 km.

34. Dilution method is more suitable for small turbulent streams, found in mountaneous areas. This method can also be used for checking the stage-discharge relationship.

35. Electromagnetic method of stream flow measurement is based on the principle of Faraday's law.

36. The minimum detectable velocity of stream flow under electromagnetic method is 0.005 m/s.

37. A commercially available electromagnetic flow meter can measure the discharge with the accuracy of ± 3%.

38. Maximum stream width that can be accommodated under electromagnetic method of stream flow measurement is 100 m.

39. Electromagnetic method is found suitable for measurement of that flow which undergoes rapid change in amount and direction, both.

40. The frequency of ultrasonic flowmeter for stream flow measurement is 500 kHZ.

41. Ultrasonic method can measure the flow upto 500 m stream flow width.

42. The indirect stream flow measurement is done by weir & flumes and slope-area method.

43. In flow measuring structures, such as notches, flumes, weirs and sluice gates, the discharge (Q) is the function of water surface elevation (H). For weirs, the form of relationship between Q and$H$ is $Q = KH^n$, in which K and n are the constant. The value of exponent n is taken as 1.5.

44. Stage-discharge relationship is in non-linear nature.

45. Stage-discharge relationship is also known as discharge rating curve.

46. A control is said to be permanent, when stage-discharge relationship remains constant *i.e.* does not change with time.

47. A control is said to be shifting if stage-discharge relationship changes with time.

48. Shifting nature of control is mainly due to (1) weed growth (2) agradation or degradation of channels (3) backwater effect (4) unsteady flow effect.

49. As per W.M.O. recommendation, the minimum and tolerable densities of hydrometry stations in flat regions of temperate, mediterrean and sub-tropical zones are 1000 to 2500 and 3000 to 10,000 km^2/station, respectively.

50. As per W.M.O. recommendation, the minimum and maximum densities of hydrometry stations in mountaneous regions of temperate, mediterrean and tropical regions are 300 to 1000 and 1000 to 5000 km^2/station, respectively.

51. As per W.M.O. recommendation, the minimum density of hydrometry station in polar and arid regions is form 5000 to 20000 km^2/satation

52. As per W.M.O. recommendation, there should be about 1700 hydrometry stations in India.

53. In India more than 542 hydrometry stations are maintained by C.W.C. Also, there are about 800 discharge measuring stations, controlled by the state governments.

REFERENCES

1. Central Water Commission, Water Resource of India, CWC Pub. No. 30/88, CWC, New Delhi, 1988.
2. Chow V.T. Handbook of Applied Hydrology, McGraw-Hill, New York, 1964.
3. Das G. Hydrology and Soil Conservation Engineering, Prentice-Hall (India), 2000.
4. Hershey R.W. Hydrometry, Wiley Interscience, Jhon Wiley, Chichester U.K., 1978.
5. Linsley, R.K., Kohler, M.A, and Paulhus J.L, Hydrology for Engineers, McGraw Hill, New York, 1958.
6. Mutreja K.N., Applied Hydrology, Tata McGraw-Hill, New Delhi 1987.
7. Subramanya K. Engineering Hydrology, Tata-McGraw-Hill, New Delhi, 2000.
8. Wisler C.O. and Brater E.F., Hydrology, Jhon Wiley, New York, 1959.

DESCRIPTIVE TYPE QUESTIONS

1. (*a*) Define stream gauging and write its importance.

(b) Describe different points to be considered for selecting the gauging site.

2. Define segmentation and write various points to be considered for it.
3. List different gauging methods and explain any one suitable method amongst them.
4. Explain area-velocity method for determining the stream discharge .
5. List different velocity measurement methods and explain any one of them.
6. Describe current meter for measuring the flow velocity.
7. (a) What is surface float and where it is used.
   (b) Describe precautions and limitations of surface float method for determining the flow velocity.
8. (a) Explain two-point method of flow velocity determination.
   (b) Determine the mean flow velocity of stream water by using two-point method, based on the following data

Depth at	*Revolutions*	*Time (s)*
0.2d	45	55
0.8d	35	60

(Assume $a = 0.3$ and $b = 0.05$.)

9. Describe the slope-area method for determining the stream flow rate.
10. Write limitations of area-velocity method and also list various points to be considered for selecting the site for this method.
11. Explain stage-discharge relationship and write the procedures to determine the value of *a*.
12. (a) Define shifting and permanent controls.
    (b) Explain various effects of shifting control on discharge rating curve.
13. Describe different methods for extending the discharge rating curve.
14. List different structures for measuring the stream flow and describe the weir.
15. List different types of tracers used for stream flow measurement and explain the salt concentration method.
16. Explain ultrasonic method for determining the stream flow and also list its various advantages.
17. Describe electromagnetic induction method of stream gauging.

OBJECTIVE TYPE QUESTIONS

1. Stream gauging determines the
   (a) stream flow (b) flood occurrence
   (c) sediment flow (d) all above
2. Most suitable gauging site is
   (a) erodible point of stream (b) non-erodible point of stream
   (c) vegetative point of stream (d) none of the above
3. Recording type gauge records the stream flow data inform of
   (a) graph (b) digit
   (c) mass curve (d) none of the above

4. Inclined staff gauge is a type of
   (*a*) non-recording type gauge (*b*) recording type gauge
   (*c*) automatic recorder (*d*) none of the above
5. The size of segment for the stream width of 90 to 180 m is recommended as
   (*a*) 1.5 m (*b*) 6.0 m
   (*c*) 15.0 m (*d*) 1.30 m
6. Suspension rods are used, when
   (*a*) velocity of stream flow is upto 1 m/s
   (*b*) flow depth ranges upto 1 m
   (*c*) both '*a*' and '*b*'
   (*d*) sufficient vegetations are in flow
7. The length of suspension rod is about
   (*a*) 3 m (*b*) 5 m
   (*c*) 15 m (*d*) 7 m
8. Sounding rod measures the stream flow depth upto
   (*a*) 6 m (*b*) 3 m
   (*c*) 10 m (*d*) 7 m
9. Floats are used for measuring the stream
   (*a*) flow velocity (*b*) flow depth
   (*c*) sediment deposition (*d*) none of the above
10. Current meters are used for measurement of
    (*a*) stream flow depth (*b*) stream flow velocity
    (*c*) sediment flow (*d*) discharge
11. The diameter of surface float for measuring the stream flow velocity, varies from
    (*a*) 5 to 10 cm (*b*) 7 to 15 cm
    (*c*) 5 to 20 cm (*d*) 1 to 1.5 m
12. Sub-surface float measures the
    (*a*) average flow velocity (*b*) stream flow depth
    (*c*) '*a*' and '*b*' both (*d*) discharge
13. The velocity rod does not measure accurately, when
    (*a*) flow depth exceeds 4.5 m
    (*b*) flow velocity exceeds 1 m/s
    (*c*) flow width is greater than 15 m
    (*d*) flow contains silts
14. Current meter records the measurements in terms of
    (*a*) revolutions for a given time
    (*b*) revolution, only
    (*c*) both '*a*' and '*b*'
    (*d*) histogram
15. The cup type current meter is also known as
    (*a*) pigmy current meter
    (*b*) optical type current meter
    (*c*) rotating cup current meter
    (*d*) Curley type current meter

16. Rating of current meter represents the
(*a*) relationship between revolution and the flow velocity
(*b*) relationship between flow velocity and time
(*c*) flow depth and velocity
(*d*) none of the above

17. Rating curve of current meter is the plot of
(*a*) flow velocity and revolution of current meter
(*b*) stream flow rate and time
(*c*) stream flow rate and revolution of meter
(*d*) none of the above

18. Slope of rating curve of current meter represents the value of
(*a*) constant '*a*'
(*b*) constant '*b*'
(*c*) mean velocity of flow
(*d*) none of the above

19. In two point method, the measurements of flow velocity are taken at
(*a*) $0.2d$ and $0.6d$ from top of water surface
(*b*) $0.2d$ and $0.8d$ from top of water surface
(*c*) $0.3d$ and $0.7d$ from top of water surface (d is the flow depth)
(*d*) at the top and bottom of the flow

20. In two-tenth method, the measurement of flow velocity is taken at the depth of
(*a*) $0.2d$ (*b*) $0.8d$
(*c*) $0.6d$ (*d*) $0.7d$

21. Pitot tube is used for measurement of flow velocity in
(*a*) stream/river (*b*) laboratory channel
(*c*) both '*a*' and '*b*' (*d*) tube flow

22. Manning's and Chezy's formula are used for determining the
(*a*) flow velocity (*b*) flow rate
(*c*) sediment load (*d*) flow depth

23. The stage-discharge curve represents the relationship between
(*a*) gauge height and stream flow rate
(*b*) gauge height and flow velocity
(*c*) both '*a*' and '*b*'
(*d*) flow depth and velocity

24. A permanent control is that, which
(*a*) does not change with time
(*b*) produces almost the same effect on stream flow
(*c*) both '*a*' and '*b*'
(*d*) consists no vegetation

25. For long term use of stage-discharge curve, the control should be
(*a*) permanent (*b*) shifting
(*c*) both '*a*' and '*b*' (*d*) equpped with weir

26. A control which is likely to change with time is called
(*a*) permanent control (*b*) shifting control
(*c*) gauging site (*d*) none of the above.

27. $\sqrt{S}/n$ method is used for
(*a*) extension of rating curve (*b*) computing stream flow
(*c*) both '*a*' and '*b*' (*d*) determining flow depth

28. The salt-concentration method is suitable for flow measurement in
(*a*) turbulent streams (*b*) laboratory channel
(*c*) both '*a*' and '*b*' (*d*) pipe flow

29. The ultrasonic signal method is used for measurement of
(*a*) flow velocity (*b*) flow rate
(*c*) sediment rate (*d*) none of the above

30. Stage-discharge relationship is in the form of
(*a*) non-linear equation (*b*) exponential equation
(*c*) logarithmic equation (*d*) quadretic equation

Answer (Objective Type Question)

1. (*a*)	**2.** (*b*)	**3.** (*a*)	**4.** (*a*)	**5.** (*a*)	**6.** (*c*)	**7.** (*a*)	**8.** (*a*)
9. (*a*)	**10.** (*b*)	**11.** (*b*)	**12.** (*a*)	**13.** (*a*)	**14.** (*a*)	**15.** (*c*)	**16.** (*a*)
17. (*a*)	**18.** (*a*)	**19.** (*b*)	**20.** (*a*)	**21.** (*b*)	**22.** (*a*)	**23.** (*a*)	**24.** (*c*)
25. (*a*)	**26.** (*b*)	**27.** (*a*)	**28.** (*a*)	**29.** (*b*)	**30.** (*a*)		

8

Flood

It is an unusual large flow of runoff resulted from rainfall or due to melting of snow, which causes very high flow stage in the river at which the excess runoff tends to over top the river bank and spread in the adjoining areas.

Flood and some specific flows through the river are not the same but are quite different. A flow at some reaches in the stream may not be flood, if it does not overtop the stream bank.

8.1. Flood Classification

Floods are classified as

1. Design flood.
2. Standard project flood.
3. Maximum probable flood.
4. Peak flood.
5. Maximum observed flood.
6. Maximum known flood.
7. Annual flood
8. Ordinary flood
9. Foundation design flood.

All these types of floods are described as under :

1. Design flood : It is also known as maximum flood, is considered for design of hydraulic structures, such as drop structures, bridge openings, flood banks etc. The design floods may be Standard Project Flood (SPF), Maximum Probable Flood (MPF) or flood of any desired recurrence interval, depending on the degree of flood protection measures employed against possibilities of failure of structures. Selection of design flood is generally done on the basis of cost-benefit ratio. The detail of design flood is described in coming section.

2. Standard Project Flood : It is also known as SPF which is defined as the flood that is likely to occur from the most severe combinations of hydrological and meteorological characteristics of the watershed, but not due to the extremely rare combinations. This flood is approximately 80% of the MPF.

3. Maximum Probable Flood (MPF). This flood is extremely rare and catastrophic. In other words, this flood is resulted from the severe most combinations of critical hydrological as well as metereological characteristics of the watershed. The design of spillway used in very high dams is done on the basis of maximum probable flood.

4. Peak Flood : It is also known as maximum intensity flood or momentary flood, is defined as the maximum instantaneous flow during flood.

5. Maximum Observed Flood : Highest flood during a specified length of record is known as maximum observed flood. The length of record may be from a week to the year or so.

6. Maximum Flood : It is the largest flood which has been occurred in the past. This type of flood is get to know by the memory of inhabitants of the locality.

7. Annual Flood : It is the highest flood that occurrs in a water year or hydrologic year. The water year is the duration of 12 months, is considered for presenting the flow data. The annual flood is either equal to or greater than the magnitude of specified flood, generally once in year.

8. Ordinary Flood : It is the flood, which occurs once or more times during project period.

8.2. Guidelines for Slection of Design Flood

This flood is considered for design of hydraulic structures. The small hydraulic structures, such as culverts and storm drainage lines are designed relatively for less severe floods, because consequences due to such floods are not very serious. On other hand, for water storage structures, such as dam, the floods producing large amount of runoff are considered for design purpose. The failure of such structures causes severe consequences in the area. Regarding safety point of view and for other requirements, the selection of floods for design and construction of hydraulic structures is very important. The guidelines for selecting the design floods for different purposes are given as under (CWC India 1973) :

1. For spillways of major and medium projects with the capacity more than 60 Mm^3 :
   (*i*) Probable maximum flood (PMF) and probable maximum precipitation (PMP) can be used as the design flood.
   (*ii*) If above design flood is not possible, then flood for the return period of 100 years should be used as the design flood.
2. For permanent barrage and minor dams with the capacity less than 60 Mm^3 :
   (*i*) SPF computed by unit hydrograph and SPS (Standard Project Storm) which is from the largest storm of the area.
   (*ii*) Flood of 100 years return period.
   (Between above two, the highest valued flood is considered as the design flood)
3. For Pickup weirs
   (*ii*) Flood with the return period of 100 or 50 years depending on the importance of project, is used as the design flood.

4. For aqueducts
   (*a*) Waterways : flood with *T* as 50 years return period.
   (*b*) Foundations and freeboard : flood of 100 years return period.
5. For project with very scanty or inadequate data : For this purpose, the design flood can be evaluated based on available empirical formula for the region.

The generalized design criterion for various water control structures have also been given by National Academy of Science, USA (1983) which are summarised in Table 8.1.

Table 8.1 : Generalized design criteria for different water control structures

S.N.	Structure	*Return period*
1.	Highway	
	(*a*) Low traffic	5 to 10
	(*b*) Intermediate traffic	10 to 25
	(*c*) High traffic	50 to 100
2.	Highway bridge	
	(*a*) Secondary system	10 to 50
	(*b*) Primary system	50 to 100
3.	Farm drainage	
	(*a*) Culverts	5 to 50
	(*b*) Ditches	5 to 50
4.	Urban drainage	
	(*a*) Storm sewers (small cities)	2 to 25
	(*b*) Storm sewers (large cities)	25 to 50
5.	Levees	
	(*a*) On farms	2 to 50
	(*b*) Around cities	50 to 200
6.	Dams (low hazard)	
	(*a*) Small	5o to 100
	(*b*) Intermediate	100+
	(*c*) Large	—
7.	Dams (significant hazard)	
	(*a*) Small	100 +
	(*b*) Intermediate	—
	(*c*) Large	—

8.3. Inflow Design Flood for Dam

The Indian Standard: IS 11223–1985 has developed guidelines fo selection of design floods for construction of dam. Under guidelines, the dam are classified according to the hydraulic head. The recommended inflov design floods for them are given in Table 8.2.

Table 8.2. Classification of dam based on hydraulic head.

Class	*Gross storage* (*Mm*^{3})	*Hydraulic head* (*m*)*	*Safe inflow design flood*
Small	0.5 to 10.0	7.5 to 20	100-year flood
Intermediate	10 to 60	12 to 30	Standard Project Flood (SPF)
Large	more than 60	more than 30	Probable Maximum Flood (PMF)

* Hydraulic head is the elevation difference between maximum water lev on u/s and the normal annual flood level on d/s.

8.4. Causes of Flood

Surface runoff is the source of flood. When volume of incoming runo becomes greater than the outflowing volume from the river or stream, the excess runoff tends to accumulate in the river course and increases the wat level. If rising of water level is continued for longer time period, then exce water starts spreading in the adjoining areas and thus resulting into occurren of flood. Floods are affected by the characteristics of precipitation ar watershed, in which precipitation characteristics are main. The type, form intensity of rainfall etc. are the main characteristics of precipitation. Th watershed characteristics, such as the soil type, texture & structure, shape size of watershed etc, affect the occurrence of flood. Amongst all above, th following three are the main cause of flood occurence,:

1. High intensity rainfall over small hilly catchment.
2. Intense rainfall over large catchment for longer duration
3. Rainfall over accumulated snow.

These causes are described as under :

1. **Occurrence of high intensity rainfall over small hilly catchment**

A high intensity rainfall is also known as intense storm, which occu for a small areal extent with greater intensity. Due to this reason greater runo volume is generated from the area, which reaches to the stream or river ve soon. If generated runoff volume is greater than the river capacity then exce water starts flooding in the nearby areas of stream. The severness of flo due to intense storm mainly depends on following points :

(*a*) Intensity and duration of rainfall.

(*b*) Land slope

(*c*) Land use

(*a*) **Intensity and duration of rainfall :** The rainfall intensity and its duration directly affect the size of flood. An intense storm occurring over small watershed results high flood, because whatever rainfall takes place in the watershed, is quickly drained to the outlet which meets to the tributaries. Similarly, if storm duration is more, then the volume of runoff becomes more and size of flood gets increase, accordingly.

(*b*) **Land slope :** Land slope also affects the runoff rate and its volume. As slope increases, the runoff also increase which resulted into occurrence of flood, provided that the out flow rate of river is less than the inflow rate of runoff from the area.

(*c*) **Land use :** The nature of land surface affects greately by affecting the runoff producing characteristics of the watershed. A land under vegetation has reduced runoff rate and affects the flood, accordingly. Similarly, the lands having less moisture content, absorb more rain water and accordingly the flood occurrence gets affected.

2. Intense rainfall over large catchment

As earlier, it has been stated that the high intensity rainfall occurs over a small area and generates high rate of runoff very quickly at the outlet, but when it is distributed on larger catchment area, a large percentage of runoff is lost due to infiltration, as result the amount of net available runoff for resulting the flood, is reduced. In addition, the runoff yield from small area draining into its tributary can cause the over flow from its bank, but as it is linked with the river or big size stream, the effect becomes negligible. On the other hand, incase of large size watershed a reverse trend is observed and thus the occurrence of flood is also affected, accordingly.

3. Occurrence of rainfall over accumulated snow :

In winter season, if there is accumulation of snow in the catchment, then there is arising of dangerous problem of occurrence of flood during spring season due to rainfalls. Because rainfall melts the snow deposits alongwith addition of rainwater to the melted water from the area, which causes flood in the area.

8.5. Estimation of Flood

Estimation of flood volume/rate is an important task for planning and design of flood regulation works and selection of suitable measures for river protection. For design of flood control structures, irrigation and hydropower projects, the magnitude of probable maximum flood volume and its corresponding stage is essential. The failure or success of structure depends on the estimation of design flood. The following methods are generally used for computing the flood discharge :

1. Empirical flood formulae
2. Probability or statistical method
3. Envelope curve method
4. Unit hydrograph method.

8.5.1. Empirical Flood Formulae

There have been developed several empirical formulae for different regions to compute the rate the flood flow; few of them are described as under :

Dicken's formula : This formula is used for computing the flood flow, resulting from small catchments of north and central Indian rivers. The formula is given as

$$Q = CA^{3/4} \qquad \text{...(8.1)}$$

where, Q = peak flood flow rate, m^3/s

C = coefficient; its values for different eatchments are given as under :

(*i*) For north Indian catchments - 11 to 14 for the mean annual rainfall of 60 to 120 cm.

(*ii*) For western ghat - 32

(*iii*) For central Indian catchments - 14 to 19.5

A = catchment area, sq.km.

Ryve's formula : It was developed on the basis of flood flow data of several rivers of southern India. The formula is given by

$$Q = CA^{2/3} \qquad \text{...(8.2)}$$

in which, the value of coefficient C is given as under :

1. Area within the distance of 80 km from the coast -6.8
2. Area 80 to 2400 km from the coast -8.3
3. Area near the hills -minimum 10.1 to maximum 40.0

Inglis formula : This formula was developed for computing the flood flow from the catchments of Maharashtra and Gujrat. The formula is given as

$$Q = \frac{124}{\sqrt{A + 10.4}} \qquad \text{...(8.3)}$$

in which, A is the area of catchment in sq km.

Nawab Jang Bahadur formula : It was developed for the watersheds of old Hyderabad state. The formula is given by

$$Q = CA^{(0.993 - 1/14 \log A)} \qquad \text{...(8.4)}$$

where, C = constant, its value varies from 48 to 69. However, for some cases it can be upto 86

A = catchment area, km^2

Creager's formula : This formula was developed for American catchments, which is given as

$$Q = 0.386\, C\, A^{0.894\,(0.86\,A)^{-0.043}} \qquad \text{...(8.5)}$$

in which, C is constant and A is the area of catchment.

Modified Myer's formula : This formula is given by

$$Q = 175\, P\sqrt{A} \qquad ...(8.6)$$

where, Q is in m^3/s, P is constant ranging from 0.002 to 1.0; usually taken as 1 and A is the area of catchment in sq km.

Dredge and Burge formula : It is given by

$$Q = 19.5 \frac{A}{L^{2/3}} \qquad ...(8.7)$$

where, $L =$ basin length (km)

$A =$ area of basin, sq. km

If B is the average width of basin, then equation (8.7) can be expressed as

$$Q = 19.5 \frac{BL}{L^{2/3}}$$

$$= 19.5\, BL^{1/3} \qquad ...(8.8)$$

Bourge's formula : This formula is given as

$$Q = 19.6 \frac{A}{L^{2/3}} \qquad ...(8.9)$$

In this formula, all parameters are the same as in equation 8.7

Rational formula : This is very popular formula for computing the peak flood discharge, resulting from small watersheds. Rational formula is the function of area of watershed and rainfall intensity, given as under :

$$Q = \frac{CIA}{36} \qquad ...(8.10)$$

where, $Q =$ peak discharge rate, m^3/s

$C =$ runoff coefficient

$I =$ rainfall intensity for the duration equal to time of concentration, cm/s

$A =$ area of watershed, ha

(A detail description has already been made in chapter 5)

8.5.2. Probability or Statistical Method

This method computes probable maximum flood. Normally, when some risks are involved regarding economic points of view in the design and construction of flood protection works, flood moderation works, embankment etc, then this method is used for computing the probable flood.

In this method, the peak flood data are arranged in descending order by their magnitude for constituting an array and distribution of each data in form of frequency of their occurrence. The annual flood series and partial duration series are the two main methods for computng the flood peak under this method.

Annual flood series method : This method deals with the consideration of highest flood (annual) and ignoring others which even exceed the annual normal flood. Probability of occurrence or return period of these floods is determined for computing the flood discharge of desired return period. The recurrence interval or return period (T) of the flood events is the reciprocal of plotting position, P (*i.e.* $T = \frac{1}{P}$). There are various formulae for computing the return period, described as under :

Weibul's formula : It involves following formula for computing the return period :

$$T = \left(\frac{n+1}{m}\right) \times 100 \qquad \text{...(8.11)}$$

where, T = return period, years

n = total number of events

m = rank number assigned to the event after arranging in descending order by their magnitude

The computation procedure of flood for different probability levels is shown under following steps :

1. Arrange the flood data in descending order.
2. Assign rank number to each flood event.
3. Determine recurrence interval (T) of each event by using equation 8.11.
4. Find out the plotting position of each event by using the following formula

$$P = \frac{1}{T} \times 100 \qquad \text{...(8.12)}$$

5. Plot the flood data and their probability and draw curve. The obtained curve is called annual flood frequency curve.
6. The obtained curve can be extended for finding the value of highest flood flow rate corresponding to the highest frequency or smallest recurrence interval. Computation procedure is shown in example 8.1.

Example 8.1. *Develop the flood frequency curve for 1-day maximum flood event by using Weibull's method. Data are as follows :*

Year	*1975*	*1976*	*1977*	*1978*	*1979*	*1980*	*1981*	*1982*	*1983*
1-day max. flood (m^3/s)	*3.50*	*8.00*	*10.35*	*2.0*	*20.5*	*13.6*	*12.0*	*25.0*	*16.3*
Year	*1984*	*1985*	*1986*	*1987*	*1988*	*1989*	*1990*	*1991*	*1992*
1-day max. flood (m^3/s)	*15.5*	*4.80*	*14.80*	*43.0*	*4.82*	*27.30*	*26.0*	*31.0*	*17.50*

Also, determine the followings :

1. 1-day maximum flood at 25, 50 and 75 years return period.

2. 1-day maximum flood at 25%, 50% and 75% probability levels.

Solution. Computation is shown in following table :

1-day max. flood (m^3/s)	*Rank number (m)*	*Recurrence interval $T = n+1/m$*	*P(%)*
43.0	1	19.00	5.25
31.0	2	9.50	10.53
27.30	3	6.33	15.79
26.0	4	4.75	21.05
25.0	5	3.80	26.32
20.5	6	3.17	33.55
17.5	7	2.71	36.90
16.3	8	2.38	42.02
15.50	9	2.11	47.39
14.8	10	1.90	52.63
13.6	11	1.73	57.78
12.0	12	1.58	63.29
10.35	13	1.46	68.49
8.0	14	1.36	73.53
4.82	15	1.27	78.74
4.80	16	1.19	84.03
3.50	17	1.12	89.29
2.0	18	1.05	95.24

Flood frequency curve is prepared by plotting 1-day maximum flood amounts and corresponding frequencies/return periods on log-log paper, as shown in Fig. 8.1.

Using the derived frequency curve, the values of flood for given frequencies or return periods are determined, directly. Determined values are given in following table.

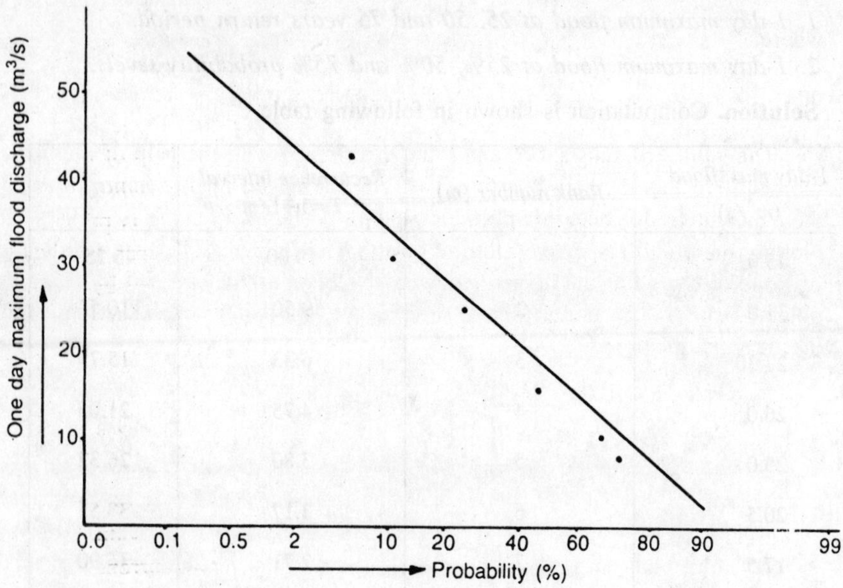

Fig. 8.1

Return period/Probability	One-day max. flood (m^3/s)
25 years } Return period	41.00
50 years } Return period	44.00
75 years } Return period	47.00
25% } Probability	27.00
50% } Probability	19.50
75% } Probability	11.00

California method : This method uses following formula for computation of return period or probability of the flood event :

$$T = \frac{n}{m} \qquad ...(8.13)$$

in which, *T*, *n* and *m* are the same as in equation 8.12. The computation procedure of flood discharge for the given return period or probability level is also the same as the Weibul's method.

Hazen's method (1930) : Under this method, the following formula is used for determining the return period :

$$T = \frac{2n}{2m - 1} \qquad ...(8.14)$$

Chow method : It follows following formula for computation of T :

$$y = a + bx \quad \text{... (8.15)}$$

where, $x = \log_{10} [\log_{10} T - \log_{10} (T - 1)]$

or

$$x = \log_{10}\left[\log_{10}\left(\frac{T}{T-1}\right)\right] \quad \text{...(8.16)}$$

The values of constants a and b are determined with the help of method of moments. In this method, the values of y are arranged in descending order by their magnitude for determining their plotting positions. A curve is prepared by plotting the y and respective plotting positions on probability paper. The values of flood discharge against given recurrence interval are determined by using the obtained curve. The probability (P) of flood event can be calculated by using the formula, given as under :

$$P = \frac{1}{T} \times 100 \quad \text{...(8.17)}$$

Stochastic method : This method follows the Gumbel's theory of extreme events, which is based on the concept of probability of event of magnitude (x), which is not being equal to or greater than the reference value (*i.e.* the probability of non-occurrence, P'). The probability of non-occurrence of flood (P^1) is given as below :

$$P' = e^{-e^{-y}} \quad \text{...(8.18)}$$

The probability of occurrence of flood $(P) = 1 - P'$

$$P = 1 - e^{-e^{-y}} \quad \text{...(8.19)}$$

in which, e is the base of natural logarithms and y is the reduced variate, which is given by the following formula :

$$y = \frac{1}{\sigma}(x - \bar{x} + 0.45) \quad \text{...(8.20)}$$

(This formula is valid for the events with more than 50 observations *i.e.* $n > 50$)

In equation 8.20, x is the magnitude of flood, $\bar{x}$ is the mean and σ is the standard deviation of the flood data. The mean ($\bar{x}$) and standard deviation (σ) are determined as under :

$$\left.\begin{aligned} \bar{x} &= \frac{\Sigma x}{n} \\ \sigma &= \sqrt{\frac{\Sigma (x - \bar{x})^2}{n-1}} \end{aligned}\right\} \quad \text{...(8.21)}$$

n is the total number of events or length of record.

After determining the value of $\bar{x}$ and σ, the recurrence interval of event (flood) can be computed as follows :

$$T = \frac{1}{P} = \frac{1}{1 - e^{-e^{-y}}} \qquad ...(8.22)$$

If x_t is flood magnitude for the recurrence interval (T) then from equation 8.22, we have

$$x_t = \bar{x} + \sigma\,(0.78\,y - 0.45) \qquad (\text{for } n > 50) \qquad ...(8.23)$$

And interms of flood discharge (Q_t) it is given as

$$Q_t = \overline{Q} + \sigma\,(0.78\,y - 0.45), \text{ for } n > 50 \qquad ...(8.24)$$

If 0.78 y is equal to 0.45, then equation 8.22 is reduced to

$Q_t = \overline{Q}$ corresponding to the return period of 2.33 years.

The flood discharge for any desired recurrence interval can also be determined by plotting the recurrence interval (T) against variate y on the Gumbel-Powell probability paper or semi-log paper. Step wise procedure is described below :

Step (1). Select atleast two recurrence intervals (say T = 25 and 50 years).

Step (2). Calculate Q_1 and Q_2 for the selected recurrence intervals by using the equation 8.24.

Step (3). Plot the values of Q and T on probability paper or semi-log paper.

Step (4). Draw line passing through the plotted points.

Step (5). Take any arbitrary recurrence interval and determine the discharge Q and plot it on the same graph paper. The plotting should lie on the line. This serves as the check point.

For finding the value of flood-discharge at highest recurrence interval (T), the derived line can be extrapolated. This method has limitation that, it does not compute the partial duration flood or rainfall. Generally, it is observed that a large number of observed data lie below the mean value and also there is large variation in the observed and mean value. Due to this reason, the curve obtained for 24-hour annual maximum flood data drawn on the log-log paper, is not in the symetrical order; this curve is called "skew curve".

The skew curve has the property that, its all the points fall on the bend line not in straight line. Slope of this curve is obtained by determing the coefficient of variation (C_v), which departure from the straight line is represented by coefficient of skewness (C_s). For determining skewness of probability curve, the following three parameters are required, which are calculated from the observed flood data, given as

1. **Coefficient of skewness** $(C_s) = \dfrac{\Sigma (x-\overline{x})^3}{(n-1)\,\sigma^3}$ ...(8.25)

It is affected by the length of record. For shorter length, its value is very less. Under this condition, C_s is adjusted by multiplying a factor equal to $\left(1+\dfrac{K}{n}\right)$, in which K is constant varies from 6 to 8.5 and n is the length of record (years).

2. **Coefficient of flood :** It is given by the following expression :

$$C_f = \frac{\overline{x}}{A^{0.8}/2.14} \quad ...(8.26)$$

where, C_f is the coefficient of flood, $\overline{x}$ is the mean of flood data and A is the area of catchment (km^2). This equation can also be used for computing the magnitude of mean flood of the watershed which has no flood record, provided that the C_f is known. In terms of mean flood, the equation 8.26 can be written as :

$$\text{Mean flood } (\overline{x}) = \frac{A^{0.8}}{2.14} C_f \quad ...(8.27)$$

3. **Coefficient of variation** (C_v) : Formula is given as :

$$C_v = \frac{\sigma}{\overline{x}} \quad ...(8.28)$$

in which, σ and $\overline{x}$ are the same as denoted in equation 8.25. C_v represents the slope of probability curve. If $C_v = 0$, then probability curve appears in horizontal form. The length of record does not affect more to C_v,

Example 8.2. *Calculate the probability of exceedance of flood for the return period of 15-years and also determine the probability of that flood which will occur in the next 10-years and 5-years return periods.*

Solution. Using the formula

$$P = \frac{1}{T} = \frac{1}{15} \times 100 = 0.066$$

Probability of exceedance = **6.7%** **Ans**

∴ Probability of flood that will not occur in next 10 years of return period

$$= (1-0.066)^{10} = 0.51 = \mathbf{51\%} \quad \textbf{Ans.}$$

Probability of the flood, which will occur in next 10 years of return period

$$= 1 - 0.51 = 0.49 = \mathbf{49\%} \quad \textbf{Ans.}$$

Similarly, probability of the flood which will not occur in 5 years of return period

$$= (1 - 0.066)^5 = 0.71\% = \mathbf{71} \quad \textbf{Ans.}$$

Probability of flood which will occur in next 5 years of return period

$$= 1 - 0.71 = .29 \text{ or } \mathbf{29\%} \quad \textbf{Ans}$$

Foster method : Frequency analysis of flood data under this method is performed by following steps :

1. Calculate the coefficient of skewness (C_s) of flood data. If length of record is shorter, then adjust C_s by multiplying the factor $\left(1 + \frac{K}{n}\right)$. In which K varies from 6 to 8.5. For Foster type-I the value of K is taken as 6 and for Foster type-III, it is 8.5. The adjusted C_s may be given as :

$$\overline{C}_s = C_s\left(1 + \frac{K}{n}\right) \qquad \text{...(8.29)}$$

2. Select arbitrary recurrence intervals, say 10,000, 1000, 100, 20, 5, 2 and 1 year.

3. Find out the skew curve factor (K) from the tables 8.3 and 8.4 for type 1 and type-III curves, respectively against selected frequency.

4. Calculate the expected flood discharge by using the following formula :

$$Q_t = \overline{Q} + K \cdot \sigma \qquad \text{...(8.30)}$$

where Q_t = expected flood discharge

$\overline{Q}$ = mean flood discharge

K = skew curve factor

σ = standard deviation of observed data

5. Plot the flood data and their recurrence intervals on log-log paper and draw curve.

6. Find out the value of flood discharge for given recurrence interval from the derived curve.

Computation procedure is explained in example 8.3.

Table 8.3. Skew curve factor (K) for Foster type curve-I

Cs	Frequency (%)										
	0.0001	*.001*	*.01*	*.1*	*1*	*5*	*20*	*50*	*80*	*95*	*99*
0	2.62	2.59	2.53	2.39	2.08	1.64	0.92	0	–0.92	–1.64	–2.08
0.2	3.00	2.94	2.83	2.66	2.25	1.72	0.89	–0.05	–0.93	–1.56	–1.91
0.4	3.44	3.35	3.18	2.95	2.42	1.79	0.87	–0.09	–0.93	–1.47	–1.75
0.6	3.92	3.80	3.59	3.24	2.58	1.85	0.85	–0.13	–0.92	–1.38	–1.59
0.8	4.43	4.27	4.00	3.55	2.75	1.90	0.83	–0.17	–0.91	–1.30	–1.44
1.0	4.95	4.75	4.42	3.85	2.92	1.95	0.80	–0.21	–0.89	–1.21	–1.30
1.2	5.50	5.25	4.83	4.15	3.09	1.99	0.77	–0.25	–0.86	–1.12	–1.17
1.4	6.05	5.75	5.25	4.45	3.25	2.03	0.73	–0.29	–0.83	–1.03	–1.06
1.6	6.65	6.25	5.67	4.75	3.40	2.07	0.69	–0.32	–0.80	–0.95	–0.96
1.8	7.20	6.75	6.08	5.05	3.54	2.10	0.64	–0.35	–0.76	–0.87	–0.87
2.0	7.80	7.25	6.50	5.35	3.67	2.13	0.58	–0.37	–0.71	–0.79	–0.80

Tale 8.4. Skew curve factor (K) for Foster type-III curve

Cs	Frequency (%)										
	0.0001	*0.001*	*0.01*	*0.1*	*1*	*5*	*20*	*50*	*80*	*95*	*99*
0	4.76	4.27	3.73	3.09	2.33	1.64	0.84	0	–0.84	–1.64	–2.33
0.2	5.48	4.84	4.16	3.08	2.48	1.69	0.83	–0.03	–0.85	–1.58	–2.18
0.4	6.24	5.42	4.60	3.67	2.62	1.74	0.82	–0.06	–0.85	–1.51	–2.03
0.6	7.02	6.01	5.04	3.96	2.77	1.79	0.80	–0.09	–0.86	–1.45	–1.88
0.8	7.82	6.61	5.48	4.25	2.90	1.83	0.78	–0.13	–0.86	–1.38	–1.74
1.0	8.63	7.22	5.92	4.54	3.03	1.87	0.76	–0.16	–0.86	–1.31	–1.59
1.2	9.45	7.85	6.37	4.82	3.15	1.90	0.74	–0.19	–0.85	–1.25	–1.45
1.4	10.28	8.50	6.82	5.11	3.28	1.93	0.71	–0.22	–0.84	–1.18	–1.32
1.6	11.12	9.17	7.28	5.39	3.40	1.96	0.68	–0.25	–0.82	–1.11	–1.19
1.8	11.96	9.84	7.75	5.66	3.50	1.98	0.64	–0.28	–0.80	–1.03	–1.08
2.0	12.81	10.51	8.21	5.91	3.60	2.00	0.61	–0.31	–0.78	–0.95	–0.99
2.2				6.20	3.70	2.01	0.58	–0.33	–0.75	–0.89	–0.90
2.4				6.47	3.78	2.01	0.54	–0.35	–0.71	–0.82	–0.83
2.6				6.73	3.87	2.01	0.51	–0.37	–0.68	–0.76	–0.77
2.8				6.99	3.95	2.02	0.47	–0.38	–0.65	–0.71	–0.71
3.0				7.25	4.02	2.02	0.42	–0.40	–0.62	–0.66	–0.67

Example 8.3. *Based on the flood data given in example 8.1, derive the flood frequency curve by using Foster method and also find out the followings :*

(i) One-day maximum flood at 25, 50 and 75 years return period.

(ii) One-day maximum flood at 25% and 75% probability levels.

Solution. (1) Computation of statistical parameters

Year	*1-day max. flood (m^3/s) (x)*	$(x-\overline{x})$	$(x-\overline{x})^2$	$(x-\overline{x})^3$	*Computation*
1975	3.50	–12.93	167.18	– 2161.70,	$\overline{x} = \frac{\Sigma x}{n} = \frac{295.67}{18}$
1976	8.00	– 8.43	71.06	– 599.07	
1977	10.35	– 6.08	36.97	– 224.76	**= 16.43**
1978	2.00	– 14.43	208.22	– 3004.68	$\sigma = \sqrt{\frac{\Sigma (x-\overline{x})^2}{n-1}}$
1979	20.50	– 4.07	16.56	67.42	
1980	13.60	– 2.83	8.00	– 22.67	**= 10.86**
1981	12.00	–4.43	19.62	– 86.94	
1982	25.00	8.57	73.44	629.42	$C_s = \frac{\Sigma (x-\overline{x})^3}{(n-1)\,\sigma^3}$
1983	16.30	– 0.13	0.017	– 0.02	
1984	15.50	– 0.93	0.86	– 0.80	$= \frac{15466.36}{(18-1) \times 10.86^3}$
1985	4.80	– 11.63	135.26	– 1573.04	**= 0.71**
1986	14.80	–1.63	2.66	– 4.33	Adjustment of C_s
1987	43.00	26.57	705.96	18757.49	$\overline{C}_s = C_s\left(1+\frac{K}{n}\right)$
1988	4.82	– 11.61	134.79	– 1564.94	
1989	27.30	10.87	118.16	1284.37	$= 0.71\left(1+\frac{6}{18}\right)$
1990	26.00	9.57	91.58	876.47	**= 0.95**
1991	31.00	14.57	212.28	3092.00	
1992	17.50	1.07	1.14	1.23	
	295.67		2003.76	15466.00	

2. Computation of expected flood : It is given in following table :

Frequency (%)	*Recurrence interval (T-yr)*	*Skew curve factor K against $\overline{C}_s = 0.95$*	*K·σ where, σ = 10.86*	*Flood $(Q_p) = \overline{Q} + K{\cdot}\sigma$*
1	2	*3*	*4*	*5*
0.01	10000	4.42	48.00	64.43
0.10	1000	3.85	41.81	58.24
1.0	100	2.92	31.71	48.14
5.0	20	1.95	21.18	37.61
20.0	5	0.80	8.69	25.12
50.0	2	– 0.21	– 2.28	14.15
100.0	1	– 1.31	–14.12	2.31

3. Preparation of flood frequency curve : It is prepared by plotting the flood discharge and corresponding frequencies/return periods on probability paper, as shown in Fig. 8.2. Using this curve, the values of expected floods for given return periods/frequencies are determined. Computed values are given as under :

Return Period/probability		*One-day max. flood (m^3/s)*
25 years	Return period	39.5
50 years		43.5
75 years		46.5
25%	Probability	24.00
5%		14.50
75%		5.00

Partial duration curve method : This method consists of plotting the flood data and their frequencies on semi-log paper. The frequency of food data can be calculated by using following formula :

$$p = \frac{m}{n} \times 100 \text{ (California method)} \qquad ...(8.31)$$

or

$$p = \frac{m}{n+1} \times 100 \text{ (Weibul's method)}$$

$$T = \frac{1}{p} \qquad ...(8.32)$$

in which, *f* is the frequency (%), *m* is the rank number of flood data after arranging in descending order by their magnitudes and *n* is the length of record. Computation procedure is described below :

1. Arrange the flood data in descending order by their magnitudes.

2. Calculate the recurrence interval of each data by using the equation 8.32.

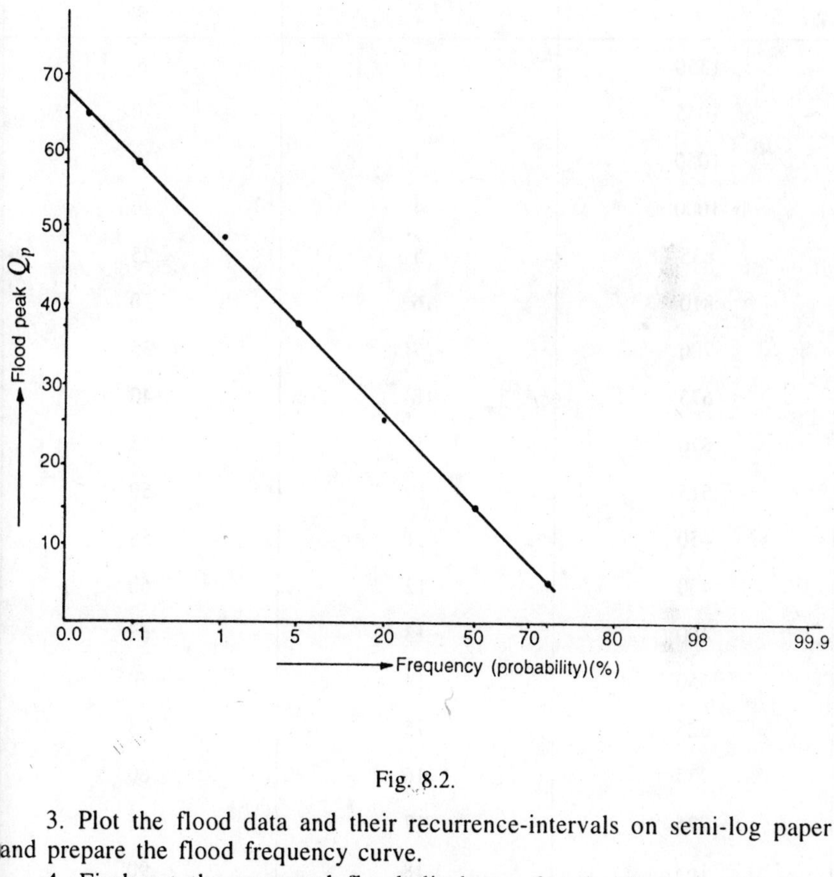

Fig. 8.2.

3. Plot the flood data and their recurrence-intervals on semi-log paper and prepare the flood frequency curve.

4. Find out the expected flood discharge for the desired recurrence interval by using the derived flood frequency curve.

Frequency method has limitation that, the prediction of higher flood discharge is not adequate, as these floods are resulted by unexpected typical storms in the watershed. The development of partial duration curve is shown in example 8.4.

Example 8.4. *One-day flood peak data of a given river for 20-years duration is given as under. Derive the partial duration curve for it.*

135, 450, 675, 1050, 1350, 325, 135, 430, 670, 810, 1055, 400, 350, 700, 1000, 515, 225, 100, 235, 835 m^3/s.

Solution. Computation is given as under :

Flood peaks after arranging in descending order, m^3/s	*Rank number (m)*	*Plotting position* $\left(p = \frac{m}{n+1} \times 100\right)$
1	2	*3*
1350	1	5
1055	2	10
1050	3	15
1000	4	20
835	5	25
810	6	30
700	7	35
675	8	40
670	9	45
515	10	50
450	11	55
430	12	60
400	13	65
350	14	70
325	15	75
235	16	80
225	17	85
165	18	90
135	19	95
100	20	100

Preparation of partial duration curve : It is prepared by plotting the frequency and corresponding flood peaks either on log-log paper or on semi-log paper. The derived curve is shown in Fig. 8.3.

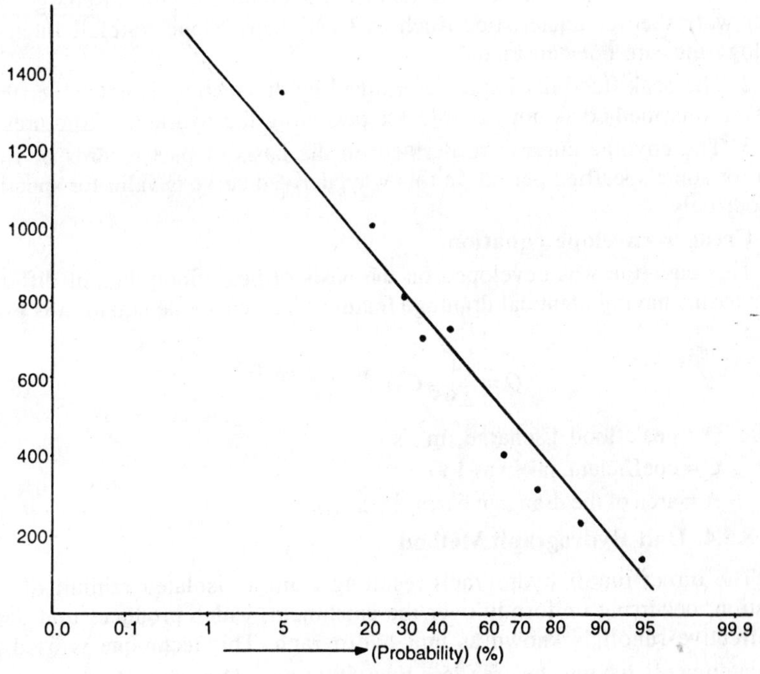

Fig. 8.3

8.5.3. Envelope Curve Method

In this method, the data on flood discharge and drainage area are collected for different identical catchments and a curve is drawn by ploting them. Obtained curve is known as envelope curve, which is used as tool for computing the flood discharge and also for compairing the design floods obtained by other methods. Kanwar et.al. have developed two envelope curves on the basis of observed floods occurring in the basins of southern and north-central Indian rivers.

World enveloping flood equation : This envelop curve was developed by J.M. Baird is given as under :

$$Q = \frac{3010\,A}{(277 + A)^{0.78}} \quad ...(8.33)$$

in which, Q is the peak flood discharge (m^3/s) and A is the area of catchment (sq.km). This method of computing the discharge, has following limitations :

1. It involves only area of watershed for computing the discharge. The other watershed characteristics, such as size, shape, slope, rainfall intensity, geology etc. are not considered.

2. The peak flood discharge determined by this method is not so accurate, causing this method is not suitable for designing the hydraulic structures.

3. The envolpe curves are derived on the basis of past records of flood data for some specified period. In this way, derived curve is valid for specified period, only.

Creager envelope equation

This equation was developed on the basis of peak flood data of different river basins having identical drainage features. The envelope equation is given by

$$Q = \frac{1}{2.95} C \cdot A^{0.864\,(A/2.95)^{-0.048}} \quad ...(8.34)$$

where, Q = peak flood discharge, m^3/s

C = coefficient, taken as 130

A = area of the drainage basin, sq. km.

8.5.4. Unit Hydrograph Method

The direct runoff hydrograph resulting from an isolated rainfall of unit duration, occurring uniformly over the catchment, which produces unit depth of effective runoff is known as unit hydrograph. This technique is used for the catchments having the area less than 5000 km^2. However, if area exceeds this limits, then entire catchment is divided into sub-catchments and individual unit hydrograph is developed for them. The total flood is obtained by adding all together.

(A detail description of unit hydrograph has already been made in chapter 6).

8.6. Flood Control Measures

The flood control measures are applied for the following two main purposes :

1. Modifying the flood, and
2. Modifying the succeptibility of flood damages.

The modifications in flood are performed by using various physical control measures and altering the land use of the watershed.

Similarly, the modifications in succeptibility of flood damage are performed by diverting the runoff, recharging into soil, etc. Various flood control measures used for this purpose are as under :

1. By constructing flood protection structures
2. By reducing flood stages
3. Storage of flood water by constructing reservoirs

4. By reducing the soil erosion from watershed
5. Reducing flood discharge by land management practices.

8.6.1. Flood Protection Structures

The flood protection structures are the levee, flood walls, close conduits, embankments, retarding basins etc. These are described as :

Levee : It is an earthen dike like structure, is one of the economical structures for protecting the flood. Its effect is immediate on the flood. The design and construction of levee is the same as the earthen dam. It is constructed, parallel to the river course as shown in Fig. 8.4. In its construction, there should be provided few curves in alignment to make the levee safe against flood water.

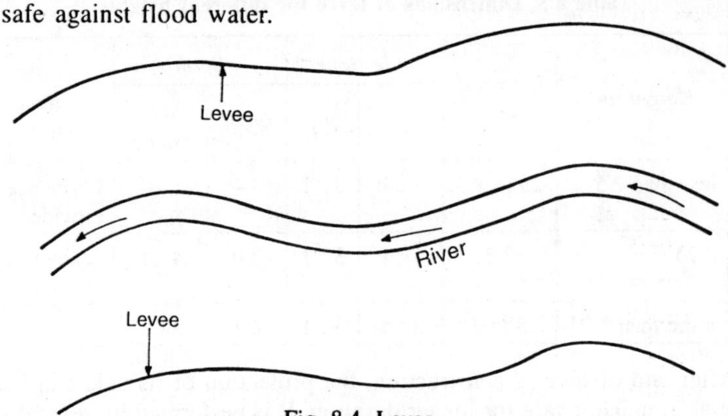

Fig. 8.4. Levee

Design of Levee : The following parameters are determined under design of levee :

1. Cross-section
2. Top width
3. Side slope
4. Bottom width
5. Muck ditch
6. Berms.

Cross-section : The cross-section of levee should be such that, it can suit the site condition and materials available at the site. However, the levee's cross-section should satisfy the following points :

1. Height should be adequate, so that overtopping of flood water may not be there.

2. It should be massive to stand against seepage.

Top width : It is decided on the basis of its purpose *i.e.* whether it is to be used as the road or for some other purposes. For movement of trucks or maintanence equipments through levee, a minimum of 3 m as top width is generally kept, but in few cases it may vary from 3 to 8 m.

Side slope : In levee, the side slopes are kept relatively flat, because the available materials at the site are not in proper quality. The side slope is mainly decided on the basis of angle of repose of the soil materials. However, varies from 3:1 to 5:1 towards upstream and from 4:1 to 7:1 towards down stream side. Height of levee is normally kept as 9m.

Muck ditch : It is provided at the back of the levee. Its purpose is to control the flow of water from the base. In addition, it also provides an additional strength to the levee's section for making safe against sliding. The width of muck ditch generally ranges from 1.5 to 3.0 m.

Berm : Its main function is to cheek the levee's bank against collapsing. It is constructed by leaving the space of 8 to 20 m width between the toe of the levee and burrow pit.

Generally, three cross-sections are widely used for construction of levee as given in Table 8.5.

Table 8.5. Dimensions of levee for different heights

S. No.	*Height (m)*	*Top width (m)*	*Side slope*		*Berm*		*Remark*
			u/s	*d/s*	*Width*	*Side slope*	
1.	less than 2.5	25 to 3.5	3 : 1	3 : 1	—	—	Berms are not provided
2.	3.25	2.5	3 : 1	3 : 1	3.0	4 : 1	A key trench is also provided
3.	more than 3.25	2.5 to 3.5	3 : 1	3 : 1	4.5	4 : 1	

After end of levee's construction, the protection of its side slope is very essential to make it safe for longer duration. It is performed by several means, such as sodding, turfing, planting of trees or shrubs, stone revettments etc. Sometimes, incase of stone revettement, the soil particles from joint places of the stones are eroded due to continuous striking of water waves over u/s side slope, causing failure of revettment and thus development of bad effect on the levee. To check such problems the joint places are planted with suitable grasses so that the stones are tightly held in position and at the same time, the soil erosion can also be eliminated.

Spacing and Height of Levee : These two parameters are decided on the basis of hit and trial technique. Initially, an arbitrary height of the levee is assumed and maximum discharge likely to be passed through the stream course for assumed height is determined. The obtained discharge is substracted from the probable maximum flood discharge to get the discharge passing through the space between the channel and levee, *i.e.* 'flood way'. The area of flood way is determined by dividing the total passing discharge through it, with the flow velocity. *i.e.*

$$\text{Area of flood way} = \frac{\text{Passing discharge}}{\text{Flow velocity}}$$

Alignment of Levee : Since the purpose of levee is to provide immediate protection to the adjacent area of the river from flood, therefore the alignment of levee is done mainly on the basis of existing properties and importance of area lying on the river bank. Sometimes, it becomes essential to align the levee much closer to the river for protecting the embankment facing the direct attack of flood water. For such situations, the river training work becomes essential which is perfomed by stone revettment, toe protection by installation of vertical wall etc.

When alingment of levee close to the river is not possible for protecting the important establishments adjacent to the river, then construction of ring bund is recommended as another protection measure. For making the ring bund more effective, the river training work for diverting the high velocity flood water away from the bund is done. The height of ring levee may be upto the embankment height. The ring levee is shown in Fig. 8.5.

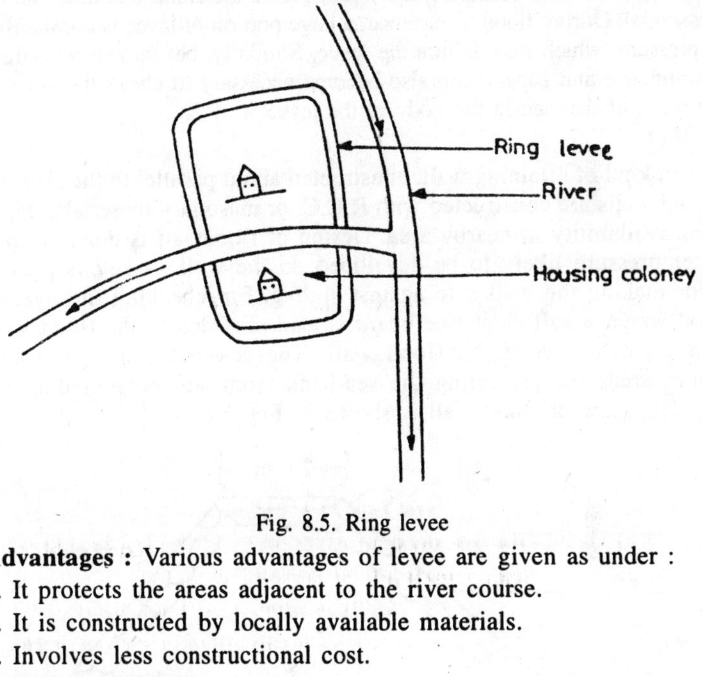

Fig. 8.5. Ring levee

Advantages : Various advantages of levee are given as under :

1. It protects the areas adjacent to the river course.
2. It is constructed by locally available materials.
3. Involves less constructional cost.
4. Easy to maintain.
5. Construction can be done, part-wise.

Disadvantages : These are as follows :

1. A large area of the land adjacent to the river is lost permanently.
2. For all places, it is not possible to construct for flood protection.
3. If proper drainage facilities are not available, then low lying areas may be infested by malaria problem.
4. Always, there is possibility of its failure due to piping etc.
5. It deteriorates the river course by high silt charge.
6. During high flood the sudden breaching of levee may lost the human lives and important properties of the area.
7. Creates the problem of rising of high water-table in the adjacent areas.

8. Large areas are sterilized by silt deposition.
9. During flood, it needs high level of inspection.

Causes of Levee's Failure

The following reasons are mainly responsible for making the failure of levee :

1. Overtopping due to wave action or high level of flood water.
2. Flow of seepage water through the section.
3. Caving action.
4. Breaching due to saturation of levee's section.
5. Direct flow of water through the cracks developed in the levee's section.

Maintenence of levee during the flood, before the flood and after the flood is most essential. During flood occurrence, a large portion of levec is constantly under water pressure, which may failure the levee. Similarly, before and after the flood, the maintinance and supervision also become necessary to check the development of any types of damage in the body of the levee.

Flood Wall

It is a kind of retaining wall, constructed about parallel to the river course. The flood walls are constructed with R.C.C. or masonary materials, depending on their availability in nearby area. Design of floodwall is done on the basis of water pressure likely to be developed on the wall. A key is provided at base for making the wall safe against sliding. For checking the overtopping of flood water, a sufficient free-board is also provided to the flood wall. Sea wall is an example of the flood wall. The sea-walls are constructed in sea-shore areas for protecting the sea-bank from soil erosion due to wave action. The view of flood wall is shown in Fig. 8.6.

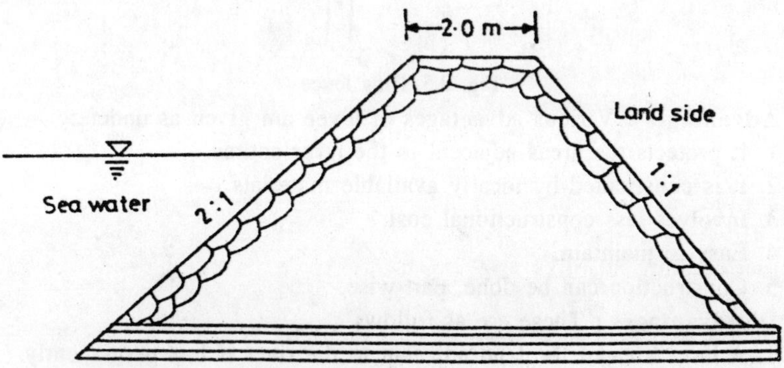

Fig. 8.6

8.6.2. Reduction of Flood Stage

The flood stage can be reduced by using the following methods :

1. Straightening and deepening the river bed.
2. Construction of by-pass channels.
3. Using cut-offs etc.

Straightening and deepening of the river bed : The discharge passing through the river's section is the product of flow velocity and cross-sectional area of the flow. Under straightening and deepening works the net carrying capacity (*i.e.*, cross-sectional area) of the river is increased, by virtue of which the flood stage gets reduced. The reduction in flood stage also depends on the gradient of the riverbed. If it is less, then reduction of the flood level will be less because of less flow velocity and discharge. Under deepening and straightening works, the bed gradient is also improved to reduce the flood stage.

Constructing by-pass channels : It is very common that, the large cities are situated on the river bank and are mostly affected by occurrence of floods during monsoon season. Sometimes, human beings of these areas are badly affected due to flood consequence. Under such condition, if construction of flood control structures is neither feasible nor economical, then alternate way to control the effect of flood is the construction of by-pass channel for diverting the flood water from that particular area. A by-pass channel is shown in Fig. 8.7.

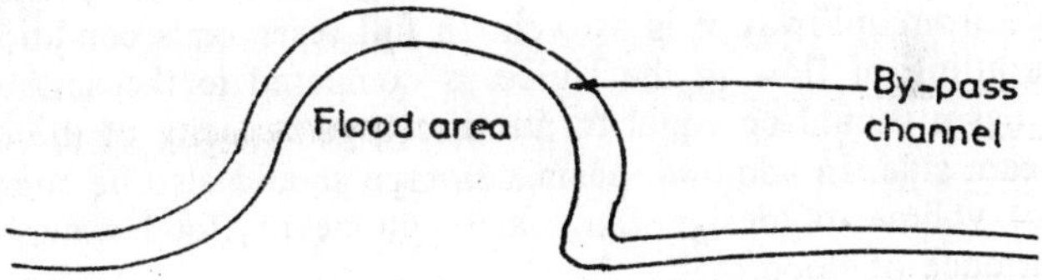

Fig. 8.7. By-pass channel.

Cut-off : Generally, when tortuosity of river is less, then slope of river bed increases towards upstream side, which causes erosion from the river bank and scouring of soil particles from the bed due to increase in flow velocity. At this situation, the cut-off plays an impressive role for reducing the flood stage and its duration, as well. Cut-off is constructed better in alluvial rivers, in the form of hair-pin bends. Under favourable conditions, these bends become in the form of large loop with narrow neck. It is shown in Fig. 8.8.

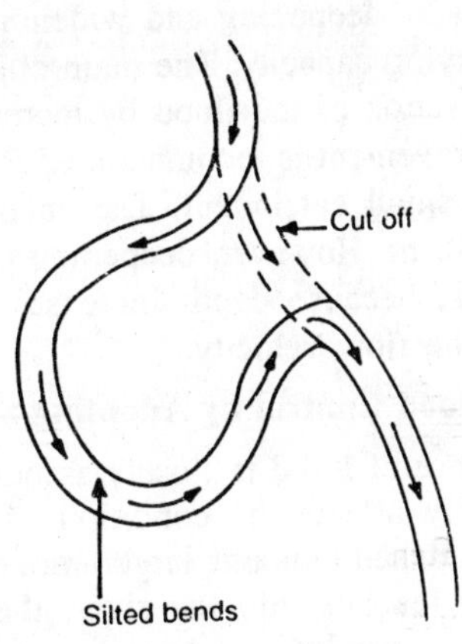

Fig. 8.8. Cut-off.

8.6.3. Flood Control By Storing Water

The reservoirs, retarding basins etc. are the structures used for controlling the flood by storing flood water. These are described as under :

Flood control by reservoirs : The reservoirs are constructed for storage of flood water to reduce the flood peaks. These are constructed at upstream end of the area, which is required to protect and from where the stored water can be safely discharged into the channel downstream side. The degree of flood reduction depends on the storage capacity of the reservoir. If reservoir's capacity is more, then reduction in flood peak will be more and vice-versa. The storage capacity of reservoir is determined by substracting the volume of water already collected in the reservoir from its total capacity. However for design of reservoir, one third area of the catchment is considered as the storage capacity of the reservoir.

Flood control by retarding basins : The retarding basins are also used as water storage structure for flood control. These are equipped with spillway as outlet and sluices. Discharge of water through sluice takes place like an orifice, while from spillway it is as weir. In full reservoir's condition, there is heavy throttling of flow in the sluice as compared to the spillway. The capacity of basin should be equal to the discharge capacity of the channels at down stream side. In addition, basin's storage should also be equal to the difference of volume of design flood and volume of flood water released during occurrence of flood.

Retarding basins have limitation that, the discharge is likely to get synchronized with the flood likely to be occured in the tributary, located at down stream side. Due to this reason these basins are not recommended to construct on small size streams.

Channel improvement : The channel improvement involves providing of proper grade, deepening and widening of the channel section, to increase the flow carrying capacity. The main objective of this work is to decrease the stage and duration of the flood by increasing the flow velocity. The work of channel improvement is recommended for narrow and shallow depth channels having very small catchment. The enlargement of width of channels varies from 30 to 40 m. However, deepening of the channel is more preferred than the widening, because depth increases the hydraulic mean radius, causing increase in the flow velocity.

8.6.4. Flood Control by Adopting Soil Conservation Measures

Occurrence of flood is closely associated to the condition of river course. Siltation badly affects the condition of river course. The runoff generated from the watershed contains large amount of soil particles in suspenson form and when it reaches into the river, then due to gradual decrease in flow velocity, the suspended soil particles tend to settle down over the bed called siltation. In long course of time, a situation arrives when silt deposition makes the river bed to the level of adjoining land. In this condition, runoff water gets spread in the adjoining area and thus causes flood occurrence.

Soil conservation measures for flood control consist of construction of contour bunds, terraces, check dams, installation of temporary and permanent gully control structures, establishment of vegetative cover, afforestation, land management practices, stream bank erosion control measures etc. All these measures check the soil erosion or soil loss by enhancing the absorbtion of water and thereby reduction in the volume of runoff from the area.

Amongst different soil conservation measures, the upstream measures (*i.e.* at watershed) are more important. The u/s measures may be agronomical or mechanical both. However, agrorcomical measures are very effective, than the mechanical measures.

8.6.5. Flood Plain Management for Flood Control

It is general recommendation that in the area adjacent to the river, where flood occurrence is common phenomena, the construction of colonies etc. is strictly prohibited but such areas are kept under other types of uses, such as in the from of parks, recreational spots etc., so that inundation of these areas may not hinder the human population.

For flood plain management, the total area in which flood is expected to occur is taken into consideration. The flood plains are divided in different zones as per degree of hazards. Generally, extent of hazard decreases away from the river. Following three zones are mainly identified under flood plain management works :

1. Warning zone
2. Restrictive zone, and
3. Prohibitive zone

In warning zone the effect of flood is more. This zone is extended from the river bank to the boundary of affected area by the flood. Since in this zone, the flood risk is more, therefore adoption of necessary measures against flood is very essential.

The restrictive zone is also referred as flood fringe zone. This is ahead of the warning zone. Effect of flood is not severe as compared to the warning zone. The construction of houses etc. is not prohibited in this zone.

Prohibitive zone is extended from middle of the river course to some distance away in the adjoining area on both sides of the river. In this zone, the effect of flood is more, causing restrictions on the development of housing apartments etc.

8.7. Economics of Flood Control

Evaluation of cost conomics of the flood control projects is an important task. It is done on the basis of type of flood protection and investment of money on that. It is evaluated in terms of cost-benefit ratio of the project, which consists of estimating the total costs invested for constructing different structures and benefits realized from them by protecting the areas against flood. Various costs involved for flood control measures and benefits obtained by them are listed as under :

Costs : It includes following :

1. Capital cost
2. Interest on capital cost
3. Depreciation and taxes
4. Operational cost
5. Repair and maintenance cost

Capital cost is the total cost incurred on investigation, planning of work, purchase of materials, payment of labours etc. The depreciation and repair & maintinance costs are estimated on the basis of capital cost *i.e.* at the rate of prescribed percent of capital cost. Generally, 4 to 5% is considered for it.

Benefits from the Project : The following benefits are realised from flood control projects :

Direct Benefits : The benefits obtained, directly by preventing the loss of land, human lives etc. are considered as the direct benefits, given as under :

1. **Benifits from levee :** The benefits from levee are calculated by multiplying the total prevented area against damage due to occurrence of flood with an assumed rate in term of rupees per hectare. Deposition of sediments in the adjoining area, if any, is also considered as the benefit.

2. **Benefits from drainage :** Since, stagnation of water badly affects the crop grown area, therefore stagnated flood water if drained from the area, must be counted as benefit. The benefit from drainage is determined as monitary value, gained from the total drained area.

3. **Benefits from anti-erosion :** The benifits from anti-erosion are evaluated as the value of land saved against erosion likely to be occurred during occurrence of flood, if flood control measures were not adopted.

Indirect Benefits : The followings are mainly accounted under indirect benefits :

1. Moeny saved under insurance
2. Benefits due to increase in yield from protected cultivable land.
3. Benefits due to not happening of epidemic disease likely to be occured in flood affected areas.
4. Money saved through work's man compensation law.

Analysis of Cost-benefit-Ratio

To determine the cost-benefit ratio and also to study the economics of flood control measures, the following steps are followed :

1. Calculate the total benefits obtained from the flood protection works. It can be given as :

Total benefits = direct benefits + indirect benefits

2. Find out total incurred cost for construction and installation of flood control structures.

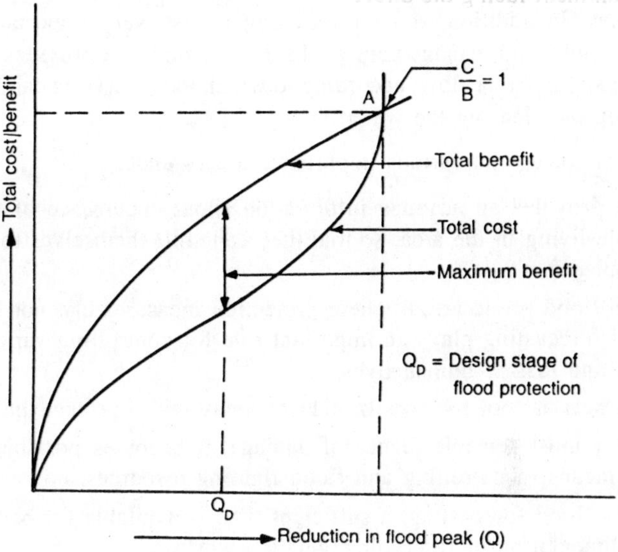

Fig. 8.9. Cost-benefit analysis.

3. Determine the reductions in the flood peak.

4. Plot the curve between total benefits, total invested costs and reductions in the flood peak by keeping the benefits and costs on *y*-axis and reductions in flood peak on *x*-axis, as shown in Fig. 8.9. In figure, the curves of total cost and benefits intersect each other at the point A, which denotes the ratio of benefit to cost $\left(i.e \, \frac{\text{benifit}}{\text{cost}} \right)$ is unity. At this point, the reduction of flood peak is maximum. Generally, the construction of flood control structures is recommended for high benefit-cost ratio. However, in the condition of rare occurrence of flood, the installation of flood protection measures is not justified, because investment of capital cost is very high to that of the benifits likely to be obtained from them.

8.8. Flood Forecasting

The occurrence of flood damages a vast tract of cultivated cropped lands, erodes the soil nutrients, ruins the households situated at the river banks, losses the human lives, spreads several diseases like malaria, typhoid etc. in the flood areas. If flood control measures have been used, then there is not possibilities of occurrence of such bad happenings. Therefore, flood forecasting plays an important role for preventing the consequences of floods by giving an advance ultimatum to the people living in the area.

By knowing the time of flood occurrence, the population living at the river's bank become alert and shift their cattles and other properties to the safe places. In addition, flood forecasting is also very important for water resources and flood management works. For example : it provides information about the stream/river flow; according to which the reservoirs can be regulated for storing or releasing the water.

Importance : Its various importance are as under :

1. It provides an advance information about occurrence of the flood to the people living in the area, so that they can shift themselves to some other suitable places.

2. In flood prone areas, where protection measures can not be installed, the flood forecasting plays an important role for controlling various kinds of damages and loss of human lives.

3. It acts as tool for arrangement of measures to protect the area.

4. For most sensible places of damage, it becomes possible to arrange suitable means of patrolling and flood fighting resources.

5. By flood forecasting, a sufficient time is available for better planning and implimentation of reservoir regulation works.

8.9. River Forecasting

If requisite data base on river flow are available and forecast of complete hydrograph is sought to have, then following steps can be followed for forecasting the flood :

1. **Evaluation of expected flow :** This is done by deriving the relationship between rainfall and runoff for different storm durations, such as hourly, daily weekly etc. The runoff is affected by various factors *i.e.* initial soil moisture level, storm duration, time of year etc., in which all the factors are easily measurable, except initial soil moisture status during storm. The initial moisture content is expressed in terms of antecedent moisture condition, called Antecedent Precipitation Index (API), which is given by the following formula :

$$\text{API} = a_1 P_1 + a_t P_2 + \ldots + a_2 P_t \qquad \ldots(8.35)$$

where,

$a_1, a_2, \ldots a_t$ = constant, which is the function of time (t). Its value is less than 'unity'

$P_1, P_2, \ldots P_t$ = depth of precipitation which has been occurred 1, 2, ... t days before the storm taken into consideration.

The constant 'a' decreases exponentially incase of daily API, given as :

$$a_t = K^t \qquad \ldots(8.36)$$

in which, K is the recession constant, which ranges from 0.25 to 0.98.

Thus, based on equation 8.36, the API can be rewriten as

$$API_t = API_o K^t \qquad ...(8.37)$$

where, API_t = antecedent precipitation index 't' days after the storm.

API_o = initial precipitation index, given as

$$API_{o1} = API_o K \quad \text{at } (t = 0) \qquad ...(8.38)$$

The relationship between runoff and antecedent precipitation index is

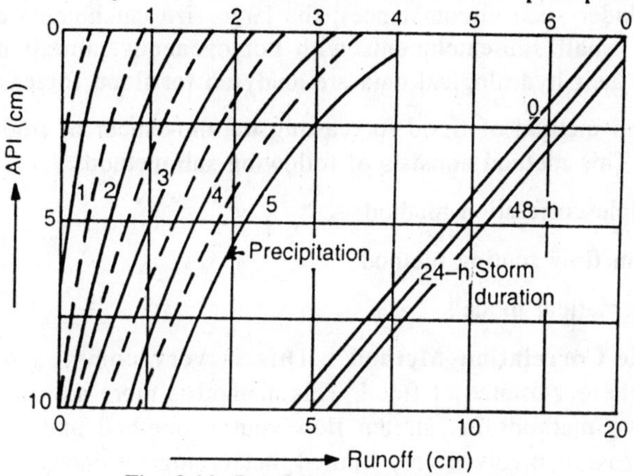

Fig. 8.10. Rainfall-runoff relation ship.

shown in Fig. 8.10.

2. **Derivation of U.H.G. and estimation of time distribution of runoff** : Unit hydrograph (U.H.G) is used for estimating the direct runoff. If distribution of runoff for the specified time is non-uniform, then unit-hydrographs for shorter durations such as 6-h, 12-h etc. should be derived as they can be derived with greater accuracy.

3. **Stream flow routing** : It is done for predicting the change in the shape of flood wave, as runoff proceeds downstream side. Stream routing is performed by using the Muskingum method, which has already been described in chapter 9.

4. The flow stages at upstream and down stream sections are determined by using the stage-discharge relationship.

Flood Forecasting Methods

The following two are the main methods for forecasting the flood :

1. Method based on the hydrological and meteorological data of the river basin.

2. Method based on the laws governing the movement of runoff through the rivers/channels.

The flood forecasting based on hydrological and meteorological informations is dealt by using water - balance approach, which includes the computation of various parameters associated to the water balânce *i.e.* precipitation amount, infiltration capacity of the soil, snow melt, depression storage, soil moisture, position of ground water etc. In hilly zones, the rivers having large catchment, are being snow bound and prediction of runoff from rainfall, snow melt etc becomes very difficult due to severity in the weather condition. Under such circumstances, the large size catchments are divided into several small sub-catchments with homogeneous rainfall distribution pattern; and their hydrological data are analysed for flood forecasting.

In second method of flood forecasting the movement of flood waves is determined. This method consists of following sub-methods.

1. Multiple correlation method

2. Stream flow routing method

3. Mathematical models

Multiple-Correlation Method : This is very common method for forecasting the occurrence of flood. This method is more advantageous than the other two methods *i.e.* stream flow routing method and mathematical models, because it involves very limited meteorological data.

In multiple - correlation method, the flood forecasting is done by using the discharge data of base station and forecasting station. The following three correlations are mainly used for the purpose :

1. Correlation between '*N*th'-hour stage of the base station and $(N + t)$ hour stage of the forecasting station, in which '*t*' is the travel time of flood wave, *i.e.*the time taken by flood wave to move from base station to the forecasting station. This type of correlation provides accurate forecasting for the streams having uniform slope and cross-section both. In lower reaches of the Sone river basin (Bihar), this correlation is found very successful for forecasting the flood. This type of correlation is shown in Fig. 8.11.

2. Correlation between change in flow stage of base and forecasting stations during the travel time (t) of flood wave. It is shown in Fig. 8.12.

This method provides accurate forecasting, when

(*i*) Rivers are large.

(*ii*) Rivers have an impressive change in discharge between forecasting and base stations.

(*iii*) Change in flood discharge between forcasting and base stations is uniform.

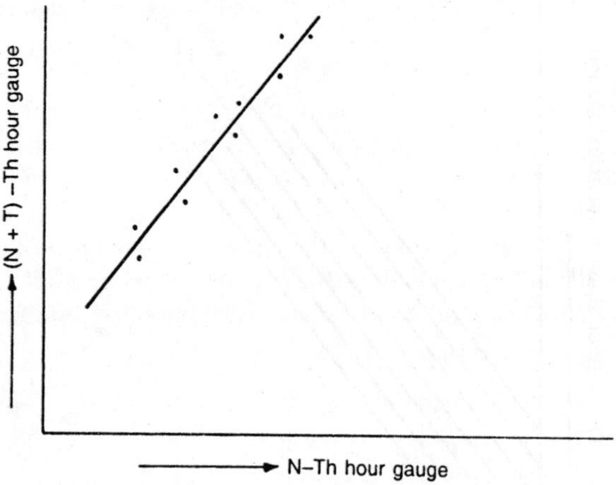

Fig. 8.11. Correlation between *N*-th hour of base station and $(N+t)$-th hour of forecasting station.

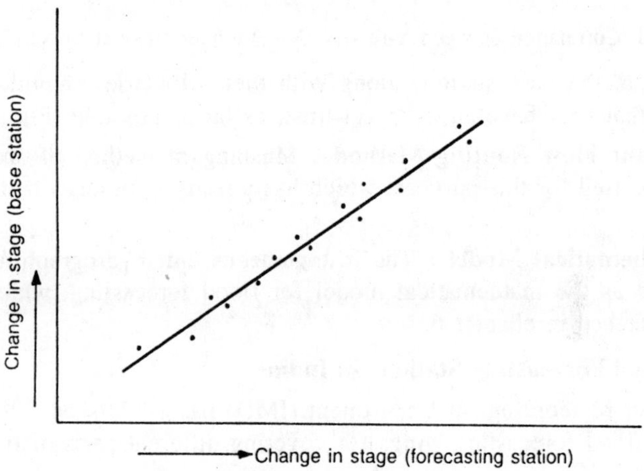

Fig. 8.12. Correlation between change in stage of base station and forecasting station.

3. Correlation between '*N*-th' hour and $(N+t)$th hour stages of forecasting station and change in storage at base station during travel time. This correlation is commonly used for flood forecasting. It is shown in Fig. 8.13.

In the use of above correlations for forecasting the flood, one point should be kept in mind that, when more than one tributaries are meeting to the main river, then change in stage of different tributaries should be taken into account.

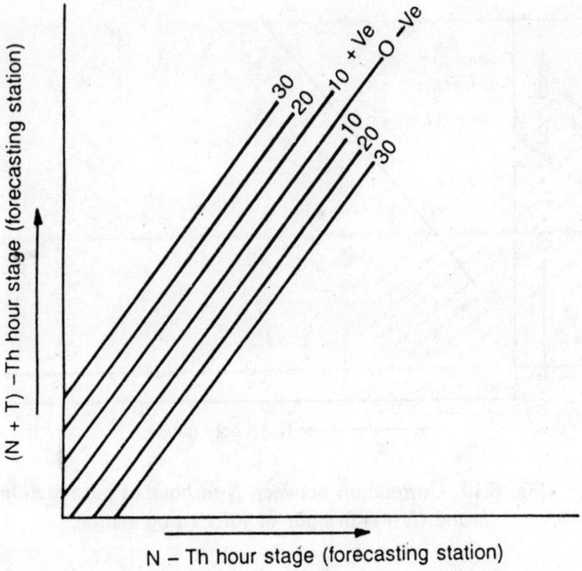

Fig. 8.13. Correlation between N-th and $(N + t)$th hour stage at forecasting station.

In addition, the base stations along with their tributaries should also be so selected that they have equal travel time, as far as possible (Fig. 8.14).

Stream Flow Routing Method : Muskingum method of channel flow routing is used for this purpose, which has already been described in chapter 9.

Mathematical Model : The instantaneous unit hydrograph approach is employed as the mathematical model for flood forecasting, which has also been described in chapter 6.

8.10. Flood Forecasting Stations In India

Indian Meteorological Department (IMD) has established following five regional flood forecasting wings for covering different parts of India :

1. **New Delhi :** It covers Himachal Pradesh, Punjab, U.P., Haryana, J & K, Rajasthan and Delhi for forecasting the flood.

2. **Calcutta :** Commands the eastern parts of India comprising the states of Bihar, Assam, Bengal, Orissa and Bay of Iceland.

3. **Madras :** This forecasting station is established for covering the southern parts of India, *i.e.*Tamilnadu, A.P., Karnataka and Kerala.

4. **Bombay :** Maharashtra and Gujrat states are covered by this forecasting station.

5. **Nagpur :** It includes M.P. and Vidarbha regions for forecasting the flood.

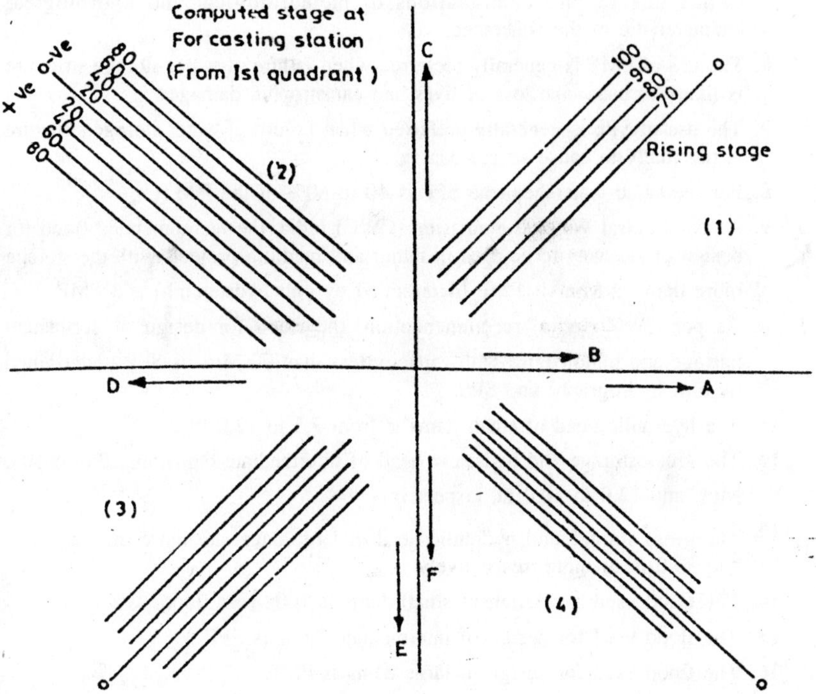

Fig. 8.14

A = observed $(N + T)$th hour gauge

B = N-th hour of forecasting station

C = $(N + T)$-th hour gauge at forecasting station

D = observed gauge of $(N + T)$-th hour of forecasting station

E = observed $(N + T)$ hour gauge

F = computed $(N + T)$-th hour gauge

IMPORTANT POINTS

1. The unusual high stage of flow in the river, at which there is overflow of runoff from the river banks is called flood.
2. The flood considered for design of hydraulic structures is called design flood.
3. The flood used for designing the spillways of water storage structure is called spillway design flood.
4. The standard project flood (SPE) is resulted from the rarely severe most combination of meteorological and hydrological characteristics of the catchment.

5. Physically possible extreme flood, which is resulted from severemost combinations is called probable maximum flood (PMF). It also includes the floods due to rare combinations of meteorological and hydrological characteristic of the watershed.
6. The use of PMF is generally preferred when failure of water storage structure is likely to cause the loss of lives and catastrophic damages.
7. The use of SPF is generally preferred when failure of water storage structure is not likely to cause severe damage.
8. For the same watershed, the SPF is 40 to 60% of the P.M.F.
9. As per Central Water Commission (CWC) India, the recommended flood for design of spillway to be used in major and medium projects with the storage more than 60 Mm^3 is PMF (determined by unit hydrograph) and PMP.
10. As per CWC (India) recommendation, the flood for design of permanent barrage and minor dams with capacity less than 60 Mm^3 is SPF (determined by unit hydrograph) and SPS.
11. The hydraulic head of small dams is from 7.5 to 12.0 m.
12. The gross storage and hydraulic head of intermediate dams are 10.0 to 60.0 Mm^3 and 12.0 to 30.0 m, respectively.
13. The gross storage and hydraulic head of large dams are more than 60 Mm^3 and 30.0 m or more, respectively.
14. The flood used for design of small dams is 100- year flood.
15. The flood used for design of intermediate dams is SPF.
16. The flood used for design of large dams is PMF.
17. The Dicken's formula for estimation of maximum flood discharge is given by $Q_p = C_D A^{3/4}$, in which C_D is the Dicken's constant which varies between 6 and 30 and A is the area of watershed (km^2)
18. Dicken's formula for computation of flood discharge is valid for the catchments of central and northern India.
19. The Ryves formula for estimating the flood discharge is given as $Q_p = C_R A^{2/3}$, in which C_R is the Ryves coefficient, which is 6.8 for the areas within 80 km from the east-coast, 8.5 for the areas between 80 to 160 km from the east coast and 10.2 for the areas close to the hills.
20. Ryves formula for estimation of flood discharge was originally developed for Tamilnadu regions.
21. Inglis formula is suitable for estimating the flood discharge of western ghats of Maharashtra.
22. The probability of occurrence of an event, r times in n successive years is given by $P_{rn} = {}^nC_r P^r \cdot q^{n-r}$, in which $q = 1 - P$.
23. Gumble's method is suitable for the probability analysis of extreme events.
24. Gumbel's method can also be used for predicting the flood peaks, maximum rainfall amounts, maximum wind velocities etc.

25. The formula for determining the frequency factor (K) for Gumbel method is given by, $K = \frac{(Y_T - 0.577)}{1.2825}$, in which Y_T is the value of y for a given T ; it is computed as $Y_T = -\left[\ln \cdot \ln \frac{T}{T-1}\right]$, T is the return period.

26. Gumbel method is applicable for analysis of infinite sample size (*i.e.* $N \to \infty$).

27. The frequency factor (K) of Gumbel method for a finite sample size is given as $K = \frac{Y_T - \overline{Y}_n}{S_n}$, in which $\overline{Y}_n$ is the reduced mean and S_n is the reduced standard deviation.

28. The Log-Pearson Type - III distribution gets reduce to Log normal distribution when $C_s = 0$

29. The recurrence interval of an event of annual series (T_A) and of the partial duration series (T_P) is related as $T_p = \frac{1}{l_n T_A - l_n (T_A - 1)}$.

30. For frequency analysis of hydrological data, the length of record should be minimum 30 years for better result. However, if it is less than 10 years, then frequency analysis should not be done.

31. The probability of occurrence of an event ($x \geq x_T$), at least once over a period of n successive years is called the risk ($\overline{R}$). It can be expressed as $\overline{R} = 1 - \left(1 - \frac{1}{T}\right)^n$, in which T is the return period (*year*).

32. The reliability of hydraulic structure can be expressed as

$$R_e = \left(1 - \frac{1}{T}\right)^n.$$

REFERENCES

1. Agrawal A and Das G., Time series model of stream flow for a catchment of Ramganga river, J. of Inst. of Engineers (India), 86, 15, 1988.
2. Anderson O.D. Time series analysis and forecasting, the Box — Approach, Butterworth and Co. London, 1976.
3. Chandra S., Seth S.M. and Rao K.B.S. Mathematical model for time series of monthly stream flow, Proscceding of National Symposion on Hydrology 13-15, Roorkee, 1975.
4. Central Water Commission, India, "Estimation of flood peak", Flood Estimation Directorate, Report No. 1/73, New Delhi, 1973.
5. Chow V.T. Handbook of Applied Hydrology, McGraw-Hill, New York, 1964.
6. Gray D.M. Principles of Hydrology, Water Inf. Centre, New York, 1970.
7. Indian Burean of Standards "Guidelines for fixing spillway capacity" IS : 11233 - 1985.
8. Neme C. J. Engineering Hydrology Tata McGraw-Hill, New Delhi, 1973.
9. Subramanya K. Engineering Hydrology, Tata McGraw-Hill, New Delhi, 2000.

10. Raghunath H.M. Hydrology, Wiley Eastern Pvt. Ltd., Delhi, 1985.
11. Mutreja K.N. Applied Hydrology, Tata McGraw Hill, New Delhi, 1986
12. Richard. The flood estimation and control Chapman and Hall, London, 1944.

DESCRIPTIVE TYPE QUESTIONS

1. Define flood and describe various types of flood.
2. Distinguish design flood and Standard Project Flood.
3. Describe the causes of flood occurrence.
4. List different methods for computation of flood and describe unit hydrograph method.
5. Describe Dicken's formula for computation of flood discharge
6. Explain Rational method for computation of peak flood.
7. Explain Weibul's method for predicting the flood discharge at different probability levels.
8. Describe Stochastic method of probability analysis.
9. Explain various measures to control the flood.
10. Describe the design of levee for flood control.
11. Write various causes of levee's failure.
12. Write short notes on followings :
    (*i*) Flood walls (*ii*) Flood stage
    (*iii*) Bypass channels (*iv*) Channel improvement.
13. Explain the economics of flood control projects.
14. Describe flood forecasting methods and its importance.
15. List various flood forecasting stations in India and explain their establishments.

OBJECTIVE TYPE QUESTIONS

1. Flood occurs, when
   (*a*) inflow > outflow (*b*) inflow < outflow
   (*c*) inflow = outflow (*d*) $I + O = S$.
2. Design flood is used for the design and construction of
   (*a*) river gauging stations (*b*) hydraulic structures
   (*c*) both '*a*' and '*b*' (*d*) gully control structures only.
3. Standard Project Flood (SPF) is approximately
   (*a*) 80% of the maximum probable flood (MPF)
   (*b*) 75% of MPF
   (*c*) 50% of MPF
   (*d*) same as the peak flood.
4. Annual flood is referred for
   (*a*) water year (*b*) particular day
   (*c*) particular month (*d*) scanty rainy period.
5. Ordinary flood occurs
   (*a*) once in the entire project period
   (*b*) once or more during project period
   (*c*) both '*a*' and '*b*'
   (*d*) at 75% probability.

6. Rivers of barren watersheds are more affected by flood occurrence, because of

(*a*) greater runoff yield (*b*) lesser water loss
(*c*) both '*a*' and '*b*' (*d*) high intiltration rate.

7. Dicken's formula for computation of flood flow is

(*a*) empirical relation (*b*) theoretical relation
(*c*) none of the above (*d*) Rational method.

8. In Dicken formula, the value of coefficient C_D for Western ghat areas is

(*a*) 32 (*b*) 45
(*c*) 85 (*d*) 18.5.

9. In Ryve's formula the value of coefficient C_R for the areas near the hill varies from

(*a*) minimum 10.1 to maximum upto 40.0
(*b*) 5.0 to 7.5
(*c*) 16.5 to 20.5
(*d*) 1 to 1.5.

10. Nawab Jang Bahadur formula is used for computation of

(*a*) discharge rate through rills
(*b*) flood flow for old Hyderabad state
(*c*) both '*a*' and '*b*'
(*d*) peak flood.

11. Return period is the reciprocal of

(*a*) plotting position (*b*) recurrence interval
(*c*) both '*a*' and '*b*' (*d*) skewness cofficient.

12. Plotting position is the reciprocal of

(*a*) recurrence interval (*b*) return period
(*c*) both '*a*' and '*b*' (*d*) probability.

13. Return period and recurrence interval represent the

(*a*) same meaning (*b*) different meaning
(*c*) none of the above (*d*) peak event.

14. If probability of occurrence of an ordinary flood is 25%, then what would be its recurrence interval.

(*a*) 4 years (*b*) 25 years
(*c*) 100 years (*d*) 50 years.

15. If $T = \frac{n+1}{m}$, then plotting position (p) will be

(*a*) $\frac{m.T}{n+1}$ (*b*) $\frac{m}{n+1}$
(*c*) $\frac{n+1}{T}$ (*d*) $\frac{m}{n}$.

16. An event of high return period has

(*a*) less probability (*b*) high plotting position
(*c*) both '*a*' and '*b*' (*d*) 50% probability.

17. An event of small magnitude involves

(*a*) high probability (*b*) less return period
(*c*) both '*a*' and '*b*' (*d*) 1% probability.

18. The probability of exceedance of flood event with the return period of 15 years will be as

(*a*) 6.6% (*b*) 15%
(*c*) 10.6% (*d*) 10 years.

19. The value of frequency factor *K* for Foster type-I distribution varies from

(*a*) 6 to 8.5 (*b*) 10 to 8.5
(*c*) 15 to 18.5. (*d*) 1 to 5.

20. Partial-duration curve is the plot of

(*a*) probability and flood discharge
(*b*) return period and flood stage
(*c*) both '*a*' and '*b*'
(*d*) rainfall and runoff.

21. The value of runoff coefficient in Nawab Jang Bahadur formula is taken as

(*a*) 48 to 69 (*b*) 10.5
(*c*) 5.5 (*d*) 23.85.

22. Levee is used for

(*a*) flood protection (*b*) control of sediment yield
(*c*) both '*a*' and '*b*' (*d*) erosion control.

23. Muck ditch is the component of

(*a*) levee (*b*) flood wall
(*c*) drop-inlet spillway (*d*) retaining wall

24. The top width of levee for more than 3.25 m height varies from

(*a*) 2.5 to 3.5 m (*b*) less than 2.5 m
(*c*) 3.5 m or more (*d*) 1.5 to 2.0 m.

25. Width of muck ditch varies from

(*a*) 1.5 to 3.0 m (*b*) 3.0 to 4.5 m
(*c*) 4.5 to 7.5 m (*d*) 0.5 to 1.0 m.

26. The overtopping of flood water compensated by providing the additional height to the hydraulic structure is called

(*a*) free board (*b*) effective height
(*c*) none of above (*d*) allowance for settlement

27. Flood walls are constructed almost

(*a*) parallel to the water course
(*b*) across the water course
(*c*) both '*a*' and '*b*'
(*d*) along the water course.

28. By-pass channels are constructed for protecting

(*a*) large cities
(*b*) valuable properties
(*c*) both '*a*' and '*b*'
(*d*) hydraulic structures.

29. The cut-off is constructed for

(*a*) reducing flood stage and its period
(*b*) reducing flow velocity
(*c*) controlling soil loss
(*d*) none of the above.

30. The warning zone involves
   (*a*) less effect of flood (*b*) much effect of flood
   (*c*) medium effect of flood (*d*) wide river course.

31 Restrictive zone is also called
   (*a*) flood fringe zone (*b*) warning zone
   (*c*) alarming area (*d*) none of the above.

32. The construction of housing colonies is allowed in
   (*a*) restrictive zone of flood plain
   (*b*) prohibitive zone of flood plain.
   (*c*) warning zone of flood plain
   (*d*) both '*a*' and '*b*'

33. Prohibitive zone is extended from
   (*a*) levee to river bank
   (*b*) middle of the river course to some distance away in the adjoining areas, both sides of river
   (*c*) both '*a*' and '*b*'
   (*d*) middle of the river course to the embankment.

34. Multiple-correlation method is used for
   (*a*) river gauging (*b*) flood forecasting
   (*c*) both '*a*' and '*b*' (*d*) derivation of UHG.

35. The flood forecasting stations in India are at
   (*a*) New Delhi, Calcutta, Madras, Bombay and Nagpur
   (*b*) New Delhi, Lucknow, Calcutta, Madras and Bombay
   (*c*) New Delhi, Lucknow, Calcutta, Madras and Bangalore
   (*d*) Patna, Lucknow, Madras, Guvahati and Udaipur.

Answer (Objective Type Question)

1. (*a*)	**2.** (*c*)	**3.** (*a*)	**4.** (*a*)	**5.** (*b*)	**6.** (*c*)	**7.** (*a*)	**8.** (*a*)
9. (*a*)	**10.** (*b*)	**11.** (*a*)	**12.** (*c*)	**13.** (*a*)	**14.** (*a*)	**15.** (*b*)	**16.** (*a*)
17. (*a*)	**18.** (*a*)	**19.** (*a*)	**20.** (*a*)	**21.** (*a*)	**22.** (*a*)	**23.** (*a*)	**24.** (*a*)
25. (*a*)	**26.** (*a*)	**27.** (*a*)	**28.** (*c*)	**29.** (*a*)	**30.** (*b*)	**31.** (*a*)	**32.** (*a*)
33. (*b*)	**34.** (*b*)	**35.** (*a*)					

9

Flood Routing

Prediction of outflow hydrograph for any station on down stream side corresponding to the known inflow hydrograph of one or more stations towards up stream side is called flood routing. It has following importance :

1. It acts as a tool for flood forecasting.
2. Provides a guide line for installation of the flood protection structures.
3. The design of reservoirs and spillways can also be performed based on the flood routing techniques.

The flood routing is of following two types :

1. Channel routing, and
2. Reservoir routing.

9.1. Channel Routing

In channel routing, the outflow hydrograph at any point towards down stream side of the gauging station is determined, based on the known inflow hydrograph of upstream side of gauging station. In other words "under channel routing the change in shape of hydrograph is determined as flood water moves from up stream to down stream side. Channel routing provides the information on flood occurrence in the river/stream.

9.2. Reservoir Routing

In this routing, the reservoir's stage and storage volume due to outflow hydrograph is determined with the helf of known inflow hydrograph. For this purpose, the following database are required :

1. Storage *Vs* elevation curve.
2. Outflow *Vs* elevation curve.
3. Inflow hydrograph
4. Initial values of storage (*S*), inflow (*I*) and outflow (*O*) rates.

9.3. Basic Equation

Continuity equation is used for all types of hydrologic routings, which states that the difference of inflow and outflow rates is equal to the rate of change of storage. If inflow rate, outflow rate and storage are I, O and S, respectively, then continuity equation is given by :

$$I - O = \frac{dS}{dt} \quad ...(9.1)$$

For a small routing time Δt, the equation 9.1 can be written as :

$$\left(\frac{I_1 + I_2}{2}\right)\Delta t - \left(\frac{O_1 + O_2}{2}\right)\Delta t = S_2 - S_1 \quad ...(9.2)$$

(**Note.** The length of routing time Δt should be very small so that, the segment of hydrograph at beginning and end of it (i.e. Δt) should be as straight line).

Differential form of continuity equation is given by :

$$\frac{\partial Q}{\partial x} + T \cdot \frac{\partial y}{\partial t} = 0 \quad ..(9.3)$$

in which, Q is the discharge rate, T is the top width of flow and 'y' is the flow depth. This equation holds good for unsteady flow condition, provided that there should not be lateral flow.

9.4. Channel Routing Techniques

There are various methods for channel routing; however followings are the main :

1. Muskingum method
2. Muskingum crest segment method, and
3. Graphical Method.

Muskingum Method

In continuity equation, the variables I_1, I_2, O_1 and S_1 are known, and O_2 and S_2 are unknown. For determining the values of these two variables, there should be two relationships, in which one is already available *i.e.* equation 9.2 and second relationship is needed. The second relationship should be in terms of O_2 and S_2, such that the O_2 is the function of S_2, *i.e.*

$$O_2 = f(S_2) \quad ...(9.4)$$

To simplify the equation 9.4, Linstey *et al* (1949) suggested that, the channel storage is the sum of two types of storages *i.e.* prism storage and wedge storage, which are explained as under :

Prism Storage : It is the storage, below the imaginary line drawn parallel to the stream bed. The prism storage is the function of outflow only *i.e.*

$$S_p = f(O) \quad ...(9.5)$$

in which, S_p is the prism storage and O is the outflow of stream.

Wedge Storage : Storage between the top water surface and imaginary line, drawn parallel to the stream bed is called wedge storage. It is shown in Fig. 9.1. The wedge storage depends on the difference of inflow and outflow

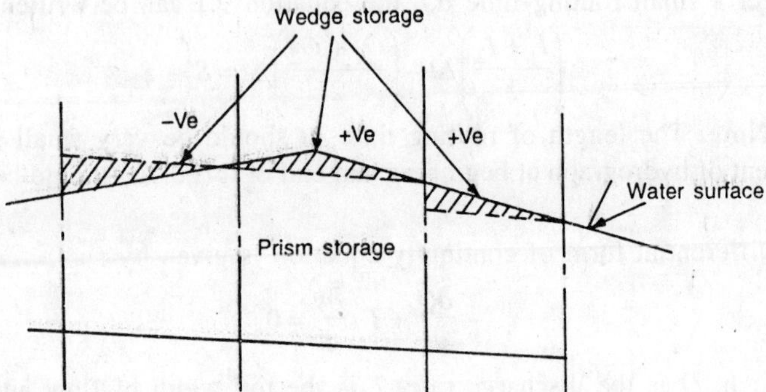

Fig. 9.1. Prism and Wedge storage.

rates of the stream flow. It gets reduced during falling stage, is taken as –ve storage, while it increases during rising stage, is counted as + ve storage. Wedge storage is expressed by the following expression :

$$S_w = f(I) \qquad ...(9.6)$$

in which, S_w is the wedge storage and I is the inflow into stream. The sum of prism storage and wedge storage is the total stream storage, given as :

$$S = S_p + S_w \qquad ...(9.7)$$

Simplified form of eqn 9.7 is given as under :

$$S = K\left[xI^m + (1-x)\,O^m\right] \qquad ...(9.8)$$

where K and x = coefficient

m = exponent; its value depends on the type of channal.

For natural channels, the m is taken as 1 and for rectangular channels it is as 0.6. For natural channel, the equation 9.8 is given by

$$S = K\,[xI + (1-x)\,O] \qquad ...(9.9)$$

This equation is known as Muskingum formula, shows a linear relationship amongst S,I and O. In equation 9.9 'x' is the *"weighing factor"* and K is the storage constant, which is very close to the travel time of channel reach. The unit of K is time and x is the dimension less. The value of x varies from 0 to 0.3 for natural channels. A channel is said to be linear, when value of x is zero. Storage equation for linear channel is given as :

$$S = K \cdot O \qquad ...(9.10)$$

In equation 9.9, the values of x and K are unknown. For routing of channel flow these two are essentially required. Procedure of K and x is described as under :

9.4.1. Determination of 'K' and 'x'

The values of 'K' and 'x' are determined by using the following steps :

1. Compute the values of 'S' for different time periods based on the given data of I and O.

2. Take an arbitrary value of x within 0 to 0.3.

3. Calculate the values of $[xI + ((1 - x) 0]$ for different time periods, for selected value of 'x'.

4. Plot S Vs $[xI + (I - x) O]$ data on graph paper. If curve is obtained as straight line, then selected value of 'x' is considered to be correct; otherwise, select another trial value of 'x' and repeat the same procedure till a straight line is obtained.

5. Find out the value of 'K', which is the inverse slope of straight line, obtained in step (4).

Example 9.1 explains the procedure for determining the K and x values.

Example 9.1. *Determine the coefficient K and weighing factor x of Muskingum equation from the following inflow and outflow hydrographs of a given watershed :*

Time (h)	*0*	*12*	*24*	*36*	*48*	*60*	*72*	*84*	*96*	*108*
Inflow (m^3/s)	25	115	565	730	446	235	134	85	57	40
Outflow((m^3/s)	29	42	277	614	628	384	225	132	83	50

Solution. Computation is shown in Table 9.1. The values of x and K are determined by plotting the storage (S) and $xI + (1 - x) O$ for different values of x (*i.e.* 0.2 and 0.25). The curve, which is in straight line is selected for the purpose. The value of 'x' for which straight line is obtained, is taken as the correct value. In this problem, the value of 'x' is obtained as 0.25. Value of K is determined as the inverse slope of the straight line, which came to be 0.32 day. Plottings are shown in Fig. 9.2. In this way, we have

$$x = 0.25$$

and $$K = 0.32 \text{ day.}$$

Tale 9.1. Computation of 'K and x

Time (h)	Inflow ($m^3/s(I)$)	Outflot m^3/s (0)	$\frac{I_1+I_2}{2} = \bar{I}$	$\frac{O_1+O_2}{2} = \bar{O}$	$\bar{I} \cdot \Delta t$	$\bar{O} \cdot \Delta t$	$S = (\bar{I}\,\Delta t - \bar{O}\,\Delta t)$ Co. 6 – Col. (7)	Cumulative storage (M.m)	x = 0.20			x = 0.25		
									XI = Col. (2) × .2	(1 – x)OCol. (3) × .8	XI + (1 – x)O Col. (10) + Col. (11)	XI = 0.25I	(1 – x) O = 0.75 O	XI + (1 – x) O
(1)	(2)	(3)	(4)	(5)	(6)	(7)	(8)	(9)	(10)	(11)	(12)	(13)	(14)	(15)
0	25	29							5.0	23.2	28.2	6.25	21.75	28.0
			70	35.5	3.02	1.53	1.50	1.50						
12	115	42							23.0	33.6	56.6	28.75	31.50	60.25
			340	159.5	14.70	6.89	7.80	9.30						
24	565	277							113.0	221.6	334.6	141.25	207.75	349.0
			647.5	445.5	27.97	19.25	8.70	18.00						
36	730	614							146.0	491.2	637.2	182.50	460.50	643.0
			588.0	621.0	25.40	26.83	-1.40	16.60						
48	446	628							89.2	502.4	591.6	111.50	471.0	582.5
			340.5	506.0	14.69	21.86	-7.20	9.40						
60	235	384							47.0	307.2	354.2	58.75	288.0	346.75
			184.5	304.5	7.97	13.15	-5.20	4.20						
72	134	225							26.8	180.0	206.8	33.50	168.75	202.25
			109.5	178.5	4.73	7.71	-3.00	1.20						
84	85	132							17.0	105.6	122.6	21.25	99.00	102.25
			71.0	107.5	3.07	4.64	-1.60	-0.40						
96	57	83							11.4	66.4	77.8	14.25	62.25	76.50
			48.5	66.5	2.10	2.87	-0.80	-1.20						
108	40	50							8.0	40.0	48.0	37.50	37.50	47.50

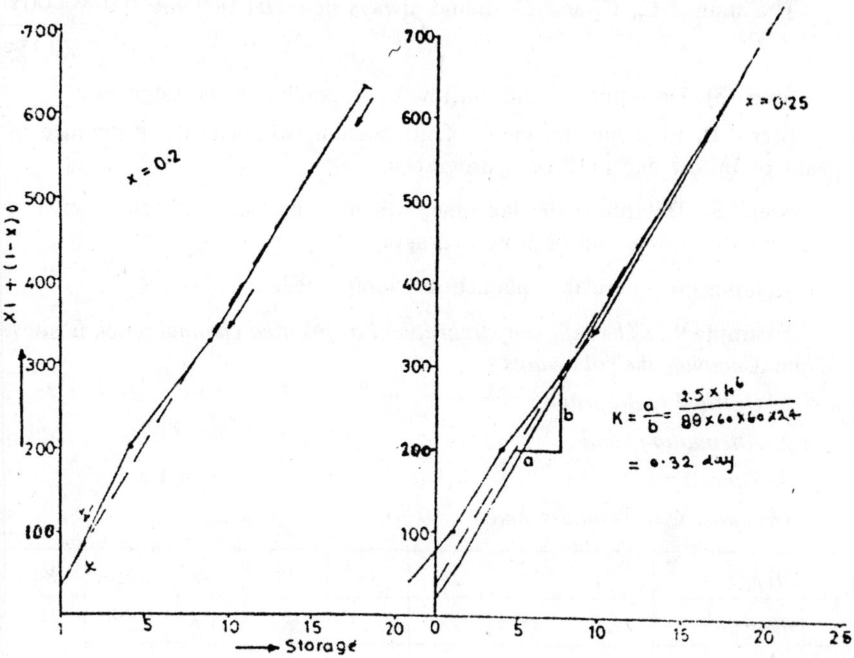

Fig. 9.2

9.4.2. Routing Procedure

It follows following steps:

Step (1). Find out the values of K and x as described earlier.

Step (2). Calculate the outflow hydrograph based on the given inflow hydrograph, by using the Muskingum routing equation, given as under:

$$O_2 = C_o I_2 + C_1 I_1 + C_2 O_1 \quad \text{...(9.11)}$$

where, O_2 = outflow of the channel

I_2 = inflow rate at the end of routing time, Δt

I_1 = inflow rate at the beginning of routing time, Δt

O_1 = outflow rate at the beginning of routing time, Δt

C_0, C_1 and C_2 = constants, which are determined by using the following formulae

$$C_0 = \frac{Kx + 0.5\,\Delta t}{K - K \cdot x + 0.5\,\Delta t} \quad \text{...(9.12)}$$

$$C_1 = \frac{-K \cdot x + 0.5\,\Delta t}{K - K \cdot x + 0.5\,\Delta t} \quad \text{...(9.13)}$$

$$C_2 = \frac{K - K \cdot x - 0.5\,\Delta t}{K - K \cdot x + 0.5\,\Delta t} \quad \text{...(9.14)}$$

The sum of C_0, C_1 and C_2 should always be equal to 1 *i.e.*

$$C_0 + C_1 + C_1 = 1 \qquad ...(9.15)$$

Step (3). Draw inflow and outflow hydrographs on the same axis.

Step (4). Find out the value of attenuation, which is the difference of peaks of inflow and outflow hydrographs.

Step (5). Determine the lag time, which is the time difference between peaks of the inflow and outflow hydrographs.

Routing procedure is explained in example 9.2.

Example 9.2. *The inflow hydrograph of a specified channel reach is given below. Compute the followings :*

1. Outflow hydrograph

2. Attenuation, and

3. Time lag

(Assume K = 24 hours and x = 0.20)

Time (h)	*0*	*12*	*24*	*36*	*48*	*60*	*72*	*84*
Inflow (m^3/s)	*32*	*35*	*78*	*262*	*332*	*278*	*230*	*188*
Time (h)	*96*	*108*	*120*	*132*	*144*	*156*	*168*	*180*
Inflow (m^3/s)	*152*	*123*	*100*	*80*	*69*	*58*	*51*	*46*

Solution. Given that the $K = 24$ hours or 1 day

$x = 0.20$

Routing period $(\Delta) = 12$ hours $= 0.5$ day

(1) Computation of C_0, C_1 and C_2 :

$$C_0 = \frac{K \cdot x + 0.5\Delta t}{K - Kx + .5\Delta t}$$

$$= \frac{1 \times .2 + .5 \times .5}{1 - 1 \times .2 + .5 \times .5}$$

$$= \mathbf{0.05}$$

$$C_1 = \frac{-K \cdot x + .5\Delta t}{K - Kx + .5\Delta t}$$

$$= \frac{1 \times .2 + .5 \times .5}{1.05} = \mathbf{0.43}$$

$$C_2 = \frac{K - Kx - .5\Delta t}{K - Kx + .5\Delta t}$$

$$= \frac{1 - 1 \times .2 - .5 \times .5}{1.05} = \mathbf{.52}$$

$$\begin{pmatrix} \textbf{Check. } C_0 + C_1 + C_2 = 1 \\ 0.05 + .43 + .52 = 1 \end{pmatrix}$$

Substitute the values of C_0, C_1, and C_2 in equation (9.11)

$$O_2 = 0.05I_2 + .43I_1 + 0.52O_1$$

(2) Computation of outflow hydrograph

Time (h)	*Inflow (m3/s)*	$0.05I_2$	$0.43I_1$	$0.52O_1$	*Outflow* (O_2) *Col (3) + Col(4) + Col (5)*	*Remarks*
(1)	*(2)*	*(3)*	*(4)*	*(5)*	*(6)*	
0	32	—	—	—	32.0 *	
12	35	1.75	13.76	16.64	32.15	
24	78	3.90	15.05	16.72	35.67	
36	262	13.10	33.54	18.55	65.19	
48	332	16.60	112.66	33.89	163.15	
60	278	13.90	142.66	84.84	241.50	* At begining O_1 is the same as inflow I_l = 32 m^3/s.
72	230	11.50	119.54	125.58	256.62	
84	188	9.40	98.90	133.44	241.74	
96	152	7.60	80.84	125.70	214.14	
108	123	6.15	65.36	113.35	184.86	
120	100	5.00	52.89	96.13	154.02	
132	80	4.00	43.00	80.10	127.10	
144	69	3.45	34.40	66.10	103.95	
156	58	2.90	29.67	54.05	86.62	
168	51	2.55	24.94	45.04	72.53	
180	46	2.30	21.93	37.72	61.95	

(3). Computation of attenuation and time lag

It is performed by plotting the inflow and outflow hydrographs on the same graph sheet, as shown in Fig. 9.3. From figure, the attenuation is obtained as 75 m^3/s and lag time as 24 hours, which indicates that the peak

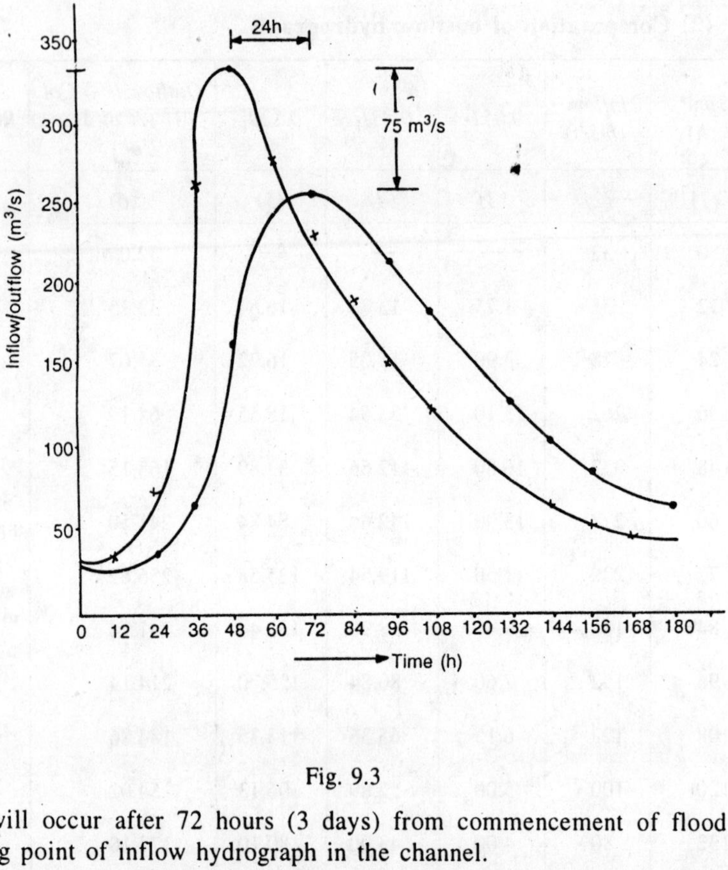

Fig. 9.3

flow will occur after 72 hours (3 days) from commencement of flood at gauging point of inflow hydrograph in the channel.

9.5. Muskingum Crest Segment Routing Method

In this method of flood routing only that portion of inflow hydrograph is routed, which is close to the crest/peak segment. Computation is performed by using the equation 9.11

$$O_n = K_1 I_n + K_2 I_{n-1} + K_3 I_{n-2} + \ldots\ldots K_n I_1 \qquad \ldots(9.16)$$

where

$$\left.\begin{aligned} K_1 &= C_0 \\ K_2 &= C_0 C_2 + C_1 \\ K_3 &= K_2 C_2 \\ K_n &= K_{n-1} C_2 \qquad \text{when } n > 2 \end{aligned}\right\} \qquad \ldots(9.17)$$

The equation 9.16 can be used for computing the routed flow at any time, without routing the entire inflow hydrograph. Example 9.3 explains the procedure of routing the channel flow by using Muskingum crest segment method.

Example 9.3. *From the inflow hydrograph given in example 9.2, calculate the outflow at 36-hour duration by using Muskingum crest segment technique.*

Solution. Given that

$n = 4$ (*i.e.* the time at which outflow is to determine)

$C = 0.05, \; C_1 = 0.43$ *and* $C_2 = 0.52.$

The outflow at $n = 4$ is given by

$$O_n = K_1 I_n + K_2 I_{n-1} + K_3 I_{n-2} + \ldots\ldots K_n I_1$$

where,

$$K_1 = C_0 = \mathbf{0.05}$$

$$K_2 = C_0 C_2 + C_1$$
$$= 0.05 \times 0.52 + 0.43 = \mathbf{0.46}$$

$$K_3 = K_2 \cdot C_2$$
$$= 0.46 \times 0.52 = \mathbf{0.24}$$

$$K_4 = K_{n-1} \cdot C_2 \qquad \text{(for } n > 2\text{)}$$
$$= K_3 \cdot C_2$$
$$= 0.24 \times 0.52 = \mathbf{0.12}$$

$\therefore$

$$O_4 = K_1 I_4 + K_2 I_3 + K_3 I_2 + K_4 I_1$$

in which,

$I_1 = 32 \text{ m}^3/\text{s} \qquad I_2 = 35 \text{ m}^3/\text{s}$

$I_3 = 78 \text{ m}^3/\text{s} \qquad I_4 = 262 \text{ m}^3/\text{s}$

$\therefore$ $\mathbf{O_4 = 61.22 \text{ m}^3/\text{s}}$ **Ans.**

Example 9.4. *Compute the outflow at 60-hour duration from the inflow hydrograph given in exmaple 9.2, by using Muskingum crest segment method.*

Solution. Given that $n = 6$

$C_0 = 0.05, \; C_1 = 0.43$ and $C_2 = 0.52$

The outflow at $n = 6$ is given as

$$O_n = K_1 I_n + K_2 I_{n-1} + K_3 I_{n-2} + \ldots\ldots K_n I_1$$

$\therefore$

$$O_6 = K_1 I_6 + K_2 I_5 + K_3 I_4 + K_4 I_3 + K_5 I_2 + K_6 I_1$$

in which,

$$K_1 = C_0 = 0.05$$

$$K_2 = C_0 \cdot C_2 + C_1$$
$$= 0.05 \times 0.52 + 0.43 = \mathbf{0.46}$$

$K_3 = \mathbf{0.24} \qquad K_6 = K_5 \cdot C_2$

$K_4 = \mathbf{0.12} \qquad\qquad = 0.06 \times 0.52 = \mathbf{0.03}$

$$K_5 = K_{n-2} \cdot C_2$$
$$= K_4 \cdot C_2$$
$$= 0.12 \times 0.52 = \mathbf{0.06}$$

and, $I_1 = 32 \text{ m}^3/\text{s}$ $I_2 = 35 \text{ m}^3/\text{s}$

$I_3 = 78 \text{ m}^3/\text{s}$ $I_4 = 262 \text{ m}^3/\text{s}$

$I_5 = 332 \text{ m}^3/\text{s}$ $I_6 = 278 \text{ m}^3/\text{s}$

Substituting these values and solving for O_6, we have

$$O_6 = \mathbf{241.92 \text{ m}^3/\text{s}} \quad \textbf{Ans.}$$

9.6. Graphical Method

This method was developed by U.S. Weather Bureau, is generally known by the name of U.S. Weather method. It is described as under :

U.S. Weather Bureau Method : This method involves following two parameters for determining under channel routing :

1. Lag time (L), and
2. Coefficient (K)

Considering the equation 9.9, *i.e.*

$$S = K[xI + (1-x)O]$$

At constant K and $x = 0$, the equation 9.9 is reduced to

$$S = K[O] \quad \text{...(9.18)}$$

Differentiating the equation 9.17 with respect to time (t), we have,

$$\frac{dS}{dt} = K \cdot \frac{dO}{dt} \quad \text{...(9.19)}$$

Left hand side term of this equation indicates the rate of change in storage, which is equal to inflow-outflow. Thus,

$$\frac{dS}{dt} = I - O \quad \text{...(9.20)}$$

Comparing the equation 9.19 and 9.20, we have,

$$K\frac{dO}{dt} = I - O$$

or

$$\frac{dO}{dt} = \frac{I-O}{K} \quad \text{...(9.21)}$$

The term $\left(\frac{I-O}{K}\right)$ is the change in outflow with respect to time. According to it, if values of I and K are known then outflow can be computed by using the inflow hydrograph of any section of river/stream. Computation procedure of I & K is described as under :

1. **Lag time** (*L*) : It is determined by drawing a horizontal line from point *A* to the previous hydrograph which cuts at point *B*, (Fig. 9.4.). The time between point *A* and *B* is taken as '*L*'.

2. **Computation of '*K*'** : It is computed by using the following steps :

1. Draw inflow hydrograph by lagging '*L*' hours, as shown in Fig. 9.5.

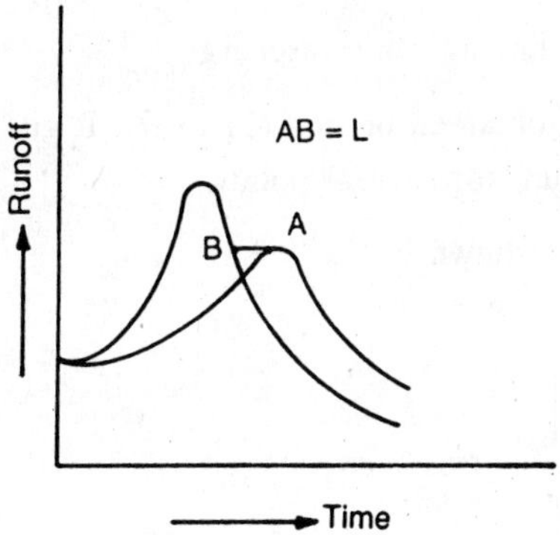

Fig. 9.4

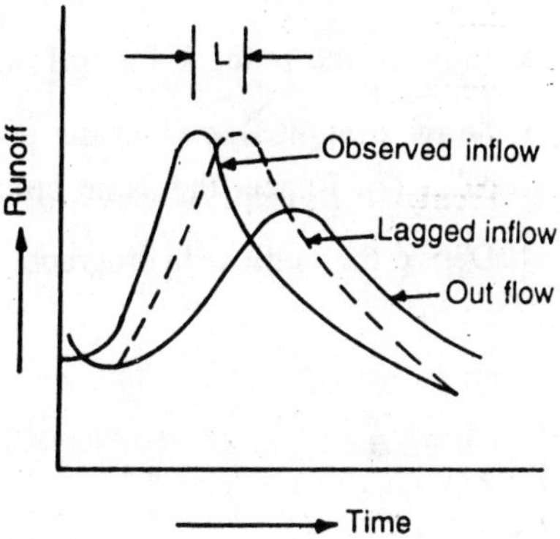

Fig. 9.5

2. Take an arbitrary point '*a*' on the rising limb of inflow hydrograph (Fig. 9.6) and draw a vertical line to cut the outflow hydrograph at point '*b*'.

3. Draw a horizontal line from point '*a*'to cut the outflow hydrograph.

4. Draw a tangential line from point '*b*' in such a way that, it cut the horizontal line at point '*z*'.

5. Measure the time from point *a* to *z*; it is the value of '*K*'.

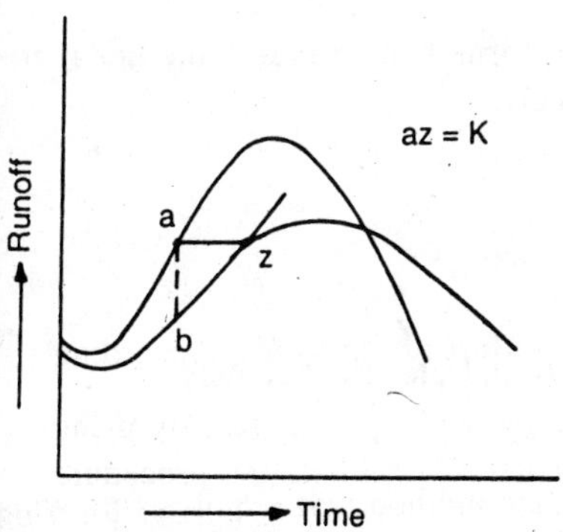

Fig. 9.6

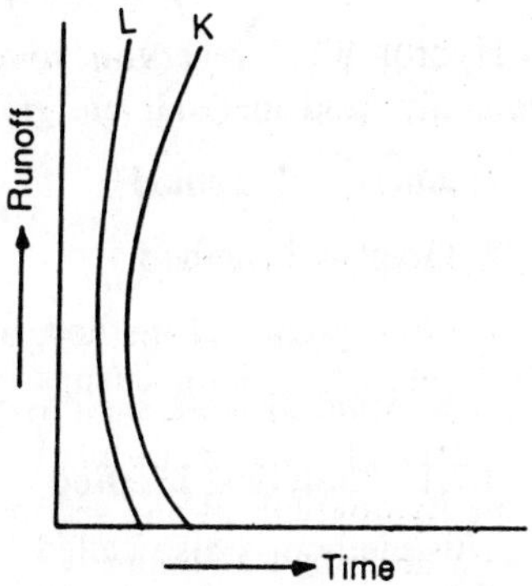

Fig. 9.7

6. By repeating the same procedure, compute several values of 'K' for different points on the inflow hydrograph and plot the same as shown in Fig. 9.7.

Derivation of Outflow Hydrograph

After determining the values of L and K, the outflow hydrograph is derived by using the following steps :

1. Lag the inflow hydrograph for the duration 'L', as shown in Fig. 9.8.

2. Indicate the point K for inflow I_2 having same discharge.

3. Draw straight line from the point obtained in step (2) to O_1. It gives the slope at O_2. Repeat the same procedure for several points.

4. Derive the outflow hydrograph. It is shown in Fig. 9.9.

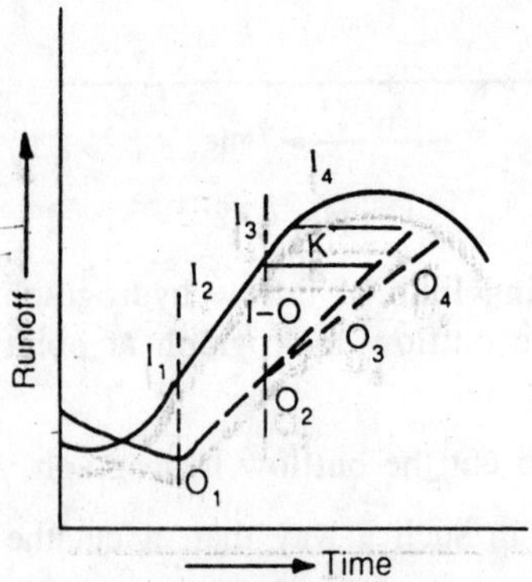

Fig. 9.8

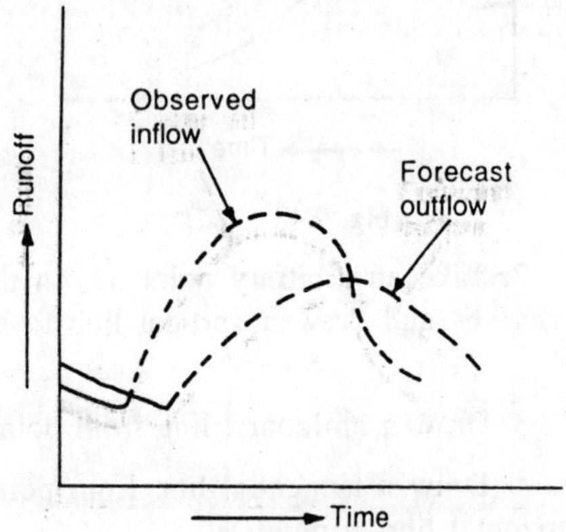

Fig. 9.9

9.7. Reservoir Routing Techniques

Hydrological reservoir routing is performed by several methods; the commonly used methods are given as under :

1. Analytical method
2. Graphical method
3. Semi-graphical method, and
4. Routing devices such as mechanical and electrical routers.

9.7.1. Analytical Method

This method is also called "Step-by-Step method". It requires following data for reservoir routing :

1. Inflow hydrograph
2. Reservoir's inflow-elevation curve.
3. Reservoirs outflow-elevation curve.

Considering the continuity equation for routing time Δt in following from

$$\left(\frac{I_1+I_2}{2}\right)\Delta t-\left(\frac{O_1+O_2}{2}\right)\Delta t=S_2-S_1 \quad \text{...(9.22)}$$

In this equation, except O_2 and S_2 all parameters are known. Rearranging the equation 9.22 in following from :

$$\left(\frac{I_1+I_2}{2}\right)\Delta t+\left(S_1-\frac{O_1}{2}\Delta t\right)=S_2+\frac{O_2}{2}\Delta t \quad \text{...(9.23)}$$

To determine the values of O_2 and S_2 there should be two equations, in which one is already available as the equation 9.22 or 9.23. The second equation should be in the form of outflow and storage. Reservoir routing under this method is performed by using the following steps :

1. Divide the inflow hydrograph into various segments in such a way that, each segment can be in straight line and time interval should also be such that the crest point of hydrograph may not be missed. Usually, 3 to 12-h interval is most appropriate.

2. At the point where inflow hydrograph impinges, fix the reservoir's level.

3. Draw discharge rating curve for the outlet and spillway.

4. Calculate $\left(\frac{I_1+I_2}{2}\right)\Delta t$ by using the given inflow hydrograph.

5. Take trial value of reservoir's final level.

6. Find out outflow for the assumed value of reservoir's level by using the discharge rating curve derived in step (3).

7. Calculate $\left(\frac{O_1+O_2}{2}\right)\Delta t$.

8. Find out the change in storage by substracting the outflow from inflow [*i.e.* step (7) – step (4)].

9. Calculate S_2, which is the sum of S_1 and change in storage obtained in step (8).

10. Determine reservoir elevation for computed value of S_2 and tally with the assumed reservoir elevation in step (5). If it is tallied, then computed reservoir elevation is O.K. Otherwise, again assume another trial value of

reservoir's elevation and repeat the same procedure upto step (10), until the computed reservoir's level exceeds the assumed value or outflow hydrograph crosses the inflow hydrograph.

11. Perform all the steps, till the level of reservoir attains the level of preflood.

A sample calculation is shown in example 9.5.

Example 9.5. *Calculate the outflow hydrograph from the following inflow hydrograph. Reservoir impinged, when it is filled to its maximum level of 550.0 m and spillway gates are kept closed.*

Inflow (m^3/s)	*Time interval(h)*	*Inflow (m^3/s)*	*Time interval (h)*
2416.67	50–55	300.00	0–5
3273.65	55–60	302.80	5–10
4224.27	60–65	312.88	10–10
5220.84	65–70	331.85	15–20
6573.51	70–75	367.16	20–25
8390.08	75–80	424.41	25–30
10,246.5	80–85	581.88	30–35
1074.6	85–90	682.22	35–40
10,994.22	90–95	1018.04	40–45
11,000.0	95–100	1641.13	45–50

Solution. Computations are shown in Table 9.2.

Table 9.2 Computations shwing the reservoir routing

Step	Time interval	Inflow (I_1)	Inflow (I_2)	$\left(\frac{I_1+I_2}{2}\right)\Delta t \times 3600 \times 10^{-6}$ ($M.m^3$)	Rservoir level	Outflow (0_1)	Outflow (0_2)	$\left(\frac{O_1+O_2}{2}\right)\Delta t$ $M.m^3$	ΔS Col. (5) – Col. (9)	Total storage at Δt time interval	Actual reservoir level
(1)	(2)	(3)	(4)	(5)	(6)	(7)	(8)	(9)	(10)	(11)	(12)
1	0—3	300.00	302.80	3.26	550.00	300.00	302.80	3.26	0.00	350.50	550.00
2	3—6	302.80	312.88	3.32	550.00	302.80	312.88	3.32	0.00	350.50	550.00
3	6—9	312.88	331.85	3.48	550.00	312.88	331.85	3.48	0.00	350.50	550.00
4	9—12	331.85	367.16	3.77	550.00	331.85	367.16	3.77	0.00	350.50	550.00
5	12—15	367.16	424.41	4.27	550.00	367.16	424.41	4.27	0.00	350.50	550.00
6	15—18	424.41	518.88	5.09	550.00	424.41	518.88	5.09	0.00	350.50	550.00
7	18—21	518.88	682.22	6.49	550.00	518.88	682.22	6.49	0.00	350.50	550.00
8	21—24	682.22	1018.04	9.18	550.00	682.22	1018.04	9.18	0.00	350.50	550.00
9	24—27	1018.04	1641.67	14.36	550.00	1018.04	1641.13	14.36	0.00	350.00	550.00
10	27—30	1641.13	2416.67	21.91	550.00	1641.13	2416.67	21.91	0.00	350.00	550.00
11	30—33	2416.67	3273.65	30.73	550.00	2416.67	3273.65	30.73	0.00	350.00	550.00
12	33—36	3273.65	4224.27	40.49	550.00	3273.65	4224.07	40.49	0.00	350.00	550.00
13	36—39	4224.27	5220.84	51.00	550.20	4224.07	4980.00	49.70	1.30	351.80	550.20
14	39—42	5220.84	6573.51	63.69	551.05	4980.00	5560.00	56.92	6.77	358.57	551.05

(contd.)

(1)	(2)	(3)	(4)	(5)	(6)	(7)	(8)	(9)	(10)	(11)	(12)
15	42—45	6573.51	8390.08	80.80	552.75	5560.00	6840.72	66.96	13.84	372.41	552.75
16	45—48	8390.08	10,246.50	100.64	554.80	6840.72	8500.00	82.84	17.80	390.21	554.80
17	48—51	10,246.50	10,740.00	113.33	555.70	8500.00	9260.00	85.90	17.43	407.64	555.70
18	51—54	10,740.00	10,994.22	117.36	556.35	9260.00	9800.00	102.92	14.44	422.08	556.35
19	54—57	10,994.22	11,000.00	118.76	556.55	9800.00	9310.00	103.19	15.57	437.65	556.55
20	57—60	11,000.00	9850.00	112.59	556.85	9310.00	8640.00	96.93	15.66	453.31	556.85
21	70—71.5	9850.00	9600.00	105.03	556.80	8640.0	7920.00	89.42	15.61	468.92	556.80
22	71.5—73	9600.00	8350.00	52.52	556.45	7920.0	6220.00	76.36	-23.84	445.08	556.45
23	73—74.5	8350.00	8756.00	46.19	556.83	6220.0	4968.00	60.41	-14.22	430.86	555.83
24	74.5—76	8756.00	5000.35	37.14	555.03	4920.0	—	—	—	—	—
25	76—77.5	5000.35	—	—	—	—	—	—	—	—	—

The inflow and outflow hydrographs are sketched by plotting the data of Col (3) and Col (8), as shown in Fig. 9.10. Finally, from figure the reservoir lag (L) is determined as 3-h and reduction in peak (*i.e.* attenuation) as 1200 m^3/s.

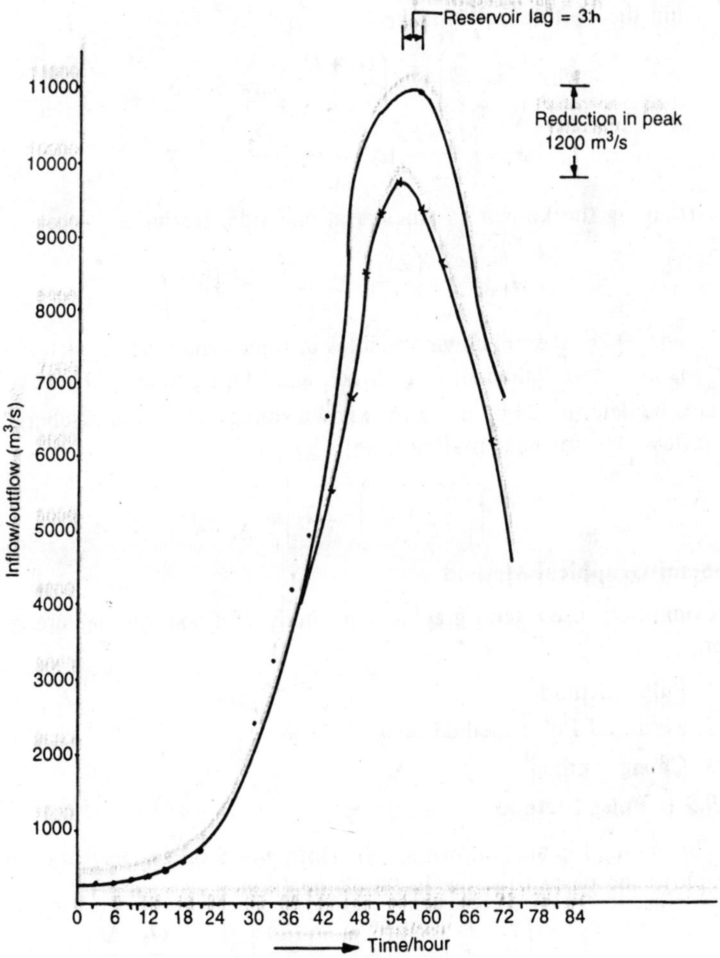

Fig. 9.10

9.8. Graphical Method

This method was developed by Goodrich (1931); due to this reason, sometimes it is also known as Goodrich Method. It requires following data for routing :

1. Inflow hydrograph.
2. Storage-elevation curve
3. Storage-discharge curve
4. Routing time (Δt), which should be very small, so that the change in inflow and out flow rates may be uniform.

Using the routing equation *i.e.*,

$$\left(\frac{I_1 + I_2}{2}\right)\Delta t - \left(\frac{O_1 + O_2}{2}\right)\Delta t = S_2 - S_1 \qquad ...(9.24)$$

or

$$S_1 + \left(\frac{I_1 + I_2}{2}\right)\Delta t - \left(\frac{O_1 + O_2}{2}\right)\Delta t = S_2 \qquad ...(9.25)$$

Arranging the known parameters at one side, we have

$$(I_1 + I_2) + \left(\frac{2S_1}{\Delta t} - O_1\right) = \left(2\frac{S_2}{\Delta t} + O_2\right) \qquad ...(9.26)$$

In eqn. 9.26, the unknown variables at right hand side are determined on the basis of known values of I_1, I_2, S_1, O_1 and routing time Δt. However, these can also be determined by using the known storage-elevation-discharge curve. The inflow rate for next routing time is given as :

$$\left[\left(\frac{2S_2}{\Delta t} + O_2\right) - 2O_2\right] = \frac{2S_1}{\Delta t} - O_1 \qquad ...(9.27)$$

9.9. Semi-Graphical Method

Commonly used semi-graphical methods of flood routing are given as under :

1. Pulse method
2. Modified Pulse method, and
3. Cheng method.

9.9.1. Pulse Method

This method is also known as ISD (Inflow – Storage-Discharge) method. It employs the basic equation in following form :

$$\left(\frac{I_1 + I_2}{2}\right)\Delta t + \left(S_1 - \frac{O_1 \cdot \Delta t}{2}\right) = \left(S_2 - \frac{O_2 \cdot \Delta t}{2}\right) \qquad ...(9.28)$$

In equation 9.27 the variables at right hand side are unknown, while at left hand side are known from the available inflow hydrograph. Under this method, the following data are required for routing the flood :

1. Inflow hydrograph/data.
2. Pool elevation *Vs* outflow curve, and
3. Pool elevation *Vs* storage curve.

The routing procedure is explained under following steps :

1. Find out outflow (O) by using pool elevation Vs outflow curve (given) for the total time period.

2. Calculate storage (S) by using pool elevation Vs storage curve (given).

3. Compute the values of $\left(S+\frac{O\cdot\Delta t}{2}\right)$ and $\left(S-\frac{O\cdot\Delta t}{2}\right)$ for computed outflows in step (1).

4. Draw the curve between discharge/outflow (O), storage (S), $\left(S+\frac{O+\Delta t}{2}\right)$ and $\left(S-\frac{O\cdot\Delta t}{2}\right)$

5. Perform routing calculations by considering the given initial pool elevation and commencement of discharge for the same elevation. It is done as follows:

(*i*) Find out the values of $\left(S_2+\frac{O_2\cdot\Delta t}{2}\right)$ which is equal to $\left(\frac{I_1+I_2}{2}\right)\Delta t+\left(S_1-\frac{O_1\cdot\Delta t}{2}\right)$ In this, the parameters I_1, I_2 and Δt are known; while $\left(S_1-\frac{O_1\,\Delta t}{2}\right)$ is determined from the available curve between outflow (O) and $\left(S-\frac{O\cdot\Delta t}{2}\right)$. $\left(S_2+\frac{O_2\cdot\Delta t}{2}\right)$ is obtained by adding the values of $\left(\frac{I_1+I_2}{2}\right)\Delta t$ and $\left(S_1-\frac{O_1\cdot\Delta t}{2}\right)$

(*ii*) Determine next outflow for the known value of $\left(S_2+\frac{O_2\cdot\Delta t}{2}\right)$ obtained in step (5i).

(*iii*) Determine the level of pool elevation against obtained outflow in step (5ii) from the curve between O and S.

(*iv*) Repeat the procedure for complete routing of reservoir.

Example 9.6 explains the Pulse method of reservoir routing.

Example 9.6. *Route the reservoir by using Pulse and modified Pulse methods for the following inflow hydrograph of reservoir :*

Time (h)	*0*	*6*	*12*	*18*	*24*	*30*	*36*	*42*
Inflow (m^3/s)	*70*	*90*	*180*	*320*	*480*	*560*	*530*	*460*
Time (h)	*48*	*54*	*60*	*66*	*72*	*78*	*84*	*90*
Inflow (m^3/s)	*350*	*260*	*200*	*170*	*130*	*80*	*50*	*40*

The pool elevation Vs storage and discharge curves of the reservoir are given in Fig. 9.11. Also, take the

1. Pool elevation at commencement = 110 m

2. Discharge at commencement = 165 m^3/s

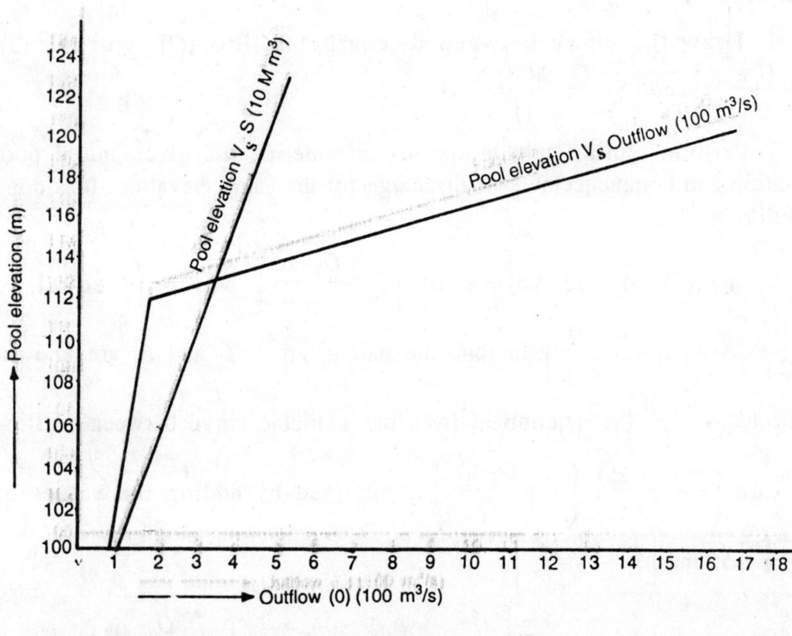

Fig. 9.11

Solution. (A) Routing By Pulse Method

The following steps are followed :

Step (1). *Determine the outflow (O) and storage (S) :* For this purpose, the available curves on pool elevation Vs outflow and storage are used. The outflow (*O*) and storage amount (*S*) are tabulated in table 9.3. The outflow and storage data are converted in the unit of cumec – 1/4 day, because of routing period 6-h.

Table 9.3

Pool elevation (m)	*Outflow (0) (m^3/s)*	*Storage*	
		M.m^3	Cumec $-\frac{1}{4}$ day*
100	80.00	10.00	463.00
102	100.00	14.00	648.20
104	118.00	18.00	833.40
106	130.00	21.50	995.45
108	150.00	25.50	1180.65
110	165.00	29.50	1365.85
112	180.00	33.50	1551.05
114	530.00	38.00	1759.40
116	885.00	41.00	1898.30
118	1240.00	45.00	2083.50
120	1600.00	48.50	2245.55
122	—	52.50	2430.75

*Cumec $-\frac{1}{4}$ day is determined by multiplying the factor 46.3 (i.e. $10^6/1660 = 46.3$) to the storage ($M\text{m}^3$).

Step 2. Computation of $\left(S+\frac{Ot}{2}\right)$ **and** $\left(S-\frac{Ot}{2}\right)$ **:** It is as below

Pool elevation (m)	*Outflow (O)*	*Storage (S) cumec - 1/4 day*	*Ot/2 cumec – 1/4 day*	$S+\frac{Ot}{2}$	$S-\frac{Ot}{2}$
100	80.00	463.00	40.00	503.00	423.00
102	100.00	648.20	50.00	698.20	598.20
104	118.00	833.40	59.00	892.40	774.40
106	130.00	995.45	65.00	1060.45	930.45
108	150.00	1180.65	75.00	1255.65	1105.65
110	165.00	1365.85	82.50	1448.35	1283.35

Contd.

112	180.00	1551.05	90.00	1641.05	1461.05
114	530.00	1759.40	265.00	2024.40	1494.40
116	885.00	1898.30	442.50	2340.80	1455.80
118	1240.00	2083.50	620.00	2703.50	1463.50
120	1600.00	2245.55	800.00	3045.55	1445.55
122	—	2430.75	—	—	—

Using the values of outflow (O), $\left(S+\frac{Ot}{2}\right)$, $\left(S-\frac{Ot}{2}\right)$ and storage (S), the curves for O Vs $\left(S+\frac{Ot}{2}\right)$, O Vs $\left(S-\frac{Ot}{2}\right)$ and O Vs S are drawn, as shown in Fig. 9.12.

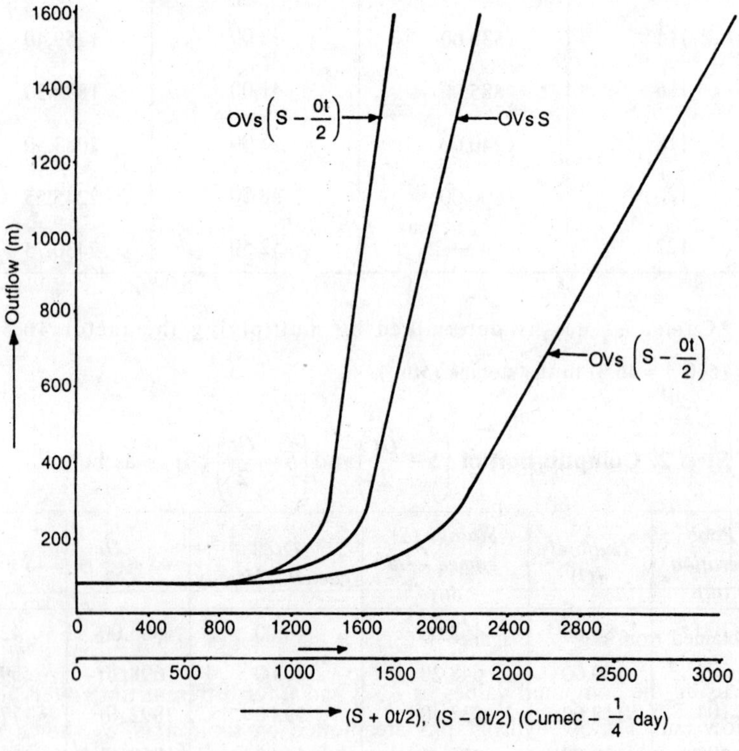

Fig. 9.12

Step 3. Routing Computation : It is as follows :-

Time *(h)*	*Inflow* (I_1)	*Inflow* (I_2)	$\frac{I_1 + I_2}{2}$	*Outflow* *(O)*	$S - \frac{Ot}{2}$	$S + \frac{Ot}{2}$
(1)	*(2)*	*(3)*	*(4)*	*(5)*	*(6)*	*(7)*
0	70.00	90.00	80.00	165.00	1083.33	1163.33
6	90.00	180.00	135.00	100.00*	716.66	851.66
12	180.00	320.00	250.00	80.00	500.00	750.00
18	320.00	480.00	400.00	110.00	833.33	1233.33
24	480.00	560.00	520.0	120.0	967.00	1487.00
30	560.00	530.00	545.0	150.00	1048.00	1593.00
36	530.00	460.00	495.0	180.00	1098.00	1593.00
42	460.00	350.00	405.00	180.00	1098.00	1503.00
48	350.00	260.00	305.0	150.00	1048.00	1353.00
54	260.00	200.00	230.0	130.00	1200.00	1430.00
60	200.00	170.00	185.00	120.00	967.00	1152.00
66	170.00	130.00	150.00	100.00	716.66	867.00
72	130.00	80.00	105.0	.80.00	500.00	605.00
78	80.00	.50,0	65.00	—	—	—
84	50.00	40.00	45.00	—	—	—
90	40.00	—	—	—	—	—

*Obtained from Fig. 9.12 against 1163.33 as the given value of $\left(S + \frac{Ot}{2}\right)$

By using the computed values of I_1, I_2 and 0 for different time intervals, the inflow and outflow hydrographs are plotted on same axis, as shown in Fig. 9.13. The reservoir lag and reduction in flood peak are determined from the plotted inflow and outflow hydrographs, which came to be :

Reservoir lag = 9.6 hour

Reduction in flood peak = 385 m^3/s

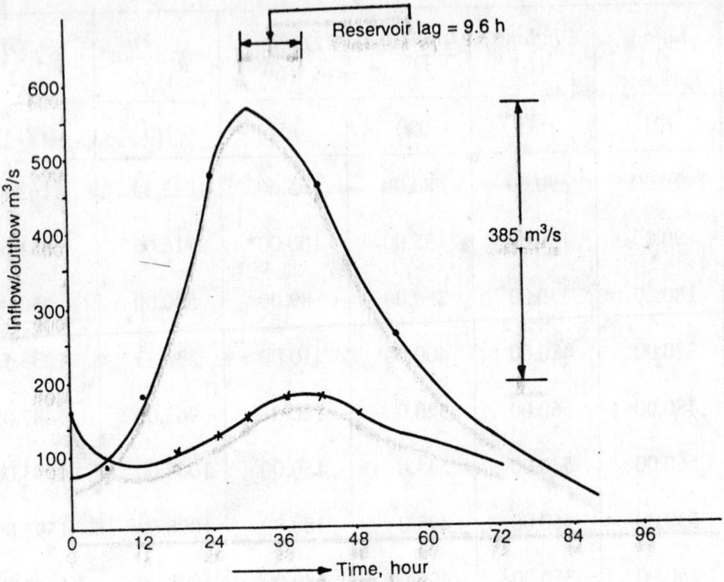

Fig. 9.13

(2) Reservoir Routing by Modified Pulse Method

Under this method, the following steps are followed :

Step 1 : Computation of Outflow and Storage : *It is done in the same way as in Pulse method. Computations are shown in Table 9.4.*

Step 2 : Computation of $(2S/t) + O$ and $(2S/t) - O$: It is as follows (Table 9.4)

Table 9.4

Pool elevation (m)	*Outflow (m^3/s)*	*Storage (S) cumec – 1/4 days*	$\frac{2S}{t}$ *cumec*	$\frac{2S}{t} + O$	$\frac{2S}{t} - O$
100	80.00	463.00	926.00	1006.00	846.00
102	100.00	648.20	1296.40	1396.40	1196.40
104	118.00	833.40	1666.80	1784.80	1548.80
106	130.00	995.45	1990.90	2120.90	1860.90
108	150.00	1180.65	2361.30	2511.30	2346.30
110	165.00	1365.85	2731.70	2896.70	2566.70
112	180.00	1551.05	3102.10	3282.10	2922.10

Contd.

114	530.00	1759.40	3518.80	4048.80	2988.80
116	885.00	1898.30	3796.60	4681.60	2911.60
118	1240.00	2083.50	4167.00	5407.00	2927.00
120	1600.00	2245.55	4490.00	6090,00	2890.90
122	—	2430.75	4861.50	—	—

Based on the computed values of $(2S/t) + O$ and $(2S/t) - O$, the curves for outflow (O) Vs $(2S/t) + O$ and outflow (O) Vs $(2S/t) - O$ are drawn as shown in Fig. 9.14.

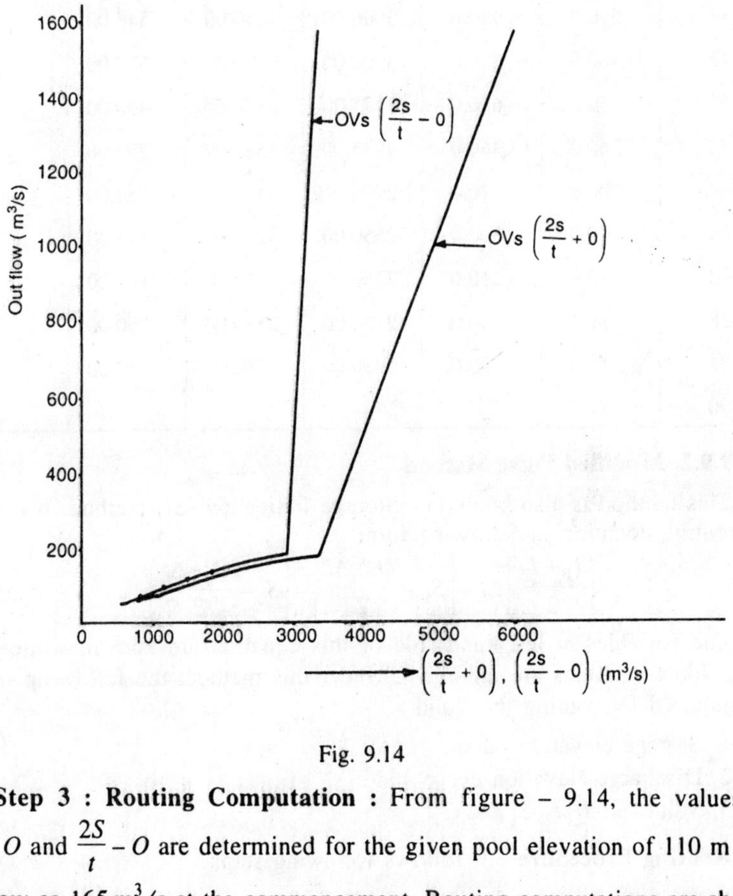

Fig. 9.14

Step 3 : Routing Computation : From figure – 9.14, the values of $\frac{2S}{t} + O$ and $\frac{2S}{t} - O$ are determined for the given pool elevation of 110 m and outflow as 165 m^3/s at the commencement. Routing computations are shown in Table 9.5.

Table–9.5

Time (h)	*Inflow (I)*	I_1+I_2	$\frac{2S}{t}-O$	$\frac{2s}{t}+O$	*Outflow (O) (m^3/s)*	*Pool elevation (m)*
0	70.0	160.0	2896.70	2566.70	165.00	110
6	90.0	27.0	2550.00	3056.70	180.00	
12	180.0	500.0	2350.00	2820.00	160.00	
18	320.0	800.0	2350.00	2850.00	160.00	
24	480.0	1040.0	2550.00	3150.00	180.00	
30	560.0	1090.0	2950.00	3590.00	300.00	
36	530.0	990.0	3000.00	4040.00	543.00	
42	460.0	810.0	3000.00	3990.00	500.00	
48	350.0	610.0	2975.00	3810.00	400.00	
54	260.0	460.0	2975.00	3585.00	299.00	
60	200.0	370.0	2900.00	3435.00	220.00	
66	170.0	300.0	2650.00	3270.00	175.00	
72	130.0	210.0	2350.00	2950.00	160.00	
78	80.0	130.0	2150.00	2560.00	150.00	
84	50.0	90.0	1950.00	2280.00	140.00	
90	40.0	—	—		—	

9.9.2. Modified Pulse Method

This method is also known as Storage Indication (SI) method. It follows the routing equation in following form :

$$\left(\frac{I_1+I_2}{2}\right)\Delta t-\left(S_1-\frac{O_1\cdot\Delta t}{2}\right)=\left(S_2-\frac{O_2\cdot\Delta t}{2}\right) \quad \text{...(9.29)}$$

The variables at left hand side of this equation are known, while right hand side's variables are unknown. Under this method, the following inputs are required for routing the flood :

1. Storage-elevation curve.
2. Discharge-elevation curve and
3. Values of I_1, I_2, S_1 and O_1.

Routing Procedure : It follows following steps :

1. Find out S_2 and O_2 by substituting the values of I_1, I_2, S_1, S_1 and O_1 in equation 9.28.

2. Plot the curve between $\left(S + \frac{O \cdot \Delta t}{2}\right)$ and elevation from the available curves on storage V_s elevation and discharge V_s elevation.

3. Also, plot another curve between outflow and elevation on the same graph paper.

4. Compute the value of outflow (O_2) at the end of time Δt by using the outflow Vs elevation curve drawn in step (3).

5. Find out the value of $\left(S_1 - \frac{\Delta t \cdot O_1}{2}\right)$ by deducting the O_2 (obtained in step 4) from $\left(S_2 - \frac{O_2 \cdot \Delta t}{2}\right)$ of next routing time.

6. Repeat the procedure for routing the entire inflow hydrograph.

The flood routing by using modified Pulse method has been explained in example 9.6.

9.10. Routing By Machines

When routing of reservoir is required to perform for large number of inflow database, then manual techniques become very time consuming and difficult. Therefore, in such condition the routing machines are very useful to save the time and get fast result. The available routing machines are given as under :

1. Mechanical machines.
2. Electronic machines.

9.10.1. Mechanical Routing Machines

These are below :

1. Flood router (F.B. Horkness)
2. Integrating router.

The integrating machines are most common; one of them is described below :

Tarpley J.F. (1939) developed an integrating router for routing the reservoir. The machine consists of five drums *A*, *B*, *C*, *D* and *E*, two motors 1 & 2. Drums are driven at constant speed with the help of motor-1. The motor-2 controls the movement of pointer. All drums are wrapped with the chart. Before starting the routing work, the pointer is placed in position on the chart. During operation, the motor-2 rotates the drum-C either in backward or forward direction, according to the amount of inflow and outflow passing through the reservoir. At the same time, the pointer of drum-C turns the drum-B depending on instantaneous elevation in the reservoir. During operation, the following observations are recorded by the machine :

1. On drum-A — inflow Vs time curve
2. On drum-B — discharge Vs elevation curve
3. On drum-C — elevation Vs storage curve

4. On drum-D — elevation Vs time curve
5. On drum-E — outflow Vs time curve

The view of integrating machine is shown in Fig. 9.15.

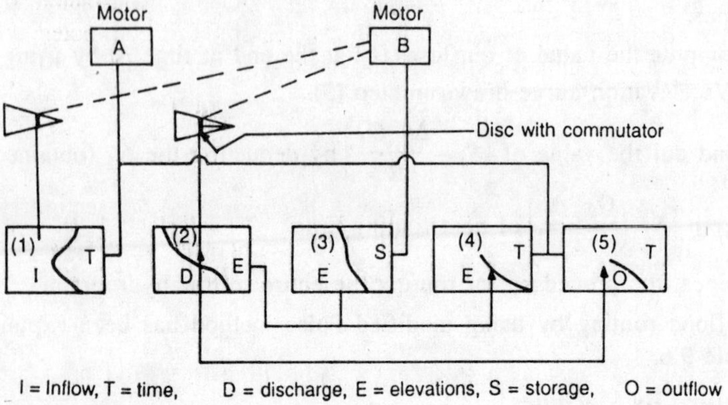

Fig. 9.15. Schematic diagram of integrating routing machine.

9.10.2. Electronic Routing Machine

It consists of two self balancing potentiometers, phototube, five resistances R_1, R_2, R_3, R_4 and R_5, 100 volt bulb, variac transformer and batteries. In this machine, the change in condensor's capacity corresponds the storage, while current denotes the inflow (I) and outflow (O). The resistance R_4 and R_5 are fixed across the self balancing potentiometer. R_5 and R_4 are very small as compared to the R_3, R_2 and R_1.

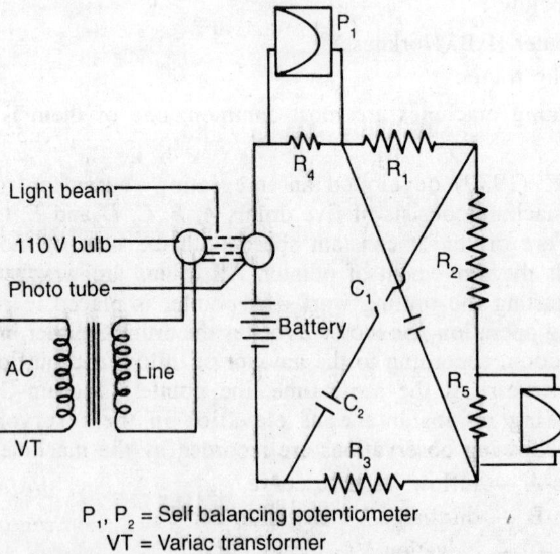

Fig. 9.16. Circuit diagram of electronic flood routing.

During operation, the inflow hydrograph is plotted on the chart of potentiometer-A. The shape of hydrograph gets change according to the variations of the current, depending on inflow rate coming into the reservoir/stream. Current is controlled by varying the voltage on lamp attached to the system. The variation in voltage affects the intensity of light falling on the photo tube and thus regulates the current to flow in the machine. The outflow hydrograph is traced automatically on the chart fixed over the potentiometer-B. Tracing speed of both potentiometer is the same. Electrical circuit of this routing machine is shown in Fig. 9.16.

IMPORTANT POINTS

1. Flood routing determines the flood hydrograph at d/s section of the river/reservoir based on the flood data of one or more stations located u/s side.
2. Flood routing is useful for flood forecasting, reservoir design, spillway design etc.
3. The hydrologic routing method follows continuity equation.
4. Hydraulic routing method follows the continuity equation and the equation of motion of unsteady flow.
5. Basic differential equation used under hydraulic method of flood routing is St. Venant equation.
6. The movement of flood hydrograph through reservoir/channel reach is gradually varied unsteady flow.
7. Differential form of continuity equation for unsteady flow through a given reach is given by $\frac{\partial O}{\partial x} + T\frac{\partial y}{\partial t} = 0$, in which T is the topwidth of flow and y is the depth of flow.
8. The equation of motion for flood wave is given as $S_0 - S_f = \frac{\partial y}{\partial x} + \frac{v}{g} \cdot \frac{\partial v}{\partial x} + \frac{1}{g} \cdot \frac{\partial v}{\partial t}$, in which v is the flow velocity at any section and S_0 & S_f are the slope of channel bed and energy line, respectively.
9. In reservoir, the outflow (O) and storage (S) are the function of reservoir elevation (h) *i.e.* $O = O\,(h)$ and $S = S\,(h)$.
10. Change in outflow hydrograph over inflow hydrograph is called attenuation.
11. Difference in time to peak of inflow and outflow hydrographs is called lag.
12. The lag and attenuation of inflow hydrograph control the storage capacity of reservoir and characteristics of spillway.
13. In channel, storage is the function of inflow and outflow.
14. Total storage of channel is the sum of prism storage and wedge storage.
15. Prism storage (S_p) is the function of outflow *i.e.* $S_p = f(O)$.
16. Wedge storage (S_w) is the function of inflow *i.e.* $S_W = f(I)$
17. Total storage in the channel is given by the expression $S = K\,[xI^m + (1-x)\,O^m]$, in which K is the storage time-constant, x is the

weighing factor which varies between 0 and 0.5 and m is exponent. For natural channels m is taken as 1 and for rectangular channels it is as 0.6.

18. For natural channels, the value of x lies between 0 and 0.3.

19. In Muskingum formula of channel routing, the value of $C_0 + C_1 + C_2 = 1$.

20. The dimension of storage constant (K) is T.

REFERENCES

1. Chow V.T. Handbook of Applied Hydrology, McGraw-Hill, New York, 1964.
2. Chow V.T. Open Channel Flow, McGraw-Hill, New York, 1985.
3. Goodric R.O., Rapid Calculation of Reservoir Discharge, Civil Engg. Vol. (1), 407-418, 1931.
4. Linsley R.K. Kohler M.A. and Paulhus J.L., Hydrology for Engineers, McGraw-Hill, New York, 1958.
5. Mutreja K.N. Applied Hydrology, Tata McGraw-Hill, New Delhi, 1986.
6. Mahmood K. and Yevjevich V. Unsteady Flow in Open Channel, vol 1 and 2, Water Rescurces Pub., Fort Collins, Colo, USA, 1975.
7. Raghunath H.M. Hydrology, WileyEastern Pvt. Ltd. Delhi, 1985.
8. Schulz E.F. Problems in Applied Hydrology, Tata McGraw-Hill, New Delhi, 1984.
9. Subramanya K. Engineering Hydrology, Tata McGraw-Hill, New Delhi, 2000.
10. Subramanya K. Flow in Open Channels, Tata McGraw-Hill, New Delhi, 1991.
11. Wilson, E.M., Engineering Hydrology, Macmillan, London, 1969.

DESCRIPTIVE TYPE QUESTIONS

1. (*a*) Define flood routing and describe channel routing.

(*b*) Write the importance of flood routing.

2. (*a*) Define reservoir routing and explain any one method for its computation.

(*b*) Explain basic equation of flood routing.

3. List channel routing techniques and describe Muskingum method.

4. (*a*) Derive Muskingum equation.

(*b*) Write the procedure to determine the value of K and x.

5. (*a*) Compute the value of K and x from the following inflow and outflow hydrographs

Time (h)	0	6	2	8	24	30	36	42	48	54
Inflow (m^3/s)	25	115	565	730	446	235	134	85	57	40
Outflow ((m^3/s)	29	42	277	614	628	384	225	132	83	50

(*b*) Explain Muskingum flood routing method.

6. Describe Muskingum Crest Segment method of flood routing.
7. Explain U.S. Weather Bureau method of flood routing.
8. List reservoir routing methods and explain Modified Pull's method.
9. Describe Pull's method of reservoir routing.
10. Explain mechanical routing machines.

OBJECTIVE TYPE QUESTIONS

1. Flood routing determines outflow hydrograph at any down stream section with the known
   (*a*) inflow hydrograph (*b*) flood storage
   (*c*) sediment load in flow (*d*) none of the above.
2. Flood routing is useful for
   (*a*) flood forecasting (*b*) sediment analysis
   (*c*) stream flow measurement (*d*) hydrograph development.
3. Channel routing is concerned with
   (*a*) reservoir
   (*b*) determination of outflow hydrograph at d/s section of channel.
   (*c*) both '*a*' and '*b*' (*d*) prism storage.
4. The continuity equation is given by
   (*a*) $O - I = \frac{dS}{dt}$ (*b*) $I - O = \frac{dS}{dt}$
   (*c*) $q = a.v$ (*d*) none of the above.
5. The differential form of continuity equation is
   (*a*) $\frac{\partial Q}{\partial x} + T\frac{\partial y}{\partial t} = 0$ (*b*) $\frac{\partial I}{\partial x} + T\frac{\partial y}{\partial t} = 0$
   (*c*) $T\frac{\partial q}{\partial x} + \frac{\partial y}{\partial t} = 0$ (*d*) $\frac{\partial v}{\partial x} + \frac{\partial v}{\partial y} = T$
6. Muskingum method is employed for
   (*a*) reservoir routing (*b*) channel routing
   (*c*) both '*a*' and '*b*' (*d*) hydrograph analysis
7. Muskingum equation is derived by considering the channel storage as the sum of
   (*a*) prism and wedge storage (*b*) prism storage, only
   (*c*) wedge storage, only (*d*) SPF and PMP
8. Prism storage is the function of
   (*a*) outflow (*b*) inflow
   (*c*) inflow and outflow (*d*) Tc.
9. Wedge storage is the function of
   (*a*) outflow (*b*) inflow
   (*c*) outflow and inflow (*d*) Tc
10. Storage constant '*K*' in Muskingum equation is the
    (*a*) inverse slope of straight line curve between S and $xI + (1 - x)0$
    (*b*) slope of curve between S and $xI + (1 - x) 0$
    (*c*) m/n
    (*d*) none of the above.

11. The 'x' of Muskingum equation is
(*a*) weighing factor (*b*) storage constant
(*c*) both '*a*' and '*b*' (*d*) lag time

12. The value of x in Muskingum equation varies from
(*a*) 0 to 0.5 (*b*) 0 to 1.0
(*c*) 0 to 1.5 (*d*) 1 to 1.5

13. A reservoir is said to be linear, when value of x is
(*a*) 0 (*b*) 0.5
(*c*) 1.0 (*d*) 1.5

14. In Muskingum routing formula, the value of $C_0 + C_1 + C_2$ is equal to
(*a*) 0 (*b*) 0.5
(*c*) 1 (*d*) 15.

15. Attenuation is the difference of
(*a*) peak of inflow and outflow hydrographs
(*b*) time to peak of inflow and outflow hydrographs
(*c*) inflow and outflow
(*d*) none of the above.

16. U.S. Weather Bureau method is used for
(*a*) reservoir routing (*b*) channel routing
(*c*) hydrograph derivation (*d*) none of the above.

17. Reservoir lag is the difference of
(*a*) time to peak of inflow and outflow hydrographs
(*b*) inflow and outflow hydrographs
(*c*) inflow and outflow
(*d*) none of the above.

18. Pulse method is also known as
(*a*) ISD method (*b*) energy balance method
(*c*) IUH method (*d*) none of the above.

19. Modified Pulse method is used for
(*a*) reservoir routing (*b*) channel routing
(*c*) both '*a*' and '*b* (*d*) hydrograph analysis

20. Modified Pulse method is also known as
(*a*) Storage Indication method
(*b*) Inflow Indication method
(*c*) Outflow Indication method
(*d*) Inflow–Outflow method.

21. The dimension of x in Muskingum equation is
(*a*) L (*b*) dimension less
(*a*) LT^{-1} (*d*) T.

22. Unit of factor K in Muskingum formula is
(*a*) λ (*b*) temperature °C
(*c*) m/s (*d*) m^3/s.

23. Nash Model is for
(*a*) channel storage (*b*) IUH
(*c*) reservoir storage (*d*) soil loss

24. Clark Model determines
(*a*) channal storage (*b*) soil loss
(*c*) IUH (*d*) sediment load.

25. Attenuation is expresed in the unit of
(*a*) m^3/s (*b*) second
(*c*) m/s (*d*) m/s^2

Answer (Objective Type Question)

1. (*a*)	**2.** (*a*)	**3.** (*b*)	**4.** (*b*)	**5.** (*a*)	**6.** (*b*)	**7.** (*a*)	**8.** (*a*)
9. (*b*)	**10.** (*a*)	**11.** (*a*)	**12.** (*a*)	**13.** (*c*)	**14.** (*c*)	**15.** (*a*)	**16.** (*b*)
17. (*a*)	**18.** (*a*)	**19.** (*a*)	**20.** (*a*)	**21.** (*b*)	**22.** (*a*)	**23.** (*b*)	**24.** (*c*)
25. (*a*)							

10

Sedimentation

Sediments are the fragmented materials, originated either due to chemical or physical disintegration of rocks. Sediments are transported by the water and air. The size of sediment may vary from big boulders to colliodal. Amongst various agents causing transportation of sediments, the flowing water is one of the main. Therefore, sediment transported by water is generally considered in general view.

For design of reservoir and channel, the data of sediment yield of contributing catchment area is very essential, because inflow of sediments in storage area of the reservoir or depositing over the channel bed affect their net capacity and accordingly an allowance is given to their design capacity to compensate the sediment deposition. A such example has been found in the reservoir of Solman river basin (U.S.A.), which was completely silted, immediately after one year of its construction.

10.1. Sources of Sediments

Various sources of sediment yield from catchment are as under:

1. Erosion due to sheet flow.
2. Soil movement due to land slide, soil creeps etc.
3. Sediment yield due to gully erosion.
4. Stream bank erosion, including bank cutting and bed scouring.
5. Sediment yield due to high wind velocity.

Amongst various sources of sediment yield, the soil erosion caused by sheet erosion, stream bank erosion etc are more pronounced, depending on the watershed and climatic characteristics. Watershed characteristics include the size, shape, soil, land slope, land use etc., while climatic characteristics include temperature, rainfall etc. to affect the sediment yield. Rainfall is more effective climatic parameter for producing the sediment yield from the watershed.

The sediment yield begins during rainfall occurrence *i.e.* when raindrops strike the soil surface from height, then soil particles are broken into finer, which are splashed upward alongwith water droplets and return back to the land surface. In the mean time, the flowing water picked the detached particles and carried away to the streams or reservoirs. The yield of sediment depends on several factors described as under :

10.2. Factors Affecting Sediment Yield

The following factors affect the sediment yield from the watershed :

1. **Watershed factors**
   (*i*) Size and shape
   (*ii*) Soil type
   (*iii*) Land slope
   (*iv*) Vegetal cover etc.
2. **Climatic factors**
   (*i*) Temperature
   (*ii*) Nature of precipitation
   (*iii*) Rainfall intensity etc.

Size and shape of watershed : The size and shape of watershed affect the sediment yield by varying the runoff amount due to a given storm. A large size watershed yields comparatively greater amount of sediment than the smaller one, because larger area contributes more runoff volume than the smaller area, if rainfall has occured uniformly throughout the watershed.

The shape of watershed is generally in two forms ; one is fan shape and other is fern shape. Fern shaped watersheds have longer axial length than the width, while fan shaped watersheds have approximately equal length and width. The time of concentration of fern shaped watershed is greater than the fan shaped, resulting into less runoff rate and sediment yield per unit area from fern shaped watershed as compared to the fan shaped watershed.

Soil type : Sediment yield from watershed is closely related to the soil types because detachment succeptibility of soil particles varies from soil to soil. A soil of coarse texture gets detach very easily by the raindrops or air current than the heavy soils. On contrast, the transportation of soil particles is less in coarse textured soils as compared to the heavy textured soils. However, once the soil particles are detached from the soil mass ; they are transported by the flowing water or blowing winds. Due to this reason, there is greater sediment yield from the coarse textured soils.

Land slope : It affects the sediment yield by affecting the velocity of sheet flow over the ground surface. High land slope increases the flow velocity as well as erosive power of flowing water. From experimental evidence, it has been found that, the erosive power of water flow varies as the square of velocity (*i.e.* V^2), while transporting power as V^6.

Vegetal cover : It is one of the dominating factors affecting the sediment yield from watershed. Vegetation creates soil cover, which dissipates the erosive power of falling rain drops and also reduces the velocity of over land flow/runoff by making hindrance in flow path. These two effects of vegetal cover minimize the sediment yield in significant way. Due to this reason, the growing of vegetation is strongly recommended for checking the sediment yield from watershed and to control the sedimentation.

Climatic factor : The climatic factors such as, temperature, nature of precipitation, rainfall intensity etc. greatly affect the sediment yield from watershed. Climatic parameters act as external force for making the soil to gets erode and production of sediment load from the watershed.

Temperature reduces the soil moisture, causing the wind erosion to come in influence to yield the sediment. The nature of precipitation reflects the forms of precipitation occuring over the ground surface. Drizzle is not effective for sediment yield, as it has very small size raindrops, by which neither soil detachment nor runoff is resulted. Snowfall is also not effective to cause sediment production in large amount than the rainfall, because it does not build the runoff, immediately after fallir̈y but after some time. It is observed that, as snow gets melted, the water is absorbed by the soil and does not available for making the surface flow. In addition, during snowfall the soil is compacted due to solid nature of snow, causing less detachment of the soil particles. While in case of rainfall, it is not so. Rainfall is only the agent, which performs the process of sediment yield due to its transporting and detaching power. Regarding rainfall intensity, an intense storm is composed of large size raindrops which yields the sediment in large amount because bigger raindrops strike the land surface with greater impacting force, resulting into breaking of coarser particles into finer which are easily carried away by the surface flow in suspension form. In addition, the finer particles are entered into the interconnected pores paces and sealed them by virtue of which surface runoff is generated very shortly during rainfall, which results greater sediment yield from the watershed.

10.3. Sediment Properties

Properties of sediment are divided into following two groups :

1. Properties of individual sediment particles, and
2. Bulk properties of sediment.

10.3.1. Individual Properties

Followings are the individual properties of sediments :

1. Size
2. Shape
3. Specific gravity
4. Fall velocity
5. Surface texture
6. Orientation.

Size of sediment : It is an important property of individual sediment. The size is a single parameter, which adequately describes the particle for different practical purposes. For spherical particles, the size is denoted by their diameter. Since there is large irregularities in the shapes, therefore, diameter is not only used as an index for indicating the size of sediment. For irregular shaped particles the size is expressed by the following parameters :

1. Volume of sediment
2. Fall velocity
3. Size of sieve mesh.

The evaluation of sediment size based on the volume and fall velocity is done by measuring the diameter of an equivalent sphere. The following terms are used to denole the size of sediment in terms of volume.

Nominal diameter : It refers to the physical size of sediment. It is defined as the diameter of spherical particle, which volume is equal to the volume of sediment. It is generally expressed as 'd_n'.

Fall velocity : The velocity of a falling spherical particle, which specific gravity is 2.65 and has the same standard falling velocity as the actual sediment is called fall velocity. The standard falling velocity is the terminal velocity of particle in distilled water of infinite extent at 24°C temperature.

Sediment diameter : It is the diameter of spherical particle existing in the same sedimentation fluid, provided that the specific gravity and terminal velocity of the spherical particle are the same as the actual sediment particle. There have been developed several relationships for computing the diameter of sediment based on nominal velocity of particles; few of them are given as under :

U.S. Government and I.I.H.R (1957) developed the following empirical formula for determining the size of particle in terms of diameter of sieve aperture *i.e.*

$$d = 0.9\, d_n \qquad \text{...(10.1)}$$

in which, d is the sieve diameter and d_n is the nominal diameter of sediment. The sieve diameter (d) of naturally born particles is always less than their nominal diameter. Similarly, another relationship between 'b' as the intermediate axis and nominal diameter (d_n) of the sediment is given as:

$$b = K \cdot d_n \qquad \text{...(10.2)}$$

where, b = intermediate axis

K = constant

d_n = nominal diameter

Approximate values of K based on shape factor are given in Table 10.1. The grade scale of different classes of sediments is given in Table 10.2

Table 10.1. Values of *K* based on shape factor

Shape factor	*K*
0.3	1.27
0.5	1.13
0.7	1.05
0.9	1.00

Source: U.S. Govt & I.I.H.R (1957)

Table 10.2. Grade scale of different classes of sediments

Class name	*Size range (mm)*
Boulders	
Very large	4096—2048
Large	2048—1024
Medium	1024—512
Small	512—256
Cobbles,	
Large	256—128
Small	128—64
Gravel,	
Very coarse	64—32
Coarse	32—16
Medium	16—8
Fine	8—4
Very fine	4—2
Sand,	
Very coarse	2—1
Coarse	1—0,5
Medium	0.5—0.25
Fine	0.25—0.125
Very fine	0.125—0625
Silt,	
Coarse	$\frac{1}{16}$ — $\frac{1}{32}$
Medium	$\frac{1}{32}$ — $\frac{1}{64}$

Contd.

Class name	*Size range (mm)*
Fine	$\frac{1}{64}-\frac{1}{128}$
Very fine	$\frac{1}{128}-\frac{1}{256}$
Clay,	
Coarse	$\frac{1}{256}-\frac{1}{512}$
Medium	$\frac{1}{512}-\frac{1}{1024}$
Fine	$\frac{1}{1024}-\frac{1}{2048}$
Very fine	$\frac{1}{2048}-\frac{1}{4096}$

Shape of sediment : Sediments are found in different shapes, depending on the environmental factors, expressions of the minerology etc. The common shapes are sphere, cone, cylinder, ellipse, cube etc. Evaluation of sediment shape is very important, because it affects the mean velocity of sediment, stability of beaches, bed load transport etc. The following terms are used to categorise the shape of sediments :

Sphericity : It is the ratio of surface area of the sphere having same volume as the sediment to the actual surface area of the sediment. It is expressed in terms of diameter, given as:

$$\text{Sphericity} = \frac{d_n}{d_s} \qquad ...(10.3)$$

$$= \frac{\text{Nominal diameter}}{\text{Diameter of circumscribing sphere}}$$

For spherical particles, the sphericity is equal to 1, while for other shapes it is always less than one.

Wadell (1953) developed following formula for computing sphericity of the particle :

$$\text{Sphericity} = \left(\frac{\text{Volume of particle}}{\text{Volume of circumscribing sphere}}\right)^{\frac{1}{3}} \qquad ...(10.4)$$

or

$$\left(\frac{d_n}{a}\right)^{1/3} \qquad ...(10.5)$$

in which, 'a' is the major axis of sediment and 'd_n' is the nominal diameter of particle.

Roundness : It is quite different to that of the sphericity. Roundness refers to the sharpness of edges and corners of the sediment, indicating the degree of wear which the particle receives. It is defined as the ratio of average radius of curvature of all the edges to the radius of maximum inscribed circle. If a sediment has four edges, which radii are r_1, r_2, r_3 and r_4, respectively (Fig. 10.1), and R is the radius of inscribed circle, then roundness is given by :

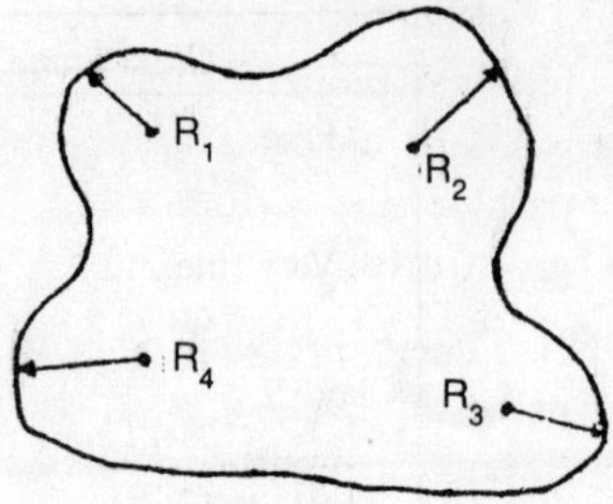

Fig. 10.1

$$\text{Roundness} = \frac{\text{Average radius of curvature of all the edges } (r_a)}{\text{Radius of maximum inscribed circle (R)}} \qquad ...(10.6)$$

where, $$r_a = \frac{r_1 + r_2 + r_3 + r_4}{4} \qquad ...(10.7)$$

The roundness of particle can also be determined by using the following coefficients

(*i*) C_{ox}^{15} coefficient of roundness $= \dfrac{r_1}{(a \cdot b \cdot c)^{1/3}}$ ...(10.8)

in which, r_1 is the smallest radius of curvature of projected area, a is the major axis, b is intermediate axis and c is shortest axis of the sediment.

(*ii*) Cailleux's coeffient of bluntness $= \dfrac{r_1}{a}$ ...(10.9)

(*iii*) Coefficient of circularity : It is also known as Tickell coefficient, given below :

$$\text{Tickell's coefficient} = \frac{\text{Projected area}}{\text{Circle area which diameter is 'a'}} \qquad ...(10.10)$$

Specific gravity : It is required to identify the source of sediments, because specific gravity of any material depends on the mineral composition of parent formation from which it was borned. It is determined by using the following formula :

$$\text{Specific gravity} = \frac{\text{Weight of sediment}}{\text{Weight of equal volume of water}} \qquad ...(10.11)$$

Specific gravity of some common sediments is listed in Table 10.3.

Table 10.3. Specific gravity of some common sediments

Sediment	*Sp. gravity*
Quartz or field spar	2,65
Garnet	3,20
Horn blende	3,20
Tourmaline	3,50-4,30
Zircon	4,60
Magnetite	5,20

Fall Velocity : Settling of particles in the fluid is influenced by the physical properties of the particles such as size, shape, specific gravity and medium characteristics like viscosity and temperature. Amongst all, the particle size is dominating factor to affect the fall velocity of sediment for a given medium.

The expression of fall velocity or settling velocity can be determined by using the Stoke's law, which states that the "falling velocity of any particle through a liquid depends on its radius"

Let, F = viscous force/resistance
d = diameter of spherical particle
μ = dynamic viscosity of the fluid
V = terminal fall velocity of the particle

Viscous resistance (F) is given by

$$F = 3\pi d\mu V \quad ...(10.12)$$

At constant fall velocity the viscous resistance (F) is balanced by the submerged weight of spherical particle.

Submerged weight of spherical particle is given by

$$= \frac{\pi d^3 (\rho_s - \rho_f)}{6} \quad ...(10.13)$$

Thus,

$$3\pi d \cdot \mu V = \frac{\pi d^3 (\rho_s - \rho_f)}{6}$$

or

$$V = \frac{2}{9\mu} r^2 (\rho_s - \rho_f) \quad ...(10.14)$$

in which, r is the radius of sphere and ρ_s & ρ_f are the specific weights of sediment and fluid, respectively.

Equation 10.14 holds good for the Reynold's number upto 0.10. However, in extreme conditions, it can also be used for the Reynold number upto 1.

Assumption : The above formula considers the following assumptions :

1. Particles size should always be greater than the molecules of the liquid.
2. Particle should be rigid, smooth and in spherical shape.
3. The fall velocity should not be impared by adjacent particles.
4. The particle falls in an infinite and calm fluid.
5. There should not be slip between fluid and particle's surface.

Surface Texture

It reflects the surface feature of sediment. The surface texture of sedment may be shining, highly polished, dull etc. Highly polished surface is mostly related to the gentle attrition or wear to sand blasting, dehydration and oxidation under desert sun or due to some other reasons. Similarly, dull surfaces is found in pebbles like sediments.

Orientation

Orientation of sediment is divided in two groups; one is while falling through the fluid and other is after depositing over the bed. The orientation while falling through the fluid is termed as "instantaneous orientation" and after deposition over the bed is called "fabric orientation". These two orientations are explained as under :

Instantaneous orientation : It depends on several factors, but inertial and viscous forces of the Reynold's number and particle's shape are most dominant. The effect of inertial force is concerned, as it increases, the Reynold's number (R_e) also increases to more than 0.10. In this condition, sediments tend to orient themselves in a stable form. On the other hand, beyond a certain R_e, the sediments do not orient in stable position but in oscillating condition when they fall over the bed. Menown (1950) reported that, when particles have high shape factor, the Reynold's number gets increase upto 100, while for low shape factor the 'R_e' decreases upto 100. A particle of low shape factor and reasonably symetrical, has stability for the R_e of 10,000 or more.

Fabric : It is of two types *i.e.* deformation and apposition fabrics. Deformation fabric is developed by external stresses, while apposition fabric takes place at the time of sediments deposition. Apposition fabric is more important than the deformation fabric regarding hydraulic point of view.

In fabric orientation, as deposition of particles takes place, the orientation gets change due to shape of the sediments. This type of orientation is developed only in coarse sediments such as pebbles, gravels etc.

10.3.2. Bulk Properties of Sediments

This property is associated to the bulk of deposited sediments. Following are the main properties considered under it :

1. **Sorting :** It is determined to identify the similarity or dissimilarity of deposited sediments. Sorting is done in respect of the particles characteristics such as size, shape, specific gravity and mineral or chemical compositions. The degree of sorting of different depositions is given below :

Glacial and Ice action deposits : The deposits made by glacial action are poorly sorted as melting glaciers contain all size of sediments, ranging from big boulders to finely ground rock fragments. However, the deposits of morains and glacial outwash are found uniform to some extent because they contain gravel, sand, silt and clay particles.

Alluvial deposits : These deposits have very wide range of deposit area, size and other characteristics. The shape of such deposits varies from narrow strip in small vallies to wide strip in large vallies. The degree of sorting differs from u/s to d/s deposits. Upstream deposits are composed of coarse particles and are poorly sorted. Middle portion also includes coarse particles and is poorly sorted. At down stream side, the deposits are formed by high percentage of finer particles, such as fine sands, silts and clay, are uniformly sorted.

Littoral deposits : Such deposits are poorly sorted. Normally, formed along the shores, which are hetrogeneous in distribution, texture and composition. This types of deposits are also found along the sea coasts and in shorelines of large size lakes. At the places of stable deposits, the sediments are relatively well sorted and uniform in distribution. But due to alteration of rising and falling tides and alternate dominance of tidal and fluvial currents result poorly sorted deposition.

Colluvial deposits : It consists of deposition of debris carried by the unconcentrated overland flow during sheet erosion. In addition, the deposits formed due to slope wash conjunction with talus and other mass-movements, are also accounted under this kind of deposits. Such deposits are poorly sorted.

Marine deposits : These deposits have very wide range of sorting, ranging from hetrogeneous gravel and big boulder deposits to wide spread zone of deep sea. At the locations, where uniform deposit exists, there is very small size distribution range. But where the conditions favour the chemical precipitation either by biological agencies or some others, the thick and extream deposits comprising limestone accumulations are found.

Sand dune : It is the sand deposit over the land surface due to wind erosion in arid and semi-arid regions. The formation of sand dune is also found in the adjacent areas of lakes and sea coasts, glacial plains etc. During high wind velocity, the silt and clay size particles are blown to the longer distance and are deposited over the ground surface due to reduction in velocity. If this action is continued for longer duration, then it leads to the formation of sand dune. Movement of sand particles is carried out by traction or saltation process. The sand dune consists of fine to medium sand particles, causing such depositis to be under well sorting.

Volcanic dust : This types of deposits are also formed due to wind movement. A large amount of volcanic dusts are transported to the longer distance by the wind currents and formed volcanic deposits, there. These deposits are well sorted, because these contain silt and clay particles, only.

Texture

Textural property of sediment deposits is the functions of size, shape and arrangement of the particlest. Difference in textures of the deposits cause a wide variation in the damage due to accelerated deposits and also modify their use for which they are suitable.

Texture of deposits changes with the kind of existing materials. A deposit containing finer particles, such as clay and silt is more uniform in texture as compared to others formed by coarse particles. Coarse deposits of alluvial lands along mountain fronts consists of mainly gravel and boulders, which result major damage if they are deposited on the agricultural land. This type of deposit involves poor texture.

Specific Weight

It is also termed as unit dry weight or volume-weight. It may be defined as the dry weight of sediment per unit volume *i.e.*

$$\text{Specific weight} = \frac{\text{Weight of dry sediment}}{\text{Total volume of sediment}}$$

The information of specific weight of sediment is verv important for reservoir construction. In addition, this property has also importance in the study of sedimentary cycle for measurement of eroded sediment, transportation of sediment load and weight or volume of sediment deposits. Specific weight of deposit is mainly affected by the percentage of voids, present. A sediment deposit in sub aqueous form involves greater voids which are filled with water, has less specific weight. While in the deposit which is exposed to the atmosphere, the voids are filled with the air, gasses or air and water, both. In such deposits, the specific weight varies significantly. Specific weights of some reservoir's sediment deposits are given in Table 10.4.

Table 10.4. Specific weight of some submerged sediment deposits formed in different reservoirs

Reservoir (location)	*Average sp.weight (lb/ft^3)*
Nizam Sagar reservoir (India)	84.0
Lake Harris (USA)	59.9
Herman lage pond (USA)	54.8
Mountain lake (USA)	54.8
Mata tila reservoir (India)	54.0
Moran reservoir (USA)	49.2
White rock (USA)	49.0
Crab orchard Lake (USA)	49.0
Lake wood Land (USA)	39.9
Lake Arthar (s. Africa)	38.0
Lake ft. Phantom hill (USA)	36.0
Lake Throckmorton	31.6

Porosity

It is another bulk property of sediment deposits, defined as the percentage of pore space of bulk volume of sediment deposits, given as under :

$$\text{Porosity} = \frac{\text{Bulk volume of sediment} - \text{volume of solid}}{\text{Bulk volume of sediment}} \times 100$$

The percentage of pore space in the sediment deposits, depends on the size distribution of fine and coarse grains, shape of the particles and their arrangement. A deposit containing sand and silt particles between coarse sand and gravel particles, the porosity of deposit reduces significantly. The reason may be explained as : the deposit of fine grained sediments is subject to compaction, causing less volume of voids, than the deposit of coarse grains or gravel. The shape and arrangement of particles also affect the porosity. The arrangement of spherical particles of non-uniform diameter, forms more porosity *i.e.* about 49%, while arrangement of sphers of uniform diameter forms about 25% pore spaces. However, the natural sedimentary deposits contain more than 50% porosity. The porosity of deposit is generally expressed interms of total porosity or effective porosity. Total porosity includes all the pore spaces of the deposit. Effective porosity refers only to the interconnected pore spaces. The porosity of unconsolidated saturated formation can be calculated by using the following formula, given by Komura (1961) :

$$P = 0.245 + 0.0864\, d_{50}^{-0.21} \qquad \text{...(10.15)}$$

in which, P is the porosity expressed in fraction and d_{50} is the median size of particle, cm. An approximate value of average porosity of some common formations is given in Table 10.5

Table 10.5. Average porosity of some formations/ depsits.

Formations/deposits	*Porosity (%)*
Granite, Basalt	45.0
Lime stone	40.0
Shale, sand stone	35.0
Gravel	25.0
Sand	18.0
Silt	10.0
Clay	1.0

Angle of Repose

It is an important property of soil mass or sediment deposits for analysis of critical tractive force and design of stable channels, hydraulic structures etc. For stable channels with non-cohesive sides, the side slope of bank is decided on the basis of angle of repose. Gibson developed following relationship for computation of angle of repose (ϕ) :

$$\tan \phi = k \cdot d^{0.125} \cdot S^{0.19} \cdot r^{0.25} \quad ...(10.16)$$

where, K = factor, taken as 0.92

d = mean grain diameter, inch

S = specific gravity of the particle under water

r = ratio of the longest to shortest diameters of grain.

This equation holds good for the 'd' ranging from 5.2×10^{-3} to 1.92×10^{-2} inch and 'S' from 0.90 to 1.63. The values of tan ϕ of different materials have been determined by Simons (1957), given in Table 10.6.

Table 10.6. Values of 'tan ϕ'

Median diameter (inch)	*Angle of repose (ϕ)*		
	Crushed edge rock	*Very angular rock*	*Very rounded rock*
0.01	32.0	31.4	29.2
0.05	34.5	32.9	29.5
0.10	36.6	33.8	29.9
0.50	40.0	37.5	32.5
1.00	40.8	39.1	34.8
5.00	42.0	41.2	38.3
10.0	42.2	41.5	39.2

Source: Simons (1957)

10.4. Sediment Transportation

The process of sediment yield and its transportation begins by the action of falling raindrops during rainfall. Process may be described as : when rain drops fall on the ground surface with some force, then break the soil particles into finer and at the same time also detach some soil particles from the ground, which are mixed in flowing water and finally reach to the streams or in the reservoirs. Detachment of soil particles due to rain drops, depends very much on the size of raindrops and soil characteristics. The size of rain drop is directly proportional to the rainfall intensity. Magnitude of impacting force exerted by the raindrop can be approximated by the following empirical relation, given by Wischemeir.

$$KE = 210.3 + 89 \log_{10} I \quad ...(10.17)$$

in which, KE is the kinetic energy, expressed in metric tones per hectare-cm and I is rainfall intensity, cm/h.

Gilbert classified the sediment transportation process in following three steps :

1. Saltation.
2. Suspenson, and
3. Surface creep.

In saltation process, the coarse sediment particles are transported either in the form of bed load slide, rolling or short skips. The saltation process gets change into suspension, when particle size becomes finer. The mechanics of saltation process has been described in detail in section 10.4.1.

Suspension process refers to the transportation of very fine particles by flowing fluids in suspension form. It is carried out due to turbulence created by flowing water or blowing winds.

In surface creep action the large size sediment particles are transported in form of creeping along the stream bed.

10.4.1. Mechanics of Saltation Process

The mechanics of saltation process during water flow has been described by several investigators, but amongst them Danel et.al (1953) have given an interesting view on saltation mechanism. According to him, the saltation mechanism is described by considering the following four conditions as per position of sediments :

1. Sediment particle rests on a reasonably plane bed, composed of similar particles [Fig. 10.2 (a)].

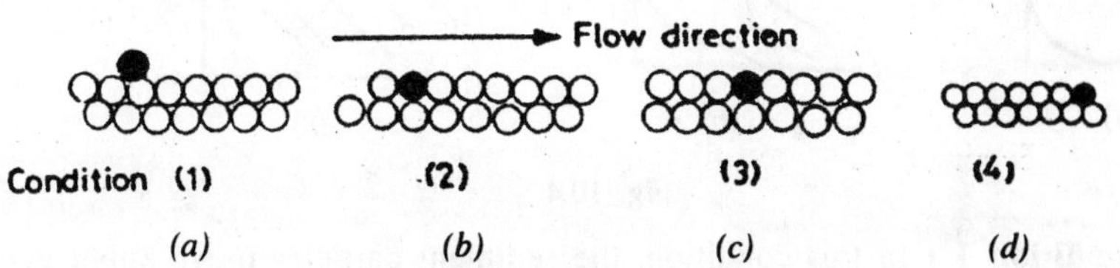

Fig. 10.2

2. Sediment particle rests on the plane bed of similar particles and supported by a layer of particles at downstream side Fig. 10.2 (*b*).

3. The particle under consideration as one of the particles which form the layer and is also surrounded by the other particles Fig. 10.2 (*c*).

4. The particle is at the down stream end of the layer Fig. 10.2 (*d*).

The saltation mechanism for above conditions is explained below. As per mode of particles movement in saltation process, it is more appropriate to start the mechanism by considering the condition (2), first.

Condition 2 : Referring, Fig. 10.3, it is seen that two forces are acting on the particle, in which one is submerged weight of the particle (W') acting vertically downward from the center of particle and other is the hydrodynamic force resulting from the uplift and drag forces. The hydrodynamic force (F) is directly proportional to the square of velocity. In this way, if 'F' increases, then there may arrive a situation, when particle is at equilibrium stage and ready to move from its original place, on increase of flow velocity. In addition, during course of stream flow, when uplift force due to water flow becomes greater than the W', then particles also tend to get lifted up [Fig. 10.4 (*a*)]. And once the particle has been lifted, the stream lines become more effective near top of the particle. Fruther more, a large area of the particle is under stagnation pressure, which also increases the lifting force. Due to these effects the particles acquire an upward velocity. During passing of particle from position '*a*' to '*b*' as shown in Fig. 10.4 (*b*), the movement of particle is might be due to rolling and sliding actions on the supporting wall located at down stream side, accompained a quick rotation about contact point of the wall and particle. At this stage, the lifting force acting on the particle gets induced. This type of effect is called "magnus effect."

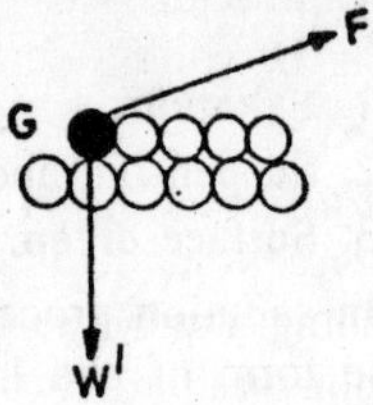

Fig. 10.3

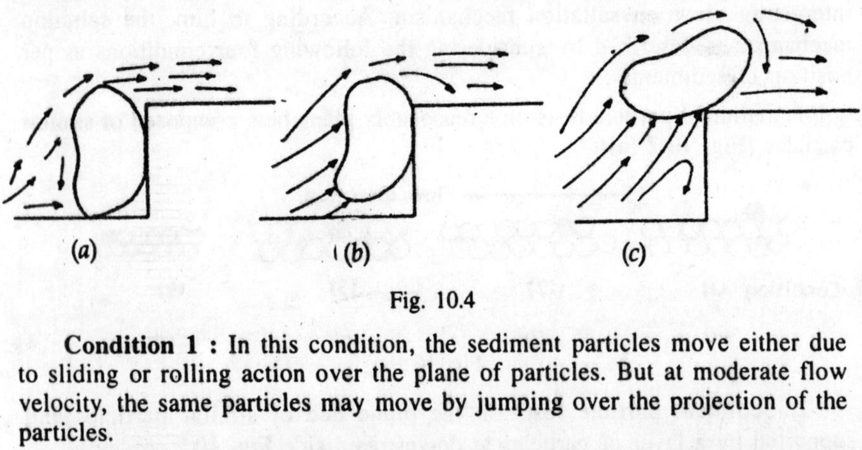

Fig. 10.4

Condition 1 : In this condition, the sediment particles move either due to sliding or rolling action over the plane of particles. But at moderate flow velocity, the same particles may move by jumping over the projection of the particles.

Condition 3 : Under this condition, the movement of particle takes place due to impacting force exerted by the other particles existing u/s side during movement.

10.5. Sediment Load

Total sediment carried by the runoff/stream flow is called sediment load. It can be in following types :

1. Contact load
2. Saltation load
3. Suspended load, and
4. Bed load.

Contact Load : The sediment load moving along the stream bed by rolling or sliding actions is called contact load. This type of sediment load is always in contact of stream bed.

Saltation Load : This is the transition load between bed load and suspended load. The movement of sediment particles is in the form of bouncing along the stream bed or movement due to direct or indirect impact of bouncing particles. Generally, small particles of sand and gravel are moved as saltation load.

Suspended Load : Very fine particles moving in suspension form along the flow is termed as suspended load. The samplers used for measuring the suspended load are called suspended load samplers. Based on the size of particles, the suspended sediments are classified into following three grades :

1. Coarse sediment — diameter more than 0.20 mm
2. Medium sediment — diameter 0.20 to 0.075 mm
3. Fine sediment — diameter less than 0.075 mm

The diameter of sediment refers to the diameter of spherical object, which has same specific weight and terminal settling velocity lying in the same sedimentation fluid.

Bed Load : It includes large size particles, which move by rolling or sliding actions on or near the stream bed. The transportation of sediments under rolling, sliding or sometimes hopping actions depends on the stream flow velocity. The sediments, which move as bed load at a particular stream section may be as suspended load at another stream section, if there is high flow velocity.

The depth-wise movement of sediment as per size of the particle is given as under :

1. Large size sediments move along the stream bed called bed load.

2. Coarse sediments move immediately above the stream bed, constitutes saltation load.

3. The layer of fine sediments, extending upto the top of water surface, constitutes suspended load. Sediment concentration of this layer increases towards downward from top of the water surface.

10.6. Estimation of Sediment Load

10.6.1. Bed load estimation

Following methods are commonly used for computing the bed load sediments :

1. Analytical method, and
2. Sampling method

Analytical Method : It involves several empirical formulae for computing the bed load movement based on the following concepts :

1. For initiation of bed load movement a minimum force is exerted by the fluid on sediment particles.

2. The force exerted by sediments on stream bed is not constant, but varies about some mean value. This concept is based on the theory of turbulent flow.

The common empirical formulae, used for computing the transportation of bed load are described as under :

Du Boy's Formula : This formula was developed on the basis of tractive force theory for the sand as sediment particle. The formula is given by

$$q_s = C_s \cdot \tau_o (\tau_o - \tau_c) \qquad ...(10.18)$$

where, q_s = rate of bed load transport per second per unit stream width

C_s = coefficient; depends on the size and shape of the sediment. It can be computed by the relationship as

$$= \frac{0.177}{d^{3/4}} \qquad ...(10.19)$$

d = diameter of sediment, mm

τ_o = average shear stress exerted on the channel boundary.

τ_c = critical shear stress.

This formula has following assumptions :

1. Sand movement is in the form of layer and subjects a uniform tractive force.

2. The gradient of vertical velocity of particle is linear.

3. Rate of sediment transport is directly proportional to the difference of average and critical shear stresses required to start the movement of sediment.

Shield's Formula : It estimates better, when bed load is composed of uniform size sediments. The formual was developed on the basis of effect of specific gravity of the sediment on transportation of bed load in addition to the tractive force, written as under :

$$\frac{q_s \cdot S_s}{q \cdot s} = \frac{(\tau_o - \tau_c)}{\gamma \cdot (S_s - 1) \cdot d} \times 100 \qquad ..(10.20)$$

where, q_s = sediment flow rate per second per unit stream width

q = discharge rate per unit stream width.

S_s = specific gravity of the sediment

S = slope of stream bed

γ = unit weight of the fluid

d = diameter of sediment

Meyer Peter's Formula : This was developed by a Swiss-engineer by considering the effect of grain diameter, bed slope and discharge characteristics of stream flow on bed load transportation. The formula is given as under :

$$G_s = \left[\tau_o \left(\frac{N'}{N}\right)^{3/2} - \tau_c\right] \times 4700 \qquad ...(10.21)$$

where, G_s = transportation rate of bed load, expressed as per unit stream width per hour

N' = Manning's roughness coefficient for plain bed

d = effective diameter of grain

N = actual Manning's roughness coefficient for rippled bed. It depends on the discharge rate. However, the following values can be taken for N

(*i*) Discharge more than 11 m^3/s — 0.020

(*ii*) Discharge less than 11 m^3/s — 0.0225

τ_o = unit tractive force exerted by the flowing water. It can be computed by using the following formula :

$$\tau_o = 0.97 \cdot \gamma \cdot R \cdot S \qquad ...(10.22)$$

in which, γ is the specific gravity of fluid, R is hydraulic mean radius of the stream flow *i.e.* $\left(\frac{A}{P}\right)$, A and P are the cross-sectional area and wetted perimeter of the stream flow, respectively and S is the slope of stream bed.

τ_c = critical shear stress required to initiate the movement of sediment, kg/m^2. It is given by

$\tau_c = 0.07\, d$, in which '*d*' is the grain diameter.

Chang Formula : It is given as under :

$$G_i = \frac{K \cdot n}{\tau_c^2}\, \tau_o (\tau_o - \tau_c) \qquad ...(10.23)$$

where, G_i = rate of bed load transport, per second/unit stream width

K = constant

n = Manning's roughness coefficient

τ_o = unit tractive force due to stream flow

τ_c = critical shear stress to displace the sediment. It is given as

$$\tau_c = 0.0175\,(1.65\, d)^x \qquad ...(10.24)$$

in which, '*d*' is the grain diameter (*mm*) and '*x*' is exponent equal to 1 or 0.5 when 1.65 *d* is more or less than 1, respectively.

The equation (10.25) holds good for computing τ_c of the sediments having specific gravity 2.65.

Schoklitsh Formula :This formula was developed on the basis of experimental data on transportation of bed loads through stream flow. The formula assumes that the bed load is composed of uniform size grains. Formula is given by :

$$G_i = \frac{4.37}{\sqrt{d}} \cdot S^{1.5} \cdot (q - q_c) \qquad ...(10.25)$$

where, G_i = rate of bed load movement (F.P.S.unit)

d = grain diameter

S = slope of stream bed

q = observed discharge rate per unit stream width

q_c = critical discharge rate, given by

$$= \frac{d}{S^{4/3}} \cdot 2.1 \times 10^{-4} \qquad ...(10.26)$$

10.6.2. Measurement of Bed Load by Using Samplers

In this method of bed load determination, the samplers are used for collecting the bed load samples from stream flow. Sampler is placed over the stream bed and samples are collected from different locations for the given time period. During sampling the sampler is kept in proper position by using the rod, particularly when stream flow depth is less. At greater stream flow depth, the sampler is suspended from boat, trolley or pully running on a cable spanned across the river/stream and sometimes from the bridge, also. Raising and lowering of sampler is done with the help of winch, provided in the system.

Types of Bed Load Sampler

The followings are the main bed load samplers for collecting the sediment samples from stream flow :

1. **Direct measuring bed load sampler**

(*a*) Early type sampler

(*i*) Basket type

(*ii*) Pan or tray type

(*iii*) Pressure difference type, and

(*iv*) Slot or pit type

(*b*) Recent type sampler

(*i*) Sphinx sampler

(*ii*) Karloyi sampler, and

(*iii*) VUN sampler

2. **Indirect bed load measuring devices**

1. Acoustic instrument, and
2. Ultrasonic method

All these are described as under.

Basket type sampler : This type of sampler consists of a box or basket, made of meshed material. For collecting sediment sample, the sampler is lowered into the stream flow to the bed, in such a way that the open end of sampler is opposite to the direction of stream flow, so that the moving sediments can be trapped by the basket, easily.

Demerit of this sampler is that, when it is lowered into the stream flow, then there is exerted an inward resistance to the flow, as result the net entrance velocity of flow coming into the sampler gets reduced. Due to this effect, few sediments are dropped before entering the sampler. In this way, the catching of sediments is not exact *i.e.* the amount of sediment caught by the sampler is less than the actual amount.

Pan or Tray type sampler : It consists of a flat pan or a tray shaped device for collecting the sediment sample from stream flow. The baffle or slots are also provided in the sampler to check the outgoing sediments from the sampler. It has same demerits as in case of basket type bed load sampler.

Pressure difference type sampler : This sampler is designed to overcome all those demerits, which are generally found in basket type and tray or pan type samplers. It consists of a pressure drop at its exit point, to eliminate the energy loss or to maintain the actual entrance flow velocity into the sampler. Sometimes, this sampler is also provided with a collecting screen in place of baffle for checking the outgoing of sediments from the sampler.

Slot or Pit type sampler : It consists of slots and a tank. The width of slot ranges from 100 to 200 times the particles diameter. For collecting sediment sample, the entire stream width is equipped with the slots; and bed load moving along the flow is dropped over the slots, which is continuousely discharged into the tank. Sediment sample is collected for a given time and transportation of bed load per unit time and per unit stream width is determined.

For use of this sampler, it is essential to maintain non-erodible stream bed at u/s and d/s sections of the slots to eliminate the problem of soil erosion during sampling.

Direct Measuring Bed Load Sampler — Recent Type

Sphinx sampler : This sampler was designed and constructed by Vinckers et.al (1953). It is suitable for measuring the sediment loads containing the particles finer than 0.4 mm diameter. Sampler consists of a rectangular nozzle at front, a wide exit at the rear end and a settling chamber. The flow enters the sampler through a nozzle and gets out from the exit point. During exit of flow, the sediment particles present in the water are dropped in the settling chamber.

The hydraulic efficiency of this sampler varies upto 90% or more and 8 to 15 percent sediments are escaped. Hydraulic efficiency of sampler is the "ratio of discharge passing through the sampler to the product of nozzle area and flow velocity *i.e.*

$$e_h = \frac{\text{Discharge through the sampler}}{\text{Nozzle area} \times \text{flow velocity}} \quad ...(10.27)$$

Karloyi sampler : It is modified form of pressure-difference type bed load sampler. A curve shape dividing wall is provided at rear end of the sampler, which is perforated length-wise in rear half portion. During sampling, as stream water enters the sampler, the suspended sediments are dropped below the dividing wall and sediment free water rises through the openings and is ultimately discharged out from the exit. Sampler is also equipped with a flexible bottom at its entrance and an automatic closing valve. The automatic valve gets open, when sampler is lowered to the stream bed for sampling. The hydraulic efficiency of this sampler is about 80%, while sampling efficiency varies upto 45 percent.

VUN Sampler : This sampler was developed by Novak in 1959. It is an improved form of Karloyi sampler, which consists of a dividing wall at its rear end. In dividing wall, there is one large and eight small mesh slots are provided. This sampler is found more suitable for measuring the bed load having the sediment size from 1 to 100 mm. At a time, this sampler can collect the sample of 65 lb or more. Sampling efficiency of VUN sampler is about 70 percent.

Indirect Measuring Bed Load Devices

These divices are comparatively recent development. The common indirect measuring bed load devices are described as under :

1. **Acoustic Instruments :** These instruments consist of following components :

1. Base plate or forked shape rod
2. Micro phone
3. Magnetic tape recorder
4. Oscilloscope
5. Head phone

For sediment sampling, when instrument is lowered to the stream bed, the sediment particles present in the stream flow, strike to the base plate or forked shaped rod and generates a kind of sound, which is recorded by the micro phone of the system. From micro phone, the recorded sound is transmitted to the oscilloscope or to a hand phone by magnetic tape recorder. Merit of this instrument is that, it is suitable to determine the relative bed load transport in the stream flow and relative variation of the same with the time, also. These informations are required for deciding the number of samples to be collected and location of sampling points. However, Hubbel (1964) reported that, the relative bed load distribution in natural streams, determined by this instrument is different to that which is determined by the slot type sampler. The acoustic instruments are more suitable for those streams, which contain coarse bed materials.

Ultrasonic method : The working principle of this instrument is based on the concept that, there is absorption of acoustic energy by the sediments mixed in water. During bed load measurement, the acoustic energy is transmitted into the stream flow. The amount of energy absorbed by the sediments in flow is calibrated in terms of bed-load movement. By using calbration curve, the bed load is determined. This method involves following assumptions :

1. Size distribution of bed load and stream bed material is the same.
2. Velocity of sediment is equal to the average velocity of stream flow.

Calibration of Bed Load Samplers

The bed load samplers described above require calibration before taking into use, because they do not yield the exact bed load movement as in the streams/rivers. Following two are the common methods, employed for calibration of bed load samplers :

1. Fixed flume method, and
2. Movable flume method

Fixed flume method : In this method, calibration of bed load sampler is performed by using fixed bed flume. The following steps are followed :

1. Install the flume at suitable or specified location.
2. Inject a known amount of sediments into the flume at uniform rate from a short distance towards upstream side of the flume. The sediment injection should be done throughout the flume width.
3. Put the sampler in the flume for taking measurement.

During experiment the observations on injection rate of sediment, width of flume & sampler and amount of sediment retained on the sampler are recorded. Based on these observations, the efficiency of sampler to catch the sediment is evaluated. The accuracy of calibration depends, very much on the uniformity in distribution of injected sediments throughout the flume width.

Limitation : This method has following limitations :

1. Rate of bed-load movement is likely to vary along the length and width of the flume, causing the measurements to be erroneous.
2. Injection of sediment in the flow at uniform rate is not possible.
3. Flow condition in the flume is not mutually related to the stream flow at equilibrium stage.

Movable flume method : This method consists of a movable flume bed, simulated to the natural stream. The used bed material in the flume is same to the river material. The sampler's efficiency is determined by comparing the injected and measured rates of sediments in the flume.

To determine the bed load movement through stream flow, the sampler is placed in the flow over the bed for collection of sediment samples The collected samples are filtered and filtered sediments are dried in sunlight. The weight of dried sediments is taken, accurately. The sediment's weight is divided by the product of time taken for measurement and stream width to get the rate of bed load movement per unit time and per unit stream width.

Sometimes, the sampling of bed load is not possible due to unforeseen reasons; under this condition, depending on characteristics of the bed load material, an amount of 2.5 to 15 percent of suspended load is added to the suspended load, to get the bed load flowing in the stream. A sample calculation for estimating the bed load is given in the example 10.1.

Example 10.1. *A watershed of 1000 ha area is equipped with a rectangular weir at its outlet. The length of weir's crest is 1.5 m. Calculate the bed load and total sediment load moving through the flow by using the following observations on suspended load :*

1. Concentration of coarse sediment = 4 g/l
2. Concentration of medium sediment = 6.5 g/l
3. Concentration of fine sediment = 1.5 g/l

Solution. Total suspended load

$$= 4 + 6.5 + 1.5 = 12 \text{ g/l}$$

or $$\frac{12}{1.4} = 8.57 \text{ c.c.}$$

(Assuming the density of sediment as 1.4 g/c.c.)

Suspended load (ha. m/m^3) $$= \frac{8.57}{100 \times 100 \times 100 \times 1000}$$

$$= \mathbf{8.57 \times 10^{-7}\ ha{\cdot}m/m^3}$$

Runoff computation : Using the weir formula (rectangular)

$$Q = 1.84\, L{\cdot}H^{3/2} \qquad \text{...(10.28)}$$

$$= 1.84 \times 1.54 \times 1^{3/2}$$

$$= \mathbf{2.76\ m^3/s}$$

Total runoff volume per day

$$= 2.76 \times 3600 \times 24$$

$$= \mathbf{23.85\ ha{\cdot}m/day}$$

Total suspended load in runoff of 238464 m^3 per day

$$= 8.57 \times 10^{-7} \times 238464$$

$$= \mathbf{0.204\ ha{\cdot}m/day}$$

Since this amount of suspended load is contributed from the area of 1000 ha or 10 km^2. Therefore, rate of flowing suspended sediment is equal to

$$= 0.204 \times \frac{100}{10} \cdot \text{ha·m}/100\ \text{km}^2/\text{day}$$

$$= 2.04\ \text{ha·m}/100\ \text{km}^2/\text{day}$$

2. **Computation of bed load :** Assuming the contribution of bed load as 10% of the suspended load. Thus, bed load is equal to $2.04 \times \frac{10}{100} = 0.204\ \text{ha·}m/100\ km^2/day.$

3. **Computation of total sediment load :** It is given by,

$$\text{Total sediment load} = \text{Suspend load} + \text{bed load}$$

$$= 2.04 + 0.204$$

$$= \mathbf{2.244\ ha·m/100\ km^2/day\ Ans}$$

10.7. Measurement of Suspended load

Suspended load is measured by suspended load sampler. The commonly used suspended load samplers are given as under :

1. Depth integrating sampler
2. Point integrating sampler
3. Automatic single stage sampler, and
4. Pumping sampler

Depth-integrating sampler : It consists of following components :

1. Metal body
2. Head
3. Tail fins
4. Container or bottle
5. Outlet tube

The tail fins are provided to the metal body. Function of fins is to align the sampler in the direction of stream flow. The container or bottle is housed in the body by its head portion. The size of bottle is same to the standard milk bottle. The inlet tube is projected out of the sampler. The size of inlet tube depends on the desired rate to fill the bottle. The outlet tube is equipped on the side of head, which function is to provide a passage for escaping the air during sediment sampling. Before lowering the sampler into stream flow, the bottle is kept in the metal body and sealed properly. The sealed connection between inlet & outlet tubes and the bottle is made by closing the head.

For sediment sampling, the sampler is traversed throughout the flow depth with uniform speed and returned back with the same speed.

A high lowering speed affects the intake of sediment load into the bottle, as result the measured sediment load is not correct. Similarly, at less lowering speed, the sampler is filled before reaching to the desired depth, causing incorrect sampling of sediment load. However, for accurate measurement, the maximum and minimum lowering as well as raising speed of sampler can be taken from the graph (TCPCM, 1969) based on stream flow depth and mean flow velocity at stream verticals.

The depth-integrating samplers are suspended into the flow by cable from bridge or some other similar types of structure. Use of cable is normally preferred, when stream flow depth is not less than 15 feet and flow velocity is more. Sometimes, wading is also used for suspending the sampler, but in shallow streams with the flow rate per unit width not more than 10 ft^2/s. The depth-integrating samplers are found in following types :

Types	*Remark*
US DH-48 (weight 4.5 lb)	Used in small streams, in which wading is possible.
US DH-59 (weight 24 lb)	Used in less stream depth along with low flow velocity.
US DH-49 (weight-62 lb)	Used in medium flow depth by cable suspension.

Point-integrating samplers : These samplers are used for collecting the sediment sample from a specified point of the stream vertical. The determined sediment load at the selected point represents the mean concentration of sediment at that point. In many samplers, it is generally observed that when sampler is lowered into the stream flow at the given point, then there is sudden inrush of water, unless air pressure of the container is equal to the hydrostatic pressure at that point. This happening affects the entry of sediments into the sampler (i.e. less than the actual amount). However, point integrating samplers are specially designed to overcome such types of effect. Main components of point-integrating samplers are given as under :

1. Inner chamber
2. Air chamber
3. Sample container
4. Rotary table
5. Intake nozzle
6. Air exhaust

Inner chamber holds the sample container which is covered by the air cnamber. The volume of air chamber is greater than the sample container.

The air chamber is permanently opened from its bottom side. The sample container and air chamber are inter-connected through a passage in between, which is closed or opened by an electrically operated rotary valve. This valve also opens and closes the intake nozzle and air exhaust port during sampling operation.

Before lowering the sampler into stream flow, the intake nozzle and air exhaust port are closed; and at the same time the pressure equalizing port is opened for making the air pressure of container equal to the hydrostatics pressure. When air pressure of the container becomes equal to the hydrostatic pressure, then stream water starts to enter in the air chamber, causing the pressure of air chamber and of the bottle/container is raised than the hydrostatic pressure. Now, pressure equalizing port is closed and intake as well as air exhaust ports are opened, simultaneously for picking the sample. At this stage the intake velocity of flow into the sampler becomes equal to the flow velocity of stream. After collecting the sample, all three ports are closed and sampler is removed from the stream flow.

The point-integrating samplers can also be used as depth- integrating samplers in following ways :

1. By opening the intake nozzle at the stream bed and integrating from there to the top of water surface.

2. By dividing the total height of verticals into different parts and integrating them. The sediment concentration obtained at the selected point of vertical indicates the average concentration of sediment.

The point-integrating samplers are of following types :

Sampler	*Remark*
P–46 (100 lb. weight)	Contains a pint milk bottle.
P–61 (100 lb. weight)	Contains a pint milk bottle.
P-63 (200 lb. weight)	Contains either a pint or a quart milk bottle.

Automatic single stage sampler : It is used for collecting the suspended load samples from flashy streams, automatically. It is used in those streams, which are not easily accessible. The automatic samplers are installed near the stream bank. For collecting the samples from different points, individual samplers are installed at respective points.

The automatic single stage sampler consists of following parts :

2. Pint milk bottle
2. Intake
   (*a*) Horizontal intake
   (*b*) Vertical intake

3. Air exhaust
4. Crown
5. Syphon

The intake and air exhaust are attached to the pint milk bottle. Two types of intake are used in this sampler *i.e.* horizontal and vertical intake, in which vertical intake is generally $\frac{3}{16}''$ to $\frac{1}{4}''$ of copper tube. The sampler with vertical intake is called vertical intake sampler, while sampler consisting horizontal intake is referred as "horizontal intake sampler". The horizontal intake samplers are used for collecting the samples of sediment coarser than 62 microns, while vertical intake samplers are used for sampling the fine sediments. The vertical intake samplers have advantage over horizontal intake samplers regarding not deposition of debris at the intake window.

When river stage reaches to the crown level, the water enters and starts to flow over the crown. Simultaneously, the syphon attached to the system gets primed and water is filled in the bottle. Normally, the entrance velocity of sediment into bottle is greater than the flow velocity of the stream, causing effect on sediment catching. The sample collected in the bottle should be upto the level of inner end of the air exhaust.

Demerits : The automatic single-stage sampler involves following demerits :

1. Since this sampler is installed near the stream bank, therefore determined sediment concentration is not correct.

2. The intake velocity of sediment into the bottle is greater than the stream flow velocity, causing the measured sediment rate to be is erroneous.

3. It collects the samples of sediment for the rising stage of flow, not for falling stage.

Pumping sampler : It is another automatic suspended load sampler. It records a continuous measurement of sediment concentration at regular interval from the selected point of the stream flow. The samples are collected by pumping the water from stream. Care is taken that, during each sampling one pint sample should be pumped from the stream and then collected in the bottle. During high flow stage the samples should be taken at every one-hour interval, while at low flow stage, it should be at 12-h intervals (TCPSM 1969).

Demerits : These are as under :

1. In pumping samplers the flow characteristics at intake do not represent the ideal condition.

2. Intake does not indicate the flow direction.

3. Intake velocity is not equal to the stream flow velocity.

Merits : This sampler provides more accurate calibration of sediment concentration corresponding to the mean concentration at stream verticals as compared to the point-integrating and depth-integrating samplers.

10.8. Aspects of Suspended Load Sampling

Following three aspects are generally followed for suspended load sampling :

1. Location of verticals
2. Position of sampling point at verticals, and
3. Frequency of sampling

In order to have correct measurement of sediment flow rate, the above aspects must be followed, carefully.

10.8.1. Sediment sampling at stream verticals

The sediment concentration greatly varies depth-wise in the stream flow *i.e.* near stream bed it is more while at the top of water surface it is less. In this way, the sediment concentration determined at any flow depth does not represent the average sediment load of stream flow. Therefore, the selection of sampling point at vertical section of stream flow is very important. The following points are generally taken care for collecting the sediment samples at stream verticals incase of point-integrating samplers :

1. In single point sampling, the sample should be collected at the depth of '0.6*d*' from the top of water surface. (*d* is the stream flow depth).

2. In two point sampling, one sample should be taken at the top of water surface approximately at 0.2*d* and other sample should be from the near of stream bed *i.e.* at '0.8*d*' from the top of water surface. The sediment concentrations obtained at these two points are equally weighted to get mean sediment concentration in stream flow.

3. In three point sampling, the samples are collected from three different points *i.e.* near the top of water surface, mid of the flow depth and near the stream bed. Sediment concentrations at these depths are equally weighted to get average suspended sediment load in stream flow.

4. Similarly, in multipoint sampling, the samples are collected from several points of stream vertical and are analysed to determine the sediment load at each point. Multipoint sampling is useful to determine the depth-wise distribution of sediment concentration in the stream flow.

10.8.2. Width-wise sediment sampling

The number of sampling points in stream width depends on the extent of stream flow width, as given in Table 10.6

Table 10.6. Number and location of sampling points in stream width

Stream width (m)	*No. of sampling points*	*Location*
< 30	3	At 25%, 50% and 75% of stream width
30—300	5	At 25%, 35%, 50%, 65% and 80% of stream width
> 300	7	At 15%, 30%, 40%, 50%, 60%, 70% and 80% of stream width

10.8.3. Sediment observation posts

The location of sediment observation posts is decided on the basis of following points :

1. As for as possible, the stream gauging site should be used as the sampling point. Most preferably, it should be located at the outlet of catchment, because it is the place where sediment yield from the catchment area comes.

2. Sampling points should be free from disturbing objects, protrusion, confluent as well as back water effect.

3. Site should be at that point of stream from where a constant soil erosion is in occurrence by turbulence effect.

4. Site should be easily asssessible and also linked with transportation facilities like road, rails and bridge.

5. At sediment monitoring station if over head plateform is available, then it should be used. It helps in sediment sampling from the entire stream width.

6. In torrent flow the cable bridge should used for taking the samples.

7. The sampling site should have a straight reach of atleast 150 m at u/s and d/s sides, both.

10.8.4. Sediment monitory station

Location of sediment monitoring station at appropriate site in the stream plays an important role for measurement of sediment load. The site selection for monitoring station should be on the basis of following points :

1. It should be at the outlet of watershed.

2. The site should be easily assessible.

3. The u/s and d/s sides of monitoring station should be straight.

4. The portrusion, confluent and back water effect should not be there.

5. If there exists road or bridge, then they should be used for collecting the sediment sample.

6. The stream point under constant soil erosion due to water turbulence should be preferred for location of sediment monitoring station.

10.9. Instruments For Sediment Monitoring Station

At sediment monitoring station the following instruments are essentially required for collecting and analysing the hydrologic data, such as rainfall, runoff, sediment yield etc., :

A. **Onsite Instruments** (For taking observations)

(*i*) Rain guage — recording and non-recording type

(*ii*) Automatic runoff recorder

(*iii*) Current meter with accessories

(*iv*) Dumpy level
(*v*) Staff gauge
(*vi*) Crane trolley
(*vii*) Cable bridge arrangement
(*viii*) Automatic stage level recorder
(*ix*) Sediment samplers - bed load and suspended load samplers
(*x*) Enamel bucket with cover

B. **Onsite Instruments** (For analysis)

(*i*) B.S.S. Sieve
(*ii*) Measuring cylinder
(*iii*) Stop watch
(*iv*) Thermometer
(*v*) Wash bottle
(*vi*) Beaker- 500 ml
(*vii*) Funnel with stand
(*viii*) Silt tube with stand
(*ix*) Jug
(*x*) China clay disc etc.

C. **Chemical Laboratory Instruments**

1. Chemical balance
2. Hot oven
3. Metalic flash and bottle.
4. Enamel bucket.

10.10. Data Collection and Analysis

(*a*) **Required data** (For stream gauging by using area-velocity method)

1. Width of segment
2. Depth of segment
3. Velocity of flow at each segment
4. Observation period etc.

(*b*) **Analysis/computation :** The method for determining runoff and sediment yield is described under following steps :

1. **Computation of runoff :** The area-velocity method is commonly used, described as under :

Using the equation,

$$Q = A \cdot V \qquad ...(10.29)$$

where, Q = runoff rate, m^3/s
$= q_1 + q_2 + \dots q_n$
A = cross–sectional area of the stream flow, m^2
V = flow velocity, m/s
$q_1, q_2 \dots q_n$ = discharge passing through segments 1, 2, ...n, respectively

Discharge passing through different segments is given by :

$$q = \text{cross-sectional area of flow segment} \times \text{flow velocity}$$

$$\therefore \left.\begin{aligned} q_1 &= a_1 \cdot v_1 \\ q_2 &= a_2 \cdot v_2 \\ &\vdots \\ q_n &= a_n \cdot v_n \end{aligned}\right\} \quad ...(10.30)$$

Thus, $Q = q_1 + q_2 + \ldots q_n$

$$= a_1 \cdot v_1 + a_2 \cdot v_2 + \ldots a_n \cdot v_n \quad ...(10.31)$$

Total volume of runoff/discharge $= Q \cdot t$ ...(10.32)

in which, 't' is the observation period.

Total runoff/discharge (m^3/day) $= Q \cdot t \times 3600 \times 24$

$$\text{Total runoff (mm/day)} = \frac{Q \cdot t \times 24 \times 3600}{10{,}000 \times \text{watershed area } (ha)}$$

$$\text{Total runoff (mm/month)} = \sum_{i=1}^{30} \frac{360 \times 24}{\text{Watershed area } (ha)} \cdot (Q \cdot t)_i \quad ...(10.33)$$

2. **Computation of rate of sediment yield**

$$\text{(1) Runoff (mm/day)} = \frac{\text{Runoff volume/day} \times 1000}{10{,}000 \times \text{watershed area } (ha)}$$

(2) Sediment yield (ha. m/day)

$$= \frac{\text{Sediment (c.c./m}^3) \times \text{runoff (m}^3\text{/day)}}{10^{10} \times \text{watershed area } (ha)}$$

3. **Sediment production rate** (ha.m/100 km^2/day)

$$= \frac{\text{Sediment yield (ha. m/day)} \times 100}{\text{Watershed area (km}^2)}$$

10.11. Analysis of Suspended load

The suspended load samples collected from stream flow/reservoir are analysed for determining the rate of sediment flow in suspension form by using the following methods :

1. Gravimetric method ; and
2. Hydrometric method

For analysis of sediment sample by using hydrometric method trained staff is required. This method is suitable for the sites where laboratory facilities are available for analysis work. For analysis of fine sediments the hydrometric method is very difficult and also does not result correct value. The gravimetric method is most suitable for determining the fine sediments and obtained result is also more reliable, is discussed below :

10.11.1. Analysis of Coarse Sediment

The collected suspended load samples from different points of stream flow are thoroughly mixed in the sample water and allowed to pass through BSS-100 (IMM-70) seive. The retained sediment particles on sieve are then thoroughly washed by clean water jet and kept for drying in oven or directly in the sun light. The weight of dry sediment is determined for the whole sampled volume. The obtained sediment is expressed in terms of g/l or ha.m per 100 sq.km area of watershed.

10.11.2. Analysis of Medium Sediment

The supernant water left during analysis of coarse sediments is collected in a enamel bucket or in a beaker for analysis of medium size sediments. If supermant water is not sufficient to make a depth of 10 cm in the beaker, then clean water is added to it. After that, the prepared sample is kept for stirring for few seconds so that uniform mixing of sediments in water can take place. It is now allowed to stand for some time to settle down the sediments. The range of settling time as per temperature of supernant water through 10 cm water column in beaker is given in Table 10.7.

Table 10.7. Settling time for medium sediments (ISI 6339:1971)

Temperature (°C)	*Settling time (sec)*
0—9	27.0
10—15	25.0
16—20	22.0
21—25	20.0
26—30	18.0
31—35	16.5

After lapse of requisite settling time the supernant is poured. This process is known as "decantation". It is repeated till the supernant water becomes clear. Now, decantated water is allowed to settle down the medium size sediments in the beaker which are transferred into a weighted beaker and dried in the oven or in sunlight. Lastly, the weight of dried sediment is determined and is expressed as g/l.

10.11.3. Analysis of Fine Sediments

During decantation process for determining the amount of medium size sediments, the residual water is again filtered through a filter paper of known weight. The fine sediments are retained on the filter paper. The wet filter paper along with fine sediments is removed from the funnel and is allowed for drying in the sun light. A precaution should be taken that the drying place should be dust free. After drying, the weight of filter paper containing fine sediments is determined, accurately. If W_1 is the weight of filter paper and W_2 is the weight of filter paper alongwith fine sediments, then weight of sediment (W) is given by

$$W = W_2 - W_1 \quad ...(10.34)$$

10.12. Sedimentation Problems in Different Soil Conservation Regions of India

For integrated planning of land resources, it is very important to delineate the entire topographical area of the country and to categorize them into different areas/zones/regions on the basis of some specified parameters representing similar problems as well as compulsons on socio-economic system. In this regard, Ministry of Agriculture, Department of Agriculture and Co-operation in collaboration with the Indian Council of Agricultural Research (I.C.A.R.) delineated the total geographical area of the country into ten (10) different soil conservation regions, given as under :

1. North-Himalayan Region
2. North-Eastern Himalayan Region
3. Assam Valley and Gangetic Delta Region
4. Desert Area Region
5. Indo-Gangetic Alluvial Plain Region.
6. Eastern-Red Soil Region
7. Southern-Red Soil Region
8. Black Soil Region
9. Mixed Black and Red-Yellow Soil Region
10. East-west coast and Ice land region.

The sedimentation problems, prominent hydrologic soil groups and areas under very high and high priority classes of different soil conservation regions are given in Table 10.8.

Table 10.8. Sedimentation problems of different soil conservation regions (India)

S. No.	*Soil conservation regions including river valley development programme catchment*	*Sediment assumed*	*Sediment production rate (ha.m/100 sq. km/year)*	*Prominent hydrologic soil group*	*Drought class*	*Percent area under very high and high priority class*
(1)	*(2)*	*(3)*	*(4)*	*(5)*	*(6)*	*(7)*
1.	North Himalayan					
	(*i*) Beas	4.29	15.10 (1975)	B	None	28.2
	(*ii*) Giri-bata	—	11.60	B	None	44.6
	(*iii*) Pohru	—	7.71	B, D	None	33.6
	(*iv*) Ram Ganga	4.29	17.30 (1973)	B	None	33.6
	(*v*) Sutlej	4.29	6.00 (1975)	B	None	43.7

Contd.

(1)	*(2)*	*(3)*	*(4)*	*(5)*	*(6)*	*(7)*
2.	North-eastern Himalayan	—				
	(*i*) Gumti	—	3.56 (1973)	B	None	76.5
	(*ii*) Teesta	—	98.20	B	None	59.0
3.	Assam valley and Gangetic delta					
	(*i*) Pagladia	—	31.40 (AV) at Nalbari	B	None	56.2
4.	Rajasthan desert and bordering Semiarid regions	—	—	B	Very severe	—
5.	Indo-Gangetic plain					
	(*i*) Danti wada	3.61	6.22 (1974)	A	Severe	24.6
	(*ii*) Sukhna lake	—	98.50 (1971)	B	Moderate	100.0
	(*iii*) Sahibi	—	—	B, C	Large	15.0 (assumed)
6.	Eastern - Red regions					
	(*i*) Hira-kund	2.52	3.55 (1977)	—	Moderate	15.0 (assumed)
	(*ii*) Sone	4.76	6.25 (1972)	—	Moderate	15.0 (assumed)
	(*iii*) Mayrakshi	3.61	20.09 (1975)	B	Moderate	40.9
	(*iv*) Kangsabati	3.27	6.73 (1972)	B	Moderate	42.0
	(*v*) Rengali-mandire	—	7.76	B	Moderate	25.7
	(vi) Much Kund	3.90	2.19 (1975)	B	None	45.0
	(*vii*) Damodar-Barkar complex					
	a) Maithon	1.62	13.02 (1971)	B	Moderate	50.5
	b) Panchet	2.47	9.92 (1974)	B	Moderate	50.5
	c) Konar	2.76	—	B	Moderate	50.5
	d) Tilaya	5.39	—	B	Moderate	50.5

Contd.

(1)	(2)	(3)	(4)	(5)	(6)	(7)
7.	Southern-Red soils					
	(*i*) Lower-Bharani	—	2.71 (1975)	B	Moderate	35.5
	(*ii*) Kundah	—	—	B	Moderate	15.0 (assumed)
8.	Black-soil regions					
	(*i*) Chambal	3.61	5.29 (1976)	D	Large	33.4
	(*ii*) Mata tila	1.43	3.50 (1972)	D	Large	30.7
	(*iii*) Ukai	1.47	4.96 (1967)	D	large	44.1
	(*iv*) Tawa	3.61	8.10 (1973)	B	Large	33.2
	(*v*) Pochampad	-	-	D	Large	41.6
	(*vi*) Nizam Sagar	0.29	6.57 (1967)	D	Severe	14.6
	(*vii*) Nagarjun Sagar	-	-	D	Severe	30.2
	(*viii*) Tung bhadra	4.29	6.11 (1972)	D	Severe	15.10 (assumed)
	(*ix*) Ghod	3.61	15.51 (1970)	C	Large	15.0 (assumed)
9.	Mixed Black-Red soil regions					
	(*i*) Mahi	1.29	8.99 (1973)	C,D	Large	41.0
10.	East West coast and Ice lands					
.	(*i*) Daman Ganga	—	15.72	B	—	49.6

(**Source : Anonymous, 1990**)

10.13. Reservoir Sedimentation

The reservoir's construction plays an important role in development of river basin by solving the problems of irrigation, power scarcity and flood control, mainly. For design and construction of reservoir, the consideration of sedimentation is one of the important parameters, because deposition of sediments in the storage area of reservoir reduces net capacity; and may arrive a time when reservoir is completely silted and aim of construction is not fulfilled. For study of sedimentation, the informations on sediment yield from river basin is very essential, because silt ladden water coming from the river basin ultimately reaches to the reservoir, where sediment deposition takes place. The measured sediment flow rate of different Indian rivers is given in Table 10.8.

The sedimentation of reservoir is started when sediment ladden water reaches into the reservoir, because velocity and turbulence of incoming flow are greatly reduced due the increased cross-sectional area of flow in the reservoir. If already stored water in the reservoir is clear and incoming water is muddy in nature, then dense fluid *i.e.* silt ladden water tends to flow to the bottom of reservoir towards dam in the form of density current or stratified flow, during which the smaller sediment particles are settled near base of the dam. It is shown in Fig. 10.5.

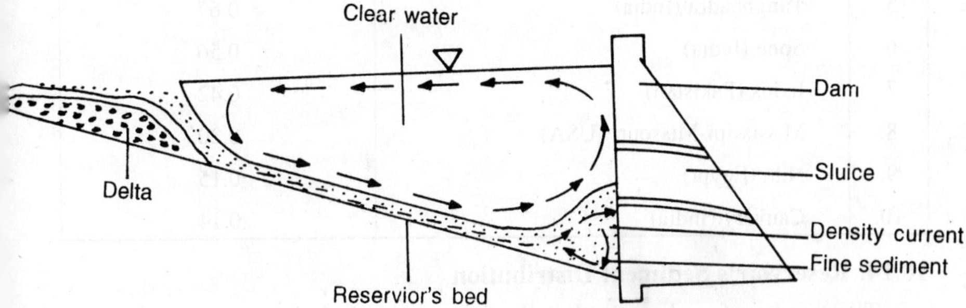

Fig. 10.5. Reservoir sedimentation.

In reservoir's design, the allowance for sediment deposition is essentially given to maintain the storage capacity of reservoir. The storage required for irrigation, power generation etc., is known as 'live storage'. Table 10.9 indicates the sedimentation rate of few Indian reservoirs; and sediment concentration of some rivers of the world in Table 10.10.

Table 10.9. Annual sedimentation rate of different Indian reservoirs.

S. No.	*Reservoir*	*Catchment area* (km^2)	*Annual sedimentation rate* (*ha.m/100 sq km*)
1.	Mayurakshi (W.B)	1860	20.09
2.	Ram ganga	—	17.30
3.	Maithon (Bihar)	6300	13.02
4.	Gandhi Sagar (M.P.)	22,600	10.05
5.	Panchet (Bihar)	11,000	9.92
6.	Tawa (M.P.)	—	8.10
7.	Nizam Sagar (A.P.)	21,694	6.57
8.	Dantiwada	—	6.32
9.	Bhakra (Punjab)	56,800	6.00
10.	Tung bhadra (Karnataka)	28,200	6.00
11.	Hirakud (Orissa)	83,000	3.89
12.	Manch Kund	—	2.33

Table 10.10. Sediment concentration of some rivers of the world

S. No.	*River*	*Silt amount (%) by weight*
1.	Yellow river (China)	4.00
2.	Sutlej river (India)	1.67
3.	Colorado (USA)	1.00
4.	Krishna (India)	0.67
5.	Tungbhadra (India)	0.67
6.	Sone (India)	0.56
7.	Indus (Pakistan)	0.42
8.	Mississipi-Missouri (USA)	0.20
9.	Nile (Egypt)	0.15
10.	Cauvery (India)	0.14

10.14. Reservoir's Sediment Distribution

The study of sediment distribution pattern of the reservoir is very important for planning and design of various components and hydraulic structures of the reservoir. However, few more are also given as under :

1. It provides a view on pattern of sediment deposition. On the basis of which, the location of outlet and penstock gates etc. can be decided for safe and proper operation of the reservoir.

2. It helps in allocation of different storages in the reservoir.

3. Region of delta formation in the reservoir and its effect on back water flow, are also possible to determine.

4. The sediment distribution pattern is also helpful for deciding the appropriate sites for development of recreational spots, such as swimming centre, boating centres etc.

10.14.1. Factors Affecting Sediment Distribution Pattern

Mode of reservoir operation greatly affects the sediment distribution. Apart from it, several other factors also affect in which few are described below :

1. **Stream/river slope :** By a stream with steep bed slope and covering longer distance to the reservoir, the deposition of sediment takes place in lower portion of the reservoir for large extent. While incase of flat slope rivers linked to the reservoir, the siltation takes place at higher elevation of the reservoir.

2. **Reservoir length.** Sediment distribution is largely affected by the length of reservoir. On the basis of several investigations, it has been found that in shorter length of reservoirs the large size sediments are deposited in lower portion, while in the reservoirs of longer length they are deposited at higher portions.

3. **Reservoir constriction :** Constriction in the reservoir's cross-section causes greater deposition of sediments at upper reaches of the reservoir. The deposition pattern of sediment is flatter at constricted portion.

4. **Size of sediment :** The size of sediment may vary from fine to big boulders. It greatly affects the sediment distribution pattern in the reservoir. If percentage of big size sediments is more in the flow, then there would be greater deposition at the centre. On the other hand, if proportion of fine particles is more, then there will be greater deposition near the dam.

5. **Inflow pattern of the stream :** Sediment distribution pattern is also affected by the inflow pattern of the connecting stream. If flood occurs in the stream at early of the monsoon season, then greater amount of sediments are charged in the flow causing more deposition of sediments in the reservoir. On the contrast, when flood occurs at the end of monsoon season, then reservoir sedimentation is comparitively less.

6. **Vegetal growth :** Vegetal growth at upstream of reservoir trapes the sediments in large amount and check them to enter the reservoir, because of appreciable reduction in the stream flow velocity. In this way, vegetal growth affects the sediment distribution in the reservoir.

7. **Sediment load in the stream flow :** The amount of sediment load carried by the stream flow is greatly affected by the watershed characteristics *i.e.* land use and climatic conditions. Combine effect of these two characteristics generates sediment yield from water shed, which ultimately enters into stream flow. If sediment load in stream flow is more, then there is greater deposition of sediments in reservoir.

8. **Capacity–inflow ratio :** This property also affects the sediment distribution pattern in the reservoir. If a small reservoir is fed by large size river, then most of the finer sediment particles do not get time to settle down in the reservoir, but are disposed off. On the other hand in large reservoirs water is retained for longer duration, as result greater deposition of suspended sediments is there.

9. **Sediment-reservoir volume ratio :** If volume of sediment inflow is greater as compared to the volume of reservoir, then there will be greater sedimentation in the reservoir.

10. **Shape of reservoir :** The shape of reservoir also affects the sediment distribution pattern. In a regular shaped reservoir the deposition of suspended sediment is more uniform. On the contrast in irregular shaped reservoirs there is large variations in the sediment deposition.

11. **Out let :** If outlet of reservoir has adequate discharging capacity and is located at lower elevation, then density currents are rapidly removed from the storage area, causing less sediment deposition.

12. **Reservoir operation :** Modes of reservoir operation affect the pattern of sediment distribution and deposition, both. The reservoirs may be single

or multipurpose. Single purpose reservoirs are operated mainly at constant level and deposition of sediment is not much affected. In case of multipurpose reservoirs the operations are carried out under wide range of outlet elevations, to fulfil various demands throughout the year; it significantly affects the sediment distribution pattern, because deposited sediments are flushed out from different elevations of live storage of the reservoir.

10.15. Computaion of Sediment Distribution

There are several methods for determining the sediment distribution pattern of the reservoir. Boreland and Miller (1960) have introduced two methods, in which one is area reduction method and other is the area-increment method. Heinman (1961) developed another method for determining the depth of sediment accumulation near the dam to decide the location of spillway. Similarly, Swamy (1977) also developed a method for estimating the sediment-distribution pattern on the basis of sedimentation data of nine Indian reservoirs.

10.15.1. Area-Reduction-Method

This method was developed on the basis of sediment distribution data of several reservoirs. Boreland and Miller (1960) divided the distribution pattern of sediment in four types of storages, namely: (1) Gorge (2) Hill (3) Flood plain-foot hill, and (4) Lake. They derived the sediment distribution curve for each of them, separately, as shown in Fig. 10.6. The equation of sediment distribution curve is given as under :

$$A_p = C \cdot p^m (1-p)^n \qquad ...(10.35)$$

where, A_p = dimensionless relative area at relative depth 'p', above the stream bed.

C, m and n = dimensionless constant, varies as per types of reservoir (Table 10.11).

p = relative depth above the stream bed.

Relative depth (dimensonless) is the height above stream bed at which determination of sediment deposition is required. For making the relative depth as dimensionless, it is divided with the total depth which is the difference of water level at full reservoir and stream bed level. The area-reduction method involves following steps for computing the area of sediment deposition at relative depth (p) :

1. Calibrate the curve 'A_p' by determining the value of constant (K) equal to $\frac{A_o}{A}$ at zero elevation. Zero elevation is the height upto which reservoir is completely silted; A_o is the area of sediment deposition at zero elevation A_p is determined corresponding to A from the curve, as shown in Fig. 10.6,

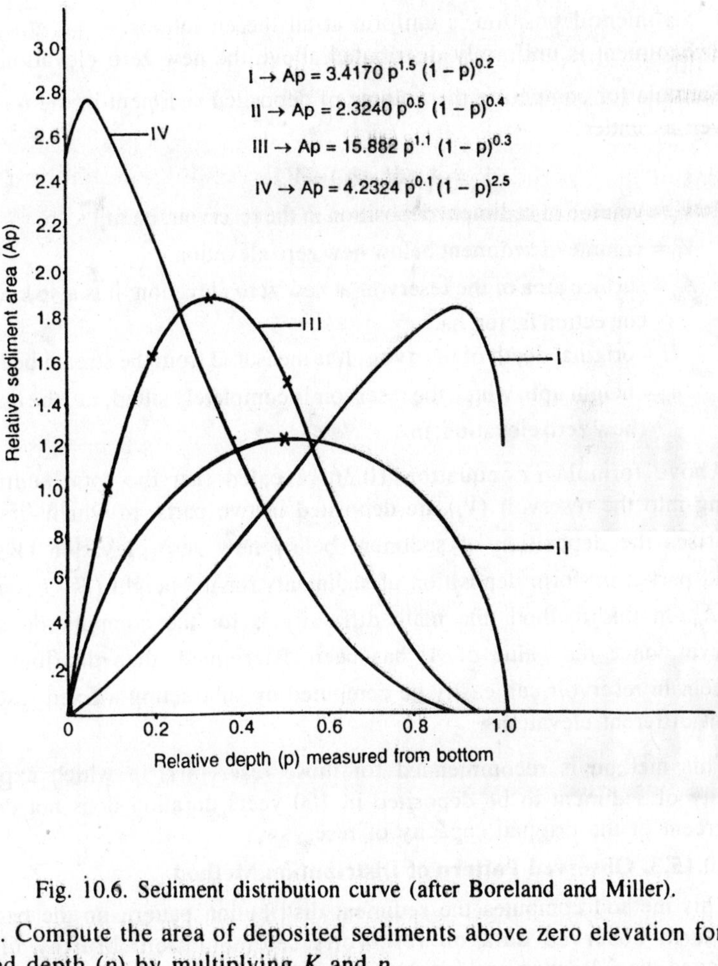

Fig. 10.6. Sediment distribution curve (after Boreland and Miller).

2. Compute the area of deposited sediments above zero elevation for any desired depth (p) by multiplying K and p.

Table 10.11. Values of *C*, *m* and *n* for different types of reservoirs.

S. No.	*Reservoir*	*C*	*m*	*n*
1.	I	3.417	1.5	0.2
2.	II	2.324	0.5	0.4
3.	III	15.882	1.1	2.3
4.	IV	4.232	0.1	2.5

10.15.2. Area-Increment Method

This method computes the sediment distribution of the reservoir on the basis of following assumptions :

1. Sediment deposition is uniform at all the elevations.
2. Sediment is uniformly distributed above the new zero elevation.

Formula for computing the volume of deposited sediment in the reservoir is given as under :

$$V_s = A_o (H - h_o) + V_o \qquad ...(10.36)$$

where, V_s = volume of sediment deposition in the reservoir, ha.m

V_0 = volume of sediment below new zero elevation.

A_o = surface area of the reservoir at new zero elevation; it is also known as correction factor, ha.

H = original depth of reservoir; it is measured from the stream bed, m

h_o = height upto which the reservoir is completely silted, *i.e.* the height of new zero elevation, m.

Above formula *i.e.* equation 10.36 revealed that the total sediments coming into the reservoir (V_s) are deposited in two parts, in which first part comprises the deposition of sediment below new zero elevation (V_o) and second part is uniform deposition of sediments for the height ($H - h_o$) on the area A_o. In this method, the main difficulty is for the computation of A_o. However, once the value of A_o has been determined, then distribution of sediment in reservoir can easily be computed by subtracting a fixed reservoir area at different elevations.

This method is recommended for those reservoirs, in which expected quantity of sediment to be deposited in 100 years duration does not exceed 15 percent of the original capacity of reservoir.

10.15.3. Observed Pattern of Distribution Method

This method computes the sediment distribution pattern on the basis of long term observed data on reservoirs sedimentation. Murthy (1977) developed the following empirical relationship for determining the deposition of sediments in dead storage area of different types of reservoir. The relationship is given as under :

$$Q_s = KC^n \qquad ...(10.37)$$

where, Q_s = percent of total deposited silts in dead storage area of reservoir

K and n = constants; their value depend on the types of reservoir (Table 10.12)

C = percentage dead storage volume of the total storage capacity of reservoir

Table 10.12. Values of *K* and *n* for use in observed pattern of sediment distribution method

Reservoir's Type	*K*	*n*
1 (Lake)	3.39	0.78
II (Flood plain, foot hill)	9.33	0.56
III (Hill)	25.12	0.35
IV (Gorge)	32.36	0.30

Example 10.1 : *Compute percentage of total deposited silts in the dead storage of reservoir, if percentage of dead storage of the total capacity of reservoir is 45%. Assume the type of reservoir as lake.*

Solution. From table 10.12, we have following values for the lake :

$$\left.\begin{aligned} K &= 3.39 \\ n &= 0.78 \end{aligned}\right\}$$
$$C = 45\%$$

∴ Using the formula, *i.e.*, $Q_s = KC^n$

$$= 3.39\,(45)^{0.78} = \mathbf{60.02\ Ans.}$$

10.15.4. Trigonametric Method

This method is used for computing the distribution of sediments of the reservoirs having their storage capacity upto 300 million m^3. The following two informations are required for computation :

1. Original capacity curve, and
2. Capacity curve of reservoir after siltation.

For determining the depth of silt deposition or final capacity of reservoir, the lines are drawn on the original capacity curve corresponding to the ordinate of maximum reservoir's level. After that, lines are reduced in the ratio of final reservoir's capacity to its original capacity. The points of reduced length of different lines are joined by a smooth curve, which represents the final capacity curve of reservoir.

10.15.5. Elevation of Sediment-Accumulation Method

Heinman (1961) developed a relationship for predicting the sediment distribution on the basis of siltation data of several reservoirs. He mentioned that the minimum accumulation of sediment takes place immediately at upstream side of the dam. The prediction equation is given as under :

$$Y = 22.6 + 0.886D - 81.2n - 0.175C + 0.494W \qquad ...(10.38)$$

where, Y = water depth after siltation

D = depth of depleted stage at the end of design period(%)

n = slope of curve which is drawn between depth and capacity of the reservoir on log–log paper

C = storage capacity remained at the end of design period (acre–ft)

W = specific weight of sediment (lb/ft^3)

10.16. Factors Affecting Reservoir Sedimentation

Various factors affecting reservoir sedimentation are given as under :

1. Quantity of silt load carried by the stream flow.

2. Reservoir's operation and nature of spillway used for disposing the water.

3. Amount of intercepted sediments at upstream of the reservoir.

4. Weight of silt per unit runoff volume coming into the reservoir.

5. Total runoff volume and peak discharge of the watershed.

6. Size and shape of watershed.

7. Slope of watershed.

8. Vegetative growth at upstream side of the reservoir.

9. Soil of catchment.

10. High intensity rainfall is more effective to cause sediment yield from the watershed, because detachment suceptibility of soil particles from ground surface is severly affected by the impacting force of falling raindrop during rainfall. Yield of sediments is greater during monsoon season, is mainly due to occurrence of intense storm.

11. Effective annual rainfall in the watershed.

12. Ratio of reservoir's capacity to the annual runoff entering the reservoir.

13. Depth and age of the deposited sediments in the reservoir.

14. Nature of deposited sediments.

10.17. Annual Silting Rates of Reservoir

As per Khosla's recommendation, earlier, the design of reservoir was performed by considering the silting rate of 0.036 Mm^3 per 100 km^2 watershed area but nowdays, this recommendation is not used because of following reasons :

1. The design capacity of reservoir is very less as compared to the actual value.

2. Only 5 points out of 38 on which enveloping curve is developed, pertain to the data of Indian reservoirs.

According to recent survey, the silting rate of reservoir is quite high as compared to the recommended rate given by Khosla.

The following formula can be used for predicting the annual silting rate of reservoir :

$$S_a = \frac{(W_1 A_1 + W_2 \cdot A_2 + \ldots W_n \cdot A_n)}{21.78 \cdot S} \cdot DR_e \, T_e \qquad \ldots(10.39)$$

where, S_a = annual rate of silt deposition (acre–ft)

$W_1, W_2, \ldots W_n$ = incremental area of the watershed, applicable to each erosion rates (acre)

$A_1, A_2, \ldots A_n$ = erosion rate (tones/acre)

DR_e = delivery ratio(%)

T_e = trap efficiency of reservoir(%)

S = specific weight of sediment

The annual loss of reservoir capacity can be computed by using the following formula for known value of S_a, *i.e.*

$$S = \frac{S_a}{C} \times 100 \qquad \ldots(10.40)$$

in which, S is the annual loss of reservoir's capacity expressed in percent; S_a is the annual silt deposition rate and C is reservoir's capacity.

Joglekar's Method : Joglekar (1960) developed an envelop curve for computing the annual silting rate of reservoirs having 100 sq km area of watershed. The curve is given as under :

$$Q = \frac{0.597}{A^{0.24}} \qquad \ldots(10.41)$$

where, Q = annual silting rate

A = catchment area (km^2)

Regional Envelope Curves : Varshney and Raichur have also developed following envelope curves :

1. For mountaneous rivers

$$Y = \frac{0.392}{A^{0.311}} \qquad \ldots(10.42)$$

2. For plain land rivers $\quad Y = \frac{0.392}{A^{0.202}} \qquad \ldots(10.43)$

3. For the reservoirs having catchment area upto 130 km^2 (south India)

$$Y = \frac{0.46}{A^{0.468}} \qquad \ldots(10.44)$$

4. For the reservoirs having catchment area more than 5000 km^2

$$Y = \frac{1.534}{A^{0.264}} \qquad \ldots(10.45)$$

Khosla Method : Khosla (1953) developed following empirical formula for computing the annual silting rate of reservoir based on the data of annual silting rate and catchment area of the reservoir :

$$Q = \frac{0.323}{A^{0.28}} \quad ...(10.46)$$

in which, Q and A are the same as mentioned in equation 10.41. He also pointed that the annual silting rate decreases with the advancement of reservoir age.

Lal Method : Lal et.al (1977) also developed an empirical formula for computing the annual silt yield per unit area by considering the capacity-inflow ratio of reservoir. The formula is given by :

$$S = \frac{\left(\frac{C}{I}\right)^{0.22} \cdot \left(\frac{I}{A}\right)^{2}}{100} \quad ...(10.47)$$

where, S = annual silt yield per unit area. It is used as an index.

$\frac{C}{I}$ = capacity–inflow ratio

C = original reservoir's capacity

I = average annual inflow rate

A = catchment area.

10.18. Problems Caused by Reservoir Sedimentation

Followings are the main problems due to deposition of sediments in the reservoir :

1. **Reduction of storage capacity :** The sediment deposition in reservoir directly reduces its storage capacity. In addition, the useful life of reservoir is also reduced because the services rendered by silt deposition gets impared.

2. **Blocking of outlets :** At the time of heavy reduction in water level of reservoir, the sediment mixed water tends to settle near the outlets and block them. Which leads to the problems on reservoir operation. Sometimes, special arrangement is required for removing the disposited sediments to perform proper reservoir's function.

3. **Creation of aggradation effect.** Deposition of sediments at the reservoir head tends to alter the stream regime and thus to affect the stream capacity to hold the flow within the juridiction of banks. For controlling this type of problem, aggradation levees and flood walls are constructed at the site.

4. **Degradation effect :** Degradation effect is developed in that condition when outflow has greater velocity, causing soil erosion from the channel below the reservoir. In addition, when outflow of clear water from the reservoir into unlined channel is continued for longer duration, also causes rapid degradation.

10.19. Control Measures For Reservoir's Sedimentation

Various control measures for reservoir's sedimentation are given as under :

1. Design aspects of reservoir.
2. Reservoir's operation technique
3. Soil erosion control
4. Sediment removal
5. Removal of flood water, etc.

Reservoir's Design Aspect : Reservoir's sedimentation can not be controlled completely, but can be minimized to a large extent by considering the following design aspects :

1. The reservoir site should be such that there is least possibilities of soil erosion either due to rainfall or stream flow.

2. The position (height) of reservoir's outlet *i.e.* sluice gate should be such that a large amount of deposited sediments in the reservoir can be removed through gate.

3. The ratio of reservoir's capacity and contributing area of catchment should be within safe limit. In this regard, USDA has suggested that the reservoir's capacity should be sufficient to store water, atleast at the rate of 3.6 ha.m per-km^2 area of catchment.

4. There should be possibility for raising the height of dam, when capacity of the reservoir is encroched by silt deposition.

5. Storage capacity of the reservoir should be less as compared to the runoff volume coming into it, because at less storage capacity the excess runoff is moved off from the reservoir, causing removal of sediments in some amounts from the reservoir.

Reservoir's Operation : Operation techniques of reservoir greatly affect the sediment deposition. The reservoir should always be filled after occurrence of peak flow. The sluice gates in dam should be located at different levels so that the water can be disposed off from different levels of the reservoir.

Soil Erosion Control

The following practices are mainly followed for controlling the soil erosion and to control the sedimentation problem :

1. **By check dam :** The check dams play a significant role for trapping the sediments from the river/stream. The working principle of check dam is to reduce the flow velocity and to check the coarse sediments at upstream end. In other words, the check dam picks the sediments from the stream flow before reaching the reservoir. In this way, the water entering the reservoir

becomes sediment free to some extent. However, the construction of check dam for sediment control is a costly measure.

2. **Vegetative screen :** It is a form of vegetative cover established at upstream end of the reservoir, through which flood water is allowed into reservoir. The function of vegetative screen is to reduce the flow velocity and trap the sediments. It is suitable and cheapest method of silt control.

3. **Soil conservation measures.** Afforestation, bunding, terracing, contour cropping, strip cropping, crop rotations, establishment of gully control structures etc. are the main soil conservation measures for controlling the soil loss/erosion from watershed. Working principle of these measures is to reduce the velocity of sediment ladden runoff by creating obstruction in the flow path. Overall, vegetative method is very effective measuere to reduce the sediment flow into the reservoir as compared to other measures such as gully control structures, check dams etc.

Removal of Sediments

Direct removal of deposited sediments from the reservoir is very costly and is not economically justified. The most common methods for removing the sediments from reservoir are given as under :

1. Excavation
2. Dredging, and
3. Flushing

Excavation is performed when sediments have been accumulated for greater depth in the reservoir which can not be removed by simple methods like flushing etc. Excavation is costly and requires mechanical equipments. Dredging is also expensive method and is not economically feasible for small storage structures.

Flushing consists of stirring the deposited sediments and sluicing them outside from the reservoir. Stirring is done by using mechanical stirrer, which disturbs the deposited sediments and mixed into the water.

Removal of Flood Water : The sediment load gets increase just after occurrence of flood. Therefore, post flood water is advocated to store in the reservoir.

IMPORTANT POINTS

1. Sediments are fragmented materials originated either due to chemical or physical disintegration of rocks which are transported by the water or air.
2. The velocity of a spherical particle which specific gravity is 2.65 and has same falling velocity as the actual sediment is called fall velocity.
3. The diameter of spherical particle which volume is equal to the volume of sediment is called nominal diameter.

4. The diameter of spherical particle existing in the same sedimentation fluid is taken as the diameter of sediment provided that the specific gravity and terminal velocity of the spherical particle is same to the sediment.
5. For the particles of spherical shape the value of sphericity is 1, while for other shapes it is always less than 1.
6. Roundness of particle is the ratio of average radius of curvature of all the edges (r_s) to the radius of longest inscribed circle (R).
7. The settling velocity of sediment particles can be determined by using the Stoke's Law.
8. The porosity of unconsolidated saturated formation can be determined by using the formula, $P = 0.245 + 0.0864\, d_{50}^{0.21}$, in which d_{50} is the mean diameter of particle.
9. In saltation process, the transportation of coarse sediment particles is either in the form of bed load slide, rolling or by short skips.
10. The saltation process gets change into suspension when particles size becomes finer.
11. The diameter of coarse sediments is more than 0.20 mm.
12. The bed load samplers are basket type, pan or tray type, pressure difference type, slot type, etc.
13. Point integrating samplers are used for collecting the sediment samples from a specified point.
14. The point integrating and depth integrating samplers are the suspended load samplers.
15. Sampling points in the stream widths of 30 to 300 m are at 25, 35, 50, 65 and 80% of stream width.
16. Sediment sampling station should have a straight reach of 150 m distance towards u/s and d/s sides, both.
17. Temperature affects the settling time of medium sediments.
18. The USDH-48 (weight 4.5 lb) sampler is used in small streams in which wading is possible.
19. Karloyi and Sphinx samplers are used for bed load sampling.
20. Sediment moving along the stream bed by rolling or sliding actions is called contact load.

REFERENCES

1. Boreland W.M. and Miller, Fluvial sediments, J.H.D, Prosc, ASCE, Vol 95, HY-5, 1960.
2. Chow V.T. Hand book of Applied Hydrology, McGraw-Hill, New York, 1964.
3. Hubbel D.W. Apparatus and Techniques for Measuring bed loads, 45CS, Water Supply paper, 1748, 1964.
4. Joglekar D.V. Life of reservoirs, Tech report No. 19, CBI & P, New Delhi, 1960.
5. Khosla A.N. Silting reservoirs, CBI & P, New Delhi, 1953.

6. Lal V.B.S., Banerjy and Narayana, Sediment yield in relation to drainage basin characteristics in some Indian Riers, Prosc of the Symposium, Publication No. - 122, Paris, 1977.
7. Murty V.V.N. Land and Water Management Engineering. Kalyani Publishers, Delhi, 1987.
8. Murthy B.N., Distribution of sediment in large reservoirs, Trans. A SCE, Vol 125 (1) : 166-180, 1977.
9. Suresh R. Soil & Water Conservation Engineering, Standard Publishers Distributors, Delhi, 2002.
10. TC PSM, Sediment measuring techniques : A fluvial sediment, JHD, Prosc, ASCE Vol 95, HY-5, 1969.
11. US Government and IIHR, A study of measurement and analysis of sediment loads in streams. The design of improved types of suspended sediment samplers. Report no 8, 1952.

DESCRIPTIVE TYPE QUESTIONS

1. (*a*) Define sediment and write various sources of sediment yield from the watershed.
   (*b*) Describe factors affecting sediment yield.
2. (*a*) Explain various properties of individual sedimentary particles.
   (*b*) Describe bulk properties of sediment.
3. (*a*) Define sphericity and compare with roundness of particles.
   (*b*) Define fall velocity and derive expression for computing the fall velocity by using Stoke's Law.
4. (*a*) Describe the process of sediment transportation.
   (*b*) Distinguish saltation and surface creep processes of sediment transportation.
5. Describe the mechanism of saltation process given by Dannel etal (1953).
6. Classify suspended loads and explain the method to analyse suspended load.
7. Define bed load and describe the methods of bed load determination.
8. Classify the samplers for determination of sediment from stream flow and explain suspended load sampler.
9. Explain Du Boy's formula for bed load computation.
10. Explain point-integrating sampler and compare with automatic single stage sampler.
11. Make the list of instruments for sediment monitoring station.
12. What is reservoir sedimentation. Describe distribution of sediment in the reservoir.
13. Describe area-increment method for predicting sediment distribution in the reservoir.
14. Describe annual silting rate of reservoir.
15. Describe various problems posed by sediment deposition in the reservoir.

16. Write short notes on followings
   (a) Sphericity
   (b) Fall velocity
   (c) Depth integrating samplers
   (d) Sediment monitoring station
   (e) Sediment control measures.

OBJECTIVE TYPE QUESTIONS

1. Size of sediment varies from
   (a) 0.01 mm to 1.0 cm
   (b) 0.01 mm to 10.0 cm
   (c) big boulder to colloidal particle
   (d) 0.1 cm to 1 cm.
2. The transporting agents of sediment are
   (a) air and water (b) only water
   (c) only air (d) cattle and human.
3. A watershed which soils include greater proportion of sands, causes
   (a) greater sediment yield (b) less sediment yield
   (c) no sediment yield (d) none of above.
4. Vegetative cover reduces the sediment yield from watershed because of
   (a) less soil erosion (b) compactness
   (c) both '*a*' and '*b*' (d) less infiltration rate.
5. A high intensity storm causes
   (a) greater sediment yield (b) less sediment yield
   (c) more infiltration loss (d) none of above.
6. Size of sediment is expressed by
   (a) fall velocity (b) volume of sediment
   (c) '*a*' and '*b*' (d) sphericity.
7. Diameter of sediment is generally taken as
   (a) 0.8 dn
   (b) 0.90 dn
   (c) 1 dn
   (d) 0.2 dn.
   (dn is the nominal diameter)
8. Size of fine sand particles varies from
   (a) 0.25 to 0.125 mm (b) 0.5 to 0.25 mm
   (c) 1 to 0.50 mm (d) 1 to 1.5 cm.
9. Size of coarse clay particles varies from
   (a) $\frac{1}{256}$ to $\frac{1}{512}$ mm (b) $\frac{1}{512}$ to $\frac{1}{1020}$ mm
   (c) $\frac{1}{128}$ to $\frac{1}{256}$ mm (d) 1 to 0.2 mm.
10. Sphericity is the ratio of
   (a) *dn* to *ds* (b) *ds* to *dn*
   (c) *dn* to *d* (d) A to P.

11. Specific gravity of magnetic sediment is
(*a*) 5.20 (*b*) 1.20
(*c*) 4.20. (*d*) 1.75

12. The formula of fall velocity is
(*a*) $\frac{2}{9\mu} d^2 (\rho_s - \rho_f)$ (*b*) $\frac{2}{9\mu} r^2 (\rho_s - \rho_f)$
(*c*) $\frac{1}{4\mu} r^2 (\rho_s - \rho_f)$ (*d*) $v = \sqrt{2gh}$.

13. Alluvial deposits involve
(*a*) uniform sorting (*b*) non uniform sorting
(*c*) fine sediments (*d*) none of above.

14. Average sp. weight of submerged sediment deposits of Mata tila reservoir is about
(*a*) 54.0 lb/ft^3 (*b*) 54.0 lb/ft^3
(*c*) 64.0 lb/ft^3 (*d*) 1.75×10^{-2} g/cm^3.

15. Average porosity of silt deposit is about
(*a*) 10.0 (*b*) 1.0
(*c*) 15.0 (*d*) about 2.205.

16. The coarse sediment particles are transported by
(*a*) saltation process (*b*) suspension process
(*c*) both '*a*' and '*b*' (*d*) surface creep.

17. The fine sediment particles are transported by
(*a*) suspension process (*b*) saltation process
(*c*) surface creep (*d*) all above.

18. Contact load moves along the stream bed due to action of
(*a*) rolling (*b*) sliding
(*c*) both '*a*' and '*b*' (*d*) saltation.

19. Du Boys formula for estimation of bed load is
(*a*) $q_s = C_s \tau_0 (\tau_o - \tau_c)$ (*b*) $q_s = \frac{1}{n} . R^{2/3} S^{1/2}, \alpha$.
(*c*) $q_s = \tau_o (\tau_o - \tau_c)$ (*d*) $q_s' = c_s \tau_0 (\tau_c - \tau_0)$

20. Basket type sampler is used as
(*a*) bed load sampler (*b*) suspended load sampler
(*c*) both '*a*' and '*b*' (*d*) saltation load sampler.

21. Depth-integrating sampler can be used as
(*a*) suspended load sampler (*b*) bed load sampler
(*c*) both '*a*' and '*b*'. (*d*) saltation load sampler.

22. In two point sampling, the samples are collected from
(*a*) 0.2*d* and 0.8*d* (*b*) 0.4*d* and 0.6*d*
(*c*) 0.3*d* and 0.7*d* (*d*) 0,4 *d* and 0.5 *d*.

23. For the stream width ranging from 30 to 300 m the number of sampling points should be
(*a*) 3 (*b*) 5
(*c*) 7 (*d*) 10.

24. A sediment sampling site should have atleast
(*a*) 100 m straight reach on u/s and d/s, both
(*b*) 200 m straight reach on u/s and d/s, both
(*c*) 150 m straight reach on u/s and d/s, both
(*d*) 50 m straight reach.

25. At 10 to 15°C water temperature, the required setlling time through 10 cm water column is
(*a*) 25 sec (*b*) 15 sec
(*c*) 16.5 sec (*d*) 5 sec.

26. Storage capacity of reservoir is reduced due to
(*a*) deposition of sediment
(*b*) less inflow of water
(*c*) less height of sluice gate in the dam
(*d*) none of above.

27. Sediment flow rate in Krishna river is
(*a*) 0.67% by weight (*b*) 0.56% by weight
(*c*) 13 *t*/sec (*d*) none of above

28. Sediment distribution pattern of reservoir is affected by
(*a*) vegetal growth (*b*) construction of reservoir
(*c*) '*a*' and '*b*' both (*d*) size of sediment.

29. Area reduction method is used for prediction of
(*a*) sediment distribution in the reservoir
(*b*) sediment deposition (*c*) out flow of sediment
(*d*) none of above.

30. The values of *c*, *m* and *n* for reservoir -III (hill) are
(*a*) 15.882, 1.1 and 2.3 (*b*) 3.417, 1.5 and 0.2
(*c*) 4.232, 0.1 and 2.5 (*d*) 1.125, 2.35 and 0.75.

31. The enveloping curve for computing annual silting rate of reservoir, given by Joglekar (1960) is
(*a*) $Q = \dfrac{0.597}{A^{0.24}}$ (*b*) $Q = \dfrac{0.507}{A^{0.24}}$
(*c*) $Q = \dfrac{0.107}{A^{.50}}$ (*d*) $\alpha = \dfrac{1.517}{A^{2.5}}$.

32. Khosla's formula for computing annual silting rate of reservoir is
(*a*) $Q = \dfrac{0.323}{A^{0.25}}$ (*b*) $Q = \dfrac{0.323}{A^{0.28}}$
(*c*) $Q = \dfrac{0.323}{A^{0.30}}$ (*d*) $\alpha = \dfrac{0.125}{A^{0.15}}$.

Answer (Objective Type Question)

1. (*c*)	**2.** (*a*)	**3.** (*a*)	**4.** (*c*)	**5.** (*a*)	**6.** (*c*)	**7.** (*a*)	**8.** (*a*)
9. (*a*)	**10.** (*a*)	**11.** (*a*)	**12.** (*b*)	**13.** (*b*)	**14.** (*a*)	**15.** (*a*)	**16.** (*a*)
17. (*a*)	**18.** (*c*)	**19.** (*a*)	**20.** (*a*)	**21.** (*a*)	**22.** (*a*)	**23.** (*b*)	**24.** (*c*)
25. (*a*)	**26.** (*a*)	**27.** (*a*)	**28.** (*c*)	**29.** (*a*)	**30.** (*a*)	**31.** (*a*)	**32.** (*b*)

11

Climatic Regions

The atmospheric variables, such as temperature, pressure, humidity, wind velocity, sunshine hour, evaporation, rainfall pattern etc. characterize the land into different climatic regions. In India, there are three climatic regions, namely: arid regions, semi-arid regions and humid regions. The hydro-meterological processes in these regions are different to each other; therefore for better utilization of water resources, the cropping systems and their planning etc. require a detail data base on climate of the area. A brief description about arid, semi-arid and humid regions is given below :

11.1. Arid-Region

Rajasthan (India) mainly falls under this climatic region. Important characteristics of arid-regions are given as under :

Rainfall : Average annual rainfall is less than 40 cm. Rainfall mostly occurs during summer season, which is generally approximated by the following formula:

$$R < (T + 14) \qquad \text{... (11.1)}$$

in which, R is the annual rainfall expressed in *cm* and T is the mean annual temperature in °C. In arid regions, there is large variation in the occurrence of rainfall, spatially and temporally, both.

Temperature : Arid zones are characterized by hot climate *i.e.* temperature is very high. The high temperature causes scarcity of water for drinking, irrigating the crops etc.

Evaporation : It is very high due to high temperature. A little rainfall does not become effective for cultivation. Due to high evaporation, there are different types of irrigation techniques are adopted for irrigating the crops and better utilization of limited available water. Usually, micro-irrigation techniques *i.e.* drip system, micro-sprinkler etc. are most suitable, as in these techniques, water loss is minimized to more than 90%. However, drip irrigation technique creates salt accumulation problem in the root zone, especially in irrigated soils.

Infiltration : It is very important factor for causing the loss of water in arid regions. Infiltration capacity of the soil remains constant throughout the year. Infiltrated water does not contribute ground water. The infiltration capacity of soil can be determined by analysing the rainfall and hydrograph. Infiltration data can be used for approximating the runoff potential of the area.

Water-table : In arid regions very deep water-table is found. It is always below the stream bed; due to this reason streams are mostly ephemeral. Ground water exploration is very costly affair for this region.

Stream flow : The stream flow is in intermittent nature *i.e.* flow is not continuous. Usually, when intense storm occurs, then stream flow starts, immediately. Discharge rate depends on the intensity of rainfall.

Sand dunes : Development of sand dunes is common feature of arid-zone. It has been reported that about 58 percent area of arid zone of Rajasthan (India) is under sand dunes.

Afforestation : It is used as one of the mechanical tools to control the wind erosion and evaporation loss from the soil. Usually, the wind breaks and shelterbelts are established under afforestation.

The suitable species of tree for afforestation in cold arid zones are given in Table 11.1.

Table 11.1. Tree species for afforestation in cold arid zones

Species	*Suitability/places*
Eucalyptus	
E. Parvifloara *E. Gunii* *E. Niphophile*	Tolerate upto 18°C temperature
E. coccifera *E. johntoni* *E. urnigera*	Tolerate upto 15°C
E. aggregata *E. delegrateusis*	Tolerate upto 12°C
Poplars ,	
P. euphratica	Doing well in Leh
P. tromuloides	Alaska, New Found Land
P. alba	Successful in Leh
P. candicansa	–do–
P. Lauri folia	Southern Siberia
P. Lasiocarpa	Central and Western India

Contd.

Species	*Suitability/places*
Shrubs ,	
Berberis vulgaris ,	
Rosa webbina	Soil binders
Hippophae rhamnoides ,	
Cotoneaster spp.	
Legumes ,	
Medicago folcata *Trifolium repens* *Astragalus spp.*	Nitrogen fixing legumes. These can be successfully planted between the pits of trees.

Source : Banerjee (1993).

Central Arid Zone Research Institute, Jodhpur (India) has introduced several exotic fast growing tree and shrub species ; few of them are given below:

1. *Accacia tortilus* (Israeli babool). It is one of the most efficient exotic species for arid zones. It produces fuel as well as fodder, both.
2. Ber : It is also an important shrub, planted as the fruit plant.
3. Neem (*Azadirachta indica*)
4. Eucalyptus
5. Beefwood (*Casuarina equistefolia*)
6. Cashewnut (*Anacardium occidentale*)
7. Sisal (*Agave americana*)

Classification of Arid region

Budyko (1958) classified the arid region into three sub-zones on the basis of "dryness ratio", which is defined as the "ratio of mean annual net radiation to the product of mean annual precipitation and latent heat of vaporization, given as

$$D = \frac{R}{P \cdot L} \qquad ...(11.2)$$

where, D = dryness ratio
R = mean annual net radiation
P = mean annual precipitation
L = latent heat of vaporization of water

The sub-divisons of arid zone are given in Table 11.2.

Table 11.2 : Division of arid zone (Budyko, 1958)

Divison of Arid zone	*Dryness ratio*
Desert	less than 3.4
Semi-desert	2.3 to 3.4
Steppe or savanna	1.1 to 2.3

Thornthwait developed a formula for computation of moisture index to identify aridity of the area. The formula is given by

$$I_m = \frac{S - d}{PET} \times 100 \qquad ...(11.3)$$

where, I_m = moisture index

S = monthly excess rainfall over PET and soil moisture storage during wet months.

d = sum of deficit rainfall and available soil moisture below PET during dry months.

PET = potential evapo transpiration.

Aridity is also used as one criteria for classifying the land into different climatic regions. For this purpose, aridity is expressed in terms of an index called "aridity index", which can be computed by using the following formula :

$$M_m = \frac{100.S - 60.d}{N} \qquad ...(11.4)$$

where, M_m = aridity index

S = soil moisture surplus

d = soil moisture deficit

N = moisture requirement

Climatic regions based on aridity index are given in Table 11.3.

Table 11.3 : Climatic regions based on aridity index.

Climatic region	*Aridity index*
Arid region	– 40 to –57
Semi-arid region	– 20 to – 40
Very arid region	less than – 57

Houerou (1973) classified the dry lands of Sahara and neighbouring regions on the basis of mean annual rainfall as shown is Table 11.4.

Table 11.4 : Climatic regions on the basis of mean annual rainfall

Climatic region	*Mean annual rainfall (mm)*	*Geographical area*
Desert	less than 100	North and south Sahara and Middle east
Arid	100-400	Mediterranean, steppe of north Africa Sahelian zone of south Sahara
Semi-arid	400-600	Mediterranean semi-arid Sudano-Sahelian zone

11.2. Semi-Arid Region

Main characteristics of semi-arid regions are as below :

Rainfall : Average annual rainfall varies from 40 to 75 cm. Winter and spring seasons usually receive majority of the rainfall. The range of precipitation can be approximated by using the following formula :

$$R = (T + 14) \text{ to } 2(T + 14) \qquad \text{...(11.5)}$$

in which, R and T are the same as in equation 11.1. The isohyetal method is found most suitable for computing mean areal precipitation than the Theissen polygon and arithmatic mean methods, because spatial and temporal distribution of rainfall is not uniform in this region.

Temperature : It is higher than the normal. Effect of temperature on water loss is the same as in arid zones, but in less amount. The use of sprinkler and drip irrigation techniques is preferred for irrigating the crops to minimize the loss and better utilize the water.

Evapotranspiration : Evaporation is the main factor to cause water loss and to make high evapotranspiration (evaporation+ transpiration) in this zone. Several years data revealed that in barren rocky areas, the ET goes upto 40 cm/year, while in dense forest areas, it is upto 90 cm/year.

Stream flow : Continuous stream flow takes place, only in rainy season. In dry or summer seasons most of the streams become dry; and whenever rainfall occurs, the stream flow starts, accordingly. The duration of stream flow is very short.

Water-table : Water-table is at moderate depth *i.e.* neither at deep nor at shallow depth.

In addition to the above characteristics, the followings are also important features of semi-arid zones :

1. Infiltration rate of the soil varies from location to location, as there is large variation in the geological conditions of the area.
2. Occurrence of drought is fixed, which is atleast once in a normal year.
3. Hydrological process is different from one river basin to another.
4. From highly elevated river basins about 90% runoff is resulted only from 10% drainage area.
5. Besides sheet erosion to charge the silt load in the stream flow, the gully and channel erosions are also effective to produce the silt load, significantly.

11.3. Humid-Regions

Important characteristics of humid regions are given below :

1. Mean annual rainfall is more than 75 cm.
2. There is not much variation about occurrence of high intensity rainfall with respect to time and space.

3. Temperature is less but humidity is very high.

4. Evaporation is less. Transpiration is one of the major causes of water loss, which ranges upto 80%.

5. Streams are perenial, in which continuous flow takes place throughout the year.

6. Ground water-table is always above the stream bed, which contributes water to the stream flow.

7. Agricultural droughts do not occur in ordinary years.

8. All crops can be satisfactorily grown throughout the year, if soil condition and water availability permit the situation.

9. A short term data can be used to predict the average annual water yield.

In addition to the above points, Hargreave (1972) also given following criteria for grouping the climatic regions on the basis of 'moisture availability index.'

Moisture-Availability-Index (MAI)

It is the measure of adequacy of precipitation in supply of moisture requirement. MAI is the ratio of dependable precipitation to the potential evapotranspiration, given as :

$$MAI = \frac{PD}{PET} \quad ...(11.6)$$

where, MAI = moisture–availability index
PD = dependable precipitation
PET = potential evapotranspiration.

Dependable precipitation is the precipitation of specified probability, which is determined on the basis of long-term precipitation data. For most of the cases, 75% probability level is taken into consideration to determine the PD. Normally, for drought sensitive & high valued crops or for special cases, consideration of high probability is more appropriate. The dependable precipitation can be computed more accurately by considering the mean precipitation value. The following formula can be used for PD :

$$PD = A + B + PM \quad ...(11.7)$$

where, A and B = factors, determined on the basis of regression analysis.
For southern states of U.S., it is given by

$A = -23$ mm
$B = 0.84$

and for Latin America

$A = -10$ mm
$B = 0.70$
PM = mean precipitation, mm.

The value of PD can not be negative, but its minimum value can be zero. In order to relate the precipitation with the crop production, it is essential to determine the rainfall at certain probability level and correlate with the dependable water supply essential to meet the potential water use.

Based on MAI, Hargreave proposed following classification of water deficiencies

MAI	*Classes*
0—0.33	Very deficient
0.34—0.67	Moderately deficient
0.68—1.00	Somewhat deficient
1.01—1.33	Adequate
1.34 and above	Excessive

Hargreave (1974) also classified the climate of north-east Brazil on the basis of precipitation, given in Table 11.5.

Table 11.5. Classification of climate based on MAI

Criteria	*Climate*
All months with MAI ranging from 0 to .33	Very arid
One or two months with MAI as 0.34 or more	Arid
Three or four months with MAI as 0.34 or more	Semi-arid
Five or more consecutive months with MAI as 0.34 or more	Wet-dry

11.4. Drought

It is the extreme of hydrologic phenomena, which represents creeping type disaster due to water deficit for longer duration. It ruins the agriculture, energy, recreational facilities, development of pollution problem and several other activities, which directly or indirectly affect the national economy.

Its occurrence causes multiplying effect and disturbs the ecological balance of the region. The arid part of Rajasthan (India) is an example of this effect, Das et.al (1980) reported that from these regions about 3 million people are migrated annually in search of food and forage.

Definition : There is no such definition of drought which can be universally accepted, because quantification of drought is still controversial; perhaps the concept is not absolute. However, as per various needs few definitions are there, e.g. Worrick (1975) defined the drought as the situation of moisture deficit sufficient to create adverse effect on vegetations, animals and human beings over the sizeable area.'' Similarly, Krishnan (1979) given the definition of drought as the general term implying the deficiency of precipitation in sufficient magnitude, so as to interfere the phases of economy. Regarding agricultural drought is concerned, prolong shortage of moisture content in the root zone of crops which is often related to the critical growth stages of the plant is referred as 'drought.' To a hydrologist, the drought indicates the situation of flow in the streams, reservoirs, ground water, lakes and soils, below average. Similarly, to an economist, it is shortage of water which significantly alters or disturbs the stabilized production base.

11.5. Drought and Rainfall

Different views on drought based on rainfall, are given as under :

1. Henry (1906), Linsley et.al (1959) defined the drought on the basis of threshold value of rainfall. They stated that those areas are subject to drought, where variation in annual rainfall is very much.

2. British Rainfall Organisation (1936) reported the drought as the period of more than 28 days having very small rainfall, each day. The drought is said to be 'absolute drought' when atleast 15 consecutive days or more with as much as 0.25 mm rainfall.

3. Tannehill (1947) reported that a consecutive period of 21 days with rainfall less than 30% of the normal rainfall at a given place and time is considered as the "drought."

4. Ramdas et.al (1948) defined the drought as the situation, when week period receives the rainfall equal to or less than half of the normal rainfall.

5. Foley (1957) developed a dimensionless index of drought severity, to indicate variation in the residual mass curve in which departure of rainfall from average for each specified period *e.g.* monthly is cumulated.

6. Goodridge (1967) developed 'drought index', which is the accumulated average daily rainfall during the period in which no effective rainfall is there. Effective rainfall is the lowest threshold value or amount of daily rainfall, which is significant to several applications.

7. Kalyansundran et.al (1969) studied the drought pattern of Bihar (India) by using "Van Roy's drought anomally index" with little modification. The Van Roy's drought index is given by,

$$I = -3\left(\frac{P-\overline{p}}{\overline{m}-\overline{p}}\right) \qquad \text{...(11.8)}$$

where, I = anomally index

P = actual precipitation

$\overline{p}$ = normal precipitation

$\overline{m}$ = mean of the ten lowest values of actual precipitation.

The $\overline{m}$ can be computed by using following formula :

$$\overline{m} = \frac{3}{4\overline{p}} \qquad \text{...(11.9)}$$

8. World Meteorological Organisation (1975) reported that for USSR a period of 10 days with total rainfall not greater than 5 mm is considered as drought period. In New Zealand, the agricultural drought is said to be occured when level of soil moisture in the root zone is either at or below the permanent wilting point.

9. Indian Meteorological Department defined the drought as the situation, when annual rainfall is less than 75% of the normal rainfall. Based on rainfall, the IMD categorized the severe drought, drought areas and chronic drought areas as below :

Severe drought : A drought is said to be severe, when deficiency of rainfall is more than 50% of the normal rainfall.

Drought areas : Areas in which drought has been occured in 20 percent of the years are considered as drought areas. Generally, for declaration of drought areas the rainfall data for the period of 60 years or more is essential.

Chronic drought areas : The areas in which drought has been occured in more than 40% of the total years considered for evaluation, are called chronic drought areas. These areas are identical to the intensely arid zones.

11.6. Drought Classification

The National Commission on Agriculture (1976) classified the drought into following three classes :

1. Meteorological drought
2. Hydrological drought; and
3. Agricultural drought

Meteorological drought is the situation, when there is very small occurrence of rainfall (usually less than 25 percent of the normal rainfall) as compared to the normal rainfall of the area.

Agricultural drought takes place, when soil moisture or rainfall is not adequate during growth stages of the crops, which causes extreme crop stress and wilting. Normally, the area which receives the annual rainfall less than 750 mm is grouped under drought prone area.

Hydrological drought is the prolong situation of meteorological drought, in which there the depletion of water level or drying of the reservoirs, lakes, streams and rivers and also declination of ground water-table in the region.

11.7. Drought, Rainfall and Temperature

There have been developed various indices for relating the rainfall and temperature for drought study; few of them are given as under :

Index of Aridity : De Martonne in 1936 developed an index for computing aridity of the area on the basis of rainfall and temperature which is called index of aridity. It is given by :

$$I = \frac{P}{t + 10} \quad ...(11.10)$$

where, I = index of aridity

P = monthly precipitation, mm

t = mean monthly temperature, °C

This index was modified by introducing the number of days (n) and replacing the monthly precipitation (P) by mean daily precipitation ($\bar{p}$). The modified aridity index is given as under :

$$I = \frac{n\bar{p}}{t + 10} \quad ...(11.11)$$

Precipitation Effectiveness Index : Thronthwait (1931) developed this index, which is the function of rainfall and mean temperature. It is used for evalutating the drought. Selyaninov (1930) also derived an index based on precipitation and temperature, given as under :

$$K = \frac{P}{(t/10)} \quad ...(11.12)$$

where, K = aridity index

P = sum of rainfall of the months, which temperature exceeds 10°C

t = sum of daily mean temperature of those months, in which mean daily temperature exceeds 0°C.

The value of K less than 0.5. indicates the drought.

Aridity index : It is defined as the ratio of annual water deficiency to the annual water required, expressed in percent. Aridity index is given as :

$$I_a = \frac{PE - AE}{PE} \times 100 \quad ...(11.13)$$

where, I_a = aridity index

PE = potential evapotranspiration

AE = actual evapotranspiration.

Potential evapotranspiration is the maximum loss of water due to combine process of evaporation and transpiration, under unristricted water supply condition. It is also termed as required PE. When magnitude of precipitation is less than PE, then total precipitation and a certain amount of soil moisture is utilized by the crop to fulfil the demand of evapotranspiration, is called actual evapotranspiration (AE). In other words, the actual evapotranspiration is the sum of precipitation and change in soil moisture, when precipitation is less than the potential evapotranspiration (*i.e.* $P < PE$). Krishnan & Thavi

(1971) classified the drought intensity of Rajasthan (India) on the basis of aridity index, given as :

Range of aridity index	*Drought intensity*
50—60	Slight
60—70	Moderate
70—80	Severe
< 80	Disastrous

Krishnan and Rao (1979) proposed following criteria to cetegorize the moderate and severe droughts on the basis of potential evapotranspiration (PE) and actual evapotranspiration (AE) :

1. **Moderate drought.** The drought is said to be moderate, when

$$\frac{PE}{2} > AE \geq \frac{PE}{4} \qquad \text{...(11.14)}$$

2. **Severe drought :** When $AE < \dfrac{PE}{4}$, then drought is said to be "severe drought".

Humidity-Index : It is the ratio of annual moisture surplus to the annual potential evapotranspiration, expressed in percent. The humidity index is given as

$$I_h = \frac{\text{Annual moisture surplus}}{\text{Annual potential evapotranspiration}} \times 100 \qquad \text{...(11.15)}$$

Moisture Adequacy Index : It was introduced by Subramanyam et.al (1963) to characterize the agricultural drought in India. Moisture adequacy index is the ratio of actual evapotranspiration to the potential evaporatranspiration, expressed in percent. It is given as under :

$$MAI = \frac{AE}{PE} \times 100 \qquad \text{...(11.16)}$$

where, MAI = moisture adequacy index
AE = actual evapotranspiration
PE = potential evapotranspiration

Based on the values of moisture adequacy index, the intensity of agricultural drought is classified as under :

Departure of MAI (%) below minimum value	*Intensity of agricultural deought*
> 10	Moderate
10—20	Large
20—30	Severe
< 30	Disastrous

11.8. Effects of Drought

Various effects of drought are described as under :

11.8.1. Effects on ground water

Availability of ground water in the area is badly affected by drought occurrence. The main source of enriching the ground water is rainwater and also to some extent the irrigation water, canal network, surface ponds, reservoirs etc, which are also affected by the drought.

The effects of drought on ground water have been evaluated by different investigators; few of them are given as under :

Chatterjee (1978) conducted studies to evaluate drought's effect on ground water in the arid zone of western Rajasthan (India) which revealed that during drought year preceeded by flood year, the available ground water does not fulfil the requirement of area. In addition, he also pointed that, during drought period the ground water recharge is badly affected (*i.e.* very less), which ultimately affected the static water level. Singhal (1979) reported that in central Maharashtra, the area occupied by Decan trap which receives the annual rainfall ranging from 400 to 500 mm, about 10% rain water is recharged into the ground water. Malik and Banerjee (1979) studied the effects of drought on ground water storage in shallow confined aquifers; and developed an exponential decay function to characterize recession characteristics of aquifer. The equation can be used to predict the position of ground water during future droughts. Equation is given by

$$h = h_o \cdot e^{-dt} \qquad ...(11.17)$$

where, h = height of water table above the mean sea level after time 't'.

h_o = initial height of water table above mean sea level.

11.8.2. Effects on water quality

Occurrence of drought also affects the ground water quality. In this regard, several investigations have been made, few of them are as : Chatterjee (1978) reported that about 65% area of arid zone of Rajasthan contains the ground water with total soluble salts more than 3000 ppm. Continuous use of this water for irrigation may render the salinity/sodicity problem. Singh and Kumar (1979) have also mentioned that in drought prone areas, where availability of irrigation water is very limited, there is increment in salinity and alkalinity levels. Similarly, Walling and Poster (1979) have also reported that due to a single severe drought, there is increase of Nitrate concentration in the stream flow.

11.8.3. Effects on socio-economic status

Consequence of drought on socio-economic condition of the population is very severe, given as below ;

1. Drought creates the scarcity of food grains and fodder for human beings and cattle feeding.

2. It poses severe problem of non-availability of drinkIng water. This happening is common in the states of Rajasthan, few parts of Maharastra, M.P., Gujrat, A.P. and Karnataka, particularly during summer season.

3. Creates severe degradation of vegetation.

4. Drought creates adverse effect on ground water position of the region, which makes the installation of ground water structures more costlier. In drought condition the water table gets lowered to the greater depth, due to which the wells are failured and require to sink for greater depth, resulting into extra expenditure of money.

5. Due to drought incidence, the wells of the area are likely to failed *i.e.* do not yield discharge; and thus posing the problems for crop cultivation and human beings, both.

6. The surface water resources, such as ponds, reservoirs, streams/rivers etc. also get dried.

7. It forces to migrate the population from one place to another to meet their requirements.

A case study was conducted by Bharata (1978) to study the effects of consequences of drought on socio-economic condition of the population, which concluded that during migration the human as well as live-stock populations face serious hardship a large number of families fall under perpetual debts and land attachments are adversely affected by agrarian disturbance. The densely populated areas are more affected as compared to the less populated area, due to drought incidence.

11.9. Drought Control

Drought control is impossible because it is not man made event which could be controlled by adopting/maintaining the precautions. It is a hydrological event, which is entirely dependent on the nature that can not be controlled, manually. However, the following measures could be fruitful to minimize the effects of drought incidence:

1. Supply oriented measures, and
2. Demand oriented measures.

11.9.1. Supply oriented drought control measures

This measure refers to the methods for using the water in such a manner, that can make possible to tolerate the drought effects upto some extent. The following measures could be adopted:

1. Adopting most suitable method for operation of surface reservoirs.
2. Constructing emergency storage structures for collecting water to supply during drought occurrence.
3. Implementing suitable operational rules to anticipate future needs.
4. Using ground water in effective manner.
5. Conjunctive use of surface and sub-surface water.

6. Inter basin or intra basin water transfer.

7. Eliminating the water loss caused by seepage from conveyance systems, reservoirs etc. It can be achieved by lining the conveyance system by using suitable materials.

8. Adopting rainfed agriculture package and practices for producing food and fooder.

9. Augmenting the water intake capacity and water storage characteristics of the soil.

10. Using improved and suitable irrigation methods.

11. Water harvesting. It was firstly done in Australia by collecting the roof water for drinking purpose. The water harvesting techniques to collect the water for supplying during drought incidence are given as under :

1. Constructing surface ponds, reservoirs, micro catchments etc.

2. Harvesting of rain water by adopting soil conservation practices, such as contour bunding, graded bunding, conservation ditching, bench terracing etc. The practice of contour bunding is done in those areas, where annual rainfall is less and soil is permeable. While graded bunding is used in the areas of relatively high rainfall and soils in impervious nature. The conservation ditching technique is suitable in black cotton soils of Karnataka. Patnaik (1981) introduced three phase approach for runoff management in Karnataka, which includes at inter-terrace level, terrace level, and farm level.

11.9.2. Demand oriented drought control measures

The following measures could be adopted under this control measure :

1. Adopting land use regulation practices to minimize the use of water during drought periods.

2. Changing cropping practices, domestic use patterns etc.

3. Using water conservation practices.

Apart from above control measures, the Working Group's Report of N.C.A. (1975) has also recommended following practices to control the drought's effect :

1. Adopting silvi-pastoral system of agroforestory in the dry areas, because it reduces the effects of drought.

2. Selecting the crops according to climate and weather variations.

3. Using flexible ratio between kharif and rabi crops, as per drought severeness.

4. Increasing the efficiencies of conveyance and distributaries of the water supply system.

5. Conserving the water at insitu.

6. Adopting suitable agronomical practices for aberrant weather.

7. Water harvesting and recycling the same in regulated manner.

Similarly, the following practices for arid zones, suggested by various investigators (reported by National Academy of Science, Washington D.C. 1974) are also used as control measures for reducing the drought's effect :

1. Collecting the rain water from hill slopes.

2. In-situ moisture conservation in rainfed farming regions. The practices, such as inter row water harvesting, water spreading dykes, contour farming etc. can be used.

3. Re-use of waste water by recharging them.

4. Reducing the water loss caused by evaporation from the open water surfaces. This type of loss can be minimized by using liquid chemicals, such as wax, catylalcohol etc.

5. Adopting those irrigation methods, which are able to save the maximum water during drought occurence. For this purpose, the drip and sprinkler irrigation methods are most suitable.

6. Reducing the loss of water due to seepage from surface water bodies. This can be achieved by using different sealant materials, like plastic sheets, asphalt, ferrocement and chemicals over bed of the water collecting bodies.

7. Adopting suitable irrigation schedulings, so that under severe condition of water scarsity the maximum crop areas can be irrigated.

8. Growing of short duration and deep rooted crops so that under severe conditions, the crop can extract the water from soil.

9. Practicing agroforestory systems with the fast growing and less spreading type tree species at the boundary of field. It reduces descicating effect of hot blowing winds on the crops.

Weather modification by artificial means is also used as one of the drought control measures. In developed countries, nowdays more concentration is given on this aspect, to get confirmed rainfall for eliminating the chances of drought occurrence and their consequences.

IMPORTANT POINTS

1. In India there are three climatic regions, namely : humid, arid and semi-arid regions.
2. Rajasthan (India) falls under arid region.
3. In arid regions, the water-table is always below the stream bed.
4. The formation of sand dunes is the common phenomena in arid zones. In Rajasthan about 58% area is covered under sand dunes.
5. Dryness ratio is the ratio of mean annual net radiation to the product of mean annual precipitation and latent heat of vaporization of water.
6. Moisture index (I_m) of a given place can be determined by using the formula, $I_m = \frac{S - d}{PET} \times 100$, in which S is the monthly excess rainfall over PET and d is

the sum of deficit rainfall and available moisture content below PET during dry months.

7. The aridity index of a given place can be determined by using the formula, $M_m = \frac{100\,S - 60d}{N}$, in which S is moisture surplus, d is moisture deficit and N is the moisture requirement.
8. Mean annual rainfall of humid-regions is more than 75 cm.
9. Moisture availability index, (MAI) is given by the formula $MAI = \frac{PD}{PET}$, in which PD is the dependable precipitation and PET is the potential evapotranspiration.
10. MAI of very arid regions varies from 0.to 0.33.
11. When magnitude of rainfall is less than 25% of the annual rainfall, then occured drought is called meteorological drought.
12. Humidity index is the ratio of annual moisture surplus to the annual potential evapotranspiration, expressed in percent.
13. Moisture adequacy index is given by the formula, $MAI = \frac{AE}{PE} \times 100$, in which AE is the actual ET and PE is the potential ET.
14. Mean annual rainfall of desert areas is less than 100 mm.
15. Aridity index of very arid regions is less than – 57.

REFERENCES

1. Chow V.T. Handbook of Applied Hydrology, McGraw-Hill, New York, 1964.
2. Murty V.V.N. Land and Water Management Engineering, Kalyani Publisher, Delhi, 1987.
3. Penman, Vegetation and Hydrology, Farnhum Royal Common Weath-Agricultural Bureaux, 1953.
4. Raghunath H.M. Hydrology, Wiley Eastern Pvt. Ltd. Delhi, 1987.
5. Subramanya K. Engineering Hydrology, Tata McGraw-Hill, New Delhi, 2000.
6. Suresh, R. Soil & Water Conservation Engineering, Standard Pub. & Distributors, Delhi, 2002.

DESCRIPTIVE TYPE QUESTIONS

1. Classify the climatic regions and explain various factors considered for their classification.
2. Describe the characteristics of arid-regions.
3. Describe the characteristics of semi-arid regions
4. What are the factors, which categorize a region to the humid climate; describe in detail.
5. Define moisture availability index (MAI) and classify the regions in different climatic regions, based on it.
6. Define drought and describe its types.
7. Describe different relationships amongst drought, rainfall and temperature.

8. Describe various effects of drought.

9. Describe various control measures of drought occurrence.

OBJECTIVE TYPE QUESTIONS

1. Climatic regions are categorized as
   (*a*) arid, semi-arid and humid regions
   (*b*) dry, humid and wet regions
   (*c*) dry, semi-dry and humid regions
   (*d*) dry and wet regions

2. Average annual rainfall of arid region is approximated by the formula
   (*a*) $R < (T + 14)$ (*b*) $R > (T + 14)$
   (*c*) $R = (T + 14)$. (*d*) $R < (T + 1)$

3. The average annual rainfall of arid zone is
   (*a*) less than 40 cm (*b*) more than 40 cm
   (*c*) equal to 40 cm. (*d*) 1150 mm

4. Temperature of arid zone is
   (*a*) very high (*b*) very low
   (*c*) moderate (*d*) about 55°C

5. The water-table in arid zones is at
   (*a*) very deep (*b*) shallow depth
   (*c*) medium depth.
   (*d*) 10 m depth from the soil surface

6. Percentage of area of Rajasthan under sand dune is
   (*a*) 58% (*b*) 85%
   (*c*) 45% (*d*) 10%

7. The 'dryness ratio' is used to classify the
   (*a*) arid zone (*b*) humid zone
   (*c*) semi-arid zone (*d*) both a & b

8. The area which dryness ratio varies from 2.3 to 3.4 is called
   (*a*) desert area (*b*) semi-desert area
   (*c*) humid area (*d*) arid area

9. Aridity-index is computed by the formula
   (*a*) $M_m = \frac{100S - 60d}{N}$ (*b*) $M_m = \frac{60d - 100s}{N}$
   (*c*) $M_n = (100s - 60d) N$. (*d*) $M_m = 0.025\, d$

10. The value of aridity index for semi-arid regions varies from
    (*a*) – 20 to – 40 (*b*) 20 to 40
    (*c*) 40 to 57 (*d*) 2 to 5

11. Average annual rainfall of semi-arid regions varies from
    (*a*) 40 to 75 cm (*b*) 40 cm or less
    (*c*) 75 cm or more (*d*) 750 to 1150 mm

12. Average annual rainfall of semi-arid regions is approximated by the formula
    (*a*) $R = (T + 14)$ to $2\,(T + 14)$ (*b*) $R = (T - 14)$ to $2\,(T + 14)$
    (*c*) $R' = (T - 14)$ to $(T + 14)$ (*d*) $R > (T + 10)$

13. Streams of arid zones are
(*a*) intermittent (*b*) perineal
(*c*) ephemeral (*d*) both *a* & *b*

14. Streams of semi-arid regions are
(*a*) ephemeral (*b*) perrineal
(*c*) intermittent (*d*) both *b* & *c*

15. Averàge annual rainfall of humid regions is generally
(*a*) less than 75 cm (*b*) more than 75 cm
(*c*) equal to 75 cm (*d*) 1000 mm

16. Perrineal streams are found in
(*a*) arid regions (*b*) semi-arid regions
(*c*) humid regions (*d*) hilly regions

17. In humid regions, the position of water-table is generally
(*a*) above the stream bed
(*b*) below the stream bed
(*c*) at 100 below the stream bed
(*d*) at 1.5 m from the soil surface

18. In humid regions there is greater
(*a*) humidity and rainfall (*b*) humidity and evaporation
(*c*) both '*a*' and '*b*' (*d*) than 100 cm of rainfall

19. Moisture Availability Index (MAI) is computed by the formula
(*a*) $MAI = \frac{PD}{PET}$ (*b*) $MAI = \frac{PET}{PD}$
(*c*) $MAI = PET \times K$ (*d*) $\frac{100}{PD}$

20. At MAI ranging from 1.01 to 1.33, the water deficiency is categorized as
(*a*) adequate (*b*) excessive
(*c*) very deficient (*d*) moderate

21. Drought represents the extreme deficient of
(*a*) water (*b*) temperature
(*c*) pressure (*d*) humidity

22. The meterological drought takes place at
(*a*) very small rainfall (*b*) very high temperature
(*c*) 70°C temperature (*d*) none of above

23. Agricultural drought is there, when
(*a*) soil moisture is not adequate during crop period.
(*b*) rainfall is not adequate during crop period.
(*c*) rainfall is 10 cm
(*d*) both '*a*' and '*b*'

24. Hydrological drought is there, when
(*a*) depletion of water level in reservoirs, lakes etc. takes place.
(*b*) prolong situation of meterological drought
(*c*) runoff is 10 mm from the area
(*d*) both '*a*' and '*b*'.

25. Ram das (1948) defined the drought as period of
(*a*) more than 28 days having very little rainfall

(*b*) more than 15 days having very little rainfall
(*c*) 30 days without rainfall
(*d*) none of above.

25. World Meteorological Organization (1975) defined the drought, as
(*a*) a period of 10 days with rainfall greater than 5 cm.
(*b*) a period of 10 days with rainfall not greater than 5 mm.
(*c*) a month without rainfall
(*d*) none of above.

26. Indian Meterological Department defined the drought as the situation when
(*a*) annual rainfall is less than 75% of normal rainfall.
(*b*) annual rainfall is less than 50% of normal rainfall.
(*c*) $T \geq 75°C$
(*d*) none of above.

27. A drought is said to be severe, when deficiency of rainfall is
(*a*) less than 50% of the normal value
(*b*) more than 50% of the normal value
(*c*) 90% of the normal value
(*d*) none of above.

28. The dryness ratio is computed by the formula
(*a*) $I = \dfrac{t+10}{P}$ (*b*) $I = \dfrac{P}{t+10}$
(*c*) $I = \dfrac{P+t}{10}$ (*d*) $D = \dfrac{R}{P \cdot L}$

29. The value of aridity index for moderate drought varies from
(*a*) 60 to 70 (*b*) 50 to 60
(*c*) 70 to 80 (*d*) 10 to 20

30. Palmer index is used for determining the
(*a*) moisture availability (*b*) drought
(*c*) flood occurence (*d*) none of above

31. The drought increases
(*a*) salinity and alkalinity levels
(*b*) moisture content (*c*) water logging
(*d*) none of above.

32. The effect of drought can be minimized by
(*a*) selecting drought tolerance crops
(*b*) using ground water in effective way
(*c*) constructing culverts
(*d*) both '*a*' and '*b*'.

Answer (Objective Type Question)

1.	(*a*)	**2.**	(*a*)	**3.**	(*a*)	**4.**	(*a*)	**5.**	(*a*)	**6.**	(*a*)	**7.**	(*a*)	**8.**	(*b*)
9.	(*a*)	**10.**	(*a*)	**11.**	(*a*)	**12.**	(*a*)	**13.**	(*a*)	**14.**	(*a*)	**15.**	(*b*)	**16.**	(*c*)
17.	(*a*)	**18.**	(*a*)	**19.**	(*a*)	**20.**	(*a*)	**21.**	(*a*)	**22.**	(*d*)	**23.**	(*d*)	**24.**	(*d*)
25.	(*b*)	**26.**	(*a*)	**27.**	(*b*)	**28.**	(*d*)	**29.**	(*a*)	**30.**	(*a*)	**31.**	(*a*)	**32.**	(*d*)

12

Statistical and Probability Analysis of Hydrologic Data

The knowledge of statistics and probability is very essential for the field of hydrology, because hydrological events are highly erratic, random and complex in nature and are not dependent on physical and chemical laws, but completely on nature. They can not be computed exactly by using any relationship, but can be predicted at different probability levels. Presentation of hydrologic data in different forms and computation of their expected values are also dealt with the help of statistical science. In hydrology, the objectives of statistics are as under :

1. Presentation of hydrologic data such as rainfall, stream flow etc. in different forms.

2. Interpretation of hydrologic data.

3. Investigation of hydrologic probabilistic regularities

4. Derivation of different relationships concerned with agriculture on the basis of available record.

12.1. Elements of Statistics

The central tendency, grouping of observations, variability, disperson, skewness, kurtosis etc. as distribution characteristics are mainly considered under statistical elements for study purposes. All these are described as under :

12.1.1. Central Tendency

It includes following parameters.

Mean : The value of population or observations which is *centrally located* is called mean.

(*a*) **Arithmatic Mean :** It is commonly used as the measure of *central tendency* of given data. The following formulae can be used for computing the mean of sampled data :

(*i*) For ungrouped data

$$\bar{x} = \frac{x_1 + x_2 + x_3 + x_4 + \dots x_n}{N}$$

or

$$\bar{x} = \sum_{i=1}^{n} x_i / N \qquad ...(12.1)$$

(*ii*) For grouped data

$$\bar{x} = \frac{\Sigma f \cdot x}{N} \qquad ...(12.2)$$

where, $\bar{x}$ = arithmatic mean of the given data

x_1, x_2, x_3 = observations of given variable

N = number of individual observations

f = frequency of observation

Advantage : Main advantages are listed below :

1. It involves very simple calculation which is easy to compute.
2. It easily reflects the meaning of central tendency.
3. Each and every data/observations are taken into consideration.
4. There is no need to arrange the data in any array.
5. It can be applied for any random data.

Disadvantage : It includes following disadvantages :

1. If a single data is missed from group, then mean value gets affected.
2. It assumes that all the variables have equal importance, while it is not so.
3. It is not possible to find the mean value of data by inspection.
4. Due to occurrence of extreme events or abnormal variations in the data series, the mean value gets badly affected.

Example 12.1 shows the computation procedure of mean by arithmatic mean method.

Example 12.1. *Calculate the following statistical parameters of annual rainfall.*

1. Arithmatic mean; and

2. Harmonic mean

Annual rainfall data is given below :

Year	*1975*	*1976*	*1977*	*1978*	*1979*	*1980*	*1981*	*1982*	*1983*
Annual rainfall (mm)	*750*	*1150*	*1030*	*650*	*750*	*1350*	*1250*	*1000*	*955*
Year	*1984*	*1985*	*1986*	*1987*	*1988*	*1989*	*1990*	*1991*	*1992*
Annual rainfall (mm)	*703*	*1018*	*1550*	*1330*	*1200*	*1030*	*950*	*1400*	*1100*

Solution.

1. Computation of mean is shown in following table.

S.No.	*Year*	*Annual rainfall (mm)*	*Computation*
1	1975	750.0	$\overline{X} = \Sigma x/N$
2	1976	1150.0	$\Sigma x = 19166.00$ mm
3	1977	1030.0	$N = 18$
4	1978	650.0	$\therefore$ Arithmatic mean
5	1979	750.0	$(\overline{X}) = \frac{\Sigma X}{N} = \frac{19166.0}{18}$
6	1980	1350.0	
7	1981	1250.0	= **1064.78 mm Ans.**
8.	1982	1000.0	
9	1983	955.0	
10	1984	703.0	
11	1985	1018.0	
12	1986	1550.0	
13	1987	1330.0	
14	1988	1200.0	
15	1989	1030.0	
16	1990	950.0	
17	1991	1400.0	
18	1992	1100.0	

2. **Harmonic mean :** It is given by the following formula :

$$\overline{x}_h = \frac{N}{\frac{1}{x_1} + \frac{1}{x_2} + \frac{1}{x_3} + \frac{1}{x_4} + \ldots \frac{1}{x_n}}$$

Computation of harmonic mean is shown as under

Year	*Annual rainfall (mm) (x)*	$\frac{1}{x}$	$\overline{X}_h$
1975	750	1.33×10^{-3}	$\Sigma \frac{1}{x_i} = 0.01686$
1976	1150	8.69×10^{-4}	$N = 18$
1977	1030	9.7×10^{-4}	$\therefore \overline{X}_h = \frac{18}{0.01686}$
1978	650	1.53×10^{-3}	= **19217.08 mm Ans.**
1979	750	1.33×10^{-3}	
1980	1350	7.40×10^{-4}	
1981	1250	8×10^{-4}	

Contd. ....

Year	Annual rainfall (mm) (x)	$\frac{1}{x}$	X_h
1982	1000	1×10^{-3}, , ,	
1983	955	1.42×10^{-3}, , ,	
1984	703	9.82×10^{-4}, , ,	
1985	1018	6.45×10^{-4}, , ,	
1986	1550	7.52×10^{-4}, , ,	
1987	1330	8.33×10^{-4}, , ,	
1988	1200	9.7×10^{-4}, , ,	
1989	1030	1.05×10^{-4}, , ,	
1990	950	1.03×10^{-3}, , ,	
1991	1400	7.14×10^{-4}, , ,	
1992	1100	9.09×10^{-4}, , ,	

Example 12.2. *Calculate arithmatic and harmonic mean of the following rainfall data :*

Rainfall (cm)	*75—100*	*100—125*	*125—150*	*150—175*	*175—200*
Frequency	*8*	*15*	*7*	*2*	*1*

Solution. Computation of mean rainfall

Class interval of rainfall (cm)	*Frequency (f)*	*Mid-point (x)*	$f \cdot x$	$\frac{1}{x}$	$f \cdot \left(\frac{1}{x}\right)$
75—100	8	87.5	700.00	0.014	0.0912
100—125	15	112.5	1687.50	0.0088	0.1320
125—150	7	137.5	962.50	0.0073	0.0511
150—175	2	162.5	325.00	0.0062	0.0124
175—200	1	187.5	187.50	0.0053	0.0053
Total	33		3862.5		0.292

$$\therefore \quad \bar{x} = \frac{\Sigma fx}{N} = \frac{3862.5}{33}$$

$$= \mathbf{117.05\ cm} \quad \textbf{Ans.}$$

$$X_h = \frac{N}{\Sigma f_i \left(\frac{1}{x_i}\right)} = \frac{23}{0.292}$$

$$= \mathbf{113.30\ cm} \quad \textbf{Ans.}$$

(*b*) **Geometric Mean :** If $x_1, x_2, x_3 \ldots x_n$ are the recorded data for '*N*' length of years then geometric mean ($\bar{x}_g$) of the given data can be determined by using the following formula :

$$\bar{x}_g = (x_1 \;\; x_2 \cdot x_3 \cdot \ldots x_n)^{1/N} \qquad \ldots(12.3)$$

Example 12.3. *The following rainfall data were recorded at 5 rain gauges stations A, B, C, D and E in a watershed of 2500 km² area. Compute geometric mean of the rainfall.*

Rain gauge station	*A*	*B*	*C*	*D*	*E*
Rainfall amount (cm)	*11.50*	*7.50*	*8.30*	*10.00*	*12.00*

Solution : The geometric mean of rainfall is given by the formula :

$$\bar{x}_g = (x_1 \cdot x_2 \cdot x_3 \ldots x_n)^{1/N}$$
$$= (11.5 \times 7.5 \times 8. \times 10.0 \times 12.0)^{1/5}$$
$$= (85905)^{1/5}$$
$$= \mathbf{9.70\ cm} \quad \textbf{Ans.}$$

(*c*) **Weighted Mean :** As it has been earlier stated, that the arithmatic mean assumes that all occurring events have equal importance, but some times this assumption is not valid due to appearance of extreme events. Under this condition, mean of the given data is determined by considering the effect of other evolved parameters, in terms of "weighted mean". Say for example : if a field has irregular slope, land use, soil characteristics etc, then mean of the land feature is determined as the weighted mean. Following formula can be used for determining the weighted mean :

$$\bar{x}_w = \frac{x_1\, w_1 + x_2 \cdot w_2 + \ldots x_n \cdot w_n}{W} \qquad \ldots(12.4)$$

where, $\bar{x}_w$ = weighted mean of the given data

W = total number of data set.

Computation procedure is shown in example 12.4.

(*d*) **Harmonic Mean :** Its use is not very common in hydrology. The mean of reciprocal of the events/items of a given series is taken as "harmonic mean". It can be computed by using the following formula :

(*i*) For grouped data, $$\bar{x}_h = \frac{\Sigma f_i}{\Sigma f_i \left(\dfrac{1}{x_i}\right)} \qquad \ldots(12.5)$$

(*ii*) For ungrouped data

$$\bar{x}_h = \frac{N}{\dfrac{1}{x_1} + \dfrac{1}{x_2} + \dfrac{1}{x_3} + \ldots \dfrac{1}{x_n}} \qquad \ldots(12.6)$$

Weighted Harmonic Mean : Mean of event after assigning the weight to each of them is known as weighted harmonic mean. It is determined in that condition, when geometric mean does not represent satisfactory result. The following formula can be used for computing the weighted harmonic mean :

$$\bar{x}_h = \frac{N}{\frac{w_1}{x_1} + \frac{w_2}{x_2} + \frac{w_3}{x_3} + \dots \frac{w_n}{x_n}} \quad \text{...(12.7)}$$

For any set of database, the accuracy of different types of mean is in following order

$$\bar{x} > \bar{x}_g > \bar{x}_h$$

Computation of weighted harmonic mean is shown in example 12.4.

Example 12.4. *For estimation of mean areal rainfall of a given watershed by using Theissen polygone method, the rainfall and area enclosed under each polygone are given as under. Calculate following statistical parameters :*

1. *Weighted mean; and*
2. *Weighted harmonic mean*

Station	*A*	*B*	*C*	*D*	*E*
Rainfall (cm)	*11.5*	*7.5*	*8.3*	*10.0*	*12.0*
Area enclosed (sq km)	*450*	*300*	*130*	*350*	*410*

Solution :

1. Weighted mean

Station	*Rainfall (cm) (x)*	*Enclosed area (km^2) (w)*	$w \cdot x$
A	11.5	450	5175.00
B	7.5	300	2250.00
C	8.3	130	1079.00
D	10.0	350	3500.00
E	12.0	410	4920.00
	Total	1640 km^2	16924 $cm.km^2$

$$\therefore \quad \text{Weighted mean } (\bar{x}_w) = \frac{x_1 w_1 + x_2 w_2 + \dots x_n w_n}{w_1 + w_2 + \dots w_n}$$

$$= \frac{16924}{1640}$$

$$= \mathbf{10.32\ cm} \quad \textbf{Ans.}$$

2. Weighted harmonic mean

Station	*Rainfall (cm)* *(x)*	*Enclosed area (w)* *(km^2)*	*w/x (km^2/cm)*
A	11.50	450.0	39.13
B	7.50	300.0	40.00
C	8.30	130.0	15.66.
D	10.00	350.0	35.00
E	12.00	410.0	34.17
	Total	1640 Km^2	163.96 km2/cm

∴ Weighted harmonic mean

$$\bar{x}_h = \frac{N}{\frac{w_1}{x_1} + \frac{w_2}{x_2} + \ldots \frac{w_n}{x_n}}$$

$$= \frac{5}{163.96}$$

$$= \mathbf{0.030\ cm/km^2} \quad \textbf{Ans.}$$

Median : The middle value "in case of odd data and average of middle two values" incase of even data are called "median". In other words "it is that value amongst data, which has 50 percent cumulative frequency. It is computed by using the following steps for ungrouped data :

1. Arrange data in ascending order.

2. Find the middle event (when data is odd) or take the average of two middle events (incase of even data), as the median of given data.

When data is in the form of group, then median is calculated by interpolation technique, given as under :

$$\text{Median} = l_1 + \frac{C}{f_m}\left[\frac{N}{2} - (\Sigma f)_1\right] \qquad \ldots(12.8)$$

where, l_1 = lower limit of median class

C = class interval

N = total number of observations

$(\Sigma f)_1$ = sum of the frequencies, lower than median class

f_m = frequency of median class

Computations of median of grouped and ungrouped data are shown in examples 12.5, 12.6 and 12.7.

Example 12.5. *Find the median value of following rainfall data, recorded at different rain gauge stations*

1.

Rain gauge station	A	B	C	D	E	F	G
Rainfall (cm)	7.5	6.5	10.0	12.0	13.5	10.5	15.0

2.

Rain gauge station	A	B	C	D	E	F	G	H
Rainfall (cm)	5.5	6.5	10.3	11.0	15.0	14.0	12.0	9.5

Solution. Computation of Median Values

1. Arranging the rainfall data in ascending order *i.e.*

6.5, 7.5, 10.0, 10.5, 12.0, 13.5, 15.0

Since data is in odd number, therefore, median is middle rainfall *i.e.*

= **10.5 cm Ans.**

2. Arranging the rainfall in ascending order *i.e.*

5.5, 6.5, 9.5, 10.3, 11.0, 12.0, 14.0, 15.0

In this case, median is average of two middle rainfall values, because of even number of data. It is given as

$$= \frac{10.3 + 11.0}{2}$$

= **10.65 cm Ans.**

Example 12.6. *Calculate the median value of following data*

Wind velocity (m/s)	7.5	8.5	3.5	6.5	10.0	9.5	13.0
Frequency	3	4	2	1	1	1	2

Solution. Computation is shown in following table :

Wind velocity (m/s)	Frequency after arranging in ascending order	Cumulative Frequency (f)
3.5	2	2
6.5	1	3
7.5	3	6
8.5	4	10
9.5	1	11
10.0	1	12
13.0	2	14

Since, there are 14 observations on wind velocity which is even number. Therefore, median will be average of two middle values, *i.e.*

7th value = 8.5 m/s
8th value = 8.5 m/s

$$\therefore \text{ Thus, median} = \frac{8.5 + 8.5}{2} = \mathbf{8.5\ m/s} \quad \textbf{Ans.}$$

Example 12.7. *Compute the median of following data.*

Rainfall (cm)	*0-5*	*5-10*	*10-15*	*15-20*	*20-25*
Frequency	*5*	*6*	*4*	*3*	*1*

Solution. Computation is shown as under :

Class interval	*Frequency*	*Cumulative frequcny*
0—5	5	5
5—10	6	11
10—15	4	15
15—20	3	18
20—25	1	19

Here, total length of record or observation is 19. Thesefore, median value will lie in that class-interval, which frequency is either 9.5 $\left(i.e. \frac{19}{2}\right)$ or more, According to it, 9.5 lies in the class-interval of 5—10, of which the cumulative frequency is 11.

Thus,
$$l_1 = 5, C = 5$$
$$N = 19, (\Sigma f)_1 = 5$$
$$f_m = 6$$

$$\therefore \text{ Median} = l_1 + \frac{C}{f_m}\left[\frac{N}{2} - (\Sigma f)_1\right]$$
$$= 5 + \frac{5}{6}\left[\frac{19}{2} - 5\right]$$
$$= \mathbf{8.75\ cm} \quad \textbf{Ans.}$$

Mode : It is that value of the variate, which has highest frequency. For moderately skewed and unimodal curve, the following formula can be used for computing the mode :

$$\text{Mean} - \text{mode} = 3\ (\text{mean} - \text{median}) \qquad ...(12.9)$$

or
$$\text{mode} = \text{mean} - 3\ (\text{mean} - \text{median})$$
$$= \text{mean} - 3\ \text{mean} + 3\ \text{median}$$
$$\text{Mode} = 3\ \text{median} - 2\ \text{mean} \qquad ...(12.10)$$

Mode is an important central value for determining the distribution of extreme events, such as occurrence of drought, flood etc. Computation of mode for grouped data is done by using the following formula :

Case 1 : Without frequency distribution of class interval

$$\text{Mode} = l + \frac{f_1 - f_2}{(f_1 - f_2) + (f_1 - f_3)} \times C \qquad \text{...(12.11)}$$

Case 2. With frequency distribution of class-interval

$$\text{Mode} = l + \frac{f_3}{f_2 + f_3} \times l \qquad \text{...(12.12)}$$

where, l = lower limit of modal class

f_1 = frequency of modal class *i.e.* maximum frequency

f_2 = frequency of preceeding class

f_3 = frequency of succeeding class

C = width of class interval

Calculation procedure of mode is shown in example 12.8.

Example 12.8. *Compute mode of the data cited in example 12.7.*

Solution. Since, data is given in the form of class-interval, therefore, the class interval bearing highest frequency is selected. In this case, the highest frequency is '6' which is of 5-10 class interval. Thus,

$$l = 5, f_1 = 6$$
$$C = 5, f_2 = 5$$
$$f_3 = 4$$

$$\therefore \quad \text{Mode} = l + \frac{f_1 - f_2}{(f_1 - f_2) + (f_1 - f_3)} C$$

$$= 5 + \frac{(6-5)\,5}{(6-5)+(6-4)}$$

$$= 5 + \frac{5}{3} = \mathbf{6.67\ cm} \quad \textbf{Ans.}$$

12.2. Variability

The variability or disperson of any data series is evaluated based on the following parameters :

1. **Mean deviation (M.D.) :** It is the mean of absolute deviation from mean value, given by the following formula :

$$M.D. = \frac{\Sigma |x - \bar{x}|}{N} \qquad \text{...(12.13)}$$

where, x = variable

$\bar{x}$ = mean of the variable

N = total number of variables.

2. **Standard deviation (S.D.) :** Square root of the mean squared deviation from the mean is the "standard deviation". The following formula can be used for computation of standard deviation :

1. For ungrouped data

$$\sigma = \sqrt{\frac{\Sigma (x - \bar{x})^2}{N - 1}} \quad ...(12.14)$$

2. For grouped data $\sigma = \sqrt{\frac{\Sigma f (x - \bar{x})^2}{N - 1}}$ ...(12.15)

where, σ = standard deviation

$\bar{x}$ = mean of the data

N = total number of observations

3. **Variance :** It is the square of standard deviation *i.e.*

$$\text{Variance} = \sigma^2 \quad ...(12.16)$$

4. **Coefficient of variation (C_v) :** It is an important disperson parameter for determining the variation amongst observations. It is computed as the ratio of standard deviation (σ) to the mean ($\bar{x}$) of given data, i.e.,

$$C_v = \frac{\sigma}{\bar{x}} \quad ...(12.17)$$

It is dimensionless statistical parameter, expressed in %.

Examples 12.9 and 12.10 show the computation procedure of S.D., variance and coefficient of variation.

Example 12.9. *Following rainfall data were recorded from a given rain gauge station.*

Year	*1982*	*1983*	*1984*	*1985*	*1986*	*1987*
Annual rainfall (cm)	*10.00*	*15.0*	*12.00*	*13.5*	*21.5*	*17.0*
Year	*1988*	*1989*	*1990*	*1991*	*1092*	*1993*
Annual rainfall (cm)	*9.5*	*7.5*	*10.5*	*13.0*	*15.5*	*16.0*

Compute the following statistical parameters :

1. Mean deviation

2. Standard deviation

3. Coefficient of variation; and

4. Variance

Solution.

Year	*Annual rainfall (x) (cm)*	$x-\bar{x}$	$\lvert x-\bar{x}\rvert$	$(x-\bar{x})^2$	*Computation*
1982	10.0	– 3.41	3.41	11.63	$\bar{X}=\frac{\Sigma x}{N}=\frac{161}{12}=\mathbf{13.41\ cm}$
1983	15.0	1.59	1.59	2.53	(1) M.D. $=\frac{\Sigma\lvert x-\bar{x}\rvert}{N}$
1984	12.0	– 1.41	1.41	1.99	
1985	13.5	0.09	0.09	0.008	$=\frac{36.0}{12}=\mathbf{3}$
1986	21.5	8.09	8.09	65.45	(2) S.D. $=\sqrt{\frac{\Sigma(x-\bar{x})^2}{N-1}}$
1987	17.0	3.59	3.59	12.89	
1988	9.5	– 3.91	3.91	15.29	$=\sqrt{\frac{166.41}{11}}=\mathbf{3.89}$
1989	7.5	– 5.91	5.91	34.93	(3) $\sigma^2=(3.89)^2=\mathbf{15.13}$
1990	10.5	– 2.91	2.91	8.47	(4) $C_V=\frac{\sigma}{\bar{x}}=\frac{3.89}{13.41}\times 100$
1991	13.0	– 0.41	0.41	0.17	$=\mathbf{29\%}$
1992	15.5	2.09	2.09	4.37	
1993	16.0	2.59	2.59	8.70	
Total	161.0	36.0	36.0	166.41	

Example 12.10. *Compute the following statistical parameters :*

1. Mean deviation *2. Standard deviation*
3. Variance *4. Coefficient of variation*

Data is given below :

Rainfall, cm	*0—3*	*3—6*	*6—9*	*9—12*	*12—15*	*15—18*	*18—21*
Frequency	*2*	*3*	*5*	*7*	*8*	*3*	*4*

Solution. Computation is as under :

Rainfall, cm	*Mid point (x)*	*Frequency (f)*	$f\cdot x$	$(x-\bar{x})$	$\lvert x-\bar{x}\rvert$	$(x-\bar{x})^2$	$f(x-\bar{x})^2$
0—3	1.5	2.0	3.0	– 9.84	9.84	96.83	193.66
3—6	4.5	3.0	13.5	– 6.84	6.84	46.79	140.37
6—9	7.5	5.0	37.5	– 3.84	3.84	14.75	73.75
9—12	10.5	7.0	73.5	– 0.84	0.84	0.71	4.97
12—15	13.5	8.0	108.0	2.16	2.16	4.67	37.36
15—18	16.5	3.0	49.5	5.16	5.16	26.63	79.89
18—21	19.5	4.0	78.0	8.16	8.16	66.59	66.59
Total		32.0	363.0	36.84	36.84	256.94	796.36

$$\bar{x} = \frac{\Sigma f_x}{N} = \frac{363}{32} = \mathbf{11.34\ cm}$$

$$M.D. = \frac{36.84}{32} = \mathbf{1.15\ cm} \quad \textbf{Ans}$$

$$S.D. = \sqrt{\frac{796.36}{31}} = \mathbf{5.07} \quad \textbf{Ans}$$

Variance $= \sigma^2 = \mathbf{25.49}$

$$C_v = \frac{5.07}{11.34} \times 100 = \mathbf{44.69\%} \quad \textbf{Ans}$$

Skewness : It is also known as asymetry, which indicates the lack of symetry in the distribution. It can be computed by using the following formula :

$$\alpha = \frac{\Sigma (x - \mu)^3}{N} \quad ...(12.18)$$

Sample skewness : It is given as,

1. For ungrouped data

$$\alpha_s = \frac{\Sigma (x - \bar{x})^3}{N - 1} \quad ...(12.19)$$

2. For grouped data

$$\alpha_s = \frac{\Sigma f (x - \bar{x})^3}{N - 1} \quad ...(12.20)$$

Coefficient of skewness : It is the degree of skewness of distribution. It can be computed by using the following formula :

$$C_s = \frac{\alpha}{\sigma_p^3} \approx \frac{\alpha_s}{\sigma^3} \quad ...(12.21)$$

Pearson's Ist coefficient of skewness : It is given by the following formula :

$$\text{Skewness } (S_{k1}) = \frac{3\,(\text{mean} - \text{mode})}{\text{S.D}} \quad ...(12.22)$$

Pearson's IInd coefficient of skewness : It is given as,

$$S_{k_2} = \frac{3\,(\text{mean} - \text{median})}{S.D} \quad ...(12.23)$$

Computation of skewness is shown in example 12.11.

Example 12.11. *For the following data of annual stream flow, calculate coefficient of skewness.*

Annual stream flow, m^3/s	*0-2*	*2-4*	*4-6*	*6-8*	*8-10*	*10-12*	*12-14*	*14-16*	*16-18*	*18-20*
Frequency	*1*	*4*	*3*	*10*	*6*	*15*	*0*	*3*	*1*	*2*

Solution. Computation is shown as under :

Annual stream flow, m^3/s	*Frequency (f)*	*Mid point (x)*	$f \cdot x$	*Cumulative frequency*	$(x - \bar{x})$	$(x - \bar{x})^2$	$f(x - \bar{x})^2$
0—2	1	1	1	1	– 8.27	68.39	68.39
2—4	4	3	12	5	– 6.27	39.31	157.24
4—6	3	5	15	8	– 4.27	18.23	54.69
6—8	10	7	70	18	– 2.27	5.15	51.50
8—10	6	9	54	24	– 0.27	0.07	0.42
10—12	15	11	165	39	1.73	2.99	44.85
12—14	0	13	0	39	3.73	13.91	0.00
14—16	3	15	45	42	5.73	32.83	98.49
16—18	1	17	17	43	7.73	59.75	59.75
18—20	2	19	38	45	9.73	94.67	189.34
Total	45		417				724.67

$$\bar{x} = \frac{\Sigma fx}{N} = \frac{417}{45} = \mathbf{9.27}$$

$$S.D. = \sqrt{\frac{\Sigma f(x-x)^2}{N-1}} = \sqrt{\frac{724.67}{44}} = \mathbf{4.06}$$

Since, median class interval is 8—10, therefore,

$$l_1 = 8, \quad (\Sigma f)_1 = 10$$

$$C = 2, \quad f_m = 6$$

$$N = 45$$

$$\therefore \textbf{ Median} = 8 + \frac{2}{6}\left[\frac{42}{2} - (2)\right]$$

$$= \mathbf{14.33}$$

$$l = 8, \quad C = 2$$

$$f_1 = 15, \quad f_2 = 6, \quad f_3 = 0$$

$$\therefore \text{ Mode} = 8 + \frac{(15-6) \times 2}{(15-6) + (15-0)}$$

$$= \mathbf{8.75}$$

Coefficient of Skewness :

(*i*) *Pearson first coefficient*

$$S_{k1} = \frac{3\ (\text{mean} - \text{mode})}{S.D}$$

$$= \frac{3\ (9.27 - 8.75)}{4.06} = \mathbf{0.384} \quad \textbf{Ans.}$$

(*ii*) *Pearson second coefficient*

$$S_{k2} = \frac{3\,(\text{mean} - \text{median})}{\text{S.D}}$$

$$= \frac{3\,(9.27 - 14.33)}{4.06} = -\mathbf{3.73} \quad \textbf{Ans.}$$

Statistical Homogeneity

The statistical homogeneity of hydrologic processes is evaluated with respect to time and space. Accordingly, it may be classified as,

1. Time homogeneity; and 2. Space homogeneity.

Time homogeneity : A process or time series is said to be time-homogeneous, if the similar or identical events which are under consideration in the series or of the series, are likely to occur at all the times. Purely random and stationary processes or time series come under this kind of homogeneity. Hydrologic data are not in time-homogeneous nature because of the effect of several variations in nature. However, the time homogeneity of hydrologic data can be analysed in following respects :

1. Trend 2. Periodicity; and 3. Persistence

The trend refers to the increasing or decreasing rate of change of mean value of the hydrologic variable in one direction.

The periodicity represents a regular or oscillatory variations in the data. The diurnal and seasonal variations, which occur frequently in the hydrological events during a year, indicates periodicity of the hydrologic phenomena. These variations are found for a fixed time span. The periodicity of event is determined by harmonic analysis.

The persistence time homogeneity refers to the linkage of successive variables of time series amongst themselves in some persistence manner. Persistency results the data into non-pure randomness. The occurrence of wet years or drought years shows the persistence, because their effect is carryover on the antecedent hydrologic conditions.

Space homogeneity : It refers to the spatial statistical meteorological homogeneity or spatial statistical hydrologic homogeneity. It is a kind of occurrence of specific meteorological or hydrologic event in a statistically homogenous region or area. This type of homogeneity can be evaluated by using regional analysis.

Trend Analysis : There have been developed various methods for removing the trend of hydrologic database, but all are not fully justify the fact that how they affect the time series of the database. The fitting of polynomial to the data is very common method of trend analysis. However, it has following objections :

1. The evolved coefficients of polynomial are determined by a high-order moment, which is unreliable because of introduction of sampling error due to consideration of small size data base.
2. The polynomial coefficients are required to recompute each time to add in the time series, as they are dependent on available data of the series.

The moving average method is another technique to eliminate the trend of time series data, in which the polynomials are determined for different parts of the record, separately by using different forms of polynomials. Advantage of this method is that, it allows to add new values without altering the previousely fitted polynomial.

If the observations on any hydroglogic event are $x_1, x_2, x_3 .... x_n$ at a given time interval, then moving average implies to determine the overlapping of m successive weighted values, for analysing the trend of time series data. The moving average for $m = 3$ is given as,

$$Y_2 = \frac{b_1x_1 + b_2x_2 + b_3x_3}{3}$$

$$Y_3 = \frac{b_1x_2 + b_2x_3 + b_3x_4}{3}$$

$$Y_4 = \frac{b_1x_3 + b_2x_4 + b_3x_5}{3}$$

$$Y_{N-1} = \frac{b_1x_{N-1} + b_2x_{N-1} + b_3x_N}{3} \qquad ...(12.24)$$

in which b_1, b_2 and b_3 are the weights of moving average; values of these coefficients are such that their sum is equal to 3. The general form of moving average for m successive weights can be expressed as,

$$\sum_{i=1}^{m} b_i = m \qquad ...(12.25)$$

The values of b_1, b_2 and b_3 may be positive or negative. When value of each weight *i.e.* b_1, b_2 and b_3 is 1, then moving average is referred as simple. Simple moving average smoothens the data, causing main features of time series and weighted moving average are changed. It is always suggested to consider the odd values of m, so that Y values could correspond the middle value of x's being averaged in the time series. The trend analysis by considering m as 2, 3 ... $N - 1$ can also be done, but it should always be kept in view that m should be small as compared to N.

The mathematical trend of time series should be in terms of simple relation.ship in the form of straight line. However, in time series the straight line relationship can not be used throughout the observation.

Once, the trend of time series has been determined, the next step is to remove the trend from data, by using any suitable technique. One method is to determine the deviation of time series from the trend line and to constitute a stationary time series. The stationary series can be obtained by dividing the deviations with their corresponding trend values. The trend of moving average is shown in Figure 12.1.

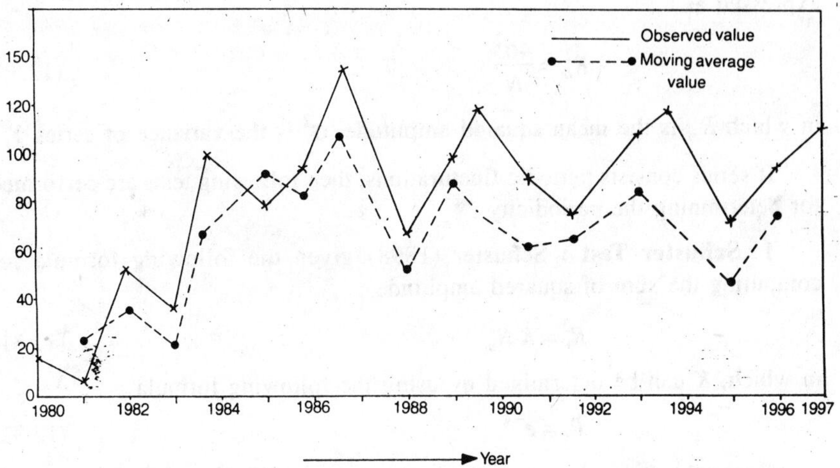

Fig. 12.1. Moving average curve.

Analysis of Periodicity : The periodicity of time series is determined by harmonic analysis, in which Fourier series is used for representing the time series.

Let, if $x_1, x_2, \ldots x_N$ are the observations of time series with T as the total length of record, then according to Fourier series,

$$x_3 = \frac{1}{2} A_0 + \sum_{J=1}^{T/2} \left(A_J \cos \frac{360\, Jt}{T} + B_J \sin \frac{360\, Jt}{T} \right) \quad \ldots(12.26)$$

in which, A_0 is the constant, t is the time, T is the total length of period and A_J & B_J are the amplitudes of harmonic series, which are given by

$$A_J = \frac{2}{N} \sum_{t=1}^{N} Y_t \cos \frac{360\, Jt}{T} \quad \ldots(12.27)$$

$$B_j = \frac{2}{N} \sum_{t=1}^{N} Y_t \sin \frac{360\, Jt}{T} \quad \ldots(12.28)$$

where Y_t is the deviation of x_t from trend line (*i.e.* straight line) for the period taken into consideration. J is the number of years of record *i.e.* $J = 1, 2, \ldots N$

Sum of squared amplitudes (R_j^2) is given as

$$R_j^2 = A_j^2 + B_j^2 \quad \ldots(12.29)$$

If series is pure random of N terms with normal distribution (*i.e.* without periodic fluctuation), then mean squared amplitude of time series can be expressed as,

$$R_m^2 = \frac{4\sigma^2}{N} \qquad \text{...(12.30)}$$

in which R_m is the mean squared amplitude, σ^2 is the variance of series Y_t.

If series consists periodic flucturations, then following tests are performed for determining the periodicity :

1. **Schuster Test :** Schuster (1898) given the following formula for computing the sum of squared amplitude :

$$R_j^2 = K\,R_m^2 \qquad \text{...(12.31)}$$

in which, K can be determined by using the following formula :

$$P_s = e^{-k} \qquad \text{...(12.32)}$$

Generally, P_s is taken as 10%. At this value of P_s, the K is equal to 2.303. Thus, substituting the K as 2.303 in equation 12.31, we have,

$$R_J^2 = 2.303\,R_m^2 \qquad \text{...(12.33)}$$

$$= \frac{9.21\,\sigma^2}{N} \qquad \left(R_m^2 = \frac{4\sigma^2}{N}\right)$$

After determining the R_J etc., the value of J can also be determined. And ultimately, the periodicity is obtained as $\frac{T}{J}$.

2. **Walker Test :** This test was developed by Walker in the year 1925. He suggested following formula for computation of factor K :

$$P_w = 1 - (1 - e^{K})^{N/2} \qquad \text{...(12.34)}$$

By considering P_w (probability) as any value, the K can be determined for given N. Substituting the K in following formula, we have

$$R_J^2 = K\,R_m^2$$

or

$$\frac{4K\,\sigma^2}{N}$$

3. **Fisher Test :** Fisher (1929) suggested the formula $R_J^2/2S^2$, which is greater than the given value of g. In which, S^2 is the unbiased estimate of σ^2. The probability of time series is given as,

$$P_f = \sum_{i=0}^{m} (-1)^i \binom{j}{i} (1 - ig)^{J-1} \qquad \text{...(12,35)}$$

in which m is the largest integer less than $1/g$ and j is the number of periods *i.e.* 1, 2 .... After determining the value of probability by using above formula, the testing of periodicity is performed same to the Schuster Test.

Hydrologic Data Series

Hydrologic data are generally presented in chronological order by their magnitudes and are expressed in an arbitrary unit. More commonly, a hydrologic data series contains following sub- series :

1. Complete-duration series
2. Partial-duration series
   (*a*) Annual exceedance series; and
   (*b*) Non-annual exceedance series
3. Extreme-value series
   (*a*) Maximum value series
      (*i*) Annual maximum series; and
      (*ii*) Non-annual maximum series
   (*b*) Minimum value series
      (*i*) Annual minimum series; and
      (*ii*) Non-annual minimum series

All these are explained as under :

Complete-duration series : It includes total available data, as shown in Figure 12.2.

Partial-duration series : It is also called partial series. In this series those observations are considered, which magnitude is greater than a certain base value. The partial series data are again classified in following two sub-series :

(*a*) **Annual exceedance series :** A partial-duration series is said to be annual exceedance series, when base value is such that the number of values in the series is equal to the number of records. It is shown in the figure – 12.2

(*b*) **Non-annual exceedance series :** If base value is such that the number of values in the series is not equal to the number of records, then series is known as non- annual exceedance series.

Extreme-value series : It includes largest or smallest values, selected from an equal time interval of the record. The time interval is taken as water year. This series is grouped as :

(*a*) **Maximum value series :** The largest values selected from an equal time interval of the record is called maximum value series. If the interval is year or water year, then series is called annual maximum series. It is shown

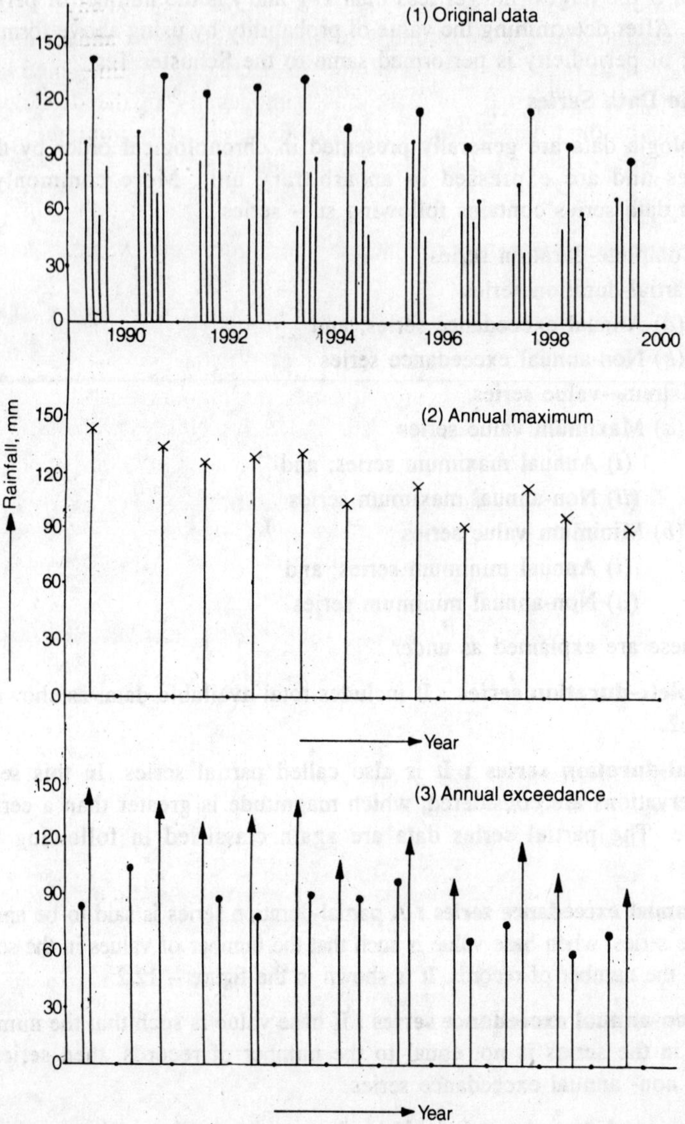

Fig. 12.2. Complete duration series.

in Figure 12.2. In annual maximum series, only annual maximum values are selected. The second largest value and others are omitted.

(*b*) **Minimum value series :** The smallest values selected from an equal time interval of the record is called minimum value series. If it is selected from the time interval of year or water year, then series is called annual minimum series. It is shown in Figure 12.2. One point should always be taken into consideration that, the dependency between observations and number of selected values increases as the time interval decreases. If time interval is less than the year, then there will be non-homogencity in the data due to variations in seasonal data. In annual minimum series, only minimum value is selected. The next lowest and others are omitted.

Probability Theory

Probability (p) of the event (X) in any set of observation is related to the return period in the following two way :

1. For each observation there is either success ($X \geq x_T$) or failure ($X < x_T$).
2. Since observations are independent, therefore probability of the recurrence interval of duration T is the product of probabilities of $T-1$ failures, followed by one success *i.e.* $(1-p)^{T-1} \cdot p$.

Probability of the event which will occur at least once in N years

Probability of such events is given by,

$$p\,(X \geq x_T \text{ at least once in N years}) = 1-(1-p)^N$$

$$= 1-\left(1-\frac{1}{T}\right)^N \qquad \text{...(12.36)}$$

Probability of most extreme event : The probability of most extreme events such as drought or largest flood, occurred during past N-years can be computed by using the following formula :

$$P\,(N, n) = \frac{n}{N+n} \qquad \text{...(12.37)}$$

where N is the years of observation and n is the year during which the extreme event either is equal to or greater than the reference value.

Probability of worst event over the past and future : It can be determined by using the following formula :

$$P\,(N, m, n) = \frac{(n-m+1)}{(N-m+1)+(n-m+1)}$$

$$= \frac{n-m+1}{N+n-2m+2} \quad \text{for } (n \geq m) \qquad \text{...(12.38)}$$

where, N = length of record (year)

m = length of critical event (year)

n = next year, when worst event will occur

Number of sequence of length (m) in N years $= N-m+1$

Number of sequence of length (n) in n years $= n-m+1$

Problem 12.12 : A 50 years record of critical drought of a given region revealed that the most severe drought was lasted 10 years. Compute the probability of most severe drought, which will likely to occur during next 15 years.

Solution: Given that, $N = 50$ years, $m = 10$ years and $n = 15$ years

Using the formula,

$$P(N, m, n) = \frac{n - m + 1}{N + n - 2m + 2}$$

$$= \frac{15 - 10 + 1}{50 + 15 - 2 \times 10 + 2} = \frac{6}{47} = \mathbf{0.127} \quad \textbf{Ans.}$$

Relationship between Probabilities of the Partial-duration Series (or annual exceedance series) and the Annual maximum Series

This relationship was developed by Lang bein (1949), which is described as under :

Let, if

1. P_E is the probability of a variate of the partial duration series which is equal to or greater than x.

2. m is the average number of events per year.

Then, (*i*) Probability of the event being equal to or greater than x will be,

$$\frac{P_E}{m} \quad \text{...(12.39)}$$

(*ii*) Probability of an event being less than x will be

$$1 - \frac{P_E}{m} \quad \text{...(12.40)}$$

(*iii*) Probability of an event of magnitude x becoming a maximum of the m events in a year will be

$$\left(1 - \frac{P_E}{m}\right)^m \quad (12.41)$$

When value of P_E is small as compared to m, then probability of the event of magnitude x becoming a maximum of the m events in a year approaches to e^{-P_E}. It is valid for most of the cases.

(*iv*) Probability of variate of annual maximum series (P_M), which is equal to or greater than x is given by

$$P_M = 1 - e^{-P_E} \quad \text{...(12.42)}$$

or

$$P_E = -\ln(1 - P_M) \quad \text{...(12.43)}$$

Relationship between Recurrence Interval of Annual Maximum Series (T_M) and Partial-duration Series (T_E)

The average time interval, within which the magnitude *y* of event is equal to or greater than *x*, once is known as recurrence interval. The return period or simple frequency also refers to the recurrence interval. Mathematically, it is given as $\frac{1}{P(X \geq x)}$, where, $P(X \geq x)$ is the probability of event (X) which is equal to or greater than *x*, once in *T* years.

Recurrence interval (T) for the event (X) less than *x* is given by

$$T = \frac{1}{1 - P(X \geq x)} \quad \text{...(12.44)}$$

Accordingly,
$$T_m = \frac{1}{P_M} \quad \text{or} \quad P_M = \frac{1}{T_M}$$

and
$$T_E = \frac{1}{P_E} \quad \text{or} \quad P_E = \frac{1}{T_E} \quad \text{...(12.45)}$$

Substituting the values of P_M and P_E in equation 12.42

$$\frac{1}{T_M} = 1 - e^{-\frac{1}{T_E}} \quad \text{...(12.46)}$$

On simplification of equation (12.46), we have

$$T_E = \frac{1}{\ln T_M - \ln (T_{M-1})} \quad \text{...(12.47)}$$

Relationship between Recurrence Interval (T) i.e. mean time interval and Actual time Interval Distribution

Recurrence interval refers to the mean time interval based on the distribution of variate *x*. The mean time interval is not the actual time interval between two events of equal amount *x*. Thom (1959) studied the distribution of actual time interval by using Poissen distribution; and derived the relationship between recurrence interval (T) and the actual time interval distribution, given as under :

$$T = \frac{r}{-\ln P(r)} \quad \text{...(12.48)}$$

in which $P(r)$ is the probability of actual time interval (r) which is to be equaled or exceeded.

Expected probability : It is the average of true exceedance probabilities of all estimated amounts for the given flood frequency. Beard (1960) stated that the estimated flood event of the given sample is approximately equal to the median of all possible estimates. In other words, there is approximately equal chance of the true amount that will be either above or below the estimated amount. On the other hand, the probability distribution of tempted value is positively skewed, causing the computed average value of many samples is larger than the median value. The expected probability of flood event in any year can be computed for the event of nominal return period (T) by using the following formula (Beard 1960) :

$$E(P_n) = P\left[t_{n-1} > Z\left(\frac{n}{n+1}\right)^{1/2}\right] \quad ...(12.49)$$

where Z is the standard normal variate of the desired probability of exceedance and t_{n-1} is Student's T-test with $n - 1$ as degree of freedom.

U.S. Water Resources Council (1981) and U.S. Army Corps of Engineers (1972) suggested the following formulae of expected probability for different return periods (Table 12.1).

Table 12.1. Formulae of expected probability.

T (Years)	*Exceedance probability*	*Expected probability* $E(P_n)$
3.33	0.30	$0.30\left(1 + \frac{0.46}{n^{0.925}}\right)$
10	0.10	$0.10\left(1 + \frac{3}{n^{1.04}}\right)$
20	0.05	$0.05\left(1 + \frac{6}{n^{1.04}}\right)$
100	0.01	$0.01\left(1 + \frac{26}{n^{1.16}}\right)$
1000	0.001	$0.001\left(1 + \frac{280}{n^{1.55}}\right)$

Problem 12.13 : Compute expected probability of 20, 100 and 1000-years return period discharge data, if sample size is 30 years.

Solution : Using the formula,

1. Expected probability for 20 year T :

$$E(P_n) = 0.05\left(1 + \frac{6}{n^{1.04}}\right)$$

$$= 0.05\left(1 + \frac{6}{(30)^{1.04}}\right) = \mathbf{0.0587} \quad \textbf{Ans.}$$

2. Expected probability for 100 year T :

$$E(P_n) = 0.01\left(1 + \frac{26}{n^{1.16}}\right)$$

$$= 0.01\left(1 + \frac{26}{(30)^{1.16}}\right) = \mathbf{0.015} \quad \textbf{Ans.}$$

3. Expected probability for 1000 year T :

$$E(P_n) = 0.001\left(\frac{1}{\frac{280}{n^{1.55}}}\right)$$

$$= 0.001\left(1 + \frac{280}{(30)^{1.55}}\right) = \mathbf{0.0024} \quad \textbf{Ans.}$$

Probability Paper

It is a kind of graph sheet designed for distribution studies. The cumulative probability of distribution can be presented graphically on probability paper. Figure 12.3 shows the format of probability paper.

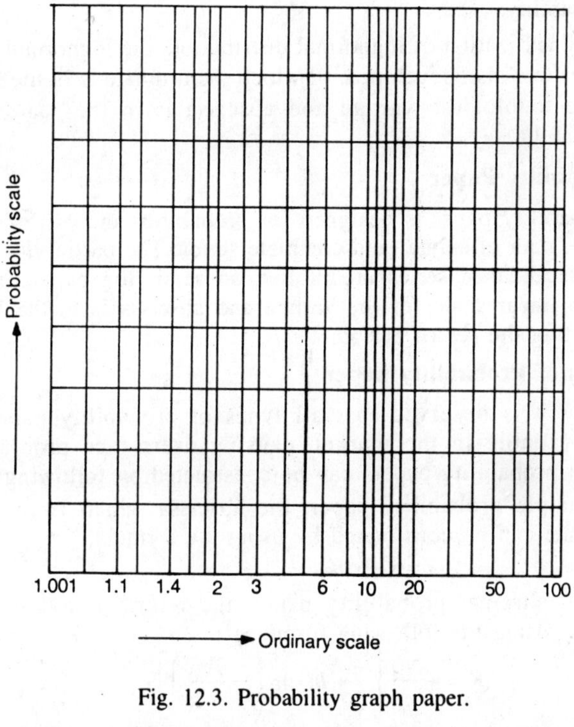

Fig. 12.3. Probability graph paper.

The Y-axis (*i.e.* ordinate) represents the value of variable (*i.e.* x) in certain scale and X-axis (*i.e.* abscissa) is probability scale ($P(X \geq x)$ or $P(X \leq x)$. On probability scale, the return period (T) is considered to plot. The two axis of the pair are so adjusted that the distribution plot is obtained in straight line. Main objective of probability graph paper is to linearize the distribution for easy extrapolation or comparison. The linearization of probability plotting was firstly proposed by Hazen in the year 1914. Since then several advances have been made in this respect, *e.g.*

(*i*) Powel (1943) developed the probability paper for Type-I extreme distribution. This paper was later named as extremal probability paper or Gumbel – Powel probability paper.

(*ii*) Court (1952) modified the extremal probability paper and named it Type-III extremal probability paper, which was used by Gumbel (1954) for drought analysis.

(*iii*) Linearization of distribution was also made by constructing log extremal probability paper or Weibull probability paper, of which the ordinate represents the logarithmic scale for plotting variate and abscissa represents a special scale for Type-I extremal distribution probability.

(*iv*) For linearization of lognormal distribution, the lognormal probability paper was also developed, of which the ordinate is in the logarithmic scale to plot the variate and abscissa is in the scale of normal probability.

Use of Probability Paper

The probability paper is designed for probability analysis of hydrologic data series *i.e.* data of annual and complete series. The partial-duration series and annual exceedance series are plotted on semi- log paper, inwhich the ordinate is in linear scale for the variate and abscissa is in the logarithmic scale for plotting the return period.

Construction of Probability paper

Generally it is observed that all types of probability papers are not commonly available in the market, causing users face problem. In this condition, the probability papers can be constructed by following ways :

1. For simple probability paper, the abscissa which is in probability $[P(X \geq x)]$ scale can be constructed by using the formula,

$$x = \bar{x} + \sigma K \qquad \text{...(12.50)}$$

2. In the extremal probability paper, the return period scale can be constructed by using the following formulae :

(*i*)
$$K = -\frac{\sqrt{6}}{\pi}\left[r + ln \cdot \ln\left(\frac{T}{T-1}\right)\right] \qquad \text{...(12.51)}$$

(*ii*)
$$T = \frac{1}{P(X \geq x)} \text{ or } \frac{1}{1 - P(X \geq x)}$$

Curve Fitting

Curve fitting can be done mathematically and graphically, both. If data are plotted on probability paper, then mathematical fitting is not require. Under graphical plotting on probability paper, the straight line is drawn to fit the plotted data just by eye-judgment. Accuracy of hand fitting depends on the person, that how he is taking the matter.

The curve fitting by mathematical methods is carried out by following three methods :

1. Method of moments
2. Method of least square; and
3. Method of maximum likelihood.

Method of Moments : This method was introduced by Gumbel (1941) to fit the Type-I extremal distribution. Under this method, the fitting of curve is theoretically exact but accuracy is largely affected by the percentage of errors involved in the used data series, especially at the tail of distribution. Because at tail end, the moment arm is more which result into magnification of errors, existing there.

In this method, the statistical parameters or moments are determined from the available data series and are substituted in the probability function of distribution technique.

Method of Least Square : In this method a regression line is derived for fitting the data series. The derived curve or regression line does not exactly represent the theoretical distribution. However, it results better curve fitting as compared to the method of moments.

3. **Method of Maximum Likelihood** : In this method, the value of concerned parameter is such that the probability of observed outcome is as high as possible. In mathematical terms it is expressed as,

$$\frac{\partial}{\partial u} p(x) = 0 \qquad ...(12.52)$$

in which $p(x)$ is the probability and u is the statistical parameter. This method of curve fitting is very complicated but provides better estimate of parameter. For curve fitting of extremal distribution, this method is found most suitable.

Goodness of fit : It is determined for evaluating the suitability of distribution technique, used for fitting the observed database. The Chi-square test (X^2 – test) is commonly used for determining the goodness of fit. The formula under this test is given by,

$$X^2 = \sum_{i=1}^{N} \frac{(y_i - y)^2}{y} \qquad ...(12.53)$$

$$= \sum_{i=1}^{N} \frac{(\Delta y_i)^2}{y} \qquad ...(12.54)$$

where y_i = observed value of variable

y = estimated value

Δy = difference between observed and estimated value.

The distribution technique with lowest X^2-value is considered as most suitable and vice-versa.

12.3. Probability Distribution

The following probability distributions are commonly employed for determining the frequencies of continuous random variables :

12.3.1. Normal Distribution

Sometimes, it is also known as Gaussian distribution. Density function of this distribution is given as under :

$$f(x) = \frac{1}{\sigma\sqrt{2\pi}} \cdot \exp\left[\frac{-(x-\mu)}{2\sigma^2}\right] \quad ...(12.55)$$

where, σ = variance

x = variable

μ = mean.

The values of σ and μ are determined from the available data. The normal frequency curve is in bell shaped and area under it is equal to 1. The following four conditions are necessary for the variables, to fit the normal probability distribution :

1. Each should be independent of the others.
2. Each should be considered separately and should have very small effect on the outcome.
3. The effect of involved factors on the outcome should be addittive.
4. The outcome of variables should be affected by causative factors.

12.3.2. Log-normal Distribution

This distribution is used in that condition, when hydrologic data involves greater skewness towards right hand side due to natural effect. In log-normal distribution, the normal data series is transformed into logarithmic scale (*i.e.* $y = \log x$) and then they are distributed. Its probability density function is given as under :

$$f(x) = \frac{1}{\sigma_y\sqrt{2\pi}} \cdot \exp\left[-\frac{(y-\mu_y)^2}{2\sigma_y}\right] \quad ...(12.56)$$

where, σ_y = standard deviation of 'y'

μ_y = mean of 'y'

$y = \ln x$.

The statistical parameters for use in Log-normal distribution have been derived by Chow, given as under :

$$\left.\begin{aligned} \mu &= exp.\ [\mu_y + \sigma_y^2/2] \\ \sigma &= \mu\ [\exp \sigma_y^2 - 1] \\ C_v &= \sqrt{exp.\ (\sigma_y)^2 - 1} \\ C_s &= 3C_v + C_v^3 \end{aligned}\right\} \quad ...(12.57)$$

12.3.3. Gumbel Distribution

This distribution is named after Gumbel (1954). The probability density function of this distribution is as below :

$$F(x) = exp.\,[-e^{-Y}] \qquad ...(12.58)$$

where,
$$Y = \frac{a + x}{c} \qquad ...(12.59)$$

$$\left.\begin{aligned} a &= \nu \cdot c \div \bar{x} \\ c &= \frac{\sqrt{b} \cdot \sigma}{\pi} \\ \nu &= 0.57721 \end{aligned}\right\} \qquad ...(12.60)$$

Substituting the values of 'a' and 'c' in equation 12.59, we have,

$$Y = \frac{(\nu \cdot c - \bar{x}) + x}{\frac{\sqrt{6}}{\pi} \cdot \sigma}$$

$$= \frac{0.57721 \frac{\sqrt{6}}{\pi} \cdot \sigma - \bar{x} + x}{\frac{\sqrt{6}}{\pi} \cdot \sigma}$$

$$= \frac{x - \bar{x} + 0.450 \cdot \sigma}{\frac{\sqrt{6}}{\pi} \cdot \sigma}$$

$$= \frac{1}{0.7797 \cdot \sigma}\,[x - \bar{x} + 0.450\,\sigma] \qquad ...(12.61)$$

12.3.4. Log-Pearson Type-IIIrd Distribution

It is a commonly used probability distribution technique for flood frequency analysis. The Log Pearson type-IIIrd distribution and Log-normal distribution become same at zero skewness. In this distribution, the natural values of variate are also converted into logarithmic form and then computations are performed. The probability density function of Log-Pearson Type-III distribution is given by,

$$f_{(x)} = f_o \left[\left(1 - \frac{x}{\alpha}\right)^{c} \cdot \exp\left(-\frac{c \cdot x}{2}\right) \right] \qquad ...(12.62)$$

where,
$$\left.\begin{aligned} C &= \frac{4}{\beta} - 1 \\ a &= \frac{C}{2} \cdot \frac{\mu_3}{\mu_2} \\ \beta &= \frac{\mu_3^2}{\mu_2^2} \end{aligned}\right\} \qquad ...(12.63)$$

and
$$f_o = \frac{n}{a} \cdot \frac{C^{C+1}}{e^{c}\,\Gamma(c+1)} \qquad ...(12.64)$$

where

μ_2 = variance

μ_3 = third moment about the mean

g = coefficient of skewness

n = length of record, year

σ = standard deviation

The above parameters are computed by using the following formulae :

(*i*) Mean $(\bar{x}) = \dfrac{\Sigma \log x}{N}$ ...(12.65)

(*ii*) Standard deviation $(\sigma) = \sqrt{\dfrac{\Sigma (\log x - \bar{x})^2}{N - 1}}$ ...(12.66)

(*iii*) Skewness coefficient $(g) = \dfrac{N \cdot \Sigma (\log x - \bar{x})^3}{(N-1)(N-2)(\sigma)^3}$ ...(12.67)

After determining the above parameters, the expected value of variate x for any return periods can be computed by using the following relationship :

$$Log\, X = \bar{x} + K \cdot \sigma$$

or $$X = \text{Anti log}\, [\bar{x} + K \cdot \sigma] \quad \text{...(12.68)}$$

in which, K is called "frequency factor," given in Table-12.2. The value of 'K' is taken against the known value of 'g' and desired return period. However, it can also be computed by using the following formula provided that the length of record must be infinite.

$$K = \frac{\sqrt{6}}{\pi}\left[0.57721 + \ln\left(\ln \frac{T}{T-1}\right)\right] \quad \text{...(12.69)}$$

in which, T is the recurrence interval or return period (year). Beard (1962) suggested that only average regional coefficient of skewness should be used in flood frequency analysis, unless the length of record exceeds 100 years period. Hazen (1930) also made modification in log Pearson type-III distribution regarding use of adjusted $\bar{C}_s$ at the place of normal skewness coefficient C_s for small samples. The adjusted $\bar{C}_s$ can be computed as follows :

$$\bar{C}_s = C_s\left(1 + \frac{8.5}{n}\right) \quad \text{...(12.70)}$$

where, $\bar{C}_s$ = adjusted skewness coefficient

C_s = normal skewness coefficient of the data

n = length of record.

Table 12.2. Frequency factor (K) for use in Log-Pearson Type-III distribution

g	Probability (%), P						
	50	20	10	4	2	1	0.5
	Recurrence interval (year), T						
	2	5	10	25	50	100	200
	(1)	(2)	(3)	(4)	(5)	(6)	(7)
3.5	– 0.396	0.420	1.180	2.278	3.152	4.051	4.970
2.5	– 0.360	0.518	1.250	2.162	3.048	3.845	4.652
2.0	– 0.307	0.609	1.302	2.219	2.912	3.605	4.298
1.8	– 0.282	0.643	1.318	2.193	2.848	3.499	4.147
1.6	– 0.254	0.675	1.329	2.163	2.780	3.388	3.990
1.4	– 0.225	0.705	1.337	2.128	2.706	3.271	3.828
1.2	– 0.195	0.732	1.340	2.087	2.626	3.149	3.661
1.0	– 0.164	0.758	1.340	2.043	2.542	3.022	3.489
0.9	– 0.148	0.769	1.339	2.018	2.498	2.957	3.401
0.8	– 0.132	0.780	1.336	1.993	2.453	2.891	3.312
0.7	– 0.116	0.790	1.333	1.967	2.407	2.824	3.223
0.6	– 0.099	0.800	1.328	1.939	2.359	2.755	3.132
0.5	– 0.083	0.808	1.323	1.910	2.311	2.686	3.041
0.4	– .066	0.816	1.317	1.880	2.261	2.615	2.949
0.3	– 0.50	0.823	1.309	1.849	2.211	2.544	2.856
0.2	– 0.033	0.830	1.301	1.818	2.159	2.472	2.763
0.1	– 0.017	0.836	1.292	1.785	2.107	2.400	2.670
0.0	– 0.000	0.841	1.282	1.751	2.054	2.326	2.576
– 0.1	0.017	0.846	1.270	1.716	2.000	2.252	2.482
– 0.2	0.033	0.850	1.258	1.680	1.945	2.178	2.388
– 0.3	0.050	0.853	1.245	1.643	1.890	2.104	2.294
– 0.4	0.066	0.855	1.231	1.606	1.834	2.029	2.201
– 0.5	0.083	0.860	1.216	1.567	1.777	1.955	2.108
– 0.6	0.099	0.857	1.200	1.528	1.720	1.880	2.016
– 0.7	0.115	0.857	1.830	1.488	1.663	1.806	1.926
– 0.8	0.132	0.856	1.166	1.448	1.606	1.733	1.837
– 0.9	0.148	0.854	1.147	1.407	1.549	1.660	1.749
– 1.0	0.164	0.852	1.128	1.366	1.492	1.588	1.664
– 1.2	0.195	0.843	1.086	1.282	1.379	1.449	1.501
– 1.4	0.225	0.832	1.041	1.198	1.270	1.318	1.351
– 1.6	0.254	0.817	0.994	1.116	1.166	1.197	1.216

Contd.

– 1.8	0.282	0.799	0.945	1.035	1.069	1.087	1.097
– 2.0	0.307	0.777	0.895	0.959	0.980	0.990	0.995
– 2.5	0.360	0.710	0.771	0.793	0.798	0.799	0.800
– 3.0	0.396	0.636	0.660	0.666	0.666	0.667	0.667

Frequency Factor

The frequency factor of given distribution technique is expressed in terms of *K–T* relationship, which is given as under :

1. **Normal Distribution** : Frequency factor (*K*) for this distribution is given by the following formula :

$$K_T = \frac{x_T - \mu}{\sigma} \qquad ...(12.71)$$

in which x_T is the variate, μ is the mean and σ is the standard deviation of sampled data.

The above formula can also be expressed in the form of

$$K_T = Z = W - \frac{2.515517 + 0.802853\,W + 0.010328\,W^2}{1 + 1.432788\,W + 0.189269\,W^2 + 0.001308\,W^3} \qquad ...(12.72)$$

where $$W = \left[\ln\left(\frac{1}{p^2}\right)\right]^{1/2} \qquad (0 < p \leq 0.5) \qquad ...(12.73)$$

Error of this formula is less than 0.00045 (Abramowitz and Stegun, 1965). For log normal distribution, this formula can be used for determining the K_T.

2. **Extreme Value Distribution** : The frequency factor (*K*) for extreme value type-I distribution can be computed by using the following formula, given by chow (1953).

$$K_T = -\frac{\sqrt{6}}{\pi}\left\{0.5772 + \ln\left[\ln\left(\frac{T}{T-1}\right)\right]\right\} \qquad ...(12.74)$$

in which, *T* is the return period.

3. **Log Pearson Type — III distribution** : Frequency factor of this distribution depends on *T* and coefficient of skewness (C_s). When $C_s = 0$, then $K = Z$ but when C_s is not 0, then K_T is approximated by the following formula, given by Kite (1977).

$$K_T = Z + (Z^2 - 1)\,K + \frac{1}{3}(Z^3 - 6Z)\,K^2 - (K^2 - 1)\,K^3 + ZK^4 + \frac{1}{3}K^5 \qquad ...(12.75)$$

where $K = \frac{C_s}{6}$

4. **Gumbel Distribution** : Frequency factor of this distribution is given as,

$$K_T = \frac{(Y_T - 0.577)}{1.2825} \qquad ...(12.76)$$

where, Y_T is the reduced variate of given return period T; it is given by

$$Y_T = -\left[Ln \cdot Ln\left(\frac{T}{T-1}\right)\right]$$

or
$$= -\left[0.834 + 2.303 \log \cdot \log\left(\frac{T}{T-1}\right)\right] \quad ...(12.77)$$

12.3.5. Plotting Distribution Method

The probability distribution of hydrologic data can also be determined by computing their plotting positions for a given length of record. There have been developed several empirical relationships for computation of plotting positions. The most common formulae are listed in Table 12.3 (Chow 1964). Amongst all, the Weibull's formula is most common and widely used, world-wide. The probability analysis by using Weibull's method is described under following steps :

Step 1 : Arrange the data in descending order by their magnitude.

Step 2 : Assign rank number to each event.

Step 3 : Calculate plotting position of each event by using the Weibull's formula, given as under :

$$p = \frac{m}{n+1} \times 100 \quad ...(12.78)$$

where, p = plotting position (percent) or relative frequency of the event, which is equal to or less than the ranked value.

m = rank number of the event, after arranging in descending order

n = total number of events.

Step 4 : Prepare frequency curve by plotting the plotting positions and corresponding event on probability graph paper.

Step 5 : Find out the expected values of event for desired frequencies or return periods/recurrence intervals $\left(i.e.\ T = \frac{1}{p}\right)$.

Table 12.3. Plotling position formulae

S.No.	*Method*	*Plotting position (p)*	*Remark*
1.	Weibull	$\frac{m}{n+1}$	m = rank number
2.	California	m/n	n = length of record
3.	Hazen	$\frac{(2m-1)}{n}$	Probability range = $P(X > x)$
4.	Beared	$[1-(0.5)^{1/n}]$	
5.	Tukey	$\frac{(3m-1)}{3n+1}$	
6.	Blom	$\left(\frac{m-\frac{3}{8}}{n+\frac{1}{4}}\right)$	

Reliability Analysis

The reliability of analysed results under frequency analysis depends on selection of probability model. It is performed by computing confidence limits of the obtained result, described as under.

Confidence Limit

Statistical results are oftenly expressed in range or confidence interval, within which the true value is expected to exist. The size of confidence interval or range is decided on the basis of confidence level. Boundary values (*i.e.* upper and lower limits) of the confidence interval are called confidence limits.

For computing the magnitudes of event for any return period T, the upper $(U_{T,\alpha})$ and lower limits $(L_{T\alpha})$ are given by,

$$U_{T\alpha} = \bar{Y} + S_y K^u_{T,\alpha} \qquad \text{...(12.79)}$$

and

$$L_{T\alpha} = \bar{Y} - S_y K^l_{T,\alpha} \qquad \text{...(12.80)}$$

where, $\bar{Y}$ is the mean of Y, S_y is standard deviation and $K^u_{T,\alpha}$ and $K^l_{T,\alpha}$ are the upper and lower confidence limit factors. Approximate values of these factors can be determined by using the following formula, given by Natrella (1963) :

$$K^u_{T,\alpha} = \frac{K_T + \sqrt{K_T^2 - ab}}{a} \qquad \text{...(12.81)}$$

$$K^l_{T,\alpha} = \frac{K_T - \sqrt{K_T^2 - ab}}{a} \qquad \text{...(12.82)}$$

where,

$$a = 1 - \frac{Z_\alpha^2}{2(n-1)} \qquad \text{...(12.83)}$$

$$b = K_T^2 - \frac{Z_\alpha^2}{n} \qquad \text{...(12.84)}$$

in which, Z_α is the standard normal variable with exceedance probability α.

The confidence level β and exceedance probability (α) are related with the following relationship :

$$\alpha = \frac{1-\beta}{2} \qquad \text{...(12.85)}$$

In Gumbel distribution the value of variate for given return period X_T is generally incorrect due to use of limited sample data. In this condition, the determination of confidence limit of estimated value of variate is essential. The confidence limit is the boundary of computed value, between which the true value of sample exists. The formula for confidence limit of estimated value by Gumbel distribution is given as under :

$$X_{1/2} = X_T \pm f(c)\, S_e \qquad \text{...(12.86)}$$

or

$$X_1 = X_T + f(c)\, S_e \qquad \text{...(12.87)}$$

$$X_2 = X_T - f(c)\, S_e \qquad \text{...(12.88)}$$

where X_1 and X_2 = upper and lower boundary values, respectively

X_T = variate

c = confidence/probability.

$f(c)$ = function of confidence/probability. It is given in Table (12.4)

Table 12.4. Value of f(c) for Gumbel distribution

c (%)	50	68	80	90	95	99
$f(c)$	0.674	1.0	1.282	1.645	1.96	2.58

S_e = standard error (equation12.86)

Standard error : It is measure of standard deviation of the event with respect to true value. The formula for standard error of estimated values of normal distribution and extreme value type-I distribution are given by Kite (1977) as,

1. For normal distribution, $S_e = \left(\dfrac{2+Z^2}{n}\right)^{1/2} \cdot S$ ...(12.89)

2. For extreme value type-I distribution,

$$S_e = \left[\frac{1}{n}\left(1 + 1.1396\,K_T + 1.1000\,K_T^2\right)\right]^{1/2} \cdot S \qquad ...(12.90)$$

where, S_e is the standard error, n is the size of original sample and S is the standard deviation of original sample.

Nemec (1973) also suggested the following formula for computing standard error of Gumbel distribution :

$$S_e = b\,\frac{J_{n-1}}{\sqrt{N}} \qquad ...(12.91)$$

where $b = (1 + 1.3\,K + 1.1\,K^2)^{1/2}$

σ_{n-1} = standard deviation of sample data

K = frequency factor of Gumbel distribution

N = sample size

Risk Analysis : The risk analysis of hydraulic structure is very essential, because if the design flow for a given return period (T) exceeds during expected life of structure, then there is possibility of failure of the structure.

The hydrologic risk of failure of structure can be determined by using the following formula :

$$\bar{R} = 1 - [1 - P\,(X \geq x_T)]^n \qquad ...(12.92)$$

where, $\bar{R}$ is the probability of event $(X \geq x_T)$ that will occur at least once in n years.

$$P\,(X \geq x_T) = \frac{1}{T}$$

n = expected life of structure.

Problem 12.14 : What design return period for construction of a culvert should be taken, if the acceptable risk of atleast one event exceeding the capacity of culvert during the design life is 15%. Assume, expected life of culvert as10 years.

Solution : Given that, $R = 15\%$, and $n = 10$ years

Using the formula, $\bar{R} = 1 - \left[1 - \frac{1}{T}\right]^n$

$$0.15 = 1 - \left[1 - \frac{1}{T}\right]^{10}$$

$$0.15 = 1 - \left[1 - \frac{1}{T}\right]^{10}$$

$$\left[1 + \frac{1}{T}\right]^{10} = 1 - 0.15 = 0.85$$

$$\left[1 - \frac{1}{T}\right] = (0.85)^{1/10} = (0.85)^{0.1}$$

$$\frac{1}{T} = 1 - (0.85)^{0.1}$$

or
$$T = \frac{1}{1 - (0.85)^{0.1}} = \mathbf{62\ years} \quad \textbf{Ans.}$$

Problem 12.15 : Determine the probability of an event for design of culvert for the return period of 62 years, that will not have its capacity exceeded during 50 years.

Solution. Given that, $T = 62$ years

Risk of failure over $n = 50$ years

Using the formula, $\bar{R} = 1 \times \left[1 - \frac{1}{T}\right]$

$$= 1 - \left[1 - \frac{1}{62}\right]^{50} = \mathbf{0.55} \quad \textbf{Ans.}$$

Sequential Generation of Hydrologic data

It refers to the generation of sequential synthetic hydrologic data.

There have been developed several techniques for sequential generation of hydrologic data; the Markov Chain Process is very common amongst them, is described as under :

Markov-Chain Process

This method generates the sequential hydrologic data based on the assumption that, the outcome of any event is the function of outcome of the preceeding event. This technique was developed during 1856 – 1922. The formula is given below.

$$x_i = r\, x_{i-1} + \varepsilon\,(y), \qquad \text{...(12.93)}$$

in which, x_i are the variables during the year i, x_{i-1} are variables during the preceeding year, r is the first- order serial correlation coefficient of the variable, also known as Markov chain coefficient, and $\varepsilon\,(y)_t$ is the random uncorrelated component of given variable. This equation indicates that the value of given variable is equal to the sum of preceding value and random component. For sequential annual runoff the formula of Markov-chain can be as

$$x_t = r\,x_{t-1} + (1-r)\,\bar{x} + k_x\,(1-r^2)\,\varepsilon \qquad ...(12.94)$$

where, x_t is the annual runoff at the year (t), $x_{(t-1)}$ is the annual runoff at preceeding year (*i.e.* $t-1$), $\bar{x}$ is the mean annual runoff, K_x is the standard deviation of the available data, r is the Markov-chain coefficient generally taken as 0.25 and ε is the random variate which is distributed with mean as 0 and standard deviation equal to 1.

In terms of monthly flow, the recursion equation of Markov-chain process can be given as,

$$Q_{i+1} = \overline{Q}_{J+1} + B_j\,(Q_i - \overline{Q}_j) + S_{j+1}\,(1-r_j^2)^{1/2}\,\varepsilon_i \qquad ...(12.95)$$

where, Q_i and Q_{i+1} are discharge during ith and $(i+1)$ months, respectively. $\overline{Q}_j$ and $\overline{Q}_{j+1}$ are the mean monthly flow during jth and $(J+1)$ months, respectively. Within a repetitive annual cycle of 12 months duration B_j is the regression coefficient for estimating flow in $(J+1)$th month from the flow in Jth month, S_{J+1} is the standard deviation of flows in $(J+1)$th month, r_j correlation coefficient between the flows of jth and $(j+1)$th months and ε_i the random normal and independent variate with mean as 0 and variance as 1.

IMPORTANT POINTS

1. The area under normal frequency curve is equal to 1.
2. The normal frequency curve is in bell shape.
3. Normal frequency distribution is also known as Gaussian distribution.
4. The Log Pearson Type-III distribution is commonly used for flood frequency analysis.
5. Hazen formula of plotting position is given by, $p = \dfrac{2m-1}{n}$, in which m is the rank number of event after arranging in descending order and n is the length of record.
6. The commonly used technique for plotting position is Weibull's method, which is given by, $p = \dfrac{m}{n+1}$.

REFERENCES

1. Chow V.T. Handbook of Applied Hydrology, Statistical and Probability Analysis of Hydrologic data, section 8-1, McGraw- Hill, New York, 1964.
2. Hazen A. Flood flows, Jhon Wiley & Sons, New York, 1930.

3. Pierce B.O. and Foster R.M. A short Tables of Integrals, Oxford & IBH, Pub, New Delhi, 1963.

DESCRIPTIVE TYPE QUESTIONS

1. Explain, why statistical and probability studies are important in hydrology.
2. Describe different elements of statistics.
3. Define skewness and write the procedure to calculate it.
4. Describe Normal distribution for computing expected rainfall amounts at different probability levels.
5. Explain plotting position method to predict the rainfall at different return periods.

OBJECTIVE TYPE QUESTIONS

1. Rainfall is a
   (*a*) random variable (*b*) discrete variable
   (*c*) both '*a*' and '*b*'. (*d*) known component of nature
2. Mean and median are
   (*a*) central tendency parameters
   (*b*) non-central tendency parameters
   (*c*) constant for any length of record
   (*d*) none of the above.
3. Mode is given by the formula,
   (*a*) mode = 3 median– 2 mean
   (*b*) mode = 3 median + 2 mean
   (*c*) mode = 2 median + 2 mean.
   (*d*) mode = $\frac{1}{2} C_s + 0.5$
4. Variance is given by
   (*a*) σ^2 (*b*) $\frac{\sigma}{c_v}$
   (*c*) C_s/σ (*d*) none of the above.
5. Pearsons Ist coefficient of skewness is
   (*a*) $C_s = \frac{\alpha}{\sigma_p^3}$ (*b*) $C_s = \frac{\sigma^3_p}{\alpha}$
   (*c*) C_s = 3 mean + 1.5 mole (*d*) none of the above.
6. Normal distribution is also known as
   (*a*) Gaussian distribution (*b*) Pearson distribution
   (*c*) both '*a*' and '*b*'. (*d*) Chow distribution
7. The log Pearson type-IIIrd distribution reduces to Log normal distribution, when
   (*a*) $C_s = 0$ (*b*) $C_s = 1$
   (*c*) $C = 0.1$. (*d*) $C_s = 100$

8. In log-Pearson type -IIIrd distribution, the factor '*K*' is determined on the basis of

(*a*) coefficient of skewness and return period
(*b*) return period and mode
(*c*) C_v and σ
(*d*) none of the above.

9. Weibull's plotting position is given by the formula,

(*a*) $p = \frac{n+1}{m}$ (*b*) $p = \frac{m}{n+1}$

(*c*) $p = \frac{m}{n} + 1$ (*d*) $p = \frac{m}{n}$

10. Hazen formula of plotting position is

(*a*) $p = \frac{n-1}{2m}$ (*b*) $p = \frac{(2m-1)}{n}$

(*c*) $p = \frac{2m}{n} + 1$ (*d*) $p = T_2$

11. Return period is given by the formula,

(*a*) $T = 2p$ (*b*) $T = 1/p$
(*c*) $T = p + n/2$ (*d*) $T = 5P - C_s$

12. Return period for design of reservoir is taken as

(*a*) 10 years (*b*) 75 years
(*c*) 125 years (*d*) 25 years.

13. Plotting position method computes

(*a*) exact amount of hydrologic event
(*b*) expected amount of hydrologic event
(*c*) hydrologic amount at 10% probability level
(*d*) hydrologic amount for 100 years T.

Answer (Objective Type Question)

1. (*b*) **2.** (*a*) **3.** (*a*) **4.** (*a*) **5.** (*a*) **6.** (*a*) **7.** (*a*) **8.** (*a*)
9. (*b*) **10.** (*b*) **11.** (*b*) **12.** (*b*) **13.** (*b*)

13

Ground Water Hydrology

As it has been earlier stated that, during occurrence of rainfall over the land surface, a part of it is returned back to the atmosphere as loss, and few part of the same directly reaches to the streams/rivers as runoff. In addition, the rest part of rainfall goes down into the soil and is stored in the voids or intergrannular space between the soil particles/aggregates of grains. In continuous rainy condition, the water retained in the voids moves down and down and accumulates over the impervious formation existing in the ground at some depth; and thus develops water storage in the ground, is called ground water.

13.1. Ground Water Resources of India

Ground water occurence is the part of hydrologic cycle; in this sense its knowledge is very important. It is assessed on the basis of various hydrological happenings, such as rainfall, movement of water into the soil by infiltration process and contribution of seepage from different surface water bodies like ponds, reservoirs, canals etc. Table 13.1 illustrates the percentage of rainfall contribution for development of ground water in different geological formations.

Table 13.1. Contribution of rainfall to develop ground water

S. No.	*Soil formation*	*Contribution (%)*
1.	Consolidated rocks	5 to 10
2.	Hard rocks	10
3.	River alluvium	10 to 15
4.	Indo - Gangetic alluvium	20
5.	Rajasthan deserts	2

Regarding ground water recharge, it has been reported that in India about 27.0 mha.m of water is recharged each year including the recharge in saline tracts. From study, it has also been estimated that in saline regions about 0.24 mha.m rain water is recharged, each year. Looking this facts, it is clear that in India, the amount of water recharged for ground water development is about 26.76 mha.m, each year. The state-wise annual of ground water recharge in India is shown in table 13.2.

Table 13.2. State-wise annual ground water recharge from different resources (mha.m)

S.No.	*State*	*From rainfall*	*From canal*	*Total recharge*	*Water lost* (%)*	*Net recharge (mha.m)*
1.	A.P	2.468	0.567	3.035	30	2.122
2.	Assam (including Nagaland, Mizoram Meghalaya etc)	5.022	0.144	5.170	60	2.061
3.	Bihar	3.319	0.543	3.862	30	2.702
4.	Delhi	0.061	-	0.061	30	0.037
5.	Gujrat	1.739	0.049	1.788	30	1.258
6.	Haryana	0.370	-	0.567	25	0.432
7.	H.P	0.283	-	0.283	60	0.111
8.	J & K	1.184	0.049	1.233	60	0.493
9.	Kerala	1.172	0.148	1.320	50	0.666
10.	Karnataka	1.826	0.222	2.048	40	1.234
11.	M.P	5.318	0.173	5.491	40	3.295
12.	Maharashtra	2.443	0.148	2.591	30	1.555
13.	Orissa	2.394	0.419	2.813	30	1.974
14.	Punjab	0.629	0.693	1.122	25	0.851
15.	Rajasthan	0.493	0.222	0714	40	0.419
16.	Tamilnadu	1.715	0.432	2.147	30	1.419
17.	U.P.	4.257	1.234	5.491	20	4.382
18.	W.B.	2.418	0.419	2.837	30	1.987
	Total	37.111	5.463	42.574	—	26.996

*Water lost includes the losses due to ET and sub-surfce flow.

13.2. Geological Formations

The sub-surface geological formations are composed of following types of formations :

1. Aquifer
2. Aquiclude
3. Aquifuse; and
4. Aquitard.

Aquifer : It is originated from the Latin word " Aquiferre", in which 'Aqui' stands for 'water' and "ferre" to bear'. In this way, the term meaning of aquifer is 'water bearing formation'. In other words, it can be defined as the geological formation which contains and yields sufficient amount of water. An aquifer easily supplies the water to the well, installed in the formation. The formations composed of sand and fine gravels are the good aquifers. Aquifers are fruther classified as per presence of impervious layer binding them, given as under :

(*a*) Confined aquifer

(*b*) Unconfined aquifer

(*c*) Semi-confined aquifer; and

(*d*) Perched-aquifer.

All these are described below

Confined Aquifer : It is one which is covered by impervious layer from its top and bottom, both the sides. In other words "it lies between two impermeable layers". A confined aquifer has following properties :

1. It is covered by impervious layer from its bottom and top sides.

2. Available ground water in this aquifer exerts an upward hydrostatic pressure to the top confining layer, which is called artesian pressure. Due to this reason, sometimes it is also known as "artesian aquifer".

3. When a well is installed in this aquifer, then level of water in the well rises above the upper confining layer. The water level in the well represents piezometric level.

4. Water pressure in confined aquifer is greater than the atmospheric pressure.

Unconfined Aquifer : This aquifer is not covered from its upper side with impervious formation, while essentially covered by an impervious layer from its bottom side. Water-table is the upper surface of this aquifer. Sometimes, it is also referred as water-table aquifer. Main properties of this aquifer are as follows :

1. Available water in this aquifer is at atmospheric pressure.

2. Water-table acts as upper boundary of this aquifer.

3. Water level in the well, installed in unconfined aquifer is in the level of ground water-table.

Semi-confined Aquifer : In this aquifer, the upper or lower layer which confines the aquifer, is in semi-permeable nature. Semi-confined aquifers are also called leaky aquifers, as there is leakage of water from the semi-pervious layer. Generally, most of the geological formations fall under this category. A semi-confined aquifer includes following main properties :

1. The top confining layer of this aquifer is essentially in semi- pervious nature, while bottom layer is either impervious or semi-pervious.

2. On lowering of water-table in the semi-confined aquifer, there begins vertical flow of water into the aquifer through semi-pervious layer, is called leakage of water.

Perched Aquifer : It is a special type of unconfined aquifer, in which water is stored to a limited areal extent.The main properties of perched aquifer are given as under :

1. The available water in this aquifer is above the main ground- water.

2. In ground, wherever impervious strata for small aerial extent occurs above the water-table, the perched aquifer is formed, there.

Aquiclude : The formation which contains sufficient amount of water, but has very small capacity to transmit the water is called aquiclude. The occurence of aquiclude in the ground is very essential because it confines the aquifer. The clay layers shales etc. are the examples of aquiclude.

Aquifuse : This is the impervious formation which neither contain nor transmit the water. Unweathered and unfractured granite and some carbonates [lime stones] are the examples of aquifuse.

Aquitard : It is semi-pervious type geological formation which has ability to transmit the water, but at very slow rate.

Fig. 13.1, illustrates different types of geological formations.

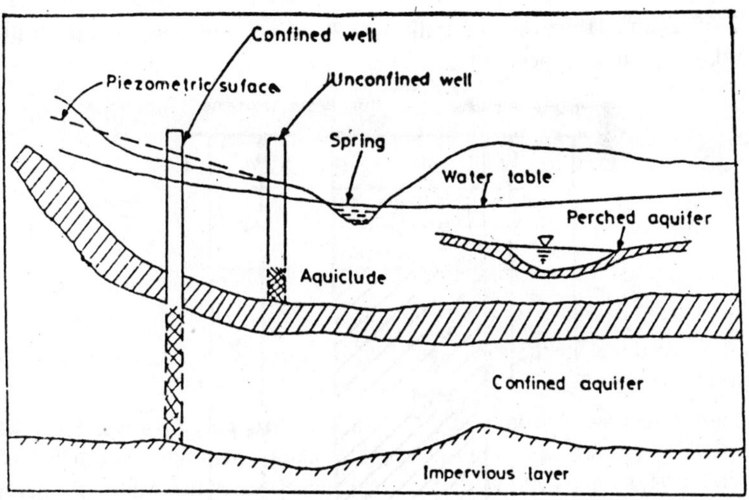

Fig. 13.1. Types of geological formations.

13.3. Properties of Aquifer

Various properties of aquifer are described as under :

Porosity : This property is related to the pore spaces of the formation. It is defined as the ratio of volume of voids to the volume of formation. It is expressed in percent. In a given formation, if V_v is the volume of voids and V is the total volume of formation, then porosity (θ) is given by :

$$\theta = \frac{V_v}{V} \times 100 \qquad ...(13.1)$$

or

$$= \frac{V - V_m}{V} \times 100$$

or

$$= \left(1 - \frac{V_m}{V}\right) \times 100 \qquad ...(13.2)$$

where, $V_v = V - V_m$, in which, V_m is the volume of soil mass (Fig. 13.2). Porosity of the aquifer is also expressed in terms of density, *i. e.*

$$\theta = \left(\frac{\gamma_m - \gamma_d}{\gamma_m}\right) \times 100 \qquad ...(13.3)$$

$$= \left(1 - \frac{\gamma_d}{\gamma_m}\right) \times 100 \qquad ...(13.4)$$

where, γ_d = mean particles density

γ_m = bulk density of the aquifer

Richard (1954) reported that the particle density of most of the soils is upto 2.65 g/cm^3. However, the bulk density of clay and sandy soils is about 1.0 and 1.8 g/cm^3, respectively.

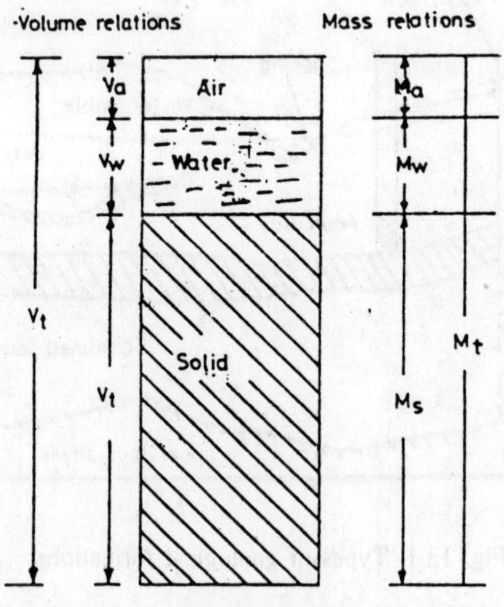

Fig. 13.2. Soil as three phase.

Example 13.1. *Determine the porosity of aquifer, if*

1. bulk density = 1.75 g/cc; and

2. particle density = 2.65 g/cc

Solution. Given that the, $\gamma_m = 2.65$ g/cc

$$\gamma_d = 1.75 \text{ g/cc}$$

$\therefore$ Porosity (θ),

$$= \left(1 - \frac{\gamma_d}{\gamma_m}\right) \times 100$$

$$= \left(1 - \frac{1.75}{2.65}\right) \times 100 = \mathbf{33.96\%} \quad \textbf{Ans.}$$

13.4. Types of Porosity

It is of following two types :

1. Primary porosity; and
2. Secondary porosity.

The porosity developed during formation of rocks is called primary porosity. It depends on the following factors :

1. Shape and arrangement of the soil particles.
2. Sorting of the particles.
3. Degree of compaction and cementation.

Secondary porosity refers to that porosity which is developed due to weathering and development of joints caused by contraction, expansion and deformation of the formation because of change in temperature and pressure in consolidated sedimentary rocks, ingneous rocks, volcanic rocks etc. The porosity of different aquifer materials is given in Table 13.3.

Table 13.3. Porosity of different aquifier materials

Aquifer material	*Porosity (%)*
Lime stone, shale	1—10
Sand stone	10—20
Sand, gravel	30—40
Clay	45—55

Void ratio : It is the ratio of volume of pores to the volume of soil particles, expressed as,

$$V_r = \frac{V_v}{V_m} \qquad ...(13.5)$$

Example 13.2. *Calculate the value of non-capillary porosity* ($\theta_{nc} = \theta - \theta_c$) *from the following data :*

1. Particle density = 2.65 g/cc
2. Bulk density = 1.5 g/cc
3. Field capacity = 20% on dry weight basis

Solution. Given that,

$$\gamma_m = 2.65 \text{ g/cc}$$
$$\gamma_d = 1.5 \text{ g/cc}$$
$$F.C. = 20\%$$

∴ Porosity (θ); by using the formula: $\theta = \left(1 - \frac{\gamma_d}{\gamma_m}\right) \times 100$

$$= \left(1 - \frac{1.5}{2.65}\right) \times 100$$
$$= \mathbf{43.40\%}$$

Capillary corosity (θ_c) $\theta_c = F{\cdot}C \cdot \gamma_d$

$$= 20 \times 1.5 = \mathbf{30\%}$$

∴ Non-capillary poarosity (θ_{nc})

$$\theta_{nc} = \theta - \theta_c$$
$$= 43.40 - 30.0 = \mathbf{13.4\%} \quad \textbf{Ans.}$$

Specific retention : It is the ratio of volume of water retained in the soil against gravity force to the total volume of soil column, expressed in percent. It is given by the following formula :

$$S_r = \frac{V_w}{V} \times 100 \qquad ...(13.6)$$

where, S_r = specific retention

V_w = volume of water retained against gravity force

V = total volume of soil column.

Specific retention also denotes the capacity of soil formation to retain the water after drainage of the soil. It is determined by centrifuge technique, in which a given soil sample is saturated with the water and centrifugal force of about 1,000 times of the gravity force is applied to the saturated sample for one hour duration. On force application, few water from saturated sample is drained and few is left in the voids of soil sample which is called centrifuge moisture equivalent. The following formula is used for computing the specific retention of soil.

$$S_r = m_e \cdot n_r \cdot \frac{\gamma_d}{\gamma_w} \qquad ...(13.7)$$

where m_e = moisture equivalent%

n_r = ratio of S_r to m_e

γ_d = dry density of soil sample

γ_w = density of the water.

The value of n_r is given as under :

For m_e ranging from 39 to 12%, the $n_r = 1$.

m_e ranging from 12 to 2%, the $n_r = 2.5$

Specific yield : It is the capacity of soil formation to drain the water contained under gravity force. The terms effective porosity and specific yield are synonymous. Specific yield is also denoted as the percentage volume of water drained by gravity force from the total volume of soil body, i.e.

$$S_y = \frac{V_y}{V} \times 100 \qquad ...(13.8)$$

where, S_y = specific yield (%)

V_y = volume of water drained

V = total volume of soil sample.

13.5. Determination of Specific Yield

There are several methods for determination of specific yield of the soil formation. The common methods, described by Meinzer (1932) are given as under :

1. Pumping method
2. Recharge method
3. Field saturation and drainage method; and
4. Sampling after lowering the water-table method.

In pumping method, a given volume of water is pumped from the soil and specific yield is determined by computing the ratio between volume of water pumped and volume of drained formation. During pumping operation, the draw-down data is also recorded by installation of observation wells at different radial distances; the draw-down data is also used for computing the specific yield.

In recharge method, the amount of seepage water from water sources such as canals, streams etc. are measured; and at the same time the rise in water-table in the surrounding formation is also measured. The specific yield is determined by computing the ratio between volume of water used and the volume of soil recharged.

The field saturation and drainage method consists of saturating the soil with water and draining the same. After drainage, the porosity and moisture contents of the soil are computed for determining the specific yield. Specific yield is the difference of moisture content and porosity of the soil. In this method, the evaporation loss is also considered.

In the method of sampling after lowering the water-table, the moisture content and porosity are determined by collecting the soil samples as in case of field saturation and drainage method. Samples are collected from the depth, just above the zone of capillary fringe when it is expected that the water-table has gone to sufficient depth. A precaution should also be maintained that there should neither absorption nor release of water by or from the soil sample. Fig. 13.3 illustrates the values of porosity, specific yield and specific retention of different types of geological formations.

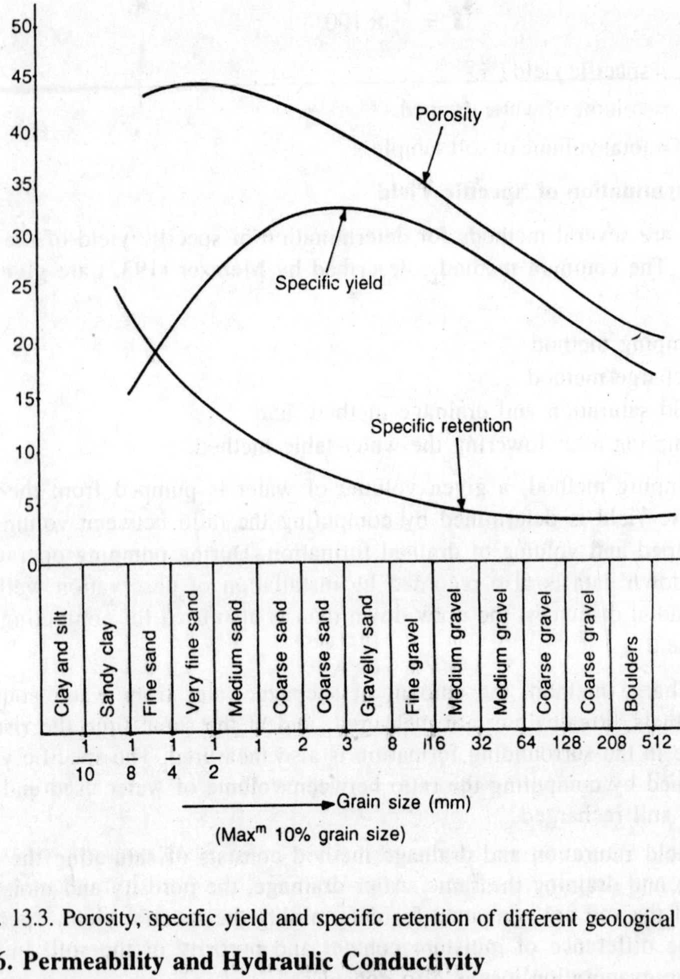

Fig. 13.3. Porosity, specific yield and specific retention of different geological formations.

13.6. Permeability and Hydraulic Conductivity

Permeability is the water transmitting capacity of the soil formation under differential pressure. It is measured in terms of rate of water transmission through the soil column having unit cross-sectional area and unit differential pressure per unit length. A formation with zero porosity is not able to transmit the water, is known as impermeable formation. However, porosity is not the measure of permeability, because most of the soil formations are even more porous but unable to yield the water such as dense clay.

Permeability is expressed in terms of coefficient, which is the rate of water movement through unit cross-sectional area of the soil column, under unit hydraulic gradient (Stearns, 1928). The permeability coefficient is also known as hydraulic conductivity, is explained as under.

Hydraulic conductivity : It is ability of soil to transmit the water. In Darcy's law, the hydraulic conductivity (*k*) is the proportionality factor, which essentially expresses an interaction between the porous media (soil) and flowing fluid (water). Hydraulic conductivity depends on the soil matrix and properties of water flowing through the soil. The soil matrix includes prosity, pore size distribution and tortuosity of the soil pores; affects the hydraulic conductivity, significantly. The fluid properties which affect the hydraulic conductivity are the density and viscosity, mainly. Various factors affecting the hydraulic conductivity are described below :

13.7. Factors Affecting Hydraulic Conductivity

Porosity : It greatly affects the hydraulic conductivity. A coarse textured soil has high porosity and greater hydraulic conductivity than the heavy soil comprising fine pores. Hydraulic conductivity varies from 10^{-2} to 10^{-7} cm/s in light to heavy textured soils, respectively. The hydraulic conductivity of different aquifer materials is given in table 13.4.

Table 13.4 : Hydraulic conductivity of different aquifer materials

Aquifer material	*K (m/day)*
Gravel	1 to 1000
Coarse sand	1 to 200
Fine sand	0.1 to 10
Silt	0.1
Clay	10^{-5} to 10^{-7}

Poor hydraulic conductivity of heavy soil containing finer pores is mainly due to drag forces offered by the wall of interconnected pore spaces on the fluid flowing through them. In fine pored soils, the fluid is much closer to the walls of the soil particles as compared to the macro pored soils. Therefore, macropored soils are good conductor of water, provided that the macro pores are interconnected and form a continuous channel through the soil. O.Neal (1952) classified the hydraulic conductivity in different classes, as shown in Table 13.5.

Table 13.5. Hydraulic conductivity classes for saturated soils.

Class	*K (cm/h)*
Very slow	less than 0.125
Slow	0.125—0.500
Moderately slow	0.500—2.0
Moderate	2.0—6.25
Moderately rapid	6.25—12.5
Rapid	12.5—25.0
Very rapid	more than 25.0

Pore space geometry : The hydraulic conductivity of porous media is also affected due to geometry of pore spaces. The pore size and its configuration affect the hydraulic conductivity to a large extant. If two porous media have similar pore spaces but their pore size distribution is different, then hydraulic conductivities of both soil media can be represented by the equation 13.9. And by using the same equation, the hydraulic conductivity of one media (soil) can be computed if hydraulic conductivity of other soil media is known.

$$K_2 = N^2 \cdot K_1 \qquad \text{...(13.9)}$$

where, K_1 = hydraulic conductivity of Ist soil

K_2 = hydraulic conductivity of IInd soil

N = factor dependent on the size of pore

Submergence : The behaviour of hydraulic conductivity is grouped into three phases based on the level of submergence, as shown in Fig. 13.4 (Allison, 1947). These phases are described as under :

Phase 1 : It is the initial phase, inwhich hydraulic conductivity decreases due to entrapment of air and downward movement of electrolytes with consequent dispersion and swelling of the soil particles and sealing of the pores, simultaneously.

Phase 2 : It is the phase of increasing hydraulic conductivity, which is due to gradual dissolution of entrapped air form the pores and reduction in the swelling of soil particles, causing downward movement of water.

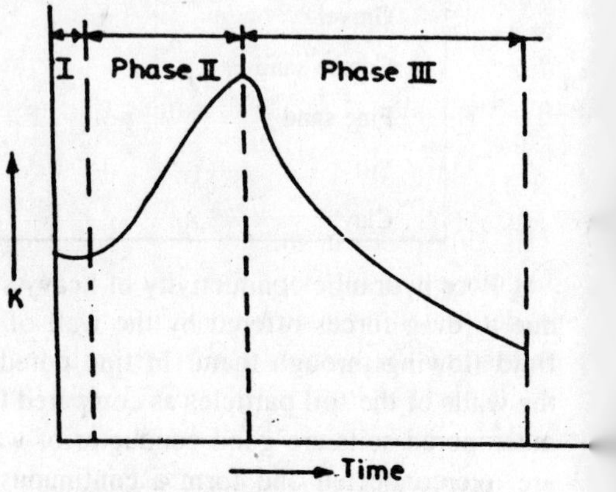

Fig. 13.4. Effect of submergence on *k*.

Phase 3 : It is the last phase, in which hydraulic conductivity gets reduce due to microbial sealing.

Tortuosity of soil pores : It is the ratio of capillary length (Lc) in a given soil column to the length of soil column (L), i.e.

$$\text{Tortuosity} = \frac{L_c}{L} \qquad ...(13.10)$$

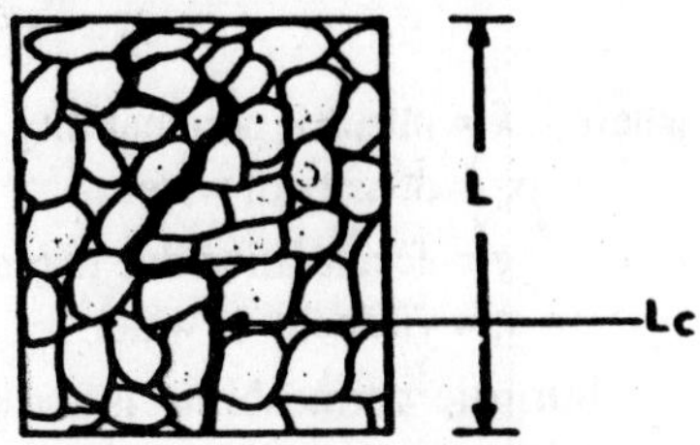

Fig. 13.5

The capillary length is the actual path traversed by the average parcel of water through the soil column as shown in Fig. 13.5. The tortuosity can also be determined by measuring the EC of soil under saturation condition and dividing the same with the resistivity (E) of water, i.e.

$$\left(\frac{L_c}{L}\right)^2 = \frac{\theta \cdot EC_s}{E} \qquad ...(13.11)$$

in which, θ is the porosity or the area of transmitting channel per unit cross-sectional area of the flow and EC_s is the electrical conductivity of soil.

Entrapped air : The entrapped air also affects hydraulic conductivity. Entrapment of air takes place when soil is allowed to saturate with water because during saturation the air already present in the pore spaces are not completly replaced by the water, but some are trapped in the pores. The trapped air in the pores is called entrapped air, which blocks the interconnected pore spaces and obstruct the water movement. In this way, the hydraulic conductivity of soil gets reduced. In addition to the above, the ability of water to dissolve the air gets change with the temperature which also affects the hydraulic conductivity. The soils containing macro pores have relatively less problem of air entrapment as compared to the soils with micro pores.

Water quality : Water quality affects the hydraulic conductivity of soil. The salt-affected soils with high exchangeable sodium content have less hydraulic conductivity. Due to this reason, the sodic soils are generally found under water stagnation condition. In addition, when saline water is used for irrigating the crops in normal soil, then there is change in the level of exchangeable ions in the soil. It also affects the hydraulic conductivity of soil.

Water characteristics : The density and viscosity are the two important characteristics of water; these two also affect hydraulic conductivity of the soil. These properties are likely to change with the temperature and electrolytic concentration of the water. The relationship among density, viscosity and hydraulic conductivity of the soil is given below:

$$K = \frac{k \cdot \rho_w \cdot g}{\eta} \qquad \text{...(13.12)}$$

where, k = intrinsic permeability

ρ_w = density of water

g = acceleration due to gravity

η = viscosity of water.

Intrinsic permeability is the property of porous medium, only.

Heavy storms : These storms are composed of big size raindrops, which strike the soil surface with greater kinetic energy and break the soil aggregates into finer particles. The finer particles enter into the pore spaces and seal them, as result the hydraulic conductivity of soil gets reduce.

13.8. Measurement of Hydraulic Conductivity

Various methods for determining the hydraulic conductivity of soil are given as under :

1. Laboratory method
   - (a) Constant head method; and
   - (b) Falling head method
2. Field method
   - (*a*) Below the water-table
     - (*i*) Piezometer method; and
     - (*ii*) Auger hole method
   - (*b*) Above the water-table
     - (*i*) Shallow well pumping method
     - (*ii*) Cylinder permeameter method; and
     - (*iii*) Double tube method

13.8.1. Laboratory Method

Under this, the following two methods are commonly used for determining the hydraulic conductivity :

(*a*) **Constant Head Method :** This method is suitable for those soils which have medium to high permeability range. The undisturbed or least disturbed soil sample is collected from the field by using core sampler and is allowed for saturation, overnight. The saturated soil sample is kept in cylindrical container provided with the apparatus. The inflow water is maintained at constant level. The following observations are recorded during experiment :

1. Amount of water discharged through the soil sample (Q)
2. Length of soil sample (l)
3. Cross-sectional area of the cylindrical container (A)

4. Duration of flow (t)

5. Head of flow (h)

6. Water temperature

Based on the above observations, the hydraulic conductivity of soil is computed by using the following formula :

$$K = C\frac{Q \cdot l}{A \cdot t \cdot h} \qquad \text{...(13.13)}$$

in which, C is the correction factor which is the ratio of viscosity of water at observed temperature during experiment to the viscosity of water at 60°F temperature *i.e.*

$$C = \frac{\text{Viscosity of water at observed temperature}}{\text{Viscosity of water at 60°F temperature}}$$

Fig. 13.6 illustrates the view of constant head permeameter.

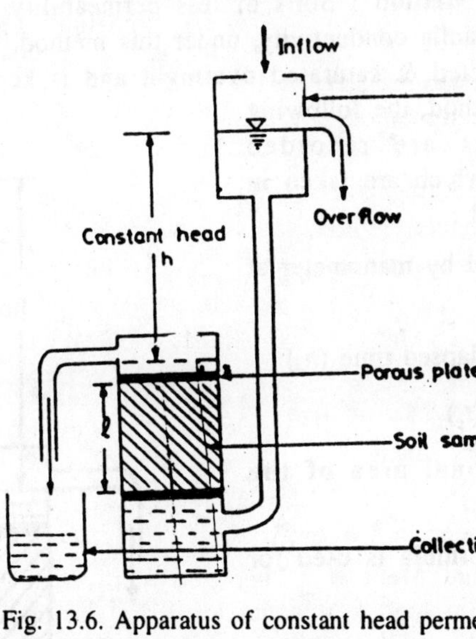

Fig. 13.6. Apparatus of constant head permemter.

Example 13.3. *The following observations were recorded under constant head permeameter method :*

(i) Diameter of soil sample = 7.0 cm

(ii) Length of soil sample = 3.5 cm

(iii) Hydraulic head = 35.0 cm

(iv) Volume of water flow = 200 cc in 1 minute and 50 seconds

Determine the hydraulic conductivity of soil. Assume C as 0.85.

Solution. Given that,

Diameter of soil sample = 7.0 cm

Radius = 3.5 cm

Cross-sectional area $(A) = \pi r^2$

$= \pi \times (3.5)^2$

$= 38.45 \text{ cm}^2$

$l = 3.5$ cm

$h = 35$ cm

$Q = 200$ cc

$t = 110$ seconds

$\therefore$ Using the formula, $K = C \dfrac{Q \cdot l}{A \cdot t \cdot h}$

$$= \frac{0.85 \times 200 \times 3.5}{38.48 \times 110 \times 35}$$

$= \mathbf{0.004 \ cm/s}$ **Ans.**

Vareable Head Method : Soils of less permeability are suitable for determining the hydraulic conductivity, under this method. The undisturbed soil sample is collected & saturated overnight and is kept in cylindrical container. In this method, the following extra observations are recorded inaddition to those which are taken in constant head method :

1. Head indicated by manometer at zero time (h_o)

2. Head at any elapsed time (h_e)

3. Elapsed time (t_e)

4. Cross-sectional area of the manometer tube (a)

The following formula is used for computing the K :

$$K = 2.3 \, C \frac{a \cdot l}{A \cdot t_e} \cdot \log \frac{h_o}{h_e} \quad ...(13.14)$$

Apparatus of vareable head permeameter is shown in Fig. 13.7.

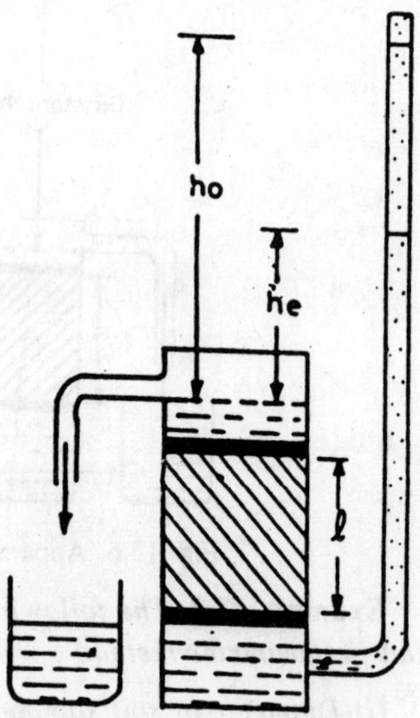

Fig. 13.7. Variable head permeameter.

Example 13.4. ***Determine the hydraulic conductivity of a given soil by using vareable head method, if***

(i) Cross-sectional area of manometer tube = 1.68 cm²

(ii) Cross-sectional area of soil sample = 688.25 cm²

(iii) Length of soil sample = 11.35 cm

(iv) Elapsed time = 5.5 hours

(v) Initial and final water levels = 350 and 275 cm, respectively

(Assume the value of C as 0.85).

Solution. Given that,

$$a = 1.68\ \text{cm}^2 \qquad h_e = 275\ \text{cm}$$
$$A = 688.25\ \text{cm}^2 \qquad t_e = 5.5\ \text{hours}$$
$$l = 11.35\ \text{cm} \qquad = 330\ \text{seconds}$$
$$h_o = 350\ \text{cm}$$

Hydraulic conductivity (K) is given by the formula,

$$K = C\frac{2.3 \times a \cdot l}{A \cdot t_e} \log \frac{h_o}{h_e}$$
$$= \frac{0.85 \times 2.3 \times 1.68 \times 11.35}{688.25 \times 330} \cdot \log \frac{350}{275}$$
$$= \mathbf{1.03 \times 10^{-3}\ cm/h} \quad \textbf{Ans.}$$

Example 13.5. *Compute the value of correction factor (C) used in hydraulic conductivity calculation. If*

1. Water flow = 150 cc

2. Length of soil sample = 4.0 cm

3. Hydraulic head = 48.0 cm

4. Elapsed time = 1 min 30 sec

5. Cross-sectional area of the sample = 38.48 cm²

6. Hydraulic conductivity of the soil = 0.0035 cm/s.

Solution. Given that,

$$Q = 150\ \text{cc} \qquad t = 90\ \text{sec}$$
$$l = 4.0\ \text{cm} \qquad A = 38.48\ \text{cm}^2$$
$$h = 48.0\ \text{cm} \qquad K = 0.0035\ \text{cm/s}$$

∴ Correction factor (C) from the formula,

$$K = C\frac{Q \cdot l}{A \cdot t \cdot h}$$

Substituting the values of K, Q, l, A, t and h and solving for C

$$0.0035 = C\frac{150 \times 4}{38.48 \times 90 \times 48}$$

$$\therefore \qquad C = \mathbf{0.96}\ \textbf{Ans.}$$

13.8.2. Field Method

In laboratory methods, *i.e.* constant head and vareable head permeameters, the used soil sample is generally disturbed, as result the determined value of hydraulic conductivity is not so correct. Therefore, to have more accurate determination of hydraulic conductivity of the soil, the insitu measurement techniques are more suitable. The common methods used under situ measurement are divided into following two main groups :

(*i*) Below the water-table; and

(*ii*) Above the water-table.

13.8.3. Field Method-below the water-table

It includes following methods :

Piezometer method : In this method, a piezometer is installed in the soil to the depth, below the water-table. At the lower end of piezometer, a cylindrical shaped cavity is developed as shown in Fig. 13.8. The length of cavity is kept about 10.2 cm and diameter equal to the diameter of piezometer, usually 4.9 cm. The bottom of cavity should not touch the impervious layer.

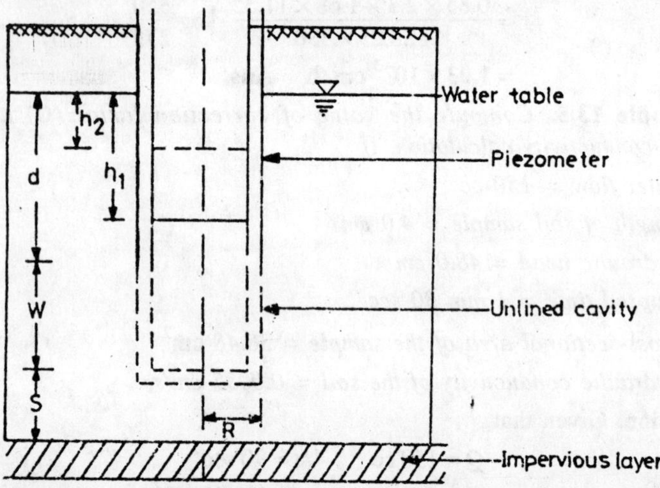

Fig. 13.8. Piezometer method of hydraulic conductivity measurement.

Prior to start measurement, the collected water in the cavity is removed time to time, to clear the inter connected pore spaces existing along the cavity wall. After that, water is allowed to rise in the cavity and left to become in equilibrium. The rising rate of water is recorded as observation. Several such observations are recorded during experiment; and the following formula given by Johnson et al (1952) is used for computing the hydraulic conductivity :

$$K = \frac{\pi R^2}{A \cdot \Delta t} \ln\left(\frac{h_1}{h_2}\right) \quad ...(13.15)$$

where, K = hydraulic conductivity of soil, cm/s

R = radius of the cavity, cm

h_1 and h_2 = height of water level in the piezometer at elapsed time t_1 and t_2, respectively.

A = factor, cm, depends on the geometry of flush system, cavity radius (R), distance between bottom of the cavity and impervious layer, cavity length and distance "d" measured from the water-table (Figure - 13.8). The value of A is taken as 43.2 cm for 'd' greater than 20.0 cm, cavity length 10.2 cm and diameter of cavity as 4.9 cm.

Piezometer method is suitable for homogeneous and isotropic layers of stratified soils. In isotropic soils, it measures only horizontal conductivity.

Demerits : Following demerits are found under this method:

1. This method introduces a considerable error, if measurements are taken closer to the impermeable layer. A correction is also required in the geometry factor 'A'. However, this demerit can be removed by maintaining the distance between bottom of the cavity and impermeable layer, atleast equal to the half of cavity length.

2. In heavy textured soils the presence of roots and worm holes results erroneous measurement of hydraulic conductivity.

3. In stony formations the installation of piezometer and development of cavity is very difficult, causing not suitable for such formations.

Auger hole method : This method consists of a hole augered to the depth below the water-table. The water is allowed to equilibriate with the water-table in the hole (Fig. 13.9). After that water is pumped from the hole and rising rate of water level in the hole is measured several times. The rate of water rising denotes the flux, while difference between water level in the hole and

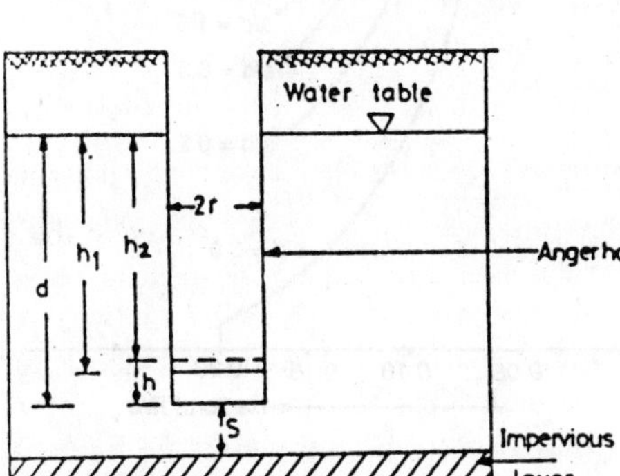

Fig. 13.9. Aujar hole method of hydraulic conductivity measurement.

water-table represents the hydraulic head. By knowing the rising rate of water level, the following formula (Johnson *etal* 1952) is used for computing the hydraulic conductivity :

$$K \; \frac{\pi R^2 \cdot \Delta h}{A' \, \Delta t \, (h_1 + h_2)/2} \qquad \text{...(13.16)}$$

where, K = hydraulic conductivity, cm/s

R = radius of hole, cm

Δh = difference in water level (*i.e.* $h_1 - h_2$) in the hole at the elapsed time from t_1 to t_2

Δt = time required to rise the water level Δh (*i.e.* $t_2 - t_1$)

A' = geometry factor, which is the function of hole radius (R), depth of hole below the water-table (d) and gap between bottom of the hole and impervious layer (S), as shown in Figure 13.9. The value of A' can be obtained from the nomograph shown in Fig. 13.10 for different ratios of S to d, corresponding to known values of R/d.

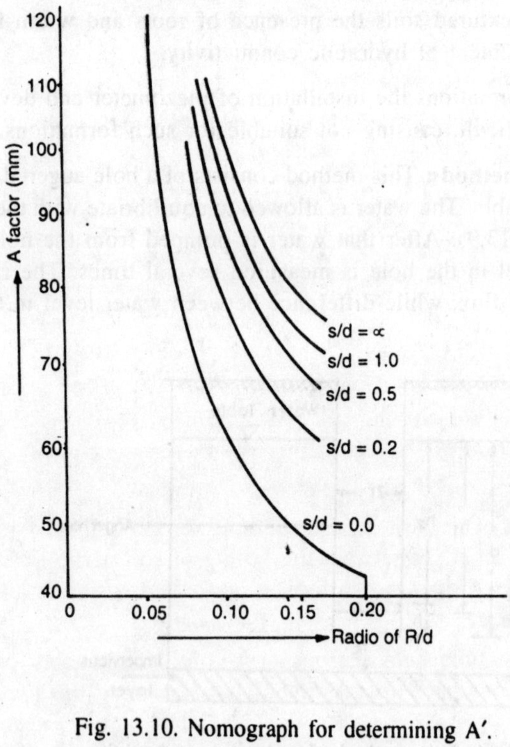

Fig. 13.10. Nomograph for determining A′.

The auger hole method is simplest amongst all the methods of insitu measurement of hydraulic conductivity. It provides an average value of hydraulic conductivity, because entry of water in the hole is resulted from all the directions, simultaneousely.

Demerits : It includes following demerits :

1. For layered soils and soils having roots & holes, this method is not found suitable.

2. Since hole is unlined, therefore, there is posibilities of partial collapse of the hole, causing inappropriate measurement of K.

3. Determination of hydraulic conductivity by using single hole is not correct. Therefore, several holes are constructed to repliciate the measurement.

4. This method is not suitable especially for gravelly soils which have very high permeability.

13.8.4. Field Method-above the water-table

Under this method, the measurement of hydraulic conductivity is done above the water-table. The lined or unlined hole of suitable size is constructed for the depth above the water-table, and water is filled to flow into the surrounding soil. The rate of declination of water level in the hole is taken as observation to evaluate the hydraulic conductivity. This method has limitation about requirement of large amount of water and time for saturating the surrounding soil and reaching at the equilibrium condition. The common methods, under this technique are described as under:

Shallow-well pump-in method : The well-piezometer method and dry auger hole method are the names of this method. The lined or unlined hole of suitable size is constructed. Water is filled in the hole and rate of declination of water level in the hole is measured when a constant water level is appeared in the hole. The set up of equipment under shallow-well pump in method is shown in Fig. 13.11. The procedure for determining the hydraulic conductivity, is described as under :

1. Construct the hole of suitable dimension and brush or scrap the wall, so that the compaction or sealing of the wall is removed.

2. Remove the scraped soil from hole.

3. Fill the sand of uniform size in the hole for the height of 15 cm below the intended water level. To prevent the falling of soil particles into the hole and thereby sealing of the sand surface, a perforated casing is also provided at the top of the sand.

4. Fill water into the hole at constant rate by using rubber pipe. A float valve can also be equipped in the hole for maintaining the constant water level.

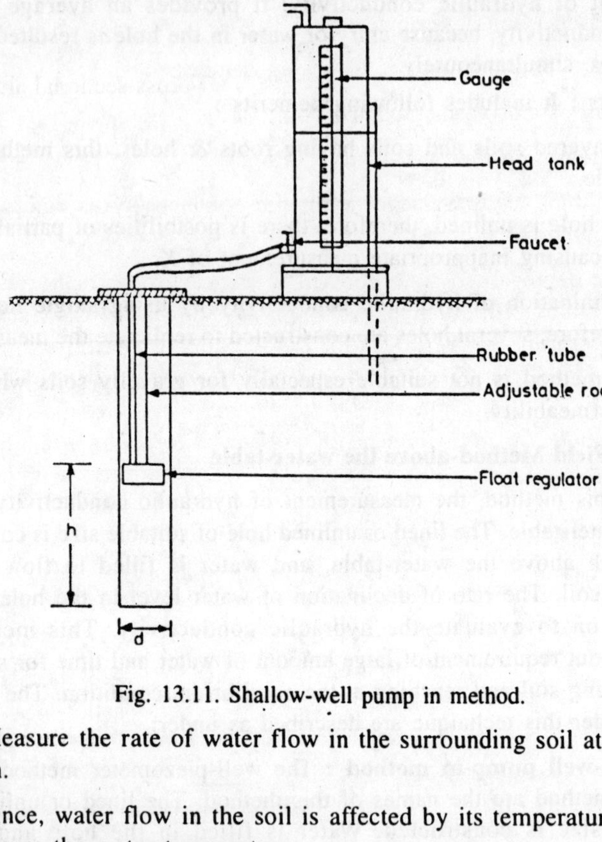

Fig. 13.11. Shallow-well pump in method.

5. Measure the rate of water flow in the surrounding soil at steady state condition.

6. Since, water flow in the soil is affected by its temperature, therefore, also measure the water temperature.

The hydraulic conductivity of soil is computed by using the following formula for two different conditions :

Condition (1). When $3h < d \le h$

$$K = \frac{\ln [h/q + \sqrt{(h/q)^2 - 1}] - 1}{2\pi h^2} \cdot q' \qquad \text{...(13.17)}$$

where, K = hydraulic conductivity, cm/h
h = depth of water in the hole, cm
q = rate of water flow in the hole, cm^3/h
q' = rate of water flow in the soil, cm^3/h

Condition (2). When $3h > d \ge h$

$$K = \frac{3 \ln (h/r)}{\pi h (h + 2d)} q' \qquad \text{...(13.18)}$$

where, K = hydraulic conductivity, cm/h
d = distance between the water level in the hole and the impervious layer, cm.

Demerits : This method has following demerits :

1. It is an expensive method.
2. Requires more time and water.
3. Determines lesser value of hydraulic conductivity as compred to the auger hole method.

Cylinder permeameter method : It is similar to the shallow-well pump in method. However, the diameter of hole is greater than the hole, used in shallow well pump in method. A 45-cm diameter cylindrical sleeve is penetrated into the soil to about 15.4 cm depth below the auger hole, as shown in Fig. 13.12. Two tensiometers and piezometers are also installed at the same depth in the hole for measurement of tension and pressure near the bottom edge of cylindrical sleeve. Tensiometer showing zero tension indicates the soil at saturation stage. The piezometer is installed to locate the presence of ristricting layer or natural water-table by measuring the positive pressure.

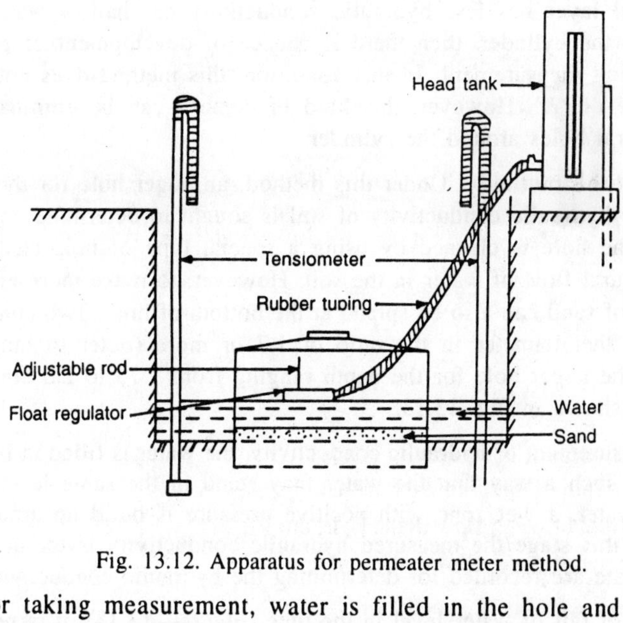

Fig. 13.12. Apparatus for permeater meter method.

For taking measurement, water is filled in the hole and outside the cylindrical sleeve; and is left for attaining the same water level, both the sides in the cylinder. Rate of water flow in the surrounding soil is measured from inner side. The hydraulic conductivity is computed by using the following formula :

$$K = \frac{L}{\Delta H \cdot A} \cdot q' \qquad ...(13.19)$$

where, K = hydraulic conductivity, cm/h

$\frac{\Delta H}{L}$ = hydraulic gradient across the soil, inside cylinder.

q' = rate of water flow, cm^3/h

A = cross–sectional area of the cylinder, cm^2

Merit of this method is that it measures the hydraulic conductivity in absense of water-table. It can also measure the 'K' of individual soil layers.

Demerits : Various demerits of this method are given as under :

1. This method measures lesser hydraulic conductivity due to development of head loss across the soil-water interface.

2. In rocky and gravelly soils, this method is not suitable.

3. It requires specialized equipments, large amount of water and time, also.

4. If soil layer has less hydraulic conductivity or shallow water-table exists below the cylinder, then there is chance of development of positive pressure during measurement. In this condition, this method does not result correct value of 'K'. However, this kind of demerit can be eliminated by making several holes around the cylinder.

Double-tube method : Under this method, an auger hole for the depth at which the hydraulic conductivity of soil is sought to determine, is made. Bottom of the hole is cleaned by using a special type of hole cleaner, to facilitate natural flow of water in the soil. However, to make more effective a thin layer of sand can also be spread at the bottom of hole. Two concentric cylinders of the diameter in the ratio of 1.7 or more (outer to inner) are inserted in the auger hole for the depth ranging from 1.75 to 2.5 cm below the hole, as shown in Fig. 13.13.

For measurement of hydraulic conductivity, the water is filled in both the cylinders in such a way that the water may stand in the same level. After filling the water, a wet zone with positive pressure is build up around the cylinder; at this stage the measured hydraulic conductivity is the actual K. Following data are recorded for determining the hydraulic conductivity :

1. Rate of fall of water level in the tube (Figure—13.13); it is recorded by stopping the water supply in the inner cylinder.

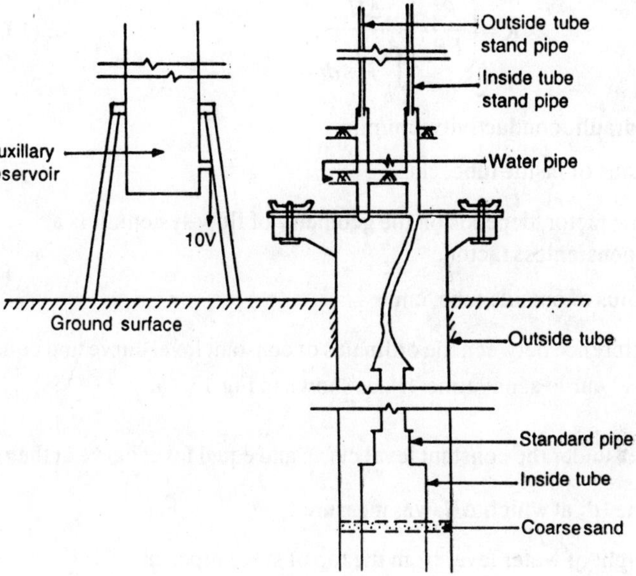

Fig. 13.13. Double tube method.

2. Drop of water level in the inner cylinder.

The data on drop of water level (H) and corresponding time (t) are plotted on simple graph paper and curves are drawn for both the sets, separately, as shown in Fig. 13.14.

The curve obtained for first set is known as constant level $H\ V_s\ t$ curve, while the curve for second set is termed as equal level $H\ V_s\ t$ curve.

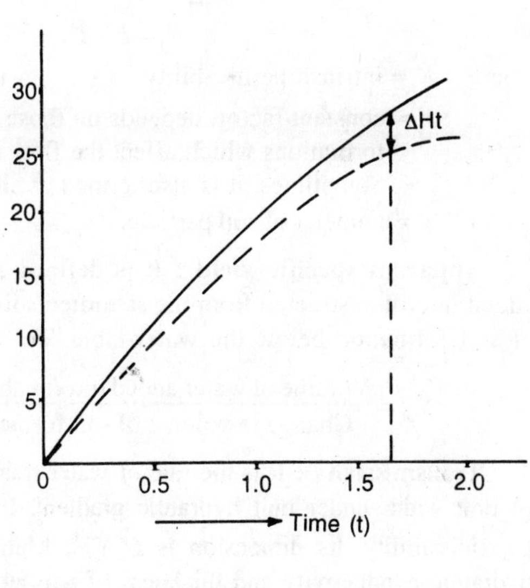

Fig. 13.14.

The following formula is used for computation of hydraulic conductivity of the soil :

$$K = \left(\frac{R_v^2}{FR_c}\right)\frac{\Delta H_t}{\int_o^t H \cdot dt} \quad \text{...(13.20)}$$

where, K = hydraulic conductivity, cm/min

R_v = radius of inside tube, cm

F = flow factor, depends on the geometry of flow system. It is a dimensionless factor.

R_c = radius of outside tube, cm

ΔH_t = difference between the ordinates of constant level curve and equal level curve at any time (t), as shown in Fig. 13.14.

$\int_o^t H \cdot dt$ = area under the constant level curve and equal level curve at the time 't', at which ΔH_t was measured.

H = height of water level from the top of stand pipe, cm.

Intrinsic permeability : The inherent characteristics of soil formation causing water transmission is known as intrinsic permeability. It is independent of viscosity and density of the water/fluid, expressed as :

$$K_i = F \cdot d^2 \quad \text{...(13.21)}$$

where K_i = intrinsic permeability

F = constant/factor, depends on those properties of soil formations which affect the flow rate, excluding the grain diameter. Sometimes, it is also termed as shape factor (dimensionless).

d = diameter of soil particle.

Apparent specific yield : It is defined as the ratio of volume of water added into/or abstracted from the saturated soil profile to the change in volume of soil formation below the water-table. *i.e.*

$$S_{ya} = \frac{\text{Volume of water added into/or abstracted from saturated layer}}{\text{Change in volume of soil formation below the water–table}}$$

Transmissivity : It is the rate of water transmission through aquifer column of unit width under unit hydraulic gradient. It is also known as coefficient of transmissibility. Its dimension is $L^2 T^{-1}$. Mathematically, it is the product of hydraulic conductivity and thickness of aquifer, given as under :

$$T = K \cdot b \quad \text{...(13.22)}$$

where, T = transmissivity of aquifer, m^2/day

K = hydraulic conductivity of aquifer, m/day

b = aquifer thickness, m

The value of transmissivity (T) ranges from less than 1.2×10^4 l/day/m to 1.2×10^6 l/day/m. An aquifer with T 1.2×10^5 l/day/m is considered satisfactory for installation of irrigation wells. Transmissivity of aquifer is determined by conducting the pumping test. Fig. 13.15 shows the view of transmissivity of an aquifer.

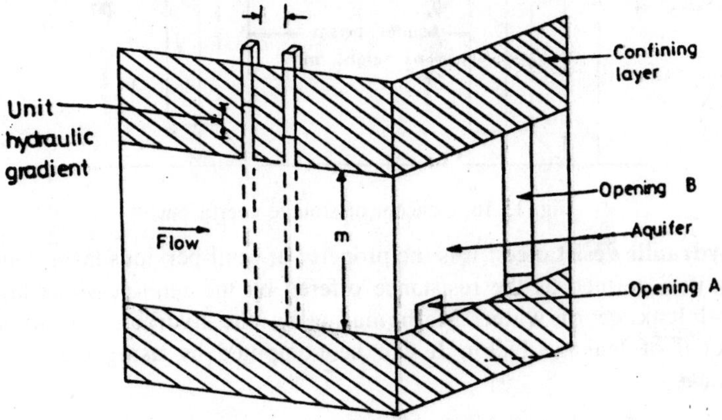

Fig. 13.15. Concept of transmissivity.

Coefficient of storage : It is the property of confined and semi-confined aquifers; defined as the volume of water released from or taken into the storage per unit surface area of the aquifer and per unit change in the component of head normal to the surface, as shown in Fig. 13.16. The concept of storage coefficient can also be explained as: when water-table is lowered for some depth, then water is released from the surrounding aquifer under gravity effect for the amount equal to the drained water. In this condition, coefficient of storage is equal to the specific yield. Coefficient of storage in confined aquifer is due to compression and expansion of water, caused by reduction in pressure due to pumping.

Generally, of confind aquifor the value of coefficient of storage varies from 1×10^{-5} to 1×10^{-3}. If coefficient of storage and fluctuation of water-table or piezometric surface are known, then amount of water released from or added into the aquifer can be computed by using the following formula :

$$V_{a/r} = S \cdot \Delta h \qquad \text{...(13.23)}$$

where, $V_{a/r}$ = volume of water added into or released from the aquifer.

S = coefficient of storage

Δh = difference in water level or piezometric surface

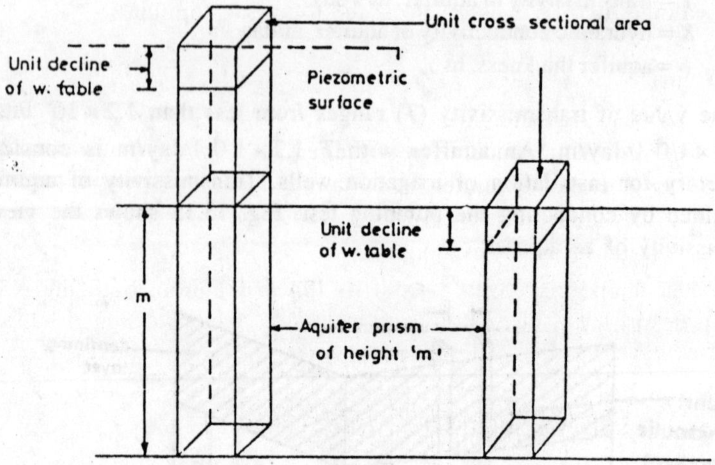

Fig. 13.16. Concept of storage coefficient.

Hydraulic resistance : It is the property of semi-pervious layer confining the aquifer; defined as the resistance offered by the semi-pervious layer on vertical leakage of water. Mathematically, the hydraulic resistance is reciprocal of leakage factor. It can be computed by using the following formula :

$$C = \frac{b'}{K'} \qquad ...(13.24)$$

where, c = hydraulic resistance, days
b' = thickness of semi-pervious layer, m
K' = hydraulic conductivity of semi-pervious layer.

Hydraulic resistance is also used as an index for semi-confined aquifer. An infinite value of 'C' of any layer indicates to be impervious formation, while C as zero or near to zero indicates to be an aquifer. For semi-pervious layer, its value ranges from 100 to 10^6 minutes.

Example 13.6. *Determine the value of hydraulic resistance of semi-pervious layer, if its thickness is 3.5 m and hydraulic conductivity is 10^{-3} m/day.*

Solution. Given that, $b' = 3.5$ m
$K' = 10^{-3}$ m/day

Therfore, hydraulic resistance of semi-pervious layer (C), we have,

$$C = \frac{b'}{K'}$$

$$= \frac{3.5}{10^{-3}} \text{ day}$$

$$= 3.5 \times 10^3 \text{ days} \quad \textbf{Ans.}$$

Leakage factor : It is given by the following formula :

$$\lambda = \sqrt{K \cdot b \cdot C} \quad ...(13.25)$$
$$= \sqrt{T \cdot C}$$

where, λ = leakage factor, m
K = hydraulic conductivity of aquifer
b = thickness of aquifer, m
C = hydraulic resistance, days
T = transmissivity of aquifer.

When aquifer is covered from its top and bottom both the sides by semi-pervious layer, then expression of leakage factor i.e. eqn. 13.25 can be modified as under :

$$\lambda = \sqrt{\frac{Kb \cdot C_1 \cdot C_2}{C_1 + C_2}} \quad ...(13.26)$$

in which, K and b are the same as in equation 13.25; and C_1 and C_2 are the hydraulic resistance of upper and lower semi-pervious layers, respectively.

Example 13.7. *An aquifer of thickness 3.5 m has hydraulic conductivity 10^{-3} m/day. The hydraulic resistance of semi-pervious layer which is at the top of aquifer is 2000 days. Compute the value of leakage factor of the aquifer.*

Solution. Given that,

Aquifer thickness (b) = 3.5 m
Hydraulic conductivity (K) = 10^{-3} m/day
Hydraulic resistance (C) = 2000 days

$\therefore$ Leakage factor (λ) from the eq. 13.25, we have

$$\lambda = \sqrt{K \cdot b \cdot C}$$
$$= \sqrt{10^{-3} \times 3.5 \times 2000}$$
$$= \mathbf{2.6\ m} \quad \textbf{Ans.}$$

Example 13.8. *An aquifer is covered by semi-pervious layer from its top and bottom both the sides. If hydraulic resistance of the top and bottom semi-pervious layer is 4000 and 3500 days, respectively, then compute the value of leakage factor. Assume,*

1. *Hydraulic conductivity of aquifer as 1.5×10^{-3} m/day*
2. *Thickness of aquifer as 4.5 m.*

Solution. Given that,

$$C_1 = 4000 \text{ days}$$
$$C_2 = 3500 \text{ days}$$
$$K = 1.5 \times 10^{-3} \text{ m/day}$$
$$b = 4.5 \text{ m}$$

∴ Leakage factor (λ) from the eq. 13.26, we have

$$\lambda = \sqrt{\frac{K \cdot b \cdot C_1 \cdot C_2}{C_1 + C_2}}$$

$$= \sqrt{\frac{1.5 \times 10^{-3} \times 4000 \times 3500}{4000 + 3500}} \text{ m}$$

$$= \mathbf{1.67\ m} \quad \textbf{Ans.}$$

Drainage factor : It is given as under :

$$B = \sqrt{\frac{(K \cdot b)}{(\alpha\, S_y)}}$$

$$= \sqrt{\frac{T}{\alpha \cdot S_y}} \qquad ...(13.27)$$

where, B = drainage factor

T = transmissivity of aquifer

$\frac{1}{\alpha}$ = Boulton's delay constant

S_y = specific yield.

Specific storage : It is the ratio of storage coefficient and thickness of aquifer, given as under :

$$S_s = \frac{S}{m} \qquad ...(13.28)$$

Specific storage can also be calculated by using the following formula :

$$S_s = \rho \cdot g \cdot \phi\, (\alpha_p + \beta) \qquad ...(13.29)$$

where, ρ = density of water/fluid

g = acceleration due to gravity

ϕ = porosity of equifer

α_p = compressibility of aquifer

β = compressibility of water.

The compressibility of aquifer (α_p) is the change in pore volume due to vertical compression per unit pore volume and per unit change in intergrannular stress. It is given by the following formula :

$$\alpha_p = \frac{1}{\Delta z\, \phi} \cdot \left[\frac{d}{dp}(\phi' \cdot \Delta z)\right] \qquad ...(13.30)$$

inwhich, Δz is the height of soil column and P is the pressure.

Example 13.9. *Calculate the value of specific storage of confined aquifer, which thickness is 15 m, porosity (φ) is 0.33 and modulus of compression is* 2.48×10^{-5} *cm³/kg. Assume* $\rho \cdot g$ *as 0.1 and* β as 4.37×10^{-5} *cm²/kg.*

Solution. Given that,

$$\phi = 0.33$$

$$b = 15 \text{ m}$$

$$\alpha_p = 2.48 \times 10^{-5} \text{ cm}^3/\text{kg}$$

$$\beta = 4.37 \times 10^{-5} \text{ cm}^2/\text{kg}$$

$$\rho \cdot g = 0.1$$

∴ Specific storage (S_s).

$$S_s = \rho \cdot g \cdot \phi (\alpha_p + \beta)$$

$$= 0.1 \times 0.33 (2.48 \times 10^{-5} + 4.37 \times 10^{-5})$$

$$= \mathbf{2.26 \times 10^{-6}} \quad \textbf{Ans.}$$

13.9. Distribution of Sub-surface Water

The subsurface water is divided into following two zones:

1. Zone of aeration; and

2. Zone of saturation.

Zone of aeration : This zone is extended from topsoil surface to the upper boundary of zone of saturation. It is very important zone for crop production. However, it does not involve the ground water flow.

The configuration and form of this zone are totally dependent on geology, topography, drainage conditions, climate etc. Inaddition, the factors affecting the position of water-table also affect the configuration of aeration zone. Generally, in highly permeable formations, in good drainage conditions, in arid climates etc, the thickness of zone of aeration is comparitively more.

Zone of aeration is fruther sub-divided into following divisions:

1. Soil water zone

2. Intermediate zone; and

3. Capillary fringe.

Water retained in these zones is called as "Vadose water".

Soil water zone : It is the top most part of zone of aeration, which lies immediately below the top soil surface and extended downward upto the root zone. Water present in this zone is used by the crops and also lost through evaporation.

For development of ground water, the soil water zone plays major role as its lithological characteristics largely affect the downward movement of water. Thickness of soil water zone depends on several factors, such as sub-surface geological conditions, crops grown and topographical features.

Intermediate zone : It is next sub-division of zone of aeration, which lies between the soil water zone and capillary fringe. Thickness of this zone depends on the depth of water-table. If water-table is very close to the ground surface, then intermediate zone is not found. On the other hand, if water-table is at greater depth, then there would be clear cut appearance of intermediate zone.

Capillary fringe : It lies immediately above the zone of saturation. The water available in this zone is termed as "capillary water". This water is drawn up through capillary action and is suspended by capillary force. Thickness of this zone depends on the texture of soil formation above the zone of saturation. If size of pores is fine then upward movement of water through soil is comparitively more, causing greater thickness of capillary fringe; and vise-versa. The height of capillary rise in different soil formations is given in Table 13.6.

Table 13.6. Extent of capillary rise in different soil formations

S.No.	*Soil formation*	*Capillary rise (cm)*
1.	Loam	100—150
2.	Fine sand	40—70
3.	Medium sand	15—40
4.	Coarse sand	5—15
5.	Gravel	less than 5
6.	Clay	150—300

Important features of capillary fringe are given as under :

1. Its lower part *i.e.* immediately above the water-table contains water in all the pores.

2. Moisture content is equal to the porosity of soil.

3. Water pressure is less as compared to the atmospheric pressure.

4. Thickness of capillary fringe tends to vary depending on the fluctuation of water-table.

Zone of saturation

It is the lower most zone of sub-surface water, which occurs over an impervious layer. Its upper surface is the water-table or phreatic surface. Sometimes, its upper surface is also covered by an impervious layer; under this condition the saturation zone acts as confined aquifer and available water is under artesian pressure. Artesian pressure reflects the piezometric level, when well is inserted in the confined aquifer. On the contrast, when water-table acts as upper layer of the zone of saturation, then water is being at the atmospheric pressure, which reflects the feature of unconfined aquifer.

If well is sunk in this zone, the water level in the well is found almost in the level of water-table.

Available water in the zone of saturation is known as ground- water. Thickness of this zone depends on the type and condition of the geological formation existing in it. Its thickness is relatively less in the formation underlain by consolidated rocks having joints and tappering at shallow depth. On the other hand, there may be several hundred meters of thickness, where formations are under lain by thick sequence of sedimentary rocks. The Gangatic plains of India are example of this kind of formation.

The vertical distribution of sub-surface water is shown in Fig. 13.17.

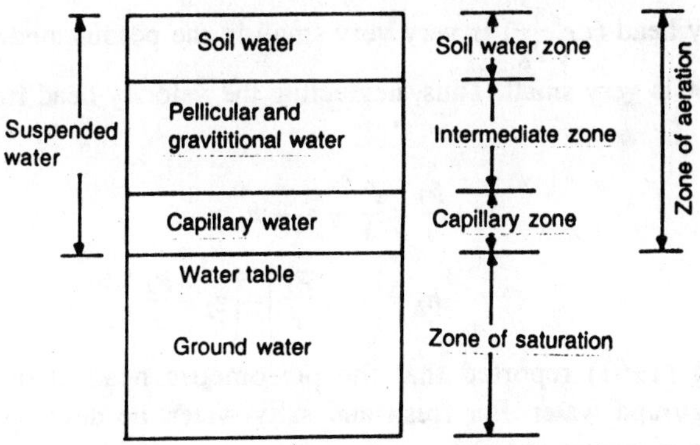

Fig. 13.17. Sub-surface distribution of water.

13.10. Ground Water Flow Equations

The basic equations to study the ground water phenomena are described as under:

13.10.1. Basic Equations

Piezometric head : Distribution of ground water head under steady state condition is governed by the Bernoullies theorum which states that at any point along the stream line, the total head is constant. Total head of ground water at any point is the sum of following energy heads :

1. Elevation head (z)
2. Pressure head $\left(\frac{p}{r}\right)$; and
3. Velocity head $\left(\frac{v^2}{2g}\right)$

Thus, total head $= z + \frac{p}{r} + \frac{v^2}{2g}$ ...(13.31)

According to Bernoullies theorum,

$$z + \frac{p}{r} + \frac{v^2}{2g} = \text{constant} \quad ...(13.32)$$

The fluid flow through any porous medium always includes some losses, which may be due to viscous deformation etc. If h_L is the head loss between two sections *A* and *B*, then equation 13.32 can be expanded as :

$$z_1 + \frac{p_1}{r} + \frac{v_1^2}{2g} = z_2 + \frac{p_2}{r} + \frac{v_2^2}{2g} + h_L \quad ...(13.33)$$

Velocity head (*i.e.* $\frac{v^2}{2g}$) is very very small in the porous media as velocity of fluid flow is very small. Thus, neglecting the velocity head from equation, we have

$$z_1 + \frac{p_1}{r} = \frac{p_2}{r} + z_2 + h_L \quad ...(13.34)$$

or

$$h_L = \left(z_1 + \frac{p_1}{r}\right) - \left(z_2 + \frac{p_2}{r}\right) \quad ...(13.35)$$

Santing (1963) reported that the piezometric head changes with the quality of ground water. For fresh and salty water, he developed following equation for piezometric head :

1. For fresh water, $h_f = z + \frac{p}{\rho_f \cdot g}$ ...(13.36)

2. For salty water, $h_s = z + \frac{p}{\rho_s \cdot g}$ ...(13.37)

Notations used in above equations are denoted as under:

p = pressure
r = specific weight of fluid
v = velocity of fluid flow in porous media
g = acceleration due to gravity
h_f = piezometric head for fresh ground water
h_s = piezometric head for salty ground water
ρ_f = density of fresh water
ρ_s = density of salty water.

Laminar and Turbulent Flow

Laminar flow : It is the flow with very less velocity. In this flow the fluid particles are moving approximately in straight line. The reason is that, at very small velocity viscous force dominates the force of inertia, causing ineffectiveness of turbulence nature of the flow. In laboratory, the nature of fluid flow can be observed by putting a drop of dye in the channel flow. If dye drop moves as a steak without mixing in the fluid, then flow is said to be laminar

The laminar flow changes into turbulent flow, when velocity of flow is increased. Laminar flow can only be steady.

Turbulent flow : It has very high flow velocity. The conduit flow, channel flow etc. may be the turbulent flow. In this flow the path of individual fluid particle is not in straight line, but interwining and crossing each other in disordering manner; consequently there is mixing of fluid particles. In brief, turbulent flow has following characteristics :

1. Fluid particles follow erratic path, *i.e.* have three dimensional movement.

2. Resultant motion of fluid is countless, irregular and haphazard.

3. Turbulent flow is very complex and can not be steady.

4. In turbulent flow through conduit, only mean flow line of the fluid is parallel to the axis of conduit.

5. Across the stream line, there is no net flow during small time interval.

In laboratory, the turbulent flow can be identified by putting a small drop of dye in the flow, if it is rapidly diffused in the flow then flow is considered to be turbulent.

13.10.2. Darcy's Equation

Darcy (1856) reported that the rate of fluid flow through porous media is

1. directly proportional to the constant cross-sectional area, (A)

2. directly proportional to the head difference, $(h_1 - h_2)$

3. inversely proportional to the length of soil formation, (L)

Thus, it can be expressed as

$$Q \propto \frac{A\,(h_1 - h_2)}{L} \qquad ...(13.38)$$

or

$$Q = K\frac{A\,(h_1 - h_2)}{L} \qquad ...(13.39)$$

where, K = coefficient of proportionality called hydraulic conductivity. Sometimes it is also known as coefficient of permeability.

Q = discharge or flow rate through soil formation.

In equation (13.39), the term $\frac{h_1 - h_2}{L}$ is the hydraulic gradient. Considering it as 'J', the equation 13.39 can be written as,

$$Q = K \cdot J \cdot A \quad ...(13.40)$$

or

$$q = \frac{Q}{A} = K \cdot J \quad ...(13.41)$$

in which, q is the specific discharge, *i.e.* discharge per unit area.

or

$$q = V = K \cdot J$$

or

$$\boxed{V \propto J} \quad ...(13.42)$$

This equation states that the velocity of fluid flow through porous media is directly proportional to the hydraulic gradient.

Validity of Darcy's Law : The Darcy's law is valid under following conditions :

1. As long as the fluid flow remains under laminar condition.

2. For the Reynold number of 0.02; however, it is acceptable upto the Re of 0.1.

Application of Darcy's Law

It has very wide range of applicability for solving the problems of ground water and drainage flow phenomenon. The description of ground water flow through layered soil based on Darcy's law is given as under.

Horizontal Flow through Layered soil : Referring Fig. 13.18, if there is no ground water flow across the boundary of individual layer, then hydraulic gradient at each layer is given by,

$$J = \frac{h_2 - h_1}{l} \quad ...(13.43)$$

where, J = hydraulic gradient

h_1 and h_2 are shown in Fig. 13.18

and l = length of flow path.

Rate of flow per unit width of layer is given by,

$$\left.\begin{aligned} q_1 &= k_1 \cdot d_1 \cdot J \\ q_2 &= k_2 \cdot d_2 \cdot J \\ q_3 &= k_3 \cdot d_3 \cdot J \end{aligned}\right\} \quad ...(13.44)$$

where, q_1, q_2, q_3 = specific discharge passing through 1st, 2nd and 3rd soil layers, respectively.

k_1, k_2, k_3 = hydraulic conductivity of 1st, 2nd, and 3rd soil layers, respectively.

d_1, d_2, d_3 = thickness of 1st, 2nd and 3rd soil layers, respectively.

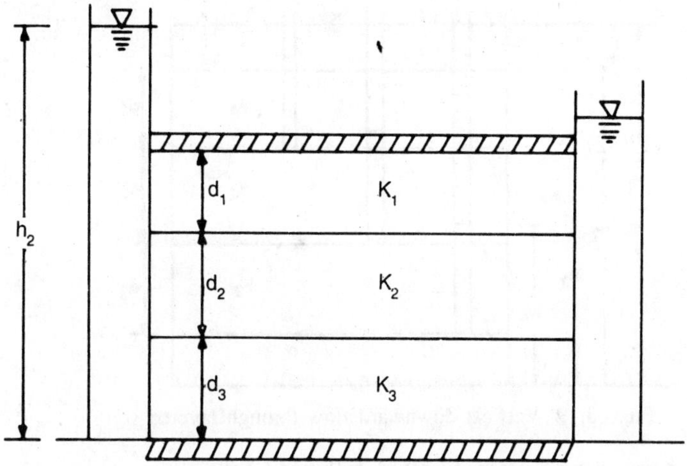

Fig. 13.18. Horizontal flow in layered soil.

Total flow through soil formation (q) is

$$q = q_1 + q_2 + q_3 \quad ...(13.45)$$

$$q = k_1\, d_1 J + k_2\, d_2\, J + k_3\, d_3 \cdot J$$

or

$$J\,(k_1 \cdot d_1 + k_2 \cdot d_2 + k_3 \cdot d_3) \quad ...(13.46)$$

If K is the equivalent hydraulic conductivity of all the layers, then specific discharge equation can be given by

$$q = K \cdot J\,(d_1 + d_2 + d_3) \quad ...(13.47)$$

or

$$K = \frac{q}{J\,(d_1 + d_2 + d_3)} \quad ...(13.48)$$

or

$$\boxed{\frac{k_1 d_1 + k_2 d_2 + k_3 d_3}{d_1 + d_2 + d_3}} \quad ...(13.49)$$

Vertical Downward Flow : Referring Fig. 13.19, if there is neither lateral flow nor water accumulation in the layers, then rate of ground water flow through unit cross-sectional area of the soil layer will be the same. It is given as under :

$$q = \begin{cases} q_1 = k_1 \dfrac{h_1 - h_2}{d_1} A \\ q_2 = k_2 \dfrac{h_2 - h_3}{d_2} A \\ q_3 = k_3 \dfrac{h_3 - h_4}{d_3} A \end{cases} \quad ...(13.50)$$

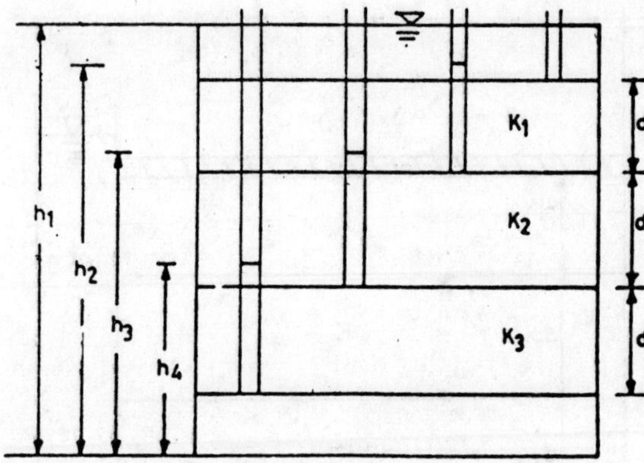

Fig. 13.19. Vertical downward flow through layered soil.

Rearranging the equation 13.50 in following form :

$$\left.\begin{aligned} q \cdot \frac{d_1}{k_1} &= (h_1 - h_2)\, A \\ q \cdot \frac{d_2}{k_2} &= (h_2 - h_3)\, A \\ q \cdot \frac{d_3}{k_3} &= (h_3 - h_4)\, A \end{aligned}\right\} \qquad \text{...(13.51)}$$

Adding all these equations, we have

$$q\left(\frac{d_1}{k_1} + \frac{d_2}{k_2} + \frac{d_3}{k_3}\right) = (h_1 - h_4)\, A$$

or

$$\boxed{q = \frac{(h_1 - h_4)}{\left(\frac{d_1}{k_1} + \frac{d_2}{k_2} + \frac{d_3}{k_3}\right)} \cdot A} \qquad \text{...(13.52)}$$

Reynold Number : Osborne Reynolds (1883) mentioned that the transition of laminar flow to turbulent flow depends not only on the mean flow velocity, but also on a dimensionless quantity $\left(\frac{V \cdot d}{\nu}\right)$, known as Reynold's number, denoted as 'R_e'. In which, V is the flow velocity, 'd' is the diameter of pipe and ν is the kinematic viscosity of fluid.

Reynold number is used for demarcating the regime of laminar and turbulent flows. The fluid flow with R_e less than 2000 is referred as laminar, while at 'R_e' greater than 4000 the flow is said to be turbulent.

Fluid Forces on Porous Media

The ground water flow is subject to following two forces :

1. Driving force; and
2. Resisting force.

Driving force is the sum of forces due to pressure difference and body weight due to gravititional effect.

The resisting force is one which resists the driving force.

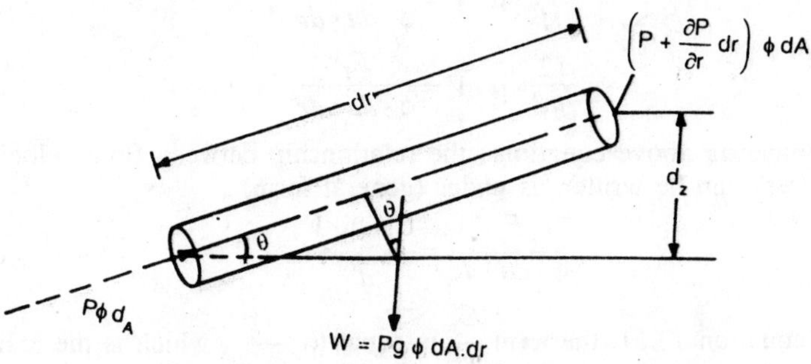

Fig. 13.20. Forces acting on flow through porous media.

Referring Fig. 13.20, let surface force is equal to

$$\left[\left(P + \frac{\partial p}{\partial r} dr\right)\phi \cdot dA - p \cdot \phi\, dA\right] \qquad ...(13.53)$$

and body weight/force is

$$W = \rho \cdot g\, \phi \cdot da \cdot dr \cdot \sin\theta \qquad ...(13.54)$$

If resisting force is F, then balancing all these forces, we have

$$\left[\left(p + \frac{\partial p}{\partial r} \cdot dr\right)\phi\, da - p \cdot \phi \cdot da\right] + \rho \cdot g\phi \cdot da \cdot dr \cdot \sin\theta = F$$

or
$$\frac{\partial p}{\partial r}\phi \cdot da \cdot dr + \rho \cdot g \cdot \phi \cdot da \cdot dr \cdot \sin\theta = F$$

$$\frac{F}{\phi \cdot da \cdot dr} = \frac{dp}{dr} + \rho \cdot g \cdot \sin\theta \qquad ...(13.55)$$

$$\therefore \quad \frac{F}{\phi \cdot da \cdot dr} = \frac{dp}{dr} + \rho \cdot g \cdot \frac{dz}{dr}$$

or
$$\frac{d}{dr}(p + \rho \cdot g \cdot z) \qquad ...(13.56)$$

If $P = p + \rho \cdot g \cdot z$, then equation 13.56 can be written as

$$\boxed{\frac{F}{\phi \cdot da \cdot dr} = \frac{dP}{dr}} \qquad ...(13.57)$$

Viscous force : The formula for viscous force can be derived by using the following relationship between driving force and mean flow velocity, through a circular capillary tube with radius R :

$$\frac{F}{\phi \cdot da \cdot dr} = \frac{8}{R^2} \mu \cdot V \qquad \text{...(13.58)}$$

The flow equation for thin film of thickness 'D' which takes place between two flat plates placed at 'b' distance apart, is written as under :

$$\frac{3}{D^2} \cdot \mu \cdot V = \frac{F_1}{\phi \cdot da \cdot dr} \qquad \text{...(13.59)}$$

and

$$\frac{12}{(b)^2} \cdot \mu \cdot V = \frac{F_1}{\phi \cdot da \cdot dr} \qquad \text{...(13.60)}$$

Comparing above equations, the relationship between flow velocity and shear stress can be written as under (general form)

$$\frac{F_1}{\phi \cdot da \cdot dr} = \frac{C_s \cdot \mu \cdot V}{d^2} \qquad \text{...(13.61)}$$

In equation 13.61, the term $\frac{C_s}{d^2}$ is equal to $\frac{1}{C \cdot d^2}$ which is the reciprocal of intrinsic permeability (k_i). In terms of intrinsic permeability the equation 13.61 can be written as :

$$\boxed{\frac{F_1}{\phi \cdot da \cdot dr} = \frac{\mu \cdot V}{k_i}} \qquad \text{...(13.62)}$$

This is the equation of viscous force, inwhich μ is the coefficient of dynamic viscosity of the fluid.

Inertial force : It is considered as the resisting force, which is due to convective acceleration of fluid elements. It is equal to the product of mass and acceleration, expressed as under :

$$\frac{dv}{dt} = \frac{\partial v}{\partial r} \cdot \frac{dr}{dt} + \frac{\partial v}{\partial t} \cdot \frac{dt}{dt} \qquad \text{...(13.63)}$$

In this equation, the term $\frac{\partial v}{\partial r} \cdot \frac{dr}{dt}$ is the convective acceleration and other term i.e. $\frac{\partial v}{\partial t} \cdot \frac{dt}{dt}$ is the local acceleration which is very small and is neglected. Thus, the inertial force per unit pore volume can be expressed as

$$\frac{F_2}{\phi \cdot da \cdot dr} = \rho \frac{\partial v}{\partial r} \cdot \frac{dr}{dt}$$

or

$$\frac{F_2}{\phi \cdot da \cdot dr} = \rho \cdot V \cdot \frac{dv}{dr} \qquad \text{...(13.64)}$$

or

$$\frac{\rho V^2}{\sqrt{k_i}}$$

$$\therefore \quad \frac{F_2}{\phi \cdot da \cdot dr} = \frac{\rho V^2}{\sqrt{k_i}} \qquad ...(13.65)$$

Adding the viscous and interial forces, we have

$$\frac{F_1}{\phi \cdot da \cdot dr} + \frac{F_2}{\phi \cdot da \cdot dr} = \frac{\mu v}{k_i} + \frac{\rho V^2}{\sqrt{k_i}} \qquad ...(13.66)$$

Total driving force, $$\frac{F}{\phi \cdot da \cdot dr} = \frac{dp}{dr} \qquad ...(13.67)$$

Equating the equations 13.66 and 13.67, we have

$$\frac{\mu \cdot V}{k_i} + \frac{\rho \cdot V^2}{\sqrt{k_i}} = \frac{dp}{dr} \qquad ...(13.68)$$

Dividing both side of the equation (13.68) with pore volume $\left(\frac{\rho \cdot V^2}{\sqrt{k_i}}\right)$, we have

$$\frac{\sqrt{k_i}}{\rho \cdot V^2}\left(\frac{dp}{dr}\right) = \frac{\mu}{\rho \cdot V\sqrt{k_i}} + 1 \qquad ...(13.69)$$

or $$f = \frac{1}{R_e} + 1 \qquad ...(13.70)$$

where, f = friction factor

$$= \frac{\sqrt{k_i}}{\rho \cdot V^2}\left(\frac{dp}{dr}\right)$$

$$\therefore \quad \boxed{\frac{1}{R_e} = \frac{\mu}{\rho \cdot V\sqrt{k_i}}}$$

13.10.3. Laplace Equation

Laplace equation is derived based on the following assumptions :

1. The formation is homogeneous and isotropic (*i.e.* $k_x = k_y = k_z$)
2. Storage coefficient is constant with time.
3. Coefficient of permeability varies with time.
4. Capillary fringe is absent.
5. Semi-pervious layers offer uniform resistance to flow.

The Laplace equation in three dimensions is given as under :

$$\frac{\partial^2 h}{\partial x^2} + \frac{\partial^2 h}{\partial y^2} + \frac{\partial^2 h}{\partial z^2} = 0 \qquad ...(13.71)$$

in which 'h' is the head causing flow. Laplace equation in terms of velocity potential (ϕ) is given by

$$\frac{\partial^2 \phi}{\partial x^2} + \frac{\partial^2 \phi}{\partial y^2} + \frac{\partial^2 \phi}{\partial z^2} = 0 \qquad ...(13.72)$$

where, $$\phi = k \cdot h \qquad ...(13.73)$$

13.10.4. Storage Equation

The storage equations for confined and unconfined aquifers are given as under:

For confined aquifer : In case of confined aquifer the change in storage is only due to elastic change in the formation. Jacob (1950) derived the following ground-water storage equation for confined aquifer :

$$S = \phi \cdot \nu \cdot b \cdot \beta \left(1 + \frac{\alpha}{\phi \cdot \beta}\right) \qquad ...(13.74)$$

where, S = storage coefficient
ϕ = porosity of aquifer
ν = specific weight of fluid
b = aquifer thickness
β = bulk modulus of compression of water
α = bulk modulus of compression of the solid part of aquifer.

For unconfined aquifer : Hantush (1964) derived the following equation for ground water storage :

$$S = S_y + \nu \cdot \phi \cdot \beta \cdot b \left(1 + \frac{\alpha}{\phi \cdot \beta}\right) \qquad ...(13.75)$$

in which, S_y is the specific yield of aquifer.

Ground Water Flow in Confined Aquifer

The flow equation for confined aquifer is derived on the basis of Darcy's law and mass balance approach. The mass balance relationship is developed by considering the inflow, outflow and change in storage made in the control volume (Fig. 13.21).

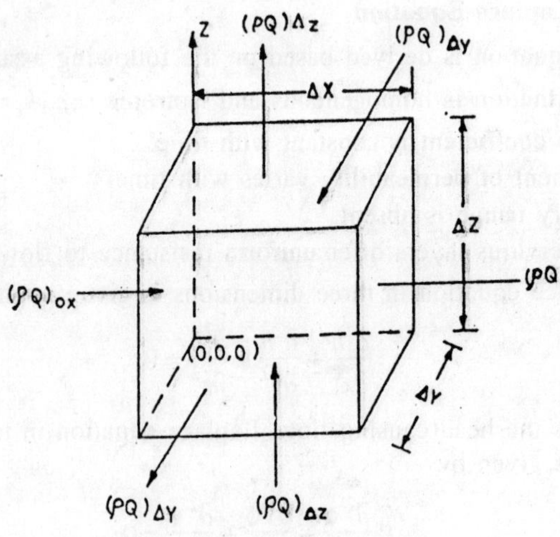

Fig. 13.21. Control volume.

Referring Fig. 13.21, the outflow and inflow equations in x-direction are given as under:

$$\left.\begin{aligned} \text{out flow} &= (\rho \cdot Q)_{\Delta x} \\ \text{and} \qquad \text{in flow} &= (\rho \cdot Q)_o \end{aligned}\right\} \qquad \text{...(13.76)}$$

in which, ρ is the fluid density, Q is the discharge passing through control volume and Δx is the horizontal length of control volume.

Expanding the outflow equation by using Taylor's series, we have

$$(\rho Q)_{\Delta x} = (\rho Q)_o + \frac{\partial}{\partial x}(\rho \cdot Q) \cdot \Delta x + \frac{\partial^2}{\partial x^2}(\rho \cdot Q) \cdot \Delta x^2 + \ldots \qquad \text{...(13.77)}$$

In this equation, the term $\frac{\partial^2}{\partial x^2}(\rho \cdot Q)\,\Delta x^2$ is very small and is neglected. Thus,

$$(\rho \cdot Q)_{\Delta x} - (\rho Q)_o = \frac{\partial}{\partial x}(\rho \cdot Q) \cdot \Delta x \qquad \text{...(13.78)}$$

This is the expression for change of storage in x-direction. Similarly, the equations of change in storage in y and z directions can also be derived as under :

$$(\rho \cdot Q)\Delta y - (\rho \cdot Q)_o = \frac{\partial}{\partial y}(\rho \cdot Q) \cdot \Delta y \qquad \text{...(13.79)}$$

and

$$(\rho \cdot Q)_{\Delta z} - (\rho \cdot Q)_o = \frac{\partial}{\partial z}(\rho \cdot Q) \cdot \Delta z \qquad \text{...(13.80)}$$

Total change in storage in control volume is given as

$$\frac{\partial}{\partial x}(\rho \cdot Q) \cdot \Delta x + \frac{\partial}{\partial y}(\rho \cdot Q) \cdot \Delta y + \frac{\partial}{\partial z}(\rho \cdot Q) \cdot \Delta z \qquad \text{...(13.81)}$$

According to Darcy's law, the discharge in x, y and z directions is given by

$$\left.\begin{aligned} Q_x &= V_x \cdot \Delta y \cdot \Delta z \\ Q_y &= V_y \cdot \Delta x \cdot \Delta z \\ Q_z &= V_z \cdot \Delta x \cdot \Delta y \end{aligned}\right\} \qquad \text{...(13.82)}$$

Substituting the values of Q_x, Q_y, Q_z in equation 13.80, we have,

$$\frac{\partial}{\partial x}(\rho \cdot V_x \cdot \Delta y \cdot \Delta z) \cdot \Delta x + \frac{\partial}{\partial y}(\rho \cdot V_y \cdot \Delta x \cdot \Delta z) \cdot \Delta y + \frac{\partial}{\partial z}(\rho \cdot V_z \cdot \Delta x \cdot \Delta y) \cdot \Delta z$$

$$\text{or} \quad \left[\frac{\partial}{\partial x}(\rho \cdot V_x) + \frac{\partial}{\partial y}(\rho \cdot V_y) + \frac{\partial}{\partial z} + (\rho \cdot V_z)\right] \cdot \Delta x \cdot \Delta y \cdot \Delta z$$

Let, the mass of flow is 'M', therefore, rate of change of mass is $\frac{\partial M}{\partial t}$ which is equal to the total change in storage of the control volume *i.e.*

$$\frac{\partial M}{\partial t}=\left[\frac{\partial}{\partial x}(\rho \cdot V_x)+\frac{\partial}{\partial y}(\rho \cdot V_y)+\frac{\partial}{\partial z}(\rho \cdot V_z)\right]\cdot \Delta x \cdot \Delta y \cdot \Delta z \quad ...(13.83)$$

Taking the Ist term of right hand side of the equation 13.83 for simplification

$$\frac{\partial}{\partial x}(\rho \cdot V_x)=\rho \frac{\partial V_x}{\partial x}+V_x \frac{\partial \rho}{\partial x} \quad ...(11.84)$$

$$=\rho \frac{\partial \cdot V_x}{\partial x}+V_x \frac{\partial \rho}{\partial p}\cdot \frac{\partial p}{\partial x}$$

or

$$\rho \frac{\partial \cdot V_x}{\partial x}+V_x \cdot \rho \cdot \beta \cdot \frac{\partial p}{\partial x} \quad ...(13.85)$$

$$\left(\frac{\partial \rho}{\partial p}=\rho \cdot \beta\right)$$

In equation 13.84, the value of β is very small, therefore, neglecting the term of β from the equation, we have

$$\frac{\partial}{\partial x}(\rho \cdot V_x)=\rho \cdot \frac{\partial V_x}{\partial x} \quad ...(13.86)$$

In the same way, the values of IInd and IIIrd terms of equation 13.83 can also be simplified as

$$\left.\begin{aligned}\frac{\partial}{\partial y}(\rho \cdot V_y)&=\rho \frac{\partial V_y}{\partial y}\\ \text{and} \quad \frac{\partial}{\partial z}(\rho \cdot V_z)&=\rho \frac{\partial V_z}{\partial z}\end{aligned}\right\} \quad ...(13.87)$$

Substituting these values in equation 13.83, we have

$$\frac{\partial M}{\partial t}=\left[\rho \frac{\partial V_x}{\partial x}+\rho \frac{\partial V_y}{\partial y}+\rho \frac{\partial V_z}{\partial z}\right]\Delta x \cdot \Delta y \cdot \Delta z$$

or

$$\rho\left[\frac{\partial V_x}{\partial x}+\frac{\partial V_y}{\partial y}+\frac{\partial V_z}{\partial z}\right]\Delta x \cdot \Delta y \cdot \Delta z$$

Again applying Darcy's law, *i.e.* $V=ki$

$$\frac{\partial M}{\partial t}=\rho\left[\frac{\partial}{\partial x}\left(k_x \cdot \frac{\partial h}{\partial x}\right)+\frac{\partial}{\partial y}\left(k_y \cdot \frac{\partial h}{\partial y}\right)+\frac{\partial}{\partial z}\left(k_z \cdot \frac{\partial h}{\partial z}\right)\right]\cdot \Delta x \cdot \Delta y \cdot \Delta z$$

or

$$\frac{\partial}{\partial x}\left(k_x \cdot \frac{\partial h}{\partial x}\right)+\frac{\partial}{\partial y}\left(k_y \cdot \frac{\partial h}{\partial y}\right)+\frac{\partial}{\partial z}\left(k_z \cdot \frac{\partial h}{\partial z}\right)=\frac{1}{\rho \cdot \Delta x \cdot \Delta y \cdot \Delta z}\cdot \frac{\partial M}{\partial t}$$

We know that, $\dfrac{\partial M}{\Delta x \cdot \Delta y \cdot \Delta z}=\rho \cdot \phi \cdot (\alpha_p+\beta)\cdot \partial p$

Therefore, $\dfrac{\partial}{\partial x}\left(k_x \cdot \dfrac{\partial h}{\partial x}\right)+\dfrac{\partial}{\partial y}\left(k_y \cdot \dfrac{\partial h}{\partial y}\right)+\dfrac{\partial}{\partial z}\left(k_z \dfrac{\partial h}{\partial z}\right)=\phi\,(\alpha_p+\beta)\dfrac{\partial p}{\partial t}$ ...(13.88)

Taking the right hand side term of equation 13.88 for simplification

$$\phi\,(\alpha_p+\beta)\frac{\partial p}{\partial t}$$

Putting the value of $p = h \cdot \rho \cdot g$, we have

$$\phi\,(\alpha_p + \beta)\,\frac{\partial}{\partial t}(h \cdot \rho \cdot g)$$

$$= \rho \cdot g \cdot \phi\,(\alpha_p + \beta)\,\frac{\partial h}{\partial t}$$

$$= S_s \cdot \frac{\partial h}{\partial t} \qquad ...(13.89)$$

Thus, the equation 13.81 becomes

$$\frac{\partial}{\partial x}\left(k_x \cdot \frac{\partial h}{\partial x}\right) + \frac{\partial}{\partial y}\left(k_y \cdot \frac{\partial h}{\partial y}\right) + \frac{\partial}{\partial z}\left(k_z \cdot \frac{\partial h}{\partial z}\right) = S_s \cdot \frac{\partial h}{\partial t}$$

or

$$k_x \frac{\partial^2 h}{\partial x^2} + k_y \frac{\partial^2 h}{\partial y^2} + k_z \frac{\partial^2 h}{\partial z^2} = S_s \cdot \frac{\partial h}{\partial t} \qquad ...(13.90)$$

For isotropic soils, in which $k_x = k_y = k_z = k$

The equation 13.90 is given by

$$\left[\frac{\partial^2 h}{\partial x^2} + \frac{\partial^2 h}{\partial y^2} + \frac{\partial^2 h}{\partial z^2}\right] = \frac{S_s}{k} \cdot \frac{\partial h}{\partial t}$$

$$\therefore \qquad \frac{\partial^2 h}{\partial x^2} + \frac{\partial^2 h}{\partial y^2} + \frac{\partial^2 h}{\partial z^2} = \frac{S}{T} \cdot \frac{\partial h}{\partial t} \qquad ...(13.91)$$

in which, T is the transmissivity ($T = m \cdot k$) of aquifer. Replacing h in terms of draw down (s) which is equal to ($h_o - h$), in which h_o is constant. Thus, the equation 13.91 can be written as

$$\boxed{\frac{\partial^2 s}{\partial x^2} + \frac{\partial^2 s}{\partial y^2} + \frac{\partial^2 s}{\partial z^2} = \frac{S}{T} \cdot \frac{\partial s}{\partial t}} \qquad ...(13.92)$$

This is the desired flow equation for confined aquifer under unsteady condition. For steady condition, the value of $\frac{\partial s}{\partial t}$ is 0.

$$\boxed{\frac{\partial^2 s}{\partial x^2} + \frac{\partial^2 s}{\partial y^2} + \frac{\partial^2 s}{\partial z^2} = 0} \qquad ...(13.93)$$

13.11. Ground Water Flow in Unconfined Aquifer

Derivation procedure of ground water flow equation for unconfined aquifer is same to the confined aquifer. The value of specific storage (S_s) of unconfined aquifer is very small and is generally neglected from the equation. The ground water flow equation for unconfined aquifer is given as :

$$\frac{\partial}{\partial x}\left(k_x \cdot \frac{\partial h}{\partial x}\right) + \frac{\partial}{\partial y}\left(k_y \cdot \frac{\partial h}{\partial y}\right) + \frac{\partial}{\partial z}\left(k_z \cdot \frac{\partial h}{\partial z}\right) = 0 \qquad ...(13.94)$$

This equation is similar to the Laplace equation for homogenous and isotropic soil. The right hand side of equation is zero because of S_s as zero; not for steady condition.

13.11.1. Boussineq Equation

Referring the Fig. 13.22, let,

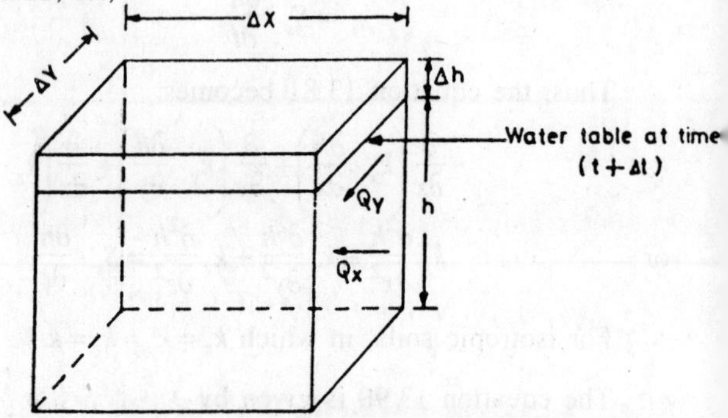

Fig. 13.22. Control volume in case of unconfined aquifer.

1. Δx, Δy and Δz are the length, breadth and height of the control volume, respectively.

2. Q_x and Q_y are the flow rates passing through the control volume in x and y-directions, respectively.

3. Position of water-table at time $t+\Delta t$ is 'h'

Change of volume flux in control volume is given by

$$\frac{\partial}{\partial x}(Q_x)\cdot\Delta x+\frac{\partial}{\partial y}(Q_y)\cdot\Delta y \qquad ...(13.95)$$

According to the Dupuit's assumption and Darcy's law, we have

$$\frac{\text{Change in volume flux}}{\Delta x\cdot\Delta y}=\frac{\partial}{\partial x}\left(k_x\cdot h\frac{\partial h}{\partial x}\right)+\frac{\partial}{\partial y}\left(k_y\cdot h\cdot\frac{\partial h}{\partial y}\right)$$

Replacing the left hand side term by apparent specific yield (S_{ya}), we have

$$\frac{\partial}{\partial x}\left(k_x\cdot h\frac{\partial h}{\partial x}\right)+\frac{\partial}{\partial y}\left(k_y\cdot h\frac{\partial h}{\partial y}\right)=S_{ya}\cdot\frac{\partial h}{\partial t} \qquad ...(13.96)$$

This equation can be simplified under following cases. (1) When aquifer is homogeneous and isotropic (*i.e.* $k_x=k_y=k$), the equation 13.96 can be written as :

$$\frac{\partial}{\partial x}\left(k\cdot h\frac{\partial h}{\partial x}\right)\cdot+\frac{\partial}{\partial y}\left(k\cdot h\cdot\frac{\partial h}{\partial y}\right)=S_{ya}\cdot\frac{\partial h}{\partial t}$$

or
$$k\left[\frac{\partial}{\partial x}\left(h\cdot\frac{\partial h}{\partial x}\right)+\frac{\partial}{\partial y}\left(h\cdot\frac{\partial h}{\partial y}\right)\right]=S_{ya}\cdot\frac{\partial h}{\partial t}$$

or
$$\frac{\partial}{\partial x}\left(h\cdot\frac{\partial h}{\partial x}\right)+\frac{\partial}{\partial y}\left(h\cdot\frac{\partial h}{\partial y}\right)=\frac{S_{ya}}{k}\cdot\frac{\partial h}{\partial t} \qquad ...(13.97)$$

or $$\frac{\partial^2 h}{\partial x^2} + \frac{\partial^2 h}{\partial y^2} = \frac{S_{ya}}{k} \cdot \frac{\partial h}{\partial t} \qquad ...(13.98)$$

This is the non-linear Boussineq equation. To linearize this equation, the notation 'h' is replaced by the aquifer's thickness as 'm'. Thus, the equation 13.98 is given by,

$$\frac{\partial^2 h}{\partial x^2} + \frac{\partial^2 h}{\partial y^2} = \frac{S_{ya}}{m \cdot k} \cdot \frac{\partial h}{\partial t}$$

or $$\frac{\partial^2 h}{\partial x^2} + \frac{\partial^2 h}{\partial y^2} = \frac{S_{ya}}{T} \cdot \frac{\partial h}{\partial t} \qquad ...(13.99)$$

For steady state condition the right hand side term of the equation will be zero. Thus,

$$\frac{\partial^2 h}{\partial x^2} + \frac{\partial^2 h}{\partial y^2} = 0 \qquad ...(13.100)$$

13.12. Ground water flow in Semi-Confined Aquifer

Ground water flow in semi-confined aquifer is described by considering the aquifer as homogeneous, isotropic and is overlain by semi-pervious layer through which the flow takes place. For derivation of flow equation, there have been developed several approaches; however the most practical approach in which horizontal flow through confined aquifer and seepage through aquitard lying at some height above the aquifer take place, is described in this section. The control volume indicating ground water flow in semi-confined aquifer is shown in Fig. 13.23.

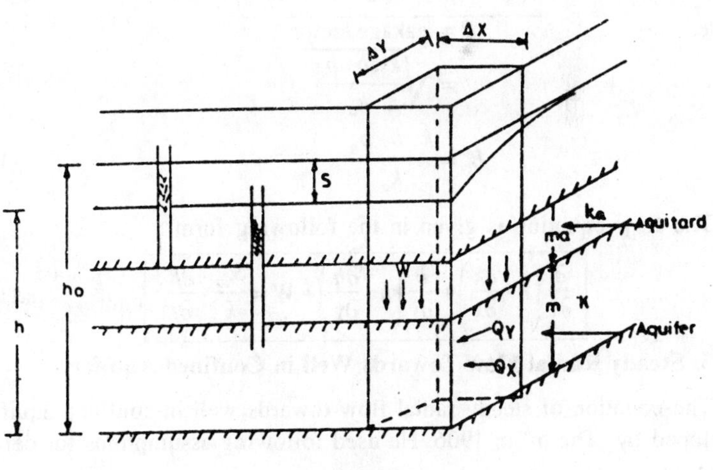

Fig. 13.23

According to the principle of mass balance, we have

$$\frac{\partial}{\partial x}(Q_x)\,\Delta x + \frac{\partial}{\partial y}(Q_y) \cdot \Delta y + W \cdot \Delta x \cdot \Delta y = S\frac{\partial h}{\partial t}\Delta x \cdot \Delta y \qquad ...(13.101)$$

Applying Darcy's law,

$$\frac{\partial}{\partial x}\left(k_x \cdot b \cdot \frac{\partial h}{\partial x}\,\Delta y\right)\Delta x+\frac{\partial}{\partial y}\left(k_y \cdot b \cdot \frac{\partial h}{\partial y}\,\Delta x\right)\Delta y+W\cdot\Delta x\cdot\Delta y=S\,\frac{\partial h}{\partial t}\,\Delta x\cdot\Delta y$$

If $k_x = k_y = k$

$$k\left[\frac{\partial}{\partial x}\left(b\cdot\frac{\partial h}{\partial x}\cdot\Delta x\cdot\Delta y\right)+\frac{\partial}{\partial y}\left(b\cdot\frac{\partial h}{\partial y}\,\Delta x\cdot\Delta Y\right)\right]+W\cdot\Delta x\cdot\Delta y=S\,\frac{\partial h}{\partial t}\,\Delta x\cdot\Delta y$$

Dividing by $b\cdot k\cdot\Delta x\,\Delta y$, we have

$$\frac{\partial}{\partial x}\left(\frac{\partial h}{\partial x}\right)+\frac{\partial}{\partial y}\left(\frac{\partial h}{\partial y}\right)+\frac{W}{b\cdot k}=\frac{S}{m\cdot k}\,\frac{\partial h}{\partial t}$$

$$\frac{\partial^2 h}{\partial x^2}+\frac{\partial^2 h}{\partial y^2}+\frac{W}{b\cdot k}=\frac{S}{T}\frac{\partial h}{\partial t} \quad ...(13.102)$$

If change in storage of aquitard is negligible, then the value of W can be computed by applying the Darcy's law, *i.e.*

$$W=k_a\left(\frac{h_o-h}{b_a}\right) \quad ...(13.103)$$

Substituting the value of W in equation 13.102

$$\frac{\partial^2 h}{\partial x^2}+\frac{\partial^2 h}{\partial y^2}+\frac{k_a\,(h_o-h)}{b_a\cdot k\cdot b}=\frac{S}{T}\frac{\partial h}{\partial t}$$

or

$$\boxed{\frac{\partial^2 h}{\partial x^2}+\frac{\partial^2 h}{\partial y^2}+\frac{h_o-h}{B}=\frac{S}{T}\frac{\partial h}{\partial t}} \quad ...(13.104)$$

where, B = leakage factor

$$=\sqrt{\frac{k\cdot b\cdot b_a}{k_a}}$$

or

$$B^2=\frac{k\cdot b\cdot b_a}{k_a} \quad ...(13.105)$$

The flow equation is given in the following form :

$$\boxed{\frac{\partial}{\partial x}\left(h\cdot\frac{\partial h}{\partial x}\right)+\frac{\partial}{\partial y}\left(h\cdot\frac{\partial h}{\partial y}\right)+W=\frac{S_{ya}}{k}\cdot\frac{\partial h}{\partial t}} \quad ...(13.106)$$

13.13. Steady Radial Flow Towards Well in Confined Aquifer

The equation of steady radial flow towards well in confined aquifer was developed by 'Theim' in 1906. He used following assumptions for derivation of the equation :

1. The well is fully penetrated.
2. Formation is homogeneous and isotropic.
3. Flow is in steady state condition.

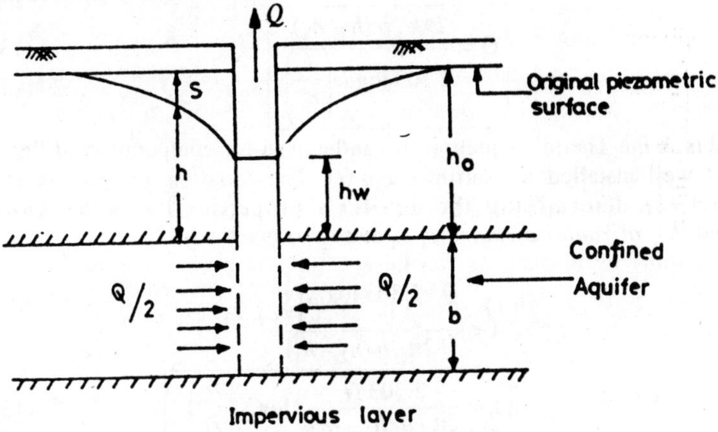

Fig. 13.24. Radial flow in confined aquifer.

Referring Fig. 13.24, let

1. Radius of well is 'r_w'.
2. Two observation wells are installed at radial distance of 'r_1' and 'r_2' from the centre of pumped well.
3. Discharge rate of well is 'Q'
4. Thickness of aquifer is 'b'
5. Piezometric head in the well is 'h_w'
6. Height of water level from the aquifer is 'h_0'

Applying cylindrical co-ordinate system for discharge 'Q' at the radial distance 'r', we have

$$Q = A \cdot V \quad \text{...(13.107)}$$

$$= -(2\pi r \cdot k \cdot b)\frac{dh}{dr} \quad \text{...(13.108)}$$

Since r is measured in outward direction from the well and inflow of water into the well is in inward direction, therefore – ve sign is omitted from the equation 13.108.

Integrating the equation (13.108) with the limits $h \to h_w$ and $r \to r_w$ *i.e.*

$$Q = \int 2\pi r \cdot k \cdot b \cdot \frac{dh}{dr} \quad \text{...(13.109)}$$

or $$Q\int_{r_w}^{r} \frac{dr}{r} = 2\pi k \cdot b \int_{h_w}^{h} dh$$

or $$Q\,[\log_e r]_{r_w}^{r} = 2\pi\, k \cdot b\, [h]_{h_w}^{h}$$

or $$Q\,[\log_e r - \log_e r_w] = 2\pi \cdot k \cdot b\,[h - h_w]$$

or $$Q = 2\pi k \cdot b\,\frac{(h - h_w)}{(\log_e r - \log_e r_w)}$$

or
$$Q = \frac{2\pi k \cdot b\,(h - h_w)}{2.303 \log_{10}\left(\frac{r}{r_w}\right)} \quad ...(13.110)$$

This is the Theim's equation. It can be used for computation of discharge rate of well installed in confined aquifer. The equation 13.110 can also be applied for determining the aquifer's properties *i.e. k by knowing* 'h_1' and 'h_2' *at radial distance of* r_1 and r_2, *respectively, i.e.*

$$k = \frac{Q \cdot 2.303 \log_{10}\left(\frac{r_2}{r_1}\right)}{2\pi \cdot b\,(h_2 - h_1)}$$

or
$$k = \frac{2.303\, Q}{2\pi \cdot b\,(h_2 - h_1)} \cdot \log_{10}\left(\frac{r_2}{r_1}\right) \quad ...(13.111)$$

In terms of draw-down the equation 13.111 can be writen as

$$k = \frac{2.303\, Q}{2\pi \cdot b\,(s_1 - s_2)} \log_{10}\left(\frac{r_2}{r_1}\right) \quad ...(13.112)$$

Example 13.10. *A fully penetrating well of 30 cm diameter is installed in confined aquifer. Compute its discharge, if*

(i) Draw-down in the piezometers located at the radial distance of 30 and 60 meters from the well is 3.0 and 1.5 m, respectively at steady state condition.

(ii) Aquifer thickness is 15 m

(iii) Hydraulic conductivity of aquifer is 9.5 m/day.

Solution. Given that,

$r_1 = 30$ m $\qquad s_1 = 3.0$ m

$r_2 = 60$ m $\qquad s_2 = 1.5$ m

Well diameter = 0.30 m

Aquifer thickness (b) = 15 m

$k = 9.5$ m/day

In confined aquifer the discharge rate of well under steady state condition is given by

$$Q = \frac{2\pi k b\,(s_1 - s_2)}{2.3 \log_{10}\left(\frac{r_2}{r_1}\right)}$$

$$= \frac{2 \times 3.14 \times 9.5 \times 15\,(3 - 1.5)}{2.3 \times \log_{10}\left(\frac{60}{30}\right)}$$

$$= \mathbf{1939.76\ m^3/day} \quad \textbf{Ans.}$$

Example 13.11. *A fully penetrating well of 30 cm diameter is installed in confined aquifer of 15 m thickness. If discharge rate of well is 56 m^3/hour, compute the hydraulic conductivity of aquifer. The draw-downs in piezometers located at the radial distance of 10 and 20 meters from the well are 2.4 and 0.75 m, respectively at steady-state condition.*

Solution. Given that,

Aquifer thickness (b) = 15 m

Discharge rate (Q) = 56 m^3/h

$r_1 = 10$ m, $s_1 = 2.4$ m

$r_2 = 20$ m $\quad s_2 = 0.75$ m

Hydraulic conductivity of the confined aquifer under steady state condition is given by

$$k = \frac{2.3 \log_{10}\left(\frac{r_2}{r_1}\right)}{2\pi \cdot b\,(s_1 - s_2)} \cdot Q$$

$$= \frac{2.3 \times \log_{10}\left(\frac{20}{10}\right)}{2 \times 3.14 \times 15\,(2.4 - 0.75)} \times 56 \text{ m/h}$$

$$= \mathbf{0.25\ m/h} \quad \textbf{Ans.}$$

13.14. Steady Flow Towards Well in Unconfined Aquifer

In unconfined aquifer the flow lines are in horizontal as well as radial direction. The ground water flow equation under steady state condition for unconfined aquifer was derived by Dupuit in 1863 on the basis of following assumptions :

1. The flow velocity is directly proportional to the tangent of hydraulic gradient.

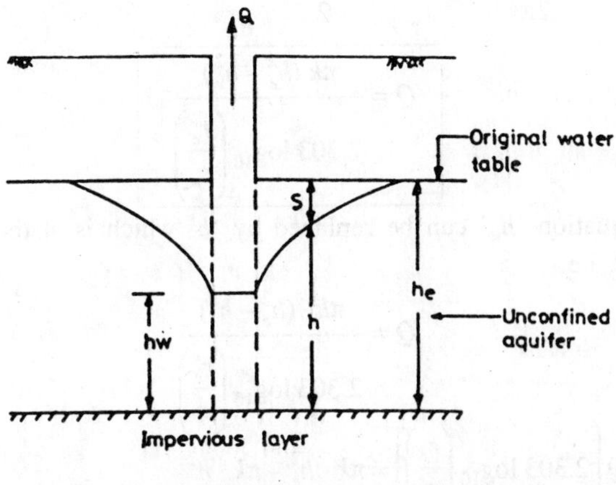

Fig. 13.25. Radial flow in unconfined aquifer.

2. The flow lines are radial and horizontal.

3. Darcy's law is applicable.

4. Aquifer is homogeneous and isotropic with constant thickness.

5. Pumping is done with constant rate for sufficient duration to attain steady state condition.

6. The well is fully penetrated.

7. There is negligible storage in the well; total water comes from the surrounding formations into the well.

Referring Fig. 13.25, the discharge (Q) of well is given by (from Darcy law),

$$Q = kiA \qquad \text{...(13.113)}$$

$$= k \cdot \frac{dh}{dr} \cdot 2\pi r \cdot h$$

or

$$2\pi r \cdot h \cdot k \cdot \frac{dh}{dr} \qquad \text{...(13.114)}$$

$$\frac{Q}{2\pi \cdot r \cdot k} dr = h \cdot dh \qquad \text{...(13.115)}$$

Integrating equation 13.115 with the limit $r_w \to r_e$ and $h_w \to h_e$, we have

$$\int_{r_w}^{r_e} \frac{Q}{2\pi \cdot r \cdot k} dr = \int_{h_w}^{h_e} h \cdot dh \qquad \text{...(13.116)}$$

or

$$\frac{Q}{2\pi k} [\log_e]_{r_w}^{r_e} = \left[\frac{h^2}{2}\right]_{h_w}^{h_e}$$

or

$$\frac{Q}{2\pi k} [\log_e r_e - \log_e r_w] = \left[\frac{h_e^2}{2} - \frac{h_w^2}{2}\right]$$

or

$$\frac{Q}{2\pi k}\left(\log_e \frac{r_e}{r_w}\right) = \frac{h_e^2 - h_2^2}{2}$$

or

$$\boxed{Q = \frac{\pi k\,(h_e^2 - h_w^2)}{2.303 \log_{10}\left(\frac{r_e}{r_w}\right)}} \qquad \text{...(13.117)}$$

In this equation 'h_w' can be replaced by 'h' which is at the distance 'r' from the well, i.e.

$$Q = \frac{\pi k \cdot (h_e^2 - h^2)}{2.303 \log_{10}\left(\frac{r_e}{r}\right)}$$

or

$$Q\left[2.303 \log_{10}\left(\frac{r_e}{r}\right)\right] = \pi k \cdot h_e^2 - \pi k \cdot h^2$$

$$\pi k h^2 = \pi k \cdot h_e^2 - Q\left[2.303 \log_{10}\left(\frac{r_e}{r}\right)\right]$$

$$h^2 = h_e^2 - \frac{Q}{\pi \cdot k}\log_e\left(\frac{r_e}{r}\right) \qquad ...(13.118)$$

Substituting the value of Q in equation (13.118)

$$h^2 = h_e^2 - \frac{(h_e^2 - h_w^2)}{\log_e\left(\frac{r_e}{r_w}\right)} \cdot \log_e\left(\frac{r_e}{r}\right) \qquad ...(13.119)$$

The equation (13.117) can also be written in term of draw-down (s), i.e.

$$Q = \frac{\pi k \cdot (h_e^2 - h_w^2)}{\log_e\left(\frac{r_e}{r_2}\right)}$$

or

$$\frac{\pi k \cdot (h_e - h_w)(h_e + h_w)}{\log_e\left(\frac{r_e}{r_w}\right)} \qquad ...(13.120)$$

Asper Fig. 13.25, the term $h_e - h_w$ represents the drawdown (s_w) in the well and $h_e + h_w$ is about to the twice of saturated thickness of aquifer (*i.e.* $2b$). Substituting these values in equation 13.120, we have

$$Q = \frac{\pi k\, s_w \cdot 2 \cdot b}{\log_e\left(\frac{r_e}{r_w}\right)}$$

$$= \frac{2\pi\, k \cdot b \cdot s_w}{\log_e\left(\frac{r_e}{r_w}\right)} \qquad ...(13.121)$$

or

$$\boxed{Q = \frac{2\pi T \cdot s_w}{\log_e\left(\frac{r_e}{r_w}\right)}} \qquad ...(13.122)$$

From equation 13.122 the draw-down in well is given by

$$\boxed{s_w = \frac{Q\left(\log_e \frac{r_e}{r_w}\right)}{2\pi T}} \qquad ...(13.123)$$

Example 13.12. *A fully penetrating well of 20 cm diameter is installed 25 m below the ground water-table and discharging the water at the rate of*

35 m^3/h. The draw-downs in the piezometers at 10 and 30 m radial distance from the well are recorded as 2.5 and 0.5 m, respectively at steady state condition. Calculate transmissivity (T) and hydraulic conductivity (k) of the unconfined aquifer.

Solution. Given that,

Diameter of well (d) = 20cm

$\therefore$ Radius (r_w) = 0.10 m

$$s_1 = 2.5 \text{ m at } r_1 = 10 \text{ m}$$

$$s_2 = 0.5 \text{ m at } r_2 = 30 \text{ m}$$

Well discharge (Q) = 35m^3/h

Aquifer thickness (b) = 25 m

Computation of T and k : Using the formula for unconfined aquifer, i.e.

$$Q = \frac{\pi k\,(h_2^2 - h_1^2)}{2.303 \log\left(\frac{r_2}{r_1}\right)}$$

in which,

$$h_1 = b - s_1 = 25 - 2.5 = 22.5 \text{ m}$$

$$h_2 = b - s_2 = 25 - 0.50 = 24.5 \text{ m}$$

$$\therefore \quad k = \frac{2.303 \times \log\left(\frac{30}{10}\right) \times 35}{\pi \times (24.5^2 - 22.5^2)} = \mathbf{0.13\ m/h} \quad \textbf{Ans.}$$

$\therefore$ And, $T = k \cdot b = 0.13 \times 25 = \mathbf{3.25\ m^2/h}$ **Ans.**

Example 13.13. *Determine hydraulic conductivity and transmissivity of the unconfined aquifer, which thickness is 20 m. For conducting pumping test, a well of 30 cm diameter is installed in the aquifer to its full thickness. The draw-down in well is 2.5 m and in the piezometer located at radial distance of 30 m is 0.50 m at steady-state condition. Assume, the discharge of well as 30 m^3/h.*

Solution. Given that,

Aquifer thickness (b) = 20 mQ = 30 m^3/h

$$s_w = 2.5 \text{ m} \qquad r_w = 0.15 \text{ m}$$

$$s_e = 0.5 \text{ m} \qquad r_e = 30 \text{ m}$$

Hydraulic conductivity (k) and transmissivity (T) of unconfined aquifer is given by the formula,

$$T = \frac{2.3\,Q \cdot \log_{10}\left(\frac{r_e}{r_w}\right)}{2\pi\, s_w}$$

$$= \frac{2.3 \times 30 \times \log_{10}\left(\frac{30}{0.15}\right)}{2\pi \times 2.5}$$

$$= \mathbf{50.54\ m^2/h} \quad \textbf{Ans.}$$

and, $$k = \frac{T}{b} = \frac{50.54}{20}$$

$$= \mathbf{2.5\ m/h} \quad \textbf{Ans.}$$

13.15. Steady Flow Toward Well in Semi-confined Aquifer

The ground water flow towards well in semi-confined aquifer is different to that of the confined or unconfined aquifers. In this aquifer, during pumping there is either recharge or leakage through the semi-pervious layer. The flow equation is derived by using the following differential equation :

$$\frac{\partial^2 h}{\partial x^2} + \frac{\partial^2 h}{\partial x^2} + \frac{W}{T} = \frac{S}{T} \cdot \frac{\partial h}{\partial t} \quad ...(13.124)$$

For steady flow condition the right hand side of above equation is taken as zero *i.e.*

$$\frac{\partial^2 h}{\partial x^2} + \frac{\partial^2 h}{\partial y^2} + \frac{W}{T} = 0 \quad ...(13.125)$$

Transforming the equation (13.125) in radial co-ordinates, we have

$$\frac{\partial^2 \phi}{\partial r^2} + \frac{1}{r}\frac{\partial \phi}{\partial r} + \frac{W}{T} = 0 \quad ...(13.126)$$

or $$\frac{1}{r} \cdot \frac{d}{dr}\left(r \cdot \frac{dh}{dr}\right) = -\frac{W}{T}$$

or $$\frac{d}{dr}\left(r \cdot \frac{dh}{dr}\right) = -\frac{W \cdot r}{T} \quad ...(13.127)$$

Integrating and symplying the equation (13.127), we have

$$r\frac{dh}{dr} = -\frac{W \cdot r^2}{2T} + C_1$$

or $$\frac{dh}{dr} = -\frac{W \cdot r}{2T} + \frac{C_1}{r} \quad ...(13.128)$$

Again integrating this equation, we have

$$h = -\frac{Wr^2}{4T} + C_1 \ln \cdot r + C_2 \quad ...(13.129)$$

Boundary conditions

(*i*) $h = h_o$ at $r = r_e$

(*ii*) $\frac{dh}{dt} = 0$ at $r = r_e$

According to boundary condition (ii), the eqn (13.128) is reduced to

$$o = -\frac{W \cdot r_e}{2T} + \frac{C_1}{r_e}$$

or $$C_1 = \frac{W \cdot r_e^2}{2T} \qquad ...(13.130)$$

Similarly, as per boundary condition (*i*) the equation 13.129 is reduced to

$$h_o = -\frac{W \cdot r_e^2}{4T} + C_1 \ln \cdot r_e + C_2 \qquad ...(13.131)$$

Substituting the value of C_1 in equation (13.131)

$$h_o = -\frac{W \cdot r_e^2}{T} + \frac{W \cdot r_e^2}{2T} \ln r_e + C_2$$

or $$C_2 = h_o + \frac{W \cdot r_e^2}{4T} - \frac{W \cdot r_e^2}{2T} \ln r_e \qquad ...(13.132)$$

Again substituting the values of C_1 and C_2 in equation 13.129

$$h = -\frac{W \cdot r^2}{4T} + \frac{W \cdot r_e^2}{2T} \ln \cdot r + h_o + \frac{W \cdot r_e^2}{4T} - \frac{W \cdot r_e^2}{2T} \ln r_e$$

or $$h - h_o = \frac{W}{4T}(r_e^2 - r^2) + \frac{W \cdot r_e^2}{2T}\left(\ln \frac{r}{r_e}\right) \qquad ...(13.133)$$

Assuming the draw-down in well as $r = r_w$

$$h - h_o = \frac{W}{4T}(r_e^2 - r_w^2) - \frac{W \cdot r_e^2}{2T}\left(\ln \frac{r_w}{r_e}\right) \qquad ...(13.134)$$

$$s_w = -\frac{W}{4T}(r_e^2 - r_w^2) - \frac{W \cdot r_e^2}{2T} \ln \cdot r_w + \frac{W \cdot r_e^2}{2T} \ln \cdot r_e$$

$$= -\frac{W}{4T}(r_e^2 - r_w^2) + \frac{W \cdot r_e^2}{2T} \ln \cdot r_e - \frac{W \cdot r_e^2}{2T} \ln \cdot r_w$$

$$= \frac{W \cdot r_e^2}{2T}\left(\ln \frac{r_e}{r_w}\right) - \frac{W}{4T}(r_e^2 - r_w^2)$$

$$= \left[\frac{W \cdot r_e^2}{2T}\left(\ln \frac{r_e}{r_w}\right) - \frac{W r_e^2}{4T}\right] + \frac{W \cdot r_w^2}{4T}$$

$$= \frac{W \cdot r_e^2}{2T}\left(\ln \frac{r_e}{r} - \frac{1}{2}\right) + \frac{W \cdot r_w^2}{4T} \qquad ...(13.135)$$

The term $\frac{W \cdot r_w^2}{4T}$ is very small, hence omitting from the equation (13.134), we have

$$s_w = \frac{W \cdot r_e^2}{2T}\left(\ln \frac{r_e}{r_w} - \frac{1}{2}\right) \quad ...(13.136)$$

At steady state condition the outflow and inflow are equal to each other, therefore,

$$Q = \pi\,(r_e^2 - r_w^2) \cdot W$$

or

$$W \cdot \pi \cdot r_e^2 - W \cdot \pi \cdot r_w^2 \quad ...(13.137)$$

The second term of equation 13.136 is very small, hence neglecting it from equation, we have

$$Q = W \cdot \pi \cdot r_e^2 \quad ...(13.138)$$

or

$$W = \frac{Q}{\pi \cdot r_e^2} \quad ...(13.139)$$

Substituting the value of W (recharge) in draw-down equation, we have

$$\boxed{s_w = \frac{Q}{2\pi T}\left(\ln \frac{r_e}{r_w} - \frac{1}{2}\right)} \quad ...(13.140)$$

The draw-down equation for semi-confined aquifer can also be derived in terms of Bessel's function of second kind by using the basic differential equation. The draw-down equation in terms of Bessel's function is given as under :

$$s_w = \frac{Q}{2\pi T} K_o\left(\frac{r}{\lambda}\right) \quad ...(13.141)$$

where, s_w = draw-down in the well
Q = discharge rate
K_o = modified Bessel's function of second kind
λ = leakage factor
r = radial distance

This equation is also known as DeGlee equation. The values of modified Bessel's function of second kind, i.e. $K_0(x)$ are given in Table 13.7.

Table 13.7. Values of $K_o(x)$ for use in DeGlee equation

N	$x = N \times 10^{0}$	$x = N \times 10^{-1}$	$x = N \times 10^{-2}$	N	$x = N \times 10^{0}$	$x = N \times 10^{-1}$	$x = N \times 10^{-2}$
1.0	0.4210	2.4271×10^{-1}	4.7212×10^{-2}	4.8	0.004597		
1.2	0.3185			5.0	0.003691	0.9244×10^{-1}	3.1142×10^{-2}
1.4	0.2437			5.2	0.002966		
1.6	0.1880			5.4	0.002385		
1.8	0.1459			5.6	0.001918		
2.0	0.1139	1.7527×10^{-1}	4.0285×10^{-2}	5.8	0.001544		
2.2	0.08927			6.0	0.001244	0.7775×10^{-1}	2.9329×10^{-2}
2.4	0.07022			6.2	0.001003		
2.6	0.05540			6.4	0.0008083		
2.8	0.04382			6.6	0.0006520		
3.0	0.03474	1.3725×10^{-1}	3.6235×10^{-2}	6.8	0.0005262		
3.2	0.02759			7.0	0.0004248	0.6605×10^{-1}	2.7798×10^{-2}
3.4	0.02196			7.2	0.0003431		
3.6	0.01750			7.4	0.0002772		
3.8	0.01397			7.6	0.0002240		
4.0	0.01116	1.1145×10^{-1}	3.3365×10^{-2}	7.8	0.0001811		
4.2	0.008927			8.0	0.0001465	0.5653×10^{-1}	2.6475×10^{-2}
4.6	0.005730			8.2	0.0001185		
				8.4	0.00009588		
				8.6	0.00007761		

Source : Ferris *et. al.* (1962).

Example 13.14. *Calculate the draw-down in a fully penetrating well installed in semi-confined aquifer of thickness 10 m, with hydraulic conductivity (k) 0.85 m/h. At steady-state condition the discharge of well was measured as 45 m^3/h. (Assume the value of* $K_o\left(\frac{r}{\lambda}\right)$ *as* 1).

Solution. Given that,

Aquifer thickness (b) = 10m

Hydraulic conductivity (k) = 0.85 m/h

Discharge of well (Q) = 45 m^3/h

$$K_o\left(\frac{r}{\lambda}\right) = 1$$

Formula of draw-down in the well for semi-confined aquifer is given by

$$s_w = \frac{Q}{2\pi T} K_o\left(\frac{r}{\lambda}\right)$$

$$= \frac{45 \times 1}{2\pi \times 0.85 \times 10}$$

$$= \mathbf{0.84\ m} \quad \textbf{Ans.}$$

13.16. Steady Flow Towards Partially Penetrating Well

Partially penetrating well is one, inwhich screen is not provided to the entire thickness of aquifer, but for a part of it. A partially penetrating well along with flow lines is shown in Fig. 13.26. In this type of well the flow lines are not in horizontal position, but they are in vertical position in the vicinity of well. For a given draw-down, a partially penetrated well has comparitively less discharge as compared to the fully penetrating well because of high head loss. From experimental evidence, it has been found that the vertical component of flow lines is more pronounced within the radial distance of $r < 2b$ or $2h_o$, where 'r' the is radius of well and 'b' is the aquifer thickness. Muskat (1937) reported that at the distance of twice of the aquifer thickness (b) the trend of water flow lines towards partially penetrating well becomes almost in radial form. While Jacob (1963) stated that in a non-isotropic formation the trend of flow line is radial at the distance of

$$r = 2 \cdot b \cdot \left(\frac{K_h}{K_v}\right)^{1/2} \quad ...(13.142)$$

where, r = distance at which the flow lines become in radial form.

b = aquifer thickness

K_h and K_v = horizontal and vertical hydraulic conductivities of the aquifer, respectively.

Kozeney (1933) derived the following relationship for computing the discharge of partially penetrating well in confined aquifer (Fig. 13.26) under steady state condition

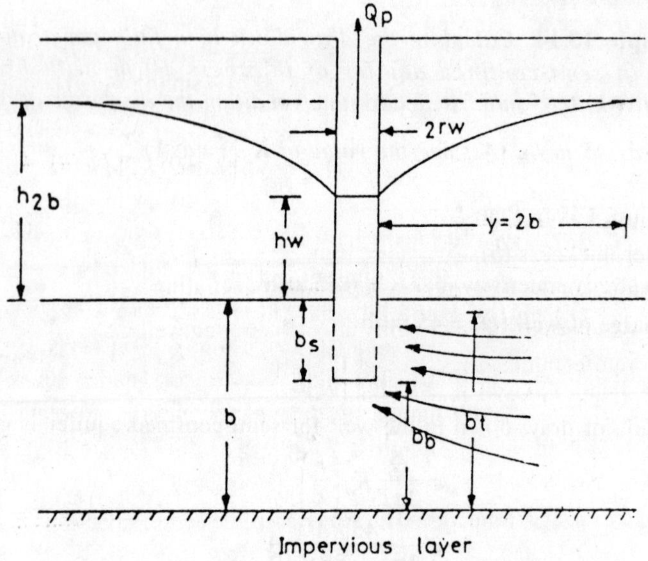

Fig. 13.26. Steady flow towards partially penetrating well.

$$Q = \frac{2\pi T \cdot s_w \cdot \alpha \left[1 + 7\left(\frac{r_w}{2\alpha \cdot b}\right)^{1/2} \cdot \cos\left(\frac{\pi\alpha}{2}\right)\right]}{\log_e\left(\frac{r_e}{r_w}\right)} \quad ...(13.143)$$

or
$$Q = Q_o \cdot \alpha \left[1 + 7\left(\frac{r_w}{2\alpha \cdot b}\right)^{1/2} \cdot \cos\left(\frac{\pi\alpha}{2}\right)\right] \quad ...(13.144)$$

where, Q = discharge rate of partially penetrating well

Q_o = discharge rate of fully penetrating well

T = transmissivity of aquifer

s_w = draw–down in fully penetrating well

r_e = distance between pumped well and locus of zero draw–down

r_w = radius of fully penetrating well

α = part of aquifer thickness, upto which the well is tapped.

b = aquifer thickness

Huisman (Anonymous, 1964) also developed the relationship for determining steady state draw-down in partially penetrating well, by making corrections in the steady state draw-down in the piezometer located at the radial distance of $r < 2b$ from partially penetrating well. The relationship is given by,

$$s_p = s + \frac{Q}{2\pi T} \cdot \frac{2b}{\pi \cdot b_s} \sum_{n=1}^{\infty} \frac{1}{n} \left[\sin(n\pi\, b_t/b) - \sin(n\pi\, b_b/b) \right]$$

$$\cdot \cos(n\pi\, bp/n) \cdot k_o \left(\frac{n\pi r}{b} \right)$$

or $$s_p - s = \frac{Q}{2\pi T} \cdot \frac{2 \cdot b}{\pi b_s} \cdot C \qquad \text{...(13.145)}$$

where, s_p = steady state draw–down in partially penetrating well

s = steady state draw–down in fully penetrating well

b = aquifer thickness

b_t = distance between the top of well screen and impervious layer (Fig. 13.26)

b_s = length of well screen

b_b = distance between the bottom of well screen and impervious layer

b_p = distance between the middle of screen and impervious layer

13.17. Unsteady Flow Towards Well in Confined Aquifer

The unsteady-state flow equation for confined aquifer is derived here with by using the basic differential equation in polar co-ordinate, given as under :

$$\frac{\partial^2 s}{\partial r^2} + \frac{1}{r}\frac{\partial s}{\partial r} = \frac{S}{T}\frac{\partial s}{\partial t} \qquad \text{...(13.146)}$$

Boundary conditions :

$$\left.\begin{array}{l} (1)\ s(r, o) = 0 \\ (2)\ s(\infty, t) = 0 \\ (3)\ \text{limit} \rightarrow \cdot\, r\dfrac{\partial s}{\partial r} = \dfrac{Q}{2\pi T} \end{array}\right\} \qquad \text{...(13.147)}$$

There have been developed several solutions for determining the well discharge and properties of aquifer for the equation 13.146 and boundary conditions *i.e.* eqn 13.147. The most common solutions amongst them are described, below :

Theis Equation : This equation is named after Theis (1935), which is given as :

$$s = \frac{Q}{4\pi T} \int_u^{\infty} \frac{e^{-u}}{u} \cdot du \qquad \text{...(13.148)}$$

where, s = draw–down, m

Q = discharge of well, m^3/day

T = transmissivity of aquifer, m^2/day

Table. 13.8. Theis well function W(u) corresponding to u and $\frac{1}{u}$

N	n	$\frac{1}{u} = n$	n(1)	n(2)	n(3)	n(4)	n(5)	n(6)	n(7)	n(8)	n(9)	n(10)
		4 = N	N (–1)	N (–2)	N (–3)	N (–4)	N (–5)	N (–6)	N (–7)	N (–8)	N (–9)	N (–10)
1.0	1.000	2.194 (-1)	1.823	4.038	6.332	8.633	1.094 (1)	1.324 (1)	1.554 (1)	1.784 (1)	2.015 (1)	2.245 (1)
1.2	0.833	1.584 (-1)	1.660	3.858	6.149	8.451	1.075(1)	1.306 (1)	1.536 (1)	1.766 (1)	1.996 (1)	2.227 (1)
1.5	0.666	1.000 (-1)	1.465	3.637	5.927	8.228	1.053 (1)	1.283 (1)	1.514 (1)	1.744 (1)	1.974 (1)	2.204 (1)
2.0	0.500	4.890 (-2)	1.223	3.355	5.639	7.940	1.024 (1)	1.255 (1)	1.485 (1)	1.715 (1)	1.945 (1)	2.176 (1)
2.5	0.400	2.491 (-2)	1.044	3.137	5.417	7.717	1.002 (1)	1.232 (1)	1.462 (1)	1.693 (1)	1.923 (1)	2.153 (1)
3.0	0.333	1.305 (-2)	9.057 (-1)	2.959	5.235	7.535	9.837	1.214 (1)	1.444 (1)	1.674 (1)	1.905 (1)	2.135 (1)
3.5	0.286	6.970 (-3)	7.942 (-1)	2.810	5.081	7.381	9.683	1.199 (1)	1.429 (1)	1.659 (1)	1.889 (1)	2.120 (1)
4.0	0.250	3.779 (-3)	7.942 (-1)	2.691	4.948	7.247	9.550	1.185 (1)	1.415 (1)	1.646 (1)	1.876 (1)	2.106 (1)
4.5	0.222	2.073 (-3)	7.024 (-1)	2.568	4.831	7.130	9.432	1.173 (1)	1.404 (1)	1.634 (1)	1.864 (1)	2.094 (1)
5.0	0.200	1.148 (-3)	5.598 (-1)	2.468	4.726	7.024	9.326	1.163 (1)	1.393 (1)	1.623 (1)	1.854 (1)	2.084 (1)
6.0	0.166	3.601 (-4)	4.544 (-1)	2.295	4.545	6.842	9.144	1.145 (1)	1.375 (1)	1.605 (1)	1.835 (1)	2.066 (1)
7.0	0.142	1.155 (-4)	3.738 (-1)	2.151	4.392	6.688	8.990	1.129 (1)	1.360 (1)	1.590 (1)	1.820 (1)	2.050 (1)
8.0	0.125	2.767 (-5)	3.106 (-1)	2.027	4.259	6.555	8.856	1.116 (1)	1.346 (1)	1.576 (1)	1.807 (1)	2.037 (1)
9.0	0.111	1.245 (-5)	2.602 (-1)	1.919	4.142	6.437	8.739	1.104 (1)	1.334 (1)	1.565 (1)	1.795 (1)	2.025 (1)

Source : Walton (1962).

$$u = \frac{r^2 \cdot S}{4t \cdot T} \quad ...(13.149)$$

r = radial distance between discharge well and piezometer, m.

S = storage coefficient, dimenson less

t = time since pumping was started, days

The solution of equation 13.148 is expressed in terms of $W(u)$, which is called well function. The solution is given by,

$$s = \frac{Q}{4\pi T} W(u) \quad ...(13.150)$$

in which,
$$W(u) = -0.5772 - \ln u + u - \frac{u^2}{2.2\,!} + \frac{u^3}{3.3\,!} - \frac{u^4}{4.4\,!} + ... \quad (13.151)$$

The values of well function W(u) are given in Table 13.8.

Assumption : Theis equation considered the following assumptions :

1. Ground water flow is analogous to the heat flow.
2. The aquifer is homogeneous, isotropic and of infinite aerial extent.
3. During pumping the well receives water from entire thickness of aquifer.
4. Well is fully penetrating.
5. Well diameter is infinitesimal.
6. Transmissivity of aquifer remains constant with time and location.
7. Aquifer is confined and in horizontal position.

Example 13.15. *A fully penetrating well is installed in confined aquifer. Thickness of aquifer is 25 m and discharge rate of well is 45 m^3/h. Calculate draw-down in the well by using Theis method. Take the value of well function W(u) as 1 and 'k' of aquifer as 0.65 m/h.*

Solution. Given that,

Aquifer thickness (b) = 25 m

Discharge rate of well (Q) = 45m^3/h

$W(u) = 1$

$k = 0.65$ m/h

Draw-down in the well at unsteady-state condition is given by the formula as

$$s_w = \frac{Q}{4\pi T} W(u)$$

$$= \frac{45}{4 \times \pi \times 0.65 \times 25}$$

$$= \mathbf{0.22\ m}$$ **Ans.**

Jacob Equation : Jacob (1946) developed the solution by making a little modification in Theis equation. He considered the first two terms of series of W(u) when value of u is less than 0.01. Thus, the equation 13.150 can be written as,

$$s = \frac{Q}{4\pi T}[-.0.5772 - \ln u] \quad ...(1.152)$$

$$= \frac{Q}{4\pi T}\left[\ln\frac{1}{u} - \ln 1.78\right]$$

$$= \frac{Q}{4\pi T}\ln\frac{2.25t \cdot T}{r^2 \cdot S}$$

or

$$s = \frac{2.303\,Q}{4\pi T}\log_{10}\frac{2.25\,t \cdot T}{r^2 \cdot S} \quad ...(13.153)$$

This equation is called Jacob equation. It can be used for computing the draw-down (s), transmissivity (T) and storage coefficient (S) of confined aquifer by conducting pumping test.

Chow Equation : Chow (1952) derived this equation for determining the aquifer's properties on the basis of Theis non equilibrium equation. He introduced a different type of function *i.e* $F(u)$, which is the function of 'u'. The values of $W(u)$ and 'u' corresponding to known draw-down (s) at any specified time (t) can be obtained against $F(u)$. The nomograph showing the

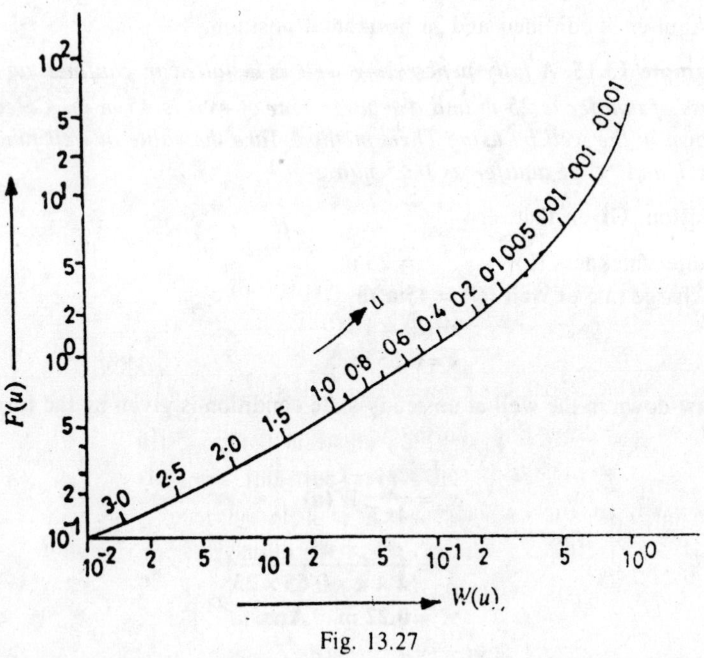

Fig. 13.27

relationship amongst $F(u)$, u and $W(u)$ is shown in Fig. 13.27. The values of $F(u)$, $W(u)$ and u are also given in Table 13.9.

The function $F(u)$ is given as under :

$$F(u) = \frac{W(u)}{2.30} e^u \quad \text{...(13.154)}$$

When u is very small then e^u approaches 1, and thus eqn (13.154) is reduced to

$$F(u) = \frac{W(u)}{2.30} \quad \text{...(13.155)}$$

Chow method is more advantageous to the Jacob's method, because it does not involve curve fitting for evaluation of aquifer's properties and can also be applied when value of 'u' is greater than 0.01. In addition, this method can also be used for analysing the short-term draw-down data.

Theis Recovery Method : Theis (1935) defined the 'residual draw-down' (s') as the difference of draw-down made during pumping at any elapsed time and recovery made at the same time, when pumping is stopped. In other words the fall of water level (draw-down) below the original static water level (before pumping) during recovery period is known as residual-draw-down. The time-draw down and time-residual draw-down curves are shown in Fig. 13.28.

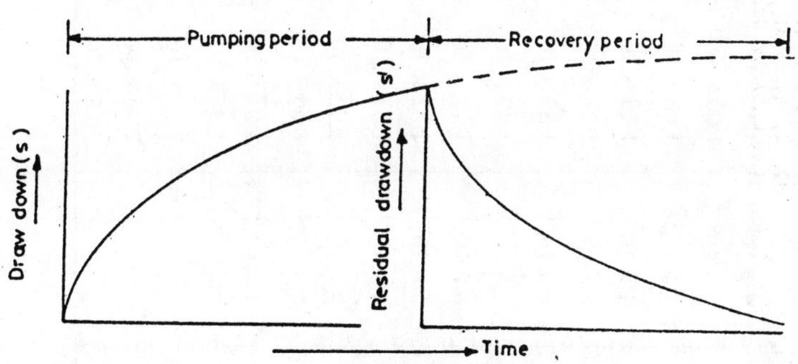

Fig. 13.28. Time drawdown/residual drawdown curve.

Let, s_p = draw–down during pumping period

s_r = recharge during recovery period

According to Theis equation,

$$s_p = \frac{Q}{4\pi T} \int_u^{\infty} \frac{e^{-u}}{u} \cdot du \quad \text{...(13.156)}$$

and

$$s_r = \frac{Q}{4\pi T} \int_{u'}^{\infty} \frac{e^{-u}}{u} \cdot du \quad \text{...(13.157)}$$

Table 13.9. Values of $F(u)$, $W(u)$ and u for use in Chow method

$F(u)$	$W(u)$	u	$F(u)$	$W(u)$	u	$F(u)$	$W(u)$	u
7.34×10^{-2}	1.14×10^{-3}	5×10^{0}	9.13×10^{-1}	1.92	9×10^{-2}		6.44	9×10^{-4}
8.98×10^{-2}	3.78×10^{-3}	4×10^{0}	9.56 × 10–1	2.03	8×10^{-2}		6.55	8×10^{-4}
1.17×10^{-1}	1.30×10^{-2}	3×10^{0}	1.00 × 100	2.15	7×10^{-2}		6.69	7×10^{-4}
1.57×10^{-1}	4.89×10^{-2}	2×10^{0}	1.06×10^{0}	2.30	6×10^{-2}	$F(u) = \frac{W(u)}{2.30}$	6.84	6×10^{-4}
2.59×10^{-1}	2.19×10^{-1}	1×10^{0}	1.13×10^{0}	2.47	5×10^{-2}		7.02	5×10^{-4}
2.76×10^{-1}	2.60×10^{-1}	9×10^{-1}	1.21×10^{0}	2.68	4×10^{-2}		7.25	4×10^{-4}
3.01×10^{-1}	3.11×10^{-1}	8×10^{-1}	1.33×10^{0}	2.96	3×10^{-2}		7.53	3×10^{-4}
3.27×10^{-1}	3.74×10^{-1}	7×10^{-1}	1.49×10^{0}	3.55	2×10^{-2}		7.94	2×10^{-4}
3.60×10^{-1}	4.54×10^{-1}	6×10^{-1}	1.77×10^{0}	4.04	1×10^{-2}		8.63	1×10^{-4}
4.01×10^{-1}	5.60×10^{-1}	5×10^{-1}	1.82×10^{0}	4.14	9×10^{-3}		8.74	9×10^{-5}
4.55×10^{-1}	7.02×10^{-1}	4×10^{-1}	1.87×10^{0}	4.26	8×10^{-3}		8.86	8×10^{-5}
5.32×10^{-1}	9.06×10^{-1}	3×10^{-1}	1.92×10^{0}	4.39	7×10^{-3}		8.99	7×10^{-5}
6.47×10^{-1}	1.22×10^{-0}	2×10^{-1}	1.99×10^{0}	4.54	6×10^{-3}		9.14	6×10^{-5}
8.74×10^{-1}	1.80×10^{-0}	1×10^{-1}	2.07×10^{0}	4.73	5×10^{-3}		9.33	5×10^{-5}
			2.16×10^{0}	4.95	4×10^{-3}			
			2.28×10^{0}	5.23	3×10^{-3}			
			2.46×10^{0}	5.64	2×10^{-3}			
			2.75×10^{0}	6.33	1×10^{-3}			

Source : Chow (1952).

where, $$u' = \frac{r^2 S'}{4t \cdot T} \qquad ...(13.158)$$

$\therefore$ Residual draw-down $(s') = s_p - s_r$

$$= \frac{Q}{4\pi T}\left[\int_u^{\infty} \frac{e^{-u}}{u}\, du - \int_{u'}^{\infty} \frac{e^{-u}}{u} \cdot du\right] \qquad ...(13.159)$$

After simplyfying the equation 13.159, we have

$$s' = \frac{Q}{4\pi T}\left[\ln\left(\frac{4t \cdot T}{r^2 S}\right) - \ln\left(\frac{4t'T}{r^2 S'}\right)\right] \qquad ...(13.160)$$

Considering s and s' as constant and equal to each other; and 'u' as very small, the equation 13.160 can be written as,

$$s' = \frac{2.303\, Q}{4\pi\, T} \log_{10} \frac{t}{t'} \qquad ...(13.161)$$

where, Q = constant discharge/recharge rate (m^3/day)
T = transmissivity of aquifer
t = time, since pumping was started (days)
t' = time, since pumping was stopped (days)

This equation can also be used for computing the properties of aquifer such as transmissivity etc. in addition to draw-down (residual).

13.18. Unsteady Flow Towards Well in Unconfined Aquifer

Boulton's Equation : Boulton (1954) derived the flow equation for computing draw-down in unconfined aquifer under unsteady-state condition by considering the following assumptions :

1. Delayed yield is significant.
2. Dewatering is negligible.
3. Vertical flow is inconsequential.

The discharge draw-down equation is given by,

$$s = \frac{Q}{4\pi T} W\left(U_{AY}, \frac{r}{B}\right) \qquad ...(13.162)$$

where, $W\left(U_{AY}, \frac{r}{B}\right)$ = Boulton's well function, given in Appendix – 9

$$U_A = \frac{r^2 S_A}{4tT}$$

$$U_y = \frac{r^2 S_y}{4t \cdot T}$$

r = radial distance of observation well from pumped well
B = drainage factor

$$= \sqrt{\frac{T}{\alpha \cdot S_y}} \qquad ...(13.163)$$

$\frac{1}{\alpha}$ = Boulton's delay index (days)

t = time, since pumping was started

S_A = storage coefficient (effective early time) corresponding to that volume of water, which is instantaneously released from the storage per unit draw–down, per unit area.

Example 13.16. *Calculate the draw-down made in fully penetrating well installed in unconfined aquifer. The other details are as follows :*

1. Discharge of well (Q) = 45 m^3/h

2. Hydraulic conductivity of aquifer (k) = 0.45 m^3/h

3. Aquifer thickness = 15 m

4. Boulton's well function $W\left(U_{AY}, \frac{r}{B}\right) = 1$

Solution. Given that $Q = 45\ m^3/h$

$k = 0.45$ m/h

$b = 15$ m

The draw-down in well is given by

$$s_w = \frac{Q}{4\pi T} W\left(U_{AY}, \frac{r}{B}\right)$$

$$= \frac{45 \times 1}{4 \times \pi \times 0.45 \times 15}$$

$$= \mathbf{0.53\ m} \quad \textbf{Ans.}$$

13.19. Unsteady Flow Towards Well in Leaky Confined Aquifer

Hantush Jacob Equation : Hantush and Jacob (1955) derived the ground water flow equation under unsteady-state condition for computing draw-down in the well installed in leaky confined aquifer. The equation is given below

$$s = \frac{Q}{4\pi T} W\left(u, \frac{r}{\lambda}\right) \quad \text{...(13.164)}$$

where, s = drawdown, m

Q = discharge rate, m^3/day

$W\left(u, \frac{r}{\lambda}\right)$ = well function for leaky confined aquifer, which is taken from table for the given values of u and $\frac{r}{\lambda}$. The values of $W\left(u, \frac{r}{\lambda}\right)$ are appended in Table 13.10 compiled by Hantush (1956).

$$u = \frac{r^2 S}{4t \cdot T}$$

and λ = leakage factor

$$= \sqrt{T \cdot C}$$

Assumptions : The Hantush and Jacob (1955) equation was derived on the basis of following assumptions :

1. Flow is unsteady.
2. Aquifer is homogeneous, isotropic and of infinite aerial extent.
3. Well is fully penetrated.
4. Water enters the well from entire thickness of aquifer and is recharged through leaky layer.

Example 13.17. *Compute discharge of fully penetrating well installed in leaky- confined aquifer under unsteady-state condition, if*

(i) Draw-down in the well is 1.6 m

(ii) Transmissivity of aquifer is 434 m^2/day

(iii) Well function, $W\left(u, \frac{r}{\lambda}\right)$ *is 10.*

Solution. Given that,

$$s_w = 1.6 \text{ m}$$
$$T = 434 \text{ m}^2/\text{day}$$
$$= 18.08 \text{ m}^2/\text{h}$$
$$W\left(u, \frac{r}{\lambda}\right) = 10$$

Discharge of well is computed by using the following formula :

$$s_w = \frac{Q}{4\pi T} W\left(u, \frac{r}{\lambda}\right)$$
$$1.6 = \frac{Q \times 10}{4 \times \pi \times 18.08}$$

Solving for Q, we have

$$10\,Q = 4\pi \times 18.08 \times 1.6$$

$\therefore$ $\mathbf{Q = 36.35\ m^3/h}$ **Ans.**

13.20. Flow Towards an Open Well

Ground water flow towards open well is quite different to that of the tubewell or small diameter well described, sofar. The flow equation for open well is derived as under :

Let,

1. Open well is constructed in unconfined aquifer.
2. 'h' is the head difference between water level in the well and the water table.

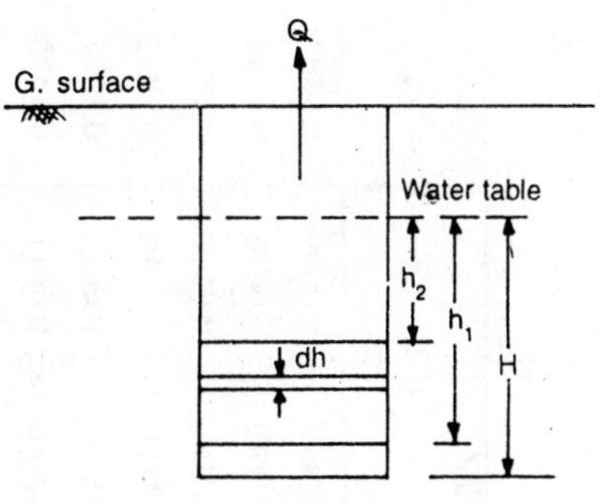

Fig. 13.29. Flow towards open well.

Table 13.10. Values of $W\left(u, \frac{r}{\lambda}\right)$

u / $\frac{r}{\lambda}$	5.0	1.0	0.5	0.1	0.105	0.101	0.005	0.001	0.005	0.0001
2.500	0.0009	0.0803	0.1174							
2.000	0.0010	0.1139	0.1944	0.2278						
1.500	0.0010	0.1509	0.3007	0.4271						
1.000	0.0010	0.1855	0.4210	0.8190	0.8409					
0.900	0.0011	0.1914	0.4440	0.9270	0.9700					
0.800	0.0011	0.1970	0.4658	1.0505	1.1210	1.1307				
0.700	0.0011	0.2020	0.4860	1.1791	1.2955	1.3210				
0.600	0.0011	0.2065	0.5044	1.3115	1.2955	1.5550				
0.500	0.0011	0.2103	0.5206	1.4422	1.4927	1.8486				
0.400	0.0011	0.2135	0.5344	1.5644	1.7075	2.2253	2.2290			
0.300	0.0011	0.2161	0.5453	1.6704	1.9283	2.7104	2.7428			
0.200	0.0011	0.2179	0.5532	1.7527	2.3110	3.2875	3.4567	3.5054		
0.150	0.0011	0.2186	0.5561	1.7829	2.3776	3.5725	3.8821	4.0595		
0.100	0.0011	0.2190	0.5581	1.8050	2.4271	3.8150	4.2960	4.8292	4.8530	
0.075	0.0011	0.2191	0.5588	1.8128	2.4448	3.9091	4.4713	5.3078	5.4062	5.4228
0.050	0.0011	0.2193	0.5594	1.8184	2.4576	3.9785	4.6084	5.7965	6.0821	6.2282

Source : Hantush (1956).

3. 'A' is the cross-sectional area of well.
4. 'Q' is the discharge rate of well.
5. $\frac{K}{A}$ is the specific yield of well.

Ground water flow in open well is essentially due to elevation difference between water-level in the well and position of water-table in the sourrounding formation, called depression head. The head at which water entry in the well dislodges the soil particles from the well wall is called critical depression head; and entrance velocity is termed as critical velocity. The well yield under unit depression head is referred as specific yield of well.

Referring Fig. 13.29 the volume of water entering the well, when water level is recuperated by small head, say 'dh' is given by

$$dv = A \cdot dh \quad ...(13.165)$$

or

$$dv = Q \cdot dt \quad ...(13.166)$$

in which, 'Q' is the discharge rate of well at any time 't' under unit depression head 'h'.

We also know, that $Q = K \cdot h$ ...(13.167)

Thus, the equation 13.166 is given by

$$dv = K \cdot h \cdot dt \quad ...(13.168)$$

Equating equations 13.167 and 13.168, we have

$$K \cdot h \cdot dt = -A \cdot dh \quad ...(13.169)$$

(Negative sign indicates that as the time increases the head 'h' decreases)

Rearranging the equation 13.169 in following form :

$$\frac{K}{A} dt = -\frac{dh}{h} \quad ...(13.170)$$

Integrating equation 13.170 with the limits 0 to T for t and h_1 to h_2 for h, i.e,

$$\int_o^T \frac{K}{A} \cdot dt = -\int_{h_1}^{h_2} \frac{dh}{h}$$

or

$$\frac{K}{A} [t]_o^T = -[ln\ h]_{h_1}^{h_2}$$

or

$$\frac{K}{A} = \frac{1}{T}\left[\ln \frac{h_1}{h_2}\right] \quad ...(13.171)$$

The term $\frac{K}{A}$ is known as "specific yield" of well expressed as m^3/h. The values of $\frac{K}{A}$ for different types of soil are listed in Table 13.11. If $\frac{K}{A}$ for a given soil is known, then discharge 'Q' of open well under depression head of 'H' can be computed as

$$Q = K \cdot H$$

or $$Q = \frac{K}{A} \cdot A \cdot H$$

or $$\frac{1}{T}\left[\ln \frac{h_1}{h_2}\right] AH$$

or $$\frac{2.303}{T} \log_{10}\left(\frac{h_1}{h_2}\right) A \cdot H \quad \text{...(13.172)}$$

In this equation, if h_1, h_2 and H are expressed in m and A in sq m., then discharge 'Q' is obtained in the unit of m^3/h.

Table 13.11. Values of $\frac{K}{A}$ for different types of soil.

Soil type	$\frac{K}{A}$ *(m^3/h)*
Clay	0.25
Fine sand	1.00
Coarse sand	0.50

Source : Bennison (1947).

13.21. Multiple Well Point System

Closely spaced wells installed for lowering the water-table or reclaiming the water-logging problem or to facilitate excavation work in case of foundation works or for some other requirements is called multiple well point system. De Ridder (1979) reported the use of multiple well point system for control of water-table and salinity problems in Indus plain of Pakistan. Suresh et.al (1991) used the same for drainage of water-logged lands of about 1000 hectares in Punjab (India). Doering *etal* (1972) suggested the use of multiple well point system for reducing artesian pressure, which is responsible for salinity development in overlying soil.

In an area with cluster of wells, the resultant draw-down at any point can be determined by using the principle of super position, described as under :

13.22. Super Position Principle

It states that for a given well system the resultant draw-down at any point in the area of influence caused by the discharge of several wells is equal to the sum of the draw-down made in the individual well. Thus, if in an area there are 'n' wells; and after pumping the well for a certain duration, the draw-downs in n wells are recorded as $s_1, s_2, s_3 \ldots s_n$, respectively. Then according to principle of superposition, the resultant draw-down (s_r) at any point is given by :

$$s_r = s_1 + s_2 + s_3 \ldots s_n$$

$$= \sum_{i=1}^{n} s_i \qquad \ldots(13.173)$$

Forchheimer (1908) developed the equation for computing draw-down in confined and unfonfined aquifers at any point (x, y) in the array of number of equally speced fully penetrating wells discharging equal amount and parallel to the line source, as shown in Fig. 13.30. The equation is given as under :

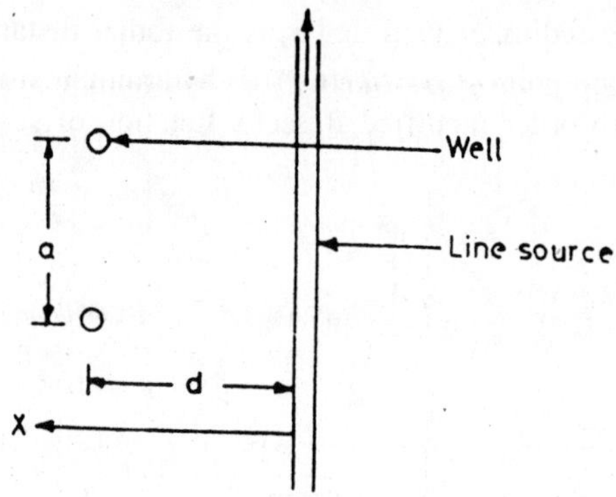

Fig. 13.30. Wells parallel to line source.

(*i*) *For confined aquifer*

$$s = H - h = \frac{Q}{2\pi k \cdot b} \log_e \frac{\cosh \frac{2\pi}{a}(x+d) - \cos \frac{2\pi y}{a}}{\cos h \frac{2\pi}{a}(x-d) - \cos \frac{2\pi y}{a}} \qquad \ldots(13.174)$$

(*ii*) *For unconfined aquifer*

$$H^2 - h^2 = \frac{Q}{\pi \cdot k} \cdot \log_e \frac{\cosh \frac{2\pi}{\alpha}(x+d) - \cos \frac{2\pi y}{a}}{\cos h \frac{2\pi}{a}(x-d) - \cos \frac{2\pi y}{a}} \qquad \ldots(13.175)$$

where, Q = discharge of well

k = hydraulic conductivity of the aquifer

b = thickness of the aquifer

a = spacing of well, arranged in a line

d = distance between the pumping point and line source

x and y = ordinate of the pumping point

Huisman (1972) developed an equation for computing resultant draw lown (s_p) at point p (x, y) as shown in Fig. 13.31 for a group of wells installed n leaky artesian aquifer of depth 'H', hydraulic conductivity 'k' and characteristics length ϕ, which are pumped with the discharge rate of 'Q'$_o$. The draw-down equation is given by

$$S_p = \frac{Q_o}{2\pi KH} K_o\left(\frac{r_o}{\phi}\right) + \frac{Q_o}{2\pi\, KH} K_O\left(\frac{x_1}{\phi}\right) + \frac{Q_o}{2\pi KH} K_o\left(\frac{x_2}{\phi}\right) + \ldots$$

$$\frac{Q_o}{2\pi KH} K_o\left(\frac{x_i}{\phi}\right) \qquad \ldots(13.176)$$

or
$$S_p = \frac{Q}{2\pi\, KH}\left\{\ln\left(\frac{1.123\,\phi}{r_o}\right) + \sum_{i=1}^{\infty} K\left(\frac{x_i}{\phi}\right)\right\} \qquad \ldots(13.177)$$

in which, r_o is the radius of well and x_i is the radial distance of well points from the observation point p, $\phi = \sqrt{kHC}$, C is hydraulic resistance of overlying layer, $K_o(\cdot)$ is zero order modified Bessel's function of second kind.

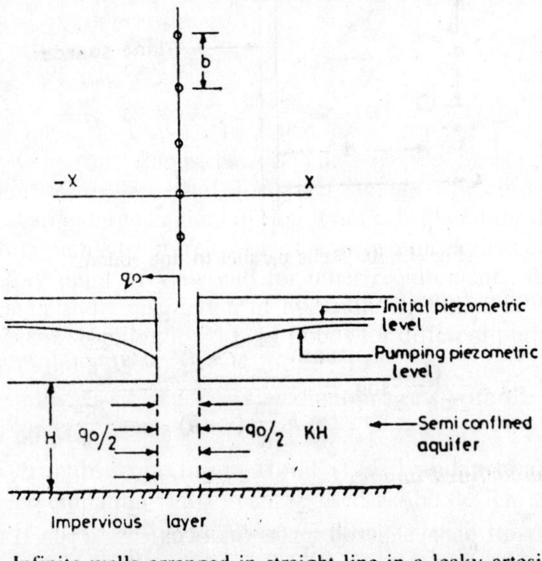

Fig. 13.31. Infinite wells arranged in straight line in a leaky artesian aquifer.

If infinite wells are installed at the distance 'b' in straight line (Fig. 13.31), then draw-down at point $p(x, y)$ considering the origin as center of the well point, can be written as :

$$S_p = \frac{Q_o}{2\pi KH} \sum_{n=-\infty}^{\infty} K_o\left(\frac{\sqrt{x^2 + (y - nb)^2}}{\phi}\right) \qquad \ldots(13.178)$$

where, n is the number of well points and x, y are the random points within infinite extent.

If $b \geq \phi$, then equation 13.176 converges rapidly and few terms are sufficient to derive the exact solution. However for this case, the computation of draw-down '*s*' by using equation 13.176 involves combersom calculation. For $b < 0.5$ to 0.75ϕ, the following formula (Huisman, 1972) can be used for computing the accurate value of draw-down :

$$S_p = \frac{Q_o}{2\pi KH}\left\{\left(\frac{\pi\phi}{b}\right)^{-\frac{x}{\phi}} - \frac{1}{2}\ln\left(1 - 2e^{\frac{-2\pi x}{b}} \cdot \cos\frac{2\pi y}{b} + e^{\frac{-4\pi x}{b}}\right)\right\} \quad ...(13.179)$$

This formula can be simplified for following cases :

Case 1 : Draw-down at longer distance from the line of well. In this case the factors $e^{\frac{-2\pi x}{b}}$ and $e^{-\frac{4\pi x}{b}}$ are rapidly approaching to zero; and accordingly the equation 13.179 is reduced to

$$S = \frac{Q_o}{2\pi KH} \cdot \frac{\pi\phi}{b} \cdot e^{-\frac{x}{\phi}}$$

or

$$\frac{1}{2}\frac{Q_o}{b} \cdot \frac{\phi}{K \cdot H} \cdot e^{-\frac{x}{\phi}} \quad ...(13.180)$$

For the equivalent gallery having same unit capacity, the discharge is given by

$$q_o = \frac{Q_o}{b} \quad ...(13.181)$$

or

$$S = \frac{q_o}{2}\frac{\phi}{kH}e^{-\frac{x}{\phi}} \quad ...(13.182)$$

Looking the equation 13.182, it can be said that the draw-down at greater distance from the line of well, is equal to that draw-down which is likely to made in the equivalent gallery.

Case 2 : Draw-down at the face of each well, *i.e.* $x = 0$ and $y = r_o + nb$; at this condition the equation 13.176 is reduced to

$$S_o = \frac{Q_o}{2b} \cdot \frac{\phi}{K \cdot H} + \frac{Q_o}{2\pi kH} \cdot \ln\frac{b}{2\pi r_o}$$

or

$$S_o = S_o' + \frac{Q_o}{2\pi kH}\ln\frac{b}{2\pi r_o} \quad ...(13.183)$$

in which, S_o' is the draw-down at the face of equivalent fully penetrating gallery and $\left(\frac{Q_o}{2\pi kH}\ln\frac{b}{2\pi r_o}\right)$ is the additional draw-down due to point abstraction (S_{pa})

Thus, $$S_o = S_o' + S_{pa} \quad ...(13.184)$$

Case 3 : Draw-down at the half way between two wells, *i.e.* at $x = 0$ and $y = \frac{b}{2} + nb$ is given as :

$$S_{b/2} = \frac{Q_o}{2b} \cdot \frac{\phi}{K \cdot H} - \frac{Q_o}{2\pi kH}(0.693)$$

or
$$S_{b/2} = S_o' - \frac{Q_o}{2\pi KH}(0.693) \qquad ...(13.185)$$

According to the cases (2) and (3), it is evident that the draw-downs made at the well face and at the distance half way between the wells are lesser than the draw-down at the face of equivalent gallery. However, some where in the line of wells ($x = 0$) the draw-down at distance 'w' from each well must be equal to the draw-down at the face of equivalent gallery.

Thus,
$$\frac{Q_o}{2b} \cdot \frac{\phi}{K \cdot H} = \frac{Q_o}{2\pi kH}\left\{\frac{\pi\phi}{b} - \frac{1}{2}\ln\left(2 - 2\cos\frac{2\pi w}{b}\right)\right\}$$

which yields,
$$\cos\frac{2\pi w}{b} = \frac{1}{2}$$

$$\frac{2\pi w}{b} = \frac{\pi}{2}$$

or
$$w = \frac{b}{6}$$

Thus,
$$S_{b/6} = S_o' \qquad ...(13.186)$$

It states that the draw-down at the line of well points speced at the distance 'b'; and at the face of equivalent gallery would be the same to the draw-down made at the distance of $b/6$.

Muskat (1973) also derived the relationships for computing well discharge under different arrangements of well, near the centre of well field of radius R (equal to the radius of influence of each well). These relationships are given as under :

Case 1 : When two wells are spaced at the distance ($a << R$) as shown in Fig. 13.32 and discharge of two wells is Q_1 and Q_2 in confined and unconfined aquifers, respectively, then discharge equations for them can be written as,

$$Q_1 = Q_2 = \frac{2\pi k \cdot b}{\log_e \frac{R^2}{r_w \cdot a}} = \frac{\pi k}{\log_e \frac{R^2}{r_w \cdot a}} \qquad ...(13.187)$$

Case 2 : When three wells are installed in such a way that they form an equilateral triangle with side 'a' ($a << R$) as shown in Fig. 13.33. Then discharge equation for the wells is given by

$$Q_1 = Q_2 = Q_3 = \frac{2\pi kb\,(H - h_w)}{\log_e \frac{R^3}{r_w \cdot a^2}} = \frac{\pi k\,(H^2 - h_w^2)}{\log_e \frac{R^3}{r_w \cdot a^2}} \qquad ...(13.188)$$

Boundery of well field ($a << R$)

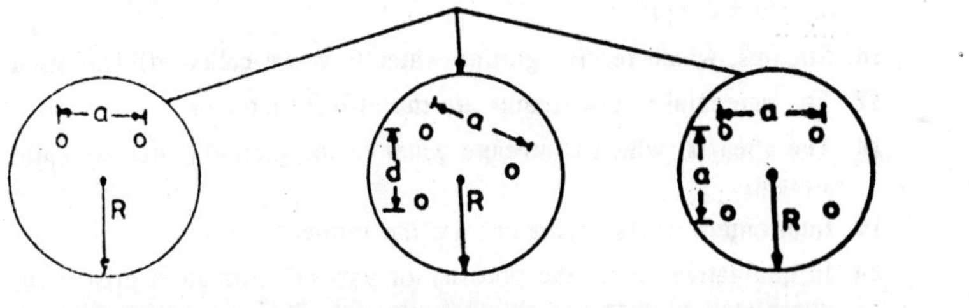

Fig. 1'3.32 Fig. 13.33 Fig. 13.34

Case 3 : When four wells are installed in such a way that they form square with the side 'a' ($a << R$) as shown in Fig. 13.34. Then discharge equation for this case is given as

$$Q_1 = Q_2 = Q_3 = Q_4 = \frac{2\pi k \cdot b\,(H - h_w)}{\log_e \sqrt{2r_w \cdot a^3}} = \frac{\pi k\,(H^2 - hw^2)}{\log_e \dfrac{R^4}{\sqrt{2r_w \cdot a^3}}} \qquad \text{...(13.189)}$$

From above relationships it is found that as the number of wells increased, the mutual interferance between the wells becomes more, which causes reduction in discharge of each well.

IMPORTANT POINTS

1. About 30% of the world's fresh water resource exists in the form of ground water.
2. The sub-surface water refers to the water available in soil mantle.
3. The saturated zone is known as ground water zone. Its upper layer is water-table, which is under atmospheric pressure.
4. Permeability of aquifer is high.
5. Aquifer appearance in sub-soil is by sand layer.
6. Aquitard allows only seepage flow. A sandy clay is aquitard.
7. Aquiclude is impermeable formation to flow. The clay is aquiclude.
8. The massive compact rock without any fracture is aquifuge.
9. Unconfined aquifer is also known as water table aquifer, which upper surface is water-table.
10. Recharge of unconfined aquifer takes place through infiltration of precipitation.
11. A confind aquifer is also known as artesian aquifer, in which water pressure is greater than the atmospheric pressure.
12. Recharge of confined aquifer takes place from the exposed area of the aquifer to the ground surface.
13. A confined aquifer is leaky, when it is confined either from one or both of its confining bed.
14. The water-table follows the topographic features of the ground surface.

15. When water table intersects the land surface, then ground water comes out and forms "spring".
16. Streams, which receive ground water flow are called effluent streams.
17. The perennial rivers/streams are the effluent streams.
18. The streams, which contribute water to the ground water are called influent streams.
19. Intermittent rivers or streams are the influent streams.
20. In qualitative terms, the porosity of any soil formation greater than 20% is considered as large porosity; between 5 to 20% as medium and less than 5% is as small porosity.
21. Porosity is the measure of water-storage capability of soil formation.
22. The actual volume of drained water by gravity force from a unit volume of aquifer is called specific yield.
23. The volume of water retained in the aquifer is called specific retention.
24. Porosity is the sum of specific yield and specific retention of soil formation.
25. The porosity and specific yield of clay formation is 45 to 55% and 1 to 10%, respectively.
26. The porosity and specific yield of sand formation is 35 to 40% and 10 to 30%, respectively.
27. Darcy's law states that the velocity of water flow through porous media is directly proportional to the hydraulic gradient.
28. Darcy's law is valid for laminar flow only.
29. Darcy's law is valid for the flow having Reynold number as 1.
30. The coefficient of permeability or hydraulic conductivity of aquifer reflects the combined effects of porous media and properties of fluid.
31. Coefficient of permeability is inversely proportional to the kinematic viscosity, which is $\frac{\mu}{\rho}$, (μ is the dynamic viscosity and ρ is the density of fluid).
32. Intrinsic permeability is the function of medium, only. Its dimension is L^2.
33. 1 Darcy = 9.87×10^{-13} m^2.
34. Transmissibility (T) of aquifer is the product of coefficient of permeability (k) and thickness of aquifer (b), *i.e.* $T = k \cdot b$.
35. A well having T as 1×10^5 lpd/m is considered to be satisfactory for irrigation point of view.
36. The intrinsic permeability of clay formation is less than 10^{-3} Darcy.
37. The intrinsic permeability of silt formation varies from 0.01 to 0.5.
38. Compressibility of water is the reciprocal of bulk modulus of elasticity.
39. The dimension of specific storage is L^{-1}. Its numerical value is very small in the order of 1×10^{-4} m^{-1}.
40. The storage coefficient (S) and transmissibility (T) are the formation constants.

41. The value of storage coefficient of confind aquifer varies from 5×10^{-5} to 5×10^{-3}.
42. In unconfined aquifers the storage coefficient is generally taken as specific yield.
43. The change of pressure in aquifer is balanced by partial compression of water and pores.
44. The ratio of change in water level to the change in pressure head is called barometric efficiency.
45. Barometric efficiency varies from 10 to 75%.
46. The bulk modules of elasticity and compressibility of loose clay soil varies from 10^2 to 5×10^2 N/cm^2 and 10^{-2} to 2×10^{-3} cm^2/N, respectively.
47. The bulk modules of elasticity and compressibility of stiff clay soil varies from 10^{-3} to 10^{-4} N/cm^2 and 10^{-3} to 10^{-4} N/cm^2, respectively.
48. The compressibility of loose sand and dense sand soils is 10^{-3} to 5×10^{-4} cm^2/N and 2×10^{-4} to 1.25×10^{-4} cm^2/N, respectively.
49. The value of bulk modulus of elasticity and compressibility of water at 0°C is 2.04×10^5 N/cm^2 and 4.90×10^{-6} cm^2/N, respectively.
50. In unconfined aquifer, the free water surface is also known as phreatic water surface.
51. Discharge per unit draw-down is known as specific capacity of well.
52. Annual utilisable ground water resource of India is about 418 km^3.
53. The Ganga basin imposes highest annual utilisable ground water resource, i.e. 41% of the total potential of India.
54. Of the total Indian geographical area, the area under consolidated rocks is about 120 M.ha.
55. Permanent withdrawal of ground water from aquifer is known as 'mining.

REFERENCES

1. Chow V.T. On the determination of transmissivity and storage coefficients from pumping test data, Trans, Am. Geophysic Union, Vol. 33 : 397-404, 1952.
2. Class note on ground water engineering, prepared by Dr A.P. Mishra and Dr B.C. Mall, College of Agricultural Engineering, R.A.U. Pusa, Bihar, 1985.
3. Darcy H. Less Fontainess Publiques de la Ville de Dijon, 1952.
4. Ferris J.G. Theory of aquifer test, U.S. Geological Surv., Water Supply paper, 1536E, p 174, 1962.
5. Garg S.P. Ground Water Engineering, Oxford & IBH Co., New Delhi, 1987.
6. Hantush M.S. Draw-down around a partially penetrating well, J. Hydrol, Div, Prosc, ASCE 127(1) : pp 268-283, 1962.
7. Jacob C.E., Radial flow in leaky artesian aquifer, Trans. Am. Geophysics, Vol. 27 : pp 198-205, 1946.

8. Jacob C.E. Corrections of drawdown caused by a pumped well, tapping less than full thicknness of aquifer, in methods of determining of permeability, transmissibility and draw-down, U.S. Geol. Survey, Water Supply paper, 1536-I, pp. 272-282, 1963.

9. Koznie J., Theorie and Brechnung der Brunnen Wasser Kraft and Wasser Writo Chaft, 28 : pp 88-116, 1933.

10. Michael A.M. Irrigation Theory and Practice, Vikash Pub. House, Delhi, 1991.

11. Raghunath H.M. Ground Water Engineering, Wiley Eastern, Pvt. Ltd., Delhi, 1990.

12. Suresh R. Steady flow towards multiple well point system, Ind. J. of Agric Engg., 1993.

13. Theis C.V. The relation between lowering of the piezometric surface and the rate and duration of discharge of well, using ground water storage, Trans. Am. Geophysics Union, 66 : p 519, 1935.

14. Walton W.C., Analytical methods for well and aquifer evaluation, Illinois state Water Survey, Urbana, Bulletin 49, p. 81, 1962.

15. Muskat M. The flow of homogeneous fluids through porous media, McGraw-Hill. Book Co. Ltd., New York, 1937.

DESCRIPTIVE TYPE QUESTIONS

1. Describe ground water resources of India.

2. List the types of geological formations and explain various features of artesian aquifer.

3. Define hydraulic conductivity and describe different methods for determining it.

4. (*a*) Define transmissivity and coefficient of storage.

(*b*) Describe distribution of ground water.

5. (*a*) Derive the equation of piezometric head.

(*b*) Define laminar and turbulent flow and also distinguish each other.

6. (*a*) Derive Darcy's equation and write its applicability.

(*b*) Derive equation for the forces acting on porous media.

7. Derive ground water flow equation in confined and unconfined aquifers.

8. Derive ground water flow equation for semi-confined aquifer.

9. Derive equation for steady radial flow towards well in confined aquifer along with assumptions, used.

10. A fully penetrating well installed in confined aquifer has 40 cm diameter. Compute discharge, if

(*a*) Drawdowns in the piezometer are 2.5 and 1.5 m located at the radial distance of 30 and 60 m, respectively

(*b*) Aquifer thickness is 20 m

(*c*) Hydraulic conductivity is 9.5 m/day.

11. Derive steady-state flow equation towards a well installed in unconfined aquifer.

12. (*a*) Define semi-confined aquifer and derive the equation of flow towards a well installed in semi-confined aquifer.

(*b*) Calculate draw-down in the well, which is fully penetrated in semi-continued aquifer of thickness 15 m. The hydraulic conductivity of aquifer is 0.085 m/h. The discharge at steady-state condition is 45 m^3/h. Assume the value of $K_0\left(\frac{r}{\lambda}\right)$ as 1.

13. Explain Theis equation and write various steps to determine the aquifer parameters.

14. Derive Jacob's equation to determine aquifer's constants.

15. Explain Chow method to determine aquifer parameters.

16. Explain Theis recovery method to determine aquifer properties.

17. Derive equation of ground water flow towards open well.

18. (*a*) Define multiple well point system.

(*b*) Explain super position principle.

19. Write short notes on

(*a*) Leakage factor (*b*) Compressibility
(*c*) Interferance of well (*d*) Partially penetrating well
(*e*) Specific yield.

OBJECTIVE TYPE QUESTIONS

1. Ground water refers to the water in
(*a*) surface ponds (*b*) aquifers
(*c*) soils (*d*) capillaries

2. Sources of ground water development are
(*a*) rainfall and surface ponds
(*b*) canal water, reservoirs etc
(*c*) both '*a*' and '*b*'
(*d*) tube wells

3. Contribution of rainfall to develop ground water in consolidated rocks varies from
(*a*) 5 to 10% (*b*) 1 to 5%
(*c*) 10 to 15% (*d*) 20 to 50%

4. In India the quantity of water recharged, each year is about
(*a*) 37 m ha-m (*b*) 27 m ha-m
(*c*) 15 m ha-m (*d*) 2×10^{10} m.ha-m

5. Aquifer is the
(*a*) water bearing formation (*b*) soil
(*c*) rock (*d*) artesian formation

6. Confined aquifer is also known as
(*a*) water-table aquifer (*b*) artesian aquifer
(*c*) both '*a*' and '*b*' (*d*) perched aquifer

7. Unconfined aquifer is also known as
(*a*) artesian aquifer (*b*) water-table aquifer
(*c*) semi-confined aquifer (*d*) perched aquifer

8. **Perched aquifer is located**
   (*a*) above the main water-table
   (*b*) below the main water-table
   (*c*) just below the water table
   (*d*) none of the above.
9. **A well installed in confined aquifer always contains**
   (*a*) greater water level than the aquifer
   (*b*) lesser water leve than aquifer
   (*c*) very less yield of water
   (*d*) none of the above.
10. **Semi-confined aquifer is also called**
   (*a*) leaky aquifer (*b*) semi-unconfined aquifer
   (*c*) perched aquifer (*d*) water table aquifer
11. **A formation, which contains sufficient water but has very small capacity to transmit the water is called**
   (*a*) aquifuge (*b*) aquitard
   (*c*) aquiclude (*d*) perched aquifer
12. **Porosity of soil formation is the ratio of**
   (*a*) volume of voids to the volume of formation
   (*b*) volume of formation to the volume of voids
   (*c*) m.c and voids
   (*d*) water volume to soil volume
13. **Porosity of clay soil varies from**
   (*a*) 1 to 10% (*b*) 45 to 55%
   (*c*) 10 to 20% (*d*) 0.1 to 1
14. **Specific retention is given by**
   (*a*) $S_r = \frac{V_w}{V}$ (*b*) $S_r = \frac{V}{V_w}$
   (*c*) $S_r = \frac{V_w - 1}{V}$ (*d*) $S_r = \frac{\theta}{S_y}$
15. **Specific yield is given by**
   (*a*) $S_y = \frac{V_y}{V} \times 100$ (*b*) $S_y = \frac{V}{V_y} \times 100$
   (*c*) $S_y = \left(\frac{V_y}{V} + 1\right) \times 100$ (*d*) $S_y = \frac{r^2 S}{4 \, . \, tT}$
16. **Hydraulic conductivity of clay soil varies from**
   (*a*) 10^{-5} to 10^{-7} m/day (*b*) 10^{-1} to 10^{-5} m^3/day
   (*c*) 10^{-7} to 10^{-15} m^3/day (*d*) 0.01 to 0.1 m^3/s
17. **Hydraulic conductivity of moderately saturated soil varies from**
   (*a*) 2.0 to 6.25 cm/h (*b*) 6.25 to 12.5 cm/h
   (*c*) 12.5 to 25.0 cm/h (*d*) 1.5 to 2.5 cm/h
18. **Tortuosity of soil pore is the ratio of**
   (*a*) capillary length to the actual length of path traversed by the water
   (*b*) capillary length to the thickness of soil formation
   (*c*) m.c. and porosity of the soil
   (*d*) both '*a*' and '*b*'

19. A saline soil contains
(*a*) high hydraulic conductivity
(*b*) less hydraulic conductivity
(*c*) zero hydraulic conductivity.
(*d*) 5×10^{-3} day/l/m as T

20. Transmissivity of aquifer is the product of
(*a*) *k* and aquifer thickness (*b*) *S* and aquifer thickness
(*c*) m.c. and voids (*d*) both '*a*' and '*b*'.

21. The unit of 'Transmissivity' is
(*a*) l/day/m (*b*) day/l/m
(*c*) m/day/l (*d*) cm/s

22. Coefficient of storage (*S*) of confined aquifer varies from
(*a*) 1×10^{-5} to 1×10^{-3} (*b*) 10^{-7} to 10^{-5}
(*c*) 10^{-1} to 10 (*d*) 0.10 to .015

23. Hydraulic resistance is the property of
(*a*) semi-pervious formation (*b*) impervious formation
(*c*) both *a* & *b* (*d*) water table

24. The hydraulic resistance of semi-pervious layer varies from
(*a*) 100 to 10^4 days (*b*) 100 to 10^6 minutes
(*c*) 100 to 10^6 days (*d*) 10 to 20 days

25. The voids are completely filled with water in
(*a*) zone of aeration (*b*) zone of saturation
(*c*) both '*a*' and '*b*' (*d*) capillary zone

26. Capilary fringe lies immediately
(*a*) below the zone of saturation
(*b*) above the zone of saturation
(*c*) just below the soil surface
(*d*) none of above.

27. The capillary rise in clay formation varies from
(*a*) 150 to 300 cm (*b*) 75 to 150 cm
(*c*) 150 to 1000 cm (*d*) 5 to 10 cm

28. The zone of aeration contains
(*a*) ground water (*b*) suspended water
(*c*) gravitional water (*d*) perched water

29. The piezometric head in saline water is
(*a*) more than the fresh water case
(*b*) less than the fresh water case
(*c*) 2.5 m (*d*) zero

30. Darcy's law is valid for
(*a*) turbulent flow (*b*) laminar flow
(*c*) both '*a*' and '*b*' (*d*) critical flow

31. Ground water flow is
(*a*) laminar (*b*) turbulent
(*c*) critical flow, only (*d*) none of the above

32. Theis equation is valid for
(*a*) confined aquifer under unsteady-state condition
(*b*) unconfined aquifer under unsteady-state condition
(*c*) perched aquifer, only
(*d*) none of the above.

33. Jacob equation is derived from
(*a*) Theis equation (*b*) DeGlee equation
(*c*) Chow equation (*d*) Darcy's law

34. The Chow function $F(u)$ is given by
(*a*) $\frac{W(u)}{2.3} e^u$ (*b*) $\frac{2.3}{W(u)} e^u$
(*c*) $\frac{W(u)}{2.3\, e^u}$ (*d*) $\frac{r^2 S}{4t \cdot T}$

35. An impervious formation contains
(*a*) very high porosity (*b*) medium porosity
(*c*) zero porosity (*d*) macro pores

36. The entrapment of air is more in
(*a*) macro pores (*b*) micro pores
(*c*) both '*a*' and '*b*' (*d*) aquitard

37. Temperature reduces the
(*a*) ground water flow towards well
(*b*) viscosity of water
(*c*) both '*a*' and '*b*'
(*d*) head loss of the well

38. A partially penetrating well involves
(*a*) more head loss (*b*) greater draw down
(*c*) both '*a*' and '*b*' (*d*) less friction loss

Answer (Objective Type Question)

1.	(*b*)	**2.**	(*c*)	**3.**	(*a*)	**4.**	(*b*)	**5.**	(*a*)	**6.**	(*b*)	**7.**	(*b*)	**8.**	(*a*)
9.	(*a*)	**10.**	(*a*)	**11.**	(*c*)	**12.**	(*a*)	**13.**	(*b*)	**14.**	(*a*)	**15.**	(*a*)	**16.**	(*a*)
17.	(*a*)	**18.**	(*b*)	**19.**	(*a*)	**20.**	(*a*)	**21.**	(*a*)	**22.**	(*a*)	**23.**	(*a*)	**24.**	(*b*)
25.	(*b*)	**26.**	(*b*)	**27.**	(*b*)	**28.**	(*b*)	**29.**	(*b*)	**30.**	(*b*)	**31.**	(*a*)	**32.**	(*a*)
33.	(*a*)	**34.**	(*a*)	**35.**	(*c*)	**36.**	(*b*)	**37.**	(*b*)	**38.**	(*a*)				

Appendix–1

Values of K, a, b and n for Different zones of India for Computing Intensity-Duration-Return period relationship.

Crop	*Station*	K	a	b	n
Northern Zone	Agra	4.911	0.1667	0.25	0.6293
	Allahaabad	8.570	0.1692	0.50	1.0190
	Amristar	14.41	0.1304	1.40	1.2963
	Dehradun	6.00	0.22	0.50	0.8000
	Jaipur	6.219	0.1026	0.50	1.1172
	Jodhpur	4.098	0.1677	0.50	1.0369
	Lucknow	6.074	0.1813	0.50	1.0331
	New Delhi	5.208	0.1574	0.50	1.1072
	Srinagar	1.503	0.2730	0.25	1.0636
	Northern zone	5.914	0.1623	0.50	1.0127
Southern zone	Bangalore	6.275	0.1262	0.50	1.1280
	Hyderabad	5.250	0.1354	0.50	1.0295
	Kodaikanal	5.914	0.1711	0.50	1.0086
	Madras	6.126	0.1664	0.50	0.8027
	Mangalore	6.744	0.1395	0.50	0.9374
	Tiruchirapalli	7.135	0.1638	0.50	0.9624
	Trivandrum	6.762	0.1536	0.50	0.8158
	Visakhapatnam	6.646	0.1692	0.50	0.9963
	Southern zone	6.311	0.1523	0.50	0.9465

Contd.

Eastern zone	Agarthala	8.097	0.1177	0.50	0.8191
	Dumdum	5.940	0.1150	0.15	0.9241
	Gauhati	7.206	0.1557	0.75	0.9401
	Gaya	7.176	0.1483	0.50	0.9459
	Imphal	4.939	0.1340	0.50	0.9719
	Jamshedpur	6.930	0.1307	0.50	9.8737
	Jharsuguda	8.596	0.1392	0.75	0.8740
	North Lakhimpur	14.070	0.1256	1.25	1.0730
	Sagar Island	16.524	0.1402	1.50	0.9635
	Shillogn	6.728	0.1502	0.75	0.9575
	Eastern Zone	6.974	0.1353	0.50	0.8801

Appendix-2

Maximum possible duration of sunshine hours in the units of 30 days of 12 hours, each

Northern hemisphere	*Jan.*	*Feb.*	*March*	*April*	*May*	*June*	*July*	*Aug.*	*Sept.*	*Oct.*	*Nov.*	*Dec.*
1	2	*3*	*4*	*5*	*6*	*7*	*8*	*9*	*10*	*11*	*12*	*13*
0	1.04	0.94	1.04	1.01	1.04	1.04	1.04	1.04	1.01	1.04	1.01	1.04
5	1.02	0.93	1.03	1.02	1.06	1.03	1.06	1.05	1.01	1.03	0.99	1.02
10	1.00	0.91	1.03	1.03	1.08	1.06	1.08	1.07	1.02	1.02	2.98	0.99
15	0.97	0.91	1.03	1.04	1.11	1.08	1.12	1.08	1.02	1.01	0.95	0.97
20	0.95	0.90	1.03	1.05	1.12	1.11	1.14	1.11	1.02	1.00	0.93	0.94
25	0.93	0.89	1.03	1.06	1.15	1.15	1.17	1.12	1.02	0.99	0.91	0.91
26	0.92	0.88	1.03	1.06	1.15	1.15	1.17	1.12	1.02	0.99	0.91	0.91
27	0.92	0.88	1.03	1.07	1.16	1.15	1.18	1.13	1.02	0.99	0.90	0.90
28	0.91	0.88	1.03	1.07	1.16	1.16	1.18	1.13	1.02	0.98	0.90	0.90
29	0.91	0.87	1.03	1.07	1.17	1.16	1.19	1.13	1.03	0.98	0.90	0.89
30	0.90	0.87	1.03	1.08	1.18	1.17	1.20	1.14	1.03	0.98	0.89	0.88
31	0.90	0.87	1.03	1.08	1.18	1.18	1.20	1.14	1.03	0.98	0.89	0.88
32	0.89	0.86	1.03	1.08	1.19	1.21	1.21	1.15	1.03	0.98	0.88	0.87
33	0.88	0.86	1.03	1.09	1.19	1.20	1.22	1.15	1.03	0.97	0.88	0.87

Contd.

Northern hemisphere	Jan.	Feb.	March	April	May	June	July	Aug.	Sept.	Oct.	Nov.	Dec.
1	2	3	4	5	6	7	8	9	10	11	12	13
34	0.88	0.85	1.03	1.09	1.20	1.20	1.22	1.16	1.03	0.97	0.87	0.86
35	0.87	0.85	1.03	1.09	1,21	1.21	1.23	1.16	1.03	0.97	0.86	0.85
36	0.87	0.85	1.03	1.10	1.21	1.22	1.24	1.16	1.04	0.97	0.86	0.84
37	0.86	0.84	1.03	1.10	1.22	1.23	1.25	1.17	1.03	0.97	0.85	0.83
38	0.85	0.84	1.03	1.10	1.23	1.24	1.25	1.17	1.04	0.96	0.84	0.83
39	0.85	0.84	1.03	1.11	1.23	1.24	1.26	1.18	1.04	0.96	0.84	0.82
40	0.84	0.83	1.03	1.11	1.24	1.25	1.27	1.18	1.04	0.96	0.83	0.81
41	0.83	0.83	1.03	1.11	1.25	1.26	1.27	1.19	1.04	0.96	0.82	0.80
42	0.82	0.83	1.03	1.12	1.26	1.27	1.28	1.19	1.04	0.95	0.82	0.79
43	0.81	0.82	1.02	1.12	1.26	1.28	1.29	1.20	1.04	0.95	0.81	0.77
44	0.81	0.82	1.02	1.13	1.27	1.29	1.30	1.20	1.04	0.95	0.80	0.76
45	0.80	0.81	1.02	1.13	1.28	1.29	1.31	1.21	1.04	0.94	0.97	0.75
46	0.97	0.81	1.02	1.13	1.29	1.31	1.32	1.22	1.04	0.94	0.79	0.74
47	0.77	0.80	1.02	1.14	1.30	1.32	1.33	1.22	1.04	0.93	0.78	0.73
48	0.76	0.80	1.02	1.14	1.31	1.33	1.34	1.23	1.05	0.93	0.77	0.72
49	0.75	0.79	1.02	1.14	1.32	1.34	1.35	1.24	1.05	0.93	0.76	0.71
50	0.74	0.78	1.02	1.15	1.33	1.36	1.37	1.25	1.06	0.92	0.76	0.70

Appendix-3

Correction factor (*f*) for use in Thornthwait formula

North latitude	*Jan*	*Feb*	*March*	*April*	*May*	*June*	*July*	*Aug.*	*Sept.*	*Oct.*	*Nov.*	*Dec.*
1	2	3	4	5	6	7	8	9	10	11	12	13
0	1.04	0.94	1.04	1.01	1.04	1.01	1.04	1.04	1.01	1.04	1.01	1.04
5	1.02	0.93	1.03	1.02	1.06	1.03	1.06	1.05	1.01	1.03	0.99	1.02
10	1.00	0.91	1.03	1.03	1.08	1.06	1.08	1.07	1.02	1.02	0.98	0.99
15	0.97	0.91	1.03	1.04	1.11	1.08	1.12	1.08	1.02	1.01	0.95	0.97
20	0.95	0.90	1.03	1.05	1.13	1.11	1.14	1.11	1.02	1.00	0.93	0.94
25	0.93	0.89	1.03	1.06	1.15	1.14	1.17	1.12	1.02	0.91	0.90	0.91
30	0.90	0.87	1.03	1.08	1.18	1.17	1.20	1.14	1.03	0.98	0.89	0.88
31	0.90	0.87	1.03	1.08	1.18	1.18	1.20	1.14	1.03	0.98	0.89	0.88
32	0.89	0.86	1.03	1.08	1.19	1.19	1.21	1.15	1.03	0.98	0.88	0.87
33	0.88	0.86	1.03	1.09	1.19	1.20	1.22	1.15	1.03	0.97	0.88	0.86
34	0.88	0.85	1.03	1.09	1.20	1.20	1.22	1.16	1.03	0.97	0.87	0.86
35	0.87	0.85	1.03	1.09	1.21	1.21	1.23	1.16	1.03	0.97	0.86	0.85
36	0.87	0.85	1.03	1.10	1.21	1.22	1.24	1.16	1.03	0.97	0.86	0.84
37	0.86	0.84	1.03	1.10	1.22	1.23	1.25	1.17	1.03	0.97	0.85	0.83
38	0.85	0.84	1.03	1.10	1.23	1.24	1.25	1.17	1.04	0.96	0.84	0.83
39	0.85	0.84	1.03	1.11	1.23	1.24	1.26	1.10	1.04	0.96	0.84	0.82
40	0.84	0.83	1.03	1.11	1.24	1.25	1.27	1.18	1.04	0.96	0.83	0.81

Contd.

North latitude	Jan	Feb	March	April	May	June	July	Aug.	Sept.	Oct.	Nov.	Dec.
1	2	3	4	5	6	7	8	9	10	11	12	13
42	0.82	0.83	1.03	1.12	1.26	1.27	1.28	1.19	1.04	0.95	0.82	0.79
44	0.81	0.83	1.02	1.13	1.27	1.28	1.30	1.20	1.04	0.95	0.80	0.76
46	0.79	0.81	1.02	1.13	1.29	1.31	1.32	1.22	1.04	0.94	0.79	0.74
48	0.76	0.80	1.02	1.14	1.31	1.33	1.34	1.23	1.05	1.93	0.77	0.72
50	0.74	0.78	1.02	1.15	1.33	1.36	1.37	1.25	1.06	0.92	0.76	0.70
South latitude												
5	1.06	0.95	1.04	1.00	1.02	0.99	1.02	1.03	1.00	1.05	1.03	1.06
10	1.08	0.97	1.05	0.99	1.01	0.96	1.00	1.01	1.00	1.06	1.05	1.10
15	1.12	0.98	1.05	0.98	0.98	0.94	0.97	1.00	1.00	1.07	1.07	1.12
20	1.14	1.00	1.05	0.97	0.96	0.91	0.95	0.99	1.00	1.08	1.09	1.15
25	1.17	1.01	1.05	0.96	0.94	0.88	0.93	0.98	1.00	1.10	1.11	1.18
30	1.20	1.03	1.06	0.95	0.92	0.85	0.90	0.96	1.00	1.12	1.14	1.21
35	1.23	1.01	1.06	0.94	0.89	0.82	0.87	0.94	1.00	1.13	1.17	1.25
40	1.27	1.06	1.07	0.93	0.86	0.78	0.84	0.92	1.00	1.15	1.20	1.29
42	1.28	1.07	1.07	0.92	0.85	0.76	0.82	0.92	1.00	1.16	1.22	1.31
44	1.30	1.06	1.07	0.92	0.83	0.74	0.81	0.91	0.99	1.17	1.23	1.33
46	1.32	1.10	1.07	0.91	0.82	0.72	0.79	0.90	0.99	1.17	1.25	1.35
48	1.34	1.10	1.08	0.90	0.80	0.70	0.76	0.89	0.99	1.18	1.27	1.37
50	1.37	1.12	1.08	0.89	0.77	0.67	0.74	0.88	0.99	1.19	1.29	1.41

Appendix-4

Monthly values of *i* corresponding to mean monthly temperature (°C)

M.M.T. (C°)	*0.0*	*0.1*	*0.2*	*0.3*	*0.4*	*0.5*	*0.6*	*0.7*	*0.8*	*0.9*
0			0.01	0.01	0.02	0.03	0.04	0.05	0.06	0.07
1	0.09	0.10	0.12	0.13	0.15	0.16	0.18	0.20	0.21	0.23
2	0.25	0.27	0.29	0.31	0.33	0.35	0.37	0.39	0.42	0.44
3	0.46	0.48	0.51	0.53	0.56	0.58	0.61	0.63	0.66	0.69
4	0.71	0.74	0.77	0.80	0.82	0.85	0.88	0.91	0.94	0.97
5	1.00	1.03	1.06	1.09	1.12	1.16	1.19	1.22	1.25	1.29
6	1.32	1.35	1.39	1.42	1.45	1.49	1.52	1.56	1.59	1.63
8	2.04	2.08	2.12	2.15	2.19	2.23	2.27	2.31	2.35	2.39
10	2.86	2.90	2.94	2.99	3.03	3.08	3.12	3.16	3.21	3.26
12	3.76	3.81	3.86	3.91	3.96	4.00	4.05	4.10	4.15	4.20
14	4.75	4.81	4.86	4.91	4.96	5.01	5.07	5.12	5.17	5.22
16	5.82	5.87	5.93	5.98	6.04.	6.10	6.15	6.21	6.26	6.32
18	6.95	7.01	7.07	7.13	7.19	7.25	7.31	7.37	7.43	7.49

Contd.

M.M.T. (C°)	0.0	0.1	0.2	0.3	0.4	0.5	0.6	0.7	0.8	0.9
20	8.16	8.22	8.28	8.34	8.41	8.47	8.53	8.59	8.66	8.72
22	9.42	9.49	9.55	9.62	9.68	9.75	9.82	9.88	9.95	10.01
24	10.75	10.82	10.89	10.95	11.02	11.09	11.16	11.23	11.30	11.37
26	12.13	12.21	12.28	12.35	12.42	12.49	12.56	12.63	12.70	12.78
28	13.58	13.65	13.72	13.80	13.87	13.94	14.02	14.09	14.17	14.24
30	15.07	15.15	15.22	15.30	15.38	15.45	15.53	15.61	16.68	15.76
31	15.84	15.92	15.99	16.07	16.15	16.23	16.30	16.38	16.46	16.54
32	16.62	16.70	16.78	16.85	16.93	17.33	17.09	17.17	17.25	17.33
33	17.41	17.49	17.57	17.65	17.73	17.81	17.89	17.97	18.05	18.13
34	18.22	18.30	18.38	18.46	18.54	18.62	18.70	18.79	18.87	18.95
35	19.03	19.91	19.20	19.28	19.36	19.45	19.53	19.61	19.69	19.78
36	19.86	19.95	20.03	20.11	20.20	20.28	20.36	20.45	20.53	20.62
37	20.70	20.79	20.87	20.96	21.04	21.13	21.21	21.30	21.38	21.47
38	21.56	21.64	21.73	21.81	21.90	21.99	22.07	22.16	22.25	22.33
39	22.42	22.51	22.59	22.68	22.77	22.86	22.95	23.03	23.12	23.21

Appendix–5

Crop coefficient (K_{co}) for use in Jensen-Haise method

Crop	*K for the period of plating to effective cover (%)*									
	10	*20*	*30*	*40*	*50*	*60*	*70*	*80*	*90*	*100*
Small grains	0.16	0.18	0.25	0.37	0.51	0.67	0.82	0.94	1.02	1.04
Beans	0.20	0.23	0.30	0.39	0.51	0.63	0.76	0.88	0.98	1.07
Pear	0.20	0.24	0.31	0.40	0.51	0.63	0.75	0.87	0.97	1.05
Potatoes	0.10	0.13	0.20	0.30	0.41	0.53	0.65	0.76	0.85	0.91
S'beet	0.10	0.13	0.20	0.30	0.41	0.53	0.65	0.76	0.85	0.96
Corn	0.20	0.23	0.29	0.38	0.49	0.61	0.72	0.82	0.91	0.96
Alfalfa	0.36	0.47	0.58	0.68	0.79	0.90	1.00	1.00	1.00	1.00
Pasture	0.87	0.87	0.87	0.87	0.87	0.87	0.87	0.87	0.87	0.87

Days after effective cover

Small grains	1.04	0.94	0.74	0.49	0.19	0.10	0.10	0.10	0.10
Beans	1.02	0.96	0.85	0.73	0.59	0.45	0.31	0.19	0.10
Pear	0.98	1.02	0.99	0.76	0.20	0.10	0.10	0.10	0.10
Potatoes	0.90	0.85	0.75	0.60	0.38	0.10	0.10	0.10	0.10
S'beets	0.90	0.90	0.90	0.90	0.90	0.90	0.90	0.90	0.90
Corn	0.99	0.99	0.93	0.82	0.68	0.54	0.40	0.20	0.17
Alfalfa	0.75	1.00	1.00	1.00	1.00	1.00	1.00	1.00	1.00
Pasture	0.87	0.87	0.87	0.87	0.87	0.87	0.87	0.87	0.87

Source : Jensen (1974)

Appendix-6

Mid-monthly solar radiation intensity (R_A)
on horizontal surface, in mm of water evaporated per day.

North hemi-sphere	Jan	Feb	March	April	May	June	July	Aug	Sept	Oct	Nov	Dec
1	2	3	4	5	6	7	8	9	10	11	12	13
0	14.5	15.0	15.2	14.7	13.9	13.4	13.5	14.2	14.9	15.0	14.6	14.3
10	12.8	13.9	14.8	15.2	15.0	14.8	14.8	15.0	14.9	14.1	13.1	12.4
20	10.8	12.3	13.9	15.2	15.7	15.8	15.7	15.3	14.4	12.9	11.2	10.3
30	8.5	10.5	12.7	14.8	16.0	16.5	16.2	15.3	13.5	11.3	9.1	7.9
40	6.0	8.3	11.0	13.9	15.9	16.7	16.3	14.8	12.2	9.3	6.7	5.5
50	3.6	5.9	9.1	12.7	15.4	16.7	16.1	13.9	10.5	7.1	4.3	3.0
60	1.3	3.5	6.8	11.1	14.6	16.5	15.7	12.7	8.5	4.7	1.9	0.9
70	—	1.1	4.3	9.1	13.6	17.0	15.8	11.4	6.8	2.4	0.1	—
80	—	—	1.8	7.8	14.6	17.8	16.5	10.6	4.0	0.2	—	—
90	—	—	—	7.9	14.9	18.1	16.8	11.2	2.6	—	—	—

Contd.

South hemisphere												
10	15.8	15.7	15.1	13.8	12.4	11.6	11.9	13.0	14.4	15.3	15.7	15.8
20	16.8	16.0	14.6	12.5	10.7	9.6	10.6	11.5	13.5	15.3	16.4	16.9
30	17.3	15.8	13.6	10.8	8.7	7.4	7.8	9.6	12.1	14.8	16.7	17.8
40	17.3	15.2	12.2	8.8	6.4	5.1	5.6	7.5	10.5	13.8	16.5	17.8
50	17.1	14.1	10.5	6.6	4.1	2.8	3.3	5.2	8.5	12.5	16.0	17.8
60	16.6	12.7	8.4	4.3	1.9	0.8	1.2	2.9	6.2	10.7	15.2	17.5
70	16.5	11.2	6.1	1.9	0.1	—	—	0.8	3.8	8.8	14.5	18.1
80	17.3	10.5	3.6	—	—	—	—	—	1.3	7.1	15.0	18.9
90	17.6	10.7	1.9	—	—	—	—	—	—	7.0	15.3	19.3

Appendix-7

Values of 'R_a' for use in modified penman equation

North latitude	Jan	Feb	March	April	May	June	July	Aug.	Sept.	Oct.	Nov.	Dec.
1	2	3	4	5	6	7	8	9	10	11	12	13
0	15.0	15.5	15.7	15.3	14.4	13.9	14.1	14.8	15.3	15.4	15.1	14.8
2	14.7	15.3	15.6	15.3	14.6	14.2	14.3	14.9	15.3	15.3	14.8	14.4
4	14.3	15.0	15.5	15.5	14.9	14.4	14.6	15.1	15.3	15.1	14.5	14.1
6	13.9	14.8	15.4	15.4	15.1	14.7	14.9	15.2	15.3	15.0	12.2	13.7
8	13.6	14.5	15.3	15.6	15.3	15.0	15.1	15.4	15.3	14.8	13.9	13.3
10	13.2	14.2	15.3	15.7	15.5	15.3	15.3	15.5	15.3	14.7	13.6	12.9
12	12.8	13.9	15.1	15.7	15.7	15.5	15.5	15.6	15.2	14.4	13.3	12.5
14	12.4	13.6	14.9	15.7	15.8	15.7	15.7	15.7	15.1	14.1	12.8	12.0
16	12.0	13.3	14.7	15.6	16.0	15.9	15.9	15.7	15.0	13.9	12.4	11.6
18	11.6	13.0	14.6	15.6	16.1	16.1	16.1	15.8	14.9	13.6	12.0	11,1
20	11.2	12.7	14.4	15.6	16.3	16.4	16.3	15.9	14.8	13.3	11.6	10.7
22	10.7	12.3	14.2	15.5	16.3	16.4	16.4	15.8	14.6	13.0	11.1	10.2
24	10.2	11.9	13.9	15.4	16.4	16.6	16.5	15.8	14.5	12.6	10.7	9.7
26	9.8	11.5	13.7	15.3	16.4	16.7	16.6	15.7	14.3	12.3	10.3	9.3
28	9.3	11.1	13.4	15.3	16.5	16.8	16.7	15.7	14.1	12.0	9.9	8.8

Contd.

North latitude	Jan	Feb	March	April	May	June	July	Aug.	Sept.	Oct.	Nov.	Dec.
1	2	3	*4*	*5*	*6*	7	*8*	*9*	*10*	*11*	*12*	*13*
30	8.8	10.7	13.1	15.2	16.5	17.0	16.8	15.7	13.9	11.6	9.5	8.3
32	8.3	10.2	12.8	15.0	16.5	17.0	16.8	15.6	13.6	11.2	9.0	7.8
34	7.9	9.8	12.4	14.8	16.5	17.1	16.8	15.5	13.4	10.8	8.5	7.2
36	7.4	9.4	12.1	14.7	16.4	17.2	16.7	15.4	13.1	10.6	8.0	6.6
38	6.9	9.0	11.8	14.5	16.4	17.2	16.7	15.3	12.8	10.0	7.5	6.1
40	6.4	8.6	11.4	14.3	16.4	17.3	16.7	15.2	12.5	9.6	7.0	5.7
42	5.9	8.1	11.0	14.0	16.2	17.3	16.7	15.0	12.2	9.1	6.5	5.2
44	5.3	7.6	10.6	13.7	16.1	17.2	16.6	14.7	11.9	8.7	6.0	4.7
46	4.9	7.1	10.2	13.3	16.0	17.2	16.6	14.5	11.5	8.3	5.5	4.3
48	4.3	6.6	9.8	13.0	15.9	17.2	16.5	14.3	11.2	7.8	5.4	3.7
50	3.8	6.1	9.4	12.7	15.8	17.1	16.4	14.1	10.9	7.4	4.5	3.2
South Latitude												
0	15.0	15.5	15.7	15.3	14.4	13.9	14.1	14.8	15.3	15.4	15.1	14.8
2	15.3	15.7	15.7	15.1	14.1	13.5	13.1	14.5	15.2	15.5	15.3	15.1
4	15.5	15.8	15.6	14.9	13.8	13.2	13.4	14.3	15.1	15.6	15.5	15.4
6	15.8	16.0	15.6	14.7	13.4	12.8	13.1	14.0	15.0	15.7	15.8	15.7
8	16.1	16.1	15.5	14.4	13.1	12.4	12.7	13.7	14.9	15.8	16.0	16.0
10	16.4	16.3	15.5	14.2	12.8	12.0	12.4	13.5	14.8	15.9	16.2	16.2
12	16.6	16.3	15.4	14.0	12.5	11.6	12.0	13.2	14.7	15.8	16.4	16.5

Contd.

North latitude	Jan	Feb	March	April	May	June	July	Aug.	Sept.	Oct.	Nov.	Dec.
1	*2*	*3*	*4*	*5*	*6*	*7*	*8*	*9*	*10*	*11*	*12*	*13*
14	16.7	16.4	15.3	13.7	12.1	11.2	11.6	12.9	14.5	15.8	15.5	16.6
16	16.9	16.4	15.2	13.5	11.7	10.8	11.2	12.6	14.3	15.8	16.7	16.8
18	17.1	16.5	15.1	13.2	11.4	10.4	10.8	12.3	14.1	15.8	16.8	17.1
20	17.3	16.5	15.0	13.0	11.0	10.0	10.4	12.0	13.9	15.8	17.0	17.4
22	17.4	16.5	14.8	12.6	10.6	9.6	10.0	11.6	13.7	15.7	17.0	17.5
24	17.5	16.5	14.6	12.3	10.2	9.1	9.5	11.2	13.4	15.6	17.1	17.7
26	17.6	16.4	14.4	12.0	9.7	8.7	9.1	10.9	13.2	15.5	17.2	17.8
28	17.7	16.4	14.3	11.6	9.3	8.2	8.6	10.4	13.0	15.4	17.2	17.9
30	17.8	16.4	14.0	11.3	8.9	7.8	8.1	10.1	12.7	15.3	17.3	18.1
32	17.8	16.2	13.8	10.9	8.5	7.3	7.7	9.6	12.4	15.1	17.2	18.1
34	17.8	16.1	13.5	10.5	8.0	6.8	7.2	9.2	12.0	14.9	17.1	18.2
36	17.9	16.0	13.2	10.1	7.5	6.3	6.8	8.8	11.7	14.6	17.0	18.2
38	17.9	15.8	12.8	9.6	7.1	5.8	6.3	8.3	11.4	14.4	17.0	18.3
40	17.9	15.7	12.5	9.2	6.6	5.3	5.9	7.9	11.0	14.2	16.9	18.3
42	17.8	15.5	12.2	8.8	6.1	4.9	5.4	7.4	10.6	14.0	16.8	18.3
44	17.8	15.3	11.9	8.4	5.7	4.4	4.9	6.9	10.2	13.7	16.7	18.3
46	17.7	15.1	11.5	7.9	5.2	4.0	4.4	6.5	9.7	13.4	16.7	18.3
48	17.6	14.9	11.2	7.5	4.7	3.5	4.0	6.0	9.3	13.2	16.6	18.2
50	17.5	14.7	10.9	7.0	4.2	3.1	3.5	5.5	8.9	12.9	16.5	18.2

Appendix-8

Correction factor for converting unadjusted ET to adjusted ET, in Modified Penman Equation.

RS mm/day	$RH_{max} = 30\%$			$RH_{max} = 60\%$			$RH_{max} = 90\%$		
	U_{day}, (m/s)								
	6	9	12	6	9	12	6	9	12
	$(U_{day}/U_{night}) = 1.0$								
0	0.90	1.00	1.00	0.98	1.05	1.05	1.06	1.10	1.10
3	0.71	0.82	0.89	0.86	0.94	0.99	0.92	1.01	1.05
6	0.53	0.68	0.79	0.70	0.84	0.93	0.82	0.95	1.00
9	0.41	0.59	0.70	0.60	0.75	0.87	0.72	0.87	0.96
	$(U_{day}/U_{night}) = 2.0$								
0	0.90	1.00	1.00	0.98	1.05	1.05	1.06	1.10	1.10
3	0.76	0.85	0.92	0.91	0.99	1.05	0.98	1.10	1.14
6	0.61	0.74	0.84	0.80	0.94	1.02	0.92	1.05	1.12
9	0.48	0.65	0.76	0.70	0.84	0.95	0.81	0.96	1.06

Contd.

RS mm/day	$RH_{max} = 30\%$			$RH_{max} = 60\%$			$RH_{max} = 90\%$		
	U_{day}, (m/s)								
	6	*9*	*12*	*6*	*9*	*12*	*6*	*9*	*12*
				$(U_{day}/U_{night}) = 3.0$					
0	0.90	1.00	1.00	0.98	1.05	1.05	1.06	1.10	1.10
3	0.81	0.88	0.94	0.96	1.06	1.12	1.04	1.18	1.28
6	0.68	0.81	0.88	0.88	1.02	1.10	1.01	1.15	1.22
9	0.56	0.72	0.82	0.76	0.88	1.05	0.92	1.06	1.18
				$(U_{day}/U_{night}) = 4.0$					
0	0.90	1.00	1.00	0.98	1.05	1.05	1.06	1.10	1.10
3	0.84	0.92	0.97	1.00	1.11	1.19	1.10	1.27	1.32
6	0.77	0.87	0.93	0.96	1.11	1.19	1.10	1.25	1.33
9	0.65	0.78	0.90	0.88	1.02	1.14	1.01	1.16	1.27

Appendix-9

Values of $W\left(U_A, \frac{r}{\lambda}\right)$ and $W\left(U_r, \frac{r}{\lambda}\right)$

$r/\lambda = 0.01$			$r/\lambda = 0.1$			$r/\lambda = 0.2$		
$1/U_A$			$1/U_A$			$1/U_A$		
N	n	$W(U_A, r/\lambda)$	N	n	$W(U_A, r/\lambda)$	N	n	$W(U_A, r/\lambda)$
1.0	1	1.82	1	1	1.80	5	0	1.19
1.0	2	4.04	5	1	3.24	1	1	1.75
1.0	3	6.31	1	2	3.81	5	1	2.96
5.0	3	7.82	2	2	4.30	1	2	3.29
1.0	4	8.40	5	2	4.71	5	2	3.50
1.0	5	9.42	1	3	4.83	1	3	3.51
1.0	6	9.44	1	4	4.85	—	—	—
$r/\lambda = 0.4$			$r/\lambda = 0.6$			$r/\lambda = 0.8$		
$1/U_A$			$1/U_A$			$1/U_A$		
N	n	$W(U_A, r/\lambda)$	N	n	$W(U_A, r/\lambda)$	N	n	$W(U_A, r/\lambda)$
1	0	0.213	1	0	0.206	5	– 1	0.046
2	0	0.534	2	0	0.504	1	0	0.197
5	0	1.11	5	0	0.996	2	0	0.466
1	1	1.56	1	1	1.31	5	0	0.857
5	1	2.18	2	1	1.49	1	1	1.05
1	2	2.22	5	1	1.55	2	1	1.12

Contd.

$r/\lambda = 1.0$			$r/\lambda = 1.5$			$r/\lambda = 2.0$			$r/\lambda = 2.5$			$r/\lambda = 3.0$		
$1/U_A$			$1/U_A$			$1/U_A$			$1/U_A$			$1/U_A$		
N	n	$W(U_A, r/\lambda)$	N	n	$W(U_A, r/\lambda)$	N	n	$W(U_A, r/\lambda)$	N	n	$W(U_A, r/\lambda)$	N	n	$W(U_A, r/\lambda)$
5	–1	0.0444	5	–1	0.0394	3.33	– 1	0.01	5	– 1	0.0271	5	– 1	0.0210
1	0	0.185	1	0	0.151	5	– 1	0.0335	1	0	0.0803	1	0	0.0534
2	0	0.421	1.25	0	0.199	1	0	0.114	1.25	0	0.0961	1.25	0	0.0607
5	0	0.715	2	0	0.301	1.25	0	0.144	2	0	0.117	2	0	0.0681
1	1	0.819	5	0	0.413	2	0	0.194	5	0	0.125	5	0	0.0695
2	1	0.481	1	1	0.427	5	0	0.227	1	1	0.125	1	1	0.0695
			2	1	0,428	1	1	0.228						
$r/\lambda = 0.01$			$r/\lambda = 0.1$			$r/\lambda = 0.2$			$r/\lambda = 0.316$			$r/\lambda = 0.4$		
$1/U_y$			$1/U_y$			$1/U_y$			$1/U_y$			$1/U_y$		
N	n	$W(U_y, r/\lambda)$,	N	n	$W(U/y, r/\lambda)$	N	n	$W(U_y, r/\lambda)$	N	n	$W(U_y, r/\lambda)$	N	n	$W(U_y, r/\lambda)$
4	2	9.45	4	0	4.86	4	– 1	3.51	4	– 1	2.66	1	– 1	2.23
4	3	9.54	4	1	4.95	4	0	3.54	4	0	2.74	1	0	2.26
4	4	10.2	4	2	5.64	2	1	3.69	4	1	3.38	5	0	2.40
4	5	12.3	4	3	7.72	4	1	3.85	4	2	5.42	1	1	2.55
4	6	14.6	4	4	10.0	1.5	2	4.55	4	3	7.72	3.75	1	3.20
						4	2	5.42				1	2	4.05

Contd.

$r/\lambda = 0.6$			$r/\lambda = 0.8$			$r/\lambda = 1.0$			$r/\lambda = 1.5$		
$1/U_y$			$1/U_y$			$1/U_y$			$1/U_y$		
4.44	−1	1.59	2.5	−2	1.13	4	−2	0.844	7.11	−2	0.444
2.22	0	1.71	2.5	−1	1.16	4	−1	0.901	3.55	−1	0.509
4.44	0	1.84	1.25	0	1.26	4	0	1.36	7.11	−1	0.587
1.67	1	2.45	2.5	0	1.39	4	1	3.14	2.67	0	0.963
4.44	1	3.26	9.37	0	1.94				7.11	0	1.57
			2.5	1	2.70						

$r/\lambda = 2.0$			$r/\lambda = 2.5$			$r/\lambda = 3.0$		
$1/U_y$			$1/U_y$			$1/U_y$		
N	n	$W(U_y, r/\lambda)$	N	n	$W(U_y, r/\lambda)$	N	n	$W(U_y, r/\lambda)$
4	−2	0.239	2.56	−2	0.132	1.78	−2	0.0743
2	−1	0.283	1.28	−1	0.162	8.89	−2	0.0939
4	−1	0.337	2.56	−1	0.199	1.78	−1	0.119
1.5	0	0.614	9.6	−1	0.399	6.67	−1	0.262
4	0	1.11	2.56	0	0.798	1.78	0	0.577

Source : Boulton (1963)

Bibiliography

Arora K.R., *Irrigation Water Power & Water Resources Engineering*, Standard Publishers Distributors, Delhi.

A class-note on Ground Water Engineering prepared by **Dr. A.P. Mishra** and **Dr. B.C. Mall,** R.A.U., Pusa (Bihar).

Boreland W.M. and Miller (1960), *Fluvial Sediment,* JHD Prose. ASCE Vol 95, Hy-5

Blaney H.F. and Criddle W.D. (1950), *Determining Water Requirements in Irrigated Areas from Climatological and Irrigation Data,* US Dept. Agriculature SCS-TP 96.

Butler S.C., *Engineering Hydrology,* Prentice Hall Inc USA.

Central Water Commission, *Water Resources of India,* CWC Pub No. 30/88, CWC, New Delhi.

Chow. V.T., *Applied Hydrology,* McGraw-Hill Book Co. 1980.

Chow V.T. (1964), *Statistical and Probability Analysis of Hyhydrologic Data,* Section 8-1. *Hand Book of Appplied Hydrology,* McGraw Hill-Co Ltd. New York.

C.C. Inglis (1940), *Technical Paper No. 30,* Public Works Department, Bombay.

Cook H.L. (1946), *The infiltration Approach to the Calculation of Surface Runoff,* Trans. Am. Geophys Union 25 ; 728

Clark C.O. (1945), *Storage and Unit Hydrographs,* Trans, ASCE, 110.

Chow V.T. (1952), *On the Determination Transmissibility and Storage Coetticients from Pumping Test Data,* Trans. Am. Geophysunion Vol 33 : 397-404

Darcy H. (1856), *Less Fontaines* Publiques de la Ville de Dijon.

Doorenbos J and Pruilt W.C. (1975), *Guidelines for Predicting Crop Water Requirements,* Irrigation and Drainage Paper 24, FAO, Rome, P : 197

Danel P.R. Durand and E Condolios (1953), *Letude de la Staltation La Houille Blache No. 2.*

Dhar O.N. and Bhattacharya B.K. (1975), *A Study of Depth-Area-Duration Statistics of the Serveremost Storm over Different Meteorological Division of North-India,* Prose. Nati Sympeseum on Hydrology, Roorkee (India) PP G-4-11.

Dhar O.N. and **Bhattacharya B.K.,** *A case study of Depth-area-duration statistics of severe most storms over different meterological divisions of North-India,* Proc. National symposium on Hydrology-Roorkee India (1975)

Ferris J.G. (1962), *Theory of Aquifer Test,* U.S. Geological Surv., Water Supply Paper 1536 E, p. 174.

Garg S.P., *Ground Water Engineering*, Oxford and IBH Co. New Delhi.

Garg S.K., *Hydrology and Water Resources Engineering*, Khanna Publishers Distributors, Delhi.

Garg D.M., *Principles of Hydrology*, Water Infoamtin Centre, Huntington New York USA.

Goodrich R.D. (1931), *Rapid Calculation of Reservoir Discharge*, Civil Engg. Vol (i) : 407-418.

Haan C.T., Jhonson H.P. and Brakensiek D.L. (1982), *Hydrologic Modelling of Small Watersheds*, ASAE Monograph No. 5.

Horton R.E. 1919, *U.S. Monthly Weather Review*, Vol. No. 47.

Horton R.E. (1935), *An Approach Towards a Physical Interpretatiion of Intiltration Capacity*, Soil Sci. Soc. Am. Prose. 5 : 339-417.

Hazen A. (1930), *Flood Hows*, John Willey & Sons. New York.

Hubbel D.W. (1964), *Apparatus and Techniques for Measuring Bed Loads*, USCS Water Supply Papper, 1748.

Hantush M.S. (1962), *Drawdown Around a Partially Penetrating Well*, Jr. Hydr, Div. Prose. ASCE 127 (i) : 268-283

Jaswant Singh (1964), *Irritational use of Rational Formula*, Paper Presented at 3rd Annual Meeting of ISAE, Allahabad (India).

Jal Vigyan Sameeksha (Hydrology Review), *Pub. of High Level Tech. Comments on Hydrology*, N.I.H. Roorkee (India) Vol. (1) No (1) June 1986.

Jacob CE (1946), *Radial Flow In Leaky Artesian Aqiuifer*, Trans. Am. Geophys Vol. 27 : 198-205.

Jacob CE (1963), *Corrections of Drawdowns Caused by a Pumped Well Tapping less than the Full Thickness of Aquiter in Methods of Determining of Permeability, Transmissibility and Draw-Down*, U.S. Geol. Survey, Water Supply Paper 1536-I, p. 272-282.

Joglekar D.V. (1960), *Life of Reservior*, Tech. Report No. 19, CBI & P, New Delhi.

Khosla A.N. (1953), *Silting of Reservoirs*, Central Board of Irrigation & Power, N. Delhi.

Kozney J. (1933), *Theorie and Brechnung der Brunnen Wasser Kraft and Wasser Writs Chaft*, 28 : 88-116.

Kirpich P.Z. (1940), *Time of Concentration of Small Agril. Watersheds*, Civil Engg. (New York) 10 : 362

Kranth. K., *Ground Water Resources Development and Management*, T.M.H. New Delhi.

Linsley R.K. etal., *Applied Hydrology*, T.M.H. New Delhi.

Linsley R.K. Kohler M.A. and Paulhus JLH (1950), *Hydrology for Engineers*, McGraw Hill-Book Co. Ltd, New York.

Linsley R.K. Kohler M.A. and Paulhus JLH (1949), *Applied Hydrology*, McGraw Hill-Book Co. Ltd, New York.

Lal V.B.S., Banerji and Narayana (1977), *Sediment Yield in Relation to Drainage Basin Characteristics in Some Indian Rivers*, Prose, of the Paris Symposium, July, Publications No.-122.

M. Tech. Class-note on Watershed Hydrology, given by **Dr. N.K. Narda,** P.A.U. Ludhiana (Punjab).

Michael A.M., *Irrigation Theory and Practice*, Vikash Pub. House, Delhi.

Murthy V.V.N., *Land and Water Management Engineering*, Kalyani Publisher, Ludhiana (Punjab).

Mutreja K.N., *Applied Hydrology*, T.M.H. New Delhi.

Mc Clloch J.S.G. (1961) : *Statistical Assesment of Rainfall*, COTA Pub. No-66, Inter-African Conf. on Hydrology, pp. 108-114 (Nairobi).

Michael A.M. Mohan S. and Swaminathan K.R., *Design and Evaluation of Irrigation Methods*, IARI Monogrph No. 1, WTC (IARI), New Delhi.

Mayer (1926) : *Trans ASCE*, Vol 89 : 985.

Murthy B.N. (1977), *Distrinution of Sediment in Large Reservoirs*, Trans ASCE, Vol. 125 (i) : 166-18.

Muskat M. (1937), *The Flow of Homogeneous Fluido Through Porous Media*, Mc Graw Hill-Book Co. Ltd. New York.

Nash J.E., *The form of Instantaneous Unit Hydrograph*, IASH Pub. No. 45, Vol 3-4, pp 114—121 (1957).

Nemec J., *Engineering Hydrology*, T.M.H. New Delhi.

Penman H.L. (1963), *Vegetation and Hydrology*, Farnham Royal Commonwealth-Agricultural Bureaux.

Penman H.L. (1948), *Natural Evaporation from Open Water*, Bare Soil nd Grass, Prose Roy. Soc. London Ser. Vol 193 : 120-145.

Pierce B.O. and **Foster R.M.,** *A short Tables of Integrals*, Oxford and IBH Pub. New Delhi (1963).

Punima B.C. and **Lal B.,** *Irrigation Engineering, Standard Publishers Distributors, Delhi.*

Raghunath H.M., *Hydrology, Willey Eastern Pvt. Ltd. Delhi.*

Raghunath H.M., *Ground Water Engineering*, Willey Eastern Pvt. Ltd. Delhi.

Rao K.N. etal, *Potential Evapotranspiration Over India*, Symposium on Water Resources II Sc Bangalore (1571).

Richard (1944), *The Flood Estimation and Control*, Chapman and Hall Ltd. London.

Subramanya, K., *Engineering Hydrology*, T.M.H. New Delhi (second edition)

Sharma, *Hydrology and Water Resources Engineering*, Dhanpat Rai and Sons, Delhi.

Suresh R., *A. Text Book of Soil and Water Conservation Engineering.* Standard Pub. Distributions, Delhi.

Suresh R., etal *Steady Flow Towards Multiple Well Point System Ind. Jr of Agric. Engg (1993).*

Simons D.B. (1957), *Theory and Design of Stable Channels in Aluuvial Materials,* Ph.D. Thesis, CSU.

Sherman L.K. (1932), *The Relation of Runoff to Size and and Character of Drainage Basin,* Trans Am Geophys Union 13 : 322-339.

Snyder F.F. (1938), *Syntheitic Unit Hydrograph,* Trans Am. Geophys Union 19 : 447-454.

Theis C.V. (1935), *The Relation between Lowering of the Piezometric Surface and the Rate and Duration of Discharge of a Well Using Ground Water Storage.* Trans. Am. Geophys Union 66 : 519.

TC PSM (1969), *Sediment Measuring Technique : A Fluvial Sediment* JHD, Prose. ASCE Vol 95, HY-5.

Tejwani K.G., Gupto S.K. and Mohan H.N. (1975), *Soil and Water Conservation Reserarch,* 1956-71, ICAR. New Delhi.

Thornthwait C.W. (1948), *An Approach Towards a Rational Classification of Climate,* Geographical Review 38 : 55-94.

Todd D.K., *Ground Water Hydrology,* John Willey and Sons New York (U.S.A.).

US Government & IIHR (1952), *A Study of Measurement and Analysis of Sediment Loads in Streams, The Design of Improved Types of Suspended Sediment Samplers,* Report No. 8.

Vinekers J.B., Bijker E.B. and Schirf J.B. (1953), *Bed Load Transport Meter*

World Meteorological Organization, *Mannual for Depth-Area Duration Analysis of Storm Precipitation, WMO No 237, T.P. 129, Genewa Switzerland. (1969).*

Wangler T.P. and **Linsley R.K.,** *Application of Stanford Watershed Model to an Indian Catchment,* Irrigation and Power Jr. of CBIP (India) Vol. 37 (4) Oct. 1975, pp 465-475.

Wisler C.O. and **E.F. Braker,** *Hydrology,* John Willey and Sons. New York (1959).

Weisner C.J., *Hydrometeorology,* Chapman and Hall Ltd. London (U.K.) (1970).

Walton W.C. (1962), **Analytical Methods for Well and Aguifer Evaluation,** Illinois State Water Survey, Urbana, Bulletin 49, p. 81.

INDEX

R

S

T

U

V

W

Z